WRITE AHEAD

Skills for Academic Success

1

Linda Robinson Fellag

Community College of Philadelphia
Philadelphia, Pennsylvania

LONGMAN ON THE **WEB**

Longman.com offers online resources for teachers and students. Access our Companion Websites, our online catalog, and our local offices around the world.

Longman English Success offers online courses to give learners flexible study options. Courses cover General English, Business English, and Exam Preparation.

Visit us at **longman.com** and **englishsuccess.com**.

Longman

Write Ahead 1: Skills for Academic Success

Pearson Education, 10 Bank Street, White Plains, NY 10606

Vice president, director of publishing: Allen Ascher
Editorial director: Louisa Hellegers
Development director: Penny Laporte
Senior acquisitions editor: Laura Le Dréan
Development editor: Mary Ann Maynard
Vice president, director of design and production: Rhea Banker
Executive managing editor: Linda Moser
Production manager: Liza Pleva
Production editor: Lynn Contrucci
Production supervisor: Melissa Leyva
Director of manufacturing: Patrice Fraccio
Senior manufacturing buyer: Edith Pullman
Photo research: Mykan White
Cover design: Ann France
Cover image: Jude Maceren/Stock Illustration Source, Inc.
Text design: Ann France
Text composition: Carlisle Communications, Ltd.
Illustrations: John Dyess Illustration
Photo credits: **1** Davis Barber/PhotoEdit. **2** top: Esbin/Anderson/Omni-Photo Communications, Inc.; bottom: Jonathan Nourok/PhotoEdit. **19** © Joe Gemignani/Corbis. **41** John Huber. **42** © Steve Chenn/Corbis. **64** © Hubert Stadler/Corbis. **65** Courtesy of the West Edmonton Mall. **77** © Tony Arruza/Corbis. **86** top left: David Young-Wolff/PhotoEdit; bottom left: A. Ramey/PhotoEdit; right: Kaluzny/Thatcher/Getty Images Inc. **89** James Carroll/Pearson Education/PH College. **94** © Jim Zuckerman/Corbis. **99** Jeff Strout. **107** Richard Lord/PhotoEdit. **129** © Charles Gupton/Stone. **130** Jeff Greenberg/PhotoEdit
Text credit: **118–119** "Tips from a Tightwad," from *The Tightwad Gazette* by Amy Dacyczyn, copyright © 1993 by Amy Dacyczyn. Used by permission of Villard Books, a division of Random House, Inc.

Library of Congress Cataloging-in-Publication Data
Fellag, Linda Robinson.
    Write Ahead / Linda Fellag
        p.   cm.
    ISBN 0-13-027256-6 (v. 1 : alk. paper)
    1. English language—Rhetoric—Problems, exercises, etc. 2. English language—Textbooks for foreign speakers. 3. Report writing—Problems, exercises, etc. I. Title
PE1413 .F45 2002
808'.042—dc21

2001050238

Printed in the United States of America
2 3 4 5 6 7 8 9 10—VHG—06 05 04 03 02

CONTENTS

SCOPE AND SEQUENCE

WRITING ASSIGNMENT	WRITING PROCESS FOCUS	GRAMMAR AND MECHANICS
A personal profile Your special qualities or characteristics A free-time activity	Brainstorming Overview of the writing process	Subjects and verbs Complete sentences Capitalization
Your family or another family you know well A family member or other person you know well	Paragraph and Topic sentence Freewriting Paragraph format Supporting sentences	Simple present tense Direct Objects Sentence end punctuation Spelling -s verbs
How you manage your time Ways to use free time Ways to save time	Listing Topic sentence Supporting sentences	Parts of speech Simple present versus present progressive Frequency adverbs Prepositions of time Commas
A shopping mall, market, or a store A public place in your town or city	Details Graphic organizers	Singular and plural nouns There is/there are Prepositions of location Object pronouns Possessive adjectives
A personal celebration in your past A community celebration that you experienced	Chronological order Concluding sentence Background information	Simple past tense Word order Spelling the -ed form
A brand-name product that you buy Your spending habits	Reasons to support an opinion Paragraph unity	And, but, so, yet, and or Comma splices Spelling similar words
Your first impressions when you met a new person Your first impressions when you saw a new place A first experience	Graphic organizers Examples of support Flowcharts Time transitions	Past and present tenses together Dependent clauses Subordinating conjunctions Punctuation marks

PREFACE

Introduction

Write Ahead is a comprehensive writing and language study series especially designed for immigrant learners of English, as well as learners who have had little formal instruction in English. The series prepares students to write fluently and accurately in academic English at these levels:

- *Write Ahead 1*   High beginning to low intermediate
- *Write Ahead 2*   Intermediate

Target Users

A growing segment of the ESL student population in the United States acquires English by immersion in English-speaking communities. Naturally, their language learning needs differ markedly from traditional international ESL students. They lack "formal, metalinguistically oriented instruction" and use non-standard English dialects, as does the subgroup of U.S. high school graduates that has been labeled "generation 1.5 learners."[1] Indeed, these students of community colleges, universities, or high schools have startling gaps in their formal knowledge of English. Many are "ear" learners who have acquired the language informally. Their oral and aural abilities far exceed their reading and writing levels, and often their formal knowledge of the language is uneven or non-existent.[2] Furthermore, many have little experience with extensive writing in English.[3] The components of *Write Ahead* were thoughtfully developed to utilize the language learning strategies and meet the pedagogical needs of such students.

Unit and Chapter Components

Chapter Goals. A list of chapter goals encourages teachers and students to preview the writing topics and language points covered in the chapter. Learning objectives are appropriate for busy immigrant English learners who need to see value and purpose in their educational tasks. At the end of each chapter, students reflect on the goals they are achieving and get extra help with goals they need more work on.

Approaching the Topic. Illustrations and questions encourage students to think about the reading theme and writing topic.

Reading for Writing. Each chapter is divided into two parts. Each part consists of a reading and a writing assignment and language activities. An opening reading models the writing assignment and provides ideas,

---

[1] Linda Harklau, Kay M. Losey, and Meryl Siegal (eds.), *Generation 1.5 Meets College Composition*, Lawrence Erlbaum Associates, Mahwah, NJ, 1999.

[2] Patricia Byrd and Joy M. Reid, *Grammar in the Composition Classroom: Essays on Teaching ESL for College-Bound Students*, Heinle & Heinle Publishers, Boston, 1998.

[3] Harklau et al., *Generation 1.5 Meets College Composition*.

vocabulary, grammar structures, and organizational features which students may apply to their writing. The readings, including student paragraphs and essays and articles, were carefully selected for high interest to students and relevance to their lives.

Language for Writing. After reading, students study and practice vocabulary and grammar that they can use in the next writing assignment. Activities include using a dictionary, finding synonyms and antonyms, studying word endings, and writing sentences. The language activities can be used immediately in student writing.

Writing Assignment. Each chapter section contains a main writing assignment. Students read the assignment and then engage in a series of writing process activities that include:

- Getting ideas by brainstorming, clustering, listing, and freewriting
- Organizing ideas into a paragraph with a topic sentence, different types of support, a conclusion, and other elements of paragraph development
- Writing a first draft
- Revising for content and development (independently and with peers)
- Editing to improve language (using an editing checklist)

The emphasis on the writing-process approach teaches students to revise and edit their writing, which they may be reluctant and ill equipped to do.[1]

Editing. In the Editing section, students study and practice grammar and mechanics that will help them edit. Features of this section include:

- Grammatical presentations that provide special attention to errors made by students with non-standard dialects of English, such as the overuse of the *be* auxiliary or missing *-s* or *-ed* verb endings
- Mechanical topics that are problematic for "ear" learners, such as spelling similar words
- Grammatical and mechanical presentations that are made accessible to learners with limited formal education by using as few metalinguistic terms as possible
- Practice with grammatical structures and mechanics appropriate for the high-beginning and low-intermediate ESL curricula, as well as practice with beginning-level structures that learners may not have acquired earlier
- Grammatical topics related to the writing assignment

Journal Writing. Students build fluency by writing journal entries on topics related to the chapter theme, often in response to reading.

On Your Own. More Writing Practice topics provide extra writing practice on topics related to the chapter theme. The Personal Spelling List encourages students to take responsibility for the accuracy of their spelling.

---

[1]Harklau et al., *Generation 1.5 Meets College Composition.*

Do It Yourself (DIY)

This section in the back of the book gives students extra practice in the grammar and mechanics presented in each chapter. The DIY also contains a handwriting guide and a Personal Editing Log. An Answer Key to the DIY exercises facilitates independent study.

Special Features of *Write Ahead*

In summary, *Write Ahead* meets the needs of immigrant English learners and those with little formal training in English through these important features:

- Writing themes and topics relate to adult immigrants' lives.
- Readings and example paragraphs provide clear models and springboards for writing.
- Students gain practice in revising and editing and other steps in the writing process.
- Language presentations are simply written with little formal grammar terminology.
- The most basic and troublesome grammar points are presented and practiced to fill in the students' learning gaps.
- Special attention is given to mechanics since these students often have little experience writing or reading formal English.
- The Do It Yourself section provides students with personalized activities.

Acknowledgments

I would especially like to thank Laura Le Dréan, senior acquisitions editor at Pearson Education, for her insightful suggestions and continual support. This series would have been impossible without her. My thanks also go to Allen Ascher, Louisa Hellegers, Penny Laporte, Michael O'Neill, Françoise Leffler, Mary Ann Maynard, Mykan White, Lynn Contrucci, and the rest of the Pearson team for their assistance.

I also appreciate the suggestions made by the following reviewers:

Victoria Badalamenti, La Guardia Community College, Long Island City, NY

Sandra Bergman, New York City Board of Education: Office of Alternative, Adult and Continuing Education, New York, NY

Sally Gearhart, Santa Rosa Junior College, Santa Rosa, CA

Kelly J. Isern, Miami Dade Community College—North Campus, Miami, FL

Kelly Kennedy-Isern, Miami Dade Community College—North Campus, Miami, FL

Charles MacMartin, Baltimore City Community College, Baltimore, MD

Judy Marasco, University of Southern California, Los Angeles, CA

Kevin McClure, ELS Language Centers, San Francisco, CA

Janet Miller, Miami Dade Community College—Kendall Campus, Miami, FL

Phoebe Rivera, Los Angeles Mission College, Sylmar, CA

Esther Robbins, Prince George's Community College, Largo, MD

Jane Selden, La Guardia Community College, Long Island City, NY

Joanne Sellen, Washington State University, Pullman, WA

Millie Stoff, Miami-Dade Community College—IAC Campus, Miami, FL

Deborah Stone, Bellevue Community College, Bellevue, WA

Steven Storla, Houston Community College, Houston, TX

Steve Striver, Miami Dade Community College—North Campus, Miami, FL

Thanks also to my family for their rational criticism and their patience. Finally, to my students at the Community College of Philadelphia, thank you for the inspiration and motivation that you continually bring to my teaching.

Linda Robinson Fellag

Getting to Know You

Chapter Goals

- Practice the steps in the writing process.
- Recognize the main parts of a sentence.
- Write complete sentences.
- Capitalize words correctly.

Approaching the Topic

Most people like to tell others about themselves. In Chapter 1, you will read and write personal stories about yourself. In this way, you'll tell others about yourself *and* improve your language skills.

1. Look at the photograph. What do you think these people do?
2. Does one of the people remind you of yourself or a friend? Which one? Why?

PART 1

Reading for Writing

The reading below includes two profiles. A profile is a short description of a person. In the profiles below two writers describe important things about themselves and what they are looking for in another person in order to get an online pen pal (a person with whom one exchanges letters through the Internet in order to become friends). Read the profiles carefully.

Profiles for Friendship

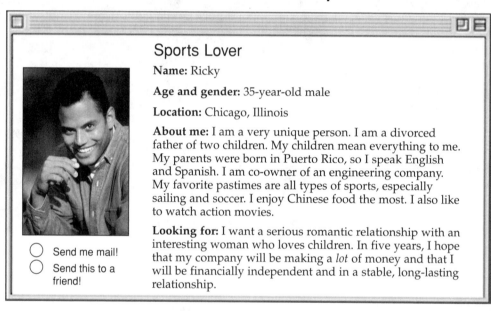

Sports Lover

Name: Ricky

Age and gender: 35-year-old male

Location: Chicago, Illinois

About me: I am a very unique person. I am a divorced father of two children. My children mean everything to me. My parents were born in Puerto Rico, so I speak English and Spanish. I am co-owner of an engineering company. My favorite pastimes are all types of sports, especially sailing and soccer. I enjoy Chinese food the most. I also like to watch action movies.

Looking for: I want a serious romantic relationship with an interesting woman who loves children. In five years, I hope that my company will be making a *lot* of money and that I will be financially independent and in a stable, long-lasting relationship.

○ Send me mail!
○ Send this to a friend!

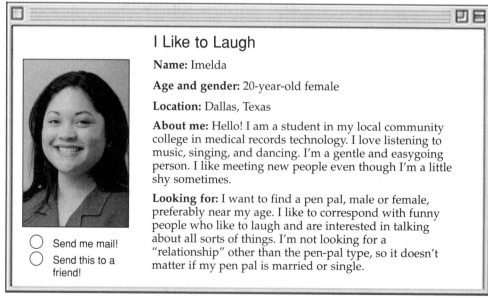

I Like to Laugh

Name: Imelda

Age and gender: 20-year-old female

Location: Dallas, Texas

About me: Hello! I am a student in my local community college in medical records technology. I love listening to music, singing, and dancing. I'm a gentle and easygoing person. I like meeting new people even though I'm a little shy sometimes.

Looking for: I want to find a pen pal, male or female, preferably near my age. I like to correspond with funny people who like to laugh and are interested in talking about all sorts of things. I'm not looking for a "relationship" other than the pen-pal type, so it doesn't matter if my pen pal is married or single.

○ Send me mail!
○ Send this to a friend!

Discussion   Discuss the following questions with a group.

1. What parts of these profiles describe you?
2. How are you different from the writers of these profiles?
3. Which profile do you like better? Why?

Language for Writing   Each of the words in the list below is an *adjective* (a word that describes a person, place, or thing). Complete the sentences with the words from the list. Use a dictionary if necessary. With your classmates, compare your answers.

unique	interesting	serious	independent	shy
gentle	romantic	single	easygoing	funny

1. My neighbor is a very _____*interesting*_____ person. He has many exciting stories to tell about his life.
2. Inna seems very _____. She's afraid to talk to people she doesn't know.
3. A _____ person is careful in the way he or she behaves so that others do not get hurt.
4. When you are _____, you can make your own decisions and take care of yourself.
5. Everyone is _____ because each person has special qualities that no other person has.
6. People who are _____ do not get nervous or worried easily.
7. Marriage is a _____ commitment.
8. I'm looking for a really _____ person—someone who tells jokes and can make me laugh.
9. Jorge is still _____, but he is thinking about getting married.
10. My boyfriend gave me roses for my birthday. He's so _____!

Writing

Assignment for Part 1

Write a short profile to describe yourself and what you are looking for in a pen pal. You will share your profile with your classmates. Write about the most important aspects, or parts, of your life. To write your profile, follow the steps below.

Getting Ideas

Brainstorming

One way to get ideas for your writing is to brainstorm, or get ideas quickly by making lists, writing sentences, or discussing ideas. When you brainstorm, you try to write down as many ideas as possible about a topic. Some of the ideas you write will be good. Others will not be useful. After you brainstorm, you should read over your ideas and choose the ones that you want to use in your writing.

1. The box below contains adjectives that describe a *quality* or *characteristic* of a person. Circle the words that describe a typical way that *you* act or feel.

2. Think of other adjectives that describe you. Write these words on the lines in the box. Use a dictionary if necessary.

3. Underline words in the box that describe what kind of pen pal you would like.

romantic	funny	***lucky***	**friendly**
amazing	**creative**	*determined*	cheerful
lazy	*honest*	confident	OUTGOING
contented	*hardworking*	shy	kind
quiet	**responsible**	serious	**caring**
_____	_____	_____	_____

4. Write sentences about yourself with at least five of the adjectives from page 5. Share your sentences with your classmates.

   Examples

   I am a very **funny** person. I love to tell jokes.

   I am **hardworking.** I study and I work part time.

5. Now make a list of your favorite leisure-time activities.

   going online _____   _____

   _____   _____

   _____   _____

6. Use your list from Exercise 5 to write five sentences. Share your sentences with your classmates.

   Example

   One of my favorite pastimes is going online.

7. Look again at the sentences you wrote in Exercise 6. Would you like your pen pal to share any of these interests? If so, which? Put a check (✔) next to them.

Organizing

It's important to organize your ideas. For this assignment, organize the ideas you got from brainstorming into two categories.

   About me:

   Looking for:

Look back at the profiles on page 2 for help.

Writing

When you have ideas for your writing and a plan for organization, you are ready to write the first draft, the first "try," of your profile. Sit down, relax, and take your time when you write. Write your online profile on a separate piece of paper, and follow the format shown on page 2.

Sharing Your Writing

1. Read your profile aloud to the class. Write your name and your native country on the board so that your classmates will remember them. After you finish, ask your classmates if they have any questions.

2. If you or someone you know has computer skills, type your profile and send it to a classmate through e-mail. Also, you can find many sites on the Internet that can connect you to people who want to write letters to each other. Search for these sites by typing in "pen pal."

Editing

Use the following explanations and activities to help you edit your writing.

Grammar

Parts of a Sentence: Subjects and Verbs

The sentence is the basic unit of writing. The most important parts of a sentence are the subject and the verb. English is a "subject-verb" language because, in most statements, the subject comes before the verb.

Subjects

The subject of a sentence names *who* or *what* the sentence is about. Here are some different types of subjects:

- **Nouns.** The subject can be a single noun.

  Ricky plays soccer every week.
  Music is one of Imelda's favorite hobbies.

- **Noun Phrases.** The subject can be a noun phrase (a noun plus other words).

  My friend Eileen has a large family.
  Some of the people in my country are not educated.

  The subject can be a noun phrase that begins with a verb ending in *-ing*.

  Playing the guitar is one of my favorite things to do.

  The noun phrase may contain two or more nouns connected by *and*.

  Mac and Kim are best friends.

- **Subject Pronouns.** The subject pronouns *I, you, he, she, it, we,* and *they* can take the place of a noun.

  Anna lives in an apartment building. **She** has good neighbors.
  Canada is a beautiful country. **It** has many natural wonders.
  Tekea and Helen are from Ethiopia. **They** are good friends.

Verbs

The verb of a sentence typically expresses an action or situation. Notice the verbs in these sentences:

VERB
Rita's brothers **live** in Hong Kong.

VERB
My parents **don't drive** a car.

Some verbs do not express action. These are called "linking verbs" because the verbs link (connect) the subject with the complement (the rest of the sentence). Some linking verbs are *be*, *seem*, *appear*, and *taste*. Notice the linking verbs in these sentences:

SUBJECT   VERB   COMPLEMENT
Dancing **is** my favorite pastime.

SUBJECT VERB COMPLEMENT
Kyi **feels** happy.

SUBJECT   VERB   COMPLEMENT
My family **is** in Puerto Rico.

1 Underline the subjects once and the verbs twice in each sentence. The subject and the verb may have more than one word.

1. <u>Learning English</u> <u>is</u> my greatest problem.
2. People do many different activities in their leisure time.
3. My classmate Anzhela likes reading books.
4. Javier and George watch action movies, but Thu likes romantic movies.
5. My math teacher often visits his family in San Francisco.
6. Bob enjoys playing with his daughter.
7. Working in a hotel is a difficult job.
8. I exercise in the college gymnasium after class.
9. Some of my friends go dancing at clubs.
10. We don't have enough time for everything.

2 Complete the following sentences. Make sure that each sentence has a subject and a verb. Share your sentences with a group.

1. *My classmates and I* _____ eat lunch in the cafeteria.
2. On the weekend, I _____.
3. My writing class _____.
4. _____ has many good qualities.
5. My best friend always _____.
6. Young people often _____.
7. _____ lives _____.
8. My parents _____.
9. A good student _____.
10. _____ spend a lot of time together.

DO IT YOURSELF
See pages 156–157 for more practice.

Complete Sentences

A sentence must have at least one subject and one complete verb and express a complete thought. Look at the sentences below.

SUBJECT   VERB
Bad storms scare me.

SUBJECT   VERB   VERB
My classmate Hoang studies and works part time.

SUBJECT   VERB
Magda and Ramon are two of my friends.

Read the two sentences below. What is missing in each sentence?

I from Vietnam.

My parents still in my native country.

The two sentences above are missing verbs. Here are correct ways to write these sentences:

I **come** from Vietnam.

OR   I **am** from Vietnam.

My parents still **live** in my native country.

OR   My parents **are** still in my native country.

Read the sentence below. Is it complete? If not, what is missing?

Is very nice to live in the United States.

This sentence is not complete. It does not have a subject. Here is a correct way to write this sentence:

It is very nice to live in the United States.

---

3 The sentences below are taken from student paragraphs. Are they complete? Write **C** if the sentence is complete. If the sentence is not complete, write **NC** and rewrite it to make it complete. Then explain why the items you rewrote were not complete.

_NC_   1. Is a nice class. _It is a nice class._   _(Subject missing.)_

_____   2. You a very nice teacher. _____

_____   3. You are very nice students. _____

_____   4. My sister in Miami. _____

_____   5. My classmate many friends. _____

_____   6. Our college very large. _____

_____   7. I a serious student. _____

_____   8. Our neighbors make noise at night. _____

4 Write complete sentences about the topics below. Make sure each sentence contains a subject and a verb and expresses a complete thought.

1. my studies
   I am studying English at Glendale Community College.

2. my free-time activity

3. my job

4. my educational goal

5. a bad habit

6. my best friend

7. my parents

8. my house

DO IT YOURSELF
See pages 159–160
for more practice.

9. my neighborhood

Language Tip ■ Using Adjectives

Use adjectives in these places in sentences:

■ Before a noun (as part of a noun phrase)

ADJECTIVE + NOUN
A **patient person** can wait calmly for a long time.

ADJECTIVE + NOUN
Alicia is a **serious student.**

■ After a linking verb

LINKING
VERB + ADJECTIVE
Tuan **is intelligent.**

LINKING
VERB + ADJECTIVE
My sister always **seems happy.**

5 Complete each of the following sentences with an appropriate adjective. In a group, compare your answers.

1. I hate to exercise. I am not a very _____ *active* _____ person.
2. Writing in English is _____.
3. If you work hard, you will be _____.
4. My best friend has _____ eyes.
5. Smoking is a _____ habit.
6. Learning English is very _____.
7. I often feel _____ after a long week of school and work.
8. A _____ college student completes all his or her homework.
9. My brother never tells a lie. He is an _____ person.
10. Her basic arithmetic class is not _____.

6 Now look one last time at your paragraph, and make sure your sentences all have subjects and verbs.

Journal Writing   A **journal** is a written record of feelings, ideas, and things that happen to you. Writing in a journal regularly gives you more practice in writing. Also, you may be able to use ideas in your journal for your writing assignments.

When you write in your journal, don't worry about how you organize your ideas. Just write whatever comes into your mind about the topic.

Write a one-page journal entry about a special person in your life. You may want to write about a family member or a friend. Give the person's name and some important information about him or her.

PART 2

Reading for Writing

The following reading is titled "Two Personal Stories" because two writers tell something important about themselves. In the first story, a young Chinese college student describes her pastime, or hobby, of visiting art museums. In the second story, a middle-aged male student writes about one of his qualities—how talkative he is. As you read, think about your own hobbies and qualities.

Two Personal Stories

Pictures of Life

Visiting art museums has become one of my favorite pastimes. As a little girl, I often visited art museums in China with my mother. My mother used to study art, so she taught me a lot about famous paintings. Now that I am older, I usually go to museums with my friends or cousins. On weekends, we spend hours examining paintings and disagreeing about the artists' techniques and the meaning of their work. I especially like the paintings of Vincent Van Gogh as well as those of many famous artists from China. If people ask me why I enjoy going to art museums so much, I tell them that I love to look at oil paintings from different times and countries and learn how people lived under different conditions. Every time I go to an art museum, I feel like I am walking through some exciting historical event or entering some peaceful environment.

Yan Li, People's Republic of China

The Real Me

Some people think that I'm a silent man, but I am really very talkative. When I was in my country, I liked to get together and talk with my friends. However, in the first month in America, I felt like an outsider. I did not talk too much. I did not want to discuss anything because of the language. Even though I had studied English in my country and I understood what I heard, I couldn't talk because I could not speak English. When I started taking English classes at my college, I still didn't talk too much with my classmates. That's why many people think I'm quiet. They don't know how I am when I'm not at school. When I have free time, I like to meet all my friends. We tell each other funny stories about our lives. We have small parties and spend a lot of time talking. I'm always the one who talks the most, but then I'm speaking in my native language. I hope that one day, when I have learned more, I will show everyone how talkative I am, even in English.

Mac Tai, Vietnam

Discussion　Discuss the following questions in a group.

1. In the first story, what does the writer do at art museums?
2. Why do you think she enjoys this pastime so much?
3. Is there any activity that makes you feel the way Yan feels about looking at paintings?
4. What do you think the title of the second story means?
5. In the second story, which sentences show that the writer is a talkative person?
6. Are you talkative? Why or why not?
7. Do you have a quality that some people do not know about? What is it?

Language for Writing　You can write about free-time activities by using:

- An *-ing* verb to name your activity

   Reading is my favorite leisure-time activity.

   I enjoy **watching TV** when I am not working or studying.

- *play* + name of sport, game, or musical instrument

   When I have free time, I **play soccer.**

- *go* + *-ing* verb

   I love to **go shopping** with my friends.

- *go* + *to* + place

   I **go to the movies** every weekend.

Complete the sentences below to make them true for you.

1. In my free time, I like to *go to the beach* _____.
2. When the weather is good, I _____.
3. My friends and I often go _____.
4. _____ is one of my favorite pastimes.
5. I enjoy _____ when I am not working or going to school.
6. Going _____ helps me to relax.

Writing

Assignment for Part 2

Write about one of your special qualities or characteristics, or write about one of your free-time activities. Follow the steps described below.

The Writing Process Writing is a process made up of several steps. You may go through these steps over and over as you write.

1. First, get ideas.
2. Next, organize your ideas.
3. Write your paper.
4. After you write, revise your writing. Read it and make changes to your ideas and organization, if necessary.
5. Last, edit your writing. Check the language and correct your punctuation and spelling.

The drawing below shows how writers typically follow these steps when they write.

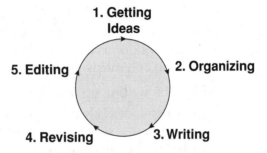

THE WRITING PROCESS

STEP 1

Getting Ideas

1. Reread your profile from page 5 and choose one quality or free-time activity to write about.
2. Answer the questions for the topic you chose and discuss your answers with a partner.

A Special Quality

What is your special quality?
When did people first notice this quality in you?
Why do you think you are like this?
Where are some examples of this quality in your behavior?

A Favorite Activity

What is your favorite activity?
When did you start to do this activity?
When do you do it? Where? With whom?
Why do you like this activity?

STEP 2

Organizing

1. Begin your composition with one sentence to introduce your special quality or favorite activity.

2. Make sure the rest of the sentences in your composition add more information about the idea in the first sentence. These sentences should support, or tell more about, your quality or activity.

Example of a first sentence: I am a very patient person.

Example of support: When I am driving in traffic, I don't get angry.

STEP 3

Writing

Write your composition on a separate piece of paper. After you write, check your writing at least twice—when you revise and when you edit.

STEP 4

Revising

Work with a partner. Read each other's compositions. Write comments on your partner's paper in the margins. Don't worry about grammar errors. Use the following checklist as a guide. Then read your partner's comments about your composition and make any necessary changes.

❏ Is the writing on the topic?

❏ Are the ideas clear? If something is not clear, put a question mark next to it. Ask your partner what he or she means and help him or her revise the composition.

❏ Are there any words you do not understand or you think are used in the wrong way? Put question marks next to them. Ask your partner what these words mean. Suggest other words.

STEP 5

Editing

Use the following explanations and activities to help you edit your writing.

Mechanics

Capitalization

A sentence begins with a capital letter. Proper nouns (specific names of people, cities, countries, companies, languages, etc.) and the pronoun *I* also begin with capital letters. Do not use a capital letter with a common noun (a general word for a place, thing, job, etc.). Look at these examples of proper and common nouns:

Proper Nouns	**Common Nouns**
City University of New York	the college
Mrs. Hedayati	my teacher
English	his native language

Turn to page 198 to review capital and lowercase letters.

1 Edit the following paragraph for errors in capitalization. Discuss your corrections with a partner. The first correction is made for you.

——————— **My Best Friend** ———————

My ♭est friend is Nega Mekonon, a Sudanese man who helped me when I really needed help. I met Nega when I first moved to Sudan. He lived there a long Time, so he helped me with a lot of Things. He even gave me a room to live in. We lived together until I got a Job. He paid the rent. also He bought all the food. After I got a Job, I started to help him, but Nega did not ask me to help Him. Nega was nice to everybody around him. He helped two other people, bely and Tadese. These Two men never worked, but They went to school. When Tadese, Bely, and I started to apply for a visa to come to the United States, I stopped working and I depended on Nega. He helped us until We left for The United States. Now i am here, but he still asks me about my Life. He calls me every month. Also he writes me letters. Nega is my best friend. I will never forget Him. If I get a chance, I will bring him here. If I don't, I will Help Him wherever he is. Nega is not only a friend in good times, but also in bad times. I haven't made any good friends since Nega, and I don't think I will ever find another friend like him.

Albert Alemu, Ethiopia

DO IT YOURSELF
See pages 195–197 for more practice.

Spelling

Some students find spelling difficult in English. The spelling and pronunciation of some words do not match. For example, you can pronounce the vowel *a* in different ways. Look at the three words with *a* in them below. Listen to a partner read them out loud.

   h<u>a</u>t   h<u>a</u>te   s<u>a</u>lt

Can you hear the differences in the *a* sound in each word?

Also, sometimes, not all letters are pronounced. Which word above has a letter that is not pronounced?

Another spelling problem in English is that one sound may have many different spellings. For example, the underlined parts of the words below are all pronounced like "ee," but they have different spellings.

   m<u>e</u>   sp<u>ea</u>k   w<u>ee</u>k   bel<u>ie</u>ve

The spelling exercises in each chapter will help you improve your spelling.

---

2 Read each pair of words below. Check (✔) the correct spelling of each word. Look in a dictionary to check your answers.

____ favorite	____ favurite	____ speack	____ speak
____ pasttime	____ pastime	____ business	____ bussiness
✔ usually	____ usualy	____ English	____ Inglish
____ enuf	____ enough	____ parent	____ parant
____ country	____ contry	____ really	____ realy
____ daughter	____ dauther	____ United States	____ United State
____ apartment	____ apartement	____ grammer	____ grammar
____ languge	____ language	____ peopel	____ people
____ does	____ dos	____ stoped	____ stopped

3 Begin a personal spelling list in a special place in your notebook. Write the title "Personal Spelling List" at the top of the page. Write the words you mispelled in Exercise 2 on your list.

4 Look over the writing you have done in Chapter 1. Find other words that you misspelled. Add these words to your Personal Spelling List.

5 Work with a partner. Study the correct spellings of the words on your Personal Spelling List. Test each other on the spelling of each word. Ask your instructor to help you pronounce the words, if necessary.

Editing Your Writing

Now you can edit your paper. Use the checklist below, and then rewrite your paper to correct any language errors you find.

Editing Checklist

❑ Do all the sentences have a subject and a verb?

❑ Are all of the sentences complete?

❑ Are the words capitalized correctly?

❑ Are all the words spelled correctly?

On Your Own

More Writing Practice

Write a composition about one of the topics below.

REMEMBER Think about the topic before you begin to write. Start with a sentence that introduces the topic and then add sentences that tell more about the idea in the first sentence. After you write, revise your paper and then edit it carefully.

1. **My Bad Habit**

   Do you have a bad habit? Describe the habit and give details such as the following: What is the habit? Why is it bad? Why do you have this habit? How can you change it?

2. **My Job**

   What is your job? Describe the work you do. Include details such as: Where do you work? When? Who do you work with? Do you like your job? Why or why not?

3. **My Best Friend**

   Who is your best friend? What do you like best about this person? In other words, what are your friend's best qualities? Where and when did you meet? What do you do or did you do together?

Chapter Goals Be responsible for your own learning by reviewing the learning goals for Chapter 1. Check (✔) the goal(s) that you are beginning to reach.

Chapter Goals Checklist

❑ Practice the steps in the writing process.

❑ Recognize the main parts of a sentence.

❑ Write complete sentences.

❑ Capitalize words correctly.

If you are having problems with one of these goals, get extra practice by writing another composition on one of the topics on page 17, or do additional language exercises in the Do It Yourself section at the back of the book. Then talk to your instructor about your writing.

Family Ties

Chapter Goals

- Follow correct paragraph format.
- Write a topic sentence.
- Write supporting sentences.
- Use simple present tense verbs.
- Recognize and use objects in sentences.
- Use sentence end punctuation.
- Learn the spelling of simple present verb endings.

Approaching the Topic

Nowadays, there are many types of families. Some children live with their parents, while others live with a single parent, a stepparent, or grandparents. In most families, however, the ties among family members are important. The readings in Chapter 2 will give you ideas for writing about families that *you* know.

1. Look at the photograph. Do you think this is a traditional family? Why or why not?

2. What responsibilities do mothers and fathers have in the families you know?

3. Think about someone in your own family. How would you describe him or her?

PART 1

Reading for Writing

The reading below describes two real-life U.S. families. The first family is traditional. The second is nontraditional because the children do not live with both their birth mother and father. As you read, think about how your own family is different from or similar to these families.

Today's Families

Meet the Dewks—today's average American family. "Dewks" is not a family name. The word stands for **d**ual-**e**mployed **w**ith **k**ids, because most U.S. families now consist of two working parents plus children.

The Martins

The Martins are typical *dewks*. Ronald Martin is a salesman, and his wife Shanelle is a secretary. They have two children: 20-year-old Jamal and 14-year-old Takia. The parents share the duties of running the household and making family decisions. Mr. Martin often travels for his work, so his wife heads the family when he is out of town. Jamal attends a local college, and his teenage sister Takia is in junior high school. Jamal lives at home, but he is becoming more independent. He drives his own car and works at a part-time job while he studies art. Takia is also busy because she participates in sports and clubs after school. The Martins are like many active families with two working parents.

The Callahan Family

Most American children are raised by two working parents, but about one-third are raised by a single parent, stepparents, or grandparents. The Callahans are an example of a nontraditional family. Lisa and Shannon Callahan live with their mother, Rose, who teaches elementary school. Lisa, 16, attends high school, and Shannon, 14, goes to middle school. Their older brother, Kevin, 19, attends college out of state. He lives in his own apartment.

Their father, Tom, lives with his new wife, Patti, and his stepdaughter, Jenny, in a nearby city about 30 minutes away. Tom works in a computer company, Patti is a housewife, and 17-year-old Jenny attends high school.

The Callahan family is especially nontraditional because it really consists of two families. Last summer, for example, Lisa and Shannon took their annual "family" vacation in Colorado with their father, their stepmother, and their stepsister. Later, Lisa and Shannon vacationed with their mother and their brother. Lisa and Shannon spend every other weekend at their father's house, and Lisa and Jenny are close friends. In fact, Jenny went to Lisa's end-of-the-year high school dance. Lisa and Shannon have a close relationship with their father. Unfortunately, they do not get along with their stepmother. Lisa and Shannon don't like their stepmother to tell them what to do. However, both girls are learning to accept their new family lives.

Discussion Discuss the following questions in a group.

1. Are the Martins similar to or different from a traditional family in your home country? In what ways?

2. What are the advantages of Lisa and Shannon's family? The disadvantages?

3. Do you know a family that is not traditional? Describe that family.

Language for Writing Read the list of vocabulary words and phrases below. Use the words to complete the sentences.

traditional	housewife	are raised by	runs the household
on his own	consists of	get along	heads

1. The Nam family ___*consists of*___ two parents and three children.

2. Usually, Mr. Nam _____ the family, but his wife takes over when he is gone.

3. Mrs. Nam does not work outside the home. She is a _____.

4. Mrs. Nam _____. She cooks, cleans, and does the shopping.

5. The Nam children _____ their parents. Both Mr. and Mrs. Nam take care of their children and teach them how to behave.

6. The Nam children like to do things together. They _____ with each other and rarely fight.

7. Mrs. Nam's brother Chong is not married. He lives _____.

8. The Nam family is a very _____ family.

▌Writing

Assignment for Part 1

Write a paragraph describing your family or another family that you know well. To write your paragraph, follow the steps of the writing process, beginning with Getting Ideas.

STEP 1

Getting Ideas

1. Reread the family descriptions in *Today's Families* on pages 20–21. Pay attention to the kinds of information the writer gives about each family.

2. To get more ideas for *your* writing, answer the questions below. Then work with a partner. Ask each other the questions, and help each other choose the information to include in your paragraph.

Questions	Answers
Is the family traditional or nontraditional?	
How many people are in the family? Give their names and ages.	
What does each family member do?	
Who makes important decisions?	
Who raises the children?	
Who runs the household? (Who does the cooking, cleaning, and other household work?)	
Do all the family members get along? Give details.	
(Your own questions)	

STEP 2

Organizing The Paragraph and Topic Sentence

Academic writing is organized into paragraphs—groups of sentences with one main idea. A paragraph usually begins with a **topic sentence**—a sentence that gives the **main idea** of the writing. The sentences after the topic sentence give information about, or support, the main idea.

Read the following student paragraph:

Topic
sentence

My Family

My family is a traditional Puerto Rican family. There are five of us—my parents, my brother, my sister, and me. My father, Ramon, owns his own grocery store. My mother, Elizabeth, works with him in the store and takes care of the house. My brother, Javier, is 21 years old. He studies pharmacy at Temple University and also works as a waiter. My sister Alma is 16. She is in eleventh grade at Olney High School. I study at my community college and work part time in the college registration office. My father is really the head of our family. If we need to make a big decision, like which college to attend, we have to ask him. However, my mother and father raise us together. They decide how late we can stay out and whether we can date. My mother also runs the household. She cooks all the meals and cleans everything. We don't help our mother very much with housework because she wants us to concentrate on our studies. We are all very busy, but we are a very close family, like many Puerto Rican families.

Sara Cortez

The first sentence is the topic sentence. It gives the main idea—that Sarah's family is a traditional Puerto Rican family. All the other sentences explain how her family is traditional.

1. Write a topic sentence for your paragraph. This sentence should state whether the family is traditional or nontraditional.

   Examples

   My family is a nontraditional family.

   The Nams are a typical Korean family.

2. Now organize the information that you chose to include in Exercise 2 of Getting Ideas. Follow the directions below.

   a. Introduce the family members by name and age.

   b. Explain what sort of work or study each family member is involved in.

   c. Give details about each person's responsibilities in the family.

   d. Give any other information about the family that fits your topic.

STEP 3

Writing

Now you are ready to write your family paragraph. Use your ideas, your topic sentence, and your organization plan to help you.

STEP 4

Revising

Read your paragraph carefully to check the ideas. Use the checklist below as a guide. Then rewrite your paragraph and make any necessary changes.

❑ Does my paragraph tell about one topic—my family or another family that I know?

❑ Does the paragraph begin with a topic sentence?

❑ Do the rest of the sentences support the main idea?

STEP 5

Editing

Use the following explanations and activities to help you edit your writing.

Grammar

Simple Present Tense

1. Use the simple present tense to write about the following:

- **A regular activity or habit**

    I **clean** my room every day.
    Working parents **lead** busy lives.

- **A belief, opinion, or preference**

    My father **believes in** hard work.
    Most children **do not like** to wake up early.

- **A general fact about a place or a person**

    Los Angeles **is not** the capital of California.
    My grandparents **live** in Colombia.

- **Ownership**

    We **own** two Ford Explorers.
    Laura and Clark **do not have** a daughter.

2. Follow these rules to form simple present tense verbs:

- Add an **-s** to the verb when the subject of the sentence is *he, she, it,* or a singular noun.

    He **drives** his wife to work every day.
    Aunt Mary always **pays** the bills in her family.
    Our family **spends** a week at the beach each summer.

    See the spelling rules for simple present tense verbs on page 37.

■ Add **not** after the verb to make forms of **be** negative.

> I **am not** the only one who works in my family.
> He **is not** lonely because he has a large family.
> My brothers **are not** in the United States. They live in France.

You can make negative contractions:

am not = *'m not*	I**'m not** the oldest child in my family.
is not = *'s not* (OR *isn't*)	My mother**'s not** lazy.
	My mother **isn't** lazy.
are not = *'re not* (OR *aren't*)	They**'re not** home right now.
	My brothers **aren't** home right now.

■ Add **do/does** + **not** before the verb to make all other verbs negative.

> I **do not have** any brothers or sisters.
> Yan **does not want** to get married right now.
> My sister and I **do not get along** with each other.

You can use negative contractions:

do not = *don't*	I **don't like** living in an apartment.
does not = *doesn't*	Sometimes my sister **doesn't do** her homework.

1 Underline the simple present tense verbs in the following paragraphs about the Callahan family, taken from the reading on pages 20–21.

The Callahans are an example of a nontraditional family. Lisa and Shannon Callahan live with their mother, Rose, who teaches elementary school. Lisa, 16, attends high school, and Shannon, 14, goes to middle school. Their older brother, Kevin, 19, attends college out of state. He lives in his own apartment. Their father, Tom, lives with his new wife, Patti, and his stepdaughter, Jenny, in a nearby city about 30 minutes away. Tom works in a computer company, Patti is a housewife, and 17-year-old Jenny attends high school.

The Callahan family is especially nontraditional because it really consists of two families. Last summer, for example, Lisa and Shannon took their annual "family" vacation in Colorado with their father, their stepmother, and their stepsister. Later, Lisa and Shannon vacationed with their mother and their brother. Lisa and Shannon spend every other weekend at their father's house, and Lisa and Jenny are close friends. In fact, Jenny went to Lisa's end-of-the-year high school dance. Lisa and Shannon have a close relationship with their father. Unfortunately, they do not get along with their stepmother. Lisa and Shannon don't like their stepmother to tell them what to do. However, both girls are learning to accept their new family lives.

2 Complete this paragraph with the simple present tense of the verbs given.

─────────────── **No Fighting!** ───────────────

John and his brother Peter often _____*fight*_____. At least once a day,
                                        1. fight

their mother _____ at them to stop fighting. Sometimes John, 5,
                2. shout

and Peter, 7, _____ to play calmly together. Everything
                 3. try

_____ quiet for a while. Then one brother _____
     4. be   5. do

something to make the other one angry, and the arguments

_____. Soon, one brother _____ the other, and a
    6. begin   7. hit

fight _____. John _____ a toy with Peter, so Peter
         8. start   9. not, share

_____ his brother on the arm. Of course, whenever their
   10. bite

mother _____ the boys which one started the fight, they both
           11. ask

_____, "He did it!" Still, the boys _____ together
   12. say   13. play

every day. They _____, but their mother _____
                    14. disagree   15. be, not

worried that the boys _____ each other. Their mother
                          16. not, love

_____ that it _____ natural for brothers to fight.
   17. know   18. be

3 Make positive or negative statements about regular activities of your family members. Use the phrases below. Change the verbs to match the subjects of your sentences.

1. take a summer vacation every year

   My family does not take a summer vacation every year.

2. do all the housework

   _____

3. work on weekends

   _____

4. share the same bedroom

   _____

5. live in an apartment

   _____

6. eat dinner together

   _____

7. spend a lot of time together

   _____

DO IT YOURSELF
See pages 164–166 for more practice.

8. drive a car

   _____

Editing Your Writing

Use the checklist below to edit your work. Then rewrite your paragraph.

> ### Editing Checklist
> ❑ Is the simple present tense used correctly?
> ❑ Are the simple present tense verbs spelled with the *–s* ending when they need it?
> ❑ Are all the sentences complete?

Journal Writing Write a journal entry about how families in a country you know well. Include details such as the following: What are the most common types of families in that country? What are the responsibilities of the family members? Are families in that country changing? In what ways?

PART 2

Reading for Writing

What makes one family member special? In the reading below, a student writer describes her Aunt Sandra. As you read, think about special qualities that *your* family members have.

My Aunt Sandra

My aunt Sandra is the most pleasant person in my family. She is in Haiti, and I live in the United States, but when we talk on the telephone, I can almost see her eyes light up and her mouth curve into a smile. Even when we speak on the phone, she always laughs. She tells me funny stories to cheer me up because I often feel homesick. For example, there's a story about her dog Auggie, who digs holes in her vegetable garden, and a story about the neighborhood children who get into trouble at school. It surprises me that Aunt Sandra is always so cheerful. In fact, she never gets depressed. Her husband died many years ago, and she doesn't have any children. Also, when she had surgery several years ago, she had a lot of pain, but she never complained. She may be lonely or feel bad, but she never shows it. When I go back home, we always have fun. Our whole family gathers at Aunt Sandra's house, and we cook a lot of dishes together. Her house is noisy with people talking and laughing. Everyone enjoys being around her. I miss Aunt Sandra so much because she is always so joyful.

Viviane Barthelmy, Haiti

Discussion   Discuss the following questions in a group.

1. What important quality does the writer's aunt have?
2. What does Aunt Sandra do that shows she has this quality?
3. Is there someone in your family like Aunt Sandra? Explain.

Language for Writing

Good writers vary the words they use in their writing. They use *synonyms* (words with similar meanings) or *antonyms* (words with opposite meanings) so that they do not repeat the same words over and over.

In the reading on page 28, the writer uses two synonyms for the word *pleasant—cheerful* and *joyful.* The writer also gives a clue to the meaning of the word *pleasant* by adding the sentence "In fact, she *never* gets *depressed*"—using a negative word, *never*, with an antonym, *depressed.*

1. Match the synonyms below. Use a dictionary, if necessary.

   __f__ 1. friendly   a. self-reliant

   ____ 2. kind   b. truthful

   ____ 3. hardworking   c. good-hearted

   ____ 4. honest   d. timid

   ____ 5. funny   e. relaxed

   ____ 6. independent   f. sociable

   ____ 7. shy   g. humorous

   ____ 8. easygoing   h. diligent

2. Next to each phrase below, write two words that have similar meanings. Use words from the list above or other words that you know. Use a dictionary if necessary.

   a. not lazy   _____   _____

   b. not nervous   _____   _____

   c. not serious   _____   _____

   d. not cruel   _____   _____

   e. not outgoing   _____   _____

Writing

Assignment for Part 2

Write a paragraph describing one member of your family or of another family that you know well. To write your paragraph, follow the steps of the writing process, beginning with Getting Ideas.

Getting Ideas

1. A good way to get ideas for writing is to freewrite. Freewriting means selecting a topic and writing whatever comes into your mind about it. You do not need to be correct when you freewrite. Read the example.

My Grandfather

My grandfather is great. He loves to laugh. He enjoys his life—watching television, going fishing. I used to go fishing with him when I was a child. He knows all the best places to fish. He always wears a hat, and my mother makes his shirts for him. He lives with my mother and father. Grandfather is always so kind and thoughtful. He takes my brothers and sisters and me out to eat. He always remembers our birthdays and gives us money for Christmas. He is so thoughtful and caring. All of us love our grandfather so much. He likes sweet things, so I often bring him candy. I love him so much. I always want to do things for him, the same way he does so many things for me. Like when I was a child, I remember my mother sometimes tried to give me a spanking, but my grandfather would convince her not to spank me. He protects and cares for me and my brothers and sisters.

2. Now freewrite for about 5 to 10 minutes about the family member you have chosen. Don't worry about grammar, spelling, or organization at this point.

3. Look at the example below. The student chose to write about her grandfather's kindness, so she kept the sentences that related to this idea and crossed out the sentences with ideas that she did not need.

My Grandfather

~~My grandfather is great. He loves to laugh. He enjoys his life—watching television, going fishing. I used to go fishing with him when I was a child. He knows all the best places to fish. He always wears a hat, and my mother makes his shirts for him. He lives with my mother and father.~~ Grandfather is always so kind and thoughtful. He takes my brothers and sisters and me out to eat. He always remembers our birthdays and gives us money for Christmas. He is so thoughtful and caring. All of us love our grandfather so much. ~~He likes sweet things, so I often bring him candy.~~ I love him so much. I always want to do things for him, the same way he does so many things for me. Like when I was a child, I remember my mother sometimes tried to give me a spanking, but my grandfather would convince her not to spank me. He protects and cares for me and my brothers and sisters.

4. Read over your freewriting. Look for ideas that you want to use in your paragraph. Cross out ideas you will not use.

Organizing

Paragraph Format

When you write a paragraph, follow this style, or format:

- **Write** your **name** and the **date** in the upper right-hand corner of the page.

- **Indent** (move to the right five spaces) the first line of the paragraph.

- **Leave margins** (blank spaces) on the left and right side.

- **Write on every other line,** or type your paper **double spaced,** so that you and your instructor can add ideas or make corrections.

- **Write a short title** that tells the main idea of your writing.

Here is an example paragraph with correct format:

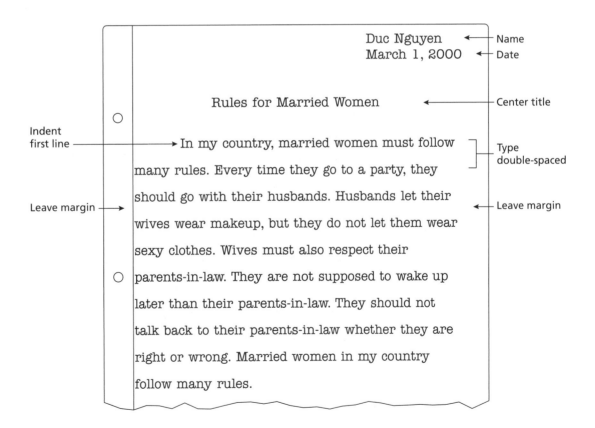

1. Rewrite the paragraphs below on a separate piece of paper. Make sure to use the correct format. With a partner, compare your paragraphs.

Mothers in My Country

In my country, most women do not work outside their home.

Most women are housewives.

They take care of children. Some families. have twelve children.

The mother cleans house and washes clothes by hand.

Mothers have very difficult lives even though they are housewives.

Paragraph A

Rich women in my country have many servants. They do not cook, clean, and take care of the house. Servants take care of everything.

Some women have two or more servants.

When they have three ser-

vants, one servant takes care of the children. The other servants clean the house.

Rich women are lucky to have servants.

Paragraph B

Supporting Sentences

The sentences that follow the topic sentence should support the main idea. Reread *My Aunt Sandra* on page 28. Notice how all the sentences in the paragraph support the topic sentence and main idea—*My Aunt Sandra is the most pleasant person in my family.*

For this assignment, the supporting sentences should show that your family member has the particular quality you have chosen.

Practice writing sentences to support each of the following topic sentences.

a. My brother Bao often gets angry.

When he plays video games, if he does not reach a high score, he gets very angry. He says the machine is broken. He jumps up and down, screams, and hits the machine.

b. My cousin Maria is very responsible.

_____

_____

_____

c. My Uncle John is a fun-loving person.

_____

_____

_____

STEP 3

Writing

1. To write your paragraph, begin by writing a topic sentence that tells an important quality of the family member you chose.

Examples

QUALITY

My mother is a **very caring person**.

QUALITY

My Uncle Charles is always **cheerful**.

_____

2. Use your freewriting ideas to write sentences that support the main idea of your topic sentence.

STEP 4

Revising

Work with a partner. Read each other's paragraph. Write comments on your partner's paper in the margins. Use the checklist below as a guide. Then read your partner's comments about your paragraph and make any necessary changes.

❏ Does the paragraph tell about one family member?

❏ Does the paragraph have a topic sentence about one of the person's qualities?

❏ Do the rest of the sentences support this main idea?

❏ Put question marks in the margin next to words you do not understand or words you think are used in the wrong way. Ask your partner what these words mean. Suggest other words.

❏ Is the paragraph written in the correct format?

Editing Use the following explanations and activities to help you edit your writing.

Grammar and Mechanics

Parts of a Sentence: Direct Objects

Many verbs in English take a direct object. The object usually comes after the verb, and it usually answers the question *what* or *whom*. Here are several types of direct objects:

- **Nouns.** The object can be a single noun.

  My father never eats **breakfast.**
  Margarita's family enjoys **parties.**
  Rudy meets **Elizabeth** every day in the library.

- **Noun Phrases.** The object can be a noun phrase.

  My sister Kerry wants **a new boyfriend.**
  The Mellons have **a very large house.**

- **Object Pronouns.** The object pronouns *me, you, him, her, it, us,* or *them* can take the place of a noun.

  I see my uncle's family once a year. I visit **them** in the summer.
  Our family bought a new car. We drove **it** to the shore.
  Jaroslav loves his mother. He calls **her** on the telephone every week.
  At the store, we all help Uncle Ron on the weekends. Sometimes we help **him** on Thursdays and Fridays, too.

Some action verbs do not have direct objects.

  We **talked** too much.
  He **lives** in a two-story house.

Linking verbs never have direct objects.

  My family **is** very traditional.
  My brother and sister **are** in Japan.
  I **feel** tired.

---

1 Identify the main parts of each sentence that follows. Write **S** above the subject, **V** above the verb, and **O** above the object. Remember that some sentences do not have objects.

    S   *V*   *O*

1. Lauren has a traditional family.

2. Lauren is already in college.

3. She has a 10-year-old brother.

4. Her mother and father work.

5. Lauren's mother and father love her.

6. The parents raise their children carefully.

7. Jim's father calls him every day.

8. Jim's wife is very nice.

9. My brother Terry lives in Ohio.

10. Terry doesn't have any children.

11. Terry and his wife Gloria own a business.

2 Fill in each blank in the paragraph below with an appropriate noun or pronoun. Make sure you know whether you need a subject or an object. With a partner, compare your paragraphs.

My Mother

My mother is a wonderful woman. ___*She*___ has all the best qualities of a good mother. We all love _____ , and she loves _____ all equally. She works hard to help support the family. Also, _____ takes care of our family. She cooks meals for my father, my brothers, my sisters, and me every day. _____ always enjoy her meals, and she makes _____ with great care. When I am sick, she helps _____ get better. When I make mistakes, she helps _____ correct them. She gives me advice gently. _____ is really like a big tree protecting my life with its shade. Being in my mother's loving arms, I always feel peaceful. I will always love _____ .

Lai Tran, Vietnam

DO IT YOURSELF
See pages 157–158 for more practice.

Language Tip ■ Telling About Age

Notice these ways to tell about the age of a person, a place, or a thing:

■ After *be*, use *months, years,* etc. (the noun form with *-s*):

> My father is **50 years old.**
> The baby is **7 months old.**

■ Before a noun, use *month, year,* etc. (the noun form without *-s*) and use hyphens:

> His **24-year-old** sister lives on her own.
> Our **five-year-old** car runs very well.

3 Write four sentences about the age of a person in your family or another family. Use the different ways you have just learned to write about age.

Examples

I have a **9-year-old** son named Tom.

My husband is **34 years old.**

1. _____

2. _____

3. _____

4. _____

Sentence End Punctuation

A sentence can end in a period (.), a question mark (?), or an exclamation point (!).

- **The period is the most common sentence end punctuation mark.**

   My grandfather was a man with unusual stories to tell.

   He had many interesting experiences in his life.

- **A question mark is used to end a question.**

   Do you have a large family?

   How many people are in your family?

- **An exclamation point is used at the end of a sentence to express a command or a strong feeling.**

   Be careful!

   My wife just had twins!

---

4 Put a period, a question mark, or an exclamation point at the end of each sentence below. The first sentence is punctuated for you.

1. Do you live in a house or an apartment?

2. My family and I live in a large apartment building

3. We plan to move next month

4. Are you a new parent

5. Watch out

6. My sister works in a pizza parlor

7. Does your brother attend college

8. That car almost hit us

9. Why do you like living at home

10. My boyfriend and I want to get married next year

5 Read the following student paragraph. Find where the sentences begin and end. Add a period at the end of each sentence. Capitalize the first letter of each new sentence.

My Grandfather's Death
---

died. We

My family was sad when my grandfather ~~died we~~ will never forget him because he was very kind to all of his family and friends when my family moved to the United States 10 years ago, my grandfather stayed in my native country of Vietnam in May 1998 we got a fax from Vietnam it said my grandfather had died of cancer he died in a hospital at the age of 78 the whole family cried for many days my grandfather is dead, but I still love him my family will always remember him

Ai Nguyen, Vietnam

DO IT YOURSELF
See pages 185–187 for more practice.

Spelling Verb Endings: The -*s* Form

For most verbs, you make the -**s** form of the simple present tense verb by adding -**s** to the base—the simplest form of the verb. However, sometimes the spelling is different. Study the spelling rules in the chart below.

Rules	Examples	
1. With most verbs, add -**s** to the base form.	work give	work**s** give**s**
2. When the base form ends in *s, x, z, ch*, or *th*, add -**es** to make the -**s** form.	watch fix	watch**es** fix**es**
3. When the base form ends in *y* preceded by a vowel, add -**s**.	pla**y**	play**s**
4. When the base form ends in *y* preceded by a consonant, change the *y* to *ie* and then add -**s**.	hurr**y**	hurr**ies**
5. Three other verbs have irregular -**s** forms:	do go have	**does** **goes** **has**

6 Complete the following sentences with the -s form of the verbs.

1. In my country, a man usually ____*marries*____ when he is about 30
   _{marry} years old.

2. My family _____ in an apartment.
   _{live}

3. My brother usually _____ work at 10 P.M.
   _{finish}

4. He _____ in a jewelry factory.
   _{work}

5. My sister _____ her two children very carefully.
   _{raise}

6. My mother _____ out for her family.
   _{watch}

7. She never _____ breakfast.
   _{eat}

8. My cousin _____ to class three days a week.
   _{go}

9. A child usually _____ his or her parents.
   _{obey}

10. My uncle _____ his own business.
    _{have}

11. My mother _____ to learn English.
    _{need}

12. My best friend _____ at Temple University.
    _{study}

DO IT YOURSELF
See pages 190–191
for more practice.

13. My mother _____ all of my clothes.
    _{wash}

14. Our father _____ too much about us.
    _{worry}

Editing Your Writing

Use the checklist below to edit your work. Then rewrite your paragraph.

Editing Checklist

❏ Is the simple present tense used correctly?

❏ Are objects used correctly in your sentences?

❏ Is the sentence end punctuation correct?

❏ Are the -s verbs spelled correctly?

On Your Own

More Editing Practice

Practice editing other students' writing so that you can find and correct your *own* language errors more effectively.

1. The student paragraph below contains three errors in simple present tense verbs and three errors in sentence end punctuation. Find the errors and correct them. In a group, compare your answers.

Living on My Own

Living on my own has brought me many problems. I didn't have so many difficulties last year I lived with my parents, and I went to school full time. I didn't have to pay any bills, and my parents gave me money for transportation. Now that I live on my own, I not have any advantages. I have to work to pay my bills and to pay for clothes, transportation, and school books. I go to school part time, but I don't study much. Sometimes when my teacher explain things to me, I not concentrate I am usually tired. This situation is very hard for me it would be better to live with my parents.

Tsehay Sisay, Ethiopia

---

2. Read over the Editing Symbols on pages 198-199 in the Do It Yourself section. Discuss the meanings of the symbols with your instructor. Add to the list any other editing symbols that your instructor uses.

Personal Spelling List

1. Look over the paragraphs you wrote in this chapter. Add misspelled words to your Personal Spelling List in your notebook.
2. Study the correct spelling of the words on your list. Work with a partner. Test each other on the spellings. Ask your instructor to help you pronounce words, if necessary.

More Writing Practice

Write a paragraph on one of the topics given on page 40.

REMEMBER Brainstorm before you begin to write. Begin your paragraph with a topic sentence. Make sure that all your sentences support the main idea. Follow correct paragraph format. After you finish, read over your paragraph and edit it.

1. **A Family Value**

   Write a paragraph about a value that parents should teach their children. Begin your paragraph with a sentence that introduces that value. Explain why it is important and how parents can teach it to children. Use examples from your own family or another family that you know well.

   ### Example Topic Sentence

   Good parents teach their children to respect older people.

2. **A Family Issue**

   Write a paragraph giving your opinion about *one* of the following family issues: divorce, remarriage, cohabitation (living together without marriage), blended families (families with children from more than one set of parents), working mothers, or single-parent families. Write a topic sentence that gives your opinion. Explain the reasons for your opinion, and support them by telling about a real family or person you know.

   ### Example Topic Sentences

   Single parents have many responsibilities.

   Divorce is necessary when a husband and wife are unhappy together.

3. **A Television or Movie Family**

   Write a paragraph about one family from a television show or movie. Begin with a topic sentence that gives the name of the show and the type of family (traditional or nontraditional). Give the names of the family members. Explain what each family member does (such as work or go to school). Describe the family members' responsibilities in the family.

   ### Example Topic Sentence

   The family on the TV show *The Emersons* is a traditional family.

Chapter Goals Think about the learning goals for Chapter 2. Check (✔) the goal(s) that you are beginning to achieve. If you are having problems with one of the areas, write another paragraph on one of the topics from More Writing Practice above, or do the language exercises in the Do It Yourself section. Talk to your instructor about your writing.

> ## Chapter Goals Checklist
>
> ❏ Follow correct paragraph format.
> ❏ Write topic sentences.
> ❏ Write supporting sentences.
> ❏ Use simple present tense verbs.
> ❏ Recognize and use objects in sentences.
> ❏ Use sentence end punctuation correctly.
> ❏ Learn the spelling of simple present verb endings.

Time Well Spent

Chapter Goals

- Write a topic sentence and supporting sentences.
- Use parts of speech correctly.
- Use simple present and present progressive verb tenses.
- Use frequency adverbs.
- Use prepositions of time.
- Use commas correctly.

Approaching the Topic

Most of us wish we had more time in each day. In Chapter 3, you will read and write paragraphs about how you use your time. You can examine your daily habits and the ways you spend your time.

1. Look at the photograph. Do you ever have days like this? Give examples.

2. What do you spend most of your time doing?

3. How do you think you spend your time: Wisely? Carelessly? Well? Wastefully?

PART 1

Reading for Writing

Many college students have trouble finding enough time for all the areas of their lives—study, work, family, and leisure activities. As you read, think about how you manage *your* time.

Managing Time in College

1   Diane Hartley has difficulties managing her time. She is a student at Duke University. As a freshman, she has become very good at wasting time. Often, she wastes a lot of time playing with her computer. She spends a lot of time in chat rooms and playing games online. She waits until the last moment to do a big class project. She often skips classes, and she  puts off studying until the last minute. Then, when she needs to study, she stays up all night and "crams" for exams. Her grade-point average is 2.0, and now Diane is afraid that she will not be able to graduate.

2   Diane is like many college students. In high school, Diane's teachers made her follow a schedule and turn in homework on time. In college, however, Diane works independently, so no one tells her to do her work. It's easy for her to fall into bad habits.

3   Colleges and universities recognize that having good study habits and using time well are important for students. Many community colleges now offer time management and study skills classes. Some schools give students lists of tips for using time wisely. The following list helps students like Diane identify the goals and important priorities in their lives and use their time to achieve those goals.

Ten Tips for Improving Time Management

1. Concentrate on one thing at a time.
2. Plan your day each morning or the night before, and set priorities.
3. Keep paper or a calendar with you to write down the things you have to do.

4. Try to avoid wasting time. Use your time wisely.

5. Reward yourself when you get things done as you had planned.

6. Set deadlines for yourself whenever possible.

7. Don't spend time regretting past failures. Instead, learn from your mistakes.

8. Remember that there is always enough time for the important things. If something is important, you should be able to make time to do it.

9. Think about your goals once a month and decide whether you need to change them. If you think about them on a monthly basis, you will be able to work on your goals on a daily basis.

10. Put up notes in your room to help you remember your goals.

Discussion   Discuss the following questions in a group.

1. What area of Diane's daily activities (work, home, or study) does the article focus on?

2. How does Diane often waste time?

3. Do you waste time? If so, explain how and when.

4. What are some things that colleges do to help students manage time? What does your school, college, or university do?

5. Look over the list of tips again. Which tips do you use to manage your time? Which of the tips might you use in the future? Explain why.

Language for Writing   1. Match each word or phrase with the correct definition. The words on the left are taken from the reading on pages 42–43. The paragraph or tip number is given in parentheses.

_h_ 1. cram (1)

____ 2. achieve (3)

____ 3. wisely (3)

____ 4. goals (3)

____ 5. priorities (3)

____ 6. reward (tip 5)

____ 7. regret (tip 7)

____ 8. on a monthly basis (tip 9)

a. to give something to someone for doing well

b. things that you think are most important and that need attention before anything else

c. happening every month

d. to feel sorry about something you have done

e. with good judgment

f. to succeed in doing or getting something as a result of your actions

g. some things that you hope to achieve in the future

h. to prepare for a test by studying a lot of information very quickly

2. Complete the paragraph with some of the words or phrases from Exercise 1.

Reaching Goals

If you want to succeed, you have to plan what you want and work hard to get it. First, ask yourself, "What are my _____ for the

1.

future? What do I want to _____ in my life?" Think about

2.

how you can reach your goals, and then make plans. Choose your goals

_____, and then work to put your goals into action. It's also

3.

important to set _____ to decide what is more important in

4.

your life and needs your attention first. _____ yourself when

5.

you do a good job in school or work; don't _____ past fail-

6.

ures. Concentrate on the present and future. It may take you a long time to

reach your goals, but when you do, you will be a success.

---

3. In English, many words are commonly used in set combinations. Here are some examples:

take a test	take a trip	make a date
take a break	reach a goal	make a deadline

Read each numbered word or phrase below and circle the word or words that go with it.

1. **set**   ~~priorities~~
                ~~goals~~
                failure

2. **stick to**   a schedule
                   a test
                   a plan

3. **achieve**   goals
                  examples
                  reasons

4. **use time**   wisely
                   poorly
                   hard

5. **cram for**   a meal
                   a quiz
                   a test

Writing

Assignment for Part 1

Write a paragraph describing how well you manage your time. To write your paragraph, follow the steps of the writing process, beginning with Getting Ideas.

STEP 1

Getting Ideas

Listing

Listing is a way to brainstorm ideas. Think about your writing topic and make a list of words or phrases that come into your mind. Then read over the list and check (✔) the items that you want to include in your writing. These items should support your main idea. Cross out items that you do not need to include.

1. Look at the example below. The student listed ideas about a typical day at school. She checked the ideas that support her main idea and crossed out the ones that don't.

My Typical School Day

○ ~~Get ready for school~~
~~6 a.m., wake up, shower, dress, have breakfast~~

○ ~~Take bus~~
Review class notes ✓
○ ~~Have coffee in cafeteria~~

10 a.m.—noon
Take reading/writing class ✓
Eat lunch and study with friends ✓

1:30—3:30
Go to the library ✓

4:00—5:00
Take algebra ✓
Ask teachers questions after class ✓
~~Take bus home, 5—6 p.m.~~

○ ~~Arrive home~~
~~Make dinner, do housework, eat dinner~~
○ ~~Relax, watch TV, spend time with family, go online~~

○ Do homework ✓

~~11 p.m.—midnight, Go to bed~~

What is her main idea? Circle the letter.

a. At school, I generally use my time well.

b. I waste a lot of time at school.

2. Make a list of the activities that you do on a typical busy day—a school day, a work day, or a weekend day.

3. Read over your list and think about the writing topic. In general, how well do you manage your time? Do you use time wisely, or do you waste much of your time? This will be your main idea. Check (✔) the items that support your main idea and cross out the ones that do not.

STEP 2

Organizing

Topic Sentence

In Chapter 2, you learned that your writing should be organized into paragraphs, each beginning with a topic sentence that expresses the main idea. Look at these examples of topic sentences:

My <u>school life</u> always seems (disorganized.)

I am (very busy) on <u>the days when I take classes</u>.

These topic sentences are effective because they do two important things: (1) They introduce the topic, and (2) They give the writer's feeling, opinion, or idea about the topic.

In each topic sentence, the topic is underlined and the writer's opinion or idea about the topic is circled.

1. Read the writing assignment topics and sample topic sentences below. Look for the sentence that both introduces the topic and expresses the writer's feeling, opinion, or idea about it. Check (✔) the better topic sentence and discuss your answers in a group.

    a. Assignment: My Weekday Schedule

    Topic Sentence 1:   I go to school and work every weekday.

    Topic Sentence 2:   I have no free time during my weekdays. ✔

    b. Assignment: My Summer Vacation

    Topic Sentence 1:   I took a vacation in Florida last summer.

    Topic Sentence 2:   My vacation in Florida was fun and relaxing.

    c. Assignment: My Job

    Topic Sentence 1:   I hate working as a cashier in a grocery store.

    Topic Sentence 2:   I work as a cashier in a grocery store.

    d. Assignment: My Place for Studying

    Topic Sentence 1:   I study in the library.

    Topic Sentence 2:   The library is a quiet place for me to study.

    e. Assignment: A Family Member's Best Quality

    Topic Sentence 1:   My brother Florian is a hardworking person.

    Topic Sentence 2:   My brother's name is Florian.

2. Write topic sentences. For each writing topic below, complete the sentence to make it true for you. Write one or more words that express your feelings, opinions, or ideas about the topic. Share your sentences in a group.

   a. My Weekend Routine

   I usually have very _____ *quiet and restful* _____ weekends.

   b. My English Class

   My English class is a _____ class.

   c. My Days Off

   My days off from school or work always seem _____.

   d. My Favorite Teacher

   My favorite teacher is _____.

   e. Learning English

   Learning English is _____.

   f. My First Day at School

   On my first day of school, I felt _____.

   g. Housework

   Doing housework is _____.

   h. My City (or Town)

   My city (or town) is a _____ place to live.

   i. My Neighbors

   My neighbors are very _____ people.

3. Write a topic sentence for the writing assignment on page 45. Make sure your topic sentence introduces the topic of managing your time and expresses an opinion, feeling, or idea about it.

   Examples

   In general, I spend my time very wisely.

   I waste a lot of time at home.

Supporting Sentences

As you learned in Chapter 2, a paragraph should contain ideas that support, or give information about, the main idea in the topic sentence. Supporting sentences explain why the main idea is true. Supporting sentences can include examples, facts, or specific details.

1. Read the student paragraph on page 48. What is the main idea? Do all of the sentences support this idea? Underline two supporting sentences.

Time Is Gold

Time is the most important thing for every person, but somehow I always seem to waste it. I know I need to manage my time more wisely, but I often waste my time by worrying about what I have to do. Usually, when I get up in the morning, I plan what I'm going to do for the day. However, I waste my time thinking about which things I have to do first, and which ones to do second. Just by thinking, I let time fly by without doing anything. For example, when I get up, I plan to go to work and then clean the house and do homework when I get home. But after I come back from work, I start thinking all over again about the things I have to do, and then I look up and I have no time left. I also waste time talking. For example, I start cleaning the kitchen, but if friends or family members call or come over, I stop and talk with them. Then it's too late to clean the kitchen. I waste all my time without doing what I planned. "Time is gold," so I should stop thinking and talking—and start doing!

Mikiyas Shewangizaw, Ethiopia

---

2. For each topic sentence below, write two possible supporting sentences.

a. Topic Sentence: I'm a working parent, so my life is always busy.
   Support: _In the mornings, I help everyone get ready for work and school._
   Support: _____

b. Topic Sentence: Participating in sports takes too much time.
   Support: _____
   Support: _____

c. Topic Sentence: My days off are busier than my work days.
   Support: _____
   Support: _____

d. Topic Sentence: I use my time well at school.
   Support: _____
   Support: _____

STEP 3

Writing

Write the first draft of your paragraph. Use your list of ideas and your topic sentence. Be sure that all the sentences in your paragraph support the topic sentence.

STEP 4

Revising

Work with a partner. Read each other's paragraph. Write comments on your partner's paragraph in the margins. Use the following checklist as a guide. Then read your partner's comments about your paragraph and make any necessary changes.

❑ Does the paragraph begin with a topic sentence that tells whether the writer spends time well or wastes time?

❑ Do the rest of the sentences support the main idea in the topic sentence?

STEP 5

Editing

Use the following explanations and activities to help you edit your writing.

Grammar

Parts of Speech

Parts of speech are the grammatical groups to which words belong. Knowing a word's part of speech helps you use that word correctly in sentences. The chart below explains what four common parts of speech do.

Notice how different parts of speech are used in the following sentences:

Part of Speech	Function
Noun	Names a person, place, thing, or idea
Verb	Tells what a person, place, thing, or idea does or is
Adjective	Describes a noun or pronoun
Adverb	Tells you how, when, or where something happens

    NOUN   VERB   ADJ NOUN ADVERB
Elizabeth uses her free time wisely.

    NOUN   VERB   NOUN   NOUN ADVERB NOUN
Jurgen takes the bus to school every day.

    NOUN VERB   ADJ   NOUN
Edward is a serious student.

More on Parts of Speech

Dictionaries print the abbreviation, or short form, for the part of speech after each word. Usually *v* stands for *verb*, *n* for *noun*, *adj* for *adjective*, and *adv* for *adverb*. Look at the following entries and abbreviations for the parts of speech from a dictionary page:

con·cen·trate /'kɑnsən,treʸt/ *v* **-trated, -trating** [I;T] **1** [*on, upon*] to keep or direct (all one's thoughts, efforts, attention, etc.): *You should concentrate on the road when you're driving. \If you don't concentrate more on your work, you'll lose your job!* **2** to (cause to) come together in or around one place: *Industrial development is concentrated in the Northeast. \The crowds concentrated in the center of the town near the stores.*

con·cen·tra·tion /,kɑnsən'treʸʃən/ *n* **1** [U] close attention: *This book will need all your concentration.* **2** [C] a close gathering: *There is a concentration of industry in the north of the country.*

1 Look up the following words in a dictionary. For each word, write the part(s) of speech and the abbreviation(s). Sometimes one word can be used as more than one part of speech.

Word	Parts of Speech	Abbreviation
schedule	*noun or verb*	*n. or v.*
free		
busy		
concentrate		
slowly		
carefully		
boring		
relax		
routine		

2 Choose the correct word to complete each sentence below. Use a dictionary if necessary to choose the correct part of speech.

1. I do my homework _____*slowly*_____.
   slow/slowly

2. I do not have enough _____ time.
   free/freedom

3. My _____ schedule sometimes gives me stress.
   busily/busy

4. I _____ when I read in English.
   concentrate/concentration

5. I do my homework very _____.
   <small>careful/carefully</small>

6. Riding on the bus _____ me.
   <small>bores/boring</small>

7. I usually _____ on the weekends.
   <small>relax/relaxing</small>

8. My daily _____ rarely changes.
   <small>routine/routinely</small>

9. She is a _____ person. She organizes her time
   <small>smartness/smart</small>

   _____.
   <small>wisely/wise</small>

Simple Present versus Present Progressive

Simple present verbs are used to describe regular activities, facts, routines, and actions that continue over time. They are commonly used in writing.

Present progressive verbs are used to describe actions that are in progress now or actions that are temporary or occur for a limited time. The present progressive is commonly used in speaking.

Simple Present	Present Progressive
Tam **lives** in an apartment.	Liu **is staying** with Tam.
His apartment **is** large.	Liu **is looking** for an apartment.
Tam **wakes** up early every day.	Liu **is sleeping** late today.
Tam **enjoys** the mornings.	Liu **is dreaming** about his new life.

Form the present progressive with a form of *be* plus the *-ing* form of the main verb. Add *not* to make negative statements.

   I **am taking** English 091 this term.
   You **are learning** more English every day.
   We **are not writing** a paragraph in English class today.

The verbs below are not commonly used in the present progressive.

Non-progressive Verbs	Example Sentences
Feelings and emotions: *like, love, hate, prefer, want, need*	Kathy **likes** to write. NOT Kathy is liking to write.
Mental states: *think, believe, understand, seem,* *forget, remember, know, mean*	She **understands** the homework. NOT She is understanding the homework.
Senses: *hear, see, smell, feel, sound*	Tom **hears** the phone. NOT Tom is hearing the phone.
Possession: *belong, own, have*	Mary **owns** her home. NOT Mary is owning her home.

3 Underline the verbs in the paragraph below. Write **PP** above present progressive verbs and **SP** above simple present verbs. In a group, tell why each is in the simple present or the present progressive.

─────────── **My Study Habits** ───────────

        SP
I <u>have</u> very good study habits. Right now I am taking two classes, algebra and English. Math class is easy. However, English 091 (writing), is difficult. My teacher gives me a lot of homework, so I am studying hard this semester. I always study by myself in my room. I use my computer and dictionary a lot. Sometimes, if I don't understand, I ask my sisters to help me. When I finish my homework, I usually write some vocabulary words that I don't know in my notebook. I am learning a lot in my writing class. That is because I have good study habits.

Tuyet Anh To, Vietnam

4 Complete the paragraph below with simple present or present progressive verbs. With a partner discuss why you chose each tense.

─────────── **Our Summer Schedule** ───────────

This summer my friend Samnang and I ____*are taking*____ summer
                             1. take

school classes. We usually _____ a long vacation, but right
                        2. have

now we _____ two classes. Every morning, I
       3. take

_____ up at 6 A.M. It usually _____ us about 45
4. wake   5. take

minutes to drive to school. Our classes _____ every day at 8
                        6. start

A.M. and _____ at 11 A.M. I _____ in the ESL
       7. end   8. be

level 1 class. I _____ a beginner. Samnang _____
         9. be   10. be

in level 3. This week the students in our class _____ the
                     11. study

present tense. Samnang _____ a computer science class, too,
            12. take

and she and her classmates _____ to make their own Web
               13. learn

DO IT YOURSELF
See pages 166–170
for more practice.
pages. I usually _____ to study in the summer, but this
          14. like, not

summer I _____ a lot.
    15. learn

Frequency Adverbs

Frequency adverbs express how often you do an action. The scale below shows the differences in the time meanings of frequency adverbs, from *always* (100 percent of the time) to *never* (0 percent of the time). Frequency adverbs are most commonly used with simple present verbs.

Always	Usually	Often/ Frequently	Sometimes	Rarely/ Seldom	Never
100%			50%		0%

I **rarely** go shopping with my husband.

I am **always** tired after a long shopping trip.

Usually I eat breakfast alone.

Put frequency adverbs after *be* but before other verbs.

I am **rarely** late to class.

I **usually** take the subway to school.

Some frequency adverbs (such as *sometimes, often, usually,* and *frequently*) can come at the beginning of a sentence.

Sometimes I eat breakfast. **Sometimes** I do not.

Often I see her jogging outside.

5 Read the following sentences and underline the frequency adverbs. Then rewrite the sentences to make them true for you by changing the frequency adverbs as necessary.

1. I ~~often~~ *rarely* spend hours watching television.

2. I never wake up early on my days off.

3. I am frequently tired after studying.

4. I sometimes forget my appointments.

5. I rarely have a lot of free time.

6. I am never afraid of being alone.

7. I often play soccer with my friends.

8. I seldom spend a long time choosing what to wear.

9. I am always happy to go shopping.

10. I never read in my free time.

6 Write sentences to describe how you spend your time. Use the words and phrases below with frequency adverbs from the chart on page 53.

1. keep my bedroom clean

   I usually keep my bedroom clean.

2. exercise every day

   _____

3. make my own dinner

   _____

4. bring my lunch to school

   _____

5. manage my time well

   _____

6. remember to do my homework

   _____

7. go to the movies

   _____

8. listen to music

   _____

DO IT YOURSELF
See pages 180–181
for more practice.

9. feel like I don't have enough time

   _____

Language Tip ■ Using *Take* to Tell About Time

The verb *take* tells how much time is needed to do an action. Use *take* in these ways:

- *It takes* + amount of time (for someone) + *to* + verb

  It takes a long time for me **to wake up** in the morning.

- *It takes* (someone) + amount of time + *to* + verb

  It takes me **two hours to travel** to my college.
  It doesn't take me **long** to eat breakfast.

- verb + *-ing* + *takes* + (someone) + amount of time

  Walking to school **takes me about an hour.**
  Doing the laundry always **takes too much time.**

7 Complete the sentences. How much time does it take you to do daily activities? Make the sentences true for you.

1. In the morning _____*it takes*_____ me about ____*45 minutes*____ to get ready to leave for work or school.

2. It doesn't _____ for me to take a shower.

3. Choosing something to wear _____.

4. Getting to school every day usually _____.

5. It _____ for me to do my homework.

6. It usually _____ to fall asleep at night.

Editing Your Writing

Use the checklist below to edit your work. Then rewrite your paragraph.

Editing Checklist

❏ Are parts of speech used correctly?

❏ Are present tense verbs used appropriately?

❏ Are frequency adverbs used correctly?

Journal Writing

Write a journal entry about two or three of the most useful tips in the reading on pages 42–43 for improving time management. Do you use these methods? Explain how and when. Do you want to try them? Explain why or why not.

PART 2

Reading for Writing

The reading on page 56, "How I Kill Time," will give you some ideas about what to do if you have extra time. As you read, think about what *you* do when you have extra time.

How I Kill Time

1   Drive-through banks, cell phones, microwave ovens—today's world is so full of time-saving devices that it's no wonder I occasionally have extra time. It's rare, but it can happen. Therefore, I created a few useful ways to kill time.

2   First of all, when I have time on my hands, I'm usually at home, so I begin by looking around for things to do. I organize my things. I fold all the clothes in my chest of drawers on one afternoon. Another morning, I reorganize the kitchen cabinets. I even alphabetize my CDs and videotapes.

3   My friend Sandy gave me a great idea. Whenever she has free time, she rearranges her furniture. Every time I visit, her living room looks different. The sofas are in a new place, or her bed is resting against another wall. I do the same, but only when there's another person who can help me.

4   I hate cleaning, but I don't mind dusting the furniture when I have free time. I'm messy, but even I don't like dust. Another thing I do is wash and wax my automobile. I love to drive through an automatic car wash and watch those big brushes washing the car.

5   If there's no good movie playing, I go shopping. I buy a lot of items that I regularly use. I buy two or three of everything: rolls of postage stamps, bars of soap, light bulbs, or paper products. I thank myself the next time that I need something.

6   If there's a child to keep me company, I have an easy way to pass the time. Every child knows how to amuse him- or herself. A park or a backyard becomes a great place to play war or look for bugs. A long bus ride to and from home feels like a great adventure. An office or apartment building is a great place to spend a day pushing buttons in an elevator.

7   Of course, if I *really* want to kill time, I can just shoot my clock!

Discussion   Discuss the following questions with a group.

1. What does the writer mean when she says she wants to *kill time*?
2. Which of her free-time activities are useful ways to spend extra time?
3. What do you do when *you* have *time to kill*?
4. What ways do you use to save time, or make the most of your time?

Language for Writing

1. Match each word with the correct definition. The words on the left are taken from the reading. The paragraph numbers are given in parentheses. Use a dictionary if necessary.

_b_ 1. devices (1)

____ 2. rare (1)

____ 3. occasionally (1)

____ 4. rearranges (3)

____ 5. items (5)

____ 6. amuse (6)

____ 7. source (6)

a. make someone laugh or smile

b. machines or tools that do special jobs

c. thing, person, or place that you get something from

d. changes the position or order of things

e. unusual

f. sometimes

g. things

2. Idioms are word groups with special meanings. English has many idioms for time. Read the list below. Look up any unfamiliar idioms under the word *time* in a dictionary.

take time off	run out of time	ahead of time
kill time	time on my hands	be on time
spare time	time flies	save time

3. Complete the sentences below with the idioms from Exercise 2. More than one idiom may be appropriate.

1. I need to ___take time off___ from work. I'm exhausted!

2. In American colleges, students should _____ for class. When they arrive late, they disrupt the lesson.

3. Whenever I have _____, I like to go to the movies.

4. _____ when you're having fun.

5. If you have any _____, read *Living up the Street* by Gary Soto.

6. Every time I take an algebra exam, I _____ before I can finish all the problems.

7. The movie starts at 5 P.M., but we plan to get there _____ so that we can get good seats.

8. To _____, I try to do all my shopping in one trip.

9. I like to _____ by going online and playing games.

Writing

Assignment for Part 2

Write a paragraph about *one* of the following topics:

■ Ways to use free time

■ Ways to save time

To write your paragraph, follow the steps of the writing process, beginning with Getting Ideas.

STEP 1

Getting Ideas

1. Brainstorm ideas in a group. One person in the group should take notes. List activities that you do when you have extra time. Then make a list of activities that are good ways to save time. Decide which topic best fits your *own* daily activities.

2. After you choose one of the two topics, freewrite for about 10 minutes. Start your freewriting with one of the following sentences:

   I enjoy many activities in my spare time.

   I have many ways to save time.

3. Read over your freewriting. Circle the sentences that relate to your topic. Cross out any sentences that are not useful. Share your freewriting with a classmate who chose the same topic. Write down any new ideas that you get from your partner.

STEP 2

Organizing

1. In your freewriting, group the sentences about each activity together. Do not jump from one activity to another.

2. Write a topic sentence that describes ways that you use extra time or ways that you save time. Your topic sentence can be general or more specific.

   General: I do many things when I have time to kill.
   Specific: When I have extra time, I listen to music or skateboard.

   General: I save time in many ways.
   Specific: Being organized at home and at school helps save me time.

3. As you did with your freewriting sentences, organize the other sentences in your paragraph into activities, such as listening to music or skateboarding. Add details about each activity.

STEP 3

Writing

Write the first draft of your paragraph. Use your topic sentence, the information from your freewriting, and your organization plan.

STEP 4

Revising

Work with a partner. Read each other's paragraph. Write comments on your partner's paper in the margins. Use the checklist below as a guide. Then read your partner's comments and make any necessary changes.

- ❏ Does the paragraph begin with a topic sentence that tells ways to use extra time or ways to save time?
- ❏ Do the rest of the sentences support this main idea?
- ❏ Are the supporting sentences organized so that they tell about one activity at a time?

STEP 5

Editing

Use the following explanations and activities to help you edit your writing.

Grammar and Mechanics

Prepositions of Time

At, on, and **in** are prepositions, another common part of speech. Use these prepositions plus nouns or noun phrases to show the time of an action.

- Use *at* + the time.

    My class starts **at 10 A.M.**

- Use *on* + names of days/*day/the weekend(s).*

    I work **on Saturday.**
    On my days off, I sleep late.
    He goes out **on the weekends.**

- Use *in* + months/years/parts of the year/parts of the day

    Sara sleeps late **in the morning.**
    Our semester ends **in May.**
    I am taking one class **in the summer.**

- Note exceptions:

    I love to read **at night/at noon/at midnight.**

1 Complete the following sentences with *at, in,* or *on.*

1. My busy school semester begins _____*in*_____ September.

2. I attend classes _____ Tuesdays and Thursdays.

3. _____ those days, I wake up _____ 5:30 A.M.

4. My first class begins _____ 8 A.M.

5. _____ noon, I eat lunch in the cafeteria.

6. _____ the afternoon, I have one class.

7. I leave college _____ 2 P.M. and go to work.

8. After work, I eat dinner, watch TV, and study. I go to bed
   _____ midnight.

9. _____ Mondays, Wednesdays, and Fridays, I do not have
   classes, so I work eight hours a day _____ those days.

10. _____ the weekends, I relax and enjoy myself.

DO IT YOURSELF
See pages 181–183
for more practice.

Commas

A comma (,) provides a brief pause, or stop, between ideas within a sentence. Notice how a student uses commas in the following paragraph:

> I work at a laundry. The name of the laundry is "Betty Brite Cleaners," and it is located on Frankford Avenue. While I am working, I am also taking courses at CCP. I came to America one year ago. At that time, I started to work there. I wash, dry, and fold clothing. I like my job, but it is sometimes tiring.

The chart below gives rules for using commas.

Rule	Example
1. Put a comma after a phrase at the beginning of a sentence.	**At that time,** I started to work at my new job.
2. Put a comma before coordinating conjunctions (*and, but, yet, so, for, or, nor*) when there is a subject and verb before and after the conjunction.	The name of the laundry is Betty Brite Cleaners**, and** it is located on Frankford Avenue. I like my job**, but** it is sometimes tiring.
3. Put a comma after a clause (a group of words with a subject and a verb) beginning with words such as *when, while, after, because, if,* or *even though.*	**While I am working,** I am also taking courses at CCP.

Rule	Example
4. Use a comma after each item in a list of three or more items.	I wash, dry, and fold clothing.
5. Put a comma after each part of a place name.	Farid lives in Washington, D.C., in a nice neighborhood.
6. Put a comma between the day and the year in a date.	Ha graduated from high school on June 1, 1999.

2 The sentences below are missing commas. Add commas using the rules from the chart above. Write the rule number(s) next to the sentence to explain your use of commas.

1. When Uyen Nguyen finished her first week at Miami-Dade Community College, she felt overwhelmed. ___Rule 3___

2. At home Uyen helps her mother shop prepare meals and do the housework. _____

3. She allows herself some leisure time but she uses the time wisely. _____

4. For example she watches television to have fun and to learn English. _____

5. When she has time she goes to the beach with friends. _____

6. She works on Thursdays and Saturdays and she has classes on Mondays Wednesdays and Fridays. _____

7. She calls her sister in Lafayette Louisiana. _____

8. Uyen started going to college on September 7 2000. _____

9. In five years she hopes to have a good job. _____

DO IT YOURSELF
See page 187 for more practice.

Editing Your Writing

Use the checklist below to edit your work. Then rewrite your paragraph.

Editing Checklist

❑ Are prepositions of time used correctly?

❑ Are commas used appropriately?

On Your Own

Personal Editing Log

Keep a record of your most common language errors so that you can find and correct your own mistakes.

1. Read over the Personal Editing Log chart at the back of the book, on page 199. Use this as a model for your own Editing Log.

2. Look over the paragraphs that you wrote in Chapters 1, 2, and 3. Record your language errors in your Personal Editing Log. Ask your instructor to help you if you are not sure which area to check. The next time you write, pay attention to these areas in order to correct your own mistakes.

Personal Spelling List

1. Work with a partner. Study the spellings of the words below. Then read each word while your partner writes it down. Ask your instructor to help you pronounce the words if necessary. Then switch roles and write down the words as your partner reads them.

_____ when	_____ frequently	_____ balance
_____ activities	_____ sometimes	_____ first
_____ schedule	_____ typical	_____ calendar
_____ routine	_____ busy	_____ evening
_____ usually	_____ a lot	_____ afternoon
_____ Saturday	_____ habit	_____ finally

2. Check (✔) the words that you misspelled. Then add these words to your Personal Spelling List.

3. Look over the writing you have done in Chapter 3. Find any other words that you misspelled. Add these words to your Personal Spelling List. Study the words before you write your next paper.

More Writing Practice

Write a paragraph on one of the following topics.

REMEMBER   Begin your paragraph with a topic sentence. Make sure all the sentences relate to the main idea. When you finish, read over your paragraph. Revise and edit it.

1. **Free Time**

   Describe how someone you know spends his or her free time. You may write about a family member, a friend, a teacher, or a co-worker. In the topic sentence, describe what the person likes to do in his or her free time. Include details such as the following: What does the person do? Where does he or she go? With whom? Why does he or she spend free time this way?

2. **A Morning Person or a Night Owl**

Are you a morning person—someone who wakes up early and can work well in the morning? Or are you a night owl who stays up late, works at night, and does not like to get up in the morning? In your topic sentence, tell which kind of person you are. Give examples of your daily activities to show that you are a morning person or a night owl.

3. **A Good or Bad Memory**

Are you good or bad at remembering things? If you have a good memory, explain how you are able to remember activities and dates, people's names, or the location of things. If you have a poor memory, write about what you forget: activities and dates, people's names, the location of things, or anything else.

Chapter Goals

Reflect on the learning goals for Chapter 3. Check the goal(s) that you have begun to reach. Ask your instructor about goals you are not reaching, or practice by writing a paragraph on one of the topics above.

Chapter Goals Checklist

❑ Write a topic sentence and supporting sentences.

❑ Use parts of speech correctly.

❑ Use simple present and present progressive verbs appropriately.

❑ Use frequency adverbs.

❑ Use prepositions of time.

❑ Use commas correctly.

On the Town

Approaching the Topic

Public places, such as parks, shopping centers, museums, restaurants, libraries, or historical buildings, make a town or city unique. In Chapter 4, you will read and write paragraphs about unique public places.

1. Look at the photograph. What public place does this scene remind you of in your town, city, or area? Tell your class.

2. When you have out-of-town visitors, where do you take them? Why?

3. Do you like to shop? What is your favorite place to shop? Why?

PART 1

Reading for Writing

The reading below describes the world's largest mall, located in Alberta, Canada. The title is "The World's Most Unusual Mall" because this place has many unusual features.

The World's Most Unusual Mall

World Waterpark at West Edmonton Mall

1   West Edmonton Mall in Alberta, Canada, is no ordinary shopping mall. It has the typical features of a mall—for example, lots of shops on different floors, all under one roof. However, with 5.3 million square feet of shopping and some very unusual attractions, it is the world's largest and most complete shopping and entertainment complex.

2   The mall is located in an area known for its natural beauty, but it is still Alberta's number one tourist attraction. How has it become so popular? For one thing, it has more than 800 stores and more than 110 restaurants. It also has some unusual attractions—the world's largest indoor amusement park, the world's largest indoor water park, an ice-skating rink, a miniature golf course, 26 movie theaters, and a Las Vegas–style casino.

3   In fact, the mall offers entertainment for people of all ages. Visitors young and old enjoy the submarine rides. Under the water, they can see colorful sea life and the remains of a ship. Children especially like swimming in the huge pools and sliding down the high water slides in the World Waterpark. A popular attraction for local teenagers is the Rock 'n Ride Dance Party, an amusement park with rock music. Bars and a casino appeal to adults.

4   West Edmonton Mall is so unique that it attracts millions of tourists from around the world each year. It even provides a hotel to encourage visitors to stay longer. At this mall, visitors can shop, eat, and enjoy a wide range of extraordinary attractions.

Discussion   Discuss the following questions in a group.

1. What makes West Edmonton Mall unusual?

2. What features of the mall are described most clearly? Which words make the description clear? Underline them.

3. How are shopping malls in your town similar to or different from this one?

Language for   1. Match each vocabulary word or phrase with the correct definition. The
Writing   words on the left are taken from the reading on page 65. The paragraph numbers are given in parentheses.

_h_ 1. features (1)

_____ 2. floors (1)

_____ 3. complex (*n.*) (1)

_____ 4. number one (2)

_____ 5. offers (3)

_____ 6. unique (4)

_____ 7. attracts (4)

_____ 8. a wide range of (4)

a. the best or most important thing or person in a group

b. makes someone interested in something

c. a large variety of

d. provides, gives to someone

e. unusual, being the only one of its kind

f. levels inside a building

g. a group of buildings or one large building used for a particular purpose

h. parts of something that you notice because they are important, or typical

2. Use the vocabulary words above to complete the paragraph.

The Galleria

The Galleria is a _____ shopping center in Houston, Texas, that has special _____ like an ice rink and a hotel. The Galleria is a _____ of office buildings and large stores connected together. With many different stores and restaurants on three different _____, the Galleria has _____ shopping and eating places—large department stores as well as small specialty shops, and fancy restaurants next to fast-food cafes. The center also _____ many services for tourists—a hotel, banks, and travel agencies. In fact, the Galleria _____ tourists from all over the world. It is the _____ shopping mall in the city.

Writing

Assignment for Part 1

Write a paragraph describing a shopping mall, a market, or a store. To write your paragraph, follow the steps of the writing process, beginning with Getting Ideas.

STEP 1

Getting Ideas

Details

Writing often includes many details. A detail is a single fact or piece of information about something. Read the two sentences. Which sentence gives you a clearer picture of an electronics store?

1. Many television sets are displayed against the walls.
2. Television sets in all sizes—from 9 to 55 inches wide—are displayed against bright red walls.

Sentence 2 gives a clearer picture of the store because it includes specific details—the television sets *in all sizes, 9 to 55 inches wide,* and *bright red walls.*

Notice how to go from a general topic to more specific detail.

■ **Names of places, people, or things**

General	*More Specific Detail*
the mall	Willow Grove Mall
stores	women's clothing stores

■ **"Sensory" details that tell what you** *see, hear, smell,* **or** *feel*

flowers	sweet-smelling yellow flowers
noise	the noisy laughter of children

■ **Dates and numbers**

many stores	more than 200 stores
a long time ago	in 1975

1. Read the descriptions of two shopping places on page 68. In a group, identify general topics and specific details.

South Street

Especially at night, South Street is like a street party. Colorful neon lights advertise the wide variety of stores and restaurants—from bars, antique shops, and bookstores, to wild clothing shops and theaters. Noisy crowds of people spill in and out of the shops and cafes. They line up outside popular clubs and restaurants. Friendly people laugh and shout as you walk by. Music comes out of a record store where live bands play on the roof. There is always a lot of fun at night.

Shopper's Paradise

Visitors to south central Texas crowd the small streets of historic Gruene for a bit of old-fashioned shopping. Gruene is a shopper's paradise. The little town is full of interesting shops such as an old-fashioned, 1800s-style general store that sells household items, several antique stores, and craft shops that display local artists' work. While you explore the main streets, your nose detects the smell of spicy barbecue and homemade baked goods. No one leaves Gruene hungry! And few people leave without buying some tempting item to help them remember their visit to historic Gruene.

2. Choose a shopping place to describe. Visit the place, and take notes about it. Include details. If you do not know the words in English, write your ideas down in your language, and translate them later. Here are a student's notes about a local produce market.

Many choices of fruit, vegetables

Low prices—most items cost $1.00 per bag
Example: 8 Delicious apples/$1.00

Popular place, always busy, but plenty of parking

Friendly service

Good selection of flowers and plants inside/outside

Lines move fast

Yard and house decorations

Good organization—easy to find items
Large chalkboard tells fruit, vegetables for sale and price

Organizing | Graphic Organizer

A *graphic organizer* is a drawing that shows ideas connected to each other in different ways. You can organize your notes with a graphic organizer like the one below.

The writer used a graphic organizer to organize his notes about Produce Junction. He wrote the name of the market in a box in the center. Then he read over his notes and put them into categories. Each category is a feature of the place, like *service* and *price.* He put a circle around each feature and drew lines off the circles to add details about each one.

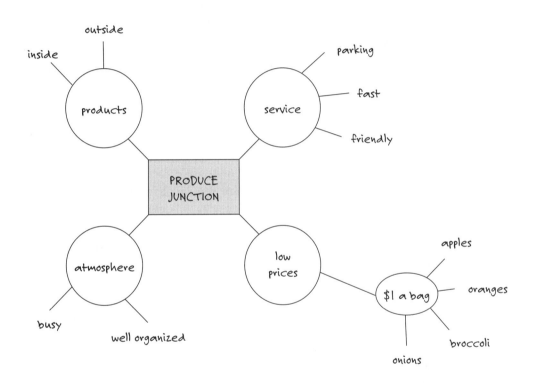

1. Work with a partner. Look at the graphic organizer and answer the questions.

   a. How many main features are there?

   b. Which features have the most details?

   c. Which features do you think the writer will include in his paragraph?

2. Now read the paragraph on page 70 and answer the questions.

Produce Junction

Produce Junction is a popular market in my town. It's always busy because it has good prices, products, and service. Inside the market, there's a long counter with a fruit line on the left and a vegetable line on the right. The sellers quickly call, "Next?" and expect customers to have their orders and money ready. The first-time customer can become confused. Still, the sellers are friendly. A large board overhead tells the produce for sale that day and the cost. One dollar buys most items—for example, 10 pounds of yellow onions, two heads of broccoli, 10 small Valencia oranges, or 8 large Golden Delicious apples. In the center of the store and outside, plants and flowers are sold by the bunch or the pot. The prices, selection, and service make this market a busy place. I'm glad that the Produce Junction is in my neighborhood.

---

   a. Did the writer organize the paragraph well? Explain.

   b. How did making the graphic organizer help the writer?

3. In your notebook, make a graphic organizer about your shopping place. Use your notes and the model on page 69. Group your ideas into the main features of the shopping place. Draw a circle around each feature. Then draw lines off each circle to add details about each feature.

4. Choose two or three of the most interesting features to include in your paragraph.

5. Write a topic sentence that introduces the shopping center by name and gives your main idea or your impression of the place.

6. In the rest of your paragraph, discuss each feature separately.

STEP 3

Writing

Write the first draft of your paragraph. Use your brainstorming notes, your graphic organizer, and your topic sentence. Remember to include specific details.

STEP 4

Revising

Work with a partner. Read each other's paragraph. Write comments on your partner's paper in the margins. Use the checklist below as a guide. Then read your partner's comments about your paragraph and make any necessary changes.

❏ Does the paragraph have a topic sentence that gives the name of the shopping place and tells something important or unusual about it?

❏ Do all the sentences in the paragraph support this main idea?

❏ Does the paragraph include specific details about the place?

STEP 5

Editing

Use the following explanations and activities to help you edit your writing.

Grammar

Singular and Plural Nouns

Common count nouns have singular and plural forms. To form the plural for most nouns, you add **-s** to the singular form.

Singular	Plural
Jacek needs a computer.	Ting has two computer**s**.
The store has one cashier.	Department stores have several cashier**s**.
The package is lying on the counter.	The packages are lying on the counter**s**.

- Some plural nouns are irregular. They do not add **-s**.

    man—men   woman—women   child—children

    person—people   fish—fish

- Non-count nouns (words for things that are not counted) do not usually have plural forms.

    milk   flour   air   homework   furniture   happiness

- Proper nouns (names of people or places) normally do not have plural forms.

    Ricardo   Miami   Almeda Mall   The Museum of Modern Art

---

1 Identify the singular and plural nouns in the paragraph below. Underline the nouns and write **S** above the singular nouns and **P** above the plural nouns.

Permanent <u>markets</u> known as <u>bazaars</u> are open every <u>day</u> in places like Damascus, Baghdad, Cairo, and Tunis. In many cases, families have sold their goods in the same spaces for generations. One of the largest and most exciting bazaars in the Middle East is in the city of Aleppo in Syria. Located in the heart of the city, this bazaar is one of the oldest in the world. The local people call their central bazaar a "city market."

Using the Plural Form

It's important to know whether a noun should be singular or plural. If you use a quantity word such as **many, some, both, several,** or **a lot of** with a count noun, you need the plural.

Incorrect	Correct
I have many friend.	I have many **friends**.
Both my parent live in Vietnam.	Both my **parents** live in Vietnam.

Some **-s** spellings of nouns are irregular. Review the spelling rules for **-s** forms of simple present tense verbs on page 37 of Chapter 2. These same rules apply to the **-s** plural forms of nouns.

Jay needs a new **watch**.	That store sells Timex **watches**.
Nora can't eat just one french **fry**.	She often buys french **fries** at the mall.

2 Correct the errors in forming plural nouns in the sentences below. With a partner, compare your answers.

1. In my opinion, there are some advantage^s of students' having part-time job^s after school.
2. Most part-time job for students are in the afternoon and nighttime.
3. They have many opportunity to meet people and open their mind.
4. They don't have to ask their parent for money.
5. How many people work in your office?
6. In some place, when you apply for a job, the first thing they ask you is if you graduated from high school.
7. Today, many company need people with several good skill.
8. My friend Baha misses too many class.

3 For each plural noun below, write a sentence about shopping.

1. bargains _____I find a lot of bargains at the dollar store._____
2. groceries _____
3. shoppers _____
4. department stores _____
5. high prices _____
6. salespeople _____
7. shopping malls _____
8. choices _____

DO IT YOURSELF
See pages 184–185 and 191–193 for more practice.

> ### *There Is* and *There Are*
>
> Sentences that start with **there is** or **there are** introduce a subject.
>
> > **There is** a well-known **zoo** in my hometown, Guangzhou. The zoo is famous because it has panda bears.
>
> In the sentence above, *there is* introduces the noun *zoo.*
>
> ■ Use *there is* when the subject is singular.
>
> > **There is** a **food court** in the shopping mall.
>
> ■ Use *there are* when the subject is plural.
>
> > **There are** many historical **places** in Boston.
>
> ■ To make sentences negative, add *not* after *be.*
>
> > There **is not (isn't)** any food in the refrigerator.
> > There **are not (aren't)** any movie theaters in my neighborhood.

4 Complete the following sentences with *there is* or *there are.*

1. _There are_____ many places to eat at my college.

2. _____ two study lounges in the Bonnell Building.

3. _____ many street food trucks outside my college.

4. _____ also a small cafeteria in the Student Life Building.

5. Sometimes my friends and I walk a few blocks to have lunch because _____ a good restaurant right next to the college.

6. _____ a diner on Spring Garden Street.

7. When _____ a special event on campus like the International Festival, we get food from the student organizations.

8. _____ also some food stands inside the college that sell drinks, bagels, muffins, and cookies.

9. If _____ no time to go to a restaurant, I buy something to eat from the snack machines.

10. _____ enough quiet places to study at my school.

5 Write sentences with *there is* and *there are* to describe your town or city.

1. skyscraper/skyscrapers *There aren't any skyscrapers in Gruene, Texas.*

2. movie theater/movie theaters _____

3. park/parks _____

4. museum/museums _____

5. library/libraries _____

6. Italian restaurant/restaurants _____

7. historical building/buildings _____

8. river/rivers _____

DO IT YOURSELF
See pages 160–161
for more practice.

Prepositions of Location

Prepositions such as **at, on,** and **in** can also indicate location.

■ **at** = general location—nearby or possibly in

Jane is **at** the airport.
The train is **at** Grand Central Station.

■ **on** = on top of, on a surface
There are flowers **on** every table.
The picture is **on** the wall.

■ **in** = inside, within an area

The food is **in** the refrigerator.
The zoo is **in** the park.

In addition, **at, on,** and **in** have some very specific uses with specific places.

■ Use **at** + address

The museum is located **at** 1700 Main Street.

■ Use **on** + street/floor

It is **on** Washington Avenue.

The store is **on** the third floor.

■ Use **in** + country/state/city

It is **in** Springfield.

Other prepositions of location are:

next to	behind	across from	beside
near	in front of	to the right/left of	between

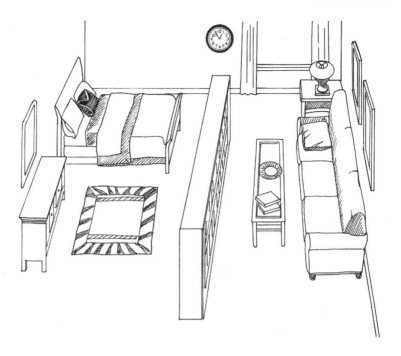

In this apartment . . .

The bed is **next to** the wall.

A chest of drawers is **near** the bed.

There is a rug **in front of** the chest of drawers.

There's a long bookcase **between** the bed and the sofa.

The sofa is **across from** the bookcase.

A small table is **beside** the sofa.

The bed is **behind** the bookcase.

A clock is on the wall **to the left of** the window.

Language Tip ■ Location Expressions

Here are two common ways to write about location:

- *Be* + preposition

    Liberty Center **is near** the train station.

    The sandwich shops **are next to** a Chinese café.

- *Be* + *located* + preposition

    The mall **is located on** Main Street.

    The Galleria and Richmond Square **are located in** southwest Houston.

6 Use a preposition of location to complete the sentences about downtown Springfield, shown below. More than one preposition may be correct.

1. The library is located _____ 1500 Broad Street _____ Springfield.

2. The bank is _____ Main Street.

3. The coffee shop is _____ the shoe store.

4. Mama's Restaurant is _____ the antique shop.

5. The flower shop is _____ the antique shop and the theater.

6. The bank is _____ Main and Broad Streets.

7. The shoe store and the coffee shop are _____ the library.

8. There are many businesses _____ Main Street.

9. Many people do their shopping _____ Springfield.

DO IT YOURSELF
See pages 183–184 for more practice.

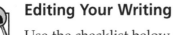 **Editing Your Writing**

Use the checklist below to edit your work. Then rewrite your paragraph.

Editing Checklist

❑ Are singular and plural nouns used correctly?

❑ Are *there is* and *there are* used correctly?

❑ Are prepositions of location used correctly?

Journal Writing   Write a journal entry about shopping habits. Include details such as the following: Do you enjoy shopping? What types of shopping do you prefer? For example, do you like clothes shopping or grocery shopping better? Do you like to shop alone or with others? Do you prefer online shopping? Explain why.

PART 2

Reading for Writing

The reading below describes a Los Angeles street fair, one of the most popular places in the city. As you read, think about how this public place compares to ones where you live.

A Los Angeles Street Fair

Santee Alley in the Garment District of downtown Los Angeles is a lively, colorful street market. It is a great place to find an incredible variety of clothing. Also, it's a fun place just to walk around and watch people. The Alley is just one part of the Garment District, a 50-block area between Broadway and Wall Streets, and Seventh and Pico Boulevard. On either side of the street, shop after shop sells jackets, shirts, dresses, skirts, pants, blue jeans, and fabrics. Every type of clothing you can imagine hangs from racks on the sidewalks. Street stands display purses, luggage, jewelry, sunglasses, toys, and watches. Vendors shout or sing to loud music to get shoppers' attention. When buyers think the prices are too high, they argue with the sellers. People can be heard discussing prices in English, Spanish, and other languages. The Alley is open daily, but the weekends are the liveliest. Many come here just to see the people, since the customers vary as much as the merchandise. Smells of hot sandwiches and fresh fruit also tempt visitors. Santee Alley is one of Los Angeles's most entertaining public places.

Discussion   Discuss the following questions in a group.

1. Which features of Santee Alley make it like a "street fair"?
2. Which details are specific names of people, places, or things?
3. Which details are things you can hear or smell?
4. Think about an outdoor market that you know. Is it similar to or different from Santee Alley? In what ways?

Language for Writing   Complete the sentences below with words from the list. In a group, compare your answers. Use a dictionary if necessary.

argue	variety	bargains	entertain
tempt	display	styles	merchandise

1. There is a large _____ of goods for sale in Santee Alley.

2. The shops in Santee Alley sell many _____ of clothing.

3. Vendors shout to get customers' attention. They want to _____ people to buy their products.

4. One seller sings about his products to _____ customers who walk by.

5. If you think a price is too high, you can _____ about it with the seller.

6. You can often find _____ at street markets—great products for lower prices than you pay in department stores.

7. Street vendors _____ their goods on tables and racks.

8. Each seller puts his _____ out carefully so that customers will look at it.

Writing

Assignment for Part 2

Write a paragraph about a public place in your town or city. To write your paragraph, follow the steps of the writing process, beginning with Getting Ideas.

STEP 1

Getting Ideas

1. Brainstorm in a group or alone. Think of public places in your town or city that are unusual, famous, or special to you, such as a restaurant, a library, a park, a museum, or a historic place. Make a list.

2. From your list, choose a place that you know well. Think about what makes the place special. Freewrite for about 10 minutes about the place. Begin your freewriting with this sentence.

    _____ is special because . . .
    <small>Name of place</small>

3. Work with a partner. Read and discuss each other's freewriting. Add notes from your discussion.

4. Read over your freewriting. Underline the sentences that you want to include in your paragraph. These sentences should support your main idea about the place. Cross out any ideas that are not useful.

STEP 2

Organizing

Topic Sentence

In a description, the topic sentence can describe your *strongest impression,* or main feeling about the place. Ask yourself these questions:

- What is the first thing that comes to mind about this place?
- Does the place have any important or unusual features?
- Is the size or activity of the place important or unusual?

Look at the examples of topic sentences below. Each sentence introduces a place and gives the writer's strongest impression about the place.

┌──── Topic ────┐   ┌─ Strongest impression ─┐
1. Pike Place Market is a busy and crowded marketplace.

┌─ Topic ─┐   ┌──────── Strongest impression ────────┐
2. Marshall's sells quality clothes and household goods at low prices.

1. Read the following descriptions. In a group, discuss each one. What is the topic sentence? What is the writer's strongest impression of the place? Do the details in the paragraph support the topic sentence?

Barbes

The Barbes quarter in Paris is a popular shopping area for North African immigrants. The people and the shops give you the feeling that you are in an Arab country. The area has fewer Westerners and more Arabs—Muslim men, typically with dark hair and mustaches, and women, many of whom wear long dresses and head coverings. The shop owners and customers speak Arabic and Berber to the predominantly Algerian and Moroccan customers. Traditional North African clothing and food are sold along with modern goods. The narrow streets and small shops remind visitors of the famous Casbah marketplace in Algiers. The sidewalks are crowded with goods from the shops. The streets are also lined with stands covered with cloth ceilings. All in all, Barbes is like a miniature Arab marketplace.

Covent Garden

Although it started as a produce market, the Covent Garden shopping area in London is now filled with many interesting shops. Established in 1661, Covent Garden soon became the market for London and the country's southeast, and all the main shops and restaurants bought their fruits, flowers, and vegetables there. In the 1920s, however, Covent Garden's market closed. For many years, the large warehouse and surrounding area remained empty. Then, in the 1960s, new shops began to open. By the 1980s, the large market building was reopened as a shopping center. Today, many stores sell fashionable clothing, perfumes, books, and gifts for the home. These stores are located inside the original market building and along the streets nearby. Once again, Covent Garden is a popular shopping area.

2. Using your freewriting from page 78, write a topic sentence stating one or two important or unusual features of your marketplace or store.

STEP 3

Writing

Write the first draft of your paragraph. Begin with your topic sentence. Use your freewriting for supporting ideas. Make sure that the sentences in your paragraph include specific details that support the main idea in the topic sentence.

STEP 4

Revising

Work with a partner. Read each other's paragraph. Write comments on your partner's paper in the margins. Use the checklist below as a guide. Then read your partner's comments and make any necessary changes.

❑ Does the topic sentence introduce the place and the writer's strongest impression about it?

❑ Do the rest of the sentences support the topic sentence?

❑ Are there specific details about the place?

❑ Are the ideas clear? If something is not clear, put a question mark next to the part you do not understand. Ask you partner to explain it. Help your partner revise the composition.

STEP 5

Editing

Use the following explanations and activities to help you edit your writing.

Grammar

Object Pronouns

As you learned in Chapter 2, many sentences have a subject, verb, and object. The object may be a noun, a noun phrase, or an object pronoun. Compare the objects in these sentences:

OBJECT NOUN PHRASE
We met **the Hatcher family** at the airport.

OBJECT PRONOUN
We saw **them** at the baggage claim area.

Compare the subject and object pronouns in the chart following and read the example sentences.

Subject Pronouns	Object Pronouns	Example Sentences
I	me	My supervisor likes **me** very much.
you	you	Sasha loves **you.**
he	him	I drove **him** to work yesterday.
she	her	Anna's mother sees **her** every night.
it	it	Give me that pen if you don't need **it.**
we	us	Please help **us.**
they	them	Don't throw away the papers. We need **them.**

Also, use object pronouns after prepositions.

My son depends **on me.**
I'm talking **to him.**
We ride **with them** to school.
She is waving **at us.**

1 Complete each sentence with the correct object pronoun.

1. Rodolfo wants to buy something. The store clerk is helping ___*him*___ .

2. Thu has many bags of groceries. She is carrying _____ in her arms.

3. Nina is buying a new TV. She plans to put _____ in her bedroom.

4. Street vendors outside my school sell Chinese food. I like _____ better than the American food in our cafeteria.

5. Rob loves homegrown tomatoes. He buys _____ from the farmer's market.

6. Susan is my roommate. She always helps _____ with the housework.

7. We are going to a flea market. Do you want to go with _____?

8. Loud music is playing in the record store. You can hear _____ from far away.

9. My husband hates to go clothes shopping. It drives _____ crazy!

10. Maria doesn't have a car. I often drive _____ when she needs to go shopping.

2 Complete the following paragraph. Use appropriate subject or object pronouns. With a partner, compare your answers.

—————————— **Arriving in a New Country** ——————————

The day that ____*I*____ arrived with my family in the United States, _____ felt very excited. _____ were in a new country. Everything around _____ was new. My family and _____ felt very happy. However, when _____ got to Florida, _____ needed help. _____ were lucky because _____ already had good friends living there. On the day _____ arrived in Miami, _____ met _____ at the airport and helped _____ rent an apartment. _____ were very glad to meet our friends again. _____ had not seen _____ for more than five years. Our friends spent a lot of time with _____. _____ told _____ what _____ should do. _____ had many problems at first, but _____ were still very happy to be in the United States.

Inna Neminskaya, Ukraine

DO IT YOURSELF
See pages 178–179 for more practice.

Possessive Adjectives

Possessive adjectives—**my, your, his, her, its, our,** and **their**—show that something belongs to someone or something.

Compare the subject pronouns and the possessive adjectives in the chart and the sentences.

Subject Pronouns	Possessive Adjectives	Example Sentences
I	my	I like to have **my** coffee before breakfast.
you	your	Do you add sugar to **your** tea?
he	his	Sendji always brings **his** water bottle to class.
she	her	Katya is enjoying **her** hot chocolate.
it	its	What a thirsty cat! It is drinking all of **its** milk.
we	our	We take **our** coffee with cream.
they	their	My children prefer to drink **their** sodas with straws.

Don't confuse possessive adjectives with contractions of subject pronouns and *be.*

CONTRACTION   POSSESSIVE ADJECTIVE
He's always happy. **His** family is happy, too.

CONTRACTION   POSSESSIVE ADJECTIVE
You're a good student. You always do **your** homework.

CONTRACTION   POSSESSIVE ADJECTIVE
They're good friends. **Their** families spend a lot of time together.

CONTRACTION   POSSESSIVE ADJECTIVE
It's important to change the oil in your car regularly. **Its** tires should be checked, too.

3 Complete each sentence with the correct possessive adjective.

1. Macy's is a well-known department store. ____*Its*____ housewares department has just about everything for the home.

2. Helen loves shopping. Every month _____ credit card bill is high.

3. The students saw many famous works of art on _____ trip to the museum.

4. Do you prefer to spend _____ money on clothes or eating out?

5. My brother bought _____ wife a diamond necklace for Christmas.

6. Roberto takes _____ mother shopping every Saturday.

7. Andres and Rudy often spend time together on the weekends. On Monday, _____ classmates always ask them what they did.

8. George's brother works in a produce market. _____ duties include packing fruit and vegetables and sweeping the floor.

9. We often find bargains at the flea market near _____ house.

DO IT YOURSELF
See pages 179–180 for more practice.

Editing Your Writing

Use the checklist below to edit your work. Then rewrite your paragraph.

Editing Checklist

❑ Do all the sentences have a subject and verb?

❑ Are object pronouns used correctly?

❑ Are possessive adjectives used correctly?

On Your Own

Personal Spelling List

1. Continue to work on your spelling problems. Look over the paragraphs you wrote in this chapter. Add misspelled words to your Personal Spelling List in your notebook.

2. Study the correct spellings of the words on your list. Work with a partner. Test each other on the spellings. Ask your instructor to help you pronounce words, if necessary.

Personal Editing Log

Continue to keep track of the types of grammar and mechanics errors that you often make. After your teacher returns your paragraphs from this chapter, read them over, and put checkmarks in your Personal Editing Log to identify the types of errors that you made.

More Writing Practice

Write a paragraph on one of the following topics.

REMEMBER   Follow correct paragraph format. Begin your paragraph with a topic sentence. Make all the sentences relate to the main idea. Include details that support your topic sentence. When you finish, read over your paragraph to revise and edit it.

1. **My Neighborhood**

   Write a paragraph describing your neighborhood. Begin with a topic sentence that tells the name of your neighborhood and its most important or interesting feature or features. Include details such as the following: the location and size of the neighborhood, the kinds of houses and other buildings. Provide details about the sights, sounds, and smells.

2. **A Center of Activity on Campus**

   Describe a busy place on your school campus, such as the library, the cafeteria, or the bookstore. Go to the place and take notes about what you see, hear, and smell. In the topic sentence, give the name of the place and your school and describe the main function or an important or unusual feature of the place.

3. **A Relaxing Place**

   Describe a place that helps you to relax. Write about a place in your home country or a place where you are living. If you cannot go to the place, take notes about what you remember. In the topic sentence, give the specific name and/or location of the place and explain why it makes you relax. Include specific details.

Chapter Goals Reflect on the learning goals for Chapter 4. Check the goal(s) that you are beginning to achieve. Ask your instructor for help about areas that you still do not understand. Write an extra paragraph, using the topics on page 84.

Chapter Goals Checklist

❑ Add details to your writing.

❑ Use graphic organizers.

❑ Use singular and plural nouns correctly.

❑ Use *there is* and *there are*.

❑ Use prepositions of location.

❑ Use object pronouns.

❑ Use possessive adjectives.

Celebrations

Chapter Goals

- Use chronological order.
- Recognize a concluding sentence.
- Use the simple past tense.
- Use correct word order.
- Give background information.
- Learn to spell verbs with the *-ed* form.

Approaching the Topic

Special celebrations—birthdays, weddings, births, graduations, and holidays—are moments that brighten our lives. In Chapter 5, you will read personal stories of celebrations and write about memorable events in your life.

1. Look at the photographs. What types of celebrations are taking place? How do you think the people are feeling?

2. Can you think of similar celebrations in your experience? Describe the events.

PART 1

Reading for Writing

The reading below relates a student's feelings about a special birthday. As you read, think about how your experience of a special day compares with that of the writer.

My Sixteenth Birthday

My sixteenth birthday was the happiest day of my life. However, the day started badly. I walked into the house, which was quiet, as usual. Even though I knew there was no one there, I still felt disappointed. I sat down on the sofa and stared at the ceiling. I was so bored. "How could everyone forget my birthday?" I wondered. My parents were still at their restaurant, so I didn't know what else I could do on this special day. Finally, I went to bed because I felt so strange. While I was sleeping, I heard a noise like someone walking around the house. I got up and went down to the living room, where I saw a dim light coming from the kitchen. I followed the light into the kitchen. At the same time, a lot of voices came out of the kitchen. "Happy birthday to you, happy birthday to you, happy birthday to Junming, happy birthday to you." It was wonderful, even though they couldn't sing well. My parents and friends were holding a birthday cake with 16 candles on it. The weak light that I had seen from the living room came from the candles. These candles flickered like fireflies. They covered my cake. My parents and friends asked me to make a wish. I closed my eyes to make a wish, and then I blew out the candles. There were no more fireflies, and someone turned on the light. I gazed steadily at the birthday cake and didn't want to cut it in pieces, but I did. I was so touched by all of these people who gave me this special day. My vision was blurred with tears. This was my sixteenth birthday, a special day I will never forget because it was the only birthday that I celebrated with both my friends and my parents.

Junming Liang, Hong Kong

Discussion Discuss the following questions in a group.

1. Underline the writer's topic sentence. What word or words tell his opinion, feelings, or idea about the day?

2. How do the writer's feelings change in the story?

3. What details does he include to show his earlier and later feelings?

4. Does this story remind you of one of your own birthdays? How?

Language for Writing In this chapter, you will write about special celebrations. Below are some expressions to describe your experiences and feelings about celebrations.

Junming's writes, "My sixteenth birthday was the happiest day of my life." Here are other ways he could express the same idea:

	Adjectives	Nouns	
My sixteenth birthday was	the happiest	day	of my life.
	the most wonderful	time	
	a special	occasion	
	a memorable	event	in my life.
	an unforgettable	experience	
	an extraordinary	moment	

1. Many combinations of the adjectives and nouns above are possible, including *a special moment, an unforgettable day,* or *a memorable event.* Use adjective + noun combinations to complete the sentences below.

a. The high school graduation ceremony was _____.

b. The birth of their baby daughter was _____

for the new parents.

c. The day that Nadia got the keys to her first automobile was

_____.

d. Moving into our first house was _____.

e. My wedding day was _____.

2. The verbs *remember* and *forget* are often used to introduce or conclude a story. Notice how they are used in the examples.

> **I'll never forget** the day that I started my first real job.
>
> Our European vacation was an experience that **I will always remember.**
>
> **I remember** my thirtieth birthday party very well.

Complete the sentences below to describe memorable events in your life.

1. I will never forget _____.

2. I remember when I _____.

3. I will never forget the day that I _____.

4. I'll always remember my _____.

5. _____ was an extraordinary experience that
   I will never forget.

Writing

Assignment for Part 1

Write a paragraph about a personal celebration in your past. To write your paragraph, follow the steps of the writing process.

STEP 1

Getting Ideas

Listing is a good way to choose a topic and get ideas. Look at the sample lists below. In List A, the writer made notes about special celebrations. Then she checked the event that she decided to write about. In List B, the writer focused on the one event and wrote down more ideas.

List A

My Personal Celebrations

○ A summer music concert—the "Feztival"

My parents' wedding anniversary party

My high school graduation ceremony

○ Senior prom

The day I got my driver's license

My nephews' christening ✓

○

List B

My Nephew's Christening

○ Arrived at the church.
Lots of white flowers.
Everyone dressed up, babies in white gowns.
Priest led the service. He wore a long, purple robe.
Parents made promises at the front of the church,
  held babies.

○ Priest put oil and water on the babies' heads.
Crying babies, nervous parents. Priest smiled.
We filmed a video.
Everyone was happy and laughing after.
A party at grandparents' house.
Priest, friends, family celebrated.

○ Lots of food and drink.
Watched video of ceremony.

1. Make a list—like List A—of special celebrations in your life, such as a party, a graduation, a wedding, a class dance, a concert, the birth of a baby, or a day when you received an award.

2. Read over your list and choose one experience to write about.

3. Next, to get more ideas, make a list—like List B—of things that happened during this special event. Include specific details.

STEP 2

Organizing

Chronological Order

Chronological, or time, order is used to write about past events. In a paragraph about a past event, begin with a topic sentence. Then write about the things that happened in the order in which they occurred.

1. Below are sentences from a student paragraph that are out of order. The topic sentence is marked **TS.** Put the events in chronological order by marking "1" next to the first event in the story, "2" next to the second event, and so on. In a group, compare your answers.

    _____ a. The day before New Year's we had to clean up everything in the house.

    _____ b. On the first day of New Year's, all of my family members went to the temple because we believe that if we go to the temple we will have good luck and good health.

    _____ c. My friends and I had a picnic. We played ball and shot off fireworks.

    _____ d. On the second and third days, I went out with my friends.

    _TS_ e. Last year we had a busy but wonderful Vietnamese New Year.

    _____ f. We just stayed home and had a big family dinner.

    _____ g. It was an unforgettable New Year's celebration.

    _____ h. After we got home from the temple, we didn't go out the rest of the day.

    _____ i. A few days before New Year's, we took time off from work to prepare.

2. Put the list of events you made in Exercise 3 in Getting Ideas in chronological order.

3. Write a topic sentence for your paragraph to introduce the event and tell your opinion, feeling, or idea about it.

    Examples

    Our vacation to the shore last summer was wonderful.

    My high school reunion was a memorable event.

Concluding Sentence

In addition to a topic sentence and supporting points, a good paragraph has a concluding sentence. The concluding sentence restates or returns to the main idea in the topic sentence.

Look back at "My Sixteenth Birthday" on page 87. Notice how the writer restates the main idea of the topic sentence in his concluding sentence by repeating key words and ideas.

Topic Sentence: My <u>sixteenth birthday</u> was the <u>happiest day</u> of my life.

Concluding Sentence: This was <u>my sixteenth birthday</u>, <u>a special day</u> I will never forget because it was the only birthday that I celebrated with both my friends and my parents.

1. In Exercise 1 of Organizing on page 90, find the concluding sentence. Does the writer restate the main idea of the topic sentence? Is this a good concluding sentence?

2. Read the two paragraphs below. After each paragraph, there are two possible concluding sentences. Circle the letter of the best concluding sentence. In a group, discuss your answers.

Moving Day

The day I moved to my new apartment was a disaster. I got up early that Saturday ready to start moving. My friends George and Michael were going to bring a truck to help me. At 9:30, George called to tell me that his truck wouldn't start, but he said he could fix it. I waited and waited. Finally, two hours later George arrived in his truck, but he was alone. Michael had gotten tired of waiting. That meant George and I had to load the truck by ourselves. When we finally got to the new apartment, the elevator was broken, so the two of us had to carry everything up three flights of stairs. After all that, I discovered that the gas and electricity were not working. My whole body was aching from lifting and carrying, and I couldn't even take a bath or cook any dinner.

    a. It felt good to finally be in my new home.

    b. I sat down and cried and promised myself I would never move again.

Teaching: Day One

I will never forget my first day of teaching. I was 24 years old, and my first job was teaching English to young soldiers in the Iranian army. That day I arrived early to set up the classroom. I had spent hours preparing my lesson. I had pictures of all the new vocabulary words and handouts of grammar exercises. I was ready to teach, but I was nervous. The students started coming in. They were all dressed in uniforms. They looked at me, and I could see they were surprised to see that the teacher was a woman.

They started asking me questions with the few words of English they knew. No matter what I said, they did not believe that I was a real teacher. I knew this was not a good start to my teaching career, so I decided to call my supervisor. He came to the class and explained to the cadets that I was a professional teacher from the United States. He finally convinced the students that I was their teacher.

> a. Even though we didn't do any of the lesson I had prepared, it was still a memorable day in my teaching career.
>
> b. Sadly, I did not teach any of the material I had prepared.

STEP 3

Writing

Write the first draft of your paragraph. Use your topic sentence, ideas from your brainstorming list, and chronological order.

STEP 4

Revising

Work with a partner. Read each other's paragraph. Write comments on your partner's paper in the margins. Use the checklist below as a guide. Then read your partner's comments and make any necessary changes.

❑ Does the paragraph have a topic sentence that introduces the event and says how you feel about it?

❑ Are the sentences in chronological order?

❑ Does the paragraph include details that support the main idea?

❑ Does the paragraph have a concluding sentence?

STEP 4

Editing

Use the following explanations and activities to help you edit your writing.

Grammar

Verbs in the Simple Past Tense
The simple past is the most commonly used verb tense to describe past actions.   When we **arrived** at the church, we **saw** all of our family members.   Everyone **had** a good time.   There **were** white flowers in the church.

■ The simple past tense of **be** has these forms:

I	was	we	were
you	were	you	were
he, she, it	was	they	were

The church **was** beautiful.

Many people **were** at the party.

■ All other verbs have the same form in the simple past tense for all subjects.

I **wore** a blue dress.

My sister **wore** a white jacket.

The little girls **wore** fancy dresses.

■ Regular verbs in the simple past tense are formed by adding **-ed** to the base form of the verb. See page 170 for the spelling rules for **-ed** verbs.

We **stayed** in the church for two hours.

Everyone **laughed** and **celebrated** together.

■ Some verbs in the simple past tense have **irregular** forms.

My sister Patti **held** her baby in her arms.

We **ate** and **drank** a lot at the celebration.

My brother-in-law Joe **felt** nervous.

See page 170 for a list of irregular verbs in the simple past tense.

Verbs in Negative Sentences

■ Add **not** after **be** to make negative statements in the simple past tense.

Junming's parents **were not** at home when he arrived.

He **was not** happy to cut the birthday cake.

■ Add **did** + **not** before the base form of the verb (the form of the verb with no endings) to make negative statements with all other verbs in the simple past tense.

My brother **did not open** his presents until midnight.

We **did not tell** him about his surprise party.

■ Make contractions with verbs in negative statements in this way:

Junming **wasn't** awake when we arrived at home.

We **weren't** tired afterwards.

He **didn't guess** about his birthday party.

Machu Picchu, Andes Mountains, Peru

1 Read the student paragraph below. Underline the verbs in the simple past tense. Mark regular verbs **R** and irregular verbs **I**.

─────────── **My Graduation Trip** ───────────

When I <u>was</u> 17 years old, my friends and I <u>celebrated</u> our high school graduation by taking a fascinating trip to the Andes Mountains. Our parents gave us this special trip as a graduation gift. We decided to visit Cuzco, the former capital of the Inca empire. We took a train there, and during our two-week vacation, we learned a lot about the culture of the ancient Incas. We hiked to the ruins of Machu Picchu, the lost city of the Incas. It is a wonderful place high in the mountains, with palaces, homes, and other old buildings. I couldn't believe that the city was so old. I also wondered how the Incas were able to build it in the mountains. The snow-topped mountains were breathtaking. We camped overnight, practiced adventure sports such as rock climbing, and drank hot water from the mountain springs. We had a wonderful time on our graduation trip.

Javier A. Aguero, Peru

2 Read the following student paragraph. Correct the errors in the simple past tense.

─────── **My Birthday Celebration in Agra** ───────

When I was 15 years old, my parents ~~give~~ *gave* me a wonderful surprise birthday party. I've always liked historical places. That's why my parents, my friends, and my relatives take me to Agra, India, for my birthday. Early in the morning we leave home to visit Agra, which is a historical place. In Agra there is one of the seven man-made wonders of the world: the Taj Mahal. We hear the history of the Taj Mahal, about how a great king, Shah Jahan, build it from marble. In the afternoon, we ate lunch. Then we start to decorate the hall that my parents had rented. After we decorate the hall, we borrowed a stereo for the birthday party that night. Later on, everyone went to the shops and buy a gift for me. After they come back to the hall, we went to change our clothes for the party. Finally, at night, we cut the cake and everybody sing "Happy Birthday" to me. Then we ate dinner. After dinner, we dance with each other. Late at night, we go to see a movie. We drove home after midnight. That was the most wonderful birthday celebration in my life. I will never forget my birthday in Agra.

Krunal Patel, India

3 Write sentences about your past experiences using the simple past tense of the verbs below. Make the verbs affirmative or negative so that they are true for you.

1. study English in my home country
   I didn't study English in my home country.

2. get good grades in elementary school
   _____

3. graduate from high school in the United States
   _____

4. take biology in high school
   _____

5. learn to drive in the United States

   _____

6. cook dinner last night

   _____

7. go to bed early last night

   _____

8. work late last night

   _____

DO IT YOURSELF
See pages 170–173
for more practice.

9. eat breakfast this morning

   _____

Word Order

As you learned in Chapter 1, the basic order of an English sentence is subject + verb. The other words in a sentence also follow a specific order. The charts below show the word order in two types of sentences.

Sentences with Action Verbs: Subject + Verb + (Object) + (Adverb)

Subject +	Verb +	(Object) +	(Adverb)
He	drove	his car	carefully.
The little boy	played	baseball	with his father.
I	worked		last semester.
The students	write	their papers	on the weekend.
We	stayed up		all night.
My manager	shouted		loudly.

An adverb or adverb phrase often comes after the verb (and the object, if there is one), but it can appear in other places in a sentence. An adverb can be one word, such as *carefully*, or a phrase, such as *with his father*.

Sentences with Linking Verbs: Subject + Verb + Complement

Subject +	Verb +	Complement
My classmate	seemed	shy. (*adj*)
Tuan	was	a good student. (*noun phrase*)
The papers	were	on the table. (*adverb phrase*)

4 Read the sentences with action verbs below. Mark subjects **S**, verbs **V**, objects **O**, and adverbs or adverb phrases **ADV**. Some sentences may not have an object or adverb.

      S   V   O   ADV

1. Henri had a party last weekend.
2. The lazy young men didn't work hard.
3. Dr. Gao won a teaching award this semester.
4. My brothers and I had many happy experiences.
5. The musicians played all night.
6. My friend took pictures all week.

5 Read the sentences with linking verbs below. Mark subjects **S**, verbs **V**, and complements **C**.

         S   V   C

1. Ruslana and her friends felt happy.
2. My friends weren't at the graduation ceremony.
3. Fonda looked shy and serious.
4. The celebration didn't seem very long.
5. Alice was the class president.

6 Put the words below into the correct order to make sentences. Write the sentences on the lines. Be sure to capitalize and punctuate where necessary.

1. drank   in   coffee   I   morning   the

   I drank coffee in the morning. _____

2. yesterday   didn't   he   bus   the   take

   _____

3. students   the   schedules   had   different

   _____

4. I   cake   made   a   last   night

   _____

5. my   help   needed   co-worker   new   some

   _____

6. feet   after   his   the   hurt   race

   _____

7. not   party   the   Sabina   happy   was   at

_____

8. tasted   the   cake   delicious

_____

9. the   Sam   library   in   was

_____

DO IT YOURSELF
See pages 175–177
for more practice.

10. did   car   George   the   not   cautiously   drive

_____

Language Tip ■ *Ago*

Ago phrases are adverb phrases that answer the question "when?" Use **ago** in sentences with past tense verbs in these ways:

- At the beginning of a sentence:

    Two years ago I didn't speak English.
    A minute ago I saw my keys, but now I can't find them.

- At the end of a sentence:

    The class started **six weeks ago.**
    We went to Canada once, but it was **a long time ago.**

---

7 Complete the sentences to describe past events in your life.

1. _I left my house_ _____ one hour ago.
2. Two weeks ago _____ .
3. _____ not long ago.
4. _____ a long time ago.
5. Five years ago _____ .
6. Just a moment ago _____ .
7. _____ one year ago.
8. Long ago _____ .
9. _____ a short while ago.

Editing Your Writing

Use the checklist below to edit your work. Then rewrite your paragraph.

> **Editing Checklist**
>
> ❑ Are simple past tense verbs used correctly?
>
> ❑ Is word order correct?
>
> ❑ Is sentence end punctuation correct?

Journal Writing Think of a special person from your past, such as a childhood friend, an old neighbor, or a relative. Write about a day you spent together, a special event you experienced together, or an activity you enjoyed together.

PART 2

Reading for Writing

The reading below describes the events of the Mardi Gras festival in New Orleans. Although it started as a Christian holy day, today Mardi Gras is more like a party than a religious event. As you read, think about how Mardi Gras compares to celebrations that you have experienced.

Mardi Gras

My trip to the Mardi Gras festival in New Orleans was an unforgettable experience. Mardi Gras is a street party where people dress in costumes, watch parades, listen to bands, and celebrate all day and night. Usually occurring in February or March, it attracts tourists from all over the world.

The first time I went to Mardi Gras, which is French for "Fat Tuesday," my friends and I woke up early on Carnival Day to find a good place to watch the parades. We took blankets, cameras, and drinks.

By the time the parade began around 11 A.M., the crowds were huge and noisy. We watched brightly decorated floats roll by, along with decorated trucks and musicians who played jazz and blues. The parade performers danced in colorful costumes. A dozen men in one group were dressed as Elvis Presley. Another group of women performers wore long gowns, white wigs, and masks.

Most people in the audience also wore costumes, makeup, and masks. My friends and I also dressed in costumes. We shouted and played a drum to get the attention of the people on the floats. We wanted them to throw us their plastic beads.

At sundown, we walked to the old French Quarter, where people in costumes walked in the street. We sang, danced, and enjoyed the music. The festivities lasted all night long, and in the early morning we headed home. We were tired and hungry, but satisfied with our wonderful Mardi Gras experience.

Discussion   Discuss the following questions in a group.

1. Is Mardi Gras similar to a celebration that you have experienced? How?
2. Which words and phrases give the writer's opinions, feelings, or ideas about Mardi Gras? Find them and underline them.
3. Which verb tense does the writer use most of the time?
4. Does the writer use chronological order? Underline the words and phrases that show time.
5. Does the writer have a concluding sentence? Underline it.

Language for Writing   1. With a partner, discuss the meanings of the words below. Then use the words to complete the paragraph.

costume	parade	wonderful	occurs
festivities	celebrated	musicians	lasted

Charro Day

Charro Day is an important celebration in Mexico because it honors Mexico's independence from Spain in 1821. The word *charro* means "cowboy" in Spanish. The celebration _____ on September 14 all across Mexico and in parts of the southwest United States. When I was 5 years old, I _____ Charro Day in Brownsville, Texas, a small town on the U.S.–Mexican border. *Charros* on horses, _____ in bands, and dancers all marched in a grand _____ down the main street. I wore a beautiful _____ and danced the Mexican hat dance. I thought it was exciting to be part of the parade, which _____ for several hours. Years later, I celebrated Charro Day in Puerto Vallarta, Mexico. The _____ included a parade and a rodeo with cowboys on horses. Charro Day is a _____ way to celebrate Mexican history.

2. Imagine a party. Write a paragraph about the party that includes all the words below. Give your story a title, and begin with a sentence like this:

   Many interesting things happened at the party last night.

had a party	lasted
huge	music
danced	the neighbors
one couple	headed home

Writing

Assignment for Part 2

Write a paragraph about a community celebration that you experienced. To write your paragraph, follow the steps of the writing process below.

STEP 1

Getting Ideas

1. Do one of the following:
   - Work in a group to brainstorm possible writing topics for the writing assignment. List topic ideas.
   - Work with classmates of your nationality or religion, if possible. Discuss important national or religious holidays that you have celebrated. List topic ideas.
2. Read over your list and choose one event to write about.
3. Make a list of the main events in the celebration.

STEP 2

Organizing

Background Information

Stories often give background information or special explanations about the story. For example, in writing about a religious, historic, or cultural celebration, a writer may need to explain the meaning of the celebration before describing the events in the story. The background information helps the reader understand the events.

Look at the example from the reading on page 99–100.

Topic sentence	My trip to the Mardi Gras festival in New Orleans was an unforgettable experience. Mardi Gras is a street party where
Background	people dress in costumes, watch parades, listen to bands, and celebrate all day and night. Usually occurring in February or March, it attracts tourists from all over the world.
Events of story	The first time I went to Mardi Gras, which is French for "Fat
Background	Tuesday," my friends and I woke up early on Carnival Day to find a good place to watch the parades. We took blankets, cameras, and drinks.

The sentences that provide background information are highlighted. The topic sentence and story events are in the simple past, but the background information is in the simple present because the information is general. If the background information refers to something that happened in the past, use the past tense.

1. Read the student paragraph below. With a partner, discuss which sentences give background information.

The Eritrean Festival

August 21–26, 1992, was a very special week in my life. It was the first time I participated in the Eritrean Festival in my country's capital city, Asmara. Eritrea got its freedom from Ethiopia on May 24, 1991. Before this date, the Eritrean people held small festivals in cities around the world to celebrate their cultural diversity. The largest one was held in Bologna, Italy, since Italy once occupied Eritrea. Because I live in a small town in the United States, I only had a chance to see a videotape of the festivals. For that reason, I always dreamed of being at the festival in Asmara in person. Finally, in August 1992, I went home to visit my family and I celebrated my first Eritrean Festival in Asmara. It was a very special event for me. During the two-day celebration, I saw exhibits and performances representing the different Eritrean cultures. We have nine different ethnic groups in my country and nine different languages. On the festival grounds, there was a tent for each group. I walked from tent to tent to learn about the different cultures—the people's food, the things they used for daily life, their musical instruments, and the way they danced. I enjoyed the festival even more because I met many friends that I hadn't seen since I left the country. The festival was an experience that I will never forget.

Helen Berhe, Eritrea

---

2. Look at the list of events you made in Exercise 3 in Getting Ideas on page 101. Make sure the list is in chronological order.

STEP 3

Writing

Write your paragraph, using your brainstorming list and organizational plan. Include any background information that will help the reader understand the event.

STEP 4

Revising

Work with a partner. Read each other's paragraph. Write comments on your partner's paper in the margins. Use the checklist below as a guide. Then read your partner's comments and make any necessary changes.

- ❑ Does the paragraph begin with a topic sentence that introduces the event and tells the writer's opinion about it?
- ❑ Do the rest of the sentences follow chronological order?
- ❑ Do the details support the main idea?
- ❑ Is there enough background information to understand the story?

STEP 5

Editing

Use the following explanations and activities to help you edit your writing.

Mechanics

Spelling the *-ed* Form

Regular simple past tense verbs are formed by adding **-ed** to the base verb. However, some **-ed** verbs have irregular spelling.

REGULAR SPELLING   IRREGULAR SPELLING

Martina **worked** at Papa John's Pizza last year, but she **stopped** working there last month.

The chart below gives the irregular spelling rules for **-ed** verbs.

Rule	Example	
1. Add *-d* when the base form ends in e.	live	**lived**
2. When the base form ends in a consonant + *y*, drop the *y* and add *-ied*.	carry	**carried**
3. Simply add *-ed* if the base form ends in a vowel + *y*.	play	**played**
4. When the base form of a one-syllable word ends in consonant + vowel + consonant, double the final consonant and add *-ed.*	step	**stepped**
5. When the last syllable of a two-syllable word is stressed, double the final consonant and add *-ed.*	occur	**occurred**

1 Test your knowledge of the -*ed* spelling rules by completing the sentences below with simple past tense of the verbs provided. With a partner, compare your answers. Then check your answers by looking back at the chart on page 103.

1. We _____*stayed*_____ home yesterday because it was raining.

stay

2. My friends and I _____ all afternoon for the exam.

study

3. Last week my parents _____ to buy a new car.

decide

4. Jayesh _____ swimming when he was a child, but he

like
   doesn't like it now.

5. Ali _____ working in the museum. Now he works in a

stop
   restaurant.

6. Lin _____ about her class grade until she learned that she

worry
   received an A.

7. I _____ my birthday party last Friday.

enjoy

8. When I was a child, I _____ to eat cereal for breakfast.

prefer

9. Trang _____ his friend's directions, but he still got lost.

follow

10. The snow _____ to fall at midnight last night.

start

11. The temperature in Dallas _____ from 90 to 75 degrees

drop
    Fahrenheit yesterday.

12. Edward _____ my telephone number and called me two

locate
    days ago.

2 Study the list of irregular past tense verbs on pages 170–172. Work with a partner. Test each other on the spellings of ten of the verbs. Use each one in a sentence. Ask your instructor to help you pronounce words, if necessary.

Example

The teacher **taught** us about simple past tense verbs.

Editing Your Writing

Use the checklist to edit your work. Then rewrite your paragraph.

Editing Checklist

❑ Are all the verbs in the correct tense?

❑ Are all the *-ed* verbs spelled correctly?

❑ Are all the irregular verbs spelled correctly?

On Your Own

Personal Spelling List

1. Continue to work on your spelling problems. Reread the spelling rules on pages 37 and 103. Look over the paragraphs you wrote in Chapter 5. Add misspelled words to your Personal Spelling list.

2. Study the correct spellings of the words on your list. Work with a partner. Test each other on the spellings. Ask your instructor to help you pronounce words, if necessary.

Personal Editing Log

Continue to keep track of the types of grammar and mechanics errors that you often make. After your teacher returns your paragraphs from this chapter, read them over, and put checkmarks in your Personal Editing Log to identify the types of errors that you made.

More Writing Practice

Write a paragraph on one of the following topics.

REMEMBER Begin your paragraph with a topic sentence. Make sure all the sentences relate to the main idea. Follow chronological order. Write a concluding sentence. When you finish, read over your paragraph to revise and edit it.

1. **Taking Responsibility**

   Write a paragraph about a specific time when you took responsibility for your actions. Begin with a topic sentence that introduces the experience and states that you acted responsibly. Include details such as the following: What happened? When? What responsible action did you take? What were the results?

2. **A Learning Experience**

   Write a paragraph to tell about your experience learning something new. Begin with a topic sentence that introduces the skill you learned and gives your opinion, feelings, or idea about the learning experience. Include details such as the following: When and where did you learn it?

Who taught you? How did this person help you? What difficulties did you face? What were the results?

3. **A Memorable Gift**

Write a paragraph about a time when you gave or received a memorable gift. On what occasion did you give or receive the gift? Who gave it to you, or to whom did you give it? When? Why do you remember it?

Chapter Goals

Reflect on what you have learned in Chapter 5. Check (✔) the point(s) that you are learning. If you are having trouble understanding one of the areas, write another paragraph on one of the topics from More Writing Practice for more practice. Ask your instructor for help.

Chapter Goals Checklist

❑ Use chronological order.

❑ Recognize a concluding sentence.

❑ Use the simple past tense.

❑ Use correct word order.

❑ Give background information.

❑ Learn to spell verbs with the -*ed* form.

CHAPTER 6

It's Your Money

Chapter Goals

- Use reasons to support an opinion.
- Write a unified paragraph.
- Write sentences with *and, but, or, so,* and *yet*.
- Write a concluding sentence.
- Avoid comma splices.
- Learn to spell similar words correctly.

Approaching the Topic

The way you spend money can affect your life in many ways. Like most people, you probably need to make careful choices about spending. In this chapter, you will read and write about some of the ways people spend and save money.

1. Do you find it easy or difficult to manage your money? Why?

2. What do you spend most of your money on?

3. Are you a careful spender or a careless spender? Give examples.

PART 1

Reading for Writing

The reading below tells about a high school student's spending habits in terms of clothes. As you read, compare your idea of the right clothes with that of the student described in the passage.

The Right Clothes

Arthur McDermott, 17, is a popular student who likes to wear fashionable clothes. He chooses his clothes for their brand names. His T-shirt has a Fast by Ferracci logo, and a loop on the side of his blue jeans reads Tommy Hilfiger. He wears Adidas sneakers and carries a backpack with a Jansport label. In Arthur's senior class, many young men display the same brand-name merchandise. The message in this big-city American high school is that if you want to be "cool," you wear the right clothes.

Arthur wasn't always popular. When he was a freshman, he did not have many friends. He realized that he had to wear cool, or stylish, clothes to fit in with the cool crowd. The most popular girls dated the boys who wore cool clothes, so he dressed that way, too. His $100 sneakers and $45 T-shirts helped make him feel important. His designer clothes separated him from the "uncool" students. His strong personality then allowed him to rise in popularity.

Since his clothes helped him gain popularity, Arthur pays a lot of attention to fashion. He buys the latest model of particular brands of sneakers such as Nike and the newest styles of jeans by JNCO or Mudd. When the fashions change and certain brands become more popular, Arthur's clothing changes, too. Wearing the right clothes keeps Arthur cool.

Discussion Discuss the following questions in a group.

1. What are the reasons that teenagers such as Arthur wear brand-name clothes?

2. Is a designer label a good reason to buy a product? Why or why not?

3. What are the right clothes for you? Why?

Language for Writing

Write the appropriate word or phrase from each group below the lines to make the sentences true for you. Compare your answers in a group.

The main factor that I consider when I buy clothes is _____.

1. fashion/comfort/cost

I like to wear _____

2. designer brands only/some brand-name and some off-brand clothes/any brand

because being in style is _____ to me. When

3. very important/somewhat important/unimportant

I go to school, I dress _____. I usually

4. comfortably/stylishly/both comfortably and stylishly

wear _____. I go clothes shopping

5. jeans/a suit/a dress/the first things I can find in my closet

about _____ a _____. I look for clothes that

6. once/twice/three times/four times   7. week/month/year

_____. In general, my main consideration in

8. last a long time/are inexpensive/are stylish

choosing clothes is _____.

9. value/style/comfort

Writing

Assignment for Part 1

Write a paragraph about a brand-name product that you buy. To write your paragraph, follow the steps of the writing process.

STEP 1

Getting Ideas

1. In a group, brainstorm products to write about. Talk about why you buy certain brand-name products. In the chart below, make a list of product brands that you have strong reasons for buying. Add your own categories to the chart.

Brand Names That I Like	
Clothes	
Soft drinks	
Electronics	

2. Choose a brand-name product from your list to write about.

Organizing **Giving Reasons to Support an Opinion**

When you give your opinion about a topic, you need to provide reasons to explain your opinion—for example, why you like a specific brand and not another.

1. Read the sample paragraphs below. For each paragraph, give the writer's opinion and the main reason or reasons for his opinion. Compare your answers with a classmate's.

Backpacks That Last

I prefer Nelson backpacks because they last a long time. Other brands tear easily, especially when you carry a lot of heavy books in them. Typically, the bottom of other backpacks I bought in the past would rip out after a short time, but this never happens with Nelson backpacks. The bottom is made of stronger fabric than the rest of the backpack. Another reason that I buy Nelson is the zipper. The zipper on a Nelson backpack is made well, so it doesn't break. The company guarantees the backpacks for life. Nelsons last a long time, so I always buy this brand of backpack.

The World's Best Pizza

Uncle John's is my favorite pizza. The main reasons I like it are that the ingredients are fresh and the crust is good. Pizzas from other fast-food places often use canned mushrooms and strange-tasting meat. Uncle John's uses fresh mushrooms and fresh-tasting meat. Also, the cheese on Uncle John's pizza tastes fresher than on other pizzas. Most important, Uncle John's crust is also tasty. At other pizza places, such as Pizza World and Giorgio's, the crust is often greasy, but Uncle John's crust is so light that it tastes like bread. I definitely like Uncle John's pizza the best.

---

2. Look at the model on page 111. The writer took notes on the features of Walters notebooks. Then she decided to write about the convenience and high quality of the notebooks, so she crossed out the points that did not fit those categories. Read the notes. Write **C** next to the notes that tell about the *convenience* of the notebooks. Write **Q** next to the notes that tell about the notebooks' *high quality*.

Walters All-Star Spiral Notebooks

Sturdy, strong	Tear-out paper
Hard, plastic covers	~~College rule lines~~
Thick paper	~~Cool colors~~
Pockets on dividing pages	~~Expensive~~

3. Below is a student's list of some of the features of Alosilk Cleansing Cream. In the table following, put each feature under one of the appropriate categories: Value, Convenience, or Quality.

Alosilk Cleansing Cream

Won't dry out my skin	Makes skin tingle after use
Isn't too greasy	Takes only a small amount to do the job
Dissolves oil	Isn't expensive
Deep cleans	Is easy to find in stores
Is easy to use	Comes in different sizes
Has an original scent	

Value	Convenience	Quality
		Won't dry out my skin.

4. Now make a list of the features of the product you chose. Make a table like the one above with the following categories: value, convenience, style, and quality. Put your features into at least two of these categories. These are the main reasons that you buy the product. Cross out the items that do not relate to these reasons.

Paragraph Unity

A paragraph has unity if it provides supporting information for only one main idea. This means that every sentence in the paragraph relates to the same main idea, including the topic sentence, supporting sentences, and concluding sentence.

1. Read the topic sentences and the "supporting" points. Check the point(s) that fit the main idea. Compare your answers with a classmate's.

   a. When I buy shoes, the main quality I look for is comfort.
      (1) The latest fashion is important.
      (2) The shoes should not be too tight or too loose.
      (3) I prefer shoes that are less than $60.00.

   b. All the shoes that I buy must be stylish.
      (1) I buy my shoes at discount stores where I save money.
      (2) I often buy my shoes at Fiora's, a store that sells the newest styles.
      (3) I like Steve Madden shoes because they are fashionable.

2. Work with a partner. Read the following topic sentence for a paragraph. Then read the list of notes about the product. Check the notes that support the topic sentence. Cross out the notes that do not fit.

   Topic Sentence: I use Ben's Toothpaste because it contains only natural ingredients.

   Notes:

Contains no chemicals	No artificial colors
Has no artificial sugar	Flavors come from plants
Only need to use a small amount	Can be found in any drug store
Comes in many tasty flavors	Not expensive
Other brands contain dyes	Other brands contain chemicals

   ---

3. Read the following paragraphs and discuss them with your partner. Draw a line through sentences that do not support the topic sentence.

   Max Walsh: A Great Place to Shop

   I prefer to shop at Max Walsh of New York because it has good prices and selection. When I compare the prices there with those at other stores, I find that Max Walsh has reasonable prices, so I buy most of my clothes at Max Walsh. I can find my size and the colors I want very easily, and the clothes are often on sale. Also, the store has nice decorations and is quiet. Every time I go there, my favorite songs are playing. Also, the fragrances of the perfume, candles, and lotion make the whole area smell great. The good prices and selection have made me a loyal shopper.

   Haimanot Anbessie, Ethiopia

Excellent Service at Buy Rite

I really like Buy Rite because the service is very good. The salespeople try to help customers and can give a lot of good advice about items. A couple of months ago, I bought a new phone in this store for $100. It's a black cordless phone with a speaker. I like it because it matches the colors in my living room. Buy Rite has a large selection of televisions. It also sells many computer products. When I came home, I saw that my phone was broken. I was really upset. I could not use this phone, but it was not my fault. I went back to Buy Rite, and the people who worked in the customer service gave me permission to exchange it. Buy Rite is really a good store that serves customers well.

Slava Aybinder, Ukraine

The Place for a Good Haircut

Haircuts Express is a good place to get a good, inexpensive haircut. I have been to many different hair salons. Sometimes I get a good haircut, but sometimes I do not. At Haircuts Express, I almost always get a good haircut. I don't come home to find that one side of my hair is shorter than the other side. The hairdressers listen to what I ask for and cut my hair the way I like it. Also, Haircuts Express is inexpensive. It costs about $15 to get a haircut and blow dry. The cost is the same for men and women. Children's haircuts are even less expensive. Haircuts Express does other things as well. For example, they can color or curl your hair. They sell shampoo and other hair products. Their prices are very reasonable, and they cut my hair well, so I prefer to go to Haircuts Express.

4. For each topic sentence below, write one or two possible supporting sentences.

   1. Balancing my budget is sometimes difficult.

     Sometimes I don't know where I spend my money.

     I always run out of money by the end of the month.

   2. Rudy Beverly is my favorite brand of designer jeans.

     _____

     _____

   3. Cell phones are very useful in my everyday life.

     _____

     _____

   4. Shopping with a friend is better than shopping alone.

     _____

     _____

5. Now, for your paragraph, write a topic sentence that names the product you chose and gives the main reason(s) why you buy it.

Example

I buy Walters All-Star Notebooks because of their high quality and convenience.

STEP 3

Writing

Write your paragraph. Use your topic sentence, your brainstorming list, and your reasons for buying the product. Make sure your paragraph has unity.

STEP 4

Revising

Work with a partner. Read each other's paragraph. Write comments on your partner's paper in the margins. Use the checklist below as a guide. Then read your partner's comments and make any necessary changes.

❏ Does the paragraph begin with a topic sentence that states the reason(s) that the writer likes the brand-name product?

❏ Do all the sentences in the paragraph explain the reasons?

❏ Does the paragraph have unity? Do all the sentences relate to the main idea?

Editing

Use the following explanations and activities to help you edit your writing.

Grammar

Sentences with *and, but, so, or,* and *yet*

A simple sentence has one subject and one complete verb. You combine simple sentences with a coordinating conjunction—**and, but, so, or, yet**—to make a compound sentence. Put a comma before the conjunction. Compound sentences follow the pattern below:

Simple sentence + , coordinating conjunction + simple sentence

Simple Sentences	**Compound Sentences**
Yesterday was cold and rainy. Today is sunny.	Yesterday was cold and rainy, **but** today is sunny.
Jennifer had a cold. She didn't go out.	Jennifer had a cold, **so** she didn't go out.

Coordinating Conjunctions and Uses		Examples
and	comes before additional information	At night I cook dinner, **and** I watch TV.
but	comes before a contrasting or different idea	I like to shop, **but** I don't have much time.
so	comes before a result	I needed some milk, **so** I went to the store.
or	comes before a choice or option	We can cook, **or** we can eat out.
yet	comes before a contrasting or different idea	I am tired, **yet** I'm going out.

---

1 Make compound sentences by combining the sentence pairs on page 116 with *and, but, so, or,* or *yet*. Choose the connecting word that best fits the meaning. Make sure your punctuation is correct.

Consumer Facts About China

1. China has 1.3 billion consumers.
    It attracts many foreign companies.

    China has 1.3 billion consumers, so it attracts many foreign companies.

2. Japanese products were once the most popular in China.
    Now U.S. products are becoming more popular.

    _____

    _____

3. China has nearly 25 percent of the world's consumers.
    Many foreign companies want to sell products there.

    _____

    _____

4. One of the biggest fast-food places in the world overlooks Tiananmen
    Square in Beijing.
    On the street, you can see Coca-Cola advertisements everywhere.

    _____

    _____

5. In the early 1990s, the Chinese economy was strong.
    Chinese consumers did not have much extra money.

    _____

    _____

6. By 2001, Chinese families had more money to spend on household goods.
    They had more products to choose from.

    _____

    _____

7. Twenty years ago, many Chinese families did not own cars.
    Today, more Chinese families own cars.

    _____

    _____

8. The number of Internet users is increasing rapidly in China.
    Chinese consumers are buying more products online.

    _____

    _____

9. Today, Chinese consumers can purchase goods made in China.
    They can buy foreign-made products.

    _____

    _____

2 Complete the sentences. For each, write an ending that is appropriate for the conjunction provided. Look at the chart on page 115 if necessary.

1. I need to go shopping, **but** *I have no money*_____.

2. Yesterday Hana went to the grocery store, **and** she _____.

3. Mary likes new styles, **so** _____.

4. Ron usually spends his money right away, **or** he _____.

5. Lilya cares a lot about how she looks, **so** _____.

6. John loves designer clothes, **but** _____.

7. Eduardo went to the bookstore, **and** he _____.

8. Usually, on the weekends, Jill goes to the mall, **or** she _____.

9. George doesn't want to buy a new car, **yet** he _____.

DO IT YOURSELF
See pages 161–162 for more practice.

Language Tip ■ *Favorite* versus *Best*

- Use **favorite** to describe the person or thing that you or someone else likes more than others of the same kind.

  Fresh is my **favorite** brand of toothpaste.

  Ana's **favorite** uncle is John.

- Use **best** to describe someone or something that is better than any others in a group.

  Fresh is **the best** brand of toothpaste.

- Don't write:

  ~~Cool Mist is **my best** brand of soap.~~

  ~~Cool Mist is **my most favorite** brand of soap.~~

  Write:

  Cool Mist is *the best* brand of soap.

  Cool Mist is *my favorite* brand of soap.

---

3 Write five sentences about your favorite products. Use *favorite* in each sentence. Then write five sentences that explain why each brand you buy is the *best*. Use *the best*. In a group, compare your sentences.

Examples

SuperSoftie is my favorite brand of tissues because they're soft.

I consider Lip Relief the best kind of lip gloss because it keeps my lips moist.

Editing Your Writing

Use the checklist below to edit your work. Then rewrite your paragraph.

Editing Checklist

❑ Are the sentences with *and, but, so, or,* and *yet* written correctly?

❑ Are commas used correctly in compound sentences?

❑ Are *favorite* and *best* used correctly?

Journal Writing   Do advertisements affect what you buy? How much do ads influence your shopping? What products do you buy because of an ad? Write a journal entry to explain.

PART 2

Reading for Writing

The reading below is titled "Tips from a Tightwad." A *tip* is a piece of advice, and a *tightwad* is someone who hates to spend or give anyone money. As you read, think about this question: Are you a tightwad?

Tips from a Tightwad

Are you a tightwad or a spendthrift? Read this list of simple tips from a tightwad. If you agree with the statements, then you probably spend your money carefully, which is what a tightwad does. If you disagree with the statements, then you may be a spendthrift—someone who spends money carelessly.

1. Don't buy things new if you don't have to. Anything you buy new becomes "used" as soon as it leaves the store. You can buy quality products at yard sales for a fraction of the cost of something new. I buy my jeans at the Salvation Army for $5, and they're like new!

2. Don't pay for expensive meals out when you can make them at home, and don't pay for entertainment when you can get it for free. Do you really need to go out to dinner tonight? Isn't there something in the fridge that will taste just as good? Are you really going to get $30 worth of satisfaction out of that meal? For entertainment, is it really worth spending money on a concert or a movie? You can take advantage of free neighborhood concerts, for example, and there are plenty of movies on TV.

3. Don't buy convenience foods or any foods that are already prepared. Making food from basic ingredients brings down your grocery bill, and it's better for you!

4. Evaluate the extra expenses in your life. Do you *really* need cable TV? Do you have to have expensive makeup? Expensive shoes? An expensive car?

5. Think before you spend. Is the satisfaction you get from spending money as great as the satisfaction you would get from something greater? When I was saving for a house, I asked myself that question before I bought anything at all. I would ask: Is it worth it to me to spend the money at a restaurant today if I have to wait longer until I can afford to buy a house? It's easy to trick yourself by saying, "It's only 5 bucks." But what about the other 10 times you already said that this week? That's more than 50 bucks!

— Adapted from *Tightwad Gazette* by Amy Dacyczyn

Discussion   Discuss the following questions in a group.

1. Are you ever a tightwad? Why?
2. Are you ever a spendthrift? In what ways?
3. Which of the writer's tips do you agree with? Why?
4. How would you like to change your spending habits?

Language for Writing   In English, many words are commonly used in specific combinations. Look at the phrases on page 120 and discuss them in a group. Then use the phrases to complete the sentences.

as soon as	agree with	it's easy to
go out to dinner/lunch	take advantage of	it's worth it
spend money on	afford to buy	get satisfaction

1. _____It's worth it_____ when you save up your money to buy something special.

2. I love to _____ with my family on the weekends.

3. I must be careful when I go shopping because I sometimes _____ things that I don't need.

4. Often, when I am shopping, I _____ sales, so I can get bargains.

5. I try to avoid spending too much, but unfortunately, _____ spend a lot of money in a short time.

6. I'm not poor, but I don't have a lot of money. I can't _____ a new car, so I'm going to buy a used one.

7. You also _____ from knowing that you paid a low price for something that you bought.

8. When I go shopping, I like to look at what I bought _____ I get home from the store.

9. Do you _____ the tips in the reading, or do you think they're not true?

Writing Assignment

Assignment for Part 2
Write a paragraph describing your spending habits. To write your paragraph, follow the steps of the writing process.

STEP 1

Getting Ideas

1. Freewrite for about 10 minutes to gather ideas for this writing assignment. Begin your freewriting with one of these sentences.

    I am a careful spender. I . . .
    I am a careless spender. I . . .

2. When you finish, read over what you wrote. Circle the best ideas to use in your paragraph. Cross out the ideas that not are useful.

3. Find a partner who started his or her freewriting with the same sentence as you. Exchange your writing and discuss your ideas. If you like ideas from your partner's paper, add notes to your own freewriting.

Organizing

1. Write a topic sentence that describes your spending habits or identifies you as a tightwad (a careful spender) or a spendthrift (a careless spender).

   Examples

   Most of the time, I spend money carefully.

   I am a careless spender because I don't think before I spend money.

   I am a real tightwad when it comes to spending my money.

2. As you learned in Chapter 5, a good paragraph has a final sentence that provides a conclusion. Read the following paragraph. Work with a partner to answer the questions below.

Saving Money on Groceries

   I have to spend a lot of money on groceries, so I pay careful attention to prices. I generally know what prices to expect. For instance, I expect to pay about $2.60 for a gallon of 2% milk and $2.99 for a pound of butter. By knowing the normal prices of food items, I don't pay too much. Also, knowing different stores helps me find the best prices. For example, Food King has good prices for baking products like flour, sugar, and oil, while Reilly's has good meat prices. I also read the sale ads from the grocery stores nearby. In one week, I may visit two or three different stores to stock up on sale items that I use regularly. For example, if Fair Market has laundry detergent and trash bags on sale, I'll buy those items there, then go to the Acme just a few blocks away to get yogurt or pasta. I find that paying attention to prices is the best way for me to spend less on groceries.

---

   a. What is the topic sentence? Write it here:

   _____

   b. What is the concluding sentence? Write it here:

   _____

   c. Does the concluding sentence repeat or rephrase a key word or idea in the topic sentence? _____. If so, circle those words or ideas.

   d. Is this a good concluding sentence?_____

3. Read each paragraph below and write a concluding sentence. Your sentence should return to the main idea by repeating or rephrasing key words or ideas from the topic sentence. Then give each paragraph an appropriate title. In a group, compare your answers.

A. _____

   It's easy to spend a lot of money while you're on vacation. First of all, you want to have fun on a vacation. You tell yourself, "I can have what I want. After all, I'm on vacation." You find yourself buying T-shirts, jewelry, or other special items to remember the place and the fun you're having. Vacation is also a time to enjoy expensive dinners or evenings out. Second, it's easy to buy without thinking when you're on vacation. Your credit card is right in your pocket, so you just pull it out and say, "Charge it!" You forget that when you return home, you're going to find bills waiting for you.

   _____

   _____.

B. _____

   Having a roommate is a good way to save money. First of all, with a roommate, you can split the rent in half. This is a big savings. On average, you can save about $300 per month. Also, you share the cost of the utilities: electricity, gas, telephone, and cable TV. This may save you up to $100 a month. In addition, you can divide the grocery costs. Finally, when you have a roommate, you aren't lonely. You can spend your free time at home because you have someone to keep you company. You don't need to go out to a restaurant or to a movie and spend money. _____

   _____

STEP 3

Writing

Write the first draft of your paragraph. Make sure that the ideas in your paragraph support the topic sentence that you wrote earlier. Include a concluding sentence that returns to this main idea.

STEP 4

Revising

Work with a partner. Read each other's paragraph. Write comments on your partner's paper in the margins. Use the checklist below as a guide. Then read your partner's comments and make any necessary changes.

- ❏ Does the paragraph have a topic sentence that tells about the writer's spending habits?
- ❏ Do all the sentences in the paragraph support this main idea?
- ❏ Is the paragraph unified; that is, do all the sentences support only one main idea?
- ❏ Does the paragraph have a concluding sentence?
- ❏ Does the paragraph have an appropriate title?

STEP 5

Editing

Use the following explanations and activities to help you edit your writing.

Grammar and Mechanics

Comma Splices

As you learned in Chapter 3 and in this chapter, commas should be used within a sentence, not at the end of a sentence. Using comma to connect sentences without a conjunction is called a comma splice error.

Look at the punctuation in these sentences:

Sentence 1	**Incorrect**

We drove to their house, we had dinner.

Sentence 2	**Correct**

We drove to their house. We had dinner.

Sentence 3	**Correct**

We drove to their house, **and** we had dinner.

Sentence 1 has a comma splice. It is incorrect because it has a comma where a period should be. Sentence 2 has correct punctuation because there is a period between the two sentences. Sentence 3 shows another way to correct a comma splice—add a coordinating conjunction like *and,* or *but* after the comma.

1 Read each pair of sentences below and check (✔) the sentence that has correct punctuation.

1. ＿＿ Every day I go grocery shopping, I buy food for my family.

   ✔ Every day I go grocery shopping, and I buy food for my family.

2. ＿＿ Sometimes I look in the newspaper. I find sale prices.

   ＿＿ Sometimes I look in the newspaper, I find sale prices.

3. ＿＿ This week the Giant is having a sale on fish, I will buy two pounds.

   ＿＿ This week the Giant is having a sale on fish, so I will buy two pounds.

4. ＿＿ Some children prefer to eat junk food, they don't like eating at home.

   ＿＿ Some children prefer to eat junk food. They don't like eating at home.

5. ＿＿ I don't enjoy crowded grocery stores, so I shop early in the morning.

   ＿＿ I don't enjoy crowded grocery stores, I shop early in the morning.

6. ＿＿ My neighborhood store doesn't have everything I need, the meat is fresh.

   ＿＿ My neighborhood store doesn't have everything I need, but the meat is fresh.

7. ＿＿ There are often good sales on cleaning products, I buy a lot of them.

   ＿＿ There are often good sales on cleaning products, so I buy a lot of them.

8. ＿＿ The cashiers are friendly, they help me put the groceries into my basket.

   ＿＿ The cashiers are friendly. They help me put the groceries into my basket.

9. ＿＿ I have to carry the groceries into my house, they are heavy.

   ＿＿ I have to carry the groceries into my house, and they are heavy.

10. ＿＿ Grocery shopping is fun, it takes a lot of time.

    ＿＿ Grocery shopping is fun, but it takes a lot of time.

2 Read the following paragraph. Find and correct the five remaining comma-splice errors. The first has been done for you.

Why People Buy Products

Researchers have studied the behavior of ~~shoppers, they~~ *shoppers. They* have found several reasons why a shopper chooses to buy particular brands. First, a buyer considers ease of use, one brand may be easier to use, another brand may be harder to use. Performance is another reason. A shopper looks for a product that works well. Long life is also important, a buyer looks for a product that will last a long time. Quality is important, but a shopper also thinks about the price of a product, is the product a good value? Finally, prestige is another important factor, prestige means the respect or admiration a product brings. In fact, a shopper may be influenced by several factors when he or she decides to buy something.

DO IT YOURSELF
See pages 188–189 for more practice.

Spelling Similar Words

English has many words with similar pronunciations and spellings, so it is easy to confuse them. For example, read the following sentence aloud and find the spelling error:

I fell very bad yesterday, so I went to the doctor.

The misspelled word is *fell.* The word *fell* is close to *felt* in spelling and pronunciation, but *felt* is the correct word for the sentence.

I felt very bad yesterday, so I went to the doctor.

1 Work with a partner. Study the pairs of words below. Read how each word is used in a sentence. Then read each sentence to your partner. Ask your partner to cover the page and write down the spelling of the word as you have used it. Switch roles, and check each other's spelling.

1. when/went
   a. **When** you called, I was not home.
   b. I **went** to the bank yesterday.

2. there/their
   a. Look over **there**!
   b. The students picked up **their** books.

3. live/leave
   a. I **live** in an apartment.
   b. Don't **leave** me alone.

4. feel/fell
   a. She **feels** sick today.
   b. He **fell** down and broke his leg.

5. to/too
   a. I am going **to** the movies.
   b. I like coffee. He does, **too**.

6. taught/thought
   a. The algebra teacher **taught** the lesson.
   b. He **thought** about his problem.

7. think/thing
   a. I **think** you are nice.
   b. You did a nice **thing**.

8. sit/seat
   a. Please **sit** down.
   b. Your **seat** is in the front row.

9. than/then
   a. Lemons taste better **than** limes.
   b. First, we will go to the park. **Then** we will have a picnic.

10. write/right
    a. I must **write** a paragraph.
    b. Did you use the **right** word?

11. where/were
    a. **Where** did you buy that shirt?
    b. They **were** very friendly to me.

12. who/how
    a. **Who** is that girl over there?
    b. Do you know **how** to spell this word?

DO IT YOURSELF
See pages 194–195 for more practice.

Editing Your Writing

Use the checklist below to edit your work. Then rewrite your paragraph.

Editing Checklist

❑ Are commas used correctly?

❑ Is the other punctuation correct?

❑ Are similar words spelled correctly?

On Your Own

Personal Spelling List

1. Continue to work on your spelling problems. Look over the paragraphs you wrote in this chapter. Add misspelled words to your Personal Spelling List in your notebook.

2. Study the correct spellings of the words on your list. Work with a partner. Test each other on the spellings.

Personal Editing Log

Continue to keep track of the types of grammar and mechanics errors that you often make. After your teacher returns your paragraphs from this chapter, read them over, and put checkmarks in your Personal Editing Log to identify the types of errors that you made.

More Writing Practice

Write a paragraph on one of the topics below.

REMEMBER Begin your paragraph with a topic sentence. Make all the sentences relate to the main idea. Be sure to include a concluding sentence that restates the main idea. When you finish, read over your paragraph to revise and edit it.

---

1. **Balancing My Budget**

   Write a paragraph to tell how well you balance your budget. Begin by explaining in general whether you balance your budget well or poorly. Do you save money? Do you owe money? Explain why.

2. **An Important Purchase**

   Write about an important purchase that you made sometime in the past. In your topic sentence, explain what you bought and the main reason you bought it. Include details such as where you made the purchase and the steps you took before and during the purchase, such as looking for sales, asking friends, or comparing different models.

3. **Celebrity Salaries**

   Movie stars and athletes often earn very high salaries. Popular movie stars may receive $20 million for making a film. Successful football and basketball players can earn more than $10 million per year. Are movie stars or athletes paid too much? Write a paragraph to give your opinion. Support your opinion with reasons.

Chapter Goals Think about what you have learned in Chapter 6. Check the goal(s) that you are reaching. If you do not understand one of the areas, ask your instructor for extra help. Get more writing practice by writing on another of the topics on page 127 and above.

Chapter Goals Checklist

❑ Use reasons to support an opinion.

❑ Write a unified paragraph.

❑ Write sentences with *and, but, or, so,* and *yet*.

❑ Write a concluding sentence.

❑ Avoid comma splices.

❑ Spell similar words correctly.

First Experiences

Chapter Goals

- Use examples to support ideas.
- Use dependent clauses.
- Create a flowchart to organize ideas.
- Use time transition words.
- Understand and use common punctuation marks.

Approaching the Topic

First experiences and impressions of new places and people are often ones that we remember for a long time. In Chapter 7, you will read and write about how people see new things in their lives and reflect on your own first experiences.

1. Look at the photograph. How would you describe these people's feelings about being in a new place?

2. Are your first impressions about places and people usually accurate or inaccurate? Give examples.

3. Think of an important first experience and describe it.

PART 1

Reading for Writing

The reading below is a student's account of her first days in the United States. The "American dream" is the belief that everyone in the United States has the opportunity to be successful if he or she works hard. As you read, think about *your own* first impressions of a new place.

My American Dream

America, the big land I had heard so much about, seemed like an exciting but scary place when I first arrived. I landed at John F. Kennedy Airport in New York on February 20, 1986. I had a private nursing job near the airport for three months, and in May 1986, I moved to Manhattan. When I got there, I was lost and scared because everyone was running all over, moving so quickly. I felt so different, and I wanted to blend in with Americans, so I started walking quickly and looking all around me.

Soon I started to feel less scared because everything was so exciting: the buildings, the churches, the apartments, the streets, and the department stores. I liked looking at the Chinese restaurants. They were very clean, and the food was delicious. I had never seen so much food and so many people. I loved going up into the Empire State Building and the twin towers of the World Trade Center, looking down on the busy city and the surrounding area. I especially liked the Statue of Liberty. It looked so powerful and strong, just standing there in the middle of the entire harbor. It gave a message of "freedom." When I went to the art museums, it felt like another dream. The beautiful paintings by the many famous artists took my breath away. I also loved sitting in Central Park and watching the people go by. Everyone was there, from poor to rich. I never thought there would be so many people. Yes, being in a new country was frightening at first, but I was so excited by the sights and sounds that it felt like a great dream.

Betty Hazan, Israel

Discussion   Discuss the following questions in a group.

1. Read the first sentence of the first paragraph again. What was the student's first impression of the United States?
2. What made her have these feelings?
3. Which parts of the city does she describe?
4. Does the writer's description of New York City remind you of your *own* first impressions of a new place? If so, what place and in what ways?

Language for Writing

Using the Word *First*

The word *first* is useful when you want to describe new experiences. Look at the following examples:

> **The first time** I visited Paris, I fell in love with it.
>
> When I **first** saw Paris, I thought it was a magnificent city.
>
> **At first**, I found Paris beautiful.
>
> My **first impression** of Paris was that it was a busy city.

Write four sentences using phrases with *first* to tell about one of your first experiences.

1. The first time I _____, _____.
2. When I first _____, _____.
3. At first, _____.
4. My first impression of _____ was that it was _____.

Verbal Adjectives

Many adjectives in English end in **-ing** or **-ed**. They are called verbal adjectives because they are verbs used as adjectives.

> Miami is an **exciting** city.
>
> I feel **excited** by all the sights and sounds of the city.

When you write about new experiences or places, use the **-ing** adjectives to describe the person or thing making an impression on you.

> My neighborhood was **boring** at first.

When you write about your feelings or reactions, use the **-ed** adjectives. These adjectives describe the person that has the impression.

> I felt **bored** because I stayed at home.

Here are some more verbal adjectives that you can use:

relaxing	frightening	depressing	surprising	interesting
relaxed	frightened	depressed	surprised	interested

Write the correct verbal adjective for each sentence below.

1. I was very _____ when I left my home country. The day I
   depressing/depressed
   said good-bye to my friends was _____.
   depressing/depressed

2. After a while, we began to feel _____ in our new
   relaxing/relaxed
   neighborhood. The parks, the woods, and the river nearby are all very

   _____ to us.
   relaxing/relaxed

3. I was _____ that very few of our neighbors talked to us.
   surprising/surprised
   Another _____ thing was the fact that no one invited us
   surprising/surprised
   into their homes.

4. My mother thought American TV was _____. I was more
   interesting/interested
   _____ in studying English.
   interesting/interested

Writing

Assignment for Part 1

Write a paragraph telling about your first impressions when you met a new person or saw a new place. To write your paragraph, follow the steps of the writing process.

STEP 1

Getting Ideas

1. Think about the first time you met a person or saw a new place. You could write about your first meeting with your husband, wife, boyfriend, or girlfriend. Or you could write about the first time you saw a new city, a new apartment or house, or a new school. Choose any meeting with a new person or new place that made a strong impression. Make sure it is a person or place that you know or remember well.

2. Next, think back on how the person or place seemed to you at first. The words in the box on page 133 may help you remember your first impressions. Circle two or three words that best describe how the person or place seemed to you at first, or write your own words on the blank lines.

interesting	attractive	*noisy*	**dirty**
pleasant	strange	**boring**	quiet
unusual	*modern*	serious	CROWDED
beautiful	*fun-loving*	inviting	run-down
dangerous	**fast-moving**	_____	_____
_____	_____	_____	_____

Graphic Organizers

Look at the graphic organizer that one student made to describe his first impressions of Washington, D.C. He started with a box. In it he wrote the topic and the central idea *diverse*. Then he wrote notes about parts of the city that related to the central idea.

The writer then wrote the following topic sentence:

When I first arrived in Washington, D.C., I was surprised to find that it was a very diverse city.

1. Make a graphic organizer for one of the words that give your first impressions of the person or place you chose to write about. In the center, make a box, and write one word that describes the person or place. Around the word, write notes that support the idea in the center. Put a circle around each set of notes.

2. Each circle of notes around the central word could be a supporting point in your paragraph. Be sure that all the notes relate to the word in the center.

3. Read over your graphic organizer. Choose the supporting points that you want to include in your paragraph. Cross out the ideas that you don't want to use, as the writer did below.

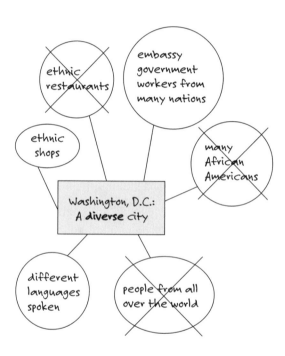

STEP 2

Organizing Examples as Support

Use specific examples to add information about the main idea and the supporting points in your writing. Examples make your writing more believable because they help to show that the opinions you express are true.

Read the student paragraph on page 135. Notice how the writer organizes his paragraph into the following parts: a topic sentence, supporting points, and examples.

A Diverse City

Topic sentence

When I first arrived in Washington, D.C., I was surprised to find that it was a very diverse city. First of all, Washington has dozens of foreign embassies. When I walked along Massachusetts Avenue, I saw many foreign people coming out of the embassies and offices. They were wearing non-American clothing representing many different nations. I was also amazed at the number of different languages I heard in the city. For instance, I sat on a park bench near Du Pont Circle and watched Russians playing chess and speaking together. In the same park, two young couples walked by speaking a foreign language, and a Spanish-speaking family ate their lunch. In addition, Washington has many stores that sell products from all over the world. In the Georgetown University area, I saw several African stores that sold leather goods from Kenya and carved stone and wood objects from Sierra Leone. There were also Indian and Caribbean food stores nearby. Cultural diversity was definitely the main thing that I noticed when I first visited Washington, D.C.

Supporting point 1

Example

Supporting point 2

Examples

Supporting point 3

Examples

Concluding sentence

This student organized his ideas into three parts (his supporting points): *embassies, languages,* and *ethnic shops.* For each supporting point, he used examples. Before he wrote, he made the graphic organizer below to organize his ideas.

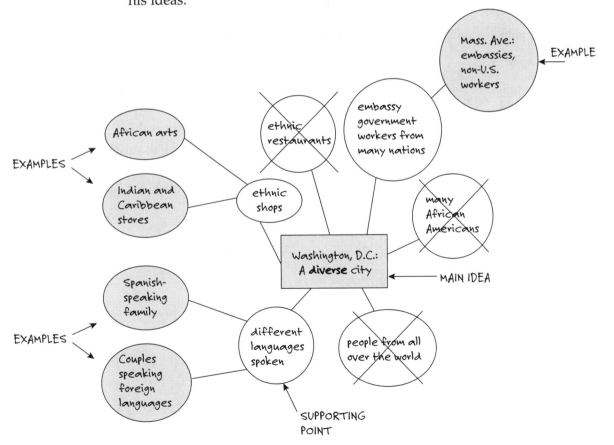

1. Look back at your graphic organizer. For each supporting point, make notes about at least one example. Put each example in a circle, and draw a line to connect it to the main point that it supports, as shown in the graphic organizer on page 135.

2. Write a topic sentence in which you introduce the person or place. Include one or two words that best describe your first impressions.

   Examples

   When I first saw my husband, I thought he was the most handsome man in the world.

   My first impression of Hong Kong was that it is a busy and crowded place.

STEP 3

Writing

Write the first draft of your paragraph. Use your topic sentence, your graphic organizer, and your outline. Be sure to include supporting points and examples.

STEP 4

Revising

Work with a partner. Read each other's paragraph. Write comments on your partner's paper in the margins. Use the checklist below as a guide. Then read your partner's comments and make any changes necessary.

❑ Does the paragraph have a topic sentence that introduces the person or place and gives a first impression?

❑ Do all the sentences in the paragraph support this first impression?

❑ Does the paragraph have supporting points about specific parts of the person or place?

❑ Does the paragraph have at least one example for each supporting point?

STEP 5

Editing

Use the following explanations and activities to help you edit your writing.

Grammar

Using Past and Present Tense Verbs Together

Verbs in the present and past tenses can be used together when you write about both past *and* present actions.

Read the start of a paragraph and notice the different verb tenses.

> I always **thought** that Boston **was** a historic city, but soon after I **arrived** there, I **discovered** that it **was** also very modern. The downtown area **has** skyscrapers . . .

The first two sentences use the past tense verbs **thought, was, arrived, discovered,** and **was** to tell about past experiences. The third sentence uses the present tense verb **has** to state a fact that is still true today.

---

1 Read the paragraph below. With a partner, underline the past and present tense verbs. Discuss why the writer uses these verbs.

My Apartment Building

When I first moved into my apartment building, I found that it was a very pleasant place to live. First of all, the neighbors were friendly. For example, the day that I moved in, my next-door neighbors, the Nams, invited me to have dinner with them. While I was moving, other neighbors came out of their apartments and introduced themselves. Now I know many of my neighbors by name. Second, I found that apartment living offered many conveniences. We were tired and busy during our first few days, so we ate at a small café in the building. The café also sold essential items like milk, bread, and toothpaste. We also found a hairdresser, dry cleaners, and travel agent in the building. It's very convenient to have all these services nearby. Finally, our new home felt very safe. My husband was out of town a lot when we first moved into the building. However, there are security guards on the first floor, and guests or delivery people have to identify themselves before the guards let them enter. Residents have to use a key to enter the building after 6 P.M. All in all, our new apartment building felt like home from the first day that we lived there, and it still does.

2 Complete the paragraph below. For each verb, choose the simple present tense or simple past tense form. Share your answers with a partner.

— **My Bad Neighborhood** —

My neighborhood ____is____ a terrible place to live. People
                    1. is

stealing, spraying graffiti on building walls, selling drugs, fighting, leaving

trash all over the place—I _____ and _____ this
                            2. see   3. hear

kind of thing every day. This _____ the neighborhood where I
                              4. be

now _____. South Philadelphia _____ the worst
     5. live   6. be

place I've ever seen in my whole life. Before I _____ here, I
                                                7. come

_____ the United States _____ a heaven. But my
8. think   9. be

thoughts _____ after I _____ to live in South
         10. change   11. come

Philadelphia. Sometimes my neighborhood _____ quiet
                                         12. be

because good people _____ afraid to drive through the
                     13. be

neighborhood. All the houses _____ like old buildings. They
                             14. look

_____ more than 100 years old. I really _____ too
15. be   16. not know

much about my neighbors, but I _____ one neighbor
                               17. know

in my block. When he _____ at me, I think he
                     18. look

_____ me. I _____ that one day my family can
19. hate   20. hope

get away from this neighborhood.

Viryol Tep, Cambodia
---

3 Complete the sentences with the simple present or simple past tense forms of the verbs given.

1. When I first ___*arrived*___ in Seattle, I _____ it _____
         arrive   think   be

   a very green city. Now, I _____ that it _____ a lot in
                                 know   rain

   Seattle, so all the plants and trees _____ very green.
                                             be

2. I _____ in an apartment building for the first time 5 years ago.
       live

   At first, it _____ strange not living in a house. But after a
                 feel

   while, I _____ used to it. Now I _____ many aspects
              become   enjoy

   of apartment life.

3. My first few months of driving in my new city _____ terrible. I
                                           be

   _____ any of the streets, so I _____ with a map on my
   not, know   drive

   lap. I often _____ on the side of the road to find out where I
                 stop

   _____. Today I _____ everywhere without a map. In
   be   go

   fact, I frequently _____ directions to other people who
                 give

   _____ lost.
   be

4. During my first weeks at work, I _____ many new people. One
                            meet

   of my co-workers, Susan, _____ like a very friendly person. We
                      seem

   _____ a lot and _____ about each other. Now, after 10
   talk   learn

   years, we _____ still good friends. My first impression of her
           be

   _____ still the same today.
   be

5. The first time I _____ my future husband, we _____ in
           see   be

   a class together at a university. I _____ sure I _____
                    not, be   like

   him then. Later we _____ out together and _____
             go   become

   friends. Now, after 20 years, he _____ still my best friend. I
                be

   _____ happy that my first impressions about him _____.
   be   change

DO IT YOURSELF
See pages 174–175
for more practice.

Sentences with Dependent Clauses

Look at the the example sentence below. It has two parts: a dependent clause and an independent clause. A clause is a group of words with a subject and a verb.

⌐———— DEPENDENT CLAUSE ————¬ ⌐ INDEPENDENT CLAUSE ¬
When **I arrived** at the airport, **my friends met** me.

- A dependent clause cannot stand alone as a complete sentence because it begins with a word like **when,** a subordinating conjunction, and is not a complete thought.

- An independent clause can stand alone as a complete sentence because it has a subject and a verb and has a complete thought.

- A dependent clause must be connected to an independent clause.

Incorrect:

I liked my next-door neighbor the first day. Because she welcomed us to the neighborhood.

Correct:

I liked my next-door neighbor the first day because she welcomed us to the neighborhood.

There are two ways to form sentences with a dependent clause. Notice the position of the subordinating conjunctions, and the punctuation, in each pattern.

1. Dependent clause, + independent clause.

   After I eat my breakfast**,** I go shopping.
   Although I am sleepy**,** I must finish my housework.

   OR

2. Independent clause + dependent clause.

   I like my neighborhood **because** it is very safe.
   We will wait for you **until** you arrive.

Subordinating Conjunctions

Subordinating conjunctions introduce dependent clauses. They show the relationship between the ideas in the clauses. Look at the chart and the different meanings of some subordinating conjunctions.

Subordinating Conjunction	Use	Example Sentence
before	Time	**Before** I left my country, I said good-bye to my friends.
after	Time	I called my mother on the telephone **after** I arrived in the United States.
when	Time	**When** we moved to France, we lived with my uncle's family.

Subordinating Conjunction	Use	Example Sentence
while	Time	I could not sleep **while** I was on the airplane.
until	Time	I wasn't happy **until** I learned enough English to communicate.
although	Contrast	**Although** I am homesick, my life is better in my new country.
even though	Contrast	I still feel lonely **even though** I have many new friends.
though	Contrast	**Though** I know the city better now, I still get lost sometimes.
because	Cause	I started taking night classes **because** I work during the day.
since	Cause	I need to work **since** I must pay my bills.
if	Condition	**If** I get my pharmacy degree in 5 years, I will be happy.

3 Read the "sentences" below. Mark the correct sentences **C**. Mark the incorrect sentences **I**. Rewrite each incorrect sentence to make it correct.

_I_ 1. Chinatown is a great place to ~~live. Because~~ *live because* it has many good restaurants and food stores in a convenient location.

____ 2. If you feel hungry at 2 A.M., you don't have to worry about cooking. That's good for me because I often work late.

____ 3. You don't have to cook because there are many good restaurants. Also, they're all inexpensive.

____ 4. In addition, you will find many grocery stores. If you want to cook at home.

____ 5. In the stores, you can find fresh food every day. When you want a home-cooked meal.

____ 6. Although I don't eat too many sweets, there are Chinese bakeries, too.

____ 7. You just need to walk two blocks when you want to use public transportation.

____ 8. You don't have to wait for a long time. Since the buses and trains run frequently.

____ 9. Although there are some problems there, living in Chinatown has many advantages. All in all, it's one of my favorite parts of the city.

4 For each item below, choose the appropriate subordinating conjunction to connect the clauses. In a group, compare your answers.

1. _____*When*_____ I read a book at night, I feel sleepy.
   Before/When

2. Call me _____ you want to go out.
   even though/if

3. I will not speak to you again _____ you say you are sorry
   until/when

   for what you did.

4. I took a shower _____ I woke up.
   before/after

5. _____ he eats too much, he often gets a stomachache.
   Since/Although

6. _____ she was very sick, she went to her classes.
   Although/Because

7. I washed and dried the dishes _____ I put them away in
   while/before

   the cabinet.

8. They decided to get married _____ they love each other.
   even though/because

DO IT YOURSELF
See pages 163–164
for more practice.

9. I cannot buy a computer _____ I save some money.
   until/if

10. _____ the telephone rang, I answered it.
    Before/When

Language Tip ■ *Very*

The following are some ways to use **very**:

- Before the adverb *much* (usually at the end of the sentence)

  I like my new city **very much**.

- Before adjectives

  When I first met John, I thought he was **very funny**.
  I had a **very bad** time on my first date with Gina.

---

5 Use *very much* or *very* + adjective to complete the following sentences. Use different adjectives in your answers.

1. The first time I tried to speak English, I was *very embarrassed* .

2. I liked my first train ride _____.

3. The first time I went sledding in the snow was _____.

4. I remember the first time I spent the night away from home. I missed
   my parents _____.

5. I was _____ the first time I saw a homeless person in the city.

6. It is _____ to move to a new place.

7. Although I often felt alone, I enjoyed my own apartment _____.

8. Students usually don't have much money, so I was _____ when I got my first job.

9. When she arrived in Chicago, she didn't go out _____. She thought the city was _____.

10. When I first started driving, I felt _____. However, now I enjoy driving _____.

Editing Your Writing

Use the checklist below to edit your work. Then rewrite your paragraph.

> ### Editing Checklist
>
> ❑ Are the simple present and simple past used correctly?
>
> ❑ Are dependent clauses correctly joined with independent clauses?
>
> ❑ Do sentences with dependent clauses have correct punctuation?
>
> ❑ Is *very* used correctly?

Journal Writing Write a journal entry about a first impression or opinion that you later changed. Explain how you first felt about a person, place, or thing. Then explain how and why your feelings changed and how you feel now.

PART 2

Reading for Writing

The reading below, "My First Plane Ride,"describes a 6-year-old child's feelings on her first airplane ride. As you read, think about your own first-time experiences.

My First Plane Ride

My first ride on an airplane was a fabulous experience that I will always remember. I was 6 years old when my mother told me that we were going to visit the Ivory Coast for vacation. I waited anxiously for the day of our trip because I knew that we had to travel by plane. On the day of our flight, I was impatient to get on the plane. I gazed out the large windows of the airport. When I finally got on the plane, I started running everywhere. I was excited by everything—the way the chairs moved forward and backward, the small lights above the seats, the window shades. I couldn't stop talking. I made remarks about all the new things to my mother and everyone around me. Naturally, the flight attendants guessed that this was my first time on a plane. One of them volunteered to show me the "kitchen," so I could see how food was served. Then she took me to the restrooms and explained how to open and lock the doors. I was fascinated when she showed us how to wear the oxygen mask in case of an emergency. Afterwards, she took me to the pilot's area where the pilots explained how to use the buttons and lights and even let me take the controls for a minute. At the end of the visit, the flight attendant gave me some candy and souvenirs from the airline, and she took me back to my seat. I was so happy that I was smiling from ear to ear. Even after so many years, thinking about those wonderful moments still makes me smile.

Nene Diallo, Guinea

Discussion   Discuss the following questions in a group.

1. How did the writer feel when she took her first plane ride?

2. What areas of the plane does she describe?

3. Do you remember your first plane (train, boat, bus) ride? Did you have an experience similar to the writer's? Explain.

Language for Writing

In the reading on page 144, the writer used a number of descriptive adjectives. Look at these examples:

> My first ride on an airplane was a **fabulous** experience.

> I was **impatient** to get on the plane; I gazed out the large windows of the airport.

When you write, try to use a variety of words instead of very common words. For example, don't overuse the following common words. Look for synonyms instead.

Overused Words

happy	excited
wonderful	good
nice	interesting
beautiful	bad

For each sentence below, circle the two words that have similar meanings to the adjectives in **boldface.** Use a dictionary if necessary.

1. I was **happy**.
   - a. cheerful *(circled)*
   - b. glad *(circled)*
   - c. gloomy

2. I had a **nice** time.
   - a. pleasant
   - b. dreadful
   - c. agreeable

3. I felt **excited**.
   - a. indifferent
   - b. thrilled
   - c. delighted

4. I had a **wonderful** day.
   - a. amazing
   - b. normal
   - c. remarkable

5. It was a **beautiful** place.
   - a. unattractive
   - b. attractive
   - c. lovely

6. The bus system is **good**.
   - a. efficient
   - b. fast
   - c. dangerous

Writing

Assignment for Part 2

Write a paragraph telling about a first experience. To write your paragraph, follow the steps of the writing process.

STEP 1

Getting Ideas

1. In a group, brainstorm possible writing topics. Read over the list below to get ideas, and add your own ideas. Discuss several of your first experiences. Then choose an experience to write about.

first time riding a horse	first time eating a type of food	first day of college
first date	first train ride	first kiss
first day of school	first day of work	first death/loss
first time driving a car		
_____	_____	_____
_____	_____	_____

2. Once you have thought of a topic, freewrite for 5 to 10 minutes. Write down everything you can think of about the experience. Don't worry about spelling, grammar, or the organization of your ideas.

STEP 2

Organizing

Flowchart

A flowchart can help you get and organize ideas for your paragraph. A flowchart is a chronological "map" of main events in a story. Look at the following flowchart.

My Sixteenth Birthday

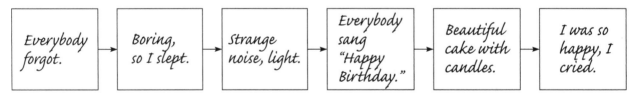

This student's flowchart shows the main events of his birthday. He wrote a few important words for each main event in the day. If you read the flowchart from left to right, you get a brief idea of the story. The flowchart helped the student write his paragraph, which appears in Chapter 5 on page 87.

1. After you have chosen a topic and done your freewriting, make a flowchart of the main events of your "first experience" paragraph. Write your topic on the top of the page. Then draw boxes that include a few words about each main event of the experience.

2. Read over your flowchart. Think about adjectives or other words that describe your feelings or the type of experience you had.

3. Discuss your first experience with a group of your classmates. Take notes and add any new ideas to your freewriting. Circle the ideas you want to include in your paragraph. Cross out ideas that are not useful.

Time Transitions

Some transition, or connecting, words indicate time order. They show the time relationship between sentences. Read the following paragraph and notice the boldfaced words. They are transitions of time.

My First Real Job

My first real job changed my life in many ways. When I graduated from college, I was ready to have a good job and a home, but I knew it would be difficult. **First**, I interviewed for nursing positions at six hospitals in the area. Fortunately, the employers liked my good grades and training experience. The largest hospital in the city offered me a high salary with benefits. I was so excited. I couldn't believe how lucky I was. **Then** I started to look for a home. I read the classified advertisements every day. I visited a real estate office. I looked at many homes. **Soon**, I found the perfect home in a safe neighborhood. It was a large home with a big yard and a garage. **Next**, I went to my bank. I had some savings in the bank because I had worked in the past, so the bank gave me a loan to buy the house. I signed all the papers. I waited for the day when I could move into my home. All of these wonderful things happened to me because of my first good job.

Here are some common transition words and phrases that show time order. These words are used when you tell a story in chronological order.

Transition	Meaning
first	initially
then	next, after
afterward	following
meanwhile	at the same time
at that moment	at that time
finally	last

1. Read the paragraph below. Fill in the blanks with appropriate time order transition words. Compare your answers with a partner's.

My Vacation in Ocean City

I had a wonderful vacation last July when I visited an American beach for the first time. My friends and I spent a week in Ocean City, New Jersey. Ocean City is a great place for relaxing and having fun. Luckily, my friend Alla's parents have a big house in that area. They let us stay there by ourselves and enjoy a week of fun. Every morning we exercised. _____, we swam in the Atlantic Ocean. _____,
          1.   2.
we jogged on the beach. _____, we had pizza or snacks and
                                        3.
walked along the beach. In the afternoon we took the trolley home.

_____, we watched some movies and planned our evenings.
          4.
One of my friends, John, had a birthday that week, so we planned a surprise evening out for him. We drove to an Italian restaurant and didn't let him open his eyes until we arrived at the door. _____, he was very
                                                                                          5.
surprised because he knew that we had chosen the restaurant especially for him. We enjoyed a good meal while a band played music.

_____, we drove to Atlantic City. We danced in the clubs and
          6.
walked along the boardwalk. _____, we gambled in the
                                          7.
casinos. _____, we went home, tired but happy. Indeed, I will
              8.
remember my first trip to an American shore for a long time.

Slava Aybinder, Ukraine

---

2. Read over your flowchart again. Write a topic sentence that introduces the experience and tells what kind of experience it was or how you felt about it. You may want to write your topic sentence in one of these ways:

   1. The first time I _____ was a _____
                              Did what?   What kind of?
   experience.

   2. I felt _____ the first time I _____.
                  How?   Did what?

STEP 3

Writing

Write the first draft of your paragraph. Use your topic sentence, your flowchart, and your freewriting ideas. Include specific details, and add time transitions between ideas where appropriate.

STEP 4

Revising

Work with a partner. Read each other's paragraph. Write comments on your partner's paper in the margins. Use the checklist below as a guide. Then read your partner's comments and make any necessary changes.

- ❏ Does the paragraph begin with a topic sentence that introduces a first-time experience and tells the writer's feeling about it?
- ❏ Do the sentences follow chronological order?
- ❏ Does the writer use time transition words appropriately?
- ❏ Are there enough specific details in the story?
- ❏ Is there a concluding sentence?

STEP 5

Editing

Use the following explanations and activities to help you edit your writing.

Mechanics

Common Punctuation Marks		
Look at the chart below. It explains a few common punctuation marks and shows how they are used in sentences.		
Punctuation Mark	**Use**	**Example Sentence**
Quotation marks (" ")	Show the exact words that someone said or wrote.	"I don't know the answer," the student said.
Long dash (—)	Often introduces a break in thought.	At first, there were many types of American food I could not eat—hamburgers, pizza, and hot dogs especially—so going to restaurants was often a problem.
Colon (:)	Introduces a list of items.	When I got to the city, there were three things that I found everywhere: old buildings, beautiful churches, and great department stores.
Semicolon (;)	Separates two related independent clauses in one sentence.	I need to find a new doctor; my current doctor's office is too far from my home.

1 Rewrite the sentences by adding the appropriate punctuation. Look back at the chart on page 149 and the punctuation rules on pages 36 and 60. You will need to use commas and sentence end punctuation.

1. Where is the train station I asked him.

   "Where is the train station?" I asked him.

2. Richard has three major hobbies playing Ping Pong listening to music and going to the movies

3. When I walked into the shop the clerk said Can I help you

4. Even though he was tired he washed his clothes did his homework and read a book before bedtime

5. My English class has students from many countries Vietnam China Cambodia Puerto Rico Russia Ethiopia and Thailand

6. In the beginning I didn't know how to say anything in English so I just smiled at people

7. I was lost so I asked for help I said Do you know the way to the train station

2 Read the paragraph below. Practice your editing skills by finding and correcting ten errors in verb tense and sentence end punctuation. The first one is done for you. With a partner, compare your answers.

My Favorite Teacher

I found a special teacher on my first day of school in the United States. I started school one week after I came to the United States. The first day of school was strange. It was a very confusing ~~day. Because~~ *day because* the people and the language were new. When I got there, first I meet my counselor. She was very friendly and kind. She comed to me with open arms, and she explained everything to me. She arrange my schedule and introduced me to each teacher. They also welcomed me with open arms. I was very happy to have a counselor like her. She treat me like my mom she was also like a friend. She used to push me to speak English and not to be scared we were very close. She was always there for me. Whenever I had a problem with anything. She also taught my American history class. I was one of her best students, she feel proud of me because she was the one who encouraged me. Every one of my teachers was kind, but she was the one who was special. I will always thank her for the difference she made in my life.

Haimanot Anbessie, Ethiopia

 Editing Your Writing

Use the checklist below to edit your work. Then rewrite your paragraph.

> ### Editing Checklist
> ❑ Are commas and periods used correctly?
> ❑ Are quotes, dashes, and other punctuation used correctly?
> ❑ Are clauses joined and punctuated correctly?
> ❑ Are all the verb forms correct?
> ❑ Are all the tenses correct?

On Your Own

Personal Spelling List

1. Continue to work on your spelling problems. Look over the paragraphs you wrote in this chapter. Add misspelled words to your Personal Spelling List in your notebook.

2. Study the correct spellings of the words on your list. Work with a partner. Test each other on the spellings.

Personal Editing Log

Always remember to check and correct the grammar, spelling, and punctuation of your work before you turn it in. Then read the marks and corrections that your teacher makes after you write. Your goal should be to edit your writing well.

After your teacher returns the paragraphs that you wrote for this chapter, read them and put checkmarks in your Personal Editing Log to identify the types of errors that you made.

More Writing Practice

Write a paragraph on one of the following topics.

REMEMBER Think about the topic before you begin to write. Organize your paragraph with a topic sentence, support, and a conclusion. Include transition words. After you finish, read over your paragraph to revise and edit it.

1. **An Important Reunion**

   Write a paragraph about seeing a place or person after a long period of time. In your topic sentence, explain how you felt at the time. Did the place or person change? Were your feelings toward the place or person different?

2. **Breaking a Rule**

   Parents everywhere have rules for their children to follow. Write a story about a time that you didn't follow your parents' rules and got into trouble. Explain what happened and include details such as the following: How did you feel at that time? How do you feel about the experience now?

3. **A Life-Changing Experience**

   Write a paragraph about an experience that changed your life. Begin with a topic sentence that states what the event was and how it changed your life. Include details such as the following: When and where did the event occur? Was the change positive or negative? How do you feel now?

Chapter Goals   Reflect on the learning goals for Chapter 7. Check the goal(s) that you are achieving. If you still have questions about one of the areas, write another paragraph on one of the topics on page 152 for more practice. Ask your instructor for help.

Chapter Goals Checklist

❑ Use examples to support ideas.

❑ Use dependent clauses.

❑ Create a flowchart to organize ideas.

❑ Use time transition words.

❑ Understand and use common punctuation marks.

Do It Yourself

"Do it yourself" means to work independently, without someone else's help. If you need extra practice with a language topic, you can do the additional exercises in this section on your own. Then check your answers on pages 200–214.

I. Sentences

A. Parts of a Sentence: Subjects and Verbs

> The subject and verb are the main parts of a sentence. Look at the subjects and verbs in the sentences below.
>
> ┌ SUBJECT ┐ VERB
> My sister lives in Canada.
>
> ┌─── SUBJECT ───┐ ┌─ VERB ─┐
> Jurgen and Charlie don't have large families.

1 Underline the subjects and circle the verbs in the sentences in the letter below.

Dear Teacher,

I like your class. It is very exciting. I am learning to write. It is not very easy, but I am doing the best I can. My weekend was okay. I worked very hard. I had to work at a wedding Saturday night until 1 A.M. I got home at 2:15 in the morning, so I was very tired. The next day, I studied all day for my other classes. I didn't go out anywhere, so it wasn't a fun weekend for me. I want to know about your weekend. Write to me soon.

2 Complete each of the following sentences with a linking verb. Use an appropriate verb from the list of common linking verbs in the box below. Add -s to the verb if necessary.

> **Common Linking Verbs**
>
> **Existence:** *be*
> **Mental states:** *think, believe, understand, seem, forget, remember, know, mean*
> **Senses:** *hear, see, smell, feel, sound*

1. Hot cocoa _____*tastes*_____ good on a cold day.
2. My books _____ in a big pile on the floor.
3. Lynne _____ a secretary in the high school.
4. You _____ very tired! Did you get any sleep last night?
5. I _____ a good cook. Everyone _____ happy to eat my food.

6. The cookies _____ delicious. Are they ready yet?

7. Richard's new car _____ very practical. It _____ a Ford Explorer with four-wheel drive.

3 Complete the sentences below. Add a subject or a verb. Use any word or words that are appropriate for the sentence.

My Neighbor Mrs. Maxwell

My neighbor Mrs. Maxwell _____ an active person. Every afternoon, she _____ a walk. _____ likes to walk, even in the winter. _____ and her friend, Mrs. Noble, often walk together. Mrs. Maxwell _____ a walking stick because she is 92 years old. Mrs. Noble _____ her a strong arm to lean on _____ keeps Mrs. Maxwell healthy. Mrs. Maxwell also _____ thick eyeglasses. She _____ very good vision. She also _____ a little trouble keeping her balance. Still, Mrs. Maxwell _____ in a house by herself. She _____ to be independent and active.

B. Parts of a Sentence: Direct Objects

Many sentences also have direct objects. Remember: Direct objects follow the verb and answer the question *what?* or *who?* Look at the subjects, verbs, and objects in the sentences below.

┌──── SUBJECT ────┐ VERB ┌── OBJECT ──┐
Chirag and Bhakti had a good time at the party.

SUBJECT VERB   OBJECT
Jim drives his sister to work every day.

SUBJECT VERB ┌──── OBJECT ────┐
Elizabeth has two dogs and a cat.

1 Underline the objects in the following sentences. Some of the sentences may have no object.

1. My family owns <u>two cars</u>.

2. We have a van and a two-door car.

3. My sister bought a car last year.

4. She doesn't like it very much.

5. My brother Liu drives too fast.

6. Her father never cooks dinner.

7. Tu and Ton share a bedroom.

8. They do not have enough space in their room.

9. My family is very happy.

10. We often take short trips on the weekend.

2 Label the subjects **S** and verbs **V** and circle the objects in the following sentences taken from student writing.

    S   *V*

1. She has (a husband and four children.)

2. She takes care of her little boy and little girl.

3. My neighborhood has many interesting places.

4. My father loses his car keys sometimes.

5. I'm going to get a good education. Then, I'm going to get a good job.

6. I don't have a full-time job.

7. I don't have too much money to spend.

8. I paid $953 for my tuition this semester.

9. My parents saved a lot of money.

10. I waste too much time.

3 Complete the following sentences by adding an appropriate object. Remember that the direct object usually answers the questions *What?* or *Who?* The first sentence is completed as an example.

My friends the Kumars are building _____*a brand-new house*_____.

Their house will have _____. Each bedroom will

have a _____. The Kumars will have

_____ for watching television and relaxing. Mrs.

Kumar wants _____ because she cooks a lot. They

can put _____ in their big basement. The large

garage will hold _____. The dining room has

_____ so that they can look out onto the backyard.

They will spend _____ on the deck in their back-

yard. The Kumars plan to have _____ to celebrate

after they move into their new house.

C. Complete Sentences

> A complete sentence must have at least one subject and one complete verb and express a complete thought.
>
> ┌ SUBJECT ┐ VERB
> Our school closed yesterday because of the snow.
>
> ┌———— SUBJECT ————┐ VERB   VERB
> My friend Melissa and I had a snowball fight and went sledding.

1 Read the following "sentences" taken from student writing. Mark the complete sentences **C** and the incomplete sentences **I**. Add or change a word or words to correct the incomplete sentences.

_I_ 1. My neighborhood is a nice place because _^*it's* very quiet.

____ 2. I live on a small street.

____ 3. Around the house very quiet.

____ 4. Near my house there so many shopping centers.

____ 5. A new building in that area.

____ 6. The houses in this area look like normal houses, not too big or too small.

____ 7. In the past, I lived with my parents.

____ 8. I didn't pay rent. When I lived with my parents.

____ 9. I think it better for me to live with my parents.

2 Complete the following linking verb sentences. After the verb, write an adjective or adjectives, a noun or noun phrase, or a prepositional phrase. Compare your answers with your classmates.

1. His backpack seems _very heavy_____.

2. Today, I feel _____.

3. The weather seems _____.

4. My teacher is _____.

5. The students in my class are _____.

6. The mountain air smells _____.

7. Your soup tastes _____.

8. In summer, the river looks _____.

9. His family is _____.

3 Complete the sentences below. Be sure each sentence has a subject and a verb and expresses a complete thought.

1. Last night I ___called my friend on the telephone___.

2. _____ and I like to spend time together.

3. _____ is my favorite pastime.

4. _____ love to go to the beach in the summertime.

5. My family _____.

6. Being with my friends and family _____.

7. After a tiring day, I _____.

8. My neighborhood _____.

9. _____ makes me afraid.

10. Every morning, the students _____.

D. *There Is* and *There Are* Sentences

> Sentences that begin with **there is** and **there are** introduce a subject.
> **There is** a table in the front of the classroom.
> **There are** several books on the table.

1 Complete the paragraph on page 161 with *there is* and *there are*. Use the drawing to help you.

Daniel's Messy Apartment

Daniel's apartment is a big mess. _____*There are*_____ things lying all over the place. _____ dirty clothes on the floor. _____ one shoe on the sofa and one under the sofa. Also, _____ dirty dishes on the coffee table. _____ a CD player in one corner of the room, but it's not working anymore. _____ CDs on the sofa and on the floor. None of them are in their cases. _____ a mirror on the wall, but it is broken. The clock doesn't work, either. _____ so much dirt on the windows that you can't see through them. _____ a telephone somewhere in the room, but Daniel can't find it. You can't sit in the chair because _____ a big dog sleeping in it. Daniel's apartment is really dirty and disorganized.

2 Write five sentences about the room where you are now. Use *there is* or *there are* to tell about things in the room.

Example

*There is a computer in my bedroom.*_____

1. _____

2. _____

3. _____

4. _____

5. _____

E. Sentences with *and, but, so, or, yet*

Combine simple sentences into compound by using a coordinating conjunction such as *and, but, so, or, yet*.	
Simple Sentences	**Compound Sentences**
Rebecca feels sick. She is going home.	Rebecca feels sick, so she is going home.
I want to buy a new car. It costs too much.	I want to buy a new car, but it costs too much.
Review the use of coordinating conjunctions in the chart on page 115.	

1 Complete the sentences with an appropriate coordinating conjunction.

1. I need some money from my bank. I can get it from the teller inside the bank, ___*or*___ I can use the automated teller machine outside.

2. Tomorrow I'll call my friend, _____ we'll decide where to go on the weekend.

3. Ron wants to become a doctor, _____ he thinks it will take too long.

4. Jessie loves to watch television shows, _____ she bought a new TV.

5. Do you want to have dinner now, _____ do you prefer to wait an hour?

6. Reyna wants to lose weight, _____ she is eating ice cream right now.

7. My brother Charles lives in Chicago, _____ my sister Joan lives in Miami.

8. Sometimes writing comes easily to me, _____ other times it is very difficult.

9. Houses in the United States are expensive, _____ I must save a lot of money.

2 Complete the sentences with *and, so, but,* or *yet.*

1. Larry spends too much money. He would like to save money, _____ he always spends it on his friends and himself.

2. He goes out to dinner every night, _____ he never cooks. His friends never have money, _____ when they go along, Larry always pays the bill.

3. Larry also goes to the movies a lot, _____ he buys gifts for his girlfriend.

4. He likes music, _____ he has to have the latest music equipment.

5. He likes to travel a lot, _____ he uses his credit card to pay for everything.

6. By the end of the month, Larry discovers that he has many bills, _____ he does not have enough money in the bank to pay them.

7. Larry wants to change his spending habits, _____ he has promised himself that next month he will cut back his spending.

F. Sentences with Dependent Clauses

> The sentences below have two parts: a dependent clause and an independent clause. The dependent clause by itself is not a complete sentence.
>
> ┌──────── DEPENDENT CLAUSE ────────┐
> English is necessary because I live in an English-speaking country.
>
> ┌─ DEPENDENT CLAUSE ─┐
> When I finish college, I hope to get a good job.
> On pages 140–141, review the subordinating conjunctions (*because*, *when*, etc.) that are used to begin dependent clauses.

1 Choose the appropriate subordinating conjunction to connect the dependent and independent clauses below to make a sentence.

1. I like to watch television ___*while*___ I eat dinner.
   (because/while)

2. _____ I was a child, I took many trips with my family.
   (When/Before)

3. _____ I have enough time, I will clean my kitchen.
   (If/Although)

4. Karen goes to the gym every day _____ she likes to
   (since/after)
   exercise.

5. Last night he read a book _____ he fell asleep.
   (until/if)

6. _____ it's raining, we are having the party inside.
   (Even though/Because)

7. I must wear my glasses _____ I hate the way they look.
   (since/though)

8. _____ I drink too much coffee, I can't sleep well.
   (Whenever/Before)

9. I locked the doors and turned off the radio _____ I left
   (after/before)
   home.

10. Every morning I take a shower _____ I wake up.
    (since/after)

2 Complete the following sentences.

1. I enjoy shopping because ___*I love to buy new things*___.

2. When _____, I take off my shoes and relax.

3. If you need help, _____.

4. _____ because I have a car.

5. Although _____, I must finish my homework.

6. Since I like to cook, _____ .

7. I can't go to the movies until _____ .

8. After I moved to my new city, _____ .

9. I feel afraid whenever _____ .

10. _____ while I was walking down the street.

II. Common Verb Tenses

A. Simple Present Tense

Be **Forms**		
I	**am**	a nice person.
He/She	**is**	my friend.
It	**is**	important.
You/They/We/ Clark and Laura	**are**	happy.

Other Verb **Forms**		
I/You/They/We	**live**	in Miami.
Patti and Michael	**live**	in Houston.
He/She	**lives**	in West Chicago.
Leo/Mary	**lives**	in a big house.
A dog	**lives**	next door.

1 Use the correct form of the verb given to complete the sentences in this paragraph. Use the simple present tense form of the verbs. The first sentence is completed as an example.

Respect for Others

Every day, my parents _____*teach*_____ me the importance of
teach

respect. My mother and father always _____ me how to
show

respect others. My father _____ me to be respectful to
tell

people who are older than I am. In the Dominican Republic, a person

_____ formal words to speak to older people. We
use

sometimes _____ an older person "aunt" or "uncle." In
call

addition, my mother always _____ respectfully to her
                                    talk

siblings even though they _____ about her age. She
                                  be

_____ at her brothers or sisters. She _____
        not scream   *pay*

attention to them when they _____. My parents
                                  speak

_____ that if you _____ respectful to others,
        know   *be*

other people will treat you the same way.

2 Complete the following sentences. Use a simple present tense verb that is appropriate for the sentence, as the first sentence illustrates.

1. Responsibility ___*is*___ a very important value to teach any child.

2. If you _____ a lot of money, it _____ easy to support your family.

3. Honesty and kindness _____ also important values for a child.

4. Being honest _____ that you _____ lies.

5. When you _____ people well, they usually _____ the same way with you.

6. If you _____ nice things for others, you _____ friends more easily.

7. A good parent _____ his or her children the best ways to behave.

8. The best parents _____ a lot of patience because it _____ time to teach a child good behavior.

3 Use the phrases to write sentences about your daily habits.

1. in the afternoon
   I usually go home in the afternoon. _____

2. in the morning
   _____

3. to school
   _____

4. during the day
   _____

5. after classes

_____

6. at night

_____

7. every week

_____

8. on the weekends

_____

9. once a month

_____

10. always

_____

11. never

_____

B. Simple Present versus Present Progressive

> Simple present tells about an action that continues over a long time. Present progressive tells about an action that is in progress now or an action that is temporary.
>
> | **Simple Present** | **Present Progressive** |
> | --- | --- |
> | Bob always **works** hard. | This year he **is working** at a grocery store. |
> | Lin **doesn't talk** very much. | Lin **is talking** to her teacher now. |

1 Complete the following sentences. Use the simple present or the present progressive tense forms of the verbs.

1. Susan ___*is taking*___ two classes this summer.
   <small>take</small>

   She usually _____ four classes during the fall and spring.
   <small>take</small>

2. Terry always _____ to learn new skills at work.
   <small>try</small>

   Right now he _____ to learn a new computer program.
   <small>try</small>

3. The weather _____ warmer this week.
   <small>get</small>

   It frequently _____ warm in the afternoon.
   <small>get</small>

4. Leigh _____ late every Saturday.
       sleep

   She _____ in her room at the moment.
      sleep

5. Usually Peter _____ close attention to everything around
         pay

   him when he _____ a car.
       drives

   Today, however, he _____ attention because he
         pay, not

   _____ on his cell phone while he _____ .
    talk   *drive*

6. Today Martina _____ too much time on the Internet.
         spend

   Normally, she _____ only a half-hour each day to check her
        spend

   e-mail.

2 Write positive or negative statements about your regular activities and habits or those of someone in your household. Use the words provided. Change the form, or ending, of the verb to match the subject of your sentence.

1. be an organized person
   I'm not an organized person.

2. cook dinner
   My mother cooks dinner for our family every day.

3. eat breakfast
   _____

4. be cheerful in the morning
   _____

5. clean my bedroom every day
   _____

6. be a lazy student
   _____

7. take a shower
   _____

8. wash my clothes
   _____

9. go out on weekends

_____

10. work full-time

_____

11. be dependable

_____

3 Use the words provided below to write positive or negative statements about the actions that you are doing now. Change the verb to the present progressive tense.

1. do math homework right now
   *I'm not doing math homework right now.*_____

2. think about my family now

_____

3. drink coffee at this moment

_____

4. look for a new job now

_____

5. learn a lot of English in this class

_____

6. take two classes this semester

_____

7. worry about my grades this term

_____

8. work long hours this week

_____

9. try to choose a college major

_____

10. live with my parents at the present time

_____

Non-Progressive Verbs

> Some verbs are not usually used in the **-ing,** or continuous, form.
>
> My mother **knows** how to cook very well.
>
> Our family **has** one car.
>
> Here is a list of some common non-continuous verbs:
>
> **Existence:** be
>
> **Feelings and emotions:** *like, love, hate, prefer, want, need*
>
> **Mental states:** *think, believe, understand, seem, forget, remember, know, mean*
>
> **Senses:** *hear, see, smell, feel, sound*
>
> **Possession:** *belong, own, have*

1 Complete the sentences with one of the non-continuous verbs in the box above. Change the form, or ending, of the verb to match the subject.

1. I _____ *hate* _____ to stay at home all the time.

2. I _____ to go shopping with my friends.

3. Do you _____ how to play the piano?

4. I often _____ people's names, but I remember their faces.

5. The word *concentrate* _____ "to think very carefully about something."

6. I _____ the telephone ringing.

7. I _____ the homework. It's very easy for me.

8. My teacher _____ that students should turn in their assignments on time.

9. Do you _____ your coffee black or with cream?

10. I _____ a car, so I ride the bus to college.

2 Write sentences about your habits, beliefs, and possessions. Use the phrases provided. Add other words to each sentence to tell more about yourself.

1. like TV shows

   I don't like to watch TV shows. _____

2. love shopping

   _____

3. prefer to eat dinner

   _____

4. remember people's names

_____

5. use the Internet

_____

6. want a lot of money

_____

7. know a lot about _____

_____

8. understand movies in English

_____

9. have _____ friends

_____

C. Simple Past Tense

Simple past tense is the most common verb tense for telling about past actions. For regular verbs, the simple past tense is formed by adding -**ed** to the base (simplest) form of the verb. However, many verbs in English have irregular past forms. Some irregular past tense verbs are listed in the chart.

Regular Past Forms

I	**worked**	very hard yesterday.
You	**worked**	on your homework last night.
John	**worked**	every day last week.
Michele and I	**worked**	at the high school last semester.
They	**worked**	all day to clean up the basement.

Irregular Past Tense Verb Chart

Base Form	Past Form	Base Form	Past Form
arise	arose	bind	bound
awake	awoke	bite	bit
be	was/were	bleed	bled
bear	bore	blow	blew
beat	beat	break	broke
become	became	breed	bred
begin	began	bring	brought
bend	bent	broadcast	broadcast
bet	bet	build	built

Base Form	Past Form	Base Form	Past Form
burst	burst	hang	hung[1]
buy	bought	have	had
cast	cast	hear	heard
catch	caught	hide	hid
choose	chose	hit	hit
cling	clung	hold	held
come	came	hurt	hurt
cost	cost	keep	kept
creep	crept	kneel	knelt
cut	cut	know	knew
deal	dealt	lay	laid
dig	dug	lead	led
do	did	leave	left
draw	drew	lend	lent
drink	drank	let	let
drive	drove	lie	lay
eat	ate	light	lit, lighted
fall	fell	lose	lost
feed	fed	make	made
feel	felt	mean	meant
fight	fought	meet	met
find	found	mistake	mistook
fit	fit	pay	paid
flee	fled	put	put
fly	flew	quit	quit
forbid	forbade	read	read
forget	forgot	ride	rode
forgive	forgave	ring	rang
freeze	froze	rise	rose
get	got	run	ran
give	gave	say	said
go	went	see	saw
grind	ground	seek	sought
grow	grew		

[1]**hung,** meaning "to hang a picture on the wall." *Hang* as in ". . . when the prisoner hanged himself in the jail" is a regular verb.

Base Form	Past Form	Base Form	Past Form
sell	sold	stick	stuck
send	sent	sting	stung
set	set	stink	stank
shake	shook	strike	struck
shed	shed	strive	strove
shine	shone	swear	swore
shoot	shot	sweep	swept
shrink	shrank	swim	swam
shut	shut	swing	swung
sing	sang	take	took
sink	sank	teach	taught
sit	sat	tear	tore
sleep	slept	tell	told
slide	slid	think	thought
speak	spoke	throw	threw
speed	sped	understand	understood
spend	spent	upset	upset
spin	spun	wake	woke
spit	spit	wear	wore
split	split	weep	wept
spread	spread	win	won
spring	sprang	wind	wound
stand	stood	withdraw	withdrew
steal	stole	write	wrote

1 Read the following student paragraph. Underline simple past tense verbs. Mark regular verbs **R** and irregular verbs **I**.

My Language Learning Experiences

When I first <u>came</u> to the United States from China, I <u>didn't know</u> how to spell, write, or read English. After one month, my father sent me to South Philadelphia High School to study English. That changed my life. In the high school, I met a lot of teachers and friends. At first I had a hard time because I didn't understand what my teachers talked about. However, all my teachers were very good. They spoke slowly and explained well. They taught me a lot of things. For example, they taught me how to spell, write, and read. They told me to use a dictionary to find the meaning of words. The first year at South Philadelphia High School helped me to improve my English.

2 Find a classmate or friend to help you study the lists of irregular simple past tense forms below. Say a sentence to your study partner, using the past tense verb. Include time words like *yesterday, last night,* or *when I was a child* to show the time.

Example

"I **cut** my finger yesterday when I was cooking."

Group A		Group B		Group C		Group D	
cut	cut	ring	rang	feel	felt	bring	brought
let	let	sing	sang	keep	kept	buy	bought
put	put	sink	sank	leave	left	think	thought
read	read	sit	sat	sleep	slept	teach	taught
set	set						

3 Read the beginning of the student essay below. Correct errors in simple past tense verbs. There are 11 errors. The first one is done for you.

Taking Responsibility

Three years ago my family had only two cars. One ~~is~~ *was* my brother's and the other was my sister's. In that year, my brother took a vacation to Vietnam and leave his car for me to take care of. That was an experience when I felt that I had to take responsibility for what I did.

One Monday, after I finished school, I went shopping with a couple of my friends. Then I went home and park my brother's car in the garage. As usual, I check the engine oil. I saw the oil level was low, so I took a can of oil from the shelf. I put it all in. I didn't realize that the oil level is that low. On Wednesday, I check the oil again before I go to school. This time the oil level was just about the same as the last time. I started to wonder how it could be because this car only holds 4 quarts of oil. But I remembered somebody say to me that old cars usually drank a lot of oil. It make me feel better. This time I put in almost a whole can of oil again. On that day, I drove around a lot and start to notice something unusual happening to the car.

D. Using Present and Past Tense Verbs Together

> Pay attention to verb tenses when you write about both present and past actions.
>
> When I first **came** to the U.S., I **didn't speak** English. Now I **speak** very well. I also **understand** what people **say** to me.

1 Complete the following sentences by using the simple present or simple past tense form of the verb in parentheses.

1. When I ___*arrived*___ home from work last night, I _____
   arrive   feel

   very tired. I _____ to sleep immediately. In the morning, I
                    go

   _____ up at 7 A.M. Now I _____ very rested, and I
      wake   feel

   _____ ready to start my new day.
      be

2. Every day Barbara _____ about a pack of cigarettes. Every time I
                          smoke

   _____ her, she _____ a cigarette in her mouth. I
      see   have

   remember when I _____ her five years ago. She _____ at
                        meet   smoke, not

   that time. She _____ to quit smoking.
                     need

3. Jack _____ an aspirin one hour ago, but he still _____
           take   have

   a headache. Ten minutes ago, he _____ a cold cloth on his
                                        put

   head, but that _____ either. His head still _____.
                     work, not   hurt

4. Five days a week Kim and Mac _____ together at Taco Cabana.
                                    work

   Kim _____ his job, but Mac _____ his. Last week Mac
          like   like, not

   _____ his hours. Now he _____ happier because he
      change   be

   _____ late at night.
      work, not

5. Rita _____ a TV show last night. It _____ a mystery
           see   be

   show about a detective, a woman, and a man. In the end, the detective

   _____ that the woman _____ the murderer, and
      find out   be

   _____ the man to find another girlfriend. Rita _____
      tell   watch

   mystery shows whenever she _____ time.
                                 have

2 Correct the errors in simple present tense and simple past tense verbs in the student paragraph below. There are eight errors.

My Spring Trip

My trip to the Dan Xie Mountains in Shao Guan, China, was very interesting. It was a spring morning. We wake up early, and we met in a hotel lobby in our city, Shen Zhen, and waited for our bus. First, we get on the bus. We sing songs and dance on the bus. After three hours, we arrive at the hills of the Dan Xie Mountains. We started to climb the mountains. Even though it was hard and tiring for us, it was interesting. On the way to the top of the mountain, we saw many kinds of birds and hear their sounds. We also see monkeys climbing the trees. We feel relaxed and happy after we saw birds and monkeys because in the city we rarely see animals or birds. We enjoyed our trip to the mountains very much.

III. Word Order in Sentences

> English is a "subject-verb" language. The subject usually comes first in the sentence before the verb. Review other rules for word order in sentences on page 96.
>
> SUBJECT VERB ⌐ OBJECT ¬ ⌐ ADVERB ¬
> We finished our work at 10 P.M.
>
> ⌐── SUBJECT ──┐ VERB ⌐ ADVERB ¬
> My friends and I went to the mall.
>
> ⌐ SUBJECT ¬ VERB COMPLEMENT
> The movie was funny.

1 Put the words in the appropriate order to make a sentence.

1. his Ting class didn't class pass
   Ting didn't pass his English class.

2. meeting a department having my is

   _____

3. holiday is a today religious

   _____

4. big they in live a apartment

   _____

5. person a I very am patient

_____

6. rain drove in Pat carefully the

_____

7. have our a neighbors dog large

_____

8. of Frank job is his tired

_____

9. old walking down man an street the is

_____

10. types secretary reports the during day the many

_____

2 Complete the action verb sentences below with appropriate words. Follow the word order below.

Subject +	Verb +	(Object) +	(Adverb)
He	drove		carefully.
The little boy	threw	the ball	to his father.
My father	works		at a supermarket.

Jean Paul is a world famous chef. He works _____. Many people _____ his special _____. He makes _____ and _____. In addition to cooking, Jean Paul _____ a cooking school. He _____ students how to cut and prepare _____. He explains his recipes very _____. All of his students _____ a lot about cooking.

3 Complete the linking verb sentences on page 177 with appropriate words. Follow the word order below.

Subject +	Verb +	Complement
My classmate	seemed	shy. (adj)
Tuan	was	a good student. (noun phrase)
The papers	were	on the table. (adverb phrase)

My friends and I felt _____ last weekend, so we went to the movies. The movie was very _____. _____ was about a 30-year-old woman with no boyfriends. She _____ sad because she wanted to get married. One day she was _____. She met one man. At first, he seemed very _____, but later he was _____ to her. In the end, _____ was happy with her new boyfriend.

IV. Pronouns

A. Subject Pronouns

> The subject pronouns *I, you, he, she, it, we,* and *they* can take the place of nouns.
>
> **Dorothy** is my next-door neighbor. **She** is 92 years old.
> **My dream car** is a red sports car. **It** can go 100 miles per hour.

1 Read the following sentences. Underline the subject pronouns. Then, draw an arrow to the noun that the pronoun stands for.

Kims' Dry Cleaners

(He 5 Mr. Kim)

Mr. Kim owns a successful dry cleaning business. He cleans and sews clothing. The shop has five large cleaning machines, three presses, and a large sewing machine. It is a noisy, busy place. Mrs. Kim helps in the family business. She works at the front counter. The Kims work six days a week, and they rarely take a holiday. They have five other employees. The customers are satisfied with the Kims' work, so they have a good business.

2 Complete the following sentences with the appropriate subject pronoun.

Planning a Vacation

Bridget and her friends are trying to decide where to go on vacation. ___*They*___ want to take an interesting but inexpensive trip. Bridget thinks _____ should visit Montreal. _____ wants to practice speaking French. Bridget also wants to visit Niagara Falls. _____ is a very famous natural wonder. Her friends, John and Charlie, would rather go to Florida. _____ want to go to Disney World. "_____ want to ride the fast rides," says John. "_____ will have a great time there." Charlie also prefers Florida. "Florida is beautiful, and _____ is not very expensive," he argues. "Also, _____ is warm." Bridget has no choice. _____ must go to Florida if _____ wants to take a vacation with her friends.

B. Object Pronouns

> Use the object pronouns **me, you, him, her, it, them,** and **us** as objects in a sentence.
>
> OBJECT
> I saw **Peter** at the mall yesterday. I met **him** near the food court.

1 Complete the following sentences with the correct object pronoun.

1. I left my bag in the library. I forgot ___*it*___ in the restroom.

2. I met Rebecca at the park. I took _____ home in my car.

3. My sisters and I saw a good movie last weekend. We enjoyed _____ very much.

4. Are your packages heavy? Let me carry _____ for you.

5. My father doesn't speak English, so I went with _____ to the doctor last week.

6. The telephone is ringing. I will answer _____.

7. Those pants look great on you. Where did you buy _____?

8. I don't have any money. Can you let _____ borrow $20?

9. I don't remember where I put my car keys. I can't find _____ anywhere.

10. Mary has a very good son. He visits his mother often and calls _____ every day.

2 Choose the appropriate object or subject pronouns to complete the sentences.

Persuasion

Our class is reading an interesting book, *Persuasion*, by Jane Austen. ___*It*___ is an adapted version, which means _____ is easier than the original book. My classmates and I like this book. In class, _____ talk about the characters in the story as if _____ were real people. The main character is Anne Elliott. _____ is a quiet, shy woman. _____

wanted to marry a captain in the Navy, but her friend, Lady Russell, persuaded _____ not to marry _____. Lady Russell said Anne was too young to marry. The captain, Frederick Wentworth, was angry at Lady Russell. _____ thought Lady Russell should not try to persuade Anne. After many years, Anne met Captain Wentworth again. _____ was nervous about meeting _____ again because she still loved _____. _____ met each other at Anne's sister's house. Soon, the captain asked Anne to marry _____. This time, Anne did not let anyone persuade _____. _____ married her captain.

C. Possessive Adjectives

> Use possessive adjectives **my, your, his, her, its, their,** and **our** to show ownership or possession.
>
> Mark works in a newspaper office. He loves **his** job.
> My family is planning a long vacation. We will take **our** trip in July.

1 Complete the sentences with the appropriate possessive adjective.

1. I like my math teacher, Mr. Rostami. ___*His*___ classes are always interesting.
2. Eric and Hung work in a computer company. _____ offices are very cold because they must keep the computers cool.
3. Martin is a serious worker. _____ job means a lot to him.
4. Tina wants to quit _____ job because she doesn't like working until midnight.
5. You can get _____ passport at the Immigration Center.
6. A community college gets most of _____ money from the government.
7. Sara is a homemaker. She takes care of _____ children and her house.
8. My friends Malu and Vaishu come from India. _____ country has many different cultures and languages.
9. Jonathan recently got married. _____ wife's name is Penny.
10. We just moved to a new apartment. _____ new place is much larger than the apartment where we lived before.

2 Correct the errors in subject pronouns, object pronouns, and possessive
adjectives in the following sentences.

   His
1. ~~He's~~ name is Romulo.

2. My friends and me are going to the movies tonight.

3. My co-workers always work hard in they jobs.

4. The dog is eating it's food.

5. Are you bored by you're work, or do you enjoy it?

6. Kathy and Doris are waiting for me. Their at the bus stop now.

7. My wife and I have been married for one year. I love she very much.

8. My best friend is a special person. She name is Maddie.

9. Jules is my brother. I don't see he often because he lives in Haiti.

10. If your tired, why don't you take a rest?

V. Parts of Speech

A. Frequency Adverbs

> Frequency adverbs tell how often you do an action. Review the chart on
> page 53 to see the differences in time meanings among common
> frequency adverbs.
>
>   I am **seldom** bored at home.
>   We **often** go the museum on the weekends.

1 Complete the sentences with an appropriate frequency adverb to make
the sentence true for you.

1. I _____*sometimes*_____ enjoy shopping.

2. I _____ have enough time in each day.

3. I _____ dream about going on vacations.

4. I am _____ tired of going to classes.

5. My friends and I are _____ busy on the weekends.

6. I _____ waste time.

7. I am _____ on time to my classes.

8. My English examinations are _____ difficult.

9. My classmates _____ speak in their native languages
   during class.

10. I am _____ angry with other people.

2 Write sentences about your daily activities. In each sentence, use the words or phrases given and a frequency adverb to tell how often you do the activity.

1. fall asleep in class
   I never fall asleep in class.

2. smoke cigarettes

3. wake up early on Saturday morning

4. wear pajamas when I sleep

5. wash my hands before eating

6. remember people's names

7. attend classes regularly

8. talk a lot on the telephone

9. clean up my own room

10. write e-mail

B. Prepositions of Time

Use **at, in,** and **on** plus nouns or noun phrases to show the time of an action. Review the rules for using **at, in,** and **on** on page 59.

Our class begins **at** 9:30 A.M.
It meets **on** Mondays, Wednesdays, and Fridays.
Our final examinations are **in** May.

1 Choose the correct preposition of time to complete each sentence.

1. I have a busy schedule _____ the summer.
   _{at/in/on}

2. I have classes _____ Mondays, Tuesdays, Wednesdays, and Thursdays.
   _{at/in/on}

3. My college is closed ﹍﹍﹍﹍ Fridays ﹍﹍﹍﹍ May, June, July, and
   _{at/in/on} _{at/in/on}
   August.

4. I work ﹍﹍﹍﹍ Fridays. I also work ﹍﹍﹍﹍ the weekends.
   _{at/in/on} _{at/in/on}

5. ﹍﹍﹍﹍ Friday, Saturday, and Sunday, I go to work ﹍﹍﹍﹍ 9 A.M.
   _{At/In/On} _{at/in/on}

6. ﹍﹍﹍﹍ these days, I get home ﹍﹍﹍﹍ the late afternoon.
   _{At/In/On} _{at/in/on}

7. ﹍﹍﹍﹍ Friday evening, I go out with my friends.
   _{At/In/On}

8. I usually go to bed ﹍﹍﹍﹍ midnight because I have to get up early
   _{at/in/on}
   ﹍﹍﹍﹍ the morning.
   _{at/in/on}

9. ﹍﹍﹍﹍ Sunday afternoon, I do my homework.
   _{At/In/On}

10. ﹍﹍﹍﹍ the weekdays, I catch the bus ﹍﹍﹍﹍
    _{At/In/On} _{at/in/on}
    8 A.M. I go to my classes, and return home ﹍﹍﹍﹍ 2 P.M.
    _{at/in/on}

2 Complete the following sentences with *at, in,* or *on.*

1. One of my favorite TV show airs ﹍﹍*at*﹍﹍ 7:30 P.M. ﹍﹍*on*﹍﹍ Mondays.
   It's called "The Simpsons."

2. I don't like to get up early ﹍﹍﹍﹍ Saturdays. I usually wake up
   ﹍﹍﹍﹍ noon. ﹍﹍﹍﹍ the summer, I sometimes get out of bed
   ﹍﹍﹍﹍ 2 P.M.

3. I usually get home ﹍﹍﹍﹍ the early afternoon and relax. I eat dinner
   ﹍﹍﹍﹍ around 7 P.M.

4. ﹍﹍﹍﹍ the summer, the days are longer. The sun usually rises
   ﹍﹍﹍﹍ about 5 A.M., and it gets dark ﹍﹍﹍﹍ 8:30 P.M.

5. ﹍﹍﹍﹍ July 4, most businesses in the United States are closed.
   Americans celebrate their independence from Great Britain ﹍﹍﹍﹍
   this day.

6. ﹍﹍﹍﹍ 2000, Paul took a trip to Greece. He arrived ﹍﹍﹍﹍
   June 20 and stayed for 10 days.

7. Mary often visits her brother ﹍﹍﹍﹍ the weekends. She leaves her
   home ﹍﹍﹍﹍ the morning and arrives at her brother's home in two
   hours. She returns home ﹍﹍﹍﹍ night.

8. _____ my birthday, we had a picnic. My friends and I played soccer in the park _____ the afternoon and had a barbeque. We returned home _____ 9 P.M.

9. _____ Saturdays, we are very busy at work. I start work _____ noon and leave _____ midnight.

C. Prepositions of Location

> Use prepositions plus nouns or noun phrases to tell about location. Review the information about prepositions of location on pages 74–75.
>
> The tire repair shop is located **at** 1500 Broad Street.
> The car dealer is **on** Trent Avenue.
> It is **in** downtown Los Angeles.

1 Look at the drawing on page 76. Complete the sentences with words from the list.

next to	near	to the left/right of	across from
on	between	in front of	at

1. The theater is _____ the bank
2. Mama's Restaurant is _____ the antique shop.
3. The coffee shop is located _____ Main Street.
4. The shoe store is located _____ Mama's Restaurant and the coffee shop.
5. The library is situated _____ Main Street and Broad Street.
6. There are some flowers _____ the flower shop.
7. The shoe store is _____ the coffee shop.
8. Many businesses are located _____ the library.

2 Write 8 sentences about the room where you are now. Use a preposition of location from Exercise 1 in each sentence.

Examples
My bed is located **next to** the closet.
There is a mirror **on** the wall.

1. _____
2. _____
3. _____
4. _____

5. _____

6. _____

7. _____

8. _____

D. Singular and Plural: Nouns

> Add **-s** to most nouns to make them plural. Follow the spelling rules on page 37 when you add **-s**. Also, refer to the list of plural nouns that do not end in **-s** on page 71.
>
> one book   two book**s**
>
> one watch   two watch**es**
>
> one person   two **people**

1 Complete the sentences with the singular or plural form of the nouns.

1. Some _____*children*_____ do not obey their parents.

⎯⎯⎯⎯ child

2. Rita's _____ live in Hong Kong. They own a business.

parent

3. One of my _____ works at Rocky's Pizza Parlor. He

friend

   usually brings a _____ home from work.

pizza

4. I have many _____ to do this weekend. I must wash my

thing

   car, clean my room, and go shopping.

5. Twenty _____ ago, I was an elementary school student.

year

6. Using a computer has a lot of _____. One

advantage

   _____ is that it works fast.

advantage

7. Before I came to the United _____, I didn't speak English

State

   well. I couldn't pronounce _____ correctly.

word

8. I want to be more independent. The main _____ is that I

reason

   want to make my own _____.

decision

9. _____ need to make many _____ in their

person   choice

   _____.

life

10. Some of my _____ say that I am very quiet. I do not ask

teacher

    many _____ in class.

question

2 Choose the appropriate noun to complete each sentence. Pay attention to whether you should use a singular or plural noun.

1. Senait is a very hard-working _____*person*_____.
<u>person/people</u>

2. She works for a large clothing _____.
<u>company/companies</u>

3. She opens many _____ of clothing every day.
<u>box/boxes</u>

4. She divides the clothing into three _____: men's,
<u>group/groups</u>

   women's, and children's clothing.

5. One of her _____ is to put a _____ on each
<u>job/jobs</u>   <u>price/prices</u>

   piece of clothing.

6. She also puts all the clothes on clothes _____.
<u>hanger/hangers</u>

7. Senait works very fast. Her _____ all look surprised at
<u>co-worker/co-workers</u>

   how quickly she works.

8. They often look at Senait's _____ to see how fast she
<u>hand/hands</u>

   moves them.

9. Her _____ sells many different _____ of
<u>company/companies</u>   <u>kind/kinds</u>

   clothing: _____, _____, _____,
      <u>shirt/shirts</u>   <u>skirt/skirts</u>   <u>pant/pants</u>

   and _____.
    <u>dress/dresses</u>

10. Senait is a very good _____.
<u>worker/workers</u>

VI. Punctuation

A. Sentence-End Punctuation

> The period (.) marks the end of a complete sentence. A question mark (?)
> ends a sentence that is a question, and an exclamation point (!) ends a
> sentence that tells a command or shows a strong feeling.
>
>   It's a beautiful day.
>
>   Do you want to go to the park?
>
>   Watch out! That skater almost ran into you.

1 Put a period, a question mark, or an exclamation point at the end of each sentence below, as the first sentence shows.

1. Do you enjoy the outdoors?

2. Then we should take a trip to the mountains

3. It's nice to take long walks in the woods

4. Do you get tired easily

5. We can go boating in the lake

6. Are you a strong swimmer

7. Be careful   The water is deep

8. I also like to go rock climbing

9. There's a good place to climb near the lake

10. Look out   Those rocks are falling

2 Read the paragraph below. Add the appropriate punctuation to mark the ends of complete sentences. Capitalize the first letter of the word that begins each sentence.

A Friend in Need

In English, they say, "A friend in need is a friend indeed" Dara is a friend who helps me when I have problems this semester I was worried about my classes I was not doing well. For example, in listening and speaking class, I couldn't understand the conversations on tape I could only understand parts of what the people were saying It was terrible Dara told me to listen to the tape over and over he also told me about some good television shows to help me with my English I think talking to him also makes my English improve because he's from Cambodia and I'm from Colombia we have to speak in English Dara showed me that I should not worry so much I'm not the only one who has trouble with English he is really a good friend to me because he helped me when I needed him

3 Read the student journal below. Then add periods to mark the end of complete sentences. Put a capital letter at the beginning of each sentence.

I am very proud of my son Dmitri he is 18, and he goes to Community College of Philadelphia this is his second year he's a very smart boy he is taking 20 credits this semester because he wants to transfer to Drexel University in the spring semester he wants to major in Management

Information Systems also, he is working at Summit Bank as a proof machine operator I hope that he will have a great future I love my children very much, and I will try to do everything that I can for them

B. The Comma

> Use a comma (,) to show a brief pause between ideas inside a sentence. Review the rules for comma use on pages 60–61.
>
>   I enjoy many hobbies. I like to read, cook, exercise, and sew.
>
>   For example, last weekend I went to the gym.

1 Add commas and periods to the following sentences.

1. When I go shopping with my family I always buy clothing
2. In our group we decided to research women's roles in the family
3. I am a very careful writer I pay attention to my spelling when I write
4. On Friday Saturday and Sunday I work from 3 P.M. to 11 P.M.
5. I want to take a vacation but I don't have enough money
6. Although I left a message on her answering machine she didn't call me back
7. My best friend lives in Detroit Michigan
8. My grandmother died on June 3 1997
9. I saw many interesting animals at the zoo last weekend for example panda bears white lions and giraffes
10. Some people do not use their money wisely they spend too much money on CDs new clothes or jewelry

2 Add commas where they are needed in each sentence. The first sentence is done for you.

At times, I would like to live in a more peaceful house. My son my daughter and my husband make a lot of noise every day. My son has many friends so he often talks on the telephone. In the evening my daughter listens to loud music or she watches TV. My favorite pastime is reading but it's sometimes too noisy to read. When I want to relax at home I look for a quiet place. For example I go outside and read in my backyard or I take a hot bath. I also take long rides in the car and I listen to music. These are the ways that I make my home life more peaceful.

C. Comma Splices

> The incorrect use of a comma—rather than a period—at the end of a sentence is called a comma splice.
>
> I'm a very hard-working person, I always do my best job. (**incorrect**)
>
> I'm a very hard-working person. I always do my best job. (**correct**)

1 Read over the following sentences from student writing. Correct any comma splice errors. Some sentences have no errors.

1. The first time that I came to the United States, I didn't know anything. I was scared of my neighbors, they made me nervous because they looked different from me. Now I have changed a lot, I'm not scared anymore.

2. When I was a child, we sometimes spent the whole day at the zoo, sometimes we also went to the movies or went fishing.

3. I have several good qualities, one quality that stands out is that I am creative.

4. When I was 8 years old, I always wanted a bike, I kept telling my father to get me one. After a few weeks, he bought me a black bike. I was so excited.

5. In 1999, my friends and I took a trip to Las Vegas. This trip was the best one that I took with my friends, it gave me a lot of memories.

6. Most people have at least one thing that they should change about themselves. I have some bad habits, for example, I am lazy. I have to become less lazy, I should be more responsible.

7. One day I saw my grandmother at school. She was crying, as a result, I realized that my grandfather was sick.

8. One reason I get angry is because of my mother, she gives me so much advice. After work, she comes back home, she starts to give me advice. She thinks I am a 10-year-old child, I don't like her giving me advice.

2 Read over the paragraph on page 189. Find and correct any comma splice errors. The first sentence is corrected for you.

Good Morals

Good morals are important for ~~children, we~~ *children. We* learn our morals from our parents. It is important for parents to teach strong morals to their children. Almost all parents teach their children not to tell lies, they tell their children that lying is a bad thing. If we are not taught these morals, we may tell lies, children also learn morals in school. We learn the right ways to act with our friends, teachers also punish children when they cheat on tests. Morality is an important value because bad morals will affect the whole world.

D. Other Punctuation Marks

Review the chart on page 149 so that you understand and use other punctuation marks correctly.	
Quotation marks (" ")	"Do you like coffee?" the girl asked.
Colon (:)	I have many hobbies: skateboarding, skiing, watching movies, and swimming.
Long dash (—)	The gymnasium has many types of equipment—rowing machines, bicycles, and weights.
Semicolon (;)	I didn't tell my parents the truth; I didn't want to hurt their feelings.

1 Add the appropriate punctuation marks to the sentences below. Write your corrected sentence on the line.

1. Do you have the time she asked

   "Do you have the time?" she asked.

2. Stereo City sells many kinds of electronic equipment televisions CD players cassette players and other items

   _____

3. When my supervisor finished explaining the work he said Do you understand

   _____

4. If you want to improve your listening watch television in English listen to the radio in English and talk with English speakers

   _____

5. Joe has traveled to many countries in Africa Egypt Tunisia Niger Kenya Rwanda and South Africa

   _____

6. At the end of our visit I didn't want to go home I will never forget you I said to my new friends

_____

7. I enjoyed my trip to the mountains I went snow sledding skiing and snowboarding

_____

8. Celia wanted to visit Canada so she went to a travel agency She asked the agent How much does a ticket to Montreal cost

_____

9. Many children's television shows especially cartoons and movies contain a lot of violence

_____

2 Correct any errors in punctuation in the student sentences below. Write your corrections on or above the line.

1. She asked me, "~~¿What are you doing?~~"   *"What are you doing?"*

2. Going online; and finding pen-pals have become my favorite pastimes.

3. Perhaps I'll see my best friend next year. Sometimes he calls me and says How are you? He is a good friend.

4. It was interesting to read your letter because reading: books and listening to music are also my favorite pastimes. I hope in the future you reach your dream and become: a doctor.

6. I am a single mother. I have three children two boys and one girl.

7. My friend encouraged me to go back to school. Don't stay home. You can do anything you want, she told me.

VI. Spelling Rules

A. Rule 1: The -*s* Form

-s on Verbs

> Some verbs have irregular **-s** spelling. Review the chart on page 37.
> wash   wash**es**   carry   carr**ies**

1 Complete these sentences with the correct form of the verbs in parentheses. Use the chart on page 37 to check your answers.

1. Mrs. Brand _____*has*_____ four children.
      have

2. Her oldest child, Emma, _____ 25 years old.
                                    be

3. Emma _____ with her husband in Chicago.
           live

4. She _____ elementary school.
         teach

5. Emma's brother Christopher _____ in a steel factory.
                                    work

6. He _____ the steel presses and other equipment.
       fix

7. The third child, Anthony, _____ to college.
                                go

8. Anthony _____ engineering.
              study

9. Laura, the "baby of the family," _____ 18 years old.
                                        be

10. Mrs. Brand _____ about all of her children even though
                   worry

    they are adults.

2 Correct the errors in the simple present tense verb forms in the student paragraph below. Write your corrections above the line. Be sure to spell the verbs correctly.

My Best Friend

My best friend Kenny is a nice person, and I enjoy being with her. She
lives
~~live~~ on Pike Street near Rising Sun Avenue. She live with her family in a
good neighborhood. She give respect to elders. She is so kind to the poor.
She knows how to sing well. She like watching movies, and she try not to
eat too much. I met her when I came to high school. My teacher introduced
her to me. She was my partner in school. That was 1999. We have been
friends for two years. We go shopping together. She come to my home and
stays the night. We go to college and we also work together. We go around,
and we have fun together. Kenny is a great person.

-s on Nouns

> Review the spelling rules for adding *-s* to verbs on page 37. Use the same
> rules when you add *-s* to make a singular noun plural.
>
> one dish   many dish**es**   **a party   many parties**

1 Read the pairs of sentences below. Complete the second sentence with the correct plural form of the underlined noun. The first sentence is completed as an example.

1. A busy <u>student</u> has many things to do.

   Busy _____*students*_____ have many things to do.

2. My <u>watch</u> keeps very good time.

   Theresa has two _____. Both of them keep very good time.

3. I can never eat just one <u>strawberry</u>.

   Sometimes I like to eat a bowl of _____ for breakfast.

4. July 13 is an important <u>date</u> because it is my son's birthday.

   I write down all my important _____ on my calendar.

5. What is your greatest <u>wish</u> for the future?

   I have many _____ for my future.

6. My niece asked me to tell her a bedtime <u>story</u>.

   I told her two _____, and then she fell asleep.

7. The biochemistry <u>laboratory</u> uses computer programs.

   The biology and biochemistry _____ have both IBM and Macintosh computers.

8. This summer I will take only one <u>class</u>.

   How many _____ do you plan to take?

9. Can I have a French <u>fry</u>?

   This restaurant makes good French _____.

10. When I was a child, I received only one <u>toy</u> for my birthday.

    My nephew has many _____.

2 Correct the errors in singular and plural nouns in the student sentences below. Be sure to spell the *-s* form correctly.

1. We are a very close family like most Turkish ~~family~~. *families.*

2. My youngest sister, Veronica, is 24 year old.

3. My stepfather has four children: Nita, Dolores, Guy, and Alton. The children are independent person.

4. Every person has many quality.

5. I have two childrens: one boy and one girl.

6. Reading book is one of my favorite pastimes. I have learned about many country, cultures, and historical things.

7. I work at Wendy's. I make sandwich and salad. I never have free time on weekend.
8. I want to write to people who like rock music and skateboarding because we have common interest.
9. I like making friends with many person.
10. When I lived in Viet Nam, I raised my two niece. It was difficult for me because I didn't have any experience raising baby.

B. Rule 2: The *-ed* Form

> Check the spelling rules for adding the **-ed** (past tense) to regular verbs on page 103.
> study   stud**ied**   stop   stop**ped**

1 Complete the sentences with the correctly spelled simple past tense form of the verb.

1. We _____worked_____ very hard on our garden last Saturday. We
   _{work}
   _____ heavy bags of dirt and plants.
   _{carry}

2. I _____ to call you yesterday, but you weren't home. I
   _{try}
   _____ to ask you to go to the movies with me.
   _{want}

3. Cesar _____ very hard for his driver's license exam. He
   _{study}
   _____ the test easily.
   _{pass}

4. Lisa _____ the vase of flowers on the table. Then she
   _{place}
   _____ back to look at it.
   _{step}

5. A shooting _____ at 10 p.m. Sunday in a grocery store in
   _{occur}
   my neighborhood. The store owner _____ the police that
   _{tell}
   the criminal was a young man in his twenties.

6. Jung _____ to play baseball when he was a child. He often
   _{love}
   _____ with his friends after school.
   _{play}

7. Carl _____ by to see you this morning. I _____
   _{drop}   _{ask}
   him to stay and wait for you, but he _____ to come back later.
   _{prefer}

2 Correct the errors in the simple past tense verbs in the student sentences. Be careful to spell the verbs correctly.

1. When I first arrived in the United States, I ~~fell~~ *felt* very shy because I couldn't speak English well.

2. At first, I just listened to my neighbors and believed everything that they sayed to me.

3. My father maked the money in the past, but now he is retired.

4. My daughter always cryed at night when she was a baby.

5. I studed English in high school in my country.

6. I tryed to stop smoking. I stoped for two weeks, but then I started again.

7. I plaied with my friends in the park when I was a child.

C. Spelling Similar Words

> Be careful to spell words correctly because English has words with similar pronunciations and spelling.

1 Choose the correct word to complete each sentence below.

1. _____ I got home from work, I had a telephone message.
   When/Went

2. I don't _____ very well, so I think I'll go to the doctor.
   fell/feel

3. Will you please _____ down?
   seat/sit

4. I _____ now. I'll see you later.
   am living/am leaving

5. The customers left _____ packages on the counter.
   there/their

6. Some people _____ that I am a funny person.
   thing/think

7. I was worried. I didn't know _____ you were.
   were/where

8. Can you tell me _____ I can register for classes?
   who/how

9. We're going to have _____ for dinner tonight.
   chicken/kitchen

10. Do you like coffee? I like it, _____ .
    too/to

11. Can I go _____ with you to the library?
    alone/along

12. I don't understand _____ I got a C on the test.
    while/why

13. Everyone should try to live his or her life in the _____ way.
    _{write/right}

14. I'll be ready in five minutes. I have to change my _____ .
    _{clothes/cloths}

15. I have a good _____ to get a promotion at work.
    _{chance/change}

2 Correct the spelling errors in the student sentences below. The number in parentheses tells the number of errors.

   cleans
1. On New Year's Day in Viet Nam, everybody ~~clears~~ their houses. (1)

2. Why I was in the bathroom, the telephone rang. (1)

3. I am leaving with my parents in an apartment right now. (1)

4. My best friend likes washing movies. (1)

5. Can you tell me who to spell the word *business*? (1)

6. Parents should teach there children that making a good living is important. (1)

7. I am married too Ramon. We have tree children. (2)

8. I though my neighborhood was save, but it is very dangerous. (2)

9. I can read my book because our classroom is very quite. (1)

10. My friends and I where ready to go. (1)

VIII. Capitalization Rules

1. Capitalize the first word of every sentence.
   My city has many interesting places to visit.

2. Capitalize the names of people, including titles.
   Mr. **S**teve **J**ones is my favorite teacher.

3. Always capitalize the pronoun *I*.
   Patti and **I** are going to the movies.

4. Capitalize family words if they are used with a name, but do not capitalize family words without a name.
   We called **U**ncle **F**arid on the telephone last night.
   My **u**ncle lives in Washington, D.C.

5. Capitalize the names of the days of the week, months of the year, and holidays, but do not capitalize the names of seasons.
   On **N**ew **Y**ear's **D**ay, we had a party.
   I came to the United States on **W**ednesday, October 7, 1998.
   In New York, there are four seasons: **s**pring, **s**ummer, **f**all, and **w**inter.

6. Capitalize names of languages, nationalities, races, and religions.
   Vietnamese   **H**aitian   **M**uslim

7. Capitalize the names of countries, states, provinces, counties, cities, and towns.

   Mexico   **Texas**   **Quebec**   **Webb County**   **Moscow**

8. Capitalize the names of oceans, lakes, rivers, islands, mountains, deserts, beaches, etc.

   the **I**ndian **O**cean   **L**ake **T**iticaca   the **Y**angtze **R**iver

   the **C**anary **I**slands   the **A**tlas **M**ountains   the **S**ahara **D**esert

   South **M**iami **B**each

9. Capitalize geographic words that refer to specific areas, but do not capitalize them if they do not refer to specific geographic areas.

   the **F**ar **E**ast   **S**outheast **A**sia   the **N**ortheast

   the **s**outhern part of my country   **n**orth of the college

10. Capitalize specific names of companies, but do not capitalize words that tell about general types of companies.

    Yevgeniy works for **U**nited **P**arcel **S**ervice.

    He wants to get a job with a **c**omputer company.

11. Capitalize specific names of courses, but do not capitalize the names of subjects of study.

    I love **m**athematics. Next semester, I will take **C**alculus 161.

---

1 Edit the following paragraph for errors in capitalization. The first sentence is corrected for you.

The Importance of Education

I know now that ~~E~~education is very important, but I didn't always have this ~~I~~idea. I remember when I was younger, I didn't like School. I thought that I would never need School in my Life because I thought that would never get me anywhere. I remember every time my Mother sent me to School, I pretended I was sick. I told Her that I couldn't go to Class. After I graduated from High School I realized that Education is one of the most important things in Life. I realize that I won't be able to get a good Job without Education. it's easy for anybody with school Knowledge to find a better Job. In Some places when you apply for a Job, the first thing they ask you is if you graduated from High School. when you are educated, you get more respect than somebody who doesn't have School Knowledge. nothing can make you succeed more than education.

2 Add the correct capitalization to the following sentences.

1. M̶y brother works at a steel factory.
2. on monday, she had a chemistry test.
3. she visited her mother in malaysia over the thanksgiving holidays.
4. my family and i crossed the pacific ocean on our trip to hawaii.
5. there are many interesting sites in the middle east.
6. dr. gary gordon is a pediatrician.
7. new year's is an important holiday in china.
8. i enjoy the fall season in the northeast because the leaves on the trees change color.

3 Complete the following sentences with a noun, a noun phrase (a noun with other words), or a pronoun. Use words that are appropriate for each sentence. Be sure to capitalize the nouns and pronouns correctly.

1. I live in *a three-bedroom apartment in the city*   .
2. _____ has two children.
3. My best friend's name is _____.
4. When I look out the window, I see _____.
5. _____ came to the United States one year ago.
6. English is a difficult _____.
7. My native language is _____.
8. I love to _____ when I have free time.
9. My favorite store is _____.
10. If I have extra money, I like to buy _____.

4 Find a short article in a newspaper or magazine. Cut the article out and paste it onto a piece of paper. Under the article, make a list of all the words with capital letters. Share your article and list with your classmates.

IX. Handwriting Guide

Study the charts on page 198 to see how to write capital and lowercase letters correctly in English.

Cursive (Handwritten) Letters
(Used in writing essays, letters, etc.)

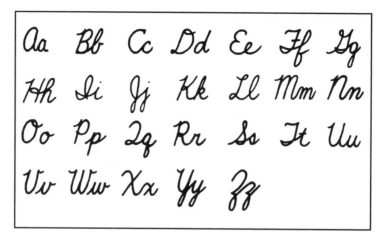

Printed Letters
(Used in writing lists, signs, etc.)

Aa	Bb	Cc	Dd	Ee	Ff	Gg
Hh	Ii	Jj	Kk	Ll	Mm	Nn
Oo	Pp	Qq	Rr	Ss	Tt	Uu
Vv	Ww	Xx	Yy	Zz		

1 Look over two or three of your compositions. Compare your cursive capital and lowercase letters with the samples in the first chart. Show your handwriting to another person to make sure that all of your letters are clearly written. Also, make sure that you use capital and lowercase letters appropriately. Rewrite any letters that look very different from the samples or seem unclear to another reader.

X. Common Editing Symbols

art.	article error	*art.* I live in <u>the</u> Chicago. (*Correct:* I live in Chicago.) *art.* I have ⌣ large family.
pl.	plural	*pl.* His <u>parent</u> own a dry cleaning business.

s-v	subject-verb agreement	My sister <u>work</u> at a Chinese restaurant. *(s-v)*
sp.	spelling error	My <u>douther's</u> name is Alina. *(sp.)*
v.t.	wrong verb tense	When I was a child, my family <u>visit</u> Agra. *(v.t.)*
v.f.	wrong verb form	I <u>am come</u> from Vietnam. *(v.f.)*
w.f.	wrong word form	I am happy to live in a <u>freedom</u> country. *(w.f.)*
w.w.	wrong word	She <u>said</u> me to go home. *(w.w.)*
◯	word or punctuation mark missing	We took a train ◯ we got lost. I bought ◯ car last summer.
⋀	insert	She ⋀going for a walk. *(v.f.)*
=	capitalize letter	<u>m</u>y classes end on <u>m</u>ay 15.
/	lowercase letter	My best *F*riend is named Joan.
⎍	wrong word order	I ⌐always⌐am⌐ late for class.
⎣	indent	Move the line to the right five spaces.

Correct the mistakes in the example sentences in the Common Editing Symbols chart above. The first sentence is corrected for you. Share your answers with your classmates.

XI. Personal Editing Log

Make a chart like the one below to record your most common grammar, spelling, and punctuation errors. Write the title and date of your paper. If you have three or more errors of one type, record the type and the number of errors, as shown in the example below.

Title of Writing	Date	Type/Number of Common Errors
"A Profile for Friendship"	Sept. 11, 2002	Verbs — 4 Capitalization — 3

Do It Yourself Answer Key

I. Sentences

A. Parts of a Sentence: Subjects and Verbs

1 I _like_ your class. It _is_ very exciting. I _am learning_ to write. It _is_ not very easy, but I _am doing_ the best I can. My weekend _was_ okay. I _worked_ very hard. I _had_ to work at a wedding Saturday night until 1 a.m. I _got_ home at 2:15 in the morning, so I _was_ very tired. The next day, I _studied_ all day for my other classes. I _didn't_ go out anywhere, so it _wasn't_ a nice weekend for me. I _want_ to know about your weekend. _Write_ to me soon.

2 Possible answers

1. Hot cocoa <u>tastes</u> good on a cold day.
2. My books <u>are</u> in a big pile on the floor.
3. Lynne <u>is</u> a secretary in the high school.
4. You <u>look</u> very tired! Did you get any sleep last night?
5. I <u>am</u> a good cook. Everyone <u>is/seems</u> happy to eat my food.
6. The cookies <u>smell/look</u> delicious. Are they ready yet?
7. Richard's new car <u>is/looks</u> very practical. It <u>is</u> a Ford Explorer with four-wheel drive.

3 Possible answers

My Neighbor Mrs. Maxwell

My neighbor Mrs. Maxwell <u>is</u> an active person. Every afternoon, she <u>takes/goes for</u> a walk. <u>She/Mrs. Maxwell</u> likes to walk, even in the winter. <u>She/Mrs. Maxwell</u> and her friend, Mrs. Noble, often walk together. Mrs. Maxwell <u>uses/needs</u> a walking stick because she is 92 years old. Mrs. Noble <u>gives/lends</u> her a strong arm to lean on. <u>Walking/Exercise</u> keeps Mrs. Maxwell healthy. Mrs. Maxwell also <u>wears/has</u> thick eyeglasses. She <u>doesn't have</u> very good vision. She also <u>has</u> a little trouble keeping her balance. Still, Mrs. Maxwell <u>lives/stays</u> in a house by herself. She <u>likes/wants</u> to be independent and active.

B. Parts of a Sentence: Direct Objects

1 1. My family owns two cars.
2. We have <u>a van</u> and <u>a two-door car</u>.
3. My sister bought <u>a car</u> last year.

4. She doesn't like <u>it</u> very much.
5. My brother Liu drives too fast.
6. Her father never cooks <u>dinner</u>.
7. Tu and Ton share <u>a bedroom.</u>
8. They do not have <u>enough space</u> in their room.
9. My family is very happy.
10. We often take <u>short trips</u> on the weekend.

2 1. S She V has _a husband and four children._
2. S She V takes care of _her little boy and little girl._
3. S My neighborhood V has _many interesting places_
4. S My father V forgets _his car keys._
5. S I'm going to get V _a good education._ Then, S I'm going to get V _a good job._
6. S I don't have V _a full-time job._
7. S I don't have V _too much money_ to spend.
8. S I paid V _$953_ for my tuition this semester.
9. S My parents saved V _a lot of money._
10. S I waste V _too much time._

3 Possible answers

My friends the Kumars are building <u>a brand-new house</u>. Their house will have <u>four bedrooms</u>. Each bedroom will have a <u>closet and a bathroom</u>. The Kumars will have <u>a living room/a den</u> for watching television and relaxing. Mrs. Kumar wants <u>a large kitchen</u> because she cooks a lot. They can put <u>all their junk/stuff/extra things</u> in their big basement. The large garage will hold <u>two cars</u>. The dining room has <u>a big window</u> so that they can look out onto the backyard. They will spend <u>a lot of time</u> on the deck in their backyard. The Kumars plan to have <u>a party</u> to celebrate after they move into their new house.

C. Complete Sentences

1 Possible answers
1. My neighborhood is a nice place because ^_it's_ very quiet. **I**

2. I live on a small street. **C**

200

3. Around the house ~~very~~ *it is very* quiet. **I**
4. Near my house ~~there~~ *there are* many shopping centers. **I**
5. ~~A~~ *There is* new building in that area. **I**
6. The houses in this area look like normal houses, not too big or too small. **C**
7. In the past, I lived with my parents. **C**
8. I didn't pay ~~rent. When~~ *rent when* I lived with my parents. **I**
9. It think ~~it~~ *it is* better for me to live with my parents. **C**

2 Possible answers

1. His backpack seems very heavy.
2. Today, I feel very sleepy.
3. The weather seems mild today.
4. My teacher is friendly.
5. The students in my class are from many countries.
6. The mountain air smells fresh.
7. Your soup tastes delicious.
8. In summer, the river looks clean.
9. His family is in Mexico/very close.

3
1. Last night, I called my friend on the telephone.
2. My best friend and I like to spend time together.
3. Reading is my favorite pastime.
4. We love to go to the beach in the summertime.
5. My family is very large.
6. Being with my friends and family makes me happy.
7. After a tiring day, I like to relax.
8. My neighborhood is dangerous.
9. Watching scary movies makes me afraid.
10. Every morning, the students have breakfast together.

A. *There Is* and *There Are* Sentences

1

Daniel's Messy Apartment

Daniel's apartment is a big mess. There are things lying all over the place. There are dirty clothes on the floor. There is one shoe on the sofa and one under the sofa. Also, there are dirty dishes on the coffee table. There is a CD player in one corner of the room, but it's not working anymore. There are CDs on the sofa and on the floor. None of them are in their cases. There is a mirror on the wall, but it is broken. The clock doesn't work, either. There is so much dirt on the windows that you can't see through them. There is a telephone somewhere in the room, but Daniel can't find it. You can't sit in the chair because there is big dog sleeping in it. Daniel's apartment is really dirty and disorganized.

2 Possible answers

1. There is a clock on the wall.
2. There is a desk near the bed.
3. There is a computer on the desk.
4. There is a television next to the desk.
5. There is a closet on one side of the wall.

E. Sentences with *and, but, so, or*

1
1. I need some money from my bank. I can get it from the teller inside the bank, or I can use the automated teller machine outside.
2. Tomorrow I'll call my friend, and we'll decide where to go on the weekend.
3. Ron wants to become a doctor, but he thinks it will take too long.
4. Jessie loves to watch television shows, so she bought a new TV.
5. Do you want to have dinner now, or do you prefer to wait an hour?
6. Reyna wants to lose weight, but she is eating ice cream right now.
7. My brother Charles lives in Chicago, and my sister Joan lives in Miami.
8. Sometimes writing comes easily to me, but other times it is very difficult.
9. Houses in the United States are expensive, so I must save a lot of money.

2
1. Larry spends too much money. He would like to save money, but he always spends it on his friends and himself.
2. He goes out to dinner every night, and/so he never cooks. His friends never have money, so/and when they go along, Larry always pays the bill.
3. Larry also goes to the movies a lot, and he buys gifts for his girlfriend.
4. He likes music, so he has to have the latest music equipment.
5. He likes to travel a lot, and/but he uses his credit card to pay for everything.

6. By the end of the month, Larry discovers that he has many bills, <u>but</u> he does not have enough money in the bank to pay them.
7. Larry wants to change his spending habits, <u>so</u> he has promised himself that next month he will cut back.

F. Sentences with Dependent Clauses

1 1. I like to watch to watch television <u>while</u> I eat dinner.
2. <u>When</u> I was a child, I took many trips with my family.
3. <u>If</u> I have enough time, I will clean my kitchen.
4. Karen goes to the gym every day <u>since</u> she likes to exercise.
5. Last night he read a book <u>until</u> he fell asleep.
6. <u>Because</u> it's raining, we are having the party inside.
7. I must wear my glasses <u>though</u> I hate the way they look.
8. <u>Whenever</u> I drink too much coffee, I can't sleep well.
9. I locked the doors and turned off the radio <u>before</u> I left home.
10. Every morning I take a shower <u>after</u> I wake up.

2 Possible answers

1. I enjoy shopping because <u>I love to buy new things</u>.
2. When <u>I get home</u>, I take off my shoes and relax.
3. If you need help, <u>you can call me</u>.
4. <u>I don't need to take the bus</u> because I have a car.
5. Although <u>I am sleepy</u>, I must finish my homework.
6. Since I like to cook, <u>I often go to the grocery store</u>.
7. I can't go to the movies until <u>I finish my work</u>.
8. After I moved to my new city, <u>I didn't have many friends</u>.
9. I feel afraid whenever <u>I walk at night</u>.
10. <u>I saw a homeless man</u> while I was walking down the street.

II. Common Verb Tenses

A. Simple Present Tense

1   Every day, my parents <u>teach</u> me the importance of respect. My mother and father always <u>show</u> me how to respect others. My father <u>tells</u> me to be respectful to people who are older than I am. In the Dominican Republic, a person <u>uses</u> formal words to speak to older people. We sometimes <u>call</u> an older person "aunt" or "uncle." In addition, my mother always <u>talks</u> respectfully to her siblings even though they <u>are</u> about her same age. She <u>does not scream</u> at her brothers or sisters. She <u>pays</u> attention to them when they <u>speak</u>. My parents <u>know</u> that if you <u>are</u> respectful to others, other people will treat you the same way.

2 Possible answers

1. Responsibility <u>is</u> a very important value to teach any child.
2. If you <u>have/make</u> a lot of money, it <u>is</u> easy to support your family.
3. Honesty and kindness <u>are</u> also important values for a child.
4. Being honest <u>means</u> that you <u>do not lie</u>.
5. When you <u>treat</u> people well, they usually <u>act/behave</u> the same way with you.
6. If you <u>do</u> nice things for others, you <u>make</u> friends more easily.
7. A good parent <u>teaches/shows</u> his or her children the best ways to behave.
8. The best parents <u>have/show</u> a lot of patience because it <u>takes</u> time to teach a child good behavior.

3 Possible answers

1. I usually go home in the afternoon.
2. I eat breakfast in the morning.
3. I go to school on Tuesdays and Thursdays.
4. I work hard during the day.
5. After classes I go to work.
6. I read books at night.
7. I wash clothes every week.
8. On the weekends I go shopping.
9. I pay my bills once a month.
10. I always wash my hands before I eat.
11. I never smoke cigarettes.

B. Simple Present versus Present Progressive

1 1. Susan <u>is taking</u> two classes this summer. She usually <u>takes</u> four classes during the fall and spring.
2. Terry always <u>tries</u> to learn new skills at work. Right now he <u>is trying</u> to learn a new computer program.

3. The weather <u>is getting</u> warmer this week.
   It frequently <u>gets</u> warm in the afternoon.
4. Leigh <u>sleeps</u> late every Saturday.
   She <u>is sleeping</u> in her room at the moment.
5. Usually Peter <u>pays</u> close attention to everything around him when he <u>drives</u> a car.
   Today, however, he <u>is not paying</u> attention because he <u>is talking</u> on his cell phone.
6. Today Martina <u>is spending</u> too much time on the Internet.
   Normally, she <u>spends</u> only a half-hour each day to check her e-mail.

2 Possible answers

1. I'm not an organized person.
2. My mother cooks dinner for our family every day.
3. I always eat breakfast in the morning.
4. I'm not always cheerful in the morning.
5. I don't clean my bedroom every day.
6. I'm not a lazy student.
7. I take a shower every day.
8. I wash my clothes every week.
9. I don't always go out on weekends.
10. I work full-time.
11. I am usually dependable.

3 Possible answers

1. I'm not doing math homework right now.
2. I'm thinking about my family now.
3. I'm not drinking coffee at this moment.
4. I'm looking for a new job now.
5. I'm learning a lot of English in this class.
6. I'm taking two classes this semester.
7. I'm not worrying about my grades this term.
8. I'm working long hours this week.
9. I'm trying to choose a college major.
10. I'm not living with my parents at the present time.

Non-Progressive Verbs

1 Possible answers

1. I <u>hate</u> to stay at home all the time.
2. I <u>(don't) like/want</u> to go shopping with my friends.
3. Do you <u>know</u> how to play the piano?
4. I often <u>forget</u> people's names, but I remember their faces.
5. The word *concentrate* <u>means</u> "to think very carefully about something."
6. I <u>hear</u> the telephone ringing.

7. I <u>understand/like</u> the homework. It's very easy for me.
8. My teacher <u>believes/thinks</u> that students should turn in their assignments on time.
9. Do you <u>prefer/like</u> your coffee black or with cream?
10. I <u>don't own/don't have</u> a car, so I ride the bus to college.

2 Possible answers

1. I don't like to watch TV shows.
2. I sometimes love shopping.
3. I prefer to eat dinner with my family.
4. I usually don't remember people's names.
5. I use the Internet every day.
6. I want a lot of money.
7. I know a lot about computers.
8. I don't understand movies in English.
9. I have a lot of friends in my home country.

C. Simple Past Tense

1   **My Language Learning Experiences**

When I first <u>came</u>[I] to the United States from China, I <u>didn't know</u>[R] how to spell, write, or read English. After one month, my father <u>sent</u>[I] me to South Philadelphia High School to study English. That <u>changed</u>[R] my life. In the high school, I <u>met</u>[I] a lot of teachers and friends. At first I <u>had</u>[I] a hard time because I <u>didn't understand</u>[R] what my teachers <u>talked</u>[R] about. However, all my teachers <u>were</u>[I] very good. They <u>spoke</u>[I] slowly and <u>explained</u>[R] well. They <u>taught</u>[I] me a lot of things. For example, they <u>taught</u>[I] me how to spell, write, and read. They <u>told</u>[I] me to use a dictionary to find the meaning of words. The first year at South Philadelphia High School <u>helped</u>[R] me to improve my English.

3   **Taking Responsibility**

Three years ago my family had only two cars. One ~~is~~ was my brother's and the other was my

sister's. In that year, my brother took a vacation to
Vietnam and ~~leave~~ *left* his car for me to take care of.

That was an experience when I felt that I had to

take responsibility for what I did.

   One Monday, after I ~~finish~~ *finished* school, I went

shopping with a couple of my friends. Then I went
home and ~~park~~ *parked* my brother's car in the garage. As

usual, I ~~check~~ *checked* the engine oil. I saw the oil level

was low, so I took a can of oil from the shelf. I put

it all in. I didn't realize that the oil level ~~is~~ *was* that low.
On Wednesday, I ~~check~~ *checked* the oil again before I ~~go~~ *went* to

school. This time the oil level was just about the

same as the last time. I ~~start~~ *started* to wonder how it

could be because this car only holds 4 quarts of oil.

But I remembered somebody ~~say~~ *said* to me that old

cars usually drank a lot of oil. It ~~make~~ *made* me feel

better. This time I put in almost a whole can of oil

again. On that day, I drove around a lot and ~~started~~

to notice something unusual happening to the car.

D. Using Present and Past Tense Verbs Together

1 1. When I <u>arrived</u> home from work last night, I
   <u>felt</u> very tired. I <u>went</u> to sleep immediately. In
   the morning, I <u>woke</u> up at 7 a.m. Now I <u>feel</u>
   very rested, and I <u>am</u> ready to start my new
   day.
   2. Barbara <u>smokes</u> about a pack of cigarettes every
   day. Every time I <u>see</u> her she <u>has</u> a cigarette in
   her mouth. I remember when I <u>met</u> her five
   years ago. She <u>did not smoke</u> at that time. She
   <u>needs</u> to quit smoking.
   3. Jack <u>took</u> an aspirin one hour ago, but he still
   <u>has</u> a headache. Ten minutes ago, he <u>put</u> a cold
   cloth on his head, but that <u>didn't work</u> either.
   His head still <u>hurts</u>.

4. Kim and Mac <u>work</u> together at Taco Cabana. Kim
   <u>likes</u> his job, but Mac <u>doesn't like</u> his. Last week
   Mac <u>changed</u> his hours. Now he <u>is</u> happier
   because he <u>does not work</u> late at night.
5. Rita <u>saw</u> a TV show last night. It <u>was</u> a mystery
   show about a detective, a woman, and a man. In
   the end, the detective <u>found out</u> that the woman
   <u>was</u> the murderer, and <u>told</u> the man to find
   another girlfriend. Rita <u>watches</u> mystery shows
   whenever she <u>has</u> time.

2   **My Spring Trip**

   My trip to the Dan Xie Mountains in Shao

Guan, China, was very interesting. It was a spring
morning. We ~~wake~~ *woke* up early, and we met in a hotel

lobby in our city, Shen Zhen, and waited for our
bus. First, we ~~get~~ *got* on the bus. We ~~sing~~ *sang* songs and
~~dance~~ *danced* on the bus. After three hours, we ~~arrive~~ *arrived* at

the hills of the Dan Xie Mountains. We started to

climb the mountains. Even though it was hard and

tiring for us, it was interesting. On the way to the

top of the mountain, we saw many kinds of birds
and ~~hear~~ *heard* their sounds. We also ~~see~~ *saw* monkeys

climbing the trees. We ~~feel~~ *felt* relaxed and happy after

we saw birds and monkeys because in the city we

rarely see animals or birds. We enjoyed our trip to

the mountains very much.

III. Word Order in Sentences

1 1. Ting didn't pass his English class.
   2. My department is having a meeting.
   3. Today is a religious holiday.
   4. They live in a big apartment.
   5. I am a very patient person.
   6. Pat drove carefully in the rain.
   7. Our neighbors have a large dog.
   8. Frank is tired of his job.
   9. An old man is walking down the street.
   10. The secretary types many reports during the
   day.

2 Possible answers

Jean Paul is a world famous chef. He works (1) <u>very hard</u>. Many people (2) <u>love/enjoy</u> his special (3) <u>food/cooking</u>. He makes (4) <u>delicious desserts</u> and (5) <u>many other types of food</u>. In addition to cooking, Jean Paul (6) <u>works at/owns</u> a cooking school. He (7) <u>teaches/shows</u> his students how to cut and prepare (8) <u>vegetables/all kinds of food</u>. He explains his recipes very (9) <u>well/clearly</u>. All of his students (10) <u>learn</u> a lot about cooking.

3 Possible answers

My friends and I felt <u>bored</u> last weekend, so we went to the movies. The movie was very <u>funny/interesting</u>. <u>It</u> was about a 30-year-old woman with no boyfriends. She <u>was/felt</u> sad because she wanted to get married. One day she was <u>at a party</u>. She met one man. At first, he seemed very <u>friendly/nice</u>, but later he was <u>mean</u> to her. In the end, <u>she/the girl</u> was happy with her new boyfriend.

IV. Pronouns

A. Subject Pronouns

1   **Kim's Dry Cleaners**

Mr. Kim owns a successful dry cleaning business. <u>He</u> cleans and sews clothing. The shop has five large cleaning machines, three presses, and a large sewing machine. <u>It</u> is a noisy, busy place. Mrs. Kim helps in the family business. <u>She</u> works at the front counter. The Kims work six days a week, and <u>they</u> rarely take a holiday. <u>They</u> have five other employees. The customers are satisfied with the Kims' work, so <u>they</u> have a good business.

2   **Planning a Vacation**

Bridget and her friends are trying to decide where to go on vacation. <u>They</u> want to take an interesting but inexpensive trip. Bridget thinks <u>they</u> should visit Montreal. <u>She</u> wants to practice speaking French. Bridget also wants to visit Niagara Falls. <u>It</u> is a very famous natural wonder.

Her friends, John and Charlie, would rather go to Florida. <u>They</u> want to go to Disney World. "<u>I</u> want to ride the fast rides," says John. "<u>We</u> will have a great time there." Charlie also prefers Florida. "Florida is beautiful, and <u>it</u> is not very expensive," he argues. "Also, <u>it</u> is warm and sunny." Bridget has no choice. <u>She</u> must go to Florida if <u>she</u> wants to take a vacation with her friends.

B. Object Pronouns

1
1. I left my bag in the library. I forgot <u>it</u> in the restroom.
2. I met Rebecca at the park. I took <u>her</u> home in my car.
3. My sisters and I saw a good movie last weekend. We enjoyed <u>it</u> very much.
4. Are your packages heavy? Let me carry <u>them</u> for you.
5. My father doesn't speak English, so I went with <u>him</u> to the doctor last week.
6. The telephone is ringing. I will answer <u>it</u>.
7. Those pants look great on you. Where did you buy <u>them</u>?
8. I don't have any money. Can you let <u>me</u> borrow $20?
9. I don't remember where I put my car keys. I can't find <u>them</u> anywhere.
10. Mary has a very good son. He visits his mother often and calls <u>her</u> every day.

2   **Persuasion**

Our class is reading an interesting book, *Persuasion*, by Jane Austen. <u>It</u> is an adapted version, which means <u>it</u> is easier than the original book. My classmates and I like this book. In class, <u>we</u> talk about the characters in the story as if <u>they</u> were real people. The main character is Anne Elliott. <u>She</u> is a quiet, shy woman. <u>She</u> wanted to marry a captain in the Navy, but her friend, Lady Russell, persuaded <u>her</u> not to marry <u>him</u>. Lady Russell said Anne was too young to marry. The captain, Frederick Wentworth, was angry at Lady Russell. <u>He</u> thought Lady Russell should not try to persuade Anne. After many years, Anne met Captain Wentworth again. <u>She</u> was nervous about meeting <u>him</u> again because she still loved <u>him</u>. <u>They</u> met each other at Anne's sister's house. Soon, the captain asked Anne to marry <u>him</u>. This time, Anne did not let anyone persuade <u>her</u>. <u>She</u> married her captain.

C. Possessive Adjectives

1 1. I like my math teacher, Mr. Rostami. <u>His</u> classes are always interesting.
2. Eric and Hung work in a computer company. <u>Their</u> offices are very cold because they must keep the computers cool.
3. Martin is a serious worker. <u>His</u> job means a lot to him.
4. Tina wants to quit <u>her</u> job because she doesn't like working until midnight.
5. You can get <u>your</u> passport at the Immigration Center.
6. A community college gets most of <u>its</u> money from the government.
7. Sara is a homemaker. She takes care of <u>her</u> children and her house.
8. My friends Malu and Vaishu come from India. <u>Their</u> country has many different cultures and languages.
9. Jonathan recently got married. <u>His</u> wife's name is Penny.
10. We just moved to a new apartment. <u>Our</u> new place is much larger than the apartment where we lived before.

2 1. ~~He's~~ ^{His} name is Romulo.
2. My friends and ~~me~~ ^I are going to the movies tonight.
3. My co-workers always work hard in ~~they~~ ^{their} jobs.
4. The dog is eating ~~it's~~ ^{its} food.
5. Are you bored by ~~you're~~ ^{your} work, or do you enjoy it?
6. Kathy and Doris are waiting for me. ~~Their~~ ^{They're} at the bus stop now.
7. My wife and I have been married for one year. I love ~~she~~ ^{her} very much.
8. My best friend is a special person. ~~She~~ ^{Her} name is Maddie.
9. Jules is my brother. I don't see ~~he~~ ^{him} often because he lives in Haiti.
10. If ~~your~~ ^{you're} tired, why don't you take a rest?

V. Parts of Speech

A. Frequency Adverbs

1 Possible answers
1. I <u>sometimes</u> enjoy shopping.
2. I <u>never</u> have enough time in each day.
3. I <u>often</u> dream about going on vacations.
4. I am <u>sometimes</u> tired of going to classes.
5. My friends and I are <u>always</u> busy on the weekends.
6. I <u>sometimes</u> waste time.
7. I am <u>usually</u> on time to my classes.
8. My English examinations are <u>rarely</u> difficult.
9. My classmates <u>sometimes</u> speak in their native languages during class.
10. I am <u>seldom</u> angry with other people.

2 Possible answers
1. I never fall asleep in class.
2. I never smoke cigarettes.
3. I usually wake up early on Saturday morning.
4. I never wear pajamas when I sleep.
5. I always wash my hands before eating.
6. I usually remember people's names.
7. I always attend classes regularly.
8. I sometimes talk a lot on the telephone.
9. I always clean up my own room.
10. I usually write e-mail every day.

B. Prepositions of Time

1 1. I have a busy schedule <u>in</u> the summer.
2. I have classes <u>on</u> Mondays, Tuesdays, Wednesdays, and Thursdays.
3. My college is closed <u>on</u> Fridays <u>in</u> May, June, July, and August.
4. I work <u>on</u> Fridays. I also work <u>on</u> the weekends.
5. <u>On</u> Friday, Saturday, and Sunday, I go to work <u>at</u> 9 A.M.
6. <u>On</u> these days, I get home <u>in</u> the late afternoon.
7. <u>On</u> Friday evening, I go out with my friends.
8. I usually go to bed <u>at</u> 10 o'clock because I have to get up early in the morning.
9. <u>On</u> Sunday afternoon, I do my homework.
10. <u>On</u> the weekdays, I catch the bus <u>at</u> 8 A.M. I go to my classes, and return home <u>at</u> 2 P.M.

2 1. One of my favorite TV show airs <u>at</u> 7:30 P.M. <u>on</u> Mondays. It's called "The Simpsons."
2. I don't like to get up early <u>on</u> Saturdays. I usually wake up <u>at</u> noon. <u>In</u> the summer, I sometimes get out of bed <u>at</u> 2 P.M.
3. I usually get home <u>in</u> the early afternoon and relax. I eat dinner <u>at</u> around 7 P.M.
4. <u>In</u> the summer, the days are longer. The sun usually rises <u>at</u> about 5 A.M., and it gets dark <u>at</u> 8:30 P.M.
5. <u>On</u> July 4, most businesses in the United States are closed. Americans celebrate their independence from Great Britain <u>on</u> this day.
6. <u>In</u> 2000, Paul took a trip to Greece. He arrived <u>on</u> June 20 and stayed for 10 days.
7. Mary often visits her brother <u>on</u> the weekends. She leaves her home <u>in</u> the morning and arrives at her brother's home in two hours. She returns home <u>at</u> night.
8. <u>On</u> my birthday, we had a picnic. My friends and I played soccer in the park <u>in</u> the afternoon and had a barbeque. We returned home <u>at</u> 9 P.M.
9. <u>On</u> Saturdays, we are very busy at work. I start work <u>at</u> noon and leave <u>at</u> midnight.

C. Prepositions of Location

1 1. The theater is <u>next to</u> the bank.
2. Mama's Restaurant is <u>across from</u> the antique shop.
3. The coffee shop is located <u>on</u> Main Street.
4. The shoe store is located <u>between</u> Mama's Restaurant and the coffee shop.
5. The library is situated <u>at</u> Main Street and Broad Street.
6. There are some flowers <u>in front of</u> the flower shop.
7. The shoe store is <u>to the right of</u> the coffee shop.
8. Many businesses are located <u>near</u> the library.

2 Answers will vary.

D. Singular and Plural: Nouns

1 1. Some <u>children</u> do not obey their parents.
2. Rita's <u>parents</u> live in Hong Kong. They own a business.
3. One of my <u>friends</u> works at Rocky's Pizza Parlor. He usually brings a <u>pizza</u> home from work.
4. I have many <u>things</u> to do this weekend. I must wash my car, clean my room, and go shopping.

5. Twenty <u>years</u> ago, I was an elementary school student.
6. Using a computer has a lot of <u>advantages</u>. One <u>advantage</u> is that it works fast.
7. Before I came to the United <u>States</u>, I didn't speak English well. I couldn't pronounce <u>words</u> correctly.
8. I want to be more independent. The main <u>reason</u> is that I want to make my own <u>decisions</u>.
9. <u>People</u> need to make many <u>choices</u> in their <u>lives</u>.
10. Some of my <u>teachers</u> say that I am very quiet. I do not ask many <u>questions</u> in class.

2 1. Senait is a very hard-working <u>person</u>.
2. She works for a large clothing <u>company</u>.
3. She opens many <u>boxes</u> of clothing every day.
4. She divides the clothing into three <u>groups</u>: men's, women's, and children's clothing.
5. One of her <u>jobs</u> is to put a price on each piece of clothing.
6. She also puts all the clothes on clothes <u>hangers</u>.
7. Senait works very fast. Her <u>co-workers</u> all look surprised at how quickly she works.
8. They often look at Senait's <u>hands</u> to see how fast she moves them.
9. Her <u>company</u> sells many different <u>kinds</u> of clothing: <u>shirts</u>, <u>skirts</u>, <u>pants</u>, and <u>dresses</u>.
10. Senait is a very good <u>worker</u>.

VI. Punctuation

A. Sentence-End Punctuation

1 1. Do you enjoy the outdoors?
2. Then we should take a trip to the mountains.
3. It's nice to take long walks in the woods.
4. Do you get tired easily?
5. We can go boating in the lake.
6. Are you a strong swimmer?
7. Be careful! The water is deep.
8. I also like to go rock climbing.
9. There's a good place to climb near the lake.
10. Look out! Those rocks are falling.

2 **A Friend in Need**

In English, they say, "A friend in need is a friend indeed." Dara is a friend who helps me when I have problems. This semester I was worried about my classes. I was not doing well. For example, in listening and speaking class, I couldn't understand the conversations on tape. **I could only understand parts of what the people were saying.** It was terrible. Dara told me to listen to the tape over and over. **He** also told me about some good television shows to help me with my English. I think talking to him also makes my English improve because he's from Cambodia and I'm from Colombia. **We** have to speak in English. Dara showed me that I should not worry so much. I'm not the only one who has trouble with English. **He** is really a good friend to me because he helped me when I needed him.

2 I am very proud of my son ~~Dmitri he~~ ^{Dimitri. He} is 18, and he goes to Community College of ~~Philadelphia this~~ ^{Philadelphia. This} is his second ~~year he's~~ ^{year. He's} a very smart ~~boy he~~ ^{boy. He} is taking 20 credits this semester because he wants to transfer to Drexel University in the spring ~~semester~~ ^{semester.} ~~he~~ ^{He} wants to major in Management Information ~~Systems also~~ ^{Systems. Also,}, he is working at Summit Bank as a proof machine ~~operator I~~ ^{operator. I} hope that he will have a great ~~future I~~ ^{future. I} love my children very much, and I will try to do everything that I can for ~~them~~ ^{them.}

B. The Comma

1
1. When I go shopping with my family, I always buy clothing.
2. In our group, we decided to research women's roles in the family.
3. I am a very careful writer. I pay attention to my spelling when I write.
4. On Friday, Saturday, and Sunday I work from 3 P.M. to 11 P.M.
5. I want to take a vacation, but I don't have enough money.
6. Although I left a message on her answering machine, she didn't call me back.
7. My best friend lives in Detroit, Michigan.
8. My grandmother died on June 3, 1997.
9. I saw many interesting animals at the zoo last weekend, for example, panda bears, white lions, and giraffes.
10. Some people do not use their money wisely. They spend too much money on CDs, new clothes, or jewelry.

2 At times, I would like to live in a more peaceful house. My son, my daughter, and my husband make a lot of noise every day. My son has many friends, so he often talks on the telephone. In the evening, my daughter listens to loud music, or she watches TV. My favorite pastime is reading, but it's sometimes too noisy to read. When I want to relax at home, I look for a quiet place. For example, I go outside and read in my backyard, or I take a hot bath. I also take long rides in the car, and I listen to music. These are the ways that I make my home life more peaceful.

C. Comma Splices

1
1. The first time that I came to the United States, I didn't know anything. I was scared of my neighbors. They made me nervous because they looked different from me. Now I have changed a lot. I'm not scared anymore.
2. When I was a child, we sometimes spent the whole day at the zoo. Sometimes we also went to the movies or went fishing.
3. I have several good qualities. One quality that stands out is that I am creative.
4. When I was eight years old, I always wanted a bike. I kept telling my father to get me one. After a few weeks, he bought me a black bike. I was so excited.
5. In 1999, my friends and I took a trip to Las Vegas. This trip was the best one that I took with my friends. It gave me a lot of memories.
6. Most people have at least one thing that they should change about themselves. I have some bad habits. For example, I am lazy. I have to become less lazy. I should be more responsible.
7. One day I saw my grandmother at school. She was crying. As a result, I realized that my grandfather was sick.
8. One reason I get angry is because of my mother. She gives me so much advice. After work, she comes back home. She starts to give me advice. She thinks I am a 10-year-old child. I don't like her giving me advice.

2   **Good Morals**

Good morals are important for ~~children, we~~ ^{children. We} learn our morals from our parents. It is important for parents to teach strong morals to their children.

Almost all parents teach their children not to tell

lies. They

~~lies, they~~ tell their children that lying is a bad

thing. If we are not taught these morals, we may

lies. Children

tell ~~lies, children~~ also learn morals in school. We

friends.

learn the right ways to act with our ~~friends,~~

Teachers

~~teachers~~ also punish children when they cheat on

tests. Morality is an important value because bad

morals will affect the whole world

D. Other Punctuation Marks

1 1. "Do you have the time?" she asked.
2. Stero City sells many kinds of electronic equipment: televisions, CD players, cassette players, and other items.
3. When my supervisor finished explaining the work, he said, "Do you understand?"
4. If you want to improve your listening, watch television in English, listen to the radio in English, and talk with English speakers.
5. Joe has traveled to many countries in Africa: Egypt, Tunisia, Niger, Kenya, Rwanda, and South Africa.
6. At the end of our visit, I didn't want to go home. "I will never forget you," I said to my new friends.
7. I enjoyed my trip to the mountains. I went snow sledding, skiing, and snowboarding.
8. Celia wanted to visit Canada, so she went to a travel agency. She asked the agent, "How much does a ticket to Montreal cost?"
9. Many children's television shows — especially cartoons and movies — contain a lot of violence.

2 1. She asked me, "What are you doing?"
2. Going online and finding pen-pals have become my favorite pastimes.
3. Perhaps I'll see my best friend next year. Sometimes he calls me and says, "How are you?" He is a good friend.
4. It was interesting to read your letter because reading books and listening to music are my favorite pastimes, too. I hope in the future you become a doctor.
6. I am a single mother. I have three children: two boys and one girl.

7. My friend encouraged me to go back to school. "Don't stay home. You can do anything you want," she told me.

VI. Spelling Rules

A. Spelling Rule 1: The -*s* Form

-*s* on Verbs

1 1. Mrs. Brand <u>has</u> four children.
2. Her oldest child, Emma, <u>is</u> 25 years old.
3. Emma <u>lives</u> with her husband in Chicago.
4. She <u>teaches</u> elementary school.
5. Emma's brother Christopher <u>works</u> in a steel factory.
6. He <u>fixes</u> the steel presses and other equipment.
7. The third child, Anthony, <u>goes</u> to college.
8. Anthony <u>studies</u> engineering.
9. Laura, the "baby of the family," <u>is</u> 18 years old.
10. Mrs. Brand <u>worries</u> about all of her children even though they are adults.

2   **My Best Friend**

My best friend Kenny is a nice person, and I

lives

enjoy being with her. She ~~live~~ on Pike Street near

lives

Rising Sun Avenue. She ~~live~~ with her family in a

gives

good neighborhood. She ~~give~~ respect to elders. She

is so kind to the poor. She knows how to sing well.

likes   tries

She ~~like~~ watching movies, and she ~~try~~ not to eat too

much. I met her when I came to high school. My

teacher introduced her to me. She was my partner

in school. That was 1999. We have been together for

comes

two years. We go shopping together. She ~~come~~ to

my home and stays the night. We go to college

together, and we also work together. We go around,

and have fun together. Kenny is a great person.

-*s* on Nouns

1 1. A busy <u>student</u> has many things to do.
   Busy <u>students</u> have many things to do.
2. My <u>watch</u> keeps very good time.
   Theresa has two <u>watches</u>. Both of them keep very good time.

3. I can never eat just one <u>strawberry</u>.
   Sometimes I like to eat a bowl of <u>strawberries</u> for breakfast.
4. July 13 is an important <u>date</u> because it is my son's birthday.
   I write down all my important <u>dates</u> on my calendar.
5. What is your greatest <u>wish</u> for the future?
   I have many <u>wishes</u> for my future.
6. My niece asked me to tell her a bedtime <u>story</u>.
   I told her two <u>stories</u>, and then she fell asleep.
7. The biochemistry <u>laboratory</u> uses computer programs.
   The biology and biochemistry <u>laboratories</u> have both IBM and Macintosh computers.
8. This summer I will take only one <u>class</u>.
   How many <u>classes</u> do you plan to take?
9. Can I have a French <u>fry</u>?
   This restaurant makes good French <u>fries</u>.
10. When I was a child, I received only one <u>toy</u> for my birthday.
    My nephew has many <u>toys</u>.

2 1. We are a very close family like most Turkish families.
       ~~family.~~ (families.)

2. My youngest sister, Veronica, is 24 ~~year~~ (years) old.

3. My stepfather has four children: Nita, Dolores, Guy, and Alton. The children are independent ~~person~~ (people.)

4. Every person has many ~~quality~~ (qualities.)

5. I have two ~~childrens:~~ (children,) one boy and one girl.

6. Reading ~~book~~ (books) is one of my favorite pastimes. I have learned about many ~~country,~~ (countries,) cultures, and historical things.

7. I work at Wendy's. I make ~~sandwich~~ (sandwiches) and ~~salad.~~ (salads.) I never have free time on weekends.

8. I want to write to people who like rock music and skateboarding because we have common ~~interest~~ (interest.)

9. I like making friends with many ~~person~~ (people.)

10. When I lived in Vietnam, I raised my two ~~niece.~~ (nieces.) It was difficult for me because I didn't have any experience raising ~~baby~~ (babies.)

B. Rule 2: The -*ed* Form

1 1. We <u>worked</u> very hard on our garden last Saturday. We <u>carried</u> heavy bags of dirt and plants.

2. I <u>tried</u> to call you yesterday, but you weren't home. I <u>wanted</u> to ask you go to the movies with me.

3. Cesar <u>studied</u> very hard for his driver's license exam. He <u>passed</u> the test easily.

4. Lisa <u>placed</u> the vase of flowers on the table. Then she <u>stepped</u> back to look at it.

5. A shooting <u>occurred</u> at 10 p.m. Sunday in a grocery store in my neighborhood. The store owner <u>told</u> the police that the criminal was a young man in his twenties.

6. Jung <u>loved</u> to play baseball when he was a child. He often <u>played</u> with his friends after school.

7. Carl <u>dropped</u> by to see you this morning. I <u>asked</u> him to stay and wait for you, but he <u>preferred</u> to come back later.

2 1. When I first arrived in the United States, I ~~fell~~ (felt) very shy because I couldn't speak English well.

2. At first, I just listened to my neighbors and believed everything that they ~~sayed~~ (said) to me.

3. My father ~~maked~~ (made) the money in the past, but now he is retired.

4. My daughter always ~~cryed~~ (cried) at night when she was a baby.

5. I ~~studed~~ (studied) English in high school in my country.

6. I ~~tryed~~ (tried) to stop smoking. I ~~stoped~~ (stopped) for two weeks, but then I started again.

7. I ~~plaied~~ (played) with my friends in the park when I was a child.

C. Spelling Similar Words

1   1. <u>When</u> I got home from work, I had a telephone message.
2. I don't <u>feel</u> very well, so I think I'll go to the doctor.
3. Will you please <u>sit</u> down?
4. I <u>am leaving</u> now. I'll see you later.
5. The customers left <u>their</u> packages on the counter.
6. Some people <u>think</u> that I am a funny person.
7. I was worried. I didn't know <u>where</u> you were.
8. Can you tell me <u>how</u> I can register for classes?
9. We're going to have <u>chicken</u> for dinner tonight.
10. Do you like coffee? I like it, <u>too.</u>
11. Can I go <u>along</u> with you to the library?
12. I don't understand <u>why</u> I got a C on the test.
13. Everyone should try to live his or her life in the <u>right</u> way.
14. I'll be ready in five minutes. I have to change my <u>clothes.</u>
15. I have a good <u>chance</u> to get a promotion at work.

2   1. On New Year's Day in Vietnam, everybody ~~clears~~ *cleans* their houses.
2. ~~Why~~ *While* I was in the bathroom, the telephone rang.
3. I am ~~leaving~~ *living* with my parents in an apartment right now.
4. My best friend likes ~~washing~~ *watching* movies.
5. Can you tell me ~~who~~ *how* to spell the word *business*?
6. Parents should teach ~~there~~ *their* children that making a good living is important.
7. I am married ~~too~~ *to* Ramon. We have ~~tree~~ *three* children.
8. I ~~though~~ *thought* my neighborhood was ~~save,~~ *safe,* but it is very dangerous.
9. I can read my book because our classroom is very ~~quite.~~ *quiet.*
10. My friends and I ~~where~~ *were* ready to go.

VIII. Capitalization Rules

1   The Importance of Education

  I know now that ~~E~~*e*ducation is very important, but I didn't always have this *I*dea. I remember when I was younger, I didn't like school. I thought that I would never need school in my life because I thought that academics would never get me anywhere. I remember every time my mother sent me to school, I pretended I was sick. I told her that I couldn't go to class. After I graduated from high school I realized that education is one of the most important things in life. I realize that I won't be able to get a good job without education. It's easy for anybody with school knowledge to find a better job. In a some places when you apply for a job, the first thing they ask you is if you graduated from high school. When you are educated, you get more respect than somebody who doesn't have school knowledge. Nothing can make you succeed more than education.

2   1. **My** brother works at a steel factory.
2. **On** Monday, she had a chemistry test.
3. **She** visited her mother in **M**alaysia over the **T**hanksgiving holidays.
4. **My** family and **I** crossed the **P**acific **O**cean on our trip to **H**awaii.
5. **There** are many interesting sites in the **M**iddle **E**ast.
6. **Dr.** **G**ary **G**ordon is a pediatrician.
7. **New** **Y**ear's is an important holiday in **C**hina.
8. **I** enjoy the fall season in the **N**ortheast because the leaves on the trees change color.

3 Possible answers
1. I live in <u>a three-bedroom apartment in the city.</u>
2. <u>My friend Beatrice</u> has two children.
3. My best friend's name is <u>Michele</u>.
4. When I look out the window, I see <u>a tree and birds</u>.
5. <u>My family</u> came to the United States one year ago.
6. English is a difficult <u>language</u>.
7. My native language is <u>Spanish</u>.
8. I love to <u>go shopping</u> when I have free time.
9. My favorite store is <u>Macy's</u>.
10. If I have extra money, I like to buy <u>new clothes</u>.

X. Common Editing Symbols

1 I live in Chicago.
I have a large family.
His parents own a dry cleaning business.
My sister works in a Chinese restaurant.
My daughter's name is Alina.
When I was a child, my family visited Agra.
I am from Vietnam. (OR I come from Vietnam.)

I am happy to live in a free country.
I like to listen to music.
We took a train. We got lost.
I bought a car last summer.
She is going for a walk.
My classes end on May 15.
My best friend is named Joan.
I am always late for class.

May 1, 1988

To Frank Armistead,
on the occasion of your
installation at
St. John's/North Prairie, Reeceville
from your colleagues
in the Yorkton Conference.

Grace and Peace to you,

Gary Schenk, Dean.

MINISTER'S PRAYER BOOK

An Order of Prayers
and
Readings

Edited with an introduction
by
JOHN W. DOBERSTEIN

FORTRESS PRESS   PHILADELPHIA

Library of Congress Cataloging-in-Publication Data

Main entry under title:

Minister's prayer book.

Includes bibliographies and index.
l. Clergy — Prayer-books and devotions — English.
I. Doberstein, John W.
BV4011.6.M56   1986   242´.692   85-16212
ISBN 0-8006-0760-0

1718H85   Printed in the United Kingdom   1-760

TO MY WIFE

'When I look at all the women in the world, I find none of whom I could boast as I boast with joyful conscience of my own. This one God himself gave to me, and I know that he and all the angels are pleased when I hold fast to her in love and fidelity.'

Luther concerning Kätie

CONTENTS

HOW TO USE THIS BOOK

This book provides a scheme and materials for the minister's daily devotions.

The basic scheme of devotions revolves about seven themes of the minister's calling and life, distributed over the seven days of the week. These themes (see Table of Contents) govern the prayers, lessons on the ministry, readings from the anthology of meditations for ministers, and intercessions provided for each day of the week.

Within each day one structure, containing twelve elements, is provided (see the Order of Devotion and Suggested Orders on page viii). Obviously, it is not expected that a pastor will use all these materials at a single sitting. It will be noted in the case of invitatories, prayers, and benedictions that three choices are given. This will provide variation from day to day for those who may wish to use the materials as a single daily devotion or for those who use them for morning, noon, and evening prayers as indicated in the Suggested Orders. In any case, the pastor should use what is possible and profitable to him and let the rest go. At the beginning, to attempt too much is as dangerous as too little.

Running concurrently with the basic seven-day scheme of the minister's calling is the scheme of the church year. The church year and its lessons govern the text, hymn, psalm, daily lessons, and the collect for the week (see the Propers for the Church year). The numbers of the suggested hymns for the week are those of the *Lutheran Book of Worship*. A two-year cycle of daily lessons is provided with three lessons for each day. The first may be used as a morning lesson and the second and third as evening lessons, or the three lessons may be used according to whatever arrangement seems appropriate.

The collection of Prayers of Preparation for Ministry provides additional materials which may also find their place in daily devotions, and the anthology, Meditations for Ministers, furnishes extra-biblical materials for meditation.

Further comments on all these materials will be found in the Introduction.

FOREWORD

Minister's Prayer Book, first published in 1959, met a clear and distinct ecumenical need for a devotional manual for pastors, relating prayer and meditation to the work of the ministry. The value of the book continues, for in an increasingly secularized society pastors more than ever need guidance in their devotional life and spirituality. Moreover, pastors need to meditate and reflect upon the nature and work of their office, continually being recalled to its center and essence. Thus *Minister's Prayer Book* has importance not only for pastors but for the health of the whole church. For this reason, and in response to continuing requests for this classic devotional volume, the publishers are pleased to bring *Minister's Prayer Book* back into print.

Users should be aware that only one section of the book has been altered in the present edition. At the request of the publishers, Philip H. Pfatteicher revised the "Propers for the Church Year" (pages 59-125) to bring these into line with current understandings reflected in the *Lutheran Book of Worship* and the two-year daily lectionary. Page xix of the editor's introduction must therefore be understood as applicable only to the original edition of *Minister's Prayer Book* and not to the present edition. The remainder of the book, however, remains unaltered, thus preserving the original and unique character of this "pastor's companion."

AN ORDER OF DEVOTION

1. Invitatory
2. Hymn for the week
3. Confession
4. Psalm
5. Creed
6. Lesson
7. Lesson on the ministry
8. Reading from the anthology
9. Collect for the week
10. Prayers, Intercessions, and the Lord's Prayer
11. Evening Commendation
12. Benediction

SUGGESTED ORDERS

for Morning, Noon, and Evening Devotions

Morning	Noon
Invitatory	Invitatory
Morning prayer	Hymn for the week
Psalm	Text for the week
Lesson from church year lectionary	Lesson on the ministry
Meditation and free prayer	Prayer
Collect for the week	Benediction
Benediction	

Evening

Invitatory
Confession
Psalm
Lesson from church year lectionary
Reading from the anthology
Evening commendation
Intercessions
Evening prayer
Benediction

I

This book, the entire content of which is concerned with the ministry, is consciously confined to the life and work of the pastor, though others whose life is wholly or partly devoted to ministering to others may find it useful, since the ministry of the pastor is only one of many ministries in the church. The compiler, however, has had seminary students in mind, along with working pastors, as he prepared this book of private devotions. It is the result of some twenty years of reading and ransacking of libraries and yet it is presented with acute consciousness of many shortcomings. To our knowledge there is no book in English that has attempted to meet the need of the evangelical pastor for an aid to a disciplined life of prayer.

There can be no question of the centrality of prayer and reading in the minister's life. And yet the constant confession we hear when ministers grow candid is that increasingly they have no time for prayer and study. Consider the life of a busy pastor in city or country and think of the traffic that runs through his day. Where will the minister, caught in a net of multitudinous responsibilities, find the quietness which will give him strength and give power and authority to his preaching and pastoral care? When will he concentrate upon prayer for the Holy Spirit, who, it is true, bids us be sensitive to the voices of the world, but also liberates us from bondage to them?

Devotional life is not a pseudo-spirituality which is too holy to concern itself with practical things. It is not morbid introspection and preoccupation with self; then it becomes a wretched, soul-destroying narcissism. This is a matter of the inmost, hidden side of a man's ministerial life, a side inaccessible to human sight, known only to ourselves and to Him who sees in secret; but it is the really determinative side. Only when we are completely alone with God do all the masks fall away, do we become utterly honest, stripped to our real and ultimate aims and ambitions. Prayer reveals whether the inmost direction of my life is really toward God and his kingdom. This is the hinterland out of which comes whatever richness there may be in a man's ministry. Out of these times of study, meditation, and prayer, of fruitful solitariness, will come the best of our testimony and we can say to our hearers, "I delivered to you that which I also received." But for many of us still the most haunting text in the Bible is this : "They made me keeper of the vineyards; but my own vineyard I have not kept!"

Pastoral care, in the full sense of one's total ministry, is always proclamation of the Word addressed to the real human situation. But I, the minister, must receive pastoral care too; I too must hear the Word of God spoken to my situation. This is prerequisite to any fruitful administration of pastoral care, since the minister must always be a witness, one of those, as Daniel T. Niles has said, "who dare to quote themselves as part of the evidence of what God has wrought." There are other prerequisites such as psychological insights based upon observation and experience, a natural gift for intuitively putting oneself in another's situation, systematic analysis, psychological or sociological, all of which may sharpen and clarify our knowledge of the spiritual situation to which the Word is to be addressed. But the experience of receiving personal pastoral care is not merely to know spiritual situations objectively, as a good psychologist or sociologist; it is to know the blessing of God's Word, heard personally in all its severity and love.

How, then, am I, the minister, to receive this pastoral care without which I cannot minister? There are a number of ways.

I may receive pastoral care from one who is appointed to be my pastor by reason of his ecclesiastical office, a synod president or bishop or other office-bearer. But the duties we have imposed upon these men who should be "pastors of pastors" actually disqualify them for the role of father confessor.

I may be ministered to by a fellow pastor or any other Christian friend. Such a person is willing to become a brother to me in the real sense of the word, one who speaks the Word of God to me, one to whom I listen because I recognize that God is speaking to me through him. In the Smalcald Articles (Part III, Art. IV) Luther speaks of the various ways in which the gospel comes to us.

First, through the spoken Word by which the forgiveness of sins is preached in the whole world; which is the peculiar office of the Gospel. Secondly, through baptism. Thirdly, through the holy sacrament of the altar. Fourthly, through the power of the keys, and also through *the mutual conversation and consolation of brethren.*

I know of no better discussions of this largely unrealized source of pastoral care than Dietrich Bonhoeffer's *Life Together* and the article, reprinted in this book, "Who Is My Pastor?" by Herman Dietzfelbinger, the present Lutheran bishop of Bavaria.

Still another source of pastoral care is my congregation and persons in it. All my theological theory is put to the test at a sickbed or a deathbed and my faith is shown up for what it really is. A great pastor once said that when he ministered to a sick person, that sick person was actually like a "professor" examining him on his theology, not the theology he had, but the theology that had him. Every real pastor has had this experience, wherein parishioners of mature and tested faith have ministered to him not only by exposing his own deepest need but by the benediction of their steadfast grip on the one thing needful.

But I can also receive pastoral care in solitariness. If the experience of pastoral care is a personal encounter with the Word of God addressed to my real situation, then whenever I listen to that Word addressed to me I am the recipient of pastoral care. And this means that I can, and must, be my own pastor. In the instance of prayer I allow God to speak to my condition through the words of the Bible and the words of witnesses. Luther's triad, *meditatio, tentatio, oratio,* a priceless pearl of our devotional heritage, sums it up. This personal "cure of soul" is prayerful, thoughtful, meditative, receptive listening to the Word of God as it speaks to me out of the words of the Bible and of witnesses (*meditatio*), the self-examination which is its necessary concomitant, as I am "taken aside, searched, challenged, smitten, and brought to decision" (*tentatio*), and finally the prayer that is my response to this Word of God that confronts me (*oratio*).

It must be understood that this is the pastor's personal and daily meeting with God; therefore preparation for preaching and teaching is not to be regarded as a substitute for regular private devotions, even though such preparation must include subjective meditation.

Our fundamental concern, however, is with evangelical meditation. It is not true that prayers and books of devotion, even the so-called "classics of devotion," can be used indiscriminately. Many of them are infused with a mystical tradition which is completely alien to the gospel and can only be confusing to the evangelical user of them. Prayer and liturgy are realized dogma, doctrine which is prayed; but if the doctrine is false, putting it into the form of devotion does not make it any less false. The Roman Catholic forms of spiritual exercises can never be a pattern for us, though they have crept into many popular Protestant manuals and discussions of prayer and meditation. The difference that separates us is that all Roman Catholic meditation rests upon the dogmatic assumption of synergism. For the Catholic, meditation and spiritual exercises are self-preparation for the reception of spiritual graces. According to Ignatius Loyola, the worshiper thus co-operates with God, serves God, and saves his soul. By employing the whole mechanical and psychological apparatus of exercises he seeks to call down divine grace. This the Evangelical must reject. I know of no better statement of the evangelical attitude than that of Paul Althaus in his dogmatics.

Nobody can induce the encounter with God by himself or induce it in another person. It is given to us only by God himself. Revelation is an event over which we have no control, an event that occurs when and where God wills. God alone reveals himself to me . . . . I know him only as He makes himself known to me.

Revelation is therefore to be attained neither by way of thought nor by way of action. It cannot be conceived or induced. We can and we should, of course, reach out for the revelation. We concentrate on the realities, concerning which others have declared to us that God has testified to them through these realities. We direct our thoughts there, we seek after His reality, we *seek* God. But this is never merely a matter of thought, of self-concentration or self-reflection, nor even of inquiring after God. It is always also a matter of one's actions, one's whole attitude of life: we seek to clear the way on our side for encounter with God, to keep ourselves open, to "understand" as we think we understand it. We can and we should *expect* an encounter in this serious sense. But we can never attain it in this way. Nor is it by any means dependent upon this preparation. It is given where God wills to give it, to those who do not expect it as well as those who do expect it. No exercises of any kind, no spiritual training, no mental cultivation, no methods ("How can we gain knowledge of higher worlds?"), no asceticism, no "fasting" in any sense, not even inquiring and seeking prayer can *coerce* it (even though it is most certainly *promised* that it will come in response to such prayerful searching!).

When the revelation is bestowed upon me it does, of course, set my thinking, willing, and acting into strong motion. Faith itself, by by which we take hold of revelation, is an act of man. We cannot appropriate it or hold on to it without thinking about it and meditating upon it and obeying it in action. But preceding this is the pure receptivity which is the primary basis of these acts. We can speak of revelation in the active voice only in so far as God is the subject. With regard to ourselves the event of revelation can be expressed only in the passive voice, which first provides the basis for our active voice. I am understood, touched, bound, addressed, known, and I recognize myself as being precisely the person to whom all this applies. All knowing rests upon being known. (*Die Christliche Wahrheit*, I, pp. 39-40.)

The theological foundation of evangelical meditation must be free of all synergistic and Pelagianistic concepts. It rejects any mysticism that puts the initiative with the worshiper. Man cannot by searching find out God. Prayer is turning to the Word of God. Prayer is nothing but response to God's Word and therefore it is nothing without the Word that precedes it. We must avoid the danger of making prayer an independent and autonomous concern of our devotional life. As Daniel Jenkins has pointed out:

Prayer is not necessarily a good thing. Unless it is directed to the right Person in the way He has laid down it can become a demonic thing and do untold damage to men and nations . . . It can be a highly dangerous thing, the most subtle and effective means of hiding man from the face of God . . . . For natural human prayer is always an attempt to have God on man's terms, an attempt, sometimes crude and sometimes profound and refined, to "square" God, to avoid the responsible decision for God, the self-committal to God, the full conformity with the will of God, which true prayer always demands. Human prayer, like human greatness and beauty and truth and indeed all human religion, needs itself to be redeemed before it can become a source of genuine blessing. (*Prayer and the Service of God*, pp. 20, 31.)

Our task is not to "practice" and "cultivate" prayer and the so-called spiritual life, but rightly to hear God's Word and give him due answer in prayer.

Another characteristic of evangelical meditation and prayer is its fundamental concern with the Scriptures. It is practical application of the evangelical principle that the Word of God speaks in, with, and under the words of the Bible. The Bible is its primary prayer book. This by no means excludes the use of other words and witnesses or meditation upon the general truths of salvation. I have never forgotten the words of Charles M. Jacobs in a chapel address: "I wish that each of us could take each day some little familiar sentence out of the Bible or, if one prefer it, *out of pure theology,* and let loose upon it all the power of imagination that he possesses." It was the italicized phrase that struck me. Nevertheless, the church of the gospel has rightly insisted that meditation and prayer be closely linked with the Bible in order that it may avoid running out into sterile, mystical brooding or unstable, unhealthy speculation. *Theologus in scripturis nascitur.* Here Adolf Köberle has put his finger on the point :

Prayer escapes the danger of disorder and confusion only when it is enkindled by the words of Scripture. From the Word proceeds its inner justification, as well as its life-giving power and the clearness of its petitions. A prayer life that does not stick to Scripture will soon become poor in ideas, poor in faith, poor in love, and will finally die. Free prayer and silent prayer require years of faithful association and training with the spirit of Scripture . . . . The more that *oratio* arises from the *meditatio* of Scripture the more moving will the prayer be. (*The Quest for Holiness,* p. 177.)

Because evangelical prayer and meditation start with the clear Word of God, and it is important that it should be heard sharply and unmistakably, stripped as far as possible of all archaic obscurity, it is suggested that the passages for the minister's meditation be read in the Revised Standard Version. This is not to be unaware of the shortcomings of this version, but in clarity and forthrightness it is doubtless far superior to the Authorized Version. The aim of evangelical devotion is perhaps best served by using several modern versions, including paraphrases like those of J. B. Phillips.

Evangelical meditation and prayer is, furthermore, a response to the imperatives in the Bible which demand and enjoin prayer and is founded upon the confident faith in God's sovereign promise that prayer will be heard and answered. So in the *Large Catechism* Luther answers quite simply, in a way that sentimental mystics may despise, the question "Why pray?" by saying : because God has commanded it and promised that he will hear. Evangelical meditation is founded upon obedience and faith. Its purpose is clearly set forth in the *Formula of Concord* :

> After God, through the Holy Ghost in baptism, has kindled and made a beginning of the true knowledge of God and faith, we should pray to him without intermission that, through the same Spirit and his grace, *by means of the daily exercise of reading, and applying to practice, God's Word,* he may preserve in us faith and his heavenly gifts, strengthen us from day to day, and support us to the end. For unless God himself be our school-teacher, we can study and learn nothing that is acceptable to him and that is salutary to ourselves and others. (Part II, chap. II, 16.)

Meditation in this broad sense of personal "soul-cure" has always been practiced, but it has never been common in the sense of being an indispensable element of the minister's day, as the breviary is in the Roman church. Voices have been raised from time to time, expressing the desire for the practice and guides for it. In 1852, Wilhelm Löhe said, "There is one practice and expression of the inner life which has been completely lost among us, namely, meditation, reflection upon divine words and truths in the presence of God." (*Der evangelische Geistliche,* I, p. 125.) In the middle of the last century there appeared in Germany a very valuable, but now completely forgotten book, the *Evangelisches Brevier* (1857) by Dieffenbach and Müller. This *Evangelical Breviary* is remarkably complete, containing a lectionary, psalter, prayers, and hymns. It is warmly recommended in the two older, standard works on pastoral care in the American Lutheran tradition, *The Evangelical Pastor* by E. T. Horn (1887) and *The Lutheran Pastor* by G. H. Gerberding (1902). Most recent is a suggestion made by a Committee on Faith and Life of the United Lutheran Church :

> In order to strengthen the pastor's devotional life, it is earnestly recommended that a pastor's office book be provided. This office book may contain a collection of Psalter selections, New Testament lections (both quoted and referenced), prayers concerned with the

pastor's needs (Luther's Sacristy Prayer), appropriate hymn texts, significant religious poetry, questions to measure and encourage faithfulness and loyalty to the ministerial office, etc. (U.L.C.A. *Minutes,* 1948, p. 304.)

As to practical directions and a method of meditation, the evangelical tradition has not been lacking, and one of the purposes of this book has been to recover something of the spiritual inheritance which lies in the Lutheran tradition, as Nathaniel Micklem has done for free churchmen in *A Book of Personal Religion* (1938). Chief among these from the Reformation period are *A Little Guide and Instructor for Future Pastors* by Caspar Huberinus, Luther's *Oratio, Meditatio, Tentatio: A Right Way to Study Theology* (in the anthology for Tuesday), Luther's *A Simple Way to Pray,* and *The Ladder of Devotion* by Caspar Calvör (Appendixes I and II). The last-named work of Luther, with its practical directions for meditation on the Lord's Prayer, the Ten Commandments, and the Creed, deserves the name of "classic" in any devotional tradition. The *Small Catechism* was, for him, not only a compendium of dogmatics or a popular handbook of Christian teaching, but, quite simply, a prayer book for the practice of daily prayer.

Learning from Luther, then, the following suggestions for the pastor's quiet hour may be helpful.

1) Prayer for the presence of God.

2) Thorough digestion of a scriptural or other passage of testimony. (What is it saying? Try to repeat the substance in your own words. What are the parallel passages? The Scriptures are their interpreter. What is the main point? Search for the inner aim of the passage.)

3) Self-examination. (What is there here that incites thanksgiving? What is the "gospel" of the passage? What sin must I confess? Regard the pangs of bad conscience stirred by the Word of God. What must I do, therefore, in my life and ministry? Be ye doers of the Word, not hearers only.)

4) Prayer on the basis of the insights gained.

5) Intercessions.

The use of an order can never be a law or an *officium* for evangelical Christians; all *opus operatum*, all merit is excluded. The editor therefore hopes that the term "breviary," with its wrong associations, will never be applied to this book. The order is only a suggestion and a guide. It seems necessary always to make this apology of "evangelical freedom" whenever a "form" of devotion is offered, but, having recognized this, we must also recognize that evangelical freedom is not freedom not to pray at all. Luther had some harsh things to say about the use of the Roman breviary; he called it "ass's worship" and "the profitless rigmarole of the seven hours." But he was equally blunt and stinging with regard to those who have forgotten that "prayer is a special exercise of faith" (*Treatise on Good Works,* Phila. Ed., I, p. 226). In the first preface of the *Large Catechism* he says:

Alas! they are shameful gluttons and ministers of their appetites, who would much more properly be swineherds and dog-fanciers than pastors and Gospel minister. And now that they are delivered from the unprofitable and burdensome babbling of the seven canonical hours, oh that instead thereof they would only, morning, noon, and night, read a page or two in the Catechism, the prayer book, the New Testament, or elsewhere in the Bible, and pray the Lord's Prayer once for themselves and their parishioners . . . and might have some little shame because like brutes they retain no more of the Gospel than such corrupt, pernicious, shameful, carnal liberty!

The question of the method of meditation leads to the question of the materials of meditation. Each pastor must use what fits his need. One may read a chapter or passage from the Bible or a hymn from the hymnal, another may use one of the countless available books of daily devotions, some will compose their own devotions, using the Bible, the hymnal, a devotional classic, and free prayer. Others may welcome a prayer book and a store of materials such as this book supplies.

This collection is based on the conviction that the pastor is best served by a selection of materials that fits his peculiar needs and responsibilities rather than a more general prayer book intended for family use.

II

The basic scheme of devotions in this book for the seven days of the week, along with the theme for each day, which governs the prayers, intercessions, and lessons on the office of the ministry, has been adapted, with some alterations, from the work of Dieffenbach and Müller.

The section which provides Propers for the Church Year requires comment and acknowledgments. Here I desire to express appreciation of and indebtedness to the following authors and books : Karl Bernhard Ritter, *Gebete für das Jahr der Kirche,* 2nd ed., Kassel, Johannes Stauda-Verlag, 1948; Rudolf Spieker, *Lesungen für das Jahr der Kirche,* 3rd ed., Kassel, Johannes Stauda-Verlag, 1950; Wilhelm Stählin, *Die Wochensprüche für das Kirchenjahr,* Kassel, Johannes Stauda-Verlag, 1954; and Ernst Glüer and Kurt Jagdmann, *Orate Fratres, Gebetsordnung für evangelisch-lutherische Pfarrer,* 2nd ed., Göttingen, Vandenhoeck & Ruprecht, 1952.

The "titles" for each Sunday and festival and the texts for the week, along with the daily lectionaries, represent one of the most fruitful Lutheran liturgical contributions of this generation, a development which makes the propers living companions for daily devotions besides providing the worshiper with greater understanding and appreciation of the church year. Apart from the enrichment of the pastor's personal devotions, the homiletical and catechetical value of these titles, texts, and lessons is apparent. In the opinion of the editor, if this book should prove to have any value, its most solid contribution will be the introduction of these materials to English-speaking readers.

The "titles" and texts for the week are not to be understood as being "thematic" in any cramping, scholastic sense.

The selection of the daily lectionaries, like the Sunday Gospel, always has a range greater than can be compressed into a "theme." The titles are intended rather to be "leading images" (*Leitbilder*), which will invite contemplation and set before the reader in an impressive picture the main concern of the week . . . They will also help to clarify the bewildering abundance of the church year. (Spieker, *Lesungen*, pp. 9 f.)

The texts for the week have been so chosen as to represent a clearly discernible connection with the Sunday Gospel (in a few cases, with the Epistle) and, along with the Gospel, the title, the hymn, and psalm for the week, indicate and recall the message of each Sunday and its place in the whole church year.

Above all, however, these texts for the week are intended to fructify the individual Christian's personal devotions. All the passages have been purposely selected to call to mind definite pictures or images and thus provide a focus for inner contemplation and meditation. Almost all the texts are brief enough to memorize, so that during the week one may turn back to "its" text and reflect upon it from ever new aspects. (Stählin, *Die Wochensprüche*.)

These texts have now been incorporated in the liturgy of the United Lutheran Church in Germany for the service without Holy Communion.

The hymns for each week have been chosen by the editor, who desires to express warm appreciation to the Rev. Dr. Luther D. Reed, esteemed teacher and friend, for making available to him in advance the texts of the new common Lutheran hymnal. The Gospel and Epistles, with some exceptions, are those of the new common liturgy. The lessons for the eve or vigil of each Sunday and festival and the Old Testament lessons are those of the *Lesungen für das Jahr der Kirche.*

The collects, with a few exceptions, are translations of prayers by Karl Bernhard Ritter in *Gebete für das Jahr der Kirche.* Like the title and text for the week, they reflect the *de tempore* or propers more clearly than do the ancient collects; they are not, however, intended to supplant these.

The Order of Prayer for the Days of the Week and the section of Prayers of Preparation for Ministry are deeply indebted to the book, *Orate Fratres,* mentioned above.

The anthology, Meditations for Ministers, is not intended to be merely "a collection of flowers of literature." Its purpose is rather to provide what is in effect a source book of pastoral theology that will point constantly to the core and center of the ministry. It contains, therefore, much that is not "devotional" in the popular sense of that term, but rather theological. No theology is much good unless it can be preached and prayed. As with many of the prayers and collects, the selections here represent an effort to recover a tradition past and present which is lost to us because of the barrier of language; therefore the many translations. Unless otherwise noted in the index of sources, all translations are the work of the editor.

The sources of materials are indicated by a number in parentheses. In the Order of Prayer the sources and authors have been relegated to the index of sources. In the Prayers of Preparation for Ministry and the anthology the source is indicated and further bibliographical data and some notes are given in the index of sources. A third index of names adds the dates of authors quoted.

It remains only to express my deep appreciation to the many authors and publishers who have permitted me to use copyrighted materials, my gratitude to my wife, to whom the book is dedicated, for her long patience, and my thanks to Miss Hope Treichler for her efficiency in preparing the typescript. My special thanks are due to my friend, the Rev. G. Elson Ruff, who lent his sure touch and fine understanding to the not inconsiderable problems of the typography and styling of the book.

For the book itself I should like to borrow from the excellent George Herbert these words from his preface to *The Country Parson:*

" The Lord prosper the intention to myself, and others, who may not despise my poor labors, but add to these points, which I have observed, until the book grow to a complete pastoral."

J. W. D.

LUTHER'S MORNING & EVENING PRAYER

In the morning, when thou risest, thou shalt say:

In the Name of the Father, and of the Son, and of the Holy Ghost. Amen.

Then, kneeling or standing, thou shalt say the Apostles' Creed and the Lord's Prayer.

Then mayest thou say this prayer:

I give thanks unto thee, heavenly Father, through Jesus Christ thy dear Son, that thou hast protected me through the night from all danger and harm; and I beseech thee to preserve and keep me this day also, from all sin and evil; that in all my thoughts, words, and deeds, I may serve and please thee. Into thy hands I commend my body and soul, and all that is mine. Let thy holy angel have charge concerning me, that the wicked one have no power over me. Amen.

And then shouldst thou go with joy to thy work, after a hymn, or the Ten Commandments, or whatever thy devotion may suggest.

In the evening, when thou goest to bed, thou shalt say:

In the Name of the Father, and of the Son, and of the Holy Ghost. Amen.

Then, kneeling or standing, thou shalt say the Apostles' Creed and the Lord's Prayer.

Then mayest thou say this prayer:

I give thanks unto thee, heavenly Father, through Jesus Christ thy dear Son, that thou hast this day so graciously protected me, and I beseech thee to forgive me all my sins, and the wrong which I have done, and by thy great mercy defend me from all the perils and dangers of this night. Into thy hands I commend my body and soul, and all that is mine. Let thy holy angel have charge concerning me, that the wicked one have no power over me. Amen.

And then lie down in peace, and sleep.

1. INVITATORY:

O satisfy us early with thy mercy: that we may rejoice and be glad all our days (Ps. 90:14).

Grace be unto you, and peace, from God our Father, and from the Lord Jesus Christ (I Cor. 1:3).

Show thy marvellous lovingkindness, O saviour of those who trust in thee; keep me as the apple of the eye; hide me in the shadow of thy wings (Ps. 17:7-8).

2. HYMN FOR THE WEEK

3. CONFESSION:

I confess to thee, Almighty and most Holy God, that I have sinned in thought, word, and deed, through my own fault, my own most grievous fault. I acknowledge my want of faithfulness in holy service, my want of discipline and obedience, my want of love. Wherefore I pray thee, O God, have mercy upon me, for the sake of Jesus Christ, thy dear Son, our Lord. Amen. (1)

Turn us, O God of our salvation, and cause thine anger toward us to cease. Make haste, O God, to deliver me; make haste to help me, O Lord. Glory be to the Father, and to the Son, and to the Holy Ghost: as it was in the beginning, is now, and ever shall be; world without end. Amen.

4. PSALM

5. CREED:

The Nicene Creed

I believe in one God, the Father Almighty, Maker of heaven and earth, And of all things visible and invisible.

And in one Lord Jesus Christ, the only-begotten Son of God, Begotten of his Father before all worlds, God of God, Light of Light, Very God of very God, Begotten, not made, Being of one substance with the Father, By whom all things were made: Who for us men, and for our salvation, came down from heaven, And was incarnate by the Holy Ghost of the

Virgin Mary, And was made man; And was crucified also for us under Pontius Pilate. He suffered and was buried; And the third day he rose again according to the Scriptures, And ascended into heaven, And sitteth on the right hand of the Father. And he shall come again with glory to judge both the quick and the dead : Whose kingdom shall have no end.

And I believe in the Holy Ghost, the Lord and Giver of Life, Who proceedeth from the Father and the Son, Who with the Father and the Son together is worshiped and glorified, Who spake by the Prophets. And I believe one Holy Christian and Apostolic Church. I acknowledge one Baptism for the remission of sins. And I look for the Resurrection of the dead, And the Life of the world to come. Amen.

6. LESSON (See lectionaries)

7. LESSON ON THE MINISTRY

The Divine Institution and Commission of the Ministry

Matthew 28:16–20	Acts 20:29–38
Luke 10:1–12, 16	I Corinthians 4:1–5
Ephesians 4:1–10	II Corinthians 5:17–21
Ephesians 4:11–16	Isaiah 6:1–13
Acts 20:24–28	Luke 5:1–11

Brief Passages for Meditation

John 7:38	I Corinthians 12:4–7
Galatians 2:20	Mark 16:15–16
Isaiah 49:4	II Timothy 1:13–14
II Corinthians 12:9–10	Isaiah 40:29–31
Matthew 10:8	

8. READING FROM THE ANTHOLOGY

9. COLLECT FOR THE WEEK

10. PRAYERS, INTERCESSIONS, AND THE LORD'S PRAYER

We give thanks to thee, heavenly Father, for the rest and peace of this holy day in which we remember all thy benefits and seek thy face;

for all the tokens of thy goodness in our homes and our lives, especially in this congregation;

for all the goodness which thou hast bestowed upon us through our brethren in the faith;

for the guarding grace with which thou hast watched over our bodies and preserved us in times of trial and trouble;

for fellowship with all who call upon thy Name;

for the goodness that continually greets and blesses us in the gifts of thy creation;

for the greatest of all gifts which thou hast bestowed upon us in Jesus Christ;

and for the hope in which we begin this great day in his Name.

For these and all other gifts, we give thee thanks, O God our heavenly Father. Amen. (2)

* * *

O Lord, my God, awaken my heart and make me wakeful to serve thee and alert to thy commands. Awaken me and root out all half-heartedness. Kindle my heart, O Lord, for I am ready for thee. Forgive my sin and discipline me. Cleanse me for the service of thy house. Come, Holy Spirit, fill my heart and mind with thy joy, thy light, thy love.

Sanctify me as thine own, sanctify me as thine instrument. Let thy Word take hold of me, speak thyself to me. Speak through my stammering words to thy people. Stir up their hearts, that thy seed may fall on good ground and bring forth fruit that will remain.

My Saviour, when I stand before thy congregation this day, hold thou my heart in thy hand.

O Lord, my God, let not this day be lost; make it thine own day. Be thou in our midst and build thy congregation.

I would be nothing; be thou all in all. Lord, I believe, help me to show forth thy praise. Amen. (3)

* * *

O God, who makest us glad with the weekly remembrance of the glorious resurrection of thy Son our Lord, vouchsafe us this day such a blessing through thy worship, that the days which follow it may be spent in thy favor; through the same Jesus Christ our Lord. Amen. (4)

* * *

Noon

O Lord, let me stand before thee. Thou art the beginning, the middle, and the end. Holy art thou, and holy is thy day, holy are all the hours of service to thee.

Lead me by thy Spirit. Help me; be thou my strength. Renew and quicken me. Give me the Bread of Life. Gather my thought, O Lord, and keep me from wandering and weariness. Preserve me from the curse of much speaking, from the death of vain busyness. Let all that I do and say be done in spirit and in truth. Keep my love ready and willing to serve thee among men. In the midst of all our labor thou art a refuge of peace. Thou dost strengthen us ever anew from the living fountain. There is no end to thy mercy.

Praise, honor, and glory be to thee, the Father, and the Son, and the Holy Spirit. By thy mercy, accept my ministry to the praise of thy glory. Amen. (5)

* * *

Evening

Eternal God, thou Father of light, we give thanks unto thee that thou hast given us the light of thy Word and let it shine upon us this day. Abide with us, for it is toward evening and the day is far spent. Be thou also our soul's light in the dark-

5

ness of this night, that we may neither be afraid nor go astray. Into thy hands we commend all whom we love, our homes, our country. Grant peace and comfort to all who are in trouble, sickness, sorrow, and other trials. Guard us, and especially our children, from spiritual perils, from temptation, sin, and shame. And may the blessing of thy Word attend us until, by thy mercy, we see the light of eternal life. Amen. (6)

* * *

Heavenly Father, we give thee thanks for this day. Thou hast met us in Thy Word, full of grace and truth; now settle thy Word in our hearts that it may direct us in the coming week. We have known afresh the fellowship of believers; now preserve and strengthen us in the joy of this fellowship and bind us together in the yoke of serving love. Above all we praise thee for thy mercy in Jesus Christ, the Lord and Saviour of our life. Be thou our safety through this night and help us in thy name to begin the work of another week to thine honor and our peace. Amen. (7)

* * *

Intercessions

" Hallowed be thy Name."

O God, whose name is holy of itself, we pray that it may be hallowed also by us. To this end help us, O blessed Father in heaven, that thy Word may be taught in truth and purity, and that we, as thy children, may lead holy lives in accordance with it; through Jesus Christ, thy Son, our Lord. Amen. (8)

* * *

Plan for Intercessions

For the congregation and the whole church; that the blessing of worship and preaching may continue through the week; for the practice of family worship; for the baptized and communicants; for those absent from worship.

Gracious Father, we humbly beseech thee for thy whole church throughout the world. Fill it with all truth, in all truth with all peace. Where it is corrupt, purge it; where it is in error, direct it; where it is superstitious, rectify it; where anything is amiss, reform it; where it is right, strengthen and confirm it; where it is in want, furnish it; where it is divided and rent asunder, make up the breaches of it; O thou Holy One of Israel, for the sake of Jesus Christ our Lord and Saviour. Amen. (9)

* * *

Eternal, merciful God, heavenly Father, I pray thee for all who have been committed to my prayers and pastoral care. Grant to all of them thy grace and Holy Spirit, that they may know thee and thy dear Son, Jesus Christ, that they may grow in true faith and fear and love, and to the end of their lives remain steadfast in the Christian life of firm hope and repentance and obedience to thy will. Give to me also, O God, grace to walk before them with pure teaching and a good life, that all of us, being preserved from unbelief and evil life, may attain to everlasting salvation, through the same Jesus Christ, thy dear Son, our Lord. Amen. (10)

* * *

We pray thee, O God, for all who proclaim and hear thy Word this day;

for all who cannot hear thy Word and join in the praise of thy church this day;

for the sick, the lonely, and the prisoners;

for all who refuse to hear thy Word and scorn thy church, that they, too, may be enlightened by thy grace;

for the lapsed, the unbelievers, and for thine unworthy servants;

for the nations, that thy name may be spread abroad among them, and for all who sit in darkness and in the shadow of death, that thy light may shine upon them. Amen. (11)

Lord Jesus Christ, thou Shepherd and Bishop of our souls, behold in mercy thy flock in this congregation where thou set me to be a pastor to feed them with Word and sacrament.

I thank thee, Lord, that I have been permitted again this day to perform this service. Now give power to thy Word, that all who have heard it may be moved to repentance, daily renewal, and sanctification of life. By thy mercy keep the baptized children in thy grace, that they may daily increase in faith toward thee and fight boldly against the world, the devil, and sin. Preserve those who have been guests at thy Table in fellowship with thee and one another.

Cause all who have been awakened from the sleep of sin by thy Word to taste and see ever more how good thou art. Preserve them from falling and keep them in thy grace, that they lead their lives in the world without offense. Let all seeking souls whom thou hast stirred to seek after thy salvation find their way to thy blessed light. To all who are indifferent to thy grace and all who resist or fall away grant repentance that they may know the things that belong unto their peace.

Be not silent to the cries of the afflicted, the sick, and the bereaved. Let thy Word be the joy and rejoicing of their hearts, and make them sure that thy thoughts toward them are thoughts of peace.

Uphold, O Lord, the whole church which thou hast purchased with thine own blood. Let not one dearly bought soul be lost, for thy mercy's sake. Amen. (12)

* * *

Grant, O Lord, that the ears which have heard the voice of thy Word may be closed to the voice of clamor and dispute; that the eyes which have seen thy great love may also behold thy blessed hope; that the tongues which have united in thy praise may speak the truth; that the feet which have walked in thy courts may walk in the ways of light; and that the bodies which have partaken of thy living body may be restored in newness of life. Glory be to thee for thine unspeakable gift. Amen. (13)

* * *

Holy Father, blessed God, who hast set me to be a watchman and pastor of thy flock, I thank thee for the blessings of this day, that I have been admitted to take part in the prayers and praises of thy church and to speak and hear thy Word. Let not thy Word be spoken in vain, nor thy mercies lost upon us. Let it accomplish in us thy purpose and bring forth faith that we may all walk worthy of our vocation and be more fruitful in every good work. Grant that those who have praised thee in thy church may openly honor thee in the sight of the world.

Confirm thy Word by the testimony of thy Spirit and so bless their worship that our prayers in common may move them to more constant prayer at the family altar, to the reading of the Scriptures, and to praise thy name in their homes, give all who have heard thy Word wisdom to understand, remembrance to consider, and watchfulness to carry it into practice, that they may do their work with peaceful hearts, a more steadfast will, and a more loving spirit, prepared in everything to honor thy will and to serve one another.

Into thy hands I commend all whom I have baptized according to thy command and promise; by thy Spirit keep them in this grace, and stir and recall those who have departed from thee. Bless all those who have communed in faith; perfect, strengthen, and establish them in thy grace and love.

Speak thou, O Lord, to all who were absent by reason of sickness or failing strength or demands of their calling, that they may not lose the sense of thy presence. Give qualms of conscience to those who neglect thy courts and withdraw themselves from thy service, to those whose faith has grown cold, to those who are deceived by follies and seduced by the customs of the world, and cause them to hunger after thy Word and find in it their provision on the way to eternal life.

Bless this congregation and all its members and bring them in strength to the morning, that they may praise thee with their work. Keep me and all of them in true faith and a godly life, that we may daily grow and increase therein, and remain steadfast to the end, through Jesus Christ, thy Son, our Lord. Amen. (14)

* * *

The Lord's Prayer

11. EVENING COMMENDATION:

Into thy hands I commend my spirit, soul, body: thou hast created, redeemed, regenerated them, O Lord of truth: and with me all mine and all things mine: thou hast bestowed them upon me, O Lord, in thy goodness. Preserve us from all evil, preserve our souls, I beseech thee, O Lord; keep us from falling and present us faultless before the presence of thy glory in that day. Let the words of my mouth and the meditation of my heart be always acceptable in thy sight, O Lord, my rock and my redeemer. (15)

12. BENEDICTION:

Grant, O Lord, by thy mercy, that we may attain unto eternal life; and when we behold thy glory as it is, let us adore thy majesty and say: Glory be to God the Father, who has created us; glory be to the Son, who has redeemed us; glory be to the Holy Spirit, who has sanctified us. Amen. (16)

* * *

Grace, mercy, and peace from God the Father, Son, and Holy Spirit, be with us henceforth and for ever. Amen.

* * *

May the almighty and merciful God, Father, Son and Holy Spirit, bless and keep us. Amen.

1. INVITATORY:

My voice shalt thou hear in the morning, O Lord: in the morning will I direct my prayer unto thee, and will look up (Ps. 5:3).

Grace to us and peace from God our Father, and the Lord Jesus Christ. Blessed be God, even the Father of our Lord Jesus Christ, the Father of mercies, and the God of all comfort. Amen (Rom. 1:7; II Cor. 1:3).

The almighty and merciful God bless us and keep us this night and for evermore. Amen.

2. HYMN FOR THE WEEK

3. CONFESSION:

Almighty Father, Lord of heaven and earth: we confess that we have sinned against thee in thought, word, and deed. Have mercy upon us, O Lord, have mercy upon us after thy great goodness; according to the multitude of thy mercies, do away our offenses; wash us thoroughly from our wickedness, and cleanse us from our sins; for Jesus Christ's sake. Amen. (17)

Turn us, O God of our salvation, and cause thine anger toward us to cease. Make haste, O God, to deliver me; make haste to help me, O Lord. Amen.

4. PSALM

5. CREED:

I believe that God has created me and all that exists; that he has given and still preserves to me my body and soul, with all my limbs and senses, my reason and all the faculties of my mind, together with my raiment, food, home, and family, and all my property; that he daily provides me abundantly with all the necessaries of life, protects me from all danger, and preserves me and guards me against all evil; all which he does out of pure, paternal, and divine goodness and mercy, without any merit or worthiness in me; for all which I am in duty bound to thank, praise, serve, and obey him. This is most certainly true. (18).

6. LESSON (SEE LECTIONARIES)

7. LESSON ON THE MINISTRY

The Promise and Responsibility of the Ministry

Ezekiel 13:1–16	II Corinthians 3:4–6
Jeremiah 20:7–13	II Corinthians 3:7–18
II Timothy 2:1–13	I Corinthians 3:1–17
Malachi 2:1–9	Matthew 5:11–19
II Corinthians 4:1–18	Luke 12:35–38

Brief Passages for Meditation

I Corinthians 9:16–17	Luke 11:23
Revelation 2:10	II Corinthians 11:13–16
Daniel 12:3	Jeremiah 6:13–15
II Corinthians 5:9–10	Matthew 12:36–37
Luke 12:32	Matthew 25:21, 30
Matthew 19:29	Revelation 22:11–12

* * *

8. READING FROM THE ANTHOLOGY

9. COLLECT FOR THE WEEK

10. PRAYERS, INTERCESSIONS, AND THE LORD'S PRAYER

Morning

Almighty God, merciful Father, who dost create and complete all things : we beseech thee on this day when the work of our calling begins anew, do thou create its beginning, direct its continuance, and bless its end, that our doings may be preserved from sin, our life hallowed, and our work in this week be wellpleasing to thee; through Jesus Christ, our Lord. Amen. (19)

Gracious God and Father, be with us this day, according to the riches of thy goodness and grace. Teach us to do thy will, not in words but in power, and do all our work in obedience alone to thee. Make us to desire nothing except that which is pleasing to thee. But grant us also to hear the friendly voice that uplifts and comforts and gives us strength to do the work to which we are called. With thee we begin, with thee continue and end. (20)

* * *

Noon

Lord God, Heavenly Father, who in thine infinite mercy didst establish thy church, thy blessed kingdom of peace, in this evil and troubled world, and didst institute thy holy ministry in the same : Grant me grace always to acknowledge this with thanksgiving and praise, that, remembering thy glorious promises, I may perform this holy ministry to thine honor and the healing of the souls committed to my care, that so thy peace may come to us and remain for evermore, through Jesus Christ, our Lord. Amen. (21)

* * *

Evening

Visit, O Lord, this dwelling, and drive from it all the snares of the enemy; let thy holy angels dwell in it to preserve us in peace, and may thy blessing be upon us evermore; through Jesus Christ, our Lord. Amen. (22)

* * *

We give thee thanks, O Lord,
    who hast preserved us through the day.
We give thee thanks,
    who wilt preserve us through the night.
Bring us in safety, we beseech thee, O Lord,
    to the morning hours,
That thou mayest receive our praise at all times;
    through Jesus Christ, our Lord. (23)

O Lord our God, who dwellest in light unapproachable, and by thy great mercy hast led us through this day, graciously accept our prayers, save us from the darkness of sin, and enlighten our minds, that abiding in thy fear and walking in thy light, we may know thy glory and praise thee for all things, thou who art the only true and gracious God, for thine is the kingdom and the power and the glory forever. Amen. (24)

* * *

Intercessions

"Thy kingdom come"

O God, everlasting Father, whose kingdom cometh of itself, we pray that it may come also unto us. To this end do thou give us thy Holy Spirit, so that by his grace we may believe thy holy Word, and live godly lives here on earth and in heaven forever. Amen. (25)

* * *

Plan for Intercession

For the missions of the church; for the proclamation of the gospel in all the world; for the younger churches; for missionary societies and missionaries; for the raising up of leaders at home and abroad; for missionary zeal at home and open doors among the nations; for oneness in Spirit and brotherly love.

For fellow-workers in the parish; vestrymen, parish workers, assistants, deaconesses, sextons, officers and leaders in the congregation.

Almighty and most merciful God, who through Jesus Christ hast begun a kingdom for the salvation of all men unto the ends of the earth; send messengers to the nations who shall bring the light of thy Word to those who sit in darkness and in the shadow of death. Make the church at home willing and ready to do thy work in prayer and generous giving.

We commend unto thee our brethren who are laboring in distant lands. Equip them with thy Spirit, that they may bear bold and faithful witness to thee. Let thy Word everywhere find open doors and receptive hearts. We commend unto thee all missionary societies, together with their leaders and teachers and those who are preparing to serve.

We pray thee for the people of Israel, that they may put away their unbelief and acknowledge and accept Jesus as their Messiah and Saviour. Have compassion upon all who follow false prophets, that they may return to the true Prophet, Jesus Christ.

Befriend, O Lord, the younger churches, their congregations, pastors, and teachers, that they may grow in the knowledge of the truth and in love toward thee and by holiness of life glorify thee among the heathen. Make them steadfast in faith in the midst of hostility and persecution.

Bring in the day when there shall be one flock and one Shepherd and we shall be united with all thy children in thine eternal kingdom. Amen. (26)

* * *

Almighty God, who by thy Son Jesus Christ didst give commandment to the apostles that they should go into all the world and preach the gospel to every creature : grant to us whom thou hast called into thy church a ready will to obey thy Word, and fill us with a hearty desire to make thy way known upon earth, thy saving health among all nations. Look with compassion upon the multitudes that are scattered abroad as sheep having no shepherd. O heavenly Father, Lord of the harvest, have respect, we beseech thee, to our prayers, and send forth laborers into thy harvest. Fit and prepare them by thy grace for the work of the ministry; give them the Spirit of power and of love and of a sound mind; strengthen them to endure hardness and grant that thy Holy Spirit may prosper their work, and that by their life and doctrine they may show forth thy glory, and set forward the salvation of all men; through Jesus Christ, our Lord. Amen. (27)

* * *

Lord God, heavenly Father, who according to thy gracious will hast established within thy church on earth, besides the ministry of the Word, other offices for the ministration of thy manifold gifts of grace : We thank thee that in this place thou hast provided men of honest report, ready to serve this congregation for thy sake; and we humbly pray thee to enrich them abundantly with thy Holy Spirit, that they may have wisdom and strength for the service unto which thou hast called them; through Jesus Christ, our Lord. Amen. (28)

* * *

Heavenly Father, who hast established all manner of offices in thy church for the work of service, whereby the Body of Christ may be built up; we commend to thy faithfulness all the workers in our parish. Give them strength to render faithful service to the children, the sick, and the lonely, and make them to be true friends of the oppressed and helpers of those that are young and in peril. Give them hearts that are compassionate and yet bold for all the tasks of their calling; through Jesus Christ, our Lord. Amen. (29)

* * *

O faithful God and Lord, who hast called the leaders of this congregation and all my fellow-workers to serve thy church and thy kingdom in this place : Grant that, remembering their calling, and made strong and fit by thy grace, they may faithfully perform the work entrusted to them in the unity of the Spirit and the power of thy love; through Jesus Christ, our Lord. Amen. (30)

* * *

O thou true light that lightest every man coming into the world, we pray thee in thy mercy to inflame the heart, and enlighten the understanding of all whom thou dost call to the service of thy church, that they may cheerfully acknowledge and readily obey thy call, to the benefit of thy people and the glory of thy holy name, who with the Father and the Holy Spirit livest and reignest, world without end. Amen. (31)

* * *

O Lord, without whom our labor is but lost, and with whom thy little ones go forth as the mighty; be present to all works in thy church which are undertaken according to thy will, and grant to thy laborers a pure intention, patient faith, sufficient success upon earth, and the bliss of serving thee in heaven; through Jesus Christ our Lord. Amen. (32)

* * *

The Lord's Prayer

11. EVENING COMMENDATION:

Into thy hands, Almighty Father, who dost will peace and purpose lovingkindness, we commend our spirits; our minds to know thee, our hearts to love thee, our wills to serve thee, for we are thine.

Into thy hands, Incarnate Saviour, who hast taught us that thou art the way, the truth, and the life, receive us and draw us after thee, that we may follow thy steps: enlighten and guide us, lest the night of sin and error overwhelm us; abide in us and quicken us by the power of thine indwelling.

Into thy hands, O Lord the Spirit, who createst good and destroyest evil, take us and fashion us after thine image: let thy comfort strengthen, thy grace renew, and thy fire cleanse us.

Soul and body, in life and in death, in this world of shadows and in thy changeless world of light eternal, now and forever, Father, Son, and Holy Spirit, into thy hands. (33)

12. BENEDICTION:

Now unto him that is able to do exceedingly abundantly above all that we ask or think, according to the power that worketh in us, to him be glory in the church by Christ Jesus, throughout all ages, world without end. Amen (Eph. 3:20).

* * *

The peace of God which passeth all understanding keep our hearts and minds through Christ Jesus (Phil. 4:7).

* * *

May the blessing of the eternal God be upon us, and upon our work and worship;

> His light to guide us,
> His presence to strengthen us,
> His love to unite us;
>> Now and always. Amen. (34)

TUESDAY

1. INVITATORY:

Thou, Lord, hast made me glad through thy work: I will triumph in the works of thy hands (Ps. 92:4).

Peace, peace to him that is far off, and to him that is near, saith the Lord. There is no peace, saith my God, to the wicked (Isa. 57:19, 21).

Grant us, almighty and merciful God, a restful night and a blessed end. Amen.

2. HYMN FOR THE WEEK

3. CONFESSION:

Almighty and most merciful God, we acknowledge and confess that we have sinned against thee in thought, word, and deed; that we have not loved thee with all our heart and soul, with all our mind and strength; and that we have not loved our neighbor as ourselves. We beseech thee, O God, to be forgiving to what we have been, to help us to amend what we are, and of thy mercy to direct what we shall be, so that the love of goodness may ever be first in our hearts, that we may always walk in thy commandments and ordinances blameless, and follow unto our life's end in the footsteps of Jesus Christ our Lord. Amen. (35)

4. PSALM

5. CREED :

I believe that Jesus Christ, true God, begotten of the Father from eternity, and also true man, born of the Virgin Mary, is my Lord : who has redeemed me, a lost and condemned creature, secured and delivered me from all sins, from death, and from the power of the devil, not with silver and gold, but with his holy and precious blood, and with his innocent sufferings and death; in order that I might be his, live under him in his kingdom, and serve him in everlasting righteousness, innocence, and blessedness; even as he is risen from the dead, and lives and reigns to all eternity. This is most certainly true. (36)

6. LESSON (SEE LECTIONARIES)

7. LESSON ON THE MINISTRY

The Minister's Life

I Timothy 3:1–7	*Matthew 23:1–12*
I Timothy 6:6–16	*Acts 8:18–24*
Ephesians 6:10–17	*Matthew 7:13–23*
Titus 2:11–15	*I Peter 4:8–11*
Philippians 3:12–21	*I Timothy 4:7b–12*

Brief Passages for Meditation

Hebrews 12:12–14	*I Thessalonians 5:5–6*
I Corinthians 9:25–27	*I Corinthians 16:13*
I Peter 3:15–16	*Hebrews 12:1–2*
I Peter 2:11–12	*Hebrews 10:26–27*
Titus 2:7	*Romans 6:3–4*
II Timothy 2:19,22	

8. READING FROM THE ANTHOLOGY

9. COLLECT FOR THE WEEK

10. PRAYERS, INTERCESSIONS, AND THE LORD'S PRAYER

Morning

Grant us, O Lord, to pass this day in gladness and peace, without stumbling and without stain, that, reaching the eventide victorious over all temptation, we may praise thee, the eternal God, who dost govern all things and art blessed for evermore; through Jesus Christ, thy Son, our Lord. Amen. (37)

* * *

We give thee hearty thanks, O Lord, for the rest of the past night, and for the gift of a new day, with its opportunities of pleasing thee. Grant that we may so pass its hours in the perfect freedom of thy service, that at eventide we may again give thanks unto thee; through Jesus Christ, our Lord. Amen. (38)

Noon

O Almighty God, thou holy and strong God, whose will it is that thy servants should walk in thy house in true holiness, in peace, simplicity, and humility; I beseech thee anoint, enlighten, and sanctify me with thy Spirit, that my walk and conversation may be to thine honor, as is fitting, that through thy servant's life thy church may be edified, thy peace increased, thy kingdom spread, and thy Name hallowed; through Jesus Christ, our Lord. Amen. (39)

* * *

O Lord, thou faithful God, I pray thee, grant thy servant the joy of laboring in the vineyard planted with sweat and tears by thy dear Son, and, until the evening comes, let me glory in the high privilege of serving thee. Amen. (40)

Evening

O Lord God, who hast been pleased to create the night for the repose of man, as thou dost appoint unto him the day for labor, grant unto us so to rest this night in the body that our souls may be awake to thee and may be uplifted in thy love. Grant that we may cast off all earthly cares, but that the thought of thy goodness and thy grace may be ever present to our minds, that while our bodies rest our consciences may find spiritual repose. May it please thee to keep us pure both in body and in spirit, that even our sleep may be to the glory of thy name. And since, being but poor sinners, we have not passed this day without offending against thee in various ways, we beseech thee that as all is now hidden by the darkness which thou sendest on the earth, so thou wouldest be pleased to bury our faults by thy compassion, so that we may not be separated from thy face. Hear us, our God, our Father and Saviour, through our Lord Jesus Christ. Amen. (41)

* * *

O thou beloved Shepherd of our souls and bodies, who slumberest not; spread thy holy protection over us as wings to cover us, that no terrors of the night may weary us, and let thy divine Majesty watch over our minds while we sleep; through Jesus Christ, our Lord. Amen. (42)

* * *

Intercessions

"Thy will be done on earth, as it is in heaven."

O God, whose will is done without our prayer, we pray that it may be done also by us. To this end do thou frustrate and bring to naught every evil counsel and purpose—such as the will of the devil, the world, and our own flesh—which would hinder the hallowing of thy name and prevent the coming of thy kingdom. Do thou strengthen and keep us steadfast in thy

Word and in faith even unto the end. Let this thy good and gracious will be done. Amen. (43)

* * *

Plan for Intercession

For the Churches of Christ in America and the Evangelical Lutheran Churches; for the congregations, clergy and laity, officers, synods, teachers and students of theology, organizations for men's, women's, and youth work.

For the children of the church; for Christian education, parish schools, teachers and helpers.

Almighty God, merciful Father, we give thee most hearty thanks that in Jesus Christ thou dost take living stones and build thy holy church as thy temple in this world, and hast called us through the preaching of the gospel to the community of believers. Keep our church upon that one foundation which is laid, which is Jesus Christ. Pour out thy Holy Spirit upon our congregations, that we may faithfully use thy gracious gifts, the Word and Sacraments, and not be among those that have the name of being alive and yet are dead. Raise up laborers after thine own heart for the manifold ministry of thy church. Give to pastors and teachers courage and joyful boldness to continue steadfast in prayer and the ministry of the Word in its purity. Equip them and all who labor in the service of mercy, the teaching of youth, and other works of the church, with power from on high, that the sleepers may be awakened, the erring converted, and the fainthearted and discouraged quickened by thy comfort.

Grant that all who have been called to thy holy work may be one in love, that they and we may labor only for the honor of thy name and seek with one accord to gather and further thy church unto the last great day. To this end, give us a sincere compassion for all the need and trouble in our congregation, that we may conquer all slothfulness and lukewarmness and joyfully accomplish what thou dost require of us.

For a Theological School

Cause thy gospel to conquer hearts wherever it is preached in our land, that all who bear the name of thy Son may find their way to one another in the unity of the Spirit, that there may be one flock with one shepherd, Jesus Christ, to whom be praise for ever and ever. Amen. (44)

* * *

O merciful God, bless this particular church in which I live; make it, and all the members of it, sound in faith, and holy in life, that they may serve thee, and thou bless them; through Jesus Christ our Lord. Amen. (45)

* * *

For a Theological School

O Lord Jesus Christ, in whom is truth and life, let thy presence abide in our school; that seeking thy truth we may find thee, and sharing thy life, may dwell together in perfect fellowship, and in days to come be found faithful servants of thee, to whom, with the Father and the Holy Spirit, be glory and praise, now and forever. Amen. (46)

* * *

Lord Jesus, who didst thyself institute the holy office of the ministry and hast commanded us to preach repentance and the forgiveness of sins in thy name, we beseech thee to set faithful watchmen upon the walls of thy church who shall guard thy towers and declare thee to the ends of the earth. Fill them whom thou sendest with true understanding of thy Word and be with their spirit that they may faithfully feed thy church which thou hast purchased with thine own blood, turn the sinful to repentance, and comfort the sorrowing, and be able by sound doctrine both to exhort and to convince the gainsayers. Give them bold hearts that they may preach thy holy word without fear, without hypocrisy, and without respect of persons, as they ought to do. (47)

We pray for them that are ministers of thy Word, whose work it is, so far as a man is able, to draw men unto thee. We pray that thou wilt bless their work, but that at the same time they themselves in this work of theirs may be drawn unto thee, that by their zeal to draw others unto thee they themselves may not be held back from thee. And we pray for the simple Christians, that being themselves drawn unto thee, they may not think poorly of themselves, as though it were not granted also unto them to draw others unto thee, in so far as a man is able.

In so far as man is able—for thou alone art able to draw unto thyself, though thou canst employ all means and all men to draw all unto thyself. Amen. (48)

* * *

Merciful God, heavenly Father, who through thine apostle Paul hast comforted and assured us that it has pleased thee to save those who believe by the foolishness of preaching the crucified Christ, I pray thee, grant unto me, and all thy servants whom thou hast called to the ministry of preaching, the gift of thy divine grace and thy Holy Spirit. May the same Spirit strengthen us against all the temptations of the devil and make us wise and able to feed thy dearly bought sheep with thy saving Word, according to thy divine will, and to the praise of thy holy name, through Jesus Christ. Amen. (49)

* * *

Holy and merciful Father, who art the true Father of the whole family in heaven and earth, we pray thee for the children of our congregation. Strengthen the parents and sponsors, that they may faithfully keep the promises they made at the baptism of their children and early lead them to thee. Grant and preserve unto us Christian schools in which the children may be instructed in thy Spirit. Bless the teachers and leaders, that they may win to saving faith the children entrusted to their care.

Grant, we beseech thee, that all the church's ministry to our children, its worship and instruction, may bring forth fruit in them. Direct especially the catechumens and their parents in quiet concentration upon the one thing needful. Stir and quicken their hearts, that they may become true disciples of Jesus and that they may bring rejoicing and honor to thy church.

Open the hearts of all children to thy Word and strengthen them in temptation. Grant that they and all of us may overcome every trial and share at last in thy resurrection, through Jesus Christ, our Lord. Amen. (50)

* * *

O Lord Jesus Christ, who art the life and light of all thy servants, we beseech thee to help and inspire those who teach in our Sunday schools, and those also who prepare them for their work. Pour out upon them the spirit of unceasing prayer and faithful service; encourage them with good success; strengthen their faith and purpose when they are weary and disheartened; and fortify them with thine assurance that they are fellow-workers together with thee; through Jesus Christ our Lord. Amen. (51)

* * *

O Lord Jesus Christ, who art the Saviour and friend of age and youth : look graciously, we beseech thee, upon those who give themselves to serve and help the young, and bless their works undertaken in thy name. Enlighten those who teach and those who learn; renew their strength that they may not grow weary in their work; let their lamps burn bright in the days of darkness; and their hearts be strong in times of disappointment. And so inspire them with thy Spirit that old and young may be builded together as living stones into the temple of thy church; who livest and reignest with the Father and the Holy Spirit, ever one God, world without end. Amen. (52)

11. Evening Commendation:

Save us, O Lord, waking; guard us sleeping; that awake we may watch with Christ, and asleep we may rest in peace. (53)

12. Benediction:

The God of all grace, who hath called us unto his eternal glory of Christ Jesus, make you perfect, stablish, strengthen, settle you. To him be glory and dominion for ever and ever. Amen (I Pet. 5:10–11).

* * *

The God of hope fill us with all joy and peace in believing, that we may abound in hope, in the power of the Holy Ghost Amen (Rom. 15:13).

* * *

May the grace of the Lord Jesus sanctify us and keep us from all evil; may he drive far from us all hurtful things, and purify both our souls and bodies; may he bind us to himself by the bond of love, and may his peace abound in our hearts Amen. (54)

WEDNESDAY

1. Invitatory:

Let the beauty of the Lord our God be upon us: and establish thou the work of our hands upon us; yea, the work of our hands establish thou it (Ps. 90:17).

* * *

Peace be to this house. Peace be with all that are in Christ Jesus (Luke 10:5 and I Pet. 5:14).

* * *

Thou wilt keep him in perfect peace, whose mind is stayed on thee: because he trusteth in thee (Isa. 26:3).

2. Hymn for the Week

3. Confession:

O Lord, with heartfelt sorrow we repent and deplore our offenses. We condemn ourselves and our evil ways, with true penitence entreating that thy grace may relieve our distress. Be pleased to have compassion upon us, O most gracious God, Father of all mercies, for the sake of thy Son, Jesus Christ our Lord. And as thou dost remove our guilt and our pollution, grant us the daily increase of the grace of thy Holy Spirit, that acknowledging from our inmost hearts our own unrighteousness, we may be touched with sorrow that shall work true repentance, and that, mortifying all sins within us, thy Spirit may produce the fruits of holiness and righteousness well-pleasing in thy sight; through Jesus Christ our Lord. Amen. (55)

4. Psalm

5. Creed:

I believe that I cannot by my own reason or strength believe in Jesus Christ my Lord, or come to him; but the Holy Ghost has called me through the gospel, enlightened me by his gifts, and sanctified and preserved me in the true faith; in like manner as he calls, gathers, enlightens, and sanctifies the whole Christian Church on earth, and preserves it in union with Jesus Christ in the true faith; in which Christian Church he daily forgives abundantly all my sins, and the sins of all believers, and will raise up me and all the dead at the last day, and will grant everlasting life to me and to all who believe in Christ. This is most certainly true. Amen. (56)

6. Lesson (see lectionaries)

7. Lesson on the Ministry

John 20:19–23	*Matthew 18:15–22*
I Corinthians 5:1–8	*Luke 7:36–50*
I Corinthians 5:9–13	*Luke 19:41–48*
II Corinthians 1:23–2:11	*Matthew 16:13–19*
Matthew 18:12–14	*II Corinthians 12:19–13:11*

Brief Passages for Meditation

Psalm 51:11–13	*Proverbs 6:23*
Colossians 3:12–13	*I Timothy 5:19–21*
II Timothy 1:6–7	*Luke 9:54–56*
Isaiah 42:3	*Isaiah 66:2*
Galatians 6:1–2	*Isaiah 5:20*
Titus 3:10–11	

8. READING FROM THE ANTHOLOGY

9. COLLECT FOR THE WEEK

10. PRAYERS, INTERCESSIONS, AND THE LORD'S PRAYER

Morning

Lord, make us bold to run the way of thy commandments and help us to stand still before thy presence, that, leading lives of quiet confidence, we may bear witness to thy grace and carry thy power into the world. Let thy light shine through us, that men may see good works in us and give glory to the Father in heaven. So direct our lives, that in the end none to whom we have failed to show mercy and love may accuse us, and we may be received into the eternal habitations; through Jesus Christ, our Lord. Amen. (57)

* * *

Lord Jesus Christ, very Sun of the world, ever arising and never going down; who by thine appearing givest health and gladness, creating, preserving, and nourishing all things in

28

heaven and in earth; I pray thee graciously to enlighten my
spirit, that the night of sin and the mists of error may be
driven away by thine inward shining; so that I may go all
my life long without stumbling, and walk as in the daytime,
pure and undefiled by the works of darkness; who with the
Father and the Holy Spirit livest and reignest for ever.
Amen. (58)

* * *

Noon

Merciful Father, who hast committed to thy servants the
keys to forgive the sins of all who are repentant and retain
those of all who repent not; grant unto me, I beseech thee, thy
Spirit and thy power, that in this congregation the secure
sinners may be shaken and the godless driven to repentance,
but that the anxious in heart may be richly comforted and
refreshed by thy blessed peace, through Jesus Christ, our Lord.
Amen. (59)

Evening

Let thy peace descend from heaven, O Lord, and rest in our
hearts, O Christ. Make us to sleep in peace and awake in thee,
that we fear no terrors of the night; who livest and reignest
with the Father and the Holy Ghost ever one God, world
without end. Amen. (60)

* * *

Watch over us, O Lord, Heavenly Father, and preserve us
from every peril which may happen to the body and soul.
Grant us grace to take our rest this night in safety beneath
thy protection. Guard and bless thy church and this thy congregation. Graciously remember, in thy mercy, those who are
in sickness, in need, and in peril. Have mercy upon all mankind; and when at length our last evening cometh grant us
then to fall asleep in thy peace, that we may awake in thy
glory; through Jesus Christ, our Lord. Amen. (61)

Abide with us, O Lord, for it is toward evening, and the day is far spent. Abide with us, for the days are hastening on, and we hasten with them, and our life is short and transient as a dream.

Abide with us, for we are weak and helpless, and if thou abide not with us, we perish by the way.

Abide with us until the Day star ariseth, and the morning light appeareth, when we shall abide forever with thee. (62)

* * *

Intercessions

"Give us this day our daily bread."

O God, who givest daily bread without our prayer, even to all the wicked, we pray thee that thou wouldst give us to acknowledge these thy benefits, and enable us to receive our daily bread with thanksgiving, through Jesus Christ our Lord. Amen. (63)

* * *

Plan for Intercession

For families, children, relatives, and friends; for Christian marriages; for the nurture of children in the gospel.

For young people and young people's work in the church.

* * *

Almighty Father, from whom every family in heaven and earth is named: I thank thee for my family and for all the relations and friends thou hast given to me.

Make me and the comrade of my way to be united to thee in serving love and faithfulness. Grant thy blessing upon our work and give us what we need for the nourishment of our bodies. Except thou build our house we labor in vain.

I pray thee for my children, that they may grow up joyfully. Give me grace to train them in thy faith, fear, and love. Preserve them from evil, from wandering and temptation. Grant that they may gain the goal here and hereafter. Lead us in thy ways by thy fatherly hand and grant unto me the joy of entering with them at last into eternal life. Through Jesus Christ, our Lord. Amen. (64)

* * *

Almighty God, our heavenly Father, who settest the solitary in families, we commend to thy continual care the homes in which thy people dwell. Put far from them, we beseech thee, every root of bitterness, the desire of vainglory, and the pride of life. Fill them with faith, virtue, knowledge, temperance, patience, godliness. Knit together in constant affection those who, in holy wedlock, have been made one flesh; turn the heart of the fathers to the children, and the heart of the children to the fathers; and so enkindle fervent charity among us all, that we be evermore kindly affectioned with brotherly love; through Jesus Christ our Lord. Amen. (65)

* * *

Almighty and merciful God and Father, I pray thee for my parents, my brothers and sisters and relations, for my friends and acquaintances, my colleagues, helpers, and benefactors, and for all who pray for me and desire my prayers for them, whose names and needs are all known unto thee. Grant them, O Lord, true faith, sincere love, and a living hope, and give them all that is needful and profitable for body and soul. Help them to remain faithful to the end in thy praise and service, that after this life they may come to thee, who art our true home, our joy, and our eternal reward. Through Jesus Christ, our Lord. Amen. (66)

* * *

O Lord Jesus Christ, the Good Shepherd, we bring before thee our young people, with all their joys, needs, and temptations. Strengthen them against the dangers and trials that threaten them in body and spirit. But in us elders, sharpen our conscience towards the great responsibility we bear for the youth among us, that we may watch over their souls with a holy concern, ward off the offenses which beset them, impel them to all that is good, and, so far as in us lies, keep them unto salvation.

To thee, merciful Father, we commend all work that is being done among young men and women, all organizations in which our youth is led to thee. Arm all leaders and teachers of youth with wisdom and patience, and fill us all with that power of love that believes all things, hopes all things, and never gives up. Raise up in our congregation fellow-workers who will become friends and helpers of youth.

Thou wilt require of us the souls of young people. Help us, O thou faithful God, to point them to thee with unwearying faithfulness and to lead them to their best friend and surest refuge, our Saviour, Jesus Christ, to whom, with thee and the Holy Ghost, be glory and honor for ever and ever. Amen. (67)

* * *

The Lord's Prayer

11. EVENING COMMENDATION:

Into thy fatherly hands, O God, we commend our spirits. Preserve us thine now and for ever; through Jesus Christ, our Lord. Amen.

12. BENEDICTION:

The Lord preserve us from all evil; the Lord preserve our souls. The Lord preserve our going out and our coming in, from this time forth, and even for evermore. Amen (Ps. 121:7–8).

* * *

The grace of our Lord Jesus Christ, and the love of God, and the communion of the Holy Ghost, be with us all. Amen (II Cor. 13:14).

The blessing of God almighty, Creator, Word, eternal Spirit, be upon us, and remain with us, now and for evermore. Amen. (68)

THURSDAY

1. INVITATORY:

Thou, Lord, art good, and ready to forgive; and plenteous in mercy unto all them that call upon thee. Give ear, O Lord, unto my prayer; and attend to the voice of my supplications (Ps. 86:5–7).

* * *

The Lord will give strength unto his people; the Lord will bless his people with peace (Ps. 29:11).

* * *

Lord Jesus, abide with us; for it is toward evening, and the day is far spent.

Lo, I am with you alway, even unto the end of the world (Luke 24:29, Matt. 28:20).

2. HYMN FOR THE WEEK

3. CONFESSION:

Forgive my sins, O Lord—forgive me the sins of my present and the sins of my past, the sins of my soul and the sins of my body; the sins which I have done to please myself, and the sins which I have done to please others. Forgive me my wanton and idle sins, forgive me my serious and deliberate sins, forgive me those sins which I know and those sins which I know not, the sins which I have labored so to hide from others that I have hid them from my own memory. Forgive them, O Lord, forgive them all. Of thy great mercy let me be absolved, and of thy bountiful goodness let me be delivered from the bonds of all that by my frailty I have committed. Grant this, O heavenly Father, for the sake of Jesus Christ, our blessed Lord and Saviour. Amen. (69)

Turn us, O God of our salvation, and cause thine anger toward us to cease (Ps. 85 : 4). Make haste, O God, to deliver me; make haste to help me, O Lord. Amen (Ps. 70 : 1).

4. PSALM

5. CREED :

The Apostles' Creed

I believe in God the Father Almighty, Maker of heaven and earth.

And in Jesus Christ his only Son our Lord, Who was conceived by the Holy Ghost, Born of the Virgin Mary, Suffered under Pontius Pilate, Was crucified, dead, and buried : He descended into hell; The third day he rose again from the dead; He ascended into heaven, And sitteth on the right hand of God the Father Almighty; From thence he shall come to judge the quick and the dead.

I believe in the Holy Ghost; The holy Christian Church, the Communion of Saints; The Forgiveness of sins; The Resurrection of the body; And the Life everlasting. Amen.

6. LESSON (SEE LECTIONARIES)

7. LESSON ON THE MINISTRY

The Minister as Pastor

John 21:15–17	*John 10:1–11*
Ezekiel 34:1–16	*John 10:12–16*
I Peter 5:1–4	*I Peter 2:1–10*
Luke 15:1–10	*Ephesians 4:11–16*
I Thessalonians 5:14–23	

Brief Passages for Meditation

Acts 20:28	*I Peter 2:25*
Isaiah 40:11	*Psalm 121:2–4*
James 1:27	*John 14:12–14*
Jeremiah 23:1–2	*Colossians 3:17; 4:2*
Hebrews 13:20–21	*Isaiah 56:10–11*
II Timothy 2:24–26	

8. Reading from the Anthology

9. Collect for the Week

10. Prayers, Intercessions, and the Lord's Prayer

Morning

O Lord, our heavenly Father, almighty and everlasting God, who hast safely brought us to the beginning of this day: Defend us in the same with thy mighty power; and grant that this day we fall into no sin, neither run into any kind of danger; but that all our doings, being ordered by thy governance, may be righteous in thy sight; through Jesus Christ, our Lord. Amen. (70)

* * *

In this hour of this day, fill us, O Lord, with thy mercy, that rejoicing throughout the whole day, we may take delight in thy praise; through Jesus Christ our Lord. Amen. (71)

* * *

Most glorious Trinity, in thy mercy we commit to thee this day our souls, our bodies, all our ways and goings, all our deeds and purposes. We pray thee so to open our hearts and mouths, that we may praise thy name, which above all names alone is holy; and since thou hast created for us the praise of thy holy name, grant that our lives may be to thine honor, and that we may serve thee in thy love and fear. Amen. (72)

Noon

Almighty and most merciful God, who art not willing that any should perish, but in thy beloved Son, Jesus Christ, hast considered the straying sheep, and also appointed shepherds to seek and lead and feed them in his holy name : be thou with me this day and always, that I may guide thy lambs and thy sheep with all gentleness and zeal, seek the lost, wait upon the sick and the weak, and lead them at length to thine eternal fold, through the same Jesus Christ, our Lord. Amen. (73)

Evening

We give thee thanks, O Lord, who hast preserved us through the day. We give thee thanks, who wilt preserve us through the night. Bring us, we beseech thee, O Lord, in safety to the morning hours; that thou mayest receive our praise at all times; through Jesus Christ our Lord. Amen. (74)

* * *

O Lord, support us all the day long of this troublous life, until the shadows lengthen and the evening comes, and the busy world is hushed, the fever of life is over, and our work done. Then, Lord, in thy mercy, grant us safe lodging, and holy rest, and peace at the last; through Jesus Christ our Lord. Amen. (75)

* * *

O Lord, my God, I thank thee that thou hast brought this day to its close. I thank thee that thou dost give rest to body and soul. Thy hand has been over me, guarding me and preserving me.

Forgive my feeble faith and all the wrong I have done this day, and help me to forgive all who have wronged me.

Grant that I may sleep in peace beneath thy care and defend me from the temptations of darkness. Into thy hands I commend my loved ones, I commend this household, I commend my body and soul. O God, thy holy name be praised. Amen. (76)

* * *

Intercessions

"And forgive us our trespasses,
as we forgive those who trespass against us."

We pray thee, our Father in heaven, that thou wouldest not regard our sins, nor deny our requests on account of them; for we are not worthy of anything that we ask, and have in no wise merited it. Grant us all through grace, though we daily commit many sins and deserve chastisement alone. Help us also on our part to forgive and readily to do good to those who offend against us; through Jesus Christ our Lord. Amen. (77)

* * *

Plan for Intercession

For our people and country; for repentance, faith, love, honesty, obedience to law; for unity, justice, and peace; for those in authority and for good citizenship.

For households and the men and women of the congregation; For enemies, the indifferent, and the lapsed.

* * *

O God, most merciful and most gracious, who hast encouraged us in thy holy Word to make supplication for all men, we beseech thee for all thy brethren of this nation, of the great cities and quiet country places, high and low, rich and poor together, that thou wouldst prosper agriculture, manufacture, commerce, and every lawful industry; that thou wouldst cleanse our national life from besetting sins, and remove all causes of division from amongst the people; that thou wouldst fill our hearts with thy love and our homes with thy peace.

And for all the nations of the human race, with their rulers, that thou in thy providence wouldst make an end of war, cruelty, oppression, and ignorance, and grant unto every land the blessings of peace and order, justice and spiritual knowledge.

We beseech thee for the church universal, throughout the world, in all its branches and in all its ministries; that thou wouldst further with thy continual favor her work in this land, and in the distant parts of the earth; that thou wouldst heal the divisions among thy Son's disciples, and hasten everywhere the coming of the kingdom of our Lord Jesus Christ: in whose name we pray. Amen. (78)

O God almighty, King of glory and Lord of heaven and earth, who dost govern all things by thy providence; we pray for the people of our land. Thou dost call them to thyself through thy Word; grant that they may know the things that belong unto their peace.

Make all our people steadfast in upholding truth, honor, and freedom, that faction and self-seeking, oppression and want may be put away, and that we may be united in a godly harmony to work that which is good. Give to the officers of the state wisdom, counsel, and strength, that they may never pervert justice, but govern us righteously in thy fear. And give to us obedient hearts that seek only thine honor in all our worldly duties.

Make haste, O Lord, to bring the day when all nations shall dwell in peace beneath thy scepter to the praise of thy just and gracious dominion; through Jesus Christ our Lord. Amen. (79)

* * *

Almighty God, from whom every family in heaven and earth is named; be thou the inhabitant and guardian of our dwellings, thy holy presence their light and good cheer, now and ever. Bless and sanctify our homes, and make them for us and our children a shelter from tempest and night. Guard us from forgetting thee, from all vain seeking after this world's goods, and unite all who live together in true discipleship of thy Son, Jesus Christ.

We pray thee for the men of the church. Thou knowest their weakness and their shortcomings. Call them to be thy disciples and bind them together in brotherhood under thy Word, that we may be armed for service to our brethren.

We commend to thee all work of the women in this congregation. Make their meetings wellsprings of life for their homes and thy church.

Merciful Saviour, who loved us when we were yet far off and granted us thy salvation, though our sins brought thee to the cross, we pray for our enemies and all who hate us. Take all bitterness from our hearts, that we may forgive our debtors as thou dost richly forgive us every day.

We pray for the ignorant, the misguided, the tempted, and all who, deceived by mammon, are vainly seeking to be satisfied in the things of this world; have mercy upon them. For all who hear thy call and do not heed it, for those who reject thy proffered grace, the careless, the indifferent, and all who are sinning their lives away; turn their hearts and save them, O Lord. For those whose faith is failing, whose love is growing cold, such as have forsaken the ways of prayer and the goodly fellowship of thy church, those who say they are thine and forget that they are thy witnesses; breathe upon these dry bones, O Lord, and turn them again to the Shepherd of souls. Forgive unto us, O God, our part in their condition, our want of love and concern and our many failures and rouse in us a hearty compassion, patience to work and to give, and faithfulness in prayer and striving for the souls of our people.

O Lord, our Shepherd, never cease to seek and to save those that are lost, that we may all praise thee together in the unity of thy Spirit. Amen. (80)

* * *

The Lord's Prayer

11. EVENING COMMENDATION:

Into thy hands, most blessed Jesus, I commend my soul and body, for thou hast redeemed both by thy most precious blood. So bless and sanctify my sleep to me, that it may be temperate, holy, and safe, a refreshment to my weary body, to enable it so to serve my soul, that both may serve thee with never-failing duty. Visit, I beseech thee, O Lord, this habitation with thy mercy, and me with thy grace and favor. Teach me to number my days, that I may apply my heart unto wisdom, and ever be mindful of my last end. Amen. (81)

12. BENEDICTION:

May the very God of peace sanctify us wholly, and our whole spirit and soul and body be preserved blameless unto the coming of our Lord Jesus Christ. Amen (I Thess. 5:23).

* * *

Now our Lord Jesus Christ himself, and God our Father, who loved us and gave us eternal comfort and good hope through grace, comfort our hearts and establish them in every good work and word (II Thess. 2:16–17).

* * *

May the love of the Lord Jesus draw us to himself;
May the power of the Lord Jesus strengthen us in his service;
May the joy of the Lord Jesus fill our souls; and
May the blessing of God Almighty, the Father, the Son, and the
Holy Ghost, be upon us and remain with us always. (82)

* * *

FRIDAY

1. INVITATORY:

O God, we do not present our supplications before thee for our righteousness, but for thy great mercies (Dan. 9:18).

* * *

Thou, O God, art as a hiding place from the wind, and a covert from the storm, as rivers of water in a dry place, as the shadow of a great rock in a weary land (Isa. 32:2).

* * *

Your light shall rise in the darkness and your gloom be as the noonday, and the Lord will guide you continually (Isa. 58:10–11).

2. Hymn for the Week

3. Confession:

O merciful God, full of compassion, longsuffering, and of great pity, who sparest when we deserve punishment, and in thy wrath thinkest upon mercy : Make me earnestly to repent, and to be heartily sorry for all my misdoings; make the remembrance so burdensome and painful, that I may flee to thee with a troubled spirit and a contrite heart; and, O merciful Lord, visit, comfort, and relieve me; cast me not out from thy presence, and take not thy Holy Spirit from me, but excite in me true repentance; give me in this world knowledge of thy truth, and confidence in thy mercy, and in the world to come life everlasting, for the sake of our Lord and Saviour, thy Son Jesus Christ. Amen. (83)

* * *

4. Psalm

5. Creed:

The Apostles' Creed

I believe in God the Father Almighty, Maker of heaven and earth.

And in Jesus Christ his only Son our Lord, Who was conceived by the Holy Ghost, Born of the Virgin Mary, Suffered under Pontius Pilate, Was crucified, dead, and buried : He descended into hell; The third day he rose again from the dead; He ascended into heaven, And sitteth on the right hand of God the Father Almighty; From thence he shall come to judge the quick and the dead.

I believe in the Holy Ghost; The holy Christian Church, the Communion of Saints; The Forgiveness of sins; The Resurrection of the body, And the Life everlasting. Amen.

6. Lesson (See lectionaries)

7. Lesson on the Ministry

Hebrews 4:14–5:14	*John 16:23–33*
Hebrews 13:10–16	*Matthew 16:21–28*
Matthew 20:25–28	*John 17:1–10*
Hebrews 7:24–27	*John 17:11–19*
John 15:1–16	*John 17:20–26*

Brief Passages for Meditation

Romans 14:7–9	*Deuteronomy 33:9–10*
Matthew 26:41	*Ephesians 5:1–2*
James 5:14–16	*Philippians 2:5–8*
John 12:25–26	*Philippians 3:8*
I John 3:16	*II Corinthians 10:3–5*
Luke 14:26–27	

8. READING FROM THE ANTHOLOGY

9. COLLECT FOR THE WEEK

10. PRAYERS, INTERCESSIONS, AND THE LORD'S PRAYER

Morning

In the name of the Lord Jesus Christ, who hast redeemed us with his precious blood, I do now arise. May he defend me against all evil, and preserve my body and soul; granting me also whatsoever shall prosper and confirm me in all good unto eternal life. Amen. (84)

* * *

Lord Jesus, who died for us upon the cross, in order that we might find rest for our souls; grant, we beseech thee, that we may gather at thy cross and be the disciples of thy cross. Enter into all who open their hearts to thee and let all who seek thee find thee. Be not silent to the cares of those who desire thee, and comfort us all with thy succor. Thou, Lord, art our life, and for thee would we live, today and for evermore. Amen. (85)

Lord Jesus Christ, who didst for me endure the horror of deep darkness, teach me by the depth of thine agony the vileness of my sin, and so bind me to thyself in bonds of gratitude and love, that I may be united with thee in thy perfect sacrifice, my Saviour, my Lord, and my God. Amen. (86)

* * *

O Lord Jesus Christ, our merciful and loving Saviour, who didst bear thy cross for us, help us to take up our cross daily and follow thee. O thou who wast lifted up for us, draw us unto thee, that we may love thee better for thy great love to us. Lord, we love thee; help thou our want of love. O heavenly Father, make us to bear in our body the marks of the Lord Jesus by a pure and holy life. O Saviour of the world, who by thy cross and precious blood hast redeemed us, save us and help us, we humbly beseech thee, O Lord, both now and evermore. Amen. (87)

* * *

Noon

Lord God, heavenly Father, who didst give thine only begotten Son to die for us sinners in order that we might have peace with thee : I praise thee and magnify thy lovingkindness and mercy. I beseech thee, O Lord, ever to remember his all-sufficient sacrifice, to impute his merit to me and all Christians, graciously to preserve us in thy peace, and finally to bring me, and the souls committed to my charge and all believers, to thine eternal peace, through Jesus Christ, our Lord. Amen. (88)

* * *

O eternal, merciful God, heavenly Father, I beseech thee for all who are committed to my cure of souls and to my prayer. Grant them all grace and thy Holy Spirit, that they may confess thee and thy dear Son Jesus Christ; grow in right faith, fear, and love; and, in unswerving hope, in a Christian, repentant life, abide in thy will and obedience faithfully to their end. Grant also to me, dear Father, grace to walk before them with a good life and to impart to them pure instruction, and grant that we all, guarded against impure faith and evil life, may come to everlasting salvation; through Jesus Christ, our Lord. Amen. (89)

* * *

Evening

Merciful God, who of thine abundant goodness towards us hast made the day to travail in, and ordained the night wherein to take our rest; grant us such rest of body that we may continually have a waking soul, to watch for the time when our Lord shall appear to deliver us from this mortal life. Let no vain or wandering fancy trouble us; let our ghostly enemies have no power over us, but let our minds be set wholly upon thy presence, to love, and fear, and rest in thee alone; that, being refreshed with a moderate and sober sleep, we may rise up again with cheerful strength and gladness to serve thee in all good works; through Jesus Christ, our Lord. Amen. (90)

* * *

Watch thou, dear Lord, with those who wake, or watch, or weep tonight, and give thine angels charge over those who sleep. Tend thy sick ones, O Lord Christ. Rest thy weary ones. Bless thy dying ones. Soothe thy suffering ones. Pity thine afflicted ones. Shield thy joyous ones. And all, for thy love's sake. Amen. (91)

* * *

Intercessions

" And lead us not into temptation."

O God, who temptest no one to sin, we pray thee so to guard and keep us, that the devil, the world, and our own flesh may not deceive us, nor lead us into error, unbelief, despair, and other great and shameful sins, and that though we be thus tempted, we may finally prevail and gain victory, through Jesus Christ, thy Son, our Lord. Amen. (92)

* * *

Plan for Intercession

For the suffering, the poor, the hungry and cold, refugees, prisoners, the oppressed, the despairing.

For social missions; workers, chaplains, doctors and nurses, institutions and hospitals, relief agencies.

For sufferers in the congregation; the aged, the sick, the dying, the bereaved, the lonely.

* * *

O Lord our God, Father of the Crucified, the comfort of the sorrowful and the strength of sufferers, we give thee thanks for him who came forth from thee, a light unto our darkness, who in divine love carried upon his own soul our sins and woes through the thick shadows, and went down the 'ways of death, so that no soul of all thy children should cry in vain for the light of thy face.

In his name, therefore, we pray:

For all who are tyrannized, ill-treated, and slain for Christ's sake: let no trial shake their faith or embitter their hearts but keep them faithful and true.

For all who are wronged, oppressed, defrauded, or betrayed: defend them from despair and anger.

For all who are downcast by fruitless toils or shattered hopes, who, hurt and bruised in spirit, serve without thanks and toil without recompense: preserve them by thy good Spirit from utter grief of heart.

For all who are friendless and homeless, the refugees, the wanderers, and the prisoners: succor them, O Lord, and have pity on every waif and child of misery.

For all who are left behind and forgotten, all who are alone and afraid, the defeated, the timid, the brokenhearted: befriend, comfort, and abide with them.

For all who are tempted to destroy themselves, the enslaved, the despairing, the victims of strong drink whose feet are caught in a net, and all who are reaping the evil they have sown: let the power of Christ break off their fetters and set them free.

For all penitents who desire to do thy will, yet falter continually; all who with doubtful feet stumble on in search of love, those who, struggling after purity, are vexed with evil imaginations; all who would fain follow thee, but fear thy cross: give strength to them that have no might and grant them victory.

For all who are disquieted and troubled in spirit, all who are in sore straits and bound in miseries, the deranged and mentally ill: loose their burden and break the yoke of evil that they may know thy peace.

For all who are sick, fevered, and worn by disease or stricken by accident, all who are deprived of sight, speech, or hearing, and all the helpless: relieve their suffering, expel their maladies, revive their spirits, heal their wounds, and make them whole.

For all old frail folk and those to whom death is drawing nigh: sustain them in unclouded faith and perfect peace.

For all the dying: let light perpetual shine upon them, that they may fall asleep in peace and awake in the light of thy face.

For all who mourn, for those bereft of those in whom their souls delighted, saddened with memories of vanished faces and loved voices stilled: give them comfort in hope of that day when heart shall find heart and those sundered on earth shall foregather in heaven.

Relieve and comfort them all, O God, and make us, too, to

rejoice in every experience, however hard, bitter, or costly, by which we are schooled in humble faith and in charity with our fellow men; through the power and mercy of Jesus Christ, our Saviour and Good Physician. Amen. (93)

* * *

O Lord Jesus Christ, who for our sake didst die upon the cross and rise again and ascend into heaven, convince us anew each day of our salvation. In every necessity grant us the sure trust that we stand in the comforting fellowship of thy suffering and that we may tread with thee the path through the suffering to glory. Grant that this may be the joy and comfort of all who are oppressed and persecuted for their faith in thee and for the sake of righteousness. Strengthen all those who are suffering from the sin and troubles of this world, the sick and aged, the hungry and cold, the homeless and imprisoned, the lonely and the sad. Thou didst bear all sin and therefore dost thou give that peace that passeth all understanding. Pour down thy peace upon hearts that are restless and rent, that each may patiently bear his cross after thee. Comfort them all with the certainty that the sufferings of this present time are not worthy to be compared with the glory which shall be revealed in us. Amen. (94)

* * *

O Lord Jesus Christ, who on the cross didst shed thy blood for us and all men, we pray thee for the church's works of mercy, and social missions. Remember, O Lord, all who give up their lives to reclaim the sinful, to lift up the degraded, and to defend the cause of the poor. Grant them fresh hope, strength, and courage, and assure them that thou hast appointed them to their task. Give them good success and finally grant them recompense.

Make to flourish all hospitals and houses of mercy and those who serve in them. Send thy blessing upon all doctors and those who wait upon the sick, all who nurse little children, care for the deluded and feeble in mind, or visit the troubled in their distress, and make them always to remember that they are fellow-workers with thee. Let all the sons of consolation and sisters of mercy be filled with the Spirit that, wherever they may go, thy power may be with them to heal; who livest and reignest with the Father and the Holy Spirit, one God, for evermore. Amen. (95)

* * *

Lord Jesus Christ, I thank thee that thou hast appointed me to serve thy church. I know, and thou knowest better than I, that I am both too slow and too hasty in my work. I miss the greatness of the need that waits for my help and in the turmoil of the day often fail to find my way back to thee. Forgive me, and restore all that I have spoiled. Heal thou the sick; guide the dying home. Let children and parents be united in faith toward thee; let the aged hope in thee. Be thou the friend of the lonely and the riches of the poor, the comforter of the sorrowing, and the strength of the tempted. Let not those who have faltered and fallen be lost. Grant opening to the words that I speak in thy name. Cause my congregation to uphold me in all faithfulness and loyalty. Be thou the center of all our church's work. Grant that my congregation may remain a member of thy holy Body and bring us at last to praise thee together for ever and ever. Amen. (96)

* * *

The Lord's Prayer

* * *

11. EVENING COMMENDATION:

Into thy hands, O God, I commend my spirit, for thou hast redeemed me, O Lord thou God of truth. Amen. (97)

12. BENEDICTION:

Almighty and merciful God, Father, Son, and Holy Spirit, vouchsafe to bless, aid, and bring us at last to the life eternal. (98)

* * *

Now unto the King eternal, immortal, invisible, the only wise God, be honor and glory for ever and ever (I Tim. 1:17).

* * *

Now unto him that is able to keep us from falling, and to present us faultless before the presence of his glory with exceeding joy, to the only wise God our Saviour, be glory and majesty, dominion and power, both now and ever (Jude 24–25).

SATURDAY

1. INVITATORY:

Lighten my eyes, O Lord, lest I sleep the sleep of death. Let me live, that I may praise thee, and let thy ordinances help me (Ps. 13:4; 119:175).

* * *

The Lord of peace give us peace at all times in all ways. The Lord be with us all (II Thess. 3:16).

* * *

Your sun shall no more go down, nor your moon withdraw itself; for the Lord will be your everlasting light (Isa. 60:20).

* * *

2. HYMN FOR THE WEEK

3. CONFESSION:

Waken my heart, O Lord, my God; make my heart watchful to serve thee and alert to thy command.

Thou hast created us full of trouble; thou hast made us strangers in this world.

49

Trouble me with the smallness of my work.

Trouble me with the greatness of thy command.

Trouble me with my unholiness and my slowness to obey.

Trouble me with time running out and every lost hour.

Trouble me with my sins and the sins of all men.

Trouble me with the troubles of thy church which are the work of men.

Trouble me, and make me to watch continually for thy judgment.

Trouble me, O Lord, and let me keep my faith in the midst of my trouble.

Let me go forth desiring the coming of thy glory. Let me go forward; for thy glory shall be revealed.

I thank thee that my work ends and thy work begins.

Lord, I believe, help thou my unbelief. Amen. (99)

* * *

4. PSALM

5. CREED:

The Apostles' Creed

I believe in God the Father Almighty, Maker of heaven and earth.

And in Jesus Christ his only Son our Lord, Who was conceived by the Holy Ghost, Born of the Virgin Mary, Suffered under Pontius Pilate, Was crucified, dead, and buried: He descended into hell; The third day he rose again from the dead; He ascended into heaven, And sitteth on the right hand of God the Father Almighty; From thence he shall come to judge the quick and the dead.

I believe in the Holy Ghost; The holy Christian Church, the Communion of Saints; The Forgiveness of sins; The Resurrection of the body, And the Life everlasting. Amen.

6. LESSON (SEE LECTIONARIES)

7. LESSON ON THE MINISTRY

The Minister as Preacher

Isaiah 61:1–3, 10–11	*I Corinthians 2:1–16*
Ezekiel 33:1–16	*Matthew 10:12–25*
II Timothy 4:1–5	*Matthew 10:26–39*
I Corinthians 1:17–31	*John 15:26–16:11*
Jeremiah 1:4–19	*Romans 10:13–17*

Brief Passages for Meditation

Jeremiah 15:19–20	*II Corinthians 2:15–17*
Galatians 1:8–9	*I Timothy 6:3–5*
II Timothy 2:15–16	*Luke 21:15*
Acts 6:4	*Isaiah 55:10–11*
Ezekiel 2:5–7	*Jeremiah 23:28–29*
John 16:33	

8. READING FROM THE ANTHOLOGY

9. COLLECT FOR THE WEEK

10. PRAYERS, INTERCESSIONS, AND THE LORD'S PRAYER

Morning

Eternal God, who committest to us the swift and solemn trust of life; since we know not what a day may bring forth, but only that the hour for serving thee is always present, may we wake to the instant claims of thy holy will, not waiting for tomorrow, but yielding today. Consecrate with thy presence the way our feet may go, and the humblest work will shine, and the roughest place be made plain. Lift us above unrighteous anger and mistrust, into faith, and hope, and charity, by a simple and steadfast reliance on thy sure will. In all things draw us to the mind of Christ, that thy lost image may be traced again, and thou mayest own us as at one with him and thee, to the glory of thy great name. Amen. (100)

Make us of quick understanding and tender conscience, O Lord; that understanding, we may obey every word of thine this day, and discerning, may follow every suggestion of thine indwelling Spirit. Speak, Lord, for thy servant heareth; through Jesus Christ our Lord. Amen. (101)

* * *

Noon

Lord, almighty God, who hast sent forth thy servants to bring peace to the restless and good tidings to the afflicted, to bind up the brokenhearted and to proclaim liberty to the captives and the opening of the prison to those who are bound; grant, I beseech thee, that I may rightly know and perform thy command. Fill my soul with thy grace and peace, that I may proclaim peace to my congregation, and prepare their hearts to receive this inestimable gift of thy mercy, through Jesus Christ our Lord. Amen. (102)

* * *

Evening

Abide with us, Lord, for it is toward evening and the day is far spent.

Abide with us and with thy whole church.

Abide with us in the end of the day, in the end of our life, in the end of the world.

Abide with us with thy grace and bounty, with thy holy Word and sacrament, with thy comfort and thy blessing.

Abide with us when over us cometh the night of affliction and temptation, the night of fear and despair, the night of bitter death.

Abide with us and with all thy faithful, through time and eternity.

We pray in this hour for all thy children : grant that they may find rest from all their labors and troubles.

We pray for all who have tasted the abundance of thy goodness: preserve their hearts from pride that they may give thee the glory.

We pray for all whom thy hand has humbled: lift them up by the word of thy love.

We pray for all the members of our congregation, for the newborn children and for those whom the hand of death has touched: lead us through this earthly life to thine eternal kingdom.

We pray for all who are dead to us, far and near: unite us with them, O Lord, in thy care and thy peace.

We pray for all who are hostile and estranged from us: destroy all that divides us and grant us reconciliation and peace.

We pray for all who are forsaken: visit those that need thee and refresh them.

Lord, we wait for thy day; let its light shine upon us and waken us to newness of life. Amen. (103)

* * *

Intercessions

"But deliver us from evil."

Our Father in heaven, deliver us, we pray thee, from all manner of evil, whether it touch our body or soul, our property or good name, and at last, when the hour of death shall come, grant us a blessed end and graciously take us from this vale of sorrow to thyself in heaven, through Jesus Christ, thy Son, our Lord. Amen. (104)

* * *

Plan for Intercession

Remembrance of the departed. Preparation of the church for the coming of Christ. Remembrance of the brevity of life and judgment to come. Prayer for a blessed death.

For the services on the morrow. For worshipers, listeners, and communicants. For other congregations, their services and ministers.

* * *

O Lord, heavenly Father, stir up our hearts and minds by thy Spirit, that we may at all times remember the end and thy righteous judgment, in order that we may lead our lives here in watchfulness and prayer and abide with thee eternally, through Jesus Christ our Lord, who liveth and reigneth with thee and the Holy Ghost, ever one God, world without end. Amen. (105)

* * *

O God, who hast appointed unto men once to die, but hast hidden from them the time of their death, help us so to live in this world that we may be ready to leave it; and that, being thine in death as in life, we may come to that rest that remaineth for thy people; through him who died and rose again for us, thy Son, Jesus Christ our Lord. Amen. (106)

* * *

Almighty, everlasting God, who through thy Son has assured forgiveness of sins and deliverance from eternal death, we pray thee, strengthen us by thy Holy Spirit, that we may daily increase in this trust in thy grace in Christ, and hold fast to the hope that we shall not die, but fall asleep and on the last day be raised to eternal life, through Jesus Christ, thy Son, our Lord, who liveth and reigneth with thee and the Holy Ghost, ever one God, world without end. Amen. (107)

* * *

Merciful Saviour, help me always to remember that I must die and give account to thee for my life and my ministry, in order that I may learn wisdom and not trifle away the time thou hast given me. Be thou to me a gracious judge.

I give thee thanks at every remembrance of those dear to our hearts who on earth trusted in thee and rejoiced in the hope of life everlasting. Spare us to them that lean upon us and spare those who are our daily prop and stay.

Uphold and strengthen us in the midst of death and danger. Refresh us, who are sinners deserving thy wrath, with the hope of eternal life and let the end of our lives be in peace. And bring us at last to thine heavenly place where is no shadow of evil, no night of pain, no grief of failure, no sadness of parting, and thy faithful dwell secure and free from care and see thee face to face; through Jesus Christ our Lord. Amen. (108)

* * *

O faithful God, merciful Father, who hast called me, thine unworthy servant, to feed thy flock, on the eve of the day when thou shalt permit me to proclaim thy Word, I bow before thee in reverence and humility and offer this my prayer :

Pour down thy Holy Spirit upon thy whole church and subject my congregation and those of my brethren to the power of thy mighty Word.

Grant unto me, and to all who are called to minister in thy church, grace and wisdom, that our preaching, being drawn from thy fountain, may refresh the souls that thirst for thy Word. Govern and guide us by thy Holy Spirit, that being furnished with thy power, we may serve thee with all boldness and faithfulness, and through our ministry true faith may be stirred and strengthened and the love of Christ grow and increase among us.

Be present, O Lord, according to thy gracious Word, with those who shall assemble themselves in thy name. Grant them teachable minds, receptive to thy Word and quick to understand it, and enable them to embrace it in singleness of heart. Open blind eyes, arouse the slothful, establish the waverers, and let the witness of life gain power over all that is dead in our midst; through Jesus Christ our Lord. Amen. (109)

* * *

Almighty God and Father, we give thee hearty thanks that thou hast sent unto us the Holy Spirit and that he has called us through the gospel, enlightened us with his gifts, and sanctified and preserved us in the true faith. Grant, we pray thee, that his power may continue to dwell richly among us. Bestow this power upon all preachers, that they may rightly proclaim thy Word, adding nothing to it and taking nothing from it, and not withholding the saving truth either from fear or to please men.

Give to thy Word on the morrow fruitful soil in our congregation and our church. Bestow thy Spirit's enlightenment upon all hearers of thy message, that they may bow before thy judgment and rejoice in thy saving gospel. Grant these gifts to all who desire Holy Baptism and receive the Lord's Supper, and give unto us all the renewal of faith and Christian life. Let the seed of thy Word grow upon earth for our salvation and so prepare us for thine eternal harvest, through Jesus Christ our Lord. Amen. (110)

* * *

The Lord's Prayer

11. EVENING COMMENDATION

Now into thy keeping, O God, I put all my doings, all my delights, all my disappointments, all my negligences, all my sins, and all my work. And to Thee, O Lord, I commit all whom thou lovest, thou Maker, Restorer, Shepherd, Healer, and Lover of our souls, through Jesus Christ our Lord. Amen. (111)

* * *

12. BENEDICTION:

May the God of peace who brought again from the dead our

Lord Jesus, the great shepherd of the sheep, equip us with everything good that we may do his will, working in us that which is pleasing in his sight, through Jesus Christ; to whom be glory for ever and ever. Amen (Heb. 13:20–21).

* * *

Bless us, O God the Father, who hast created us,
Bless us, O God the Son, who hast redeemed us,
Bless us, O God the Holy Ghost, who sanctifieth us.
O Blessed Trinity, keep us in body, soul, and spirit unto everlasting life. Amen. (112)

* * *

Blessing and honor and thanksgiving and praise, more than we can utter, more than we can conceive, be unto thee, O holy and glorious Trinity, Father, Son, and Holy Ghost, by all angels, all men, all creatures, for ever and ever. Amen. (113)

ADVENT	SATURDAY	SUNDAY	MONDAY	TUESDAY	WEDNESDAY	THURSDAY	FRIDAY	SATURDAY
Morning		24, 150	122, 145	33, 146	80, 147:1-12	18:1-20; 147:13-21	102, 148	90, 149
Evening	80, 72	25, 110	40, 67	85, 94	53, 17	126, 62	130, 16	

CHRISTMAS

December 24
Evening Prayer — 132, 114

December 25
Morning Prayer — 2, Laudate Psalm*
Evening Prayer — 98, 96

December 26
Morning Prayer — 116, Laudate Psalm*
Evening Prayer — 119:1-24; 27

December 27
Morning Prayer — 34, Laudate Psalm*
Evening Prayer — 19, 121

December 28
Morning Prayer — 2, Laudate Psalm*
Evening Prayer — 110, 111

December 29
Morning Prayer — 96, Laudate Psalm*
Evening Prayer — 132, 97

December 30
Morning Prayer — 93, Laudate Psalm*
Evening Prayer — 89:1-18; 89:19-52

December 31
Morning Prayer — 98, Laudate Psalm*
Evening Prayer — 45, 96

January 1
Morning Prayer — 98, Laudate Psalm*
Evening Prayer — 99, 8

January 2
Morning Prayer — 48, Laudate Psalm*
Evening Prayer — 9, 29

January 3
Morning Prayer — 111, Laudate Psalm*
Evening Prayer — 107, 15

January 4
Morning Prayer — 20, Laudate Psalm*
Evening Prayer — 93, 97

January 5
Morning Prayer — 99, Laudate Psalm*
Evening Prayer — 96, 110

January 6
Morning Prayer — 72, Laudate Psalm*
Evening Prayer — 100, 67

EPIPHANY

see General on facing page

*Sunday = 150, Monday = 145, Tuesday = 146, Wednesday = 147:1-12, Thursday = 147:13-21, Friday = 148, Saturday = 149

DAILY PRAYER

	SATURDAY	SUNDAY	MONDAY	TUESDAY	WEDNESDAY	THURSDAY	FRIDAY	SATURDAY
LENT Morning		84, 150	119:73-80; 145	34, 146	5, 147:1-12	27, 147:13-21	22, 148	43, 149
Evening	31, 143	42, 32	121, 6	25, 91	27, 51	126, 102	105, 130	
EASTER Morning		93, 150	97, 145	98, 146	99, 147:1-12	47, 147:13-21	96, 148	92, 149
Evening	23, 114	136, 117	124, 115	66, 116	9, 118	68, 113	49, 138	
GENERAL *Week 1* Morning		103, 150	5, 145	42, 146	89:1-18; 147:1-12	97, 147:13-21	51, 148	104, 149
Evening	138, 98	117, 139	82, 29	102, 133	1, 33	16, 62	142, 65	
Week 2 Morning		19, 150	135, 145	123, 146	15, 147:1-12	36, 147:13-21	130, 148	56, 149
Evening	118, 111	81, 113	97, 112	30, 86	48, 4	80, 27	32, 139	
Week 3 Morning		67, 150	57, 145	54, 146	65, 147:1-12	143, 147:13-21	88, 148	122, 149
Evening	100, 63	46, 93	85, 47	28, 99	125, 91	81, 116	6, 20	
Week 4 Morning		80, 150	62, 145	12, 146	96, 147:1-12	116, 147:13-21	84, 148	63, 149
Evening	125, 90	66, 23	73, 9	36, 7	132, 134	26, 130	25, 40	

PROPERS FOR THE CHURCH YEAR

Title and Text for the Week
Proper Psalms
Hymn for the Week
Lectionary
Collects and Prayers

I SUNDAY IN ADVENT
THE COMING LORD

"Lo, your king comes to you; triumphant and victorious is he."
Zechariah 9:9

PSALMS FOR THE WEEK: (see table, pp. 58-59, Advent)

HYMN FOR THE WEEK

"Savior of the nations, come" (28)

LESSONS		*Year 1*	
S.	Isa. 1:1-9	II Peter 3:1-10	Matt. 25:1-13
M.	Isa. 1:10-20	I Thess. 1:1-10	Luke 20:1-8
T.	Isa. 1:21-31	I Thess. 2:1-12	Luke 20:9-18
W.	Isa. 2:1-4	I Thess. 2:13-20	Luke 20:19-26
Th.	Isa. 2:5-22	I Thess. 3:1-13	Luke 20:27-40
F.	Isa. 3:1-4:1	I Thess. 4:1-12	Luke 20:41-21:4
S.	Isa. 4:2-6	I Thess. 4:13-18	Luke 21:5-19

		Year 2	
S.	Amos 1:1-5; 13-2:8	I Thess. 5:1-11	Luke 21:5-19
M.	Amos 2:6-16	II Peter 1:1-11	Matt. 21:1-11
T.	Amos 3:1-11	II Peter 1:12-21	Matt. 21:12-22
W.	Amos 3:12-4:5	II Peter 3:1-10	Matt. 21:23-32
Th.	Amos 4:6-13	II Peter 3:11-18	Matt. 21:33-46
F.	Amos 5:1-17	Jude 1-16	Matt. 22:1-14
S.	Amos 5:18-27	Jude 17-25	Matt. 22:15-22

Almighty God and Lord, come to us with all your power and help us who are anxious and troubled. Send us the Savior, that he may enter our hearts, and with your light illumine our night, through Jesus Christ our Lord. (114)

II SUNDAY IN ADVENT
The Coming Deliverer

"Prepare the way of the Lord ... behold, the Lord God comes with might."

Isaiah 40:3, 10

PSALMS FOR THE WEEK: (see table, pp. 58-59, Advent)

HYMN FOR THE WEEK

"On Jordan's banks the Baptist's cry" (36)

LESSONS

Year 1

S.	Isa. 5:1-7	II Peter 3:11-18	Luke 7:28-35
M.	Isa. 5:8-17	I Thess. 5:1-11	Luke 21:20-28
T.	Isa. 5:18-25	I Thess. 5:12-28	Luke 21:29-38
W.	Isa. 6:1-13	II Thess. 1:1-12	John 7:53-8:11
Th.	Isa. 7:1-9	II Thess. 2:1-12	Luke 22:1-13
F.	Isa. 7:10-25	II Thess. 2:13-3:5	Luke 22:14-30
S.	Isa. 8:1-15	II Thess. 3:6-18	Luke 22:31-38

Year 2

S.	Amos 6:1-14	II Thess. 6:5-12	Luke 1:57-68
M.	Amos 7:1-9	Rev. 1:1-8	Matt. 22:22-33
T.	Amos 7:10-17	Rev. 1:9-16	Matt. 22:34-46
W.	Amos 8:1-14	Rev. 1:17-2:7	Matt. 23:1-12
Th.	Amos 9:1-10	Rev. 2:8-17	Matt. 23:13-26
F.	Hag. 1:1-15	Rev. 2:18-29	Matt. 23:27-39
S.	Hag. 2:1-9	Rev. 3:1-6	Matt. 24:1-14

Lord, accept our prayer and supplication, and grant that we may heed the call of John to prepare the way for your Son, and receive him into our hearts, that we may become your children; through Jesus Christ our Lord. (115)

III SUNDAY IN ADVENT

The Forerunner of the Lord

"Behold, I send my messenger to prepare the way before me." Malachi 3:1

PSALMS FOR THE WEEK: (see table, pp. 58-59, Advent)

HYMN FOR THE WEEK

"Hark! a thrilling voice is sounding!" (37)

LESSONS		*Year 1*	
S.	*Isa.* 13:1-13	*Heb.* 12:18-29	*John* 3:22-40
M.	*Isa.* 8:16-9:1	*II Peter* 1:1-11	*Luke* 22:39-53
T.	*Isa.* 9:2-7	*II Peter* 1:12-21	*Luke* 22:54-69
W.	*Isa.* 9:8-17	*II Peter* 2:1-10a	*Mark* 1:1-8
Th.	*Isa.* 9:18-10:4	*II Peter* 2:10b-16	*Matt.* 3:1-12
F.	*Isa.* 10:5-19	*II Peter* 2:17-22	*Matt.* 11:2-15
S.	*Isa.* 10:20-27	*Jude* 17-25	*Luke* 3:1-9

		Year 2	
S.	*Amos* 9:11-15	*II Thess.* 2:1-3, 13-17	*John* 5:30-47
M.	*Zech.* 1:7-17	*Rev.* 3:7-13	*Matt.* 24:15-31
T.	*Zech.* 2:1-13	*Rev.* 3:14-22	*Matt.* 24:32-44
W.	*Zech.* 3:1-10	*Rev.* 4:1-8	*Matt.* 42:45-51
Th.	*Zech.* 4:1-14	*Rev.* 4:9-5:5	*Matt.* 25:1-13
F.	*Zech.* 7:8-8:8	*Rev.* 5:6-14	*Matt.* 25:14-30
S.	*Zech.* 8:9-17	*Rev.* 6:1-17	*Matt.* 25:31-46

Lord Jesus, our Light and our Salvation, you alone are the one who was to come to save us. We thank you for your coming and for your will to perform in us again your saving work. Rule us by your Holy Spirit, that henceforth we may wait for none other and put our trust in nothing in heaven or earth except you alone, our Lord. (116)

IV SUNDAY IN ADVENT
THE COMING JOY

"My soul magnifies the Lord, and my spirit rejoices in God my Savior."   Luke 1:46-47

PSALMS FOR THE WEEK: (see table, pp. 58-59, Advent)

HYMN FOR THE WEEK

"Oh Come, Oh Come, Emmanuel" (34)

LESSONS		*Year 1*	
S.	Isa. 11:1-9	Eph. 6:10-20	John 3:16-21
M.	Isa. 11:10-16	Rev. 20:1-10	John 5:30-47
T.	Isa. 28:9-22	Rev. 20:11-21:8	Luke 1:5-25
W.	Isa. 29:9-24	Rev. 21:9-21	Luke 1:26-38
Th.	Isa. 31:1-9	Rev. 21:22-22:5	Luke 1:39-48a (48b-56)
F.	Isa. 33:17-22	Rev. 22:6-11, 18-20	Luke 1:57-66
S.	Isa. 35:1-10	Rev. 22:12-17, 21	Luke 1:67-80

		Year 2	
S.	Gen. 3:8-15	Rev. 12:1-10	John 3:16-21
M.	Zeph. 3:14-20	Titus 1:1-16	Luke 1:1-25
T.	II Sam. 2:1b-10	Titus 2:1-10	Luke 1:26-38
W.	II Sam. 7:1-17	Titus 2:11-3:8a	Luke 1:39-48a (48b-56)
Th.	II Sam. 7:18-29	Gal. 3:1-14	Luke 1:57-66
F.	Jer. 31:10-14	Gal. 3:15-22	Luke 1:67-80 or Matt. 1:1-17
S.	Isa. 60:1-6	Gal. 3:23-4:7	Matt. 1:18-25

Lord, purify our hearts that they may be worthy to become your dwelling place. Let us never fail to find room for you, but come and abide with us that we also may abide in you, for you were born into the world for us and now live and reign, King of kings and Lord of lords, for evermore. (117)

THE NATIVITY OF OUR LORD

CHRISTMAS EVE/CHRISTMAS DAY

"The Word became flesh and dwelt among us." John 1:14

PSALMS: (see table, pp. 58-59, Christmas)

HYMN OF THE DAY

"Of the Father's love begotten" (42)

LESSONS	*Year 1*	
Eve Isa. 35:1-10	*Rev.* 22:12-17, 21	*Luke* 1:67-80
Day Zech. 2:10-13	*I John* 4:7-16	*John* 3:31-36

	Year 2	
Eve Isa. 60:1-6	*Gal.* 3:23-4:7	*Matt.* 1:18-25
Day Micah 4:1-5; 5:2-4	*I John* 4:7-16	*John* 3:31-36

Christmas Eve

O Lord, heavenly Father, through your angels you bade poor shepherds of the field not to fear but rejoice that Christ the Savior was born. Drive away all fear from our hearts and stir up in us this true and rightful joy, that, though here on earth we may be despised, miserable, poor, and forlorn, we may nevertheless be comforted and rejoice that we have your dear Son, Christ our Lord, as our Savior, who for our sake became man, that he might defend us from death and evil and save us forever. (118)

Christmas Day

O Son of God, from the beginning you were with the Father, and for us and for our salvation you came down from heaven. Grant us more and more to receive of your fullness and to accept from you the power to become the children of God; for you are the true light of everyone who comes into the world, now and forever. (119)

ST. STEPHEN, DEACON AND MARTYR
DECEMBER 26

PSALMS: (see table, pp. 58-59, Christmas)

HYMN OF THE DAY

"The Son of God goes forth to war" (183)

LESSONS

Wisd. 4:7-15   Acts 6:1-7   Acts 7:59-8:8
or II Chron. 24:17-22

Merciful God and Father, you gave your Son to reconcile us, your enemies, to you. Grant that we too may learn to pray for our enemies, as your servant Stephen prayed for his persecutors, and, like him, be permitted to see your glory; through Jesus Christ our Lord. (120)

ST. JOHN, APOSTLE AND EVANGELIST
DECEMBER 27

PSALMS: (see table, pp. 58-59, Christmas)

HYMN OF THE DAY

"O word of God incarnate" (231)

LESSONS

Prov. 8:22-30   I John 5:1-12   John 13:20-35

Most merciful God, who in the apostle John raised up in your church a pure witness of the truth, continue graciously to enlighten it, that through your light it may be led to fullness of life; through Jesus Christ our Lord. (121)

THE HOLY INNOCENTS, MARTYRS
DECEMBER 28

PSALMS: (see table, pp. 58-59, Christmas)

HYMN OF THE DAY

"Your little ones, dear Lord" (52)

LESSONS

| Isa. 49:13-23 | Isa. 54:1-13 | Matt. 18:1-14 |

O Lord, on this day when innocent children proclaimed your praise by their death and were made martyrs of your Son, slay in us everything that resists you, that we, who have been called to be your children, may be witnesses both in word and life to your salvation; through Jesus Christ, your Son, our Lord. (122)

I SUNDAY AFTER CHRISTMAS
IN GOD'S KEEPING

"From his fullness have we all received, grace upon grace." John 1:16

PSALMS FOR THE WEEK: (see table, pp. 58-59, Christmas)

HYMN FOR THE WEEK

"Let all together praise our God" (47)

LESSONS

		Year 1	
Sun.	Isa. 62:6-7, 10-12	Heb. 2:10-18	Matt. 1:18-25
Dec. 29	Isa. 12:1-6	Rev. 1:1-8	John 7:37-52
Dec. 30	Isa. 25:1-9	Rev. 1:9-20	John 7:53-8:11
Dec. 31	Isa. 26:1-6	II Cor. 5:16-6:2	John 8:12-19

		Year 2	
Sun.	I Sam. 1:1-2, 7b-28	Col. 1:9-20	Luke 2:22-40
Dec. 29	II Sam 23:13-17b	II John 1-13	John 2:1-11
Dec. 30	I Kings 17:17-24	III John 1-15	John 4:46-54
Dec. 31	I Kings 3:5-14	James 4:13-17; 5:7-11	John 5:1-15

Almighty and everlasting God, you glorified yourself through your Son, Jesus Christ, from his youth up. Bestow upon us your Spirit, that we too may walk in your sight as your children, and bring forth the fruits of righteousness; through Jesus Christ our Lord. (123)

THE NAME OF JESUS

JANUARY 1

"Whatever you do, in word or deed, do everything in the name of the Lord Jesus, giving thanks to God the Father through him."   Colossians 3:17

PSALMS: (see table, pp. 58-59, Christmas)

HYMN OF THE DAY

"O Jesus, King most wonderful" (537)

LESSONS   *Year* 1

   Gen. 17:1-12a,   *Col.* 2:6-12   *John* 16:23b-30
   15-16

                        Year 2

   Isa. 62:1-5, 10-12 *Rev.* 19:11-16   *Matt.* 1:18-25

O God our heavenly Father, we give thanks that you have sent your Son to us, that he might save his people from their sins. Grant us your grace, that in this new year we may begin all that we do, in word and deed, in the name of Jesus, and through him give praise to you, our Father; and continue and increase therein all the days of our life until at last, when time is ended, we may praise and adore you in eternity; through Jesus Christ our Lord. (124)

II SUNDAY AFTER CHRISTMAS

LIGHT OF LIGHT

"God is light and in him is no darkness at all." I John 1:5

PSALMS FOR THE WEEK: (see table, pp. 58-59, Christmas)

HYMN FOR THE WEEK

"Of the Father's love begotten" (42)

LESSONS		Year 1	
Jan. 2	Gen. 12:1-7	Heb. 11:1-12	John 6:35-42, 48-51
Jan. 3	Gen. 28:10-22	Heb. 11:13-22	John 10:7-17
Jan. 4	Exod. 3:1-15	Heb. 11:23-31	John 14:6-14
Jan. 5	Josh. 1:1-9	Heb. 11:32-12:2	John 15:1-16
Sun.	Eccles. 3:3-9, 14-17	I John 2:12-17	John 6:41-47
	or Deut. 33:1-5		

		Year 2	
Jan. 2	I Kings 19:1-8	Eph. 4:1-16	John 6:1-14
Jan. 3	I Kings 19:9-18	Eph. 4:17-32	John 6:15-27
Jan. 4	Josh. 3:14-4:7	Eph. 5:1-20	John 9:1-12, 35-38
Jan. 5	Jonah 2:2-9	Eph. 6:10-20	John 11:17-27, 38-44
Sun.	I Kings 3:5-14	Col. 3:12-17	John 6:41-47

Gracious Lord and God, we magnify the wisdom of your ways and in childlike trust commit ourselves to your fatherly guidance. Uphold us by your hand, guide us with your counsel, and receive us at last into glory; through Jesus Christ, your Son, our Lord. (125)

69

THE EPIPHANY OF OUR LORD

JANUARY 6

THE GLORY OF CHRIST

"The darkness is passing away, and the true light is already shining."

I John 2:8

PSALMS: (see table, pp. 58-59, January 6, General Week 1 for January 6-12)

HYMN FOR THE WEEK

"Oh Morning Star, how fair and bright" (76)

LESSONS		*Year 1*	
Jan. 6	Isa. 52:7-10	Rev. 21:22-27	Matt. 12:14-21
Jan. 7	Isa. 52:3-6	Rev. 2:1-7	John 2:1-11
Jan. 8	Isa. 59:15b-21	Rev. 2:8-17	John 4:46-54
Jan. 9	Isa. 63:1-5	Rev. 2:18-29	John 5:1-15
Jan. 10	Isa. 65:1-9	Rev. 3:1-6	John 6:1-14
Jan. 11	Isa. 65:13-16	Rev. 3:7-13	John 6:15-27
Jan. 12	Isa. 66:1-2, 22-23	Rev. 3:14-22	John 9:1-12, 35-38

		Year 2	
Jan. 6	Isa. 49:1-7	Rev. 21:22-27	Matt. 12:14-21
Jan. 7	Deut. 8:1-3	Col. 1:1-14	John 6:30-33, 48-51
Jan. 8	Exod. 17:1-7	Col. 1:15-23	John 7:37-52
Jan. 9	Isa. 45:14-19	Col. 1:24-2:7	John 8:12-19
Jan. 10	Jer. 23:1-8	Col. 2:8-23	John 10:7-17
Jan. 11	Isa. 55:3-9	Col. 3:1-17	John 14:6-14
Jan. 12	Gen. 49:1-2. 8-12	Col. 3:18-4:6	John 15:1-16

Lord God you guided the wise men to the manger by the light of a star and permitted them there to see your only Son. Grant us also the grace to behold your glory and to present to you the gift of our hearts; through Jesus Christ our Lord.(126)

THE BAPTISM OF OUR LORD

I Sunday after the Epiphany

The Son of God

"We have beheld his glory, glory as of the only Son from the Father." John 1:14

PSALMS FOR THE WEEK: (see table, pp. 58-59, General Week 2)

HYMN FOR THE WEEK

"To Jordan came the Christ, our Lord" (79)

LESSONS	*Year 1*	
S.	*Isa.* 40:1-11	*Heb.* 1:1-12	*John* 1:1-7, 19-20, 29-34
M.	*Isa.* 40:12-24	*Eph.* 1:1-14	*Mark* 1:1-13
T.	*Isa.* 40:25-31	*Eph.* 1:15-23	*Mark* 1:14-28
W.	*Isa.* 41:1-16	*Eph.* 2:1-10	*Mark* 1:29-45
Th.	*Isa.* 41:17-29	*Eph.* 2:11-22	*Mark* 2:1-12
F.	*Isa.* 42:(1-9) 10-17	*Eph.* 3:1-13	*Mark* 2:13-22
S.	*Isa.* (42:18-25) 43:1-13	*Eph.* 3:14-21	*Mark* 2:23-3:6

	Year 2	
S.	*Gen.* 1:1-2:3	*Eph.* 1:3-14	*John* 1:29-34
M.	*Gen.* 2:4-9(10-15) 16-25	*Heb.* 1:1-14	*John* 1:1-18
T.	*Gen.* 3:1-24	*Heb.* 2:1-10	*John* 1:19-28
W.	*Gen.* 4:1-16	*Heb.* 2:11-18	*John* 1:(29-34) 35-42
Th.	*Gen.* 4:17-26	*Heb.* 3:1-11	*John* 1:43-51
F.	*Gen.* 6:1-8	*Heb.* 3:12-19	*John* 2:1-12
S.	*Gen.* 6:9-22	*Heb.* 4:1-13	*John* 2:13-22

Almighty God, at the baptism of your blessed Son Jesus Christ in the Jordan you manifested his glorious divinity. Grant that the brightness of his presence may shine in our hearts and his glory be set forth in our lives; through Jesus Christ our Lord. (127)

II SUNDAY AFTER THE EPIPHANY

"The law was given through Moses; grace and truth came through Jesus Christ."   John 1:17

PSALMS FOR THE WEEK: (see table, pp. 58–59, General Week 3)

HYMN FOR THE WEEK

"The only Son from heaven" (86)

LESSONS   *Year 1*

S.	Isa. 43:14–44:5	Heb. 6:17–7:10	John 4:27–42
M.	Isa. 44:6–8, 21–23	Eph. 4:1–16	Mark 3:7–19a
T.	Isa. 44:9–20	Eph. 4:17–32	Mark 3:19b–35
W.	Isa. 44:24–45:7	Eph. 5:1–14	Mark 4:1–20
Th.	Isa. 45:5–17	Eph. 5:15–33	Mark 4:21–34
F.	Isa. 45:18–25	Eph. 6:1–9	Mark 4:35–41
S.	Isa. 46:1–13	Eph. 6:10–24	Mark 5:1–20

                           Year 2

S.	Gen. 7:1–10, 17–23	Eph. 4:1–16	Mark 3:7–19
M.	Gen. 8:6–22	Heb. 4:14–5:6	John 2:23–3:15
T.	Gen. 9:1–17	Heb. 5:7–14	John 3:16–21
W.	Gen. 9:18–29	Heb. 6:1–12	John 3:22–36
Th.	Gen. 11:1–9	Heb. 6:13–20	John 4:1–15
F.	Gen. 11:27–12:8	Heb. 7:1–17	John 4:16–26
S.	Gen. 12:9–13:1	Heb. 7:18–28	John 4:27–42

Merciful God, loving Father, you govern all things in heaven and earth and make all things new through your almighty word. Transform our sinful nature and all our doings by the power of your Holy Spirit, that we may please you and attain perfect joy, through Jesus Christ our Lord. (128)

III SUNDAY AFTER THE EPIPHANY

"The Spirit of the Lord God is upon me."   Isaiah 61:1

PSALMS FOR THE WEEK: (see table, pp. 58-59, General Week 4)

HYMN FOR THE WEEK

"O Christ, our light, O Radiance true" (380)

LESSONS		*Year 1*	
S.	*Isa.* 47:1-15	*Heb.* 10:19-31	*John* 5:2-18
M.	*Isa.* 48:1-11	*Gal.* 1:1-17	*Mark* 5:21-43
T.	*Isa.* 48:12-21(22)	*Gal.* 1:18-2:10	*Mark* 6:1-13
W.	*Isa.* 49:1-12	*Gal.* 2:11-21	*Mark* 6:13-29
Th.	*Isa.* 49:13-23 (24-26)	*Gal.* 3:1-14	*Mark* 6:30-46
F.	*Isa.* 50:1-11	*Gal.* 3:15-22	*Mark* 6:47-56
S.	*Isa.* 51:1-8	*Gal.* 3:23-29	*Mark* 7:1-23

		Year 2	
S.	*Gen.* 13:2-18	*Gal.* 2:1-10	*Mark* 7:31-37
M.	*Gen.* 14:(1-7)8-24	*Heb.* 8:1-13	*John* 4:43-54
T.	*Gen.* 15:1-11, 17-21	*Heb.* 9:1-14	*John* 5:1-18
W.	*Gen.* 16:1-14	*Heb.* 9:15-28	*John* 5:19-29
Th.	*Gen.* 16:15-17:14	*Heb.* 10:1-10	*John* 5:30-47
F.	*Gen.* 17:15-27	*Heb.* 10:11-25	*John* 6:1-15
S.	*Gen.* 18:1-16	*Heb.* 10:26-39	*John* 6:16-27

Lord, open our ears and hearts, that we may heed your hidden wisdom and let your word be a light to our path. Speak to us through your living word, that we may obey your call and follow him whom you have sent, Jesus Christ our Savior, who lives and reigns with you and the Holy Spirit, one God, now and forever. (129)

"Make me understand the way of your commandments,
that I may meditate on your marvelous works."

Psalm 119:27

PSALMS FOR THE WEEK: (see table, pp. 58-59, General Week 1)

HYMN FOR THE WEEK

"Hope of the world, thou Christ of great compassion" (493)

LESSONS		*Year 1*	
S.	*Isa.* 51:9-16	*Heb.* 11:8-16	*John* 7:14-31
M.	*Isa.* 51:17-23	*Gal.* 4:1-11	*Mark* 7:24-37
T.	*Isa.* 52:1-12	*Gal.* 4:12-20	*Mark* 8:1-10
W.	*Isa.* 52:13-53:12	*Gal.* 4:21-31	*Mark* 8:11-26
Th.	*Isa.* 54:1-10(11-17)	*Gal.* 5:1-15	*Mark* 8:27-9:1
F.	*Isa.* 55:1-13	*Gal.* 5:16-24	*Mark* 9:2-13
S.	*Isa.* 56:1-8	*Gal.* 5:25-6:10	*Mark* 9:14-29

		Year 2	
S.	*Gen.* 18:16-33	*Gal.* 5:13-25	*Mark* 8:22-30
M.	*Gen.* 19:1-17	*Heb.* 11:1-12	*John* 6:27-40
	(18-23)24-29		
T.	*Gen.* 21:1-21	*Heb.* 11:13-22	*John* 6:41-51
W.	*Gen.* 22:1-18	*Heb.* 11:23-31	*John* 6:52-59
Th.	*Gen.* 23:1-20	*Heb.* 11:32-12:2	*John* 6:60-71
F.	*Gen.* 24:1-27	*Heb.* 12:3-11	*John* 7:1-13
S.	*Gen.* 24:28-38,	*Heb.* 12:12-29	*John* 7:14-36
	49-51		

Almighty God, you set your Son over the works of your
hands, so that even the rebellious spirits must obey him. Give
power to your word that your kingdom may grow and increase
in power and all creation be delivered into the glorious liberty
of your children; through Jesus Christ our Lord. (130)

"This is my comfort in my trouble,
  that your promise gives me life."

Psalm 119:50

PSALMS FOR THE WEEK: (see table, pp. 58-59, General Week 2)

HYMN FOR THE WEEK

  "Hail to the Lord's anointed" (87)

LESSONS

Year 1

S.	Isa. 57:1-13	Heb. 12:1-6	John 7:37-46
M.	Isa. 57:14-21	Gal. 6:11-18	Mark 9:30-41
T.	Isa. 58:1-12	II Tim. 1:1-14	Mark 9:42-50
W.	Isa. 59:1-21	II Tim. 1:15-2:13	Mark 10:1-16
Th.	Isa. 60:1-22	II Tim. 2:14-26	Mark 10:17-31
F.	Isa. 61:1-9	II Tim. 3:1-17	Mark 10:32-45
S.	Isa. 61:10-62:5	II Tim. 4:1-8	Mark 10:46-52

Year 2

S.	Gen. 24:50-67	II Tim. 2:14-21	Mark 10:13-22
M.	Gen. 25:19-34	Heb. 13:1-16	John 7:37-52
T.	Gen. 26:1-6; 12-33	Heb. 13:17-25	John 7:53-8:11
W.	Gen. 27:1-29	Rom. 12:1-8	John 8:12-20
Th.	Gen. 27:30-45	Rom. 12:9-21	John 8:21-32
F.	Gen. 27:46-28:4, 10-22	Rom. 13:1-14	John 8:33-47
S.	Gen. 29:1-20	Rom. 14:1-23	John 8:47-59

O God, you have called and gathered a people from the ends of the earth to serve you. Grant the increase of your government among us and give us your Holy Spirit, that your name may be glorified to all who sit in darkness and the shadow of death; through Jesus Christ our Lord. (131)

"The creation waits with eager longing for the revealing of the children of God."   Romans 8:19

PSALMS FOR THE WEEK: (see table, pp. 58-59, General Week 3)

HYMN FOR THE WEEK

"O Christ, our hope, our hearts' desire" (300)

LESSONS		*Year* 1	
S.	Isa. 62:6-12	I John 2:3-11	John 8:12-19
M.	Isa. 63:1-6	I Tim. 1:1-17	Mark 11:1-11
T.	Isa. 63:7-14	I Tim. 1:18-2:8 (9-15)	Mark 11:12-26
W.	Isa. 63:15-64:9	I Tim. 3:1-16	Mark 11:27-12:12
Th.	Isa. 65:1-12	I Tim. 4:1-16	Mark 12:13-27
F.	Isa. 65:17-25	I Tim. 5:(1-16) 17-22(23-25)	Mark 12:28-34
S.	Isa. 66:1-6	I Tim. 6:(1-5)6-21	Mark 12:35-44

		Year 2	
S.	Gen. 29:20-35	I Tim. 3:14-4:10	Mark 10:23-31
M.	Gen. 30:1-24	I John 1:1-10	John 9:1-17
T.	Gen. 31:1-24	I John 2:1-11	John 9:18-41
W.	Gen. 31:25-50	I John 2:12-17	John 10:1-18
Th.	Gen. 32:3-21	I John 2:18-29	John 10:19-30
F.	Gen. 32:22-33:17	I John 3:1-10	John 10:31-42
S.	Gen. 35:1-20	I John 3:11-18	John 11:1-16

O God, our heavenly Father, since we cannot stand before you with our own works, send your Holy Spirit into our hearts that we may be comforted by your mercy and by your help overcome all that torments us because of our sins; through Jesus Christ our Lord. (132)

VII SUNDAY AFTER THE EPIPHANY

"Be kind to one another, tenderhearted, forgiving one another, as God in Christ forgave you." Ephesians 4:32

PSALMS FOR THE WEEK: (see table, pp. 58-59, General Week 4)

HYMN FOR THE WEEK

"O God, O Lord of heaven and earth" (396)

LESSONS		*Year 1*	
S.	Isa. 66:7-14	I John 3:4-10	John 10:7-16
M.	Ruth 1:1-14	II Cor. 1:1-11	Matt. 5:1-12
T.	Ruth 1:15-22	II Cor. 1:12-22	Matt. 5:13-20
W.	Ruth 2:1-13	II Cor. 1:23-2:17	Matt. 5:21-26
Th.	Ruth 2:14-23	II Cor. 3:1-18	Matt. 5:27-37
F.	Ruth 3:1-18	II Cor. 4:1-12	Matt. 5:38-48
S.	Ruth 4:1-22	II Cor. 4:13-5:10	Matt. 6:1-6

		Year 2	
S.	Prov. 1:20-33	II Cor. 5:11-21	Mark 10:35-45
M.	Prov. 3:11-20	I John 3:18-4:6	John 11:17-29
T.	Prov. 4:1-27	I John 4:7-21	John 11:30-44
W.	Prov. 6:1-19	I John 5:1-12	John 11:45-54
Th.	Prov. 7:1-27	I John 5:13-21	John 11:55-12:8
F.	Prov. 8:1-21	Phlm. 1-25	John 12:9-19
S.	Prov. 8:22-36	II Tim. 1:1-14	John 12:20-26

O God, you sent forth your commandment upon earth, and your word runs very swiftly. Let your Holy Spirit so prepare our minds and wills for your teaching, that no carelessness or shallowness of love or ease may hinder us from bringing forth the fruits of righteousness, by which the world may know that we are followers of your blessed Son, Jesus Christ our Lord. (133)

VIII SUNDAY AFTER THE EPIPHANY

"Remember not the former things, nor consider the things of old. Behold I am doing a new thing; now it springs forth, do you not perceive it?" Isaiah 43:18-19A

PSALMS FOR THE WEEK: (see table, pp. 58-59, General Week 1)

HYMN FOR THE WEEK

"Sing praise to God, the highest good" (542)

LESSONS		Year 1	
S.	Deut. 4:1-9	II Tim. 4:1-8	John 12:1-8
M.	Deut. 4:9-14	II Cor. 10:1-18	Matt. 6:7-15
T.	Deut. 4:15-24	II Cor. 11:1-21a	Matt. 6:16-23
W.	Deut. 4:25-31	II Cor. 11:21b-33	Matt. 6:24-34
Th.	Deut. 4:32-40	II Cor. 12:1-10	Matt. 7:1-12
F.	Deut. 5:1-22	II Cor. 12:11-21	Matt. 7:13-21
S.	Deut. 5:22-33	II Cor. 13:1-14	Matt. 7:22-29

		Year 2	
S.	Prov. 9:1-12	II Cor. 9:6b-15	Mark 10:46-52
M.	Prov. 10:1-12	II Tim. 1:15-2:13	John 12:27-36a
T.	Prov. 15:16-33	II Tim. 2:14-26	John 12:36b-50
W.	Prov. 17:1-20	II Tim. 3:1-17	John 13:1-20
Th.	Prov. 21:30-22:6	II Tim. 4:1-8	John 13:21-30
F.	Prov. 23:19-21, 29-24:2	II Tim. 4:9-22	John 13:31-38
S.	Prov. 25:15-28	Phil. 1:1-11	John 18:1-14

Most loving Father, whose will it is for us to give thanks for all things, to fear nothing but the loss of you, and to cast all our care on you who care for us: Preserve us from faithless fears and worldly anxieties, that no clouds of this mortal life may hide from us the light of that love which is immortal, and which you have manifested to us in your Son, Jesus Christ our Lord. (134)

THE TRANSFIGURATION OF OUR LORD
LAST SUNDAY AFTER THE EPIPHANY
THE HIDDEN GLORY

"God who said, 'Let light shine out of darkness,' . . . has shone in our hearts to give the light of the knowledge of the glory of God in the face of Christ."   II Corinthians 4:6

PSALMS FOR THE WEEK: (see table, pp. 58-59, General Week 2)

HYMN FOR THE WEEK

"Oh, wondrous type! Oh, vision fair" (80)

LESSONS		*Year 1*
S.	Dan. 7:9-10, 13-14	*II Cor.* 3:1-9	*John* 12:27-36a
M.	*Deut.* 6:1-15	*Heb.* 1:1-14	*John* 1:1-18
T.	*Deut.* 6:16-25	*Heb.* 2:1-10	*John* 1:19-28

		Year 2	
S.	*Mal.* 4:1-6	*II Cor.* 3:7-18	*Luke* 9:18-27
M.	*Prov.* 27:1-6, 10-12	*Phil.* 2:1-13	*John* 18:15-18, 25-27
T.	*Prov.* 30:1-4, 24-33	*Phil.* 3:1-11	*John* 18:28-38

Christ our God, you were transfigured on the mountain and manifested your glory to your disciples as they were able to bear it. Shed your everlasting light upon us, that we may behold your glory and enter into your sufferings, and proclaim you to the world, for you give light in the darkness and are yourself the light, now and forever. (135)

ASH WEDNESDAY

"You are dust, and to dust you shall return." Genesis 3:19b

PSALMS FOR THE WEEK: (see table, pp. 58-59, Lent)

HYMN FOR THE WEEK

"Out of the depths I cry to you" (295)

LESSONS		Year 1	
W.	Jonah 3:1-4:11	Heb. 12:1-14	Luke 18:9-14
Th.	Deut. 7:6-11	Titus 1:1-16	John 1:29-34
F.	Deut. 7:12-16	Titus 2:1-15	John 1:35-42
S.	Deut. 7:17-26	Titus 3:1-15	John 1:43-51

		Year 2	
W.	Amos 5:6-15	Heb. 12:1-14	Luke 18:9-14
Th.	Hab. 3:1-10 (11-15)16-18	Phil. 3:12-21	John 17:1-8
F.	Ezek. 18:1-4, 25-32	Phil. 4:1-9	John 17:9-19
S.	Ezek. 39:21-29	Phil. 4:10.20	John 17:20-26

Help us, Lord, to observe this season with wholesome sacrifice and cheerful self-denial, that the time of need may find us willing and ready to fight against all the forces of evil and that, by your grace, your visitations may prove blessings to us; through Jesus Christ our Lord. (136)

I SUNDAY IN LENT

TEMPTATION

"The reason the Son of God appeared was to destroy the works of the devil." I John 3:8

PSALMS FOR THE WEEK: (see table, pp. 58-59, Lent)

HYMN FOR THE WEEK

"God the Father, be our stay" (308)

LESSONS	Year 1		
S.	Jer. 9:23-24	I Cor. 1:18-31	Mark 2:18-22
M.	Deut. 8:1-20	Heb. 2:11-18	John 2:1-12
T.	Deut. 9:(1-3)4-12	Heb. 3:1-11	John 2:13-22
W.	Deut. 9:13-21	Heb. 3:12-19	John 2:23-3:15
Th.	Deut. 9:23-10:5	Heb. 4:1-10	John 3:16-21
F.	Deut. 10:12-22	Heb. 4:11-16	John 3:22-36
S.	Deut. 11:18-28	Heb. 5:1-10	John 4:1-26

	Year 2		
S.	Dan. 9:3-10	Heb. 2:10-18	John 12:44-50
M.	Gen. 37:1-11	I Cor. 1:1-19	Mark 1:1-13
T.	Gen. 37:12-24	I Cor. 1:20-31	Mark 1:14-28
W.	Gen. 37:25-36	I Cor. 2:1-13	Mark 1:29-45
Th.	Gen. 39:1-23	I Cor. 2:14-3:15	Mark 2:1-12
F.	Gen. 40:1-23	I Cor. 3:16-23	Mark 2:13-22
S.	Gen. 41:1-13	I Cor. 4:1-7	Mark 2:23-3:6

O God, by whose Spirit we are led into the wilderness of trial, grant that, standing in your strength against the powers of darkness, we may so win the victory over all evil suggestions that with singleness of heart we may ever serve you and you alone; through him who was in all points tempted as we are, your Son, Jesus Christ our Lord. (137)

II SUNDAY IN LENT

WORSHIP IN SPIRIT AND TRUTH

"Ho, every one who thirsts, come to the waters; and he who has no money, come, buy and eat." Isaiah 55:1

PSALMS FOR THE WEEK: (see table, pp. 58-59, Lent)

HYMN FOR THE WEEK

"Lord, thee I love with all my heart" (325)

LESSONS		*Year 1*	
S.	Jer. 1:10	I Cor. 3:11-23	Mark 3:31-4:9
M.	Jer. 1:11-19	Rom. 1:1-15	John 4:27-42
T.	Jer. 2:1-13, 29-32	Rom. 1:16-25	John 4:43-54
W.	Jer. 3:6-18	Rom. 1:(26-27) 28-2:11	John 5:1-18
Th.	Jer. 4:9-10, 19-28	Rom. 2:12-24	John 5:19-29
F.	Jer. 5:1-9	Rom. 2:25-3:18	John 5:30-47
S.	Jer. 5:20-31	Rom. 3:19-31	John 7:1-13

		Year 2	
S.	Gen. 41:14-45	Rom. 6:3-14	John 5:19-24
M.	Gen. 41:46-57	I Cor. 4:8-20(21)	Mark 3:7-19a
T.	Gen. 42:1-17	I Cor. 5:1-8	Mark 3:19b-35
W.	Gen. 42:18-28	I Cor. 5:9-6:11	Mark 4:1-20
Th.	Gen. 42:29-38	I Cor. 6:12-20	Mark 4:21-34
F.	Gen. 43:1-15	I Cor. 7:1-9	Mark 4:35-41
S.	Gen. 43:16-34	I Cor. 7:10-24	Mark 5:1-20

Lord Jesus Christ, you walked the way of the cross as the obedient servant of God. Open our ears and teach us by your Spirit, that we may not rebel but walk in the obedience of disciples who have learned from you, who with the Father and the Holy Spirit live and reign, one God, now and forever. (138)

RECONCILIATION

"In Christ God was reconciling the world to himself, not counting their trespasses against them." II Corinthians 5:19

PSALMS FOR THE WEEK: (see table, pp. 58-59, Lent)

HYMN FOR THE WEEK

"May God bestow on us his grace" (335)

LESSONS *Year 1*

S.	Jer. 6:9-15	I Cor. 6:12-20	Mark 5:1-20
M.	Jer. 7:1-15	Rom. 4:1-12	John 7:14-36
T.	Jer. 7:21-34	Rom. 4:13-25	John 7:37-52
W.	Jer. 8:4-7, 18-9:6	Rom. 5:1-11	John 8:12-20
Th.	Jer. 10:11-24	Rom. 5:12-21	John 8:21-32
F.	Jer. 11:1-8, 14-17	Rom. 6:1-11	John 8:33-47
S.	Jer. 13:1-11	Rom. 6:12-23	John 8:47-59

Year 2

S.	Gen. 44:1-17	Rom. 8:1-10	John 5:25-29
M.	Gen. 44:18-34	I Cor. 7:25-31	Mark 5:21-43
T.	Gen. 45:1-15	I Cor. 7:32-40	Mark 6:1-13
W.	Gen. 45:16-28	I Cor. 8:1-13	Mark 6:13-29
Th.	Gen. 46:1-7, 28-34	I Cor. 9:1-15	Mark 6:30-46
F.	Gen. 47:1-26	I Cor. 9:16-27	Mark 6:47-56
S.	Gen. 47:27-48:7	I Cor. 10:1-13	Mark 7:1-23

Heavenly Father, you sent your Son to us and laid on him the burden of the cross that we might see and know the glory of your holy love. Grant that our faith in him may not be shaken by adversity or daunted by the threat of it, but that we may ever follow steadfastly the way that leads to perfect fellowship with him, and so with you; through Jesus Christ our Lord. (139)

IV SUNDAY IN LENT
FAITH AND LIFE

"The Son of man came not to be served but to serve, and to give his life as a ransom for many." Matthew 20:28

PSALMS FOR THE WEEK: (see table, pp. 58-59, Lent)

HYMN FOR THE WEEK

"I trust, O Christ, in you alone" (395)

LESSONS	*Year* 1	
S.	*Jer.* 14:1-9(10-16) *Gal.* 4:21-5:1	*Mark* 8:11-21
	17-22	
M.	*Jer.* 16:(1-9)10-21 *Rom.* 7:1-12	*John* 6:1-15
T.	*Jer.* 17:19-27 *Rom.* 7:13-25	*John* 6:16-27
W.	*Jer.* 18:1-11 *Rom.* 8:1-11	*John* 6:27-40
Th.	*Jer.* 22:13-23 *Rom.* 8:12-27	*John* 6:41-51
F.	*Jer.* 23:1-8 *Rom.* 8:28-39	*John* 6:52-59
S.	*Jer.* 23:9-15 *Rom.* 9:1-18	*John* 6:60-71

  | *Year* 2 | |
--- | --- | ---
S. | *Gen.* 48:8-22 *Rom.* 8:11-25 | *John* 6:27-40
M. | *Gen.* 49:1-28 *I Cor.* 10:14-11:1 | *Mark* 7:24-37
T. | *Gen.* 49:29-50:14 *I Cor.* 11:2-34 | *Mark* 8:1-10
W. | *Gen.* 50:15-26 *I Cor.* 12:1-11 | *Mark* 8:11-26
Th. | *Exod.* 1:6-22 *I Cor.* 12:12-26 | *Mark* 8:27-9:1
F. | *Exod.* 2:1-22 *I Cor.* 12:27-13:3 | *Mark* 9:2-13
S. | *Exod.* 2:23-3:15 *I Cor.* 13:1-13 | *Mark* 9:14-29

Lord God, heavenly Father, in your Son you have given the world a pioneer of salvation and made him the true and eternal priest and mediator of his people. Grant that we may hold fast to him in love, learn obedience in his discipleship, and so be brought into the heavenly sanctuary through him, who lives and reigns with you and the Holy Spirit, one God, now and forever. (140)

V SUNDAY IN LENT

THE NEW LIFE

"You are not your own; you were bought with a price."
$\qquad$ I Corinthians 6:19-20

PSALMS FOR THE WEEK: (see table, pp. 58-59, Lent)

HYMN FOR THE WEEK

"My song is love unknown" (94)

LESSONS		*Year 1*	
S.	*Jer.* 23:16-32	*I Cor.* 9:19-27	*Mark* 8:31-9:1
M.	*Jer.* 24:1-10	*Rom.* 9:19-33	*John* 9:1-17
T.	*Jer.* 25:8-17	*Rom.* 10:1-13	*John* 9:18-41
W.	*Jer.* 25:30-38	*Rom.* 10:14-21	*John* 10:1-18
Th.	*Jer.* 26:1-16(17-24)	*Rom.* 11:1-12	*John* 10:19-42
F.	*Jer.* 29:1(2-3)4-14	*Rom.* 11:13-24	*John* 11:1-27 or *John* 12:1-10
S.	*Jer.* 31:27-34	*Rom.* 11:25-36	*John* 11:28-44 or *John* 12:37-50

		Year 2	
S.	*Exod.* 3:16-4:12	*Rom.* 12:1-21	*John* 8:46-59
M.	*Exod.* 4:10-20 (21-26)27-31	*I Cor.* 14:1-19	*Mark* 9:30-41
T.	*Exod.* 5:1-6:1	*I Cor.* 14:20-33a, 39-40	*Mark* 9:42-50
W.	*Exod.* 7:8-24	*II Cor.* 2:14-3:6	*Mark* 10:1-16
Th.	*Exod.* 7:25-8:19	*II Cor.* 3:7-18	*Mark* 10:17-31
F.	*Exod.* 9:13-35	*II Cor.* 4:1-12	*Mark* 10:32-45
S.	*Exod.* 10:21-11:8	*II Cor.* 4:13-18	*Mark* 10:46-52

O Lord, mercifully assist us in our supplications and prayers. Direct the lives of your servants toward the goal of everlasting salvation, that, surrounded by all the changes and uncertainties of life, we may be defended by your gracious and ready help in Jesus Christ our Lord. (141)

SUNDAY OF THE PASSION
THE MAN OF SORROWS

"He shall divide the spoil with the strong; because he poured out his soul to death and ... bore the sins of many." Isaiah 53:12

PSALMS FOR THE WEEK: (see table, pp. 58-59, Lent)

HYMN FOR THE WEEK

"A Lamb goes uncomplaining forth" (105)

LESSONS		*Year* 1	
S.	Zech. 9:9-12 or Zech. 12:9-11; 13:1, 7-9	*I Tim.* 6:12-16	*Matt.* 21:12-17
M.	Jer. 11:18-20; 12:1-16(17)	*Phil.* 3:1-14	*John* 12:9-19
T.	Jer. 15:10-21	*Phil.* 3:15-21	*John* 12:20-26
W.	Jer. 17:5-10, 14-17(18)	*Phil.* 4:1-13	*John* 12:27-36

		Year 2	
S.	Zech. 9:9-12 or Zech. 12:9-11; 13:1, 7-9	*I Tim.* 6:12-16	*Luke* 19:41-48
M.	Lam. 1:1-2, 6-12	*II Cor.* 1:1-7	*Mark* 11:12-25
T.	Lam. 1:17-22	*II Cor.* 1:8-22	*Mark* 11:27-33
W.	Lam. 2:1-9	*II Cor.* 1:23-2:11	*Mark* 12:1-11

O God, holy and eternal, you permit us to enter into the fellowship of that holy suffering by which your dear Son, our Savior, conquered sin and death. Grant that we may celebrate the remembrance of his passion with true devotion, accept the cross as his disciples, and thus fulfill your holy will; through Jesus Christ our Lord. (142)

MAUNDY THURSDAY
The New Commandment

"A new commandment I give to you, that you love one another."   John 13:34

PSALMS FOR THE DAY: (see table, pp. 58-59, Lent)

HYMN FOR THE DAY

"O Lord, we praise you, bless you, and adore you!" (215)

LESSONS   *Year* 1

   Jer. 20:7-11(12-13)   *I Cor.* 10:14-17;   *John* 17:1-11
   14-18   11:27-32   (12-26)

                Year 2

   Lam. 2:10-18   *I Cor.* 10:14-17;   *Mark* 14:12-25
                11:27-32

Lord God, of your fatherly mercy you spared not your only Son but gave him up to death and the cross. Send your Holy Spirit into our hearts, that we may be comforted by this grace, henceforth be on guard against sin, and patiently bear whatever you send us to suffer, that through him we may live for ever with you. (143)

GOOD FRIDAY
The Perfect Sacrifice

"By a single offering Christ has perfected for all time those who are sanctified."   Hebrews 10:14

PSALMS FOR THE DAY: (see table, pp. 58-59, Lent)

HYMN FOR THE DAY

"Sing, my tongue, the glorious battle" (118)

LESSONS   *Year* 1

   Wisd. 1:16-2:1, 12-22   *I Peter* 1:10-20   *John* 13:36-38
   or *Gen.* 22:1-4   or *John* 19:38-42

                Year 2

   Lam. 3:1-9, 19-33   *I Peter* 1:10-20   *John* 13:36-38
                                or *John* 19:38-42

Almighty God, we ask you to look with mercy on your family, for whom our Lord Jesus Christ was willing to be betrayed and to be given over to the hands of sinners and to suffer death on the cross; who now lives and reigns with you and the Holy Spirit, one God, forever and ever. (144)

HOLY SATURDAY
THE GREAT SABBATH

"There remains a sabbath rest for the people of God; for whoever enters God's rest also ceases from his labors as God did from his." Hebrews 4:9-10

PSALMS FOR THE DAY: (see table, pp. 58-59, Lent)

HYMN FOR THE DAY

"Alas! And did my Savior bleed" (98)

LESSONS	Year 1	
Job 19:21-27a	*Heb.* 4:1-16	*Rom.* 8:1-11

	Year 2	
Lam. 3:37-58	*Heb.* 4:1-16	*Rom.* 8:1-11

Oh God, Creator of heaven and earth: Grant that, as the crucified body of your dear Son was laid in the tomb and rested on this holy Sabbath, so we may await with him the coming of the third day, and rise with him to newness of life; who now lives and reigns with you and the Holy Spirit, one God, for ever and ever. (145)

THE RESURRECTION OF OUR LORD

EASTER DAY

THE EMPTY TOMB

"I am the living one; I died, and behold I am alive for evermore, and I have the keys of Death and Hades."

Revelation 1:18

PSALMS FOR THE WEEK: (see table, pp. 58-59, Easter)

HYMN FOR THE WEEK

"Christ Jesus lay in death's strong bands" (134)

LESSONS		*Year 1*	
S.	Exod. 12:1-14	Isa. 51:9-11	Luke 24:13-35 or John 20:19-23
M.	Jonah 2:1-10	Acts 2:14, 22-32	John 14:1-14
T.	Isa. 30:18-26	Acts 2:36-41 (42-47)	John 14:15-31
W.	Micah 7:7-15	Acts 3:1-10	John 15:1-11
Th.	Ezek. 37:1-14	Acts 3:11-26	John 15:12-27
F.	Dan. 12:1-4, 13	Acts 4:1-12	John 16:1-15
S.	Isa. 25:1-9	Acts 4:13-21 (22-31)	John 16:16-33

		Year 2	
S.	Exod. 12:1-14 or Isa. 51:9-11	John 1:1-18	Luke 24:13-35 or John 20:19-23
M.	Exod. 12:14-27	I Cor. 15:1-11	Mark 16:1-8
T.	Exod. 12:28-39	I Cor. 15:12-28	Mark 16:9-20
W.	Exod. 12:40-51	I Cor. 15:(29)30-41	Matt. 28:1-16
Th.	Exod. 13:3-10	I Cor. 15:41-50	Matt. 28:16-20
F.	Exod. 13:1-2, 11-16	I Cor. 15:51-58	Luke 24:1-12
S.	Exod. 13:17-14:4	II Cor. 4:16-5:10	Mark 12:18-27

Almighty God, by the death of your Son you have destroyed sin and death, and by his resurrection you have restored innocence and everlasting life, in order that, delivered from the power of the devil, we may live in your kingdom. Grant that we may believe this with our whole heart, and, steadfast in this faith, may praise and thank you evermore; through Jesus Christ our Lord. (146)

II SUNDAY OF EASTER

BELIEVING WITHOUT SEEING

"Like newborn babes, long for the pure spiritual milk, that by it you may grow up to salvation; for you have tasted the kindness of the Lord." I Peter 2:2-3

PSALMS FOR THE WEEK: (see table, pp. 58-59, Easter)

HYMN FOR THE WEEK

"O sons and daughters of the King" (139)

LESSONS		*Year 1*	
S.	Isa. 43:8-13	I Peter 2:2-10	John 14:1-7
M.	Dan. 1:1-21	I John 1:1-10	John 17:1-11
T.	Dan. 2:1-16	I John 2:1-11	John 17:12-19
W.	Dan. 2:17-30	I John 2:12-17	John 17:20-26
Th.	Dan. 2:31-49	I John 2:18-29	Luke 3:1-14
F.	Dan. 3:1-18	I John 3:1-10	Luke 3:15-22
S.	Dan. 3:19-30	I John 3:11-18	Luke 4:1-13

		Year 2	
S.	Exod. 14:5-22	I John 1:1-7	John 14:1-7
M.	Exod. 14:21-31	I Peter 1:1-12	John 14:(1-7) 8-17
T.	Exod. 15:1-21	I Peter 1:13-25	John 14:18-31
W.	Exod. 15:22-16:10	I Peter 2:1-10	John 15:1-11
Th.	Exod. 16:10-22	I Peter 2:11-3:12	John 15:12-27
F.	Exod. 16:23-36	I Peter 3:13-4:6	John 16:1-15
S.	Exod. 17:1-16	I Peter 4:7-19	John 16:16-33

Lord God almighty, every year you renew the face of the earth, and it is your will to renew the world fallen into sin and death. Grant that we may discern in your Son the dawning of the true life and in him share in this new creation; for he lives and reigns with you and the Holy Spirit, one God, now and forever. (147)

III SUNDAY OF EASTER
The Risen Lord Appears to His Disciples

"God raised him on the third day and made him manifest; not to all the people but to us who were chosen by God as witnesses, who ate and drank with him after he rose from the dead."

Acts 10:40-41

Psalms for the Week: (see table, pp. 58-59, Easter)

Hymn for the Week

"With high delight let us unite" (140)

Lessons		Year 1	
S.	Dan. 4:1-18	I Peter 4:7-11	John 21:15-25
M.	Dan. 4:19-27	I John 3:19-4:6	Luke 4:14-30
T.	Dan. 4:28-37	I John 4:7-21	Luke 4:31-37
W.	Dan. 5:1-12	I John 5:1-12	Luke 4:38-44
Th.	Dan. 5:13-30	I John 5:13-20(21)	Luke 5:1-11
F.	Dan. 6:1-15	II John 1-13	Luke 5:12-26
S.	Dan. 6:16-28	III John 1-15	Luke 5:27-39

		Year 2	
S.	Exod. 18:1-12	I John 2:7-17	Mark 16:9-20
M.	Exod. 18:13-27	I Peter 5:1-14	Matt. (1:1-17) 3:1-6
T.	Exod. 19:1-16	Col. 1:1-14	Matt. 3:7-12
W.	Exod. 19:16-25	Col. 1:15-23	Matt. 3:13-17
Th.	Exod. 20:1-21	Col. 1:24-2:7	Matt. 4:1-11
F.	Exod. 24:1-18	Col. 2:8-23	Matt. 4:12-17
S.	Exod. 25:1-22	Col. 3:1-17	Matt. 4:18-25

Almighty and everlasting God, through the death and resurrection of your Son you have proclaimed to us the gospel of peace. Grant that by the power of his resurrection we may be born anew to a living hope, and so overcome the world; through Jesus Christ our Lord. (148)

IV SUNDAY OF EASTER

THE GOOD SHEPHERD

"I am the good shepherd. . . . My sheep hear my voice, and I know them, and they follow me; and I give them eternal life." John 10:11, 27-28

PSALMS FOR THE WEEK: (see table, pp. 58-59, Easter)

HYMN FOR THE WEEK

"The King of love my shepherd is" (456)

LESSONS		*Year 1*	
S.	Wisd. 1:1-15 or Gen. 18:22-33	I Peter 5:1-11	Matt. 7:15-29
M.	Wisd. 1:16-2:11, 21-24 or Jer. 30:1-9	Col. 1:1-14	Luke 6:1-11
T.	Wisd. 3:1-9 or Jer. 30:10-17	Col. 1:15-23	Luke 6:12-26
W.	Wisd. 4:16-5:8 or Jer. 30:18-22	Col. 1:24-2:7	Luke 6:27-38
Th.	Wisd. 5:9-23 or Jer. 31:1-14	Col. 2:8-23	Luke 6:39-49
F.	Wisd. 6:12-23 or Jer. 31:15-22	Col. 3:1-11	Luke 7:1-17
S.	Wisd. 7:1-14 or Jer. 31:23-25	Col. 3:12-17	Luke 7:18-28(29-30) 31-35

		Year 2	
S.	Exod. 28:1-4, 30-38	I John 2:18-29	Mark 6:30-44
M.	Exod. 32:1-20	Col. 3:18-4:6(7-18)	Matt. 5:1-10
T.	Exod. 32:21-34	I Thess. 1:1-10	Matt. 5:11-16
W.	Exod. 33:1-23	I Thess. 2:1-12	Matt. 5:17-20
Th.	Exod. 34:1-17	I Thess. 2:13-20	Matt. 5:21-26
F.	Exod. 34:18-35	I Thess. 3:1-13	Matt. 5:27-37
S.	Exod. 40:18-38	I Thess. 4:1-12	Matt. 5:38-48

O Savior Christ, you lead to immortal happiness those who commit themselves to you. Grant that we, being weak, presume not to trust in ourselves, but may always have you before our eyes, to follow you, our guide; that you, who only know the way, may lead us to our heavenly desires. To you with the Father and the Holy Spirit be glory forever. (149)

V SUNDAY OF EASTER

THE NEW LIFE

"If we walk in the light, as he is in the light, we have fellowship with one another, and the blood of Jesus his Son cleanses us from all sin." I John 1:7

PSALMS FOR THE WEEK: (see table, pp. 58-59, Easter)

HYMN FOR THE WEEK

"At the Lamb's high feast we sing" (210)

LESSONS

Year 1

S.	Wisd. 7:22-8:1 or Isa. 32:1-8	II Thess. 2:13-17	Matt. 7:7-14
M.	Wisd. 9:1, 7-8 or Jer. 32:1-15	Col. 3:18-4:18	Luke 7:36-50
T.	Wisd. 10:1-4(5-12) 13-21 or Jer. 32:16-25	Rom. 12:1-21	Luke 8:1-15
W.	Wisd. 13:1-9 or Jer. 32:36-44	Rom. 13:1-14	Luke 8:16-25
Th.	Wisd. 14:27-15:3 or Jer. 33:1-13	Rom. 14:1-12	Luke 8:26-39
F.	Wisd. 16:15-17:1 or Deut. 31:30-32:14	Rom. 14:13-23	Luke 8:40-56
S.	Wisd. 19:1-8, 18-22 or Deut. 32:34-41(42)43	Rom. 15:1-13	Luke 9:1-17

Year 2

S.	Lev. 8:1-13, 30-36	Heb. 12:1-14	Luke 4:16-30
M.	Lev. 16:1-19	I Thess. 4:13-18	Matt. 6:1-6, 16-18
T.	Lev. 16:20-34	I Thess. 5:1-11	Matt. 6:7-15
W.	Lev. 19:1-18	I Thess 5:12-28	Matt. 6:19-24
Th.	Lev. 19:26-37	II Thess. 1:1-12	Matt. 6:25-34
F.	Lev. 23:1-22	II Thess. 2:1-17	Matt. 7:1-12
S.	Lev. 23:23-44	II Thess. 3:1-18	Matt. 7:13-21

Almighty and everlasting God, who in the Easter mystery established the new covenant of reconciliation: Grant that all who have been reborn into the fellowship of Christ's body may show forth in their lives what they profess by their faith; through Jesus Christ our Lord, who lives and reigns with you and the Holy Spirit, one God, for ever and ever. (150)

VI SUNDAY OF EASTER

THE SPIRIT AND THE CHURCH

"I will pour out a spirit of compassion and supplication."

Zechariah 12:10

PSALMS FOR THE WEEK: (see table, pp. 58-59, Easter)

HYMN FOR THE WEEK

"Dear Christians one and all rejoice" (299)

LESSONS		*Year* 1	
S.	Ecclus. 43:1-12, 27-32	*I Tim.* 3:14-4:5	*Matt.* 13:24-34a
	or *Deut.* 15:1-11		
M.	Deut. 8:1-10	*James* 1:1-15	*Luke* 9:18-27
	or *Deut.* 18:9-14		
T.	Deut. 8:11-20	*James* 1:16-27	*Luke* 11:1-13
	or *Deut.* 18:15-22		
W.	Bar. 3:24-37	*James* 5:13-18	*Luke* 12:22-31
	or *Deut.* 19:1-7		

		Year 2	
S.	Lev. 25:1-17	*James* 1:2-8, 16-18	*Luke* 12:13-21
M.	Lev. 25:35-55	*Col.* 1:9-14	*Matt.* 13:1-16
T.	Lev. 26:1-20	*I Tim.* 2:1-6	*Matt.* 13:18-23
W.	Lev. 26:27-42	*Eph.* 1:1-10	*Matt.* 22:41-46

God, our heavenly Father, through your Son you have promised us the Holy Spirit. Send down upon us that Spirit, that he may teach us to show forth your praise, not only here on earth in weakness, since we know your power and glory only from afar, but also in power and glory on that day when, united with the choir of angels, we shall see you face to face; through Jesus Christ, your Son, our Lord. (151)

THE ASCENSION OF OUR LORD

THE CORONATION OF CHRIST

"We see Jesus, who for a little while was made lower than the angels, crowned with glory and honor because of the suffering of death."   Hebrews 2:9

PSALMS FOR THE WEEK: (see table, pp. 58-59, Easter)

HYMN FOR THE WEEK

"Up through endless ranks of angels" (159)

LESSONS		Year 1	
Th.	Ezek. 1:1-14, 24-28b	Heb. 2:5-8	Matt. 28:16-20
F.	Ezek. 1:28-3:3	Heb. 4:14-5:6	Luke 9:28-36
S.	Ezek. 3:4-17	Heb. 5:7-14	Luke 9:37-50

		Year 2	
Th.	Dan. 7:9-14	Heb. 2:5-18	Matt. 28:16-20
F.	I Sam. 2:1-10	Eph. 2:1-10	Matt. 7:22-27
S.	Num. 11:16-17, 24-29	Eph. 2:11-22	Matt. 7:28-8:4

Lord Jesus Christ, after your resurrection you gloriously ascended into heaven. Grant us the help of your grace, that as you promised to dwell with us always on earth, so in heart and mind we may never cease to dwell with you in heaven, where with the Father and the Holy Spirit you live and reign, one God, now and forever. (152)

VII SUNDAY OF EASTER
CHRIST THE INTERCESSOR

"Since then we have a great high priest who has passed through the heavens, Jesus, the Son of God, let us hold fast our confession." *Hebrews 4:14*

PSALMS FOR THE WEEK: (see table, pp. 58-59, Easter)

HYMN FOR THE WEEK

"O love, how deep, how broad, how high" (88)

LESSONS		*Year 1*	
S.	*Ezek.* 3:16-27	*Eph.* 2:1-10	*Matt.* 10:24-33, 40-42
M.	*Ezek.* 4:1-17	*Heb.* 6:1-12	*Luke* 9:51-62
T.	*Ezek.* 7:10-15, 23b-27	*Heb.* 6:13-20	*Luke* 10:1-17
W.	*Ezek.* 11:14-25	*Heb.* 7:1-17	*Luke* 10:17-24
Th.	*Ezek.* 18:1-4, 19-32	*Heb.* 7:18-28	*Luke* 10:25-37
F.	*Ezek.* 34:17-31	*Heb.* 8:1-13	*Luke* 10:38-42
S.	*Ezek.* 43:1-12	*Heb.* 9:1-14	*Luke* 11:14-23

		Year 2	
S.	*Exod.* 3:1-12	*Heb.* 12:18-29	*Luke* 10:17-24
M.	*Josh.* 1:1-9	*Eph.* 3:1-13	*Matt.* 8:5-17
T.	*I Sam.* 16:1-13a	*Eph.* 3:14-21	*Matt.* 8:18-27
W.	*Isa.* 4:2-6	*Eph.* 4:1-16	*Matt.* 8:28-34
Th.	*Zech.* 4:1-14	*Eph.* 4:17-32	*Matt.* 9:1-8
F.	*Jer.* 31:27-34	*Eph.* 5:1-32	*Matt.* 9:9-17
S.	*Ezek.* 36:22-27	*Eph.* 6:1-24	*Matt.* 9:18-26

Almighty, everlasting God, hear the prayers of your church which waits for you, and grant that the splendor of your glory may shine upon it and illumine the hearts of your reborn children. Prepare us by your grace to receive your Holy Spirit; through Jesus Christ our Lord. (153)

THE DAY OF PENTECOST
The Soul of the Church

"Not by might, nor by power, but by my Spirit, says the Lord of hosts." Zechariah 4:6

PSALMS FOR THE WEEK: (see table, pp. 58-59, Easter, for Sunday; General Week 1 for Monday-Saturday)

HYMN FOR THE WEEK

"Come, Holy Ghost, God and Lord" (163)

LESSONS		Year 1	
S.	Isa. 11:1-9	I Cor. 2:1-13	John 14:21-29
M.	Isa. 63:7-14	II Tim. 1:1-14	Luke 11:24-36
T.	Isa. 63:15-64:9	II Tim. 1:15-2:13	Luke 11:37-52
W.	Isa. 65:1-12	II Tim. 2:14-26	Luke 11:53-12:12
Th.	Isa. 65:17-25	II Tim. 3:1-17	Luke 12:13-31
F.	Isa. 66:1-6	II Tim. 4:1-8	Luke 12:32-48
S.	Isa. 66:7-14	II Tim. 4:9-22	Luke 12:49-59

		Year 2	
S.	Deut. 16:9-12	Acts 4:18-21, 23-33	John 4:19-26
M.	Ezek. 33:1-11	I John 1:1-10	Matt. 9:27-34
T.	Ezek. 33:21-33	I John 2:1-11	Matt. 9:35-10:4
W.	Ezek. 34:1-16	I John 2:12-17	Matt. 10:5-15
Th.	Ezek. 37:21b-28	I John 2:18-29	Matt. 10:16-23
F.	Ezek. 39:21-29	I John 3:1-10	Matt. 10:24-33
S.	Ezek. 47:1-12	I John 3:11-18	Matt. 10:34-42

Lord Jesus Christ, Son of the almighty God, send your Holy Spirit into our hearts through your blessed word, that he may rule and guide us according to your will; strengthen us in every trial and need; and lead us, past all error, into your truth; that we may stand fast in faith, increase in love and all good works, and by the sure hope of your grace, which you have obtained for us by your death, be saved eternally; for you live and reign with the Father and the Holy Spirit for ever and ever. (154)

THE HOLY TRINITY
I SUNDAY AFTER PENTECOST
THE MYSTERY OF GOD

"Holy, holy, holy is the Lord of hosts; the whole earth is full of his glory." Isaiah 6:3

PSALMS FOR THE WEEK: (see table, pp. 58-59, General Week 2)

HYMN FOR THE WEEK

"Creator Spirit, heavenly dove" (284)

LESSONS		*Year* 1	
S.	*Ecclus.* 43:1-12 (27-33) *or Deut.* 6:1-9(10-15)	*Eph.* 4:1-16	*John* 1:1-18
M.	*Ruth* 1:1-18	*I Tim.* 1:1-17	*Luke* 13:1-9
T.	*Ruth* 1:19-2:13	*I Tim.* 1:18-2:8	*Luke* 13:10-17
W.	*Ruth* 2:14-23	*I Tim.* 3:1-16	*Luke* 13:18-30
Th.	*Ruth* 3:1-18	*I Tim.* 4:1-16	*Luke* 13:31-35
F.	*Ruth* 4:1-22	*I Tim.* 5:17-22 (23-25)	*Luke* 14:1-11
S.	*Deut.* 1:1-8	*I Tim.* 6:6-21	*Luke* 14:12-24

		Year 2	
S.	*Job* 38:1-11; 42:1-5	*Rev.* 19:4-16	*John* 1:29-34
M.	*Prov.* 3:11-20	*I John* 3:18-4:6	*Matt.* 11:1-6
T.	*Prov.* 4:1-27	*I John* 4:7-21	*Matt.* 11:7-15
W.	*Prov.* 6:1-19	*I John* 5:1-12	*Matt.* 11:16-24
Th.	*Prov.* 7:1-27	*I John* 5:13-21	*Matt.* 11:25-30
F.	*Prov.* 8:1-21	*II John* 1-13	*Matt.* 12:1-14
S.	*Prov.* 8:22-36	*III John* 1-15	*Matt.* 12:15-21

Lord God, almighty, immortal, invisible, the mysteries of whose being are unsearchable: Accept our praises for the revelation which you have made of yourself, Father, Son, and Holy Spirit, three persons and one God; and mercifully grant that, ever holding fast this faith, we may magnify your glorious name; for you live and reign, one God, now and forever. (155)

"God has made him both Lord and Christ, this Jesus whom you crucified."   Acts 2:36

PSALMS FOR THE WEEK: (see table, pp. 58-59, General Week 3)

HYMN FOR THE WEEK

"To God the Holy Spirit let us pray" (317)

LESSONS	Year 1		
S.	*Deut.* 4:1-9	*Rev.* 7:1-4, 9-17	*Matt.* 12:33-45
M.	*Deut.* 4:9-14	*II Cor.* 1:1-11	*Luke* 14:25-35
T.	*Deut.* 4:15-24	*II Cor.* 1:12-22	*Luke* 15:1-10
W.	*Deut.* 4:25-31	*II Cor.* 1:23-2:17	*Luke* 15:1-2, 11-32
Th.	*Deut.* 4:32-40	*II Cor.* 3:1-18	*Luke* 16:1-9
F.	*Deut.* 5:1-22	*II Cor.* 4:1-12	*Luke* 16:10-17(18)
S.	*Deut.* 5:22-33	*II Cor.* 4:13-5:10	*Luke* 16:19-31

	Year 2		
S.	*Prov.* 9:1-12	*Acts* 8:14-25	*Luke* 10:25-28, 38-42
M.	*Prov.* 10:1-12	*I Tim.* 1:1-17	*Matt.* 12:22-32
T.	*Prov.* 15:16-33	*I Tim.* 1:18-2:15	*Matt.* 12:33-42
W.	*Prov.* 17:1-20	*I Tim.* 3:1-16	*Matt.* 12:43-50
Th.	*Prov.* 21:30-22:6	*I Tim.* 4:1-16	*Matt.* 13:24-30
F.	*Prov.* 23:19-21, 29-24:2	*I Tim.* 5:17-22 (23-25)	*Matt.* 13:31-35
S.	*Prov.* 25:15-28	*I Tim.* 6:6-21	*Matt.* 13:36-43

Almighty, everlasting God, you have given us the promise of your divine life. Bestow upon us your Holy Spirit, that, quickened by your word, we may lay hold on eternal life by strong faith in your Son, and in him be saved; through Jesus Christ, your Son, our Lord. (156)

III SUNDAY AFTER PENTECOST

"Come to me, all who labor and are heavy-laden, and I will give you rest."   Matthew 11:28

PSALMS FOR THE WEEK: (see table, pp. 58-59, General Week 4)

HYMN FOR THE WEEK

"When in the hour of deepest need" (303)

LESSONS		Year I	
S.	Deut. 11:1-12	Rev. 10:1-11	Matt. 13:44-58
M.	Deut. 11:13-19	II Cor. 5:11-6:2	Luke 17:1-10
T.	Deut. 12:1-12	II Cor. 6:3-13 (14-7:1)	Luke 17:11-19
W.	Deut. 13:1-11	II Cor. 7:2-16	Luke 17:20-37
Th.	Deut. 16:18-20; 17:14-20	II Cor. 8:1-16	Luke 18:1-8
F.	Deut. 26:1-11	II Cor. 8:16-24	Luke 18:9-14
S.	Deut. 29:2-15	II Cor. 9:1-15	Luke 18:15-30

		Year 2	
S.	Eccles. 1:1-11	Acts 8:26-40	Luke 11:1-13
M.	Eccles. 2:1-15	Gal. 1:1-17	Matt. 13:44-52
T.	Eccles. 2:16-26	Gal. 1:18-2:10	Matt. 13:53-58
W.	Eccles. 3:1-15	Gal. 2:11-21	Matt. 14:1-12
Th.	Eccles. 3:16-4:3	Gal. 3:1-14	Matt. 14:13-21
F.	Eccles. 5:1-7	Gal. 3:15-22	Matt. 14:22-36
S.	Eccles. 5:8-20	Gal. 3:23-4:11	Matt. 15:1-20

Almighty God, grant to your Church your Holy Spirit and the wisdom which comes down from heaven, that your word may not be bound but have free course and be preached to the joy and edifying of Christ's holy people, that in steadfast faith we may serve you and in the confession of your name abide to the end; through Jesus Christ our Lord. (157)

IV SUNDAY AFTER PENTECOST

"The Son of man came to seek and to save the lost."

Luke 19:10

PSALMS FOR THE WEEK: (see table, pp. 58-59, General Week 1)

HYMN FOR THE WEEK

"O God, O Lord of heaven and earth" (396)

LESSONS	Year 1		
S.	Deut. 29:16-29	Rev. 12:1-12	Matt. 15:29-39
M.	Deut. 30:1-10	II Cor. 10:1-18	Luke 18:31-43
T.	Deut. 30:11-20	II Cor. 11:1-21a	Luke 19:1-10
W.	Deut. 31:30-32:14	II Cor. 11:21b-33	Luke 19:11-27
Th.	Ecclus. 44:19-45:5 or Song of Sol. 1:1-3, 9-11, 15-16a; 2:1-3a	II Cor. 12:1-10	Luke 19:28-40
F.	Ecclus. 45:6-16 or Song of Sol. 2:8-13, 4:1-4a, 5-7, 9-11	II Cor. 12:11-21	Luke 19:41-48
S.	Ecclus. 46:1-10 or Song of Sol. 5:10-16; 7:1-2(3-5) 6-7a(9); 8:6-7	II Cor. 13:1-14	Luke 20:1-8

	Year 2		
S.	Eccles. 6:1-12	Acts 10:9-23	Luke 12:32-40
M.	Eccles. 7:1-14	Gal. 4:12-20	Matt. 15:21-28
T.	Eccles. 8:14-9:10	Gal. 4:21-31	Matt. 15:29-39
W.	Eccles. 9:11-18	Gal. 5:1-15	Matt. 16:1-12
Th.	Eccles. 11:1-8	Gal. 5:16-24	Matt. 16:13-20
F.	Eccles. 11:9-12:14	Gal. 5:25-6:10	Matt. 16:21-28
S.	Num. 3:1-13	Gal. 6:11-18	Matt. 17:1-13

Almighty and merciful God, you are not willing that any should perish, but that all should come to repentance. Grant that by your word we may again and again be convicted of our many sins, but also fervently grasp anew the comfort of your Spirit and of faith, in order that we may be justified in your Son and be saved through him, Jesus Christ our Lord. (158)

V SUNDAY AFTER PENTECOST

"Fear not, for I have redeemed you; I have called you by
name, you are mine."   Isaiah 43:1

PSALMS FOR THE WEEK: (see table, pp. 58-59, General Week 2)

HYMN FOR THE WEEK

"Lord of our life, and God of our salvation" (366)

LESSONS   *Year* 1

S.	*Ecclus.* 46:11-20 or *Exod.* 6:2-13; 7:1-6	*Rev.* 15:1-8	*Matt.* 18:1-14
M.	*I Sam.* 1:1-20	*Acts* 1:1-14	*Luke* 20:9-19
T.	*I Sam.* 1:21-2:11	*Acts* 1:15-26	*Luke* 20:19-26
W.	*I Sam.* 2:12-26	*Acts* 2:1-21	*Luke* 20:27-40
Th.	*I Sam.* 2:27-36	*Acts* 2:22-36	*Luke* 20:41-21:4
F.	*I Sam.* 3:1-21	*Acts* 2:37-47	*Luke* 21:5-19
S.	*I Sam.* 4:1b-11	*Acts* 4:32-5:11	*Luke* 21:20-28

Year 2

S.	*Num.* 6:22-27	*Acts* 13:1-12	*Luke* 12:41-48
M.	*Num.* 9:15-23; 10:29-36	*Rom.* 1:1-15	*Matt.* 17:14-21
T.	*Num.* 11:1-23	*Rom.* 1:16-25	*Matt.* 17:22-27
W.	*Num.* 11:24-33 (34-35)	*Rom.* 1:28-2:11	*Matt.* 18:1-9
Th.	*Num.* 12:1-16	*Rom.* 2:12-24	*Matt.* 18:10-20
F.	*Num.* 13:1-3, 21-30	*Rom.* 2:25-3:8	*Matt.* 18:21-35
S.	*Num.* 13:31-14:25	*Rom.* 3:9-20	*Matt.* 19:1-12

O most loving Father, you want us to give thanks for all
things, to fear nothing except losing you, and to lay all our cares
on you, knowing that you care for us. Protect us from faithless
fears and worldly anxieties, and grant that no clouds in this
mortal life may hide from us the light of your immortal love
shown to us in your Son, Jesus Christ our Lord. (159)

"One thing is needful. Mary has chosen the good portion, which shall not be taken away from her." Luke 10:42

PSALMS FOR THE WEEK: (see table, pp. 58-59, General Week 3)

HYMN FOR THE WEEK

"Even as we live each day" (350)

LESSONS Year 1

S.	I Sam. 4:12-22	James 1:1-18	Matt. 19:23-30
M.	I Sam. 5:1-12	Acts 5:12-26	Luke 21:29-36
T.	I Sam. 6:1-16	Acts 5:27-42	Luke 21:37-22:13
W.	I Sam. 7:2-17	Acts 6:1-15	Luke 22:14-23
Th.	I Sam. 8:1-22	Acts 6:15-7:16	Luke 22:24-30
F.	I Sam. 9:1-14	Acts 7:17-29	Luke 22:31-38
S.	I Sam. 9:15-10:1	Acts 7:30-43	Luke 22:39-51

Year 2

S.	Num. 14:26-45	Acts 15:1-12	Luke 12:49-56
M.	Num. 16:1-19	Rom. 3:21-31	Matt. 19:13-22
T.	Num. 16:20-35	Rom. 4:1-12	Matt. 19:23-30
W.	Num. 16:36-50	Rom. 4:13-25	Matt. 20:1-16
Th.	Num. 17:1-11	Rom. 5:1-11	Matt. 20:17-28
F.	Num. 20:1-13	Rom. 5:12-21	Matt. 20:29-34
S.	Num. 20:14-29	Rom. 6:1-11	Matt. 21:1-11

Almighty and everlasting God, through your Son you have assured forgiveness of sins and deliverance from eternal death. Strengthen us by your Holy Spirit, that we may daily increase in this faith and hold fast the hope that we shall not die, but fall asleep and on the last day be raised to everlasting life; through Jesus Christ our Lord. (160)

VII SUNDAY AFTER PENTECOST

"Whoever hears you hears me, and whoever rejects you rejects me, and whoever rejects me rejects him who sent me."

Luke 10:16

PSALMS FOR THE WEEK: (see table, pp. 58-59, General Week 4)

HYMN FOR THE WEEK

"O Christ our light, O Radiance true" (380)

LESSONS

Year 1

S.	I Sam. 10:1-16	Rom. 4:13-25	Matt. 21:23-32
M.	I Sam. 10:17-27	Acts 7:44-8:1a	Luke 22:52-62
T.	I Sam. 11:1-15	Acts 8:1b-13	Luke 22:63-71
W.	I Sam. 12:1-6 (7-15)16-25	Acts 8:14-25	Luke 23:1-12
Th.	I Sam. 13:5-18	Acts 8:26-40	Luke 23:13-25
F.	I Sam. 13:19-14:15	Acts 9:1-9	Luke 23:26-31
S.	I Sam. 14:16-30	Acts 9:10-19a	Luke 23:32-43

Year 2

S.	Num. 21:4-9, 21-35	Acts 17:(12-21) 22-34	Luke 13:10-17
M.	Num. 22:1-21	Rom. 6:12-23	Matt. 21:12-22
T.	Num. 22:21-38	Rom. 7:1-12	Matt. 21:23-32
W.	Num. 22:41-23:12	Rom. 7:13-25	Matt. 21:33-46
Th.	Num. 23:11-26	Rom. 8:1-11	Matt. 22:1-14
F.	Num. 24:1-13	Rom. 8:12-17	Matt. 22:15-22
S.	Num. 24:12-25	Rom. 8:18-25	Matt. 22:23-40

Lord God, heavenly Father, you have bound us together in one body through your Holy Spirit. Help us to serve one another willingly and forgive one another from our hearts; through Jesus Christ our Lord. (161)

"Bear one another's burdens, and so fulfill the law of Christ." Galatians 6:2

PSALMS FOR THE WEEK: (see table, pp. 58-59, General Week I)

HYMN FOR THE WEEK

"Forth in thy name, O Lord I go" (505)

LESSONS

		Year 1	
S.	I Sam. 14:36-45	Rom. 5:1-11	Matt. 22:1-14
M.	I Sam. 15:1-3, 7-23	Acts 9:19b-31	Luke 23:44-56a
T.	I Sam. 15:24-35	Acts 9:32-43	Luke 23:56b-24:11(12)
W.	I Sam. 16:1-13	Acts 10:1-16	Luke 24:13-35
Th.	I Sam. 16:14-17:11	Acts 10:17-33	Luke 24:36-53
F.	I Sam. 17:17-30	Acts 10:34-48	Mark 1:1-13
S.	I Sam. 17:31-49	Acts 11:1-18	Mark 1:14-28

		Year 2	
S.	Num. 27:12-23	Acts 19:11-20	Mark 1:14-20
M.	Num. 32:1-6, 16-27	Rom. 8:26-30	Matt. 23:1-12
T.	Num. 35:1-3, 9-15, 30-34	Rom. 8:31-39	Matt. 23:13-26
W.	Deut. 1:1-18	Rom. 9:1-18	Matt. 23:27-39
Th.	Deut. 3:18-28	Rom. 9:19-33	Matt. 24:1-14
F.	Deut. 31:7-13, 24-32:4	Rom. 10:1-13	Matt. 24:15-31
S.	Deut. 34:1-12	Rom. 10:14-21	Matt. 24:32-51

Lord, take our bodies and our minds and make them wholly yours. So increase your grace in us that not our own desires but your holy will may rule us all in all; through Jesus Christ our Lord. (162)

IX SUNDAY AFTER PENTECOST

"Walk as children of light, for the fruit of light is found in all that is good and right and true."   Ephesians 5:8-9

PSALMS FOR THE WEEK: (see table, pp. 58-59, General Week 2)

HYMN FOR THE WEEK

"O Holy Spirit, enter in" (459)

LESSONS	Year 1		
S.	I Sam. 17:50-18:4	Rom. 10:4-17	Matt. 23:29-39
M.	I Sam. 18:5-16 (17-27a)27b-30	Acts 11:19-30	Mark 1:29-45
T.	I Sam. 19:1-18 (19-24)	Acts 12:1-17	Mark: 2:1-12
W.	I Sam. 20:1-23	Acts 12:18-25	Mark 2:13-22
Th.	I Sam. 20:24-42	Acts 13:1-12	Mark 2:23-3:6
F.	I Sam. 21:1-15	Acts 13:13-25	Mark 3:7-19a
S.	I Sam. 22:1-23	Acts 13:26-43	Mark 3:19b-35

	Year 2		
S.	Josh. 1:1-18	Acts 21:3-15	Mark 1:21-27
M.	Josh. 2:1-14	Rom. 11:1-12	Matt. 25:1-13
T.	Josh. 2:15-24	Rom. 11:13-24	Matt. 25:14-30
W.	Josh. 3:1-13	Rom. 11:25-36	Matt. 25:31-46
Th.	Josh. 3:14-4:7	Rom. 12:1-8	Matt. 26:1-16
F.	Josh. 4:19-5:1, 10-15	Rom. 12:9-21	Matt. 26:17-25
S.	Josh. 6:1-14	Rom. 13:1-7	Matt. 26:26-35

Lord God, whose strength is sufficient for all who lay hold on it, grant us in you to comfort our hearts and be strong. Humility, meekness, temperance, purity, largeheartedness, sympathy, zeal—grant us these evidences of faith, servants of hope, fruits of love; for the sake of Jesus Christ, our strength, our righteousness, and our hope of glory. (163)

X SUNDAY AFTER PENTECOST

"Behold, the kingdom of God is within you."

Luke 17:21 (KJV)

PSALMS FOR THE WEEK: (see table, pp. 58-59, General Week 3)

HYMN FOR THE WEEK

"From God can nothing move me" (468)

LESSONS		Year 1	
S.	I Sam. 23:7-18	Rom. 11:33-12:2	Matt. 25:14-30
M.	I Sam. 24:1-22	Acts 13:44-52	Mark 4:1-20
T.	I Sam. 25:1-22	Acts 14:1-18	Mark 4:21-34
W.	I Sam. 25:23-44	Acts 14:19-28	Mark 4:35-41
Th.	I Sam. 28:3-20	Acts 15:1-11	Mark 5:1-20
F.	I Sam. 31:1-13	Acts 15:12-21	Mark 5:21-43
S.	II Sam. 1:1-16	Acts 15:22-35	Mark 6:1-13

		Year 2	
S.	Josh. 6:15-27	Acts 22:30-23:11	Mark 2:1-12
M.	Josh. 7:1-13	Rom. 13:8-14	Matt. 26:36-46
T.	Josh. 8:1-22	Rom. 14:1-12	Matt. 26:47-56
W.	Josh. 8:30-35	Rom. 14:13-23	Matt. 26:57-68
Th.	Josh. 9:3-21	Rom. 15:1-13	Matt. 26:69-75
F.	Josh. 9:22-10:15	Rom. 15:14-24	Matt. 27:1-10
S.	Josh. 23:1-16	Rom. 15:25-33	Matt. 27:11-23

Lord, you have promised to grant what we pray in the name of your Son. Teach us to pray aright and to laud and praise you with all your saints in the fullness of life everlasting; through Jesus Christ our Lord. (164)

XI SUNDAY AFTER PENTECOST

"God opposes the proud, but gives grace to the humble."

I Peter 5:5

PSALMS FOR THE WEEK: (see table, pp. 58-59, General Week 4)

HYMN FOR THE WEEK

"Jesus, priceless treasure" (457, 458)

LESSONS		Year 1	
S.	II Sam. 1:17-27	Rom. 12:9-21	Matt. 25:31-46
M.	II Sam. 2:1-11	Acts 15:36-16:5	Mark 6:14-29
T.	II Sam. 3:6-21	Acts 16:6-15	Mark 6:30-46
W.	II Sam. 3:22-39	Acts 16:16-24	Mark 6:47-56
Th.	II Sam. 4:1-12	Acts 16:25-40	Mark 7:1-23
F.	II Sam. 5:1-12	Acts 17:1-15	Mark 7:24-37
S.	II Sam. 5:22-6:11	Acts 17:16-34	Mark 8:1-10

		Year 2	
S.	Josh. 24:1-15	Acts 28:23-31	Mark 2:23-28
M.	Josh. 24:16-33	Rom. 16:1-16	Matt. 27:24-31
T.	Judg. 2:1-5, 11-23	Rom. 16:17-27	Matt. 27:32-44
W.	Judg. 3:12-30	Acts 1:1-14	Matt. 27:45-54
Th.	Judg. 4:4-23	Acts 1:15-26	Matt. 27:55-56
F.	Judg. 5:1-18	Acts 2:1-21	Matt. 28:1-10
S.	Judg. 5:19-31	Acts 2:22-36	Matt. 28:11-20

Almighty, everlasting God, mercifully behold us who have been made your children through baptism and, according to your grace, grant that your promises may be fulfilled in us; through Jesus Christ our Lord. (165)

XII SUNDAY AFTER PENTECOST

"How great is your goodness, O Lord . . . which you have done in the sight of all for those who put their trust in you."

Psalm 31:19

PSALMS FOR THE WEEK: (see table, pp. 58-59, General Week 1)

HYMN FOR THE WEEK

"If God himself be for me" (454)

LESSONS		Year 1	
S.	II Sam. 6:12-23	Rom. 14:7-12	John 1:43-51
M.	II Sam. 7:1-17	Acts 18:1-11	Mark 8:11-21
T.	II Sam. 7:18-29	Acts 18:12-28	Mark 8:22-33
W.	II Sam. 9:1-13	Acts 19:1-10	Mark 8:34-9:1
Th.	II Sam. 11:1-27	Acts 19:11-20	Mark 9:2-13
F.	II Sam. 12:1-14	Acts 19:21-41	Mark 9:14-29
S.	II Sam. 12:15-31	Acts 20:1-16	Mark 9:30-41

		Year 2	
S.	Judg. 6:1-24	II Cor. 9:6-15	Mark 3:20-30
M.	Judg. 6:25-40	Acts 2:37-47	John 1:1-18
T.	Judg. 7:1-18	Acts 3:1-11	John 1:19-28
W.	Judg. 7:19-8:12	Acts 3:12-26	John 1:29-42
Th.	Judg. 8:22-35	Acts 4:1-12	John 1:43-51
F.	Judg. 9:1-16, 19-21	Acts 4:13-31	John 2:1-12
S.	Judg. 9:22-25, 50-57	Acts 4:32-5:11	John 2:13-25

Merciful God, you resist the proud but give grace to the humble. Help us to trust you utterly, to rest our hope and confidence in you, and to serve you with pure hearts; through Jesus Christ our Lord. (166)

XIII SUNDAY AFTER PENTECOST

"He will not break a bruised reed or quench a smoldering wick."   Matthew 12:20

PSALMS FOR THE WEEK: (see table, pp. 58-59, General Week 2)

HYMN FOR THE WEEK

"When in the hour of deepest need" (303)

LESSONS		*Year 1*	
S.	II Sam. 13:1-22	Rom. 15:1-13	John 3:22-36
M.	II Sam. 13:23-39	Acts 20:17-38	Mark 9:42-50
T.	II Sam. 14:1-20	Acts 21:1-14	Mark 10:1-16
W.	II Sam. 14:21-33	Acts 21:15-26	Mark 10:17-31
Th.	II Sam. 15:1-18	Acts 21:27-36	Mark 10:32-45
F.	II Sam. 15:19-37	Acts 21:37-22:16	Mark 10:46-52
S.	II Sam. 16:1-23	Acts 22:17-29	Mark 11:1-11

		Year 2	
S.	Judg. 11:1-11, 29-40	II Cor. 11:21b-31	Mark 4:35-41
M.	Judg. 12:1-7	Acts 5:12-26	John 3:1-21
T.	Judg. 13:1-15	Acts 5:27-42	John 3:22-36
W.	Judg. 13:15-24	Acts 6:1-15	John 4:1-26
Th.	Judg. 14:1-19	Acts 6:15-7:16	John 4:27-42
F.	Judg. 14:20-15:20	Acts 7:17-29	John 4:43-54
S.	Judg. 16:1-14	Acts 7:30-43	John 5:1-18

Lord God, heavenly Father, you desire not the death of sinners, but rather that they should turn from sin and live. Mercifully turn away the punishment of our iniquities and, that we may be edified, grant us your Spirit and your power; through Jesus Christ our Lord. (167)

XIV SUNDAY AFTER PENTECOST

"As you did it to one of the least of these my brethren, you did it to me."   Matthew 25:40

PSALMS FOR THE WEEK: (see table, pp. 58-59, General Week 3)

HYMN FOR THE WEEK

"A multitude comes from the east and the west" (313)

LESSONS		*Year 1*	
S.	II Sam. 17:1-23	Gal. 3:6-14	John 5:30-47
M.	II Sam. 17:24-18:8	Acts 22:30-23:11	Mark 11:12-26
T.	II Sam. 18:9-18	Acts 23:12-24	Mark 11:27-12:12
W.	II Sam. 18:19-33	Acts 23:23-25	Mark 12:13-27
Th.	II Sam. 19:1-23	Acts 24:1-23	Mark 12:28-34
F.	II Sam. 19:24-43	Acts 24:24-25:12	Mark 12:35-44
S.	II Sam. 23:1-7, 13-17	Acts 25:13-27	Mark 13:1-13

		Year 2	
S.	Judg. 16:15-31	II Cor. 13:1-11	Mark 5:25-34
M.	Judg. 17:1-13	Acts 7:44-8:1a	John 5:19-29
T.	Judg. 18:1-15	Acts 8:1-13	John 5:30-47
W.	Judg. 18:16-31	Acts 8:14-25	John 6:1-15
Th.	Job 1:1-22	Acts 8:26-40	John 6:16-27
F.	Job 2:1-13	Acts 9:1-9	John 6:27-40
S.	Job 3:1-26	Acts 9:10-19a	John 6:41-51

Merciful God, kindle in our hearts the fire of your love, that we may serve you and our neighbor according to your will; through Jesus Christ our Lord. (168)

XV SUNDAY AFTER PENTECOST

"What does the Lord your God require of you, but to fear the Lord your God, to walk in all his ways, to love him, to serve the Lord your God with all your heart and with all your soul."

Deuteronomy 10:12

PSALMS FOR THE WEEK: (see table, pp. 58-59, General Week 4)

HYMN FOR THE WEEK

"Son of God, eternal Savior" (364)

LESSONS   *Year 1*

S.	II Sam. 24:1-2, 10-25	Gal. 3:23-4:7	John 8:12-20
M.	I Kings 1:(1-4)5-31	Acts 26:1-23	Mark 13:14-27
T.	I Kings 1:32-2:4 (5-46a)46b	Acts 26:24-27:8	Mark 13:28-37
W.	I Kings 3:1-15	Acts 27:9-26	Mark 14:1-11
Th.	I Kings 3:16-28	Acts 27:27-44	Mark 14:12-26
F.	I Kings 5:1-6:1, 7	Acts 28:1-16	Mark 14:27-42
S.	I Kings 7:51-8:21	Acts 28:17-31	Mark 14:43-52

Year 2

S.	Job. 4:1-6, 12-21	Rev. 4:1-11	Mark 6:1-6a
M.	Job 4:1; 5:1-11, 17-21, 26-27	Acts 9:19b-31	John 6:52-59
T.	Job 6:1-4, 8-15, 21	Acts 9:32-43	John 6:60-71
W.	Job 6:1; 7:1-21	Acts 10:1-16	John 7:1-13
Th.	Job 8:1-10, 20-22	Acts 10:17-33	John 7:14-36
F.	Job 9:1-15, 32-35	Acts 10:34-48	John 7:37-52
S.	Job 9:1; 10:1-9, 16-22	Acts 11:1-18	John 8:12-20

Almighty God, you richly and unceasingly furnish us with all good things and preserve us day by day. Make us to acknowledge this with our whole heart, that we may thank and praise you for your lovingkindness and mercy here and for evermore; through Jesus Christ our Lord. (169)

XVI SUNDAY AFTER PENTECOST

"Cast all your anxieties on him, for he cares about you."

I Peter 5:7

PSALMS FOR THE WEEK: (see table, pp. 58-59, General Week 1)

HYMN FOR THE WEEK

"Praise the almighty, my soul adore him!" (539)

LESSONS		Year 1	
S.	I Kings 8:22-30 (31-40)	I Tim. 4:7b-16	John 8:47-59
M.	II Chron. 6:32-7:7	James 2:1-13	Mark 14:53-65
T.	I Kings 8:65-9:9	James 2:14-26	Mark 14:66-72
W.	I Kings 9:24-10:13	James 3:1-12	Mark 15:1-11
Th.	I Kings 11:1-13	James 3:13-4:12	Mark 15:12-21
F.	I Kings 11:26-43	James 4:13-5:6	Mark 15:22-32
S.	I Kings 12:1-20	James 5:7-20	Mark 15:33-39

		Year 2	
S.	Job 11:1-9, 13-20	Rev. 5:1-14	Matt. 5:1-12
M.	Job 12:1-6, 13-25	Acts 11:19-30	John 8:21-32
T.	Job 12:1; 13:3-17, 21-27	Acts 12:1-17	John 8:33-47
W.	Job 12:1; 14:1-22	Acts 12:18-25	John 8:47-59
Th.	Job 16:16-22; 17:1, 13-16	Acts 13:1-12	John 9:1-17
F.	Job 19:1-7, 14-27	Acts 13:13-25	John 9:18-41
S.	Job 22:1-4, 21-23:7	Acts 13:26-43	John 10:1-18

Grant us, O Lord, not to mind earthly things, but to love things heavenly, and while we now dwell among things that are passing away, to cleave to those that shall abide forever; through Jesus Christ our Lord. (170)

XVII SUNDAY AFTER PENTECOST

"Our Savior Christ Jesus . . . abolished death and brought
life and immortality to light."   II Timothy 1:10

PSALMS FOR THE WEEK: (see table, pp. 58-59, General Week 2)

HYMN FOR THE WEEK

"Forgive our sins as we forgive" (307)

LESSONS   *Year* 1
S.	I Kings 12:21-33	Acts 4:18-31	John 10:31-42
M.	I Kings 13:1-10	Phil. 1:1-11	Mark 15:40-47
T.	I Kings 16:23-34	Phil. 1:12-30	Mark 16:1-8(9-20)
W.	I Kings 17:1-24	Phil. 2:1-11	Matt. 2:1-12
Th.	I Kings 18:1-19	Phil. 2:12-30	Matt. 2:13-23
F.	I Kings 18:20-40	Phil. 3:1-16	Matt. 3:1-12
S.	I Kings 18:41-19:8	Phil. 3:17-4:7	Matt. 3:13-17

Year 2
S.	Job 25:1-6; 27:1-6	Rev. 14:1-7, 13	Matt. 5:13-20
M.	Job 32:1-10, 19-33:1, 19-28	Acts 13:44-52	John 10:19-30
T.	Job 29:1-20	Acts 14:1-18	John 10:31-42
W.	Job 29:1; 30:1-2, 16-31	Acts 14:19-28	John 11:1-16
Th.	Job 29:1; 31:1-23	Acts 15:1-11	John 11:17-29
F.	Job 29:1; 31:24-40	Acts 15:12-21	John 11:30-44
S.	Job 38:1-17	Acts 15:22-35	John 11:45-54

Almighty and everlasting God, comfort of the sad and
strength to those who suffer: Let the prayers of your children
who are in any trouble rise to you. To everyone in distress grant
mercy, grant relief, grant refreshment; through Jesus Christ
our Lord. (171)

XVIII SUNDAY AFTER PENTECOST

"What does the Lord require of you but to do justice, and to love kindness, and to walk humbly with your God?" Micah 6:8

PSALMS FOR THE WEEK: (see table, pp. 58–59, General Week 3)

HYMN FOR THE WEEK

"Salvation unto us has come" (297)

LESSONS		Year 1	
S.	I Kings 19:8–21	Acts 5:34–42	John 11:45–57
M.	I Kings 21:1–16	I Cor. 1:1–19	Matt. 4:1–11
T.	I Kings 21:17–29	I Cor. 1:20–31	Matt. 4:12–17
W.	I Kings 22:1–28	I Cor. 2:1–13	Matt. 4:18–25
Th.	I Kings 22:29–45	I Cor. 2:14–3:15	Matt. 5:1–10
F.	II Kings 1:2–17	I Cor. 3:16–23	Matt. 5:11–16
S.	II Kings 2:1–18	I Cor. 4:1–7	Matt. 5:17–20

		Year 2	
S.	Job 38:1, 18–41	Rev. 18:1–8	Matt. 5:21–26
M.	Job 40:1–24	Acts 15:36–16:5	John 11:55–12:8
T.	Job 40:1; 41:1–11	Acts 16:6–15	John 12:9–19
W.	Job 42:1–17	Acts 16:16–24	John 12:20–26
Th.	Job 28:1–28	Acts 16:25–40	John 12:27–36a
F.	Esther 1:1–4, 10–19	Acts 17:1–15	John 12:36b–43
S.	Esther 2:5–8, 15–23	Acts 17:16–34	John 12:44–50

Lord God, grant unto us your Holy Spirit that we may hear and accept your word, in order that, being cleansed in mind and renewed in life, we may live to you, here and hereafter; through Jesus Christ our Lord. (172)

"This commandment we have from him, that he who loves God should love his brother also."   I John 4:21

PSALMS FOR THE WEEK: (see table, pp. 58-59, General Week 4)

HYMN FOR THE WEEK

"Lord, keep us steadfast in your word" (230)

LESSONS		*Year* 1	
S.	II Kings 4:8-37	Acts 9:10-31	Luke 3:7-18
M.	II Kings 5:1-19	I Cor. 4:8-21	Matt. 5:21-26
T.	II Kings 5:19-27	I Cor. 5:1-8	Matt. 5:27-37
W.	II Kings 6:1-23	I Cor. 5:9-6:11	Matt. 5:38-48
Th.	II Kings 9:1-16	I Cor. 6:12-20	Matt. 6:1-6, 16-18
F.	II Kings 9:17-37	I Cor. 7:1-9	Matt. 6:7-15
S.	II Kings 11:1-20a	I Cor. 7:10-24	Matt. 6:19-24

		Year 2	
S.	Esther 3:1-4:3	James 1:19-27	Matt. 6:1-6, 16-18
M.	Esther 4:4-17	Acts 18:1-11	Luke (1:1-4) 3:1-14
T.	Esther 5:1-14	Acts 18:12-28	Luke 3:15-22
W.	Esther 6:1-14	Acts 19:1-10	Luke 4:1-13
Th.	Esther 7:1-10	Acts 19:11-20	Luke 4:14-30
F.	Esther 8:1-8, 15-17	Acts 19:21-41	Luke 4:31-37
S.	Esther 9:1-32	Acts 20:1-16	Luke 4:38-44

Dear Father in heaven, you have revealed your love to us in Jesus Christ. Grant us your Holy Spirit, that we may love you with our whole heart and our neighbors as ourselves; through Jesus Christ our Lord. (173)

"God chose what is foolish in the world to shame the wise, God chose what is weak in the world to shame the strong."

I Corinthians 1:27

PSALMS FOR THE WEEK: (see table, pp. 58-59, General Week 1)

HYMN FOR THE WEEK

"The Church of Christ, in every age" (433)

LESSONS		Year 1	
S.	II Kings 17:1-18	Acts 9:36-43	Luke 5:1-11
M.	II Kings 17:24-41	I Cor. 7:25-31	Matt. 6:25-34
T.	II Chron. 29:1-3; 30:1(2-9)10-27	I Cor. 7:32-40	Matt. 7:1-12
W.	II Kings 18:9-25	I Cor. 8:1-13	Matt. 7:13-21
Th.	II Kings 18:28-37	I Cor. 9:1-15	Matt. 7:22-29
F.	II Kings 19:1-20	I Cor. 9:16-27	Matt. 8:1-17
S.	II Kings 19:21-36	I Cor. 10:1-13	Matt. 8:18-27

		Year 2	
S.	Hos. 1:1-2:1	James 3:1-13	Matt. 13:44-52
M.	Hos. 2:2-15	Acts 20:17-38	Luke 5:1-11
T.	Hos. 2:16-23	Acts 21:1-14	Luke 5:12-26
W.	Hos. 3:1-5	Acts 21:15-26	Luke 5:27-39
Th.	Hos. 4:1-10	Acts 21:27-36	Luke 6:1-11
F.	Hos. 4:11-19	Acts 21:37-22:16	Luke 6:12-26
S.	Hos. 5:1-7	Acts 22:17-29	Luke 6:27-38

Almighty and merciful God, for your mercy's sake, keep far from us all that opposes you, that, unhindered in body and soul, we may serve you with hearts set free; through Jesus Christ our Lord. (174)

"'The Lord knows those who are his,' and 'let every one who names the name of the Lord depart from iniquity.'"

II Timothy 2:19

PSALMS FOR THE WEEK: (see table, pp. 58-59, General Week 2)

HYMN FOR THE WEEK

"All who believe and are baptized" (194)

LESSONS

Year 1

S.	II Kings 20:1-21	Acts 12:1-17	Luke 7:11-17
M.	II Kings 21:1-18	I Cor. 10:14-11:1	Matt. 8:28-34
T.	II Kings 22:1-13	I Cor. 11:2(3-16) 17-22	Matt. 9:1-8
W.	II Kings 22:14-23:3	I Cor. 11:23-34	Matt. 9:9-17
Th.	II Kings 23:4-25	I Cor. 12:1-11	Matt. 9:18-26
F.	II Kings 23:36-24:17	I Cor. 12:12-26	Matt. 9:27-34
S.	Jer. 35:1-19	I Cor. 12:27-13:3	Matt. 9:35-10:4

Year 2

S.	Hos. 5:8-6:6	I Cor. 2:6-16	Matt. 14:1-12
M.	Hos. 6:7-7:7	Acts 22:30-23:11	Luke 6:39-49
T.	Hos. 7:8-16	Acts 23:12-24	Luke 7:1-17
W.	Hos. 8:1-14	Acts 23:23-35	Luke 7:18-35
Th.	Hos. 9:1-9	Acts 24:1-23	Luke 7:36-50
F.	Hos. 9:10-17	Acts 24:24-25:12	Luke 8:1-15
S.	Hos. 10:1-15	Acts 25:13-27	Acts 8:16-25

Almighty and merciful God, fulfill in us your promises and grant that when that day shall come we may sit down with all the redeemed at the heavenly feast and praise you in eternal light; through Jesus Christ our Lord. (175)

XXII SUNDAY AFTER PENTECOST

"I am the Lord your God; you shall have no other gods before me."   Exodus 20:2-3

PSALMS FOR THE WEEK: (see table, pp. 58-59, General Week 3)

HYMN FOR THE WEEK

"Father eternal, ruler of creation" (413)

LESSONS		Year 1	
S.	Jer. 36:1-10	Acts 14:8-18	Luke 7:36-50
M.	Jer. 36:11-26	I Cor. 13:(1-3)4-13	Matt. 10:5-15
T.	Jer. 36:27-37:2	I Cor. 14:1-12	Matt. 10:16-23
W.	Jer. 37:3-21	I Cor. 14:13-25	Matt. 10:24-33
Th.	Jer. 38:1-13	I Cor. 14:26-33a (33b-36)37-40	Matt. 10:34-42
F.	Jer. 38:14-28	I Cor. 15:1-11	Matt. 11:1-6
S.	Jer. 52:1-34	I. Cor. 15:12-29	Matt. 11:7-15

		Year 2	
S.	Hos. 11:1-11	I Cor. 4:9-16	Matt. 15:21-28
M.	Hos. 11:12-12:1	Acts 26:1-23	Luke 8:26-39
T.	Hos. 12:2-14	Acts 26:24-27:8	Luke 8:40-56
W.	Hos. 13:1-3	Acts 27:9-26	Luke 9:1-17
Th.	Hos. 13:4-8	Acts 27:27-44	Luke 9:18-27
F.	Hos. 13:9-16	Acts 28:1-16	Luke 9:28-36
S.	Hos. 14:1-9	Acts 28:17-31	Luke 9:37-50

Almighty, everlasting God, graciously look upon your church, for you alone are our strength and our salvation. Uphold us with your hand, that we may not stumble and fall; through Jesus Christ our Lord. (176)

XXIII SUNDAY AFTER PENTECOST

"Have mercy upon us, O Lord, have mercy." Psalm 123:4

PSALMS FOR THE WEEK: (see table, pp. 58-59, General Week 4)

HYMN FOR THE WEEK

"Lord, teach us how to pray aright" (438)

LESSONS		*Year 1*	
S.	Jer. 29:1, 4-14 or Jer. 39:11-40:6	Acts 16:6-15	Luke 10:1-12, 17-20
M.	Jer. 44:1-14 or Jer. 29:1, 4-14	I Cor. 15:30-41	Matt. 11:16-24
T.	Lam. 1:1-5(6-9) 10-12 or Jer. 40:7-41:3	I Cor. 15:41-50	Matt. 11:25-30
W.	Lam. 2:8-15 or Jer. 41:4-18	I Cor. 15:51-58	Matt. 12:1-14
Th.	Ezra 1:1-11 or Jer. 42:1-22	I Cor. 16:1-9	Matt. 12:15-21
F.	Ezra 3:1-13 or Jer. 43:1-13	I Cor. 16:10-24	Matt. 12:22-32
S.	Ezra 4:7, 11-24 or Jer. 44:1-14	Phlm. 1-25	Matt. 12:33-42

		Year 2	
S.	Ecclus. 4:1-10 or Mic. 1:1-9	I Cor. 10:1-13	Matt. 16:13-20
M.	Ecclus. 4:20-5:7 or Mic. 2:1-13	Rev. 7:1-8	Luke 9:51-62
T.	Ecclus. 6:5-17 or Mic. 3:1-8	Rev. 7:9-17	Luke 10:1-16
W.	Ecclus. 7:4-14 or Mic. 3:9-4:5	Rev. 8:1-13	Luke 10:17-24
Th.	Ecclus. 10:1-18 or Mic. 5:1-4, 10-15	Rev. 9:1-12	Luke 10:25-37
F.	Ecclus. 11:2-20 or Mic. 6:1-8	Rev. 9:13-21	Luke 10:38-42
S.	Ecclus. 15:9-20 or Mic. 7:1-7	Rev. 10:1-11	Luke 11:1-13

Almighty, everlasting God, abundantly and daily you forgive all our sins. Grant us your Holy Spirit, that he may inscribe your mercy in our hearts, in order that we too may willingly forgive others; through Jesus Christ our Lord. (177)

XXIV SUNDAY AFTER PENTECOST

"Let your loins be girded and your lamps burning."

Luke 12:35

PSALMS FOR THE WEEK: (see table, pp. 58-59, General Week 1)

HYMN FOR THE WEEK

"Love divine, all loves excelling" (315)

LESSONS		Year 1	
S.	Hag. 1:1-2:9 or Jer. 44:15-30	Acts 18:24-19:7	Luke 10:25-37
M.	Zech. 1:7-17 or Jer. 45:1-5	Rev. 1:4-20	Matt. 12:43-50
T.	Ezra 5:1-17 or Lam. 1:1-5(6-9)10-12	Rev. 4:1-11	Matt. 13:1-9
W.	Ezra 6:1-22 or Lam. 2:5-18	Rev. 5:1-10	Matt. 13:10-17
Th.	Neh. 1:1-11 or Lam. 2:16-22	Rev. 5:11-6:11	Matt. 13:18-23
F.	Neh. 2:1-20 or Lam. 4:1-22	Rev. 6:12-7:4	Matt. 13:24-30
S.	Neh. 4:1-23 or Lam. 5:1-22	Rev. 7:(4-8)9-17	Matt. 13:31-35

		Year 2	
S.	Ecclus. 18:19-33 or Jon. 1:1-17a	I Cor. 10:15-24	Matt. 18:15-20
M.	Ecclus. 19:4-17 or Jon. 1:17-2:10	Rev. 11:1-14	Luke 11:14-26
T.	Ecclus. 24:1-12 or Jon. 3:1-4:11	Rev. 11:14-19	Luke 11:27-36
W.	Ecclus. 28:14-26 or Nah. 1:1-14	Rev. 12:1-6	Luke 11:37-52
Th.	Ecclus. 31:12-18, 25-32:2 or Nah. 1:15-2:12	Rev. 12:7-17	Luke 11:53-12:12
F.	Ecclus. 34:1-8, 18-22 or Nah. 2:13-3:7	Rev. 13:1-10	Luke 12:13-31
S.	Ecclus. 35:1-17 or Nah. 3:8-19	Rev. 13:11-18	Luke 12:32-48

Almighty, everlasting God, you have promised us a new heaven and a new earth in which righteousness dwells. Direct us by your Spirit, that we may wait watchfully for the coming of your Son, and with holy lives go forth to meet him, Jesus Christ our Lord. (178)

XXV SUNDAY AFTER PENTECOST

"Give thanks to the Father, who has qualified us to share in the inheritance of the saints in light." Colossians 1:12

PSALMS FOR THE WEEK: (see table, pp. 58-59, General Week 2)

HYMN FOR THE WEEK

"Rejoice, angelic choirs, rejoice!" (146)

LESSONS

Year 1

S.	Neh. 5:1-19 or Ezra 1:1-11	Acts 20:7-12	Luke 12:22-31
M.	Neh. 6:1-19 or Ezra 3:1-13	Rev. 10:1-11	Matt. 13:36-43
T.	Neh. 12:27-31a, 42b-47 or Ezra 4:7, 11-24	Rev. 11:1-19	Matt. 13:44-52
W.	Neh. 13:4-22 or Hag. 1:1-2:9	Rev. 12:1-12	Matt. 13:53-58
Th.	Ezra 7:(1-10)11-26 or Zech. 1:7-17	Rev. 14:1-13	Matt. 14:1-12
F.	Ezra 7:27-28; 8:21-36 or Ezra 5:1-17	Rev. 15:1-8	Matt. 14:13-21
S.	Ezra 9:1-15 or Ezra 6:1-22	Rev. 17:1-14	Matt. 14:22-36

Year 2

S.	Ecclus. 36:1-17 or Zeph. 1:1-6	I Cor. 12:27-13:13	Matt. 18:21-35
M.	Ecclus. 38:24-34 or Zeph. 1:7-13	Rev. 14:1-13	Luke 12:49-59
T.	Ecclus. 43:1-22 or Zeph. 1:14-18	Rev. 14:14-15:8	Luke 13:1-9
W.	Ecclus. 43:23-33 or Zeph. 2:1-15	Rev. 16:1-11	Luke 13:10-17
Th.	Ecclus. 44:1-15 or Zeph. 3:1-7	Rev. 16:12-21	Luke 13:18-30
F.	Ecclus. 50:1, 11-24 or Zeph. 3:8-13	Rev. 17:1-18	Luke 13:31-35
S.	Ecclus. 51:1-12 or Zeph. 3:14-20	Rev. 18:1-14	Luke 14:1-11

Almighty God, draw our hearts to you, guide our minds, fill our imaginations, control our wills, so that we may be wholly yours. Use us as you will, always to your glory and the welfare of your people; through our Lord and Saviour Jesus Christ.(179)

"Whoever endures to the end will be saved." Matthew 24:13

PSALMS FOR THE WEEK: (see table, pp. 58-59, General Week 3)

HYMN FOR THE WEEK

"O God of earth and altar" (428)

LESSONS

Year 1

S.	Ezra 10:1-17 or Neh. 1:1-11	Acts 24:10-21	Luke 14:12-24
M.	Neh. 9:1-15(16-25) or Neh. 2:1-20	Rev. 18:1-8	Matt. 15:1-20
T.	Neh. 9:26-38 or Neh. 4:1-23	Rev. 18:9-20	Matt. 15:21-28
W.	Neh. 7:73B-8:3, 5-18 or Neh. 5:1-19	Rev. 18:21-24	Matt. 15:29-39
Th.	I Macc. 1:1-28 or Neh. 6:1-19	Rev. 19:1-10	Matt. 16:1-12
F.	I Macc. 1:41-63 or Neh. 12:27-31A, 42B-47	Rev. 19:11-16	Matt. 16:13-20
S.	I Macc. 2:1-28 or Neh. 13:4-22	Rev. 20:1-6	Matt 16:21-28

Year 2

S.	Ecclus. 51:13-22 or Joel 1:1-13	I Cor. 14:1-12	Matt. 20:1-16
M.	Joel 1:1-13 or Joel 1:15-2:2	Rev. 18:15-24	Luke 14:12-24
T.	Joel 1:15-2:2(3-11) or Joel 2:3-11	Rev. 19:1-10	Luke 14:25-35
W.	Joel 2:12-19	Rev. 19:11-21	Luke 15:1-10
Th.	Joel 2:21-27	James 1:1-15	Luke 15:1-2, 11-32
F.	Joel 2:28-3:8	James 1:16-27	Luke 16:1-9
S.	Joel 3:9-17	James 2:1-13	Luke 16:10-17(18)

Lord God, heavenly Father, through your Son you have revealed to us that heaven and earth shall pass away. Keep us steadfast in your word and in true faith; graciously guard us from all sin and preserve us amid all temptations, so that our hearts may not be overcharged with the cares of life, but at all times in watchfulness and prayer we may await the return of your Son and joyfully cherish the expectation of our eternal salvation; through Jesus Christ our Lord. (180)

XXVII SUNDAY AFTER PENTECOST

"We must all appear before the judgment seat of Christ."

II Corinthians 5:10

PSALMS FOR THE WEEK: (see table, pp. 58-59, General Week 4)

HYMN FOR THE WEEK

"The day is surely drawing near" (321)

LESSONS   *Year 1*

S.	I Macc. 2:29-43 (44-48) or Ezra 7:(1-10)11-26	Acts 28:14B-23	Luke 16:1-13
M.	I Macc. 2:49-70 or Ezra 7:27-28; 8:21-36	Rev. 20:7-15	Matt. 17:1-13
T.	I Macc. 3:1-24 or Ezra 9:1-15	Rev. 21:1-8	Matt. 17:14-21
W.	I Macc. 3:25-41 or Ezra 10:1-17	Rev. 21:9-21	Matt. 17:22-27
Th.	I Macc. 3:42-60 or Neh. 9:1-15(16-25)	Rev. 21:22-22:5	Matt. 18:1-9
F.	I Macc. 4:1-25 or Neh. 9:26-38	Rev. 22:6-13	Matt. 18:10-20
S.	I Macc. 4:36-59 or Neh. 7:73b-8:3, 5-18	Rev. 22:14-21	Matt. 18:21-35

Year 2

S.	Hab. 1:1-4(5-11) 12-2:1	Phil. 3:13-4:1	Matt. 23:13-24
M.	Hab. 2:1-4, 9-20	James 2:14-26	Luke 16:19-31
T.	Hab. 3:1-10(11-15) 16-18	James 3:1-12	Luke 17:1-10
W.	Mal. 1:1, 6-14	James 3:13-4:12	Luke 17:11-19
Th.	Mal. 2:1-16	James 4:13-5:6	Luke 17:20-37
F.	Mal. 3:1-12	James 5:7-12	Luke 18:1-8
S.	Mal. 3:13-4:6	James 5:13-20	Luke 18:9-14

Lord Jesus Christ, before whose judgment seat we must all appear and give account of the things done in the body: grant that, when the books are opened on that day, the faces of your servants may not be ashamed; through your merits, O blessed Savior, for you live and reign with the Father and the Holy Spirit, one God, now and forever. (181)

CHRIST THE KING

LAST SUNDAY AFTER PENTECOST

"The King of kings and Lord of lords, who alone has immortality, to him be honor and eternal dominion."

I Timothy 6:15-16

PSALMS FOR THE WEEK: (see table, pp. 58-59, General Week 1)

HYMN FOR THE WEEK

"At the name of Jesus" (179)

LESSONS

Year 1

S.	Isa. 19:19-25	Rom. 15:5-13	Luke 19:11-27
M.	Joel 3:1-2, 9-17	I Pet. 1:1-12	Matt. 19:1-12
T.	Nah. 1:1-13	I Pet. 1:13-25	Matt. 19:13-22
W.	Obad. 15:21	I Pet. 2:1-10	Matt. 19:23-30
Th.	Zeph. 3:1-13	I Pet. 2:11-25	Matt. 20:1-16
F.	Isa. 24:14-23	I Pet. 3:13-4:6	Matt. 20:17-28
S.	Mic. 7:11-20	I Pet. 4:7-19	Matt. 20:29-34

Year 2

S.	Zech. 9:9-16	I Pet. 3:13-22	Matt. 21:1-13
M.	Zech. 10:1-12	Gal. 6:1-10	Luke 18:15-30
T.	Zech. 11:4-17	I Cor. 3:10-23	Luke 18:31-43
W.	Zech. 12:1-10	Eph. 1:3-14	Luke 19:1-10
Th.	Zech. 13:1-9	Eph. 1:15-23	Luke 19:11-27
F.	Zech. 14:1-11	Rom. 15:7-13	Luke 19:28-40
S.	Zech. 14:12-21	Phil. 2:1-11	Luke 19:41-48

O Lord, our most gracious Redeemer and King, dwell and reign within us, take possession of us by your Spirit, and reign where you have a right to reign, and spread your kingdom throughout the world, now and forever. (182)

Almighty God, through your Son Jesus Christ you gave the holy apostles many gifts and commanded them to feed your flock. Inspire all pastors to preach your Word diligently and your people to receive it willingly, that finally we may receive the crown of eternal glory; through Jesus Christ our Lord. (183)

PRAYERS OF PREPARATION FOR
MINISTRY

SATURDAY EVENING

O God, Father, Son, and Holy Spirit, my Lord and my God, I humbly pray thee to pardon all my sins. Look not upon my great unworthiness but upon thy great mercy, by which thou hast appointed me to be thine ambassador in Christ's stead. Put thy Word in my mouth and on the morrow speak thou with my tongue. Bring forth fruit through me, thine unworthy servant, and let not the preaching of thy Word be without effect among us. May all that I utter be in accord with thy Word and the confession of thy church, that thy name may be glorified, thy congregation truly awakened, and thus, through me, thine unworthy servant, thy church be edified.

As thou didst inhabit the praises of Israel, dwell thou in the praises of this our church. Let the sacrifice of our praise be acceptable to thee, and preserve us from vain babbling and lying lip service.

Incline thine ear to our prayer, O God of Jacob; hear the voice of our supplications and help us.

Preserve unto us thy holy Word, that it may be joyfully and boldly proclaimed in its purity, and guard us in the right use of the sacrament in accord with the institution of Jesus Christ, our Saviour. Restrain all who would destroy us and turn them to thyself.

Be thou our God and our children's God, now and henceforth, and hear my prayer, O Father, for the sake of thy dear Son, O Jesus Christ, thou blessed Saviour, O Holy Spirit, thou Comforter divine. Amen.

—Joachim Embden (184)

* * *

O Lord, our God, who wouldst have all men to be saved and to come to the knowledge of the truth, let the miracle of thy grace come to pass in the services of the morrow, that the hearts of the hearers may be opened, that members may come to a living faith, that sinners be converted, the unrepentant shaken, the weary and heavy-laden comforted, but that in all things thy church may be edified, to thy glory, O Lord, through Jesus Christ. Amen.

—Orate Fratres (185)

ON SUNDAY

Ever blessed Trinity, to thy mercy I commit this day, my body and soul, together with all my ways and undertakings. I beseech thee to be gracious unto me; enlarge my heart and open my lips, that I may praise and magnify thy name which alone is holy. And as thou hast made me for the praise of thy holy name, grant that I may yield my life a sacrifice to thy honor in humble love and fear. —*Löhe's Liturgy* (186)

ON GOING TO CHURCH

Almighty God, our heavenly Father, by thy great goodness I am permitted to go to thy house, to worship toward thy holy temple. Lead me, gracious Lord, in righteousness, and prepare thy way before me. Keep me in the path of thy commandments, for thou art the God of my salvation. Thy dwellings are my delight, and I rejoice to be in the congregation of the saints, who confess and praise thy name. How amiable are thy tabernacles, O Lord of hosts! My soul longeth, yea, even fainteth for the courts of the Lord. O come, let us worship and bow down; let us kneel before the Lord our Maker. For he is our God, and we are the people of his pasture, and the sheep of his hand. Exalt the Lord our God. Worship at his footstool, for he is holy. I cry unto thee in an acceptable time. Hear me, O Lord, for the sake of thy great goodness, and grant me thy blessing. Amen.

—*Löhe's Liturgy* (187)

SACRISTY PRAYERS

Luther's Sacristy Prayer

O Lord God, dear Father in heaven, I am indeed unworthy of the office and ministry in which I am to make known thy glory and to nurture and to serve this congregation.

But since thou hast appointed me to be a pastor and teacher, and the people are in need of the teaching and the instruction, O be thou my helper and let thy holy angels attend me.

Then if thou art pleased to accomplish anything through me, to thy glory and not to mine or to the praise of men, grant me, out of thy pure grace and mercy, a right understanding of thy Word and that I may also diligently perform it.

O Lord Jesus Christ, Son of the living God, thou shepherd and bishop of our souls, send thy Holy Spirit that he may work with me, yea, that he may work in me to will and to do through thy divine strength according to thy good pleasure. Amen.

–Attributed to Luther (188)

* * *

Lord God, thou has appointed me to be a bishop and pastor in thy church. Thou seest how unfit I am to undertake this great and difficult office, and were it not for thy help, I would long since have ruined it all. Therefore I cry unto thee; I will assuredly apply my mouth and my heart to thy service. I desire to teach the people and I myself would learn ever more and diligently meditate thy Word. Use thou me as thine instrument, only do not thou forsake me, for if I am left alone I shall easily bring it all to destruction. Amen.

–Luther (189)

* * *

Since I am coming to that holy room
　　Where with the choir of saints for evermore,
I shall be made Thy music; as I come
　　I tune the instrument here at the door,
　　And what I must do then, think here before.

–John Donne (190)

O Lord God almighty, who didst endue thine apostles with singular gifts of the Holy Spirit, so that they proclaimed thy Word with power, grant unto me, who am set to minister and teach in thy holy name, the same Spirit of wisdom and love and power; that the truth thou givest me to declare may search the conscience, convince the mind, and win the heart of those who hear it, and the glory of thy kingdom be advanced; through Jesus Christ my Lord. Amen.

—Book of Common Order (191)

* * *

O thou who hast called us to this holy ministry and set us in the blessed fellowship of all who serve thee in the church of thy Son, accept our thanksgiving for the high privilege which is ours. Teach us diligence, humility, and kindness in our ministry. Grant that through faithful study of thy Word in the Scriptures and in the events of our time, through constant prayer, blameless living, and self-giving service we may come to understand the ways of men and of society. As we lead thy people in their worship of thee, and interpret to them the truth from thee, may we be led to the altar of thy holy love, and linger often near the cross where thou makest thyself known as Redeemer. As we shepherd thy people, fill our hearts with love for them, and may their growth into the likeness of Christ be our chief concern.

For our brothers in the service of Christ, we ask thy continuing favor. Empower them to be the prophets of thy purpose and the priests of thy grace. Guard and guide them and their dear ones, giving them thy peace in their going out and their coming in, till we all come at last to our Father's house, to go no more out for ever. Amen.

—David A. MacLennan (192)

* * *

Veni spiritus, pasce pastorum, duc ducem, aperi aperturo, da daturo, Christe Kyrie, Herr, erbarme dich unser.

Come, Holy Spirit, shepherd him who is to shepherd others; guide him who is to guide others; discover to him [the Scriptures] who is to discover them to others; give to him who is to give to others, Lord Christ, have mercy upon us!

—Ancient pastoral prayer

* * *

Send forth, O God, thy Holy Spirit into my soul; that whatsoever I have done, desired, or considered of wrong may be pardoned, and I may be cleansed for this service. Send forth thy Spirit into my heart, that I may rightly love both thee and the congregation. Send forth thy Spirit into my mind, that I may wisely understand the needs of these thy people, and the truth of thy gospel. Send forth thy Spirit into my words; that I may worthily represent these men and women in my prayers, and Christ Jesus in my speech. And, when this service shall be done, take not, O Lord, thy Holy Spirit from me; but mercifully suffer him henceforth to guide and strengthen me; through the same Jesus Christ our Lord. Amen.

—John Underwood Stephens (193)

* * *

Lord, at thy word opens yon door, inviting
Teacher and taught to feast this hour with thee:
Opens a book where God in human writing
Thinks his deep thoughts, and dead tongues live for me.

Too dread the task, too great the duty calling,
Too heavy far the weight is laid on me!
Oh, if mine own thought should on thy words falling
Mar the great message, and men hear not thee!

Give me thy voice to speak, thine ear to listen,
Give me thy mind to grasp the mystery;
So shall my heart throb and my glad eyes glisten,
Rapt with the wonders thou dost show to me.

—J. H. Moulton (194)

Almighty God, heavenly Father, I will come into thy house in the multitude of thy mercy and in thy fear will I worship toward thy holy temple. Lead me, O Lord, in thy righteousness; make thy way straight before my face. Make me to go in the path of thy commandments, for thou art the God of my salvation. O Lord, I love the habitation of thy house, the congregation of saints who praise and confess thee. How lovely is thy dwelling place, O Lord of hosts. My soul longs, yea, faints for the courts of the Lord. O come, let us worship and bow down; let us kneel before the Lord our maker, for he is our God, and we are the people of his pasture and the sheep of his hand. Exalt the Lord our God, and worship at his footstool, for he is holy. My prayer is unto thee, O Lord, in an acceptable time; in the abundance of thy steadfast love, answer me, O God. Amen.

–Psalms (195)

* * *

O Lord, take away from us all coldness, all wanderings of the thoughts, and fix our souls upon thee and thy love, O merciful Lord and Saviour, in this our hour of prayer. Amen.

–Edward White Benson (196)

* * *

Lord Jesus, it is thine office which I hold,
    it is thy work I am doing;
    it is thy people whom I would build up;
    it is thy glory that I seek.

Help me, therefore, in this hour, that I, poor sinner, may do and perform it all according to thy most holy will. Amen.

–G. C. Dieffenbach (197)

* * *

O Lord, my God, without whom I can do nothing as I ought; go with me, I beseech thee, into thy house, and so guide me by thy Holy Spirit that I may devoutly lead the worship of thy people, worthily proclaim thy gospel, and show forth thy truth and grace to all who wait upon thee; through Jesus Christ our Lord. Amen.

—Book of Common Order (198)

* * *

O God most high, who hast called me to minister to thy people in holy things; give me such grace this day that wisely and charitably, prudently and acceptably, I may proclaim thy Word, and so give guidance to the blind, comfort to the sad and weary, strength to the weak, and confirmation to the strong; and that by all my words and actions I may minister to the spiritual welfare of those who wait upon thee, and show forth the honor of my Lord; for his name's sake. Amen.

—Book of Common Order (199)

* * *

WHEN SEVERAL PREPARE TOGETHER FOR A SERVICE
I (200)

Lord, remember not my sins nor my transgressions:
*According to thy mercy remember thou me for thy goodness'
sake, O Lord.*

Lord, hear my voice:
Let thine ears be attentive to the voice of my supplications.

If thou, Lord, shouldest mark iniquities:
O Lord, who shall stand?

But there is forgiveness with thee:
That thou mayest be feared.

I wait for the Lord:
My soul doth wait, and in his word do I hope.

My soul waiteth for the Lord:
More than they that watch for the morning.

For with the Lord there is mercy:
And with him is plenteous redemption.

And he shall redeem Israel:
From all his iniquities.

Glory be to the Father, and to the Son, and to the Holy Ghost :

As it was in the beginning, is now, and ever shall be, world without end. Amen.

Lord, remember not my sins nor my transgressions :

According to thy mercy remember thou me for thy goodness' sake, O Lord.

Lord, have mercy upon us.

Christ, have mercy upon us. Lord, have mercy upon us.

Let us pray : O merciful Lord, incline thine ears to our prayer and enlighten our hearts by the grace of thy Holy Spirit, that we may be worthy stewards of thy mysteries, and may love thee with an everlasting love; through Jesus Christ our Lord. (201)

Amen.

Almighty God, unto whom all hearts are open, all desires known, and from whom no secrets are hid : Cleanse the thoughts of our hearts by the inspiration of thy Holy Spirit, that we may perfectly love thee, and worthily magnify thy holy name; through Jesus Christ, thy Son, our Lord. (202)

Amen.

Enlighten our minds, we beseech thee, O God, by thy Spirit who proceedeth from thee, that, as thy Son hath promised, we may be led into all truth; through the same Jesus Christ, thy Son, our Lord. (203)

Amen.

Cleanse our consciences, we beseech thee, O Lord, by thy visitation, that thy Son, our Lord Jesus Christ, when he cometh, may find in us a mansion prepared for himself; through the same Jesus Christ, thy Son, our Lord, who liveth and reigneth with thee and the Holy Ghost, ever one God, world without end. (204)

Amen.

The Lord is nigh unto all that call upon him:
To all that call upon him in truth.
My mouth shall speak the praise of the Lord:
Let all flesh bless his holy name for ever and ever.
Let us pray: Prepare us, O Lord, for thy service:
Open thou our lips to praise thy name.

Cleanse, enlighten, and kindle us, that we, with all the faithful, may call upon thee in true devotion, laud and praise thee, and magnify thy wonders with all thy creatures, rejoicing in the abundance of thy salvation; through Jesus Christ our Lord.

Amen.

Grant that we may glorify thy name with heart and mouth and hands:

To thine honor, to the salvation of thy people, in the power of thy Holy Spirit. Amen.

III (206)

The Lord is nigh unto all that call upon him:
To all that call upon him in truth.
My mouth shall speak the praise of the Lord:
Let all flesh bless his holy name for ever and ever.

Let us pray: Lord, prepare us for thy service. Let us come before thee with eager and humble hearts and disciplined minds. Cleanse us, enlighten us, and kindle us. Bind us together in love, obedience, and faithfulness; through Jesus Christ our Lord.

Amen.

Help us, thy servants, O Lord, and build thy kingdom. By thy mercy, accept our service to the praise of thy glory.

Amen.

O Lord, open thou our lips and purify our hearts, that we may worthily magnify thy holy name; through Jesus Christ our Lord. Amen.   (207)

* * *

O Lord, our God and Father, dispose our hearts and guide us by thy Holy Spirit, that our prayers and praises may be acceptable in thy sight; through Jesus Christ our Lord. Amen.   (208)

* * *

Cleanse our hearts, we humbly beseech thee, O Lord, from all vain and wandering thoughts, that we may joyfully praise thee in thy holy house; through Jesus Christ our Lord. Amen.   (209)

* * *

Open thou our lips, O Lord, and our mouths shall show forth thy praise. Inspire these thy choristers who have consecrated to thy service the gift of song wherewith thou hast endowed them. And so sustain them in their guidance of the congregation who are now met to praise thee, that thy holy name may be glorified, and thy people truly rejoice in thy presence. Help them so to bear themselves as they worship thee in thy sanctuary and lead the songs of Zion, that they shall be acceptable to thee in this their office, and make all thy people joyful; through Jesus Christ our Lord. Amen.

—Hubert L. Simpson (210)

* * *

O God, our heavenly Father, who hast called us to the sacred ministry of praise in the service of thy church, make us ready now to worship thee in spirit and in truth. Teach us to understand and love thy holy service, and help us to be reverent and attentive, guarding us from all wandering thoughts and unseemly actions, and make all that we shall say and do acceptable unto thee; through Jesus Christ our Lord. Amen.   *—Book of Common Worship* (211)

* * *

Grant us, O Lord, the help of thy Spirit in our hearts, that we may enter into thy holy presence with reverence and gladness and render a service acceptable unto thee; through Jesus Christ our Lord. Amen.

—Book of Offices and Prayers (212)

AT THE ALTAR

Lord Jesus, we are not worthy that thou shouldest come under our roof, but in thy wondrous mercy come and be with us in this hour. Have mercy upon thy humble servant, and fill my soul with thy peace.

Behold, I give heart and mouth and hand to thy service. By thy grace, use me as a lowly and unworthy instrument of thy mercy to the salvation of thy congregation. Amen.

—G. C. Dieffenbach (213)

* * *

Praise, glory, and honor be to thee, Father, Son, and Holy Spirit. Through thy mercy, accept my ministry to the praise of thy glory. Amen. (214)

* * *

O God, Father, Son, and Holy Spirit, open thou my heart and lips, that I may worthily call upon thy holy name, and pray and praise and thank thee. Amen.

—Pfarrgebete zum Gottesdienst (215)

BEFORE PREACHING

Lord Jesus, teach thou me, that I may teach them; sanctify and enable all my powers, that in their full strength they may deliver thy message reverently, readily, faithfully, and fruitfully. O make thy word a swift word, passing from the ear to the heart, from the heart to life and conversation; that as the rain returns not empty, so neither may thy word, but accomplish that for which it is given. O Lord, hear; O Lord, forgive; O Lord, hearken; and do so for thy blessed Son's sake, in whose sweet and pleasing words we say, "Our Father," etc.

—George Herbert (216)

* * *

Remember, O Lord, thy covenant and remember me, thy servant, and inspire what I should think and say. Give me thy Holy Spirit. O Lord, God of Israel, strengthen me in this hour, and graciously help me to do the work which I have undertaken, trusting only in thy grace, to the glory of thy name and the salvation of all who hear, for the sake of thy dear Son, Jesus Christ. Amen.

—Thomas Schmidt (217)

* * *

O Christ, our God, rule thou my heart and spirit and tongue. Come, Holy Spirit, thou giver of all the gifts of grace, grant me utterance and wisdom that I may show forth thy praise. Forbid that I should utter any unwise word that would do hurt to my conscience or the honor of thy holy name. Give fruit to the seed of thy Word. Kindle the hearts of the hearers, that they may give heed to thy Word in quietness and holy reverence and thus be edified henceforth and finally be saved, through our Lord Jesus Christ. Amen.

—Friedrich Balduin (218)

* * *

With a humbled spirit will I draw near to thee; in the much hope and strength which thou hast given me will I speak to thee. Therefore, O Son of David, who wast revealed in a mystery and didst come down to us in human flesh, do thou with the key of thy cross open up the secrets of my heart; send one of the seraphim that with a burning coal from off the altar he may cleanse my soiled lips, uncloud my mind, and supply that which I shall teach; that my tongue, in the loving service of my neighbor's good, may not fall into tones of error but may re-echo and proclaim truth without ceasing.

–Julian of Toledo (219)

* * *

We pray thee, almighty God, open the hearts of thy people to thy law and give them humble minds to receive thy heavenly commandments. Whatever our mortal tongue shall utter for the salvation of their souls, do thou in thy heavenly pity make acceptable to them. Speak thou from heaven through us and give them life; and may they and we who watch over them be counted worthy to attain to Christ unharmed.

–Mozarabic

* * *

O my Master! on whose errand I come, let me hold my peace, and do thou speak thyself, for thou art Love, and when thou teachest, all are scholars.

–George Herbert (220)

* * *

Lord Jesus, dear Master, I come to thee now: Give to me out of thy hands the bread of life, that at thy command I may carry it to thy hungry people. See, I have nothing of my own, nothing at all; I am a beggar; but thou art rich and hast the fulness of grace and truth. Lord, to whom shall we go? Thou alone hast words of life. Give to thy poor servants the bread of life, and today, according to thy grace, fill my hands that I may distribute it at thy bidding. O, thou loving Saviour, suffer not thy poor disciples to go away empty, but give to us some fragments, that our souls may be satisfied with life and peace. Amen.

–G. C. Dieffenbach (221)

O Lord, send out thy light and thy truth; let them lead me.
Psalm 43:3

* * *

O Lord, open thou my lips, and my mouth shall show forth thy praise.
Psalm 51:15

* * *

O Lord, graciously defend me, that I may not preach to others and be myself a castaway.
I Cor. 9:27

* * *

O Lord, grant to thy servant to speak thy Word with all boldness.
Acts 4:29

* * *

Grant me, O Lord, to do what is right and preach what is true, that my acts and teaching may instruct thy people. For thy name's sake.
—Priest's Prayer Book (222)

* * *

Lord, uphold me that I may uplift thee. (223)

Lord Jesus, speak thou in my heart and through my lips.

Grant, O Lord, that in speaking the truth of Christ with plainness, I may deserve to be heard for the sake of Christ.
—Use of Sarum

Fill me, O Christ, with wonder, love, and praise, that I may exalt thee, God with us.

O Lord, be thou my light and my strength.

O Lord, in my weakness perfect thy strength.

O Lord, make me thy messenger.

O Lord, arm me with the sword of thy Spirit.

Lord Jesus, speak to me that I may speak for thee.

Lord, help me to speak the truth, the whole truth, and nothing but the truth.

Lord, give me power to be thy witness.

Lord, open my lips, and open the hearts of this people.

* * *

> *Fac ut possim demonstrare*
> *Quam sit dulce te amare,*
> *Tecum pati, tecum flere,*
> *Tecum semper congaudere.*

> Enable me to show how sweet it is
> > To love thee,
> > To bear with thee,
> > To weep with thee,
> > Forever to rejoice with thee.

—Unknown (224)

* * *

BEFORE HOLY COMMUNION

O Lord, graciously accept my ministry at thine altar, that as a faithful steward of thy mysteries I may rightly administer thy body and blood to thy glory and the salvation of those who share in thy Supper. Amen.

—Pfarrgebete zum Gottesdienst (225)

* * *

O Lord Jesus Christ, grant that I may administer thy Holy Sacrament with clean hands and present thy body and blood unto eternal life; who livest and reignest, world without end. Amen. *—Pfarrgebete zum Gottesdienst* (226)

* * *

Almighty God, Father of mercies, who hast called us this day to the Communion of thy blessed Son, our Lord; make thy grace sufficient for me, I humbly beseech thee, that I may acceptably celebrate thy most high worship, and without condemnation have part in ministering before thee; and grant such faith unto all thy people, that in the Holy Sacrament they may behold thy love which passeth knowledge, and be made partakers of thy heavenly grace; through Jesus Christ our Lord. Amen.

—Book of Common Order (227)

* * *

O most merciful God, incline thy loving ears to my prayers, and illuminate my heart with the grace of the Holy Spirit, that I may be enabled worthily to minister to thy mysteries, and to love thee with an everlasting love, and to attain everlasting joys, through Jesus Christ our Lord. Amen.

—Gallican (228)

* * *

O Lord and heavenly Father, who hast given unto us thy people the true Bread that cometh down from heaven, even thy Son Jesus Christ; grant that our souls may so be fed by him who giveth life unto the world, that we may abide in him and he in us, and thy church be filled with the power of his unending life; through Jesus Christ our Lord. Amen.

—A New Prayer Book (229)

* * *

O Lord Jesus Christ, thou true and only High Priest, who on the altar of the cross has offered thyself to thy heavenly Father as a ransom for us poor sinners, and as a memorial of thy sacrifice hast instituted this holy Sacrament, in which thou givest us thy Body to eat and thy Blood to drink; I beseech thee, for the sake of thy boundless love and mercy, to grant that I, thine unworthy servant, may celebrate this Sacrament with such devotion and fear as are acceptable to thee. I know indeed that on account of my sins and transgressions I am not worthy to approach thine altar, O Lord. But I know, too, and acknowledge and confess, that thou canst make me worthy, O thou who redeemest and savest sinners. Deliver me from all unholy, vain, and hurtful thoughts, that I may serve thee with a clean heart and in humble faith. Take this heart of stone, and give me a heart of flesh, that I may love and serve thee and have all my joy in thee. Bless unto me and to all who approach this holy Table, this salutary gift of thy Body and Blood, that it may be to us the strength of body and soul, keeping us in the paths of righteousness, so that we may finally be permitted to see thee face to face, and be admitted to the great Communion on high, when thou drinkest the fruit of the vine anew with thy disciples in thy Father's kingdom. Amen.

—Löhe's Liturgy (230)

* * *

WHEN THE MINISTER COMMUNICATES HIMSELF

Lord, I am not worthy that thou shouldest come under my roof; but speak the word only, and my soul shall be healed. I will take the bread of heaven, and call upon the name of the Lord. The Body of Christ preserve me unto everlasting life.

What shall I render unto the Lord for all his benefits toward me? I will take the cup of salvation, and call upon the name of the Lord. The Blood of Christ preserve me unto everlasting life.

—Pfarrgebete zum Gottesdienst (231)

* * *

AFTER HOLY COMMUNION

Grant, O Lord, that what we have received with our mouth we may take and keep with believing hearts, that this temporal gift may help us to eternal salvation; through Jesus Christ our Lord. Amen.

—Leonine Sacramentary

* * *

Holy Father, I thank thee for thine unspeakable love, revealed anew at the table of the Lord, give to me and to all thy people grace to abide in fellowship with thee; and fence round my heart with thy love and purity, that no selfishness or guile or sloth may stain the ministry committed to my trust, but that in singleness of heart I may serve thee to the end; through Jesus Christ our Lord. Amen.

–Book of Common Order (232)

* * *

O Lord Jesus Christ, thou Everlasting Son of the Father, I give thanks unto thee, that thou hast given me, thine unworthy servant, grace to fulfil thy ministry and to distribute and receive the life-giving gift of thy Body and Blood. I beseech thee that this feast may not minister to the condemnation but to the salvation of those whom thou hast admitted to it. Grant that it may be unto me a shield of faith and the power of a right and holy life. Destroy in me all evil, and implant and nourish that which is good; subdue the passions and mortify the deeds of the flesh, so that I may ever cling to thee, and with an acceptable walk and conversation magnify thy name. And finally when my course on earth is ended, receive me into the habitations of light, to feast with the true Light and Joy of thine elect: O thou who livest and reignest with the Father and the Holy Ghost, one God, forever and ever. Amen.

–Löhe's Liturgy (233)

* * *

AFTER THE SERVICE WITH THE CHOIR

Grant, O Lord God, that what we have heard with our ears and sung with our lips, we may believe in our hearts and practice in our lives; for Jesus Christ's sake. Amen.

–Traditional (234)

* * *

Preserve in peace, O Lord, us thy servants; and grant that we whom thou hast called to sing thy praises on earth may

be made partakers of thy heavenly glory, through Jesus Christ
our Lord. Amen. —*Traditional*

* * *

Grant, we beseech thee, merciful God, that we who worship
thee in thy church may be witnesses unto thee in the world;
through the might of Jesus Christ our Lord. Amen.

—*A. Campbell Fraser* (235)

* * *

AFTER THE SERVICE

Merciful Lord, who by thy grace art able to do exceeding
abundantly above all that we ask or think; confirm and make
effectual by thy power what has been wrought this day by
my ministrations in the name and faith of thine ever blessed
Son; that thy Word may not return unto thee void, but may
quicken all in love to thee and in devotion to thy cause, and
bring forth fruit to thy glory; through Jesus Christ our Lord.
Amen. —*Book of Common Order* (236)

* * *

THANKSGIVING AFTER THE SERVICE

Praise, O ye servants of the Lord,
 praise the name of the Lord.
Blessed be the name of the Lord
 from this time forth and for evermore.
From the rising of the sun unto the going
 down of the same
The Lord's name is to be praised.

Let us pray:

Eternal God, we give thee thanks that thou hast vouchsafed
unto us to hear and to proclaim thy Word, to call upon thee
and praise thee, and to serve thee in this holy ministry. Amen.

We pray thee to pardon all remissness and sin, all thought-
lessness and all fleshly zeal.

Look not upon what we have done wrongly, but grant that the seed of thy Word may strike root, grow and increase. Ward off the evil one that he may not choke or snatch it away altogether. Grant that both teachers and hearers may keep faith and a good conscience and continue in thy truth to the end, that we may finally appear in thy presence with glory and receive the crown that fadeth not away; through Jesus Christ our Lord. Amen.

To God be glory in the church and in Christ Jesus to all generations, for ever and ever. Amen.

–Gebete für das Jahr der Kirche (237)

* * *

THE MINISTER TEACHING

Before Instructing Children

Lord Jesus Christ our Saviour, we give thee thanks that thou hast called the children unto thyself and blessed them. I pray that thou wouldst bless these children also. Put thy saving Word into their hearts and grant them the power gladly to live in accord with it, that when thou shalt call them they may come to thee in heaven. But to us, who proclaim thy Word to thy children, grant also joy and wisdom, that thy church may be built and bring forth the fruit of everlasting life. Amen.   *–Petersburger Agende, 1898 (238)*

* * *

Catechumens

Jesus, my dear Master, teach me how to teach; draw me to thee, that I may bring to thee these whom thou hast given to me. Our children have been baptized at thy bidding; O, now give me grace to teach them to keep what thou hast commanded. Testify thou to their souls; and awaken their hearts to a living faith, that they may embrace thee and give themselves wholly to thee. Prepare them by the power of

thy Holy Spirit and also through the instruction and prayer
of thy servant for a worthy reception of the Holy Supper.
Make them willing to renew their vows to thee and more and
more to renounce the devil. Defend them against the evil one,
that these souls, redeemed by thy blood, may not be lost nor
go astray. They are thine, Lord Jesus; therefore keep them
in thy love; stablish, strengthen, settle them even in this hour,
and keep them by thy power and grace unto eternal life.
Amen.   —*G. C. Dieffenbach* (239)

* * *

Lord God, heavenly Father, who dost send thy Holy Spirit
to all who pray for him and hast confirmed this and all other
blessed promises to us and our children, grant to all of us thy
Spirit's power, wisdom, and light, that I may rightly teach
the way of salvation, and our youth, together with the whole
congregation, be made willing to be led to the fountains of
living water, and thus be filled with salvation and eternal
life, through Jesus Christ, thy Son, our Lord. Amen.

—*G. C. Dieffenbach* (240)

* * *

After Instruction

O God, heavenly Father, the giver of every good and perfect gift, I have sown thy Word in weakness; now give thou
the increase, that it may prosper and these young people grow
up to thine honor and bring forth fruit unto the day of
harvest. Grant this, O Lord, for the sake of Jesus Christ, thy
dear Son, our Lord. Amen.   —*G. C. Dieffenbach* (241)

* * *

BEFORE A BAPTISM

Lord, I thank thee that thou art willing to receive this child
through Holy Baptism as thy child. Be thou in the midst of us
according to thy promise. Grant that this child may learn to
grasp thy great gift in faith of heart and live as a thankful

and joyful child of God. Grant this anew every day also to me and all the congregation of the baptized, that thy name may be glorified and thy kingdom come; through Jesus Christ our Lord. Amen.

—Neues Gebet (242)

* * *

Be present, O Lord, to our supplications; and graciously hearken unto me, who am the first to need thy mercy; and as thou hast made me the minister of this work, not by choosing me on account of merit, but by the gift of thy grace, so give me confidence to perform thine office, and do thou thyself by our ministration carry out the act of thine own loving-kindness; through our Lord. Amen.

—Gelasian Sacramentary (243)

* * *

Before a Marriage

O Lord, who hast promised thy blessing upon marriage, grant that I may so proclaim thy commands and promises to this young couple that, being forgiven of thee, they may live together in love and peace and serve thee in gratitude and joy. Give them day by day the strength to bear each other's burden, that they may grow together in every need and joy and become a blessing one to the other. Be thou a strong helper in every troubled marriage in our congregation, and watch thou also over my marriage. I am thine; save me for I have sought thy precepts. Amen.

—Neues Gebet (244)

* * *

Before a Funeral

O Lord, make me to stand in awe of the power thou hast given to death. O Lord, have mercy upon us.

Help me in this hour to speak the right word concerning the pilgrimage of this man (this woman). Help me in this hour to bear witness to thy power over life and death, the severity of thy judgment, and the abundance of thy mercy. Unite us with all those who have gone before us in the fellowship of faith, the fellowship of love, the fellowship of hope.

The world passeth away; may thy kingdom come. Amen.

—Pfarrgebete (245)

* * *

Before Calling on the Bereaved

O thou in whose house are many mansions, speak thou through me to these, whose loved one has gone from their sight, but not from thine. There is naught in me to heal the wounded heart or fill the aching void. But let thy words of comfort and truth be given me to speak, that these sorrowing ones may find their peace in thee. Amen.

—Prayers for the Minister's Day (246)

* * *

Before Visiting the Sick

Lord Jesus, our Saviour, who hast compassion upon all the sick and afflicted, be with me, thy servant, in this hour, that I may rightly comfort, strengthen, encourage, admonish, and prepare the sick for a blessed death. Grant unto me thy Holy Spirit, that all that I say may be blessed and my prayers and supplications be pleasing unto thee. Into thy hands I commend myself; at thy bidding I go: thou wilt preserve me, for I trust in thee. Blessed be thy holy name. Amen.

—G. C. Dieffenbach (247)

* * *

Before Making a Call

O thou who hast thine own message for those whom I shall meet this afternoon, give me such openness toward thee, that through me thy love may be made known, thy help bestowed, and the next step for each be made plain, through Jesus Christ our Lord. Amen. *—Prayers for the Minister's Day* (248)

Before Any Ministry of Comfort

Let not, O Lord, my lips perform this office, but let thy Holy Spirit work within and through me; that thy comfort may descend with power, and thy glory may be made known, through Jesus Christ our Lord. Amen.

–John Underwood Stephens (249)

* * *

Before any Ministry

O God, who raisest up in the hearts of faithful pastors the Spirit of thy Son to preach the gospel to the poor and to relieve the distresses of the sick and sorrowful, grant unto me, I beseech thee, a full portion of the same Spirit, that in humility and love I may so minister unto their necessities, as with them to be a partaker of everlasting consolation, through Jesus Christ our Lord. Amen.

–The Priest's Prayer Book (250)

* * *

For Any Meeting or Interview

O God, the Father of our Lord Jesus Christ, give us the spirit of wisdom and revelation, that we may know the hope of our calling, the riches of thine inheritance, the greatness of thy power. Make us ready to hear the truth, not as we would have it, but as it is. Close the springs of error and open the door of light. Let us know and proclaim the ordinances of thy love, thy salvation, in Jesus Christ our Lord. Amen.

–Pfarrgebete (251)

* * *

For a Retreat

O Lord Jesus Christ, who didst say to thine apostles, "Come ye apart into a desert place and rest a while," for there were many coming and going; grant, we beseech thee, to thy servants here gathered together, that they may rest awhile at this present time with thee. May they so seek thee, whom their souls desire to love, that they may both find thee and be found of thee. And grant such love and wisdom to accompany the words which shall be spoken in thy name, that they may not fall to the ground, but may be helpful in leading us onward through the toils of our pilgrimage to that rest which remaineth to the people of God; where, nevertheless, they rest not day and night from thy perfect service; who with the Father and the Holy Ghost livest and reignest ever one God, world without end. Amen.

—Prayers for All Occasions (252)

* * *

FOR A VESTRY MEETING

Blessed Lord, who hast called us to this office in thy church, guide us, we beseech thee, in our deliberations, so that all our aims and purposes may be to the strengthening of the work in this parish and the support of the church's mission throughout the world; through Jesus Christ our Lord. Amen.

* * *

FOR PARISH ORGANIZATIONS

O Lord, whose holy apostle has taught us that as members of thy body we all have our part to play in the whole life of thy church, we thank thee for this work which thou hast given us to do together; and we pray thee to give us grace to persevere in it, and through it to serve thee to thy honor and glory. Amen.

* * *

FOR THE EVERY-MEMBER CANVASS

O God, who hast been pleased to call us to be workers together with thee, make us now of one heart and mind to pray and work and give for the up-building and strengthening of thy church at home and abroad. Bless our Every-Member

Canvass, and stir up the wills of all our people to do according to their ability as good stewards in thy service; through Jesus Christ our Lord. Amen.

* * *

FOR AN ANNUAL PARISH MEETING

Grant, O Lord, that thy Holy Spirit may preside over us now in all our concerns and deliberations for the welfare of this parish. We thank thee for all the blessings of the past year, and pray that we may go together from strength to strength in the year before us. Help us all to dedicate ourselves to thee, and to be ready to make sacrifice of time and money for the extension of thy kingdom. Amen.

* * *

FOR A MEETING OF MINISTERS

O Lord Jesus Christ, Head of the church which is thy body, by whom we have been chosen as ambassadors and ministers of reconciliation, direct us, we beseech thee, in all our doings with thy most gracious favor; let all our plans and purposes be in accordance with thy holy will, our aim only that we may serve thee and our people faithfully as good shepherds of thy flock. Enlighten us by thy Holy Spirit as we consider together the meaning and obligations of our sacred calling, and the opportunities and responsibilities of the church in these times. Inspire our minds, assist our wills, and strengthen our hands, that we may not falter or fail in the work thou hast given us to do, to thine honor and glory. Amen.

* * *

O God our Father, of whose holy mysteries we are the ministers and stewards; grant that in all things we may be found faithful. Warm our hearts and confirm our wills in loyal devotion to thee and to thy kingdom. Strengthen us to endure hardness that we may never sleep at our posts. And vouchsafe us at the end the blessing of thy praise. Grant this, O Father, for the sake of Jesus Christ our Lord. Amen.

Open thou mine eyes, that I may behold wondrous things out of thy law. Make me to understand the way of thy precepts: so shall I talk of thy wondrous works. Turn away mine eyes from beholding vanity; and quicken thou me in thy way. Stablish thy word unto thy servant, who is devoted to thy fear. I am thy servant; give me understanding that I may know thy testimonies. Make thy face to shine upon thy servant; and teach me thy statutes. My lips shall utter praise, when thou hast taught me thy statutes. My tongue shall speak of thy word; for all thy commandments are righteousness. Let thine hand help me; for I have chosen thy precepts. Thy word is true from the beginning; give me understanding according to thy word.

—From Psalm 119 (253)

* * *

O God, the fountain of all wisdom, in a deep sense of my own ignorance, and of that great charge which lies upon me, I am constrained to come often before thee, from whom I have learned whatever I know, to ask that help without which I shall disquiet myself in vain; most humbly beseeching thee to guide me with thine eye; to enlighten my mind, that I may see myself, and teach others the wonders of thy law; that I may learn from thee what I ought to think and speak concerning thee. Direct and bless all the labors of my mind, give me a discerning spirit, a sound judgment, and an honest and religious heart. And grant that, in all my studies, my first aim may be to set forth thy glory, and to set forward the salvation of mankind; that I may give a comfortable account of my time at the great day, when all our labors shall be tried.

And if thou art pleased that by my ministry sinners shall be converted, and thy kingdom enlarged, give me the grace of humility, that I may never ascribe the success to myself, but to thy Holy Spirit, which enables me to will and to do according to thy good pleasure. Grant this, O Father of all light and truth, for the sake of Jesus Christ. Amen.

—Thomas Wilson (254)

* * *

O Lord, I humbly beseech and implore thee, grant me always the humble knowledge that edifies. Give unto me that gentle and wise eloquence which is innocent of all arrogance and exaltation of one's own gifts above the brethren. Put into my mouth, I pray thee, the word of consolation and edification and exhortation through thy Holy Spirit, that I may exhort those that are good to be better and, by word and example, recall those who are going contrary to thy straight path. May the words which thou shalt grant to thy servant be as sharp javelins and burning arrows which will pierce the hearts of the hearers and kindle them to fear and love thee. Amen.

—Ambrose (255)

* * *

Almighty, everlasting God, Lord, heavenly Father, whose Word is a lamp to our feet and a light on our way: Open and enlighten my mind that I may understand thy Word purely, clearly, and devoutly, and then, having understood it aright, fashion my life in accord with it, in order that I may never displease thy majesty; through Jesus Christ, thy Son, our dear Lord, who liveth and reigneth with thee and the Holy Ghost, ever one God, world without end. Amen.

—Johannes Bugenhagen (256)

Lord Jesus Christ, open the ears and eyes of my heart, that I may hear and understand thy Word and do thy will. I am a pilgrim on earth; hide not thy commandments from me. Take away the covering from mine eyes, that I may see wonderful things in thy law.
—Ephraem of Edessa (257)

Almighty and most merciful God, who hast sent this book to be the revelation of thy great love to man, and of thy power and will to save him, grant that our study of it may not be made in vain by the callousness or carelessness of our hearts, but that by it we may be confirmed in penitence, lifted in hope, made strong for service, and above all filled with the true knowledge of thee and of thy Son Jesus Christ. Amen.

–George Adam Smith (258)

* * *

Grant me, I beseech thee, O merciful God, ardently to desire, prudently to study, rightly to understand, and perfectly to fulfil that which is pleasing to thee, to the praise and glory of thy name.

–Thomas Aquinas (259)

* * *

O Lord Jesus Christ, who art the Truth incarnate and the Teacher of the faithful; let thy Spirit overshadow us in the reading of thy Word, and conform our thoughts to thy revelation; that learning of thee with honest hearts, we may be rooted and built up in thee, who livest and reignest with the Father and the Holy Spirit, world without end.

–William Bright (260)

* * *

Let not thy Word, O Lord, become a judgment upon us, that we hear it and do it not, that we know it and love it not, that we believe it and obey it not: O thou, who with the Father and the Holy Spirit livest and reignest, world without end. Amen.

–Thomas à Kempis (261)

* * *

Ever blessed God, who art Light and in whom is no darkness at all, and who hast vouchsafed to a dark world the light of the knowledge of thy glory in the face of Jesus Christ, thine Eternal Son, our only Saviour, prosper and sanctify our study of thy sacred Word, the precious record of this thy marvellous revelation; and as all our human wisdom is but foolishness without the illumination of the Holy Spirit, grant us his continual aid, that, being taught of God, we may attain daily unto fuller knowledge of the truth and be fitted ever more and more for the holy ministry whereunto it has pleased thee to call us; through Jesus Christ our Lord. Amen.   —*David Smith* (262)

* * *

Good Master, my only Master, thou who from my youth up hast taught me until this day all that I ever learned of the truth, and all that, as thy pen, I have ever written of it, send down upon me also now of thy great goodness, thy light, so that thou, who hast led me into the profoundest depths, mayest also lead me up to the mountain heights of this inaccessible truth. Thou who hast brought me into this great and wide sea, bring me also into thy haven. Thou who hast conducted me into this wide and pathless desert, thou, my Way, my End, lead me also unto thy end. Show to thy child how to solve the knot of thy Word.

—*Thomas Bradwardine* (263)

* * *

O thou in whom peace abides from age to age, give me now a quiet mind and a listening heart, that the word which thou wouldest speak in this church thou mayest make known to me, and the will which thou wouldest reveal to thy people here thou mayest lodge in my soul this day and for evermore, through Jesus Christ our Lord. Amen.

—*Prayers for the Minister's Day* (264)

FOR SELF AND FLOCK

Remembrance of Baptism

O God, who hast taught us by thy holy apostle that we are buried with Christ by baptism into death; that like as he was raised up from the dead by the glory of the Father, even so we also should walk in newness of life; grant that I may walk in the grace of my baptism, so that the old Adam in me may be drowned and destroyed by daily sorrow and repentance, together with all the sins and evil lusts; and that again a new man may daily come forth and rise, who shall live in the presence of God in righteousness and purity forever; through Jesus Christ, thy well-beloved Son, our Saviour, who liveth and reigneth with thee and the Holy Ghost, one God, world without end. Amen.

—*Luther* (265)

* * *

O God, thou art my God;
I belong to thee; I long for thee.
All my springs are in thee.
In thee is the meaning of my existence.
Toward thee is the deepest intention of my soul,
    The set direction of my life.
To thee I offer myself anew, and all my powers, and
    All the work of this day.
I put myself completely into thy hands to be used
    for thy purposes.
I would have no other desire than to accomplish thy will.
Grant me the help of thy Holy Spirit that I may
    Live this day as unto thee.
Through Jesus Christ our Lord. Amen.

—*Walter S. Davidson* (266)

* * *

Prayer for Faith

God in heaven, I thank thee that thou hast not required of man that he should comprehend Christianity; for if that were required, I should be of all men most miserable. The more I seek to comprehend it, the more incomprehensible it appears to me, and the more I discover merely the possibility of offense. Therefore I thank thee that thou dost only require faith, and I pray thee to increase it more and more. Amen.

–Søren Kierkegaard (267)

* * *

For Courage and Trust

O God, heavenly Father, who desirest all men to be saved and to come to the knowledge of the truth, give me thy Spirit and strengthen my heart that I may never despair, but labor in hope, look unto Christ, endure his cross, and finally have part in his joy. Give me grace to proclaim the truth wisely, charitably, and acceptably, and so to present the Lord Jesus Christ in word and deed, that people may hear him gladly. Be thou my strength and embolden me to serve thee, that, renouncing every worldly ambition and unworthy method, I may trust only in the power of thy Word and thy Spirit and never shrink from declaring thy saving Word of truth, through Jesus Christ our Lord. Amen.

–J.W.D.

* * *

For Courage

Dear heavenly Father, I thank thee that thou hast not hidden from me thy holy Word. Help me to live by it, to withstand every trial and overcome every temptation. Teach me to be a real father to those in my home, to manage my household well, and lead them to eternal life.

Bless me also in the ministry which thou hast committed to me, that I may rightly preach the gospel to the souls entrusted to my care. When undue timidity prevents me from speaking, do thou overrule it; but when I am too facile with thy Word, close thou my mouth.

Give me a genuine compassion for all who suffer and go astray. Teach me to meet thine enemies in the right way. Help me to co-operate with them insofar as this is Christian and to resist them where resistance is due.

Bless also the church which I serve. Give to our leaders a simple trust in thy Word and wisdom, courage, and firmness over against the world. Grant to all our pastors that they may stand together and as brothers bear the church's sorrows and joys. Defend them from contentiousness and from unworthy peaceableness. Above all, graciously befriend all who are suffering persecution. Teach thy church to give thanks for those who suffer for thy name's sake and preserve it from the great sin of leaving them in the lurch.

And now give me diligence, watchfulness, faithfulness, and courage in the office committed to me. Bless the work of my hands and grant me good success. Amen.

—Hans Asmussen (268)

* * *

I need thee to teach me day by day, according to each day's opportunities and needs. Give me, O my Lord, that purity of conscience which alone can receive, which alone can improve thy inspiration. My ears are dull, so that I cannot hear thy voice. My eyes are dim, so that I cannot see thy tokens. Thou alone canst quicken my hearing, and purge my sight, and cleanse and renew my heart. Teach me to sit at thy feet and to hear thy Word. Amen.

—John Henry Newman (269)

O Christ, my Master, let me keep very close to thee. When I am tempted to be undisciplined or self-indulgent, let me remember thy forty days of prayer and fasting. When the fires of my spirit burn low, let me remember thee continuing all night in prayer. When I flinch from hardship, let me go with thee to thy Gethsemane. When I am lonely, let me turn to thee, my risen Lord. Whatever the outer facts may be, grant me thy gift of inner joy; in thy name and through thy grace. Amen.

—Walter Russell Bowie (270)

O Lord, make me the instrument of thy peace.
Where there is hatred, let me sow love;
   Where there is injury, pardon;
   Where there is discord, union;
   Where there is doubt, faith;
   Where there is despair, hope;
   Where there is darkness, light;
   Where there is sadness, joy;
O Lord, grant that we seek
   not to be consoled, but to console;
   not to be understood, but to understand;
   not to be loved, but to love.
For it is in giving that we receive,
   in forgetting that we find ourselves,
   in pardoning that we are pardoned,
   and in dying that we are born to eternal life. Amen.

—Francis of Assisi (271)

* * *

The Busy Pastor

Teach me, good Lord:

Not to murmur at multitude of business or shortness of time.

Not to magnify undertaken duties by seeming to suffer under them, but to treat all as liberties and gladnesses.

Not to call attention to crowded work, or petty fatigues.

Not to gather encouragement from appreciation by others, lest this should interfere with purity of motive.

Not to seek praise, respect, gratitude, or regard from superiors or equals on account of age or past service.

Not to let myself be placed in favorable contrast with another.
       —Edward White Benson (272)

O Lord, give, I beseech thee, in the name of Jesus Christ thy Son, my God, that love which never faileth, that my light may be kindled and never quenched; that it may burn in me and give light to others. And thou, O Christ, our dearest Saviour, do thou thyself constantly kindle our lamps that they may shine evermore in thy temple, that they may receive unquenchable light from thee, the unquenchable Light; that our darkness may be enlightened while the darkness of the world flies from us. My Jesus, I beseech thee, give thy light to my lamp, that in its light may be manifested to me that Holy of Holies, in which thou, the eternal Priest, dost dwell: that I may continually contemplate thee only, long for thee, gaze on thee, and yearn for thee in love, O Saviour full of love! show thyself to us that knock, that we may perceive and love thee alone, think of thee day and night; that thy love, which many waters cannot quench, may possess our whole souls, and nevermore be quenched by the waters of the earth; to the praise of thy holy name. Amen.

—The Call to Worship (273)

* * *

O Lord God, merciful and mighty:
Help those whom I have neglected to help,
Set aright those whom I have caused to stumble;
Visit those whom I have neglected to visit;
Bring back those whom I have led astray;
Cheer the hearts of those whom I have made sad;
Draw with the cords of thy love those for whom
    my love has grown cold.
Save them all, O Lord, and have mercy upon me, the chief
    of sinners, lest after that I have preached to others, I myself
    should be a castaway.
Hear me, O Father, for the sake of Christ, my Lord.
    Amen.

—Unknown

O thou faithful God, merciful Father, who hast called me, thy poor, unworthy servant, to the holy ministry and made me a fisher of men, that I might draw many souls into the kingdom of heaven, and hast set me apart by thine own proper means to preach the gospel to this my flock: I beseech thee, by thy grace, to fit me, thine unworthy servant, for the ministry of the New Testament. Grant that I may be a faithful minister and steward of the mysteries of God and wait upon mine office cheerfully, not for the sake of shameful gain, but with all my heart and for love of thy holy name. Grant that I may faithfully feed the flock thou hast entrusted to me with wholesome doctrine; wait upon the weak, heal the sick, bind up the wounded, restore the erring, seek the lost, and with gentle spirit correct those who have been overtaken in a fault. Bestow upon me thy Holy Spirit, who giveth my lips wisdom rightly to divide thy Word. Suffer me not to be an empty vessel of thy grace, but work thou abundantly through me and give thy blessing richly. Thou hast made me a watchman over thy people, help me, O Lord, that I may warn the wicked and teach transgressors thy ways, that sinners may be converted unto thee and many won into thy kingdom. Vouchsafe also that I myself may live in conformity to thy Word and be an example to the flock, lest when I have preached to others I myself should be a castaway, or lest by an ungodly life I give cause to thine enemies to blaspheme thy name, or otherwise give offense. Grant unto me and all my hearers thy Holy Spirit, that we may know thee, the only true God, and Jesus Christ, continue in penitence and steadfast hope unto the end, and thus together receive the incorruptible crown of glory when the great Shepherd shall appear, even Jesus Christ our Saviour, who liveth and reigneth with thee and the Holy Ghost, world without end. Amen.

—Johann Habermann (274)

I do not ask
That crowds may throng the temple,
    That standing room be priced;
I only ask that as I voice the message
    They may see Christ!

I do not ask
For church by pomp or pageant,
    Or music such as wealth alone can buy;
I only ask that as I voice the message
    He may be nigh!

I do not ask
That men may sound my praises,
    Or headlines spread my name abroad;
I only pray that as I voice the message
    Hearts may find God!

I do not ask
For earthly place or laurel,
    Or of this world's distinctions any part;
I only ask, when I have voiced the message,
    My Saviour's heart!   —*Ralph S. Cushman* (275)

* * *

For Forgiveness

O Lord, we are not worthy of the least of all thy mercies
and all the truth which thou hast showed unto thy servants.
But thou, by thy great compassion, forgive us, O Lord:

Our little faith, our lack of vision,

The sin of knowing thy word and not proclaiming it with
boldness and passion,

Our readiness to accept half-truths and to be carried away
by every wind of doctrine,

Our many sins against thy love and thy mercy in our
daily relationships,

Our many driftings into ease and compromise, our slackness in the fight against evil,

The prejudice and pride which often obscures our sense of oneness in thee.

Forgive us, O Lord.

Lord, have mercy upon us.

Christ, have mercy upon us.

Lord, have mercy upon us. Amen.

—Suzanne de Dietrich (276)

* * *

Dedication

Lord, we would be thy instruments. We have nothing to offer except the desire to be workers in thy harvest. But since thou hast chosen the weak things of this world and the things which are not, wilt thou not also choose us to be thy servants? We cannot of ourselves speak thy message to man. But we pray that thou wilt grant us not to speak our own words but thy Word, through which men come to know and love thee.

Give us courage to confess the name of Jesus Christ before men. Help us to care for them, to act as neighbors unto them and to share with them what thou hast given to us. We do not ask to see the results of our work. We would only know that thou art using us in thy work of salvation and that thy kingdom is coming among us. Send us, Lord, as witnesses of the good news of thy love made known in Jesus Christ. Amen.

—W. A. Visser 't Hooft (277)

* * *

FOR FIRMNESS

O God, who hast given us the grace to carry the sword of thy kingdom of peace; who hast made us messengers of peace in a world of strife, and messengers of strife in a world of false peace: make strong our hand, make clear our voice, give us humility with firmness and insight with passion that we may fight not to conquer, but to redeem.

O God, who hast given us the grace to be the instruments of love in its work of healing and judgment; who hast commissioned us to proclaim forgiveness and condemnation, deliverance to the captive and captivity to the proud; give us the patience of those who understand, and the impatience of those who love: that the might of thy gentleness may work through us, and the mercy of thy wrath may speak through us.

O God, who hast set us upon a hill, a city of light that cannot be hid; and dost bid us shine forth in all places, uncover the hidden works of darkness, and make plain the lies of greed and self-esteem; grant us thy power, that we spare not ourselves or others, but send forth thy light without fear or favor, to those who seek it and to those who fear it.

O God of truth and love and peace, we thank thee for thy constraint upon us, for work undone which we must do, for truth unspoken which we must speak. Possess us. Be strong in us, that we may be strong to do thy will. In the name of him who calls us to thy kingdom of peace and love and truth. Amen.

—Gregory Vlastos (278)

* * *

Almighty God, heavenly Father, who hast called us too into the work of thy vineyard and lavished upon us thy grace and all manner of spiritual and eternal gifts, help us to live unto thee in humility and patience, to hope in thy pure grace and faithfulness, to abide in thy house, and praise and magnify thy glorious grace for ever, through Christ our Lord. Amen.

—Hermann Bezzel (279)

* * *

O Sovereign Pastor, who gavest thy life for thy sheep, grant that I may never sacrifice thy flock to my own ease, convenience, profit, or pleasure. But grant that I may employ my time, my substance, my care, my labors, my prayers, for their welfare continually, and thus, at least, "give my life for my sheep." Amen.

—Thomas Wilson (280)

* * *

Grant us, O Lord of the church, living congregations in which thy Spirit shall speak and work and make me also ready to serve thee in thy church with the gift thou hast given me, not to please men and not for worldly honor, but for gratitude and love. Amen.

—Otto Riethmüller (281)

* * *

O God, who hast brought us into the church of thy dear Son, make all in our parish a family of one heart and mind in love toward thee; and grant that our common life and work may help to bring in thy kingdom; through Jesus Christ our Lord.

—Prayers for All Occasions (282)

* * *

PRAYERS FOR THEOLOGICAL STUDENTS

O Lord Jesus Christ, give me thy blessing in my preparation for the work of the ministry in thy holy church. Remove far from me the spirit of worldliness and give me grace, that I may continually grow in that holiness of life which is required of those who bear the vessels of the Lord. Give me that wisdom which cometh from above, and that gentleness which becometh the gospel of peace. Make me diligent in the study of thy Word, and teach me by thy Spirit so that I may be enabled to teach others. And so bless me in these years of preparation that I may be thoroughly furnished unto every good work, doing all things unto thy glory, who with the Father and the Holy Ghost are one God, world without end. Amen.

—John Wright (283)

O God, who hast kindled in me the desire to dedicate my life to thy service as a minister of the gospel: Grant me an abundant measure of thy grace during these years of my preparation that I may use profitably the opportunities to study and walk worthy of the calling of one to whom shall be entrusted the ministry of sacred things; through Jesus Christ my Lord. Amen.

—Emil E. Fischer (284)

* * *

Let thy blessing, O Lord, rest upon those who are seeking to prepare themselves to be ministers of thy Word. Give them a true understanding of the needs of the human heart and a sure faith in the adequacy of Jesus Christ to fulfil those needs. Keep them steadfast in the determination to devote their lives to bringing Christ to men, and help them so to use the time of their preparation that all their studies may be made to contribute toward the fulfilment of their holy calling; through the same Jesus Christ, our Lord. Amen.

—Emil E. Fischer (285)

* * *

ORDINATION AND ANNIVERSARY OF ORDINATION

Dedication before Ordination

O Lord, I give myself to thee, thine ever, only thine to be. This day I consecrate all that I have or hope to be to thy service. All that I have been I lay at the foot of thy cross. O crucified Lord, forgive the sins of my past life; fold me in the embrace of thine all-prevailing sacrifice; purify me by thy Passion: raise me by thy perfect submission. Son of Man, hallow all my emotions and affections; gather them to thyself and make them strong only for thy service, enduring through thy Presence. Eternal Word, sanctify my thoughts; make them free with the freedom of thy Spirit. Son of God, consecrate my will to thyself; unite it with thine; and so fill me with thine own abundant life. King of glory, my Lord and

Master, take my whole being; redeem it by thy blood; engird it with thy power; use it in thy service; and draw it ever closer to thyself. From this day forth, O Master, take my life and let it be ever only all for thee. Amen.

—Cosmo Gordon Lang (286)

* * *

O Lord, in the simplicity of my heart, I offer myself to thee today, to be thy servant for ever, to obey thee, and to be a sacrifice of perpetual praise. Amen.

—Thomas à Kempis

* * *

O Lord, I give myself to thee, I trust thee wholly. Thou art wiser than I, more loving to me than I myself. Deign to fulfil thy high purposes in me whatever they be; work in me and through me. I am born to serve thee, to be thine, to be thy instrument. Let me be thy blind instrument. I ask not to see, I ask not to know, I ask simply to be used. Amen.

—John Henry Newman (287)

* * *

Remember, O Lord, what thou hast wrought in us, and not what we deserve; and as thou hast called us to thy service, make us worthy of our calling.

—Leonine Sacramentary

* * *

Prayer at an Ordination

O Jesus, we thy ministers bow before thee to confess the common sins of our calling. Thou knowest all things; thou knowest that we love thee and that our heart's desire is to serve thee in faithfulness; and yet, like Peter, we have so often failed thee in the hour of thy need. If ever we have loved our own leadership and power when we sought to lead our people to thee, we pray thee to forgive. If we have been engrossed in narrow duties and little questions, when the vast needs of humanity called aloud for prophetic vision and apostolic sympathy, we pray thee to forgive. If in our loyalty to the church of the past we have distrusted thy living voice and have suffered thee to pass from our door unheard, we pray thee to forgive. If ever we have been more concerned for the strong and the rich than for the shepherdless throngs of the people for whom thy soul grieved, we pray thee to forgive.

O Master, amidst our failures we cast ourselves upon thee in humility and contrition. We need new light and a new message. We need the ancient spirit of prophecy and the leaping fire and joy of a new conviction, and thou alone canst give it. Inspire the ministry of thy church with dauntless courage to face the vast needs of the future. Free us from all entanglements that have hushed our voice and bound our action. Grant us grace to look upon the veiled sins of the rich and the coarse vices of the poor through thine eyes. Give us thine inflexible sternness against sin, and thine inexhaustible compassion for the frailty and tragedy of those who do sin. Make us faithful shepherds of thy flock, true seers of God, and true followers of Jesus. Amen.

—The Call to Worship (288)

Anniversary of Ordination

Almighty and most merciful God, thou hast called me to be a shepherd of thy people, whom thou hast purchased with the innocent and precious blood of thy Son, Jesus Christ. It is not men who have called me, but thou thyself hast done it through the mouth of men, and for this office hast given me thy Holy Spirit with the laying on of human hands. Thanks be to thee for thine unspeakable gift of grace.

In that thou hast called me, thou hast set before me a great promise. Thou hast promised unto me for my ministry, that thine own saving Word would go forth in my words to the church and the world, and that thou thyself wouldst grant forgiveness and life when my hands administer baptism and communion and I grant absolution. In my calling thou hast most certainly promised that Jesus Christ, the crucified and risen Lord, would himself be present and active in my ministry.

Thanks be to thee for this immeasurable promise. It is greater than any man can fathom. By this promise thou hast freed me from struggling to perform my own works, liberated me to share in the works of thy victorious power.

O holy and righteous God, I confess that I am not worthy to remain in thy service, not worthy to be called a shepherd of thy flock. I have neglected thy promise in a thousand ways. Forgive my sins for the sake of Jesus Christ the Good Shepherd. Requite not my guilt upon those whom thou hast entrusted to me. Account not unto me the words by which I have denied thee and the silences by which I have led astray thy flock.

Look not in judgment upon those who testify against me, the sinners whom I have not warned, the sick I have not visited, the betrayed whose cause I have not defended, the children whom I have not led to thee. Look not upon my wrongdoing, but look upon thy dear Son, Jesus Christ, the Shepherd and the Lamb who bore the sins of the world. By thy grace, reckon unto me his obedience.

Almighty and merciful God, take not thy ministry from me, but grant unto me once more thy Holy Spirit. Stir up in me thy gift of grace that it may be a leaping flame to burn up my proud and deceitful spirit and transform my whole being to the praise of thy glory. Amen.

—*Orate Fratres* (289)

* * *

In Commemoration of the Day of Ordination

Unto the King eternal, immortal, invisible, the only wise God, be honor and glory for ever and ever. Hellelujah.

Thus saith the Lord to his apostle who thrice denied him: Simon, son of Jonas, lovest thou me more than these? He saith unto him, yea, Lord, thou knowest that I love thee. He saith unto him, Feed my lambs. He saith to him again the second time, Simon, son of Jonas, lovest thou me? He saith unto him, yea, Lord; thou knowest that I love thee. He saith to him, Feed my sheep. He saith unto him the third time, Simon, son of Jonas, lovest thou me? Peter was grieved, because he said unto him the third time, Lovest thou me? And he said unto him, Lord, thou knowest all things; thou knowest that I love thee. Jesus saith unto him, Feed my sheep.

* * *

Almighty and most merciful God! thou hast called me to the office of shepherd and servant of thy church, which thou hast purchased for thyself through the innocent and precious blood of thy Son Jesus Christ. It is not men who have called me, but thou thyself hast called me through the lips of men and given me the Holy Spirit for this office by the laying on of human hands. Thanks be to thee for thine unspeakable gift of grace.

In that thou didst call me, O Lord, thou didst set before me a great promise. With my office thou gavest me the promise that in my words thine own saving Word would go out to the congregation and the world, and that when my hands administered baptism and the Lord's Supper, thou thyself would grant forgiveness and life. Through my call thou didst promise most surely, that, in my ministry, Jesus Christ the Crucified and Risen would himself be present and active.

Thanks be to thee for this immeasurable promise. It is greater than any man can ever fathom. By that promise thou hast freed me from the limitations of mine own efforts and made me free to participate in the works of thy victorious power.

Most holy and righteous God, I confess unto thee that I am not worthy that thou shouldst let me remain in thy ministry. I am not meet to be called a shepherd of thy flock. A thousand times have I neglected thy promise.

How often have I despaired at the terrors of this world and the impenitence of my congregation. How often have I become weary and sick of the indifference of those committed to my care. The manifest fruitlessness of my work and my own unworthiness have often influenced me more strongly than thy promise, and joylessly and slow of heart I performed my ministry like a profession.

But when thou didst glorify thy name in the sight of the world; when thou didst gather and waken and comfort men through my words, when thou didst break through the spell of indifference and self-trust in my congregation, I was all too ready to take the credit myself and be conscious of my own efforts and accomplishments.

By littleness of faith and pride I have stood in the way of thy Word. Instead of being only a mouth through which thou didst daily speak thy Word anew to men; instead of being a quietness through which thy mighty Word sounded forth, I have spoken myself and dealt out wrath and reconciliation, sorrow and joy, presuming to administer thy wrath and thy grace, thy godly sorrow and thy heavenly joy. Driven by the pressures of this world and shunning the silence of listening for thy Word, I have busied myself with the empty running of machinery, quite confident that I already knew what thou wouldst speak to men. But thus have I neglected thy promise and failed to reach the real persons to whom thou hast sent me.

Most holy and merciful God, forgive my sins for the sake of Jesus Christ the Good Shepherd.

Remember not in thy judgment, O Lord, the words with which I have preached judgment when I should have given comfort, or with which I have comforted when I should have proclaimed thy wrath. Visit not my sin upon the people thou hast entrusted to me. Forgive them, for often they could not

173

know what they were doing because I did not tell them. Remember not the words by which I have denied thee and the silences by which I have misled thy flock.

Look not in thy judgment to them that testify against me, the sinners I did not admonish, the sick I did not visit, the helpless whose cause I did not plead, the children I did not lead to thee. Look not upon my wrongdoing but look to thy dear Son Jesus Christ, who as Shepherd and Lamb alike bore the sins of the world. By thy grace impute unto me his obedience.

Almighty and most merciful God, take not thy charge, the holy ministry, from me, but grant me again thy Holy Spirit. Enkindle within me the gift of thy Spirit to a blazing fire, that my pride and despair may be burned away and I, the whole man, may be changed to an offering of praise to thy glory.

Come, Holy Spirit, thou Spirit of the Father and the Son, make God's Word great for me; make me desire it and delight in it, that nothing may be more joyful to me than to listen to it speaking still to me today. Sanctify me, that I may be nothing but the mouth of God's speech. Open my eyes that I may see the flock entrusted to me with the eyes of the Good Shepherd, that I may recognize and lift up the bruised reed. Awaken within me the image of the one High Priest, Jesus Christ.

Come, Holy Spirit, pour down thyself upon thy church. Raise up in her men and women to serve with me in common priestly ministry. Cleanse in us what is unclean. Water and sprinkle what is parched. Restore what is wrong. Warm what is cold. Direct what is rebellious. Grant us great power to do that which is good and avoid that which is evil.

Come down also, Holy Spirit, upon the members of my family. Make them thine own living temples. Sanctify our marriage, that we may be one in praise of thy grace and in thy service. Stir up my children to be witnesses to thy wonderful works.

Creator Spirit, come thou also upon my brethren whom thou hast set over me for the leadership of thy church. So rule these thy servants that thou shalt thyself be the Leader of thy church. Help me to see in their guidance thine own divine governance, that we may all be one body and grow up into him who is our Head, even Jesus Christ, our crucified and risen Lord, to whom be glory for ever and ever. Amen.

* * *

Thus saith the Lord : Thou hast burdened me with thy sins, thou hast wearied me with thine iniquities. I, even I, am he that blotteth out thy transgressions for mine own sake; and I will not remember thy sins. And again he saith : I will put a new spirit within you and I will take the stony heart out of your flesh.

* * *

Praise, glory, and honor be unto thee, the Father, and the Son, and the Holy Ghost. Amen.   *—Edmund Schlink* (290)

* * *

O God, by whose command the order of all time runs its course, look graciously upon me thy servant, whom thou hast been pleased to call to thy service, and that my service may be pleasing to thee, do thou mercifully preserve in me thy gifts; through Jesus Christ our Lord. Amen.

—Gelasian Sacramentary (291)

MEDITATIONS FOR MINISTERS

AN ANTHOLOGY

SUNDAY

The Divine Institution and Mission of the Ministry

* * *

I heard the voice of the Lord saying, "Whom shall I send, and who will go for us?" Then I said, "Here I am! Send me." —Isaiah 6:8

———

Take heed to yourselves and to all the flock, in which the Holy Spirit has made you guardians, to feed the church of the Lord which he obtained with his own blood. —Acts 20:28

THE INSTITUTION OF THE MINISTRY

Article IV

Of Justification

Also they teach, that men cannot be justified before God by their own strength, merits, or works, but are freely justified for Christ's sake through faith, when they believe that they are received into favor, and their sins are forgiven for Christ's sake, who, by his death, hath made satisfaction for our sins. This faith God imputes for righteousness in his sight. Rom. 3 and 4.

Article V

Of the Ministry of the Church

That we may obtain this faith, the office of teaching the gospel and administering the sacraments was instituted.

For through the Word and sacraments, as through instruments, the Holy Ghost is given, who worketh faith where and when it pleaseth God in those that hear the gospel, to wit, that God, not for our own merits, but for Christ's sake, justified those who believe that they are received into favor for Christ's sake.

—The Augsburg Confession, 1530 (1)

* * *

The church has God's command to appoint ministers and deacons. And because it is so great a consolation that we know that he will preach and work through men and those who have been chosen by men, it is good that this choosing of men be highly praised and honored.

—Apology of the Augsburg Confession (2)

The twelve apostles were the followers and representatives of their Lord, clothed with the authority to speak like him in his name, to forgive sins, and to continue his work. Following the apostles, other men receive the commission to be pastors and teachers of the church of God. The church is an organism in which all the members do not have the same function. In this church, God has appointed "first apostles, second prophets, third teachers" to feed the flock and constantly continue their instruction. The ministry is therefore one of the means by which he continues his work and still speaks and acts on earth. —*Bo Giertz* (3)

* * *

The Second Epistle to the Corinthians is a minister's discussion with a congregation that is not satisfied with him. And in it the Apostle shows himself to be a witness of the mercy of God in that he does not defend and justify himself; neither does he pity himself and neither does he fulminate. He says in the fourth chapter, "Therefore, having this ministry by the mercy of God, we do not lose heart." Here "mercy" and "ministry" (*diakonia*) are juxtaposed. Paul is saying, because I know that my ministry stems from mercy, none of you can put me out of countenance. This "countenance" I owe to God.

Is not this the one comfort that is given to us when we are assailed by the world? . . . Always it is a firm consolation to know whence we have received our office and ministry. We hold it in an order instituted by God. This order has its origin in mercy. Because we have received mercy, because this happened and still goes on happening, we can serve. This mercy does not stand only at the beginning of our ministry, it accompanies us always, even into every doubt and difficulty. Only he who makes mercy in this sense the foundation of his ministry can go on working confidently. —*Georg Merz* (4)

The ministry is not to be unduly exalted above other callings. All callings which, in the order of creation, contribute to community are equally holy. It is not, therefore, a degradation or a sign of unfaithfulness, if a man leaves the ministry for another calling. What is decisive, and what may be disgraceful, is his reason for doing so. But equally disgraceful may be his reason for coveting the prerogatives of the ministry (cf. Simon Magus). In either case a man must feel himself called of God to that specific function.

On the other hand, the ministry is not to be degraded and made common. The office of Word and sacrament not only lends dignity and authority, but also makes exacting demands. It is not a man's gifts, his learning, his efficiency, or the charm of his personality which make him a minister, but the gospel which he is called upon and ordained to preach. This makes him "minister" (servant), "bishop" (overseer), "pastor" (shepherd), "priest" (a Christ to his neighbor), "parson" (representative person). This, which he is, he must constantly become. He must, therefore, stand before his people as one of them, a fellow-sinner, and yet in the full dignity and authority of his office, which he "strives to adorn with a holy life and conversation." The high estimate which the laity puts upon the office of the ministry is not to be disappointed. The dialectic of the situation cannot be avoided. The minister is not a priest with an indelible character upon whose ministrations in the sacraments the layman is dependent. Neither is he just another member of the congregation. But he stands before the congregation as the bearer of the office of Word and sacraments upon which the congregation is dependent. It is, however, the living Word upon which the congregation is dependent, and it is this which empowers the sacraments. It is, therefore, the living Christ who must be brought to men in the "mediated immediacy" of Word and sacrament. This differs from a sacramental view which thinks of substantial powers infused.

—*The Doctrine of the Ministry* (5)

To ordain does not mean to consecrate. Accordingly if we know of a godly man, we choose him and, on the strength of the Word which is ours, we give him authority to preach the Word and administer the sacraments. This is what it means to ordain. They [Catholics] explained the word *bestellen*, which comes from the apostles, with the word *weihen*, but we who are gathered together in Christ's name and possess the Word are indifferent to those things which pertain to orders. If, then, we are in agreement that this man or some other should be ordained, surely he is ordained. But this is opposed because it is something new. He is a priest who is a brother of Christ and is anointed by the Holy Spirit to be as Christ; he is a priest by virtue of his baptism. Consequently whoever tries to make a priest, as a minister of the Word is made, blasphemes God who has already done this. "By ordination" means "by choice," that there may be an order or arrangement to prevent everybody from preaching who wishes to do so. By the same token one ought to exercise one's ministry, but not forever, for it can be committed to a man today and taken away from him again tomorrow. The priesthood which we receive from Christ, on the other hand, continues forever. Such is the ministry. To be sure, this is only a formula; it needs to be expounded at greater length. At all events, it is the Word that makes priests, . . . not any outward anointing or tonsure.

—Luther (6)

* * *

Remember that, however much ordination pledges us to a particular profession, it imposes upon us no additional obligation to holiness. It is a great privilege to be a minister of the church, but it is a far greater privilege to be a member of it; he who most magnifies the solemnity of baptism will most rightly value the far inferior solemnity of ordination.

—Arthur Penrhyn Stanley (7)

I like to think of the minister as only one of the congregation set apart by the rest for a particular purpose. They say to him: Look, brother, we are busy with our daily toils, and confused with cares, but we eagerly long for peace and light to illuminate our life, and we have heard there is a land where these are to be found, a land of repose and joy, full of thoughts that breathe and words that burn, but we cannot go thither ourselves. We are too embroiled in daily cares. Come, we will elect you, and set you free from toil, and you shall go thither for us and week by week trade with that land and bring us its treasures and its spoils. *—James Stalker* (8)

* * *

You are the servants and ministers of the Crucified. He on high is your Master. You may be the ministers of the highest earthly blessing to men; but it is the blessings of the world unseen, blessings for weary and endangered souls, blessings purchased by the Eternal Sacrifice, and running on through death into an everlasting life—it is with these that you are specially charged. Do nothing, admit nothing in what you allow to yourselves, which shall confuse or obscure that yours is a spiritual ministry, and that you, as your Master, have to do with souls. *—Richard William Church* (9)

* * *

In Praise of the Ministry

Who can tell all the glory and the virtue that a real and faithful pastor has in the eyes of God? There is no dearer treasure, nor any more precious thing on earth or in this life than a real and faithful pastor or preacher.

Reckon for yourself the profit which the preaching office and the care of souls produce; your son is assuredly producing this profit, if he is conducting this office faithfully. For example, so many souls are daily taught by him, converted, baptized, and brought to Christ and saved, redeemed from sins, death, hell, and the devil, and through him come to everlasting righteousness, to everlasting life and heaven. As Daniel says, "They that teach others shall shine as the heavens, and they that turn many to righteousness shall be as the stars in eternity." Because God's Word and office, when they are rightly administered, must without ceasing do great things, and work actual miracles, so your son must without ceasing do great miracles before God, such as raising the dead, driving out devils, making the blind to see, the deaf to hear, the lepers clean, the dumb to speak. Though these things may not happen in a bodily way, yet they do happen spiritually in the soul, where the miracles are even greater. Christ says, in John 14, "He that believeth on me shall do the works that I do, and do still greater works." If a believer can do this to single individuals, how much more will a public preacher do it to a great crowd? Not that he does this as a man! It is his office, ordained by God for this purpose, that does it, that and the Word of God which he teaches; he is the instrument for this.

But for the world, too, he does great and mighty works. He informs and instructs all classes how they are to conduct themselves outwardly in their offices and ranks, so that they may do what is right before God; he can comfort and advise those who are troubled, compose difficulties, relieve troubled consciences, help to maintain peace and to settle and remove differences, doing innumerable works of this kind every day. For a preacher confirms and strengthens and helps to maintain government, and temporal peace of all kinds. He checks the rebellious; teaches obedience, morals, discipline, and honor; instructs fathers and mothers and children and servants in their duties; in a word, he is the teacher of all secular offices and ranks. These are, indeed, the smallest good works of a pastor, and yet they are so high and noble that no wise men among all the heathen have either known them or understood them, still less been able to do them. Nay more, even today no jurist, no university, foundation, or monastery knows these works, and they are not taught either in canon law or secular law. For in these spheres there is no one who calls these offices God's greatest gifts or his gracious ordinances; it is only the Word of God and the preachers that praise and honor them so highly.

A true pastor, then, serves men in body and soul, in property and honor. See now how he serves God and what a glorious sacrifice, or service, he renders; for by his work and his word the kingdom of God is maintained in the world; so, too, are kept the name and the honor and the glory of God, the true knowledge of God, the right faith and understanding of Christ, the fruits of the suffering and blood and death of Christ, the gifts and works and power of the Holy Spirit, the true and saving use of baptism and the sacrament, the right and pure doctrine of the gospel, the right way of disciplining and crucifying the body. Who could ever give high enough praise to any one of these things? What more can be said about them? The more one does with these things, the more he carries on the battle against the devil, the world's wisdom, and the imaginations of the flesh; the more victories he wins; the more he puts down error and prevents heresy. For he must strive and fight against the gates of hell and overcome the devil. He does it, too; and yet not he, but his work and his word. These are the innumerable and unspeakable works and miracles of the preaching office. In a word, if one would praise God to the uttermost, one must praise his Word and the preaching of it; for it is God's Word, and the preaching of it is his. —*Luther* (10)

* * *

Only in one respect dare you put yourself beside the apostle : you have the same Lord to preach, the same baptism to administer, to forgive and to retain sins in the same way. Take heed diligently that none may rob you of this treasure! It is not harder for him who hears your words to come to Christ than for those who heard the preaching of the apostle. He whom you baptize is no less baptized than those whom the apostle baptized. He who receives the forgiveness of sins from you receives it as surely as one who received it from the apostle. This is the highest honor of your ministry.

—*Hans Asmussen* (11)

* * *

There are greater honors and higher ranks, but there is no other office that refreshes the weariness of the heart and brings comfort to the poor and speaks peace to the dying and shows a lost world the way home.   —*Hermann Bezzel* (12)

* * *

Saumur is an old provincial town in France on the banks of the Loire. At the end of the sixteenth century it was one of the chief strongholds of Protestantism in France, and a Protestant church still exists there. Today the town is chiefly important because of a large *"École de Cavalerie"* established as long ago as 1768. At the entrance of the ancient Roman Catholic Church of St. Pierre, in the prewar days, the traveler might have seen a placard urging French youth to enter the priesthood. It read in part: "There are just four days in anyone's life: birth, confirmation, marriage, death. Would you not like to be one who would be needed on all four of those days?"   —*Raymond Calkins* (13)

* * *

There is no romance in the world comparable to that of the Christian ministry. In part . . . that romance is to be found in the dealing with human lives, which present to the minister untold spiritual opportunities which appeal to his interest, his imagination, his sympathetic understanding. His quiet work of parish ministration deepens and broadens every year. He finds himself content even in the smallest parish, with every ambition satisfied. To see the signs of inner progress; to watch over the growing lives; to meet the sorrows of many people; to be persuaded of the reality of the influence he can wield; to find himself drawn by the deep ties of spiritual affection; to have his days filled with duties that are perpetually fresh with all their sameness; to have the right of entrance to many homes and to many hearts; to be known by all whom he meets; to be able to speak freely on the deepest things in life; to find himself always confronted by tasks which are too great to be measured; and all the time to know the blessedness of human love, to have the memory of happy years—what more romantic life on earth can be lived than that? He may have a baptismal service, a wedding, a funeral service on the same day, certainly within the same week. Let one ponder the infinite significance of each one of these, and who touches life at its very center more intimately, more constantly than he? And his whole life is made up of these things. He deals with human nature in its spiritual relationships. What business on earth is so meaningful as that?

The ministry may be the most arduous, the most difficult, the most precarious of the professions, but it is the most rewarding. It yields deeper and more lasting happiness and satisfaction than any other. "Always in time of stress, I turn to you." So wrote a young woman to her minister. To know that people in time of trouble will want you, need you : can there be anything more beautiful than that?

And beneath all of this, there is the knowledge that his work is not, cannot be in vain. Always he can see even in time of apparent failure the rod of the almond tree (Jer. 1:11–12). Others may despair; he never. When all looks like winter, he knows that there are infinite forces at work that can and will bring to life all that is best in man and in the world. He has the romantic hope that is not based on a secular appraisal of life, but rather has its source in the energizing powers of God, the travail of whose soul shall not be satisfied until the kingdoms of this world become the kingdoms of our Lord and of his Christ.

So the parish minister goes his way day by day, rejoicing in the very diversity of interests and activities that fill his days, dealing with almost every type of problem known to human experience, and filled with a hope that never grows dim. Looking back upon it all, he says, I would like to live it all over again. For my life has been pure poetry, real romance from first to last. There is no more romantic career than that of a minister of Jesus Christ.

—Raymond Calkins (14)

* * *

The Laborers are Few

The most incomprehensible thing about our calling is that God can and should use us men as co-workers at all! What a fathomless ocean of mercy we gaze into, that God should call such as you and me to be ministers of his holy, almighty, and merciful Word! That the Lord for whom it would be a little thing to achieve his purpose without us, should seek laborers for his harvest and be willing to take us into his service—this is so incomprehensible that we can only credit it in gratitude and obedience.

The secret of this calling lies not least in the opening of our eyes to see the field that is white for harvest, to see all the uncomforted need and guilt that, whether knowingly or not, is hungering and thirsting for the gospel. "The harvest is plentiful, but the laborers are few." The truth is, indeed, that it is high time to pray the Lord to send laborers into his harvest. How little we pray for this! In any case I believe that this will be of more help in clarifying the question of whether one has been called than all our brooding: ". . . but the laborers are few."

—Heinrich Vogel (15)

Speaking the Gospel Joyfully

Whenever we are together we ought to magnify not only the mercy of God which has forgiven us, but also his goodness in using us for his work. I hope there are among us many brethren, who, though they may have been led into the ministry through various accidents, nevertheless gain the courage to say, "I have been called," or at least, "This has been committed to me." We should strengthen and encourage one another in this. Often we are such timidhearted persons, and the burden of the ministry lies heavy upon us. Many a time we would be glad to shake it off and take leave of the ministry, and yet, inwardly, we cannot take leave, and we go on, groaning and grieving. I meet many a whimpering brother, members of the church's troop of groaning laborers. They surely cannot exert much attractive force in the community. Is the reason for much of the fruitlessness of our preaching that we appear in the pulpit and in the congregation with such gloomy faces? Is not this so often a hindrance for the children and young people of our congregations? I trust that we give them faithful and stout instruction; but surely much of what we say to them will be forgotten. Much would be gained if they simply took with them this impression: A young man, or an old man, stood up before us; what he told us we did not always understand; but there must be something wonderfully lovely about the gospel if a person can talk about it so joyfully!

—*Friedrich von Bodelschwingh* (16)

ON FITNESS FOR THE MINISTRY

One of the most certain marks of a divine call is, when it is the full purpose of a man's heart to live for Jesus Christ and his church.
—Thomas Wilson (17)

* * *

Gifts and office make no men sons of God; as so, they are but servants; though these, as ministers and apostles, were servants of the highest form. It is the church, as such, that is the lady, a queen, the bride, the Lamb's wife; and prophets, apostles, and ministers are but servants, stewards, laborers for her good.

As therefore the lady is above the servant, the queen above the steward, or the wife above all her husband's officers, so is the church, as such, above these officers.

—John Bunyan (18)

* * *

Two reassurances come at once to the support of one who enters thus by divine summons upon the work of the ministry. The first it that the fundamental qualities needed for the performance of his task are not those of the exceptional man. They are within the reach of every consecrated man. It is not required that he should be a man of unusual intellectual ability, that he should have outstanding traits that at once command attention and compel admiration, or that he should be gifted in any special fashion. What is demanded is virtue that is inherent in manhood as such, all touched and quickened and sweetened by the spirit of Jesus Christ. The spiritualization of average capacities rather than the possession of unusual powers is the needful element.

The second great ground of hope is that ordinary abilities, when touched by the Spirit of God, become extraordinary. The disciples were not ready and furnished for their apostolic work until they had had their pentecostal experience. Then see what manner of men they became! And today let a minister with no special gifts of mind or character be baptized as by fire with the Holy Spirit, and his life is given unimagined influence over the lives of other men. Nothing on earth is more romantic than the unsuspected powers thus released in themselves and to others who have only moderate human ability. Whom God chooses to be his prophet he equips for the task.

—Raymond Calkins (19)

* * *

An office-bearer who wants something other than to obey his King is unfit to bear his office. —Abraham Kuyper (20)

* * *

> Give me the priest these graces shall possess;
> Of an ambassador, the just address,
> A Father's tenderness, a Shepherd's care,
> A Leader's courage, which the cross can bear,
> A Ruler's arm, a Watchman's wakeful eye,
> A Pilot's skill, the helm in storms to ply,
> A Fisher's patience, and a Labourer's toil,
> A Guide's dexterity to disembroil,
> A Prophet's inspiration from above,
> A Teacher's knowledge, and a Saviour's love.
> Give me a priest, a light upon a hill,
> Whose rays his whole circumference can fill,
> In God's own Word and Sacred Learning versed,
> Deep in the study of the heart immersed,
> Who in such souls can the disease descry,
> And wisely fair restoratives supply.

—Thomas Ken (21)

* * *

Then said the Interpreter, "Come in; I will show thee that which will be profitable to thee." So he commanded his man to light the candle, and bid Christian follow him; so he had him into a private room, and bid his man open a door; the which when he had done, Christian saw the picture of a very grave person hang up against the wall; and this was the fashion of it: it had eyes lifted up to heaven, the best of books in his hand, the law of truth was written upon his lips, the world was behind its back; it stood as if it pleaded with men, and a crown of gold did hang over its head.

Then said Christian, "What means this?"

"The man whose picture this is," replied the Interpreter, "is one of a thousand. He can beget children, travail in birth with children, and nurse them himself when they are born. And whereas thou seest him with his eyes lift up to heaven, the best of books in his hand, and the law of truth writ on his lips; it is to show thee, that his work is to know, and unfold dark things to sinners; even as also thou seest the world as cast behind him, and that a crown hangs over his head; that is to show thee, that slighting and despising the things that are present, for the love that he hath to his Master's service, he is sure in the world that comes next to have glory for his reward. Now," said the Interpreter, "I have showed thee this picture first, because the man whose picture this is, is the only man whom the Lord of the place whither thou art going hath authorized to be thy guide, in all difficult places thou mayest meet with in the way: wherefore take good heed to what I have showed thee, and bear well in thy mind what thou hast seen, lest in thy journey thou meet with some that pretend to lead thee right, but their way goes down to death." —*John Bunyan* (22)

* * *

He must not be himself a babe in knowledge, that will teach men all those mysterious things that are to be known in order to salvation. O what qualifications are necessary for that man that hath such a charge upon him as we have! How many difficulties in divinity to be opened! yea, about the fundamentals that must needs be known! How many obscure texts of Scripture to be expounded! How many duties to be done, wherein ourselves and others may miscarry, if in the matter, and end, and manner, and circumstances they be not well informed! How many sins to be avoided, which without understanding and foresight cannot be done! How many weighty and yet intricate cases of conscience have we almost daily to resolve! Can so much work, and such work as this, be done by raw, unqualified men?

−*Richard Baxter* (23)

* * *

Will a common measure of holy skill and ability of prudence, and other qualifications serve for such a task as this? I know necessity may cause the church to tolerate the weak; but woe to us if we tolerate and indulge our own weakness. Doth not reason and conscience tell you, that if you dare venture on so high a work as this, you should spare no pains to be fitted to perform it? It is not now and then an idle snatch or taste of studies that will serve to make a sound divine.

−*Richard Baxter* (24)

* * *

If we will be divines only in tongues and title, and have not the divine image upon our souls, nor give up ourselves to the divine honor and will, no wonder if we be separated from the divine presence, and denied the fruition of God for ever. Believe it, sirs, God is no respecter of persons: he saveth not men for their coats or callings; a holy calling will not save an unholy man. If you stand at the door of the kingdom of grace, to light others in, and will not go in yourselves, when you are burnt to the snuff, you will go out with a stink, and shall knock in vain at the gates of glory, that would not enter at the door of grace. You shall then find that your lamps should have had the oil of grace as well as of ministerial gifts; of holiness as well as of doctrine, if you would have had a part in the glory which you preached. Do I need to tell you that preachers of the gospel must be judged by the gospel; and stand at the same bar, and be sentenced on the same terms, and dealt with as severely as any other men? Can you think to be saved then by your clergy; and to come off by a *legit ut clericus*, when there is wanting the *credidit ex vixit ut Christianus?* Alas, it will not be; you know it will not! Take heed therefore to yourselves for your own sakes; seeing you have souls to save or lose as well as others. —*Richard Baxter* (25)

* * *

Smaller strength may serve for lighter works and burdens. But if you venture on the great undertakings of the ministry, if you will lead on the troops of Christ against the face of Satan and his followers; if you will engage yourselves against principalities and powers, and spiritual wickedness in high places; if you undertake to rescue captivated sinners, and to fetch men out of the devil's paws; do not think that a heedless, careless minister is fit for so great a work as this. You must look to come off with greater shame, and deeper wounds of conscience, than if you had lived a common life, if you will think to go through such things as these with a careless soul. It is not only the work that calls for heed, but the workman also, that he may be fit for business of such weight. —*Richard Baxter* (26)

* * *

I Timothy 3:2-7

My God, what qualifications are these! and how rash was I to undertake such a work, without sitting down and counting the cost, whether I was able to finish it! Thou only canst supply all my defeats, which I beseech thee to do.

Enable me, I beseech thee, to come as near as possible to this character; that I may teach the mysteries, defend the faith, maintain the truths of the gospel; that I may be a

195

pattern to my flock, edify the church, both by my discourses and example, and hearty zeal for the salvation of souls; and a care to secure my flock from the corruptions of the age. Amen.

–*Thomas Wilson* (27)

* * *

Ministers are like trumpets, which make no sound if breath be not breathed into them. Or like Ezekiel's wheels, which move not unless the Spirit move them. Or like Elisha's servants whose presence does no good unless Elisha's spirit be there also.

–*John Flavel*

* * *

We want the new song of those who stand upon the rock, taken from the fearful pit and the miry clay, with the trembling still upon them and the slime still moist. We want the devotion of men whom grace found, and scarcely saved from the jaws of death, and took from the belly of hell. We want more joy, but more of the joy of men who have tasted death either in their own conscience or in the communion of their Redeemer's. We need it to make faith what in some of its popular forms it is ceasing in any imperial way to be, a power and a passion in authority among the passions and powers of the race.

–*Peter Taylor Forsyth* (28)

* * *

Take heed to yourselves. Do not saunter into the life of the ministry with half-open eyes. Count the cost of the work upon which you are entering. . . . You have seen men fail in the work which you are about to undertake, men who somehow or other have missed their vocation and have become a burden to themselves and their people. The time was when they were young men, fresh from college, inspired with high ideals, full of hope like yourself. Then they as little dreamed of failure as you do today. Why did they fail? Because the cost of the work proved more than they had calculated. They began to build, but they were not able to finish. "Be not high-minded but fear." What has happened to them may happen to you. If you would avoid the same result, sit down while you yet have time, and count the cost. What is the cost? I answer, your life, yourself, all that you have, all that you are. You must spend all or nothing. The Master demands every fraction of your life, and demands it every hour. Each of your faculties must be placed at his absolute disposal. You are no longer your own. You belong to him, body, mind, and soul. These are the conditions, the indispensable conditions of his service. Sit down and count the cost and ask yourself: Can I undertake it?

Undertake it? No; not by yourself. You are too weak. You will fail before the day is out. But what you cannot do yourself Another can do for you. His iron will can work through your feeble will, and strengthen it with a strength which is not your own. "Without me," says the Master, "ye can do nothing." "I can do all things," says the disciple, "through Christ which strengtheneth me."

—Forbes Robinson (29)

* * *

The Pastors We Need

Pastors who are in possession of a much-to-be-desired scientific training, not so much in the scientific exercise of one, two, three, but rather in struggle, in spiritual confrontation with the decisive thing, in the struggle, not so much against the attacks and questions of science, but rather against human passions. Pastors who can split up the "crowd" and turn it into individuals. Pastors who are not too much occupied with study and who have no desire whatsoever to dominate. Pastors who, though able to speak, will be no less able to keep silent and be patient. Pastors who, though they may know men's hearts, have no less learned temperance in judgment and condemnation. Pastors who understand how to exercise authority, through the art of sacrifice. Pastors who have been prepared, trained, and educated to obedience and suffering, so that they will be able to correct, admonish, edify, move, and also constrain, not by force, anything but that, but rather through their own obedience; and above all be able to put up with all the rudeness of the sick person without letting it upset him, any more than a physician allows himself to be disturbed by the curses and kicks of a patient during an operation.   —*Søren Kierkegaard* (30)

* * *

If the church is called a flock, the minister is the pastor to seek that which is lost, to strengthen the diseased, to heal the sick, to bring again that which was driven away; in a word, to shepherd the flock in all the exercises of tenderness, consideration, and care, that connect themselves with this endearing character (Ezek. 39:4). If the family of Christ are an household, the minister is the steward faithful and wise (Luke 12:42), dispensing the provision of the house according to the necessities of its several members. If the church of God be a city, he is the watchman (Ezek. 33:7) to wake and warn slumberers of their peril. If it be a husbandry, he is the laborer (I Cor. 3:9) to plant and water the soil, to cleanse the earth, to watch the growth of the plant, and instrumentally to bring forward the harvest. If it be a building, he is the master-builder (I Cor. 3:10) to build upon the "sure foundation" lively stones—a spiritual house—"growing into an holy temple of the Lord, builded together for an habitation of God through the Spirit" (I Pet. 2:5; Eph. 2:20, 22). If there be a treaty of peace to be negotiated between the Majesty of heaven and a world of rebels, he is the ambassador entrusted with "the ministry of reconciliation," and praying then in Christ's stead, "Be ye reconciled unto God" (II Cor. 5:20).   —*Charles Bridges* (31)

Good Ministers of Christ

True ministers know that Christ is Lord and that they are only servants. Therefore it is not they themselves who prepare the way to men's hearts, but Christ their Lord. It matters not to them whether they have anything or count for anything themselves or not, so long as the way is prepared for Christ to enter unhindered into the souls of men. That they are servants of Christ serves to humble them, but that they are servants of the Lord of lords serves to encourage them. He is a rich Lord and will provide for his servants when they have nothing. He is a mighty Lord and will protect them when they are persecuted by the world. A great lord does not forsake his servants, nor does Christ his own. But those who depart from him in life and teaching are not his servants. They are the servants of men; they seek to be pleasing to men. Whom shall they seek when men turn from friends into enemies and depart from them? Then they shall be forsaken of God and men. Christ's servants turn to Christ. They turn to him as disciples to their master and learn from him what they would teach others. They turn to him as their Leader and tread in the footsteps of his holy life. I am a follower of Christ, Paul exults. They turn to him as their Comforter when they are in trouble and anxiety. They turn to him as Counsellor when they know not how to counsel themselves or others. In every need they go to him in prayer in the Spirit and tell him their trouble. To him they have free access. Servants of Christ are called faithful teachers because they are called of Christ, not to rule, but to serve. A good minister forgets himself; he seeks only Christ and souls. Christ is his only goal, he seeks only to preach and glorify Christ with his heart, mouth, and whole life. He serves with labor and care; he is a galley slave who rows with terrible exertion the little ship of Christ.

This complexion must he have who would be a good servant of Christ. First, he must receive his office and ministry from Christ and by it lead the people to the obedience of Christ, seeking to win them not to himself but to Christ, as a servant of his Lord. Then he must shun no labor, fear no discomfort; he is full of cares and anxieties. Pastors are spiritual mothers. They feel the travail of a mother's heart and must say with Paul (Gal. 4): "My little children, of whom I travail in birth again until Christ be formed in you." A pastor must also row with care, that he may bring the ship of Christ unharmed through the rocks of self-confidence and despair. On one side he must row with the strong hand of Moses, on the other with the mild and gentle hand of Christ. Finally, a faithful servant of Christ must have no fear of the world's scorn and persecution, for the world has as little right in the ministry as the devil in the kingdom of heaven. After all we are not the world's, but Christ's servants.

—Heinrich Müller (32)

* * *

The Call

The ministry is a matter of pure grace and favor; who then will dare to enter into it without a divine call! There is nothing in which a king would willingly be more absolute than in the choice of his ministers. And shall we dare to contest and take away this right from the King of kings?

—Pasquier Quesnel (33)

* * *

You must feel, if you are the man I take you for, how unworthy you are to be what you are called to be. Now there are two ways of dealing with this feeling. You may say, "I am not called to be an absolute saint; but I will try to reach a fairly high standard"; or you may say, "Yes, I am called to be an absolute saint. I will not lower my ideal. I will comfort myself with that single word 'called.' If he has called me, he will do in me and for me what he wills."

This second way is the true way of dealing with feelings of unworthiness and unfitness. You and I are utterly unfit. But we are both called, called from our mother's womb, called to be saints and to be ministers. He who called us will help us. With man the call seems quixotic, impossible; with Him all things are possible. At times when the call is loudest we can but reply, "Ah! Lord, I am but a little child." We are intensely conscious of feebleness and, what is worse, of treachery and meanness within; we half love what we are called upon to denounce; we play with the sin we are to teach men to abhor. Yet the call is sure, is definite, is perpetual, and again and again you will in all probability find what a help it is to look back to that day in which the call took formal shape. You have that as a definite fact to rest upon, to reprove, to encourage, to urge to renewed effort, to force you to be true and energetic.

—Forbes Robinson (34)

* * *

The sermons of a man without vocation are apt to be little better than unconscious soliloquies.

—William Malcolm Macgregor (35)

* * *

Certainty of Calling

This certainty of calling, which was St. Paul's, may be the possession of every minister of God's Word, if he learn it well, and preach it wholly, and deliver the message as he receives it, even as a king's ambassador. For such an ambassador speaks not of himself, or as a private person, but for his king and in the king's name. As representing the king he is honored and set in a place he would not occupy as a private person. Wherefore let the preacher of the gospel be certain that his calling is from God. . . .

Calling is not to be despised, for it is not enough for a man to have the Word and pure doctrine, but also he must be assured of his calling, and he that entereth without this assurance, entereth but to kill and destroy. For God never prospereth the labors of those that are not called. This is therefore our comfort which are in the ministry of the Word, "that we have an office which is heavenly and holy," to the which we, being lawfully called, do triumph against the gates of hell.

—Luther (36)

* * *

There are many amongst us who believe within themselves that they can never become good theologians, that they could do better in almost any other realm. Yet they cannot imagine that their existence could be anything other than theological existence. Even if they had to give up theology as their vocational work, they would never cease to ask the theological question. It would pursue them into every realm. They would be bound to it, actually, if not vocationally. They could not be sure that they could fulfil its demands, but they would be sure that they were in its bondage. They who believe those things in their hearts belong to the assembly of God. They are grasped by the Divine Spirit. They have received the gift of knowledge. They are theologians.

—Paul Tillich (37)

* * *

Vocation and Priesthood

Vocation is one of the lordliest of words, as it implies that the man thus impressed for service is now God's man, that in the only true sense he is a priest of God. In the New Testament we are frequently reminded that the merely official and technical priesthood is of very small account, with almost fierce reiteration the writer to the Hebrews maintains that, in its nature, it is a human ordinance and at best a shadow and image of the true. Triumphantly he notes that if Jesus were still on earth he could not be a priest at all, for he lacked all the formal qualifications; but that technical defect did not infringe upon his real priesthood just as a technical completeness would never have enriched it. Priesthood, as that writer discerned, attaches to man's nature, not to the correctness of ceremonial; so Carlyle speaks of an old Seceder minister in Ecclefechan as "the priestliest man I ever under any ecclesiastical guise was privileged to look upon," and, in the mercy of God, such men are found alike in all the churches. When a man awakens to his task there stirs in him a pitying sense of human need and trouble and of the frustration of human lives; so as a friend he seeks to get near to men, putting himself at their disposal for all good, and thus exhibiting the elementary qualification of a high priest who must (Heb. 5 :2) be "able to deal gently with the ignorant and the straying." But there is more than this in the priest's office, for he stands also in God's council and knows his mind, and thus can bring God and his blessings to men just as he brings men and their needs to God. It is in this that a ministry reaches its height, and the full priestly authority is attained through the humble and reverent sense of a divine vocation.

—William Malcolm Macgregor (38)

* * *

I think I have told you of my father's words spoken during his last illness: "If I had a thousand lives, I would give them all, all to the ministry." You will not regret your decision. If angels could envy, how they would envy us our splendid chance, to be able, in a world where everything unseen must be taken on sheer faith, in a world where the contest between the flesh and the spirit is being decided for the universe, not only to win the battle ourselves but also to win it for others! To help a brother up the mountain while you yourself are only just able to keep your foothold, to struggle through the mist together, that surely is better than to stand at the summit and beckon. You will have a hard time of it, I know; and I would like to make it smoother and to "let you down" easier; but I am sure that God, who loves you even more than I do, and has absolute wisdom, will not tax you beyond your strength. . . . I'll pray for you, like the widow in the parable, and I have immense belief in prayer. . . . You remember what was said of Maurice, "He always impressed me as a man who was naturally weak in his will; but an iron will seemed to work through him." That Will can work through you and transform you, but for God's sake don't trust to your own will.

—Forbes Robinson (39)

* * *

Signs of a True Call

The decisive sign of a real call is the pastor's own faith. It is the root of that inner compulsion that is operative in all genuine cure of souls. From it grow the zeal and patience, the willingness to make haste and to wait, the search for one's neighbor, the sympathy for him, and above all the certainty with which we administer the Word to him and which wins him to the Word. It may be a weak faith, a tempted and struggling faith (and where is there ever real faith without doubt and struggle?); but it must be faith, one's own personal knowledge of grace and sin, of repentance and rebirth, one's own existence in prayer and supplication. The tepid, but also the secure and satisfied, cannot really be called. Ultimately, this means simply that the pastor of souls must himself be a living member of the congregation that gathers about the Word and sacraments and lives in and by faith. One cannot be a pastor of souls apart from the fellowship. For what other meaning and substance can the cure of souls have except the gathering of the lost into the fellowship of the people of God? And how can a man gather if he himself is living in isolation?

Then, a second sign; back of pastoral care is a call. But this call is not only being called *through* the Word; it means also being called *to* the Word. That is, the pastor of souls who is to lead others to the Word must himself be one who is led by the Word, grounded and practiced in the Word. Therefore meditation of the Word of God is the most important requirement of the pastor. He must be steeped in the Word. . . . In the good sense, he must be a "scribe," learned in the Scriptures. Don't shy away from the title of "scribe." After all, according to Jesus himself there are "scribes who have been trained of the kingdom" (Matt. 13:52). In other words, don't be ashamed to call yourself a theologian, in so far, that is, as true theology is always a theology of the Word.

—*Eduard Thurneysen* (40)

* * *

For Self-examination

Wouldst thou have a picture of life in Christendom, showing how it compares with the Christian life? Then I will present to thee such a picture, to show how it is we live Christianly, and how our life compares with Christianity, the absolute. And be not disturbed by the notion that the form of presentation is perhaps not serious and solemn enough, for, believe me, the solemnity of solemn Sunday discourses is so far, in a Christian sense, from being real seriousness that it rather diverts attention from the one really serious question, what reality looks like, what our life is, where we are. And do not by any means suppose that I speak as I do because I feel myself to be better than others; no, no, already I have made the admission about myself, and I here repeat it, that I am coddled like all the others; and, on the other hand, my life has always expressed sincere sympathy with the experience of being tried by the bothers and cares which are capable of tormenting so greatly a poor human being. But nevertheless Christianity requires us to be spirit, to strive thereafter, and the serious question is, what life we lead. So then, I hope, thou also wilt willingly, honestly, and candidly, with seriousness and with due attention (not mocking me, which would divert attention), apply thyself to this investigation.

Imagine a candidate in theology. Let it be me, I also indeed am a candidate in theology. He has already been a candidate for some few years, and now he enters upon that period of life when it is said of him that "he is seeking." "A candidate in theology"—"seeks": when the riddle is proposed in these terms, one does not need a particularly lively imagination to guess at once what it is he "seeks"—of course it is the kingdom of God (Matt. 6:33). However, thy guess is wrong; no, he seeks something else, a parish, a living—he seeks this almost absolutely; in other respects the affair has nothing to do with the absolute, nor does it betray any impression of the absolute. He seeks. In his search he runs from Herod to Pilate, recommends himself before ministers and secretaries, he writes and writes, one sheet of stamped paper after another—for the supplication must be written on paper which bears the stamp of the government, perhaps one might call this the impression of the absolute, otherwise there is nothing of the sort here. A year passes; he had almost worn himself out with his running and seeking, which can hardly be said to be in the service of the absolute, except (as has been remarked) that he seeks "absolutely everything."

Finally he gets what he sought; he finds the scriptural text confirmed, "Seek and ye shall find"; but the absolute he did not find, it was only a small living—but after all it was not the absolute he was seeking. Still, he is at peace; and indeed he is now in need of repose, so that he can rest himself and his legs after the much seeking.

However, when he makes himself more precisely acquainted with the income of the living, he discovers to his dismay that it is a few hundred dollars less than he had supposed. This is exceedingly calamitous for him, as, humanly speaking, one can well understand and can agree with him about it. It is doubly unpleasant for him because at the same time he has found something else which he sought concurrently, namely, a wife, which quite obviously is related to a living, and may be each year more so. He loses heart. He buys again a sheet of stamped paper, is already afoot to put in a supplication to be allowed to withdraw. However, some of his friends get him to give this up. So the thing is decided. He becomes a parson.

Now he is to be installed by the Dean and is himself to deliver the inaugural address. The Dean is a man of intelligence and learning, not without an eye for world history, much to his own profit and that of the congregation. He presents the new parson to the congregation, makes an address, and chooses for his text the words of the Apostle, "Lo, we have left all and followed thee." Upon this text he speaks pithily and forcefully; he shows that, especially in view of the movements of these times, the minister of the Word must now be prepared to sacrifice everything, though it were life and blood—and the very reverend speaker knows that the young man he installs (yes, as I have said, we can very well understand the young man, for that is human; but we cannot so well understand the Dean) happened to be desirous of withdrawing because the living was a few hundred dollars too little.

Thereupon the new parson mounts the pulpit. And the Gospel for the day, upon which he is to preach, is—very opportunely!—"Seek ye first the kingdom of God." Truly, when one recalls what this young man had to go through with during the laborious years of seeking, this "seek first" is the last thing one would be likely to think of!

So he preaches. And it was in every respect a good sermon; even the Bishop, who was present, said: "It was a capital sermon, and excellently delivered, he is really an orator."—

"Yes, but then, if it were to be judged Christianly."—"Good gracious, it was an entirely Christian sermon, it was the sound, unalloyed doctrine, and the stress he laid upon *first* to seek God's kingdom was not without thrilling effect."— "Yes, but now, Christianly judged, I mean, how far was there here a correspondence between the preacher's life and his discourse? I could hardly free myself entirely from the thought that the speaker—who for me is a true picture of us all—cannot precisely be said with truth to have sought first God's kingdom."—"That's not at all required."—"Oh, excuse me, but that is what he preached about, that we first should seek God's kingdom."—"Quite so, that is exactly the way he should preach, that is what is required of him. It is the doctrine that has to be attended to, the doctrine has to be preached pure and unalloyed."

This represents about the way Christendom stands related to Christianity, the absolute. After running round about on a score of errands (alas, humanly speaking, after having had to put up with a great deal) one gets one's finite existence made secure, and then we get a sermon about seeking first the kingdom of God.   —*Søren Kierkegaard* (41)

* * *

The First Parish

He is likely to find himself at the beginning of his ministry in a small and inconspicuous parish, which may seem to present scant opportunity for the exercise of his powers. In this he is mistaken, for the smallest parish presents opportunities beyond the powers of those most richly endowed. He could labor there all his life and perform a work of vast significance. . . . To it he will apply himself with all his God-given powers and exercise all the talents he possesses. His congregation may be small and unlearned, but he will prepare his sermons with the utmost care and fashion them according to the needs of his people. The funds may be limited; all the more he will seek to have them used to the best advantage. The equipment may be poor; he will study how it may be improved. The parish may be composed of only a few hundred souls; he will remember that each one of these has its need of sacramental grace. The children may be few, yet not one of them but may grow beyond all human reckoning in character and influence. In a word, he idealizes the whole situation, sees in it the possibilities of spiritual romance, and devotes to it every capacity of mind and soul.

Thus he learns the essential technique of a spiritual ministry. Indeed there is a sense in which "pastoral care" can be learned not in a school of theology but only in the care of a parish. He acquires skill in the use of his tools; in methods of administration; in the ways of the religious training of the young; in parish visitation. The smallest parish offers a minister an invaluable opportunity of learning his trade. And to the degree to which he devotes himself wholeheartedly and with interest and imagination to his work, does he acquire competency and efficiency. He becomes disciplined in every aspect of his task.

So also does he prepare himself for the summons that may come to him for a position which cannot be more useful, but may be more prominent and lucrative. . . . The minister who is wanted is the one who has proved that he can do good work. The one who feels that his parish is so small that it does not deserve his best efforts, who regards it only as a steppingstone, and almost at once looks for what he calls a better chance, never gets very far. But the man who devotes himself with energy, imagination, and interest to the parish that is his prepares for future opportunities which often disclose themselves only by force of zeal and thoroughness. The small task often can be marvelously transformed into an open way if a man performs it with competency. . . . It does not always happen that competency has its visible rewards. Yet nothing short of it ever qualifies for advancement in the ministry. —*Raymond Calkins* (42)

Restlessness

There is no more common illusion in our profession than the conviction that we could be a shining success anywhere else than in the sphere which we happen to be occupying. . . . The charge that is without its discouragements has yet to be discovered. Get it wrought into the fibers of your being that the sphere in which you find yourself is the arena in which you are to win your soul. —*George Johnstone Jeffrey* (43)

* * *

The Place God Gives Me

To his son in his first parish.

I beg you, do not look upon Dortmund as a steppingstone, but rather say: Here I shall stay as long as it pleases God; if it be his will, until I die. Look upon every child, your confirmands, every member of the congregation as if you will have to give account for every soul on the day of the Lord Jesus. Every day commit all these human souls from the worst and weakest of hands, namely, your own, into the best and strongest of hands. Then you will be able to carry on your ministry not only without care but also with joy overflowing and joyful hope. —*Friedrich von Bodelschwingh* (44)

* * *

Bishop Walpole, the father of Hugh Walpole, the novelist, once said to a friend who was weighing a call:

"If you are uncertain of which of two paths to take, choose the one on which the shadow of the cross falls." —(45)

* * *

The Long Pastorate

One's heart goes back from this eager, restless, ambitious age to the former days, and recalls with fond recollection the pastor of his youth, who had lived all his ministry in one place, and was buried where he was ordained—who had baptized a child, and admitted her to the sacrament, and married her and baptized her children—who knew all the ins and outs of his people's character, and carried family history for generations in his head—who was ever thinking of his people, watching over them, visiting their homes, till his familiar figure on the street linked together the past and the present, and heaven and earth, and opened a treasure house of sacred memories. He prayed with a lad before he went away—his mother could almost repeat the words; he was constantly inquiring about his welfare, so binding him to his faith and home by silken ties; he was in the house on the day of his return, to see how it had fared with him in the outer world. People turned to him as by an instinct in their joys and sorrows; men consulted him in the crises of life, and, as they lay a-dying, committed their wives and children to his care. He was a head to every widow, and a father to the orphans, and the friend of all lowly, discouraged, unsuccessful souls. Ten miles away people did not know his name, but his own congregation regarded no other, and in the Lord's presence it was well known, it was often mentioned; when he laid down his trust, and arrived on the other side, many whom he had fed and guided, and restored and comforted, till he saw them through the gates, were waiting to receive their shepherd-minister, and as they stood around him before the Lord, he, of all men, could say without shame, 'Behold, Lord, thine under-shepherd, and the flock thou didst give me."

—John Watson (46)

* * *

Ordination

When Doctor Martin ordained Magister Benedict Schumann on Jubilate Sunday, April 22, 1540, he read the passage, Acts 13 [:3], which relates how hands were laid upon the two apostles, Paul and Barnabas; also Acts 20 [:29] in which Paul warns the bishops and pastors at Miletus to guard themselves against the wolves; as well as the third chapter of I Timothy (v. 1 ff) and Titus 1 (v. 6) on how a bishop should be called and conduct himself.

In addition he said: "My dear brother, you have been ordained by God to be a faithful servant of Jesus Christ in N., to further his holy name by the pure teaching of the gospel, to which we call and send by the power of God, just as God has sent us. Therefore, watch earnestly, be diligent, pray God that he may preserve you in this high calling, that you may not fall away by reason of false doctrine, heresy, sectarianism, or your own thoughts, but rather begin it in the fear of God, faithful diligence, and constant prayer and rightly accomplish it in Christ." This was the main content of his prayer.

Afterwards he laid his hands upon him and, kneeling, prayed the Lord's Prayer aloud. When he had risen to his feet, he lifted up his eyes and hands to heaven and said: "Lord God, heavenly, merciful Father, who hast commanded us to ask and seek and knock, and also promised to hear us when we call upon thee in the name of thy Son: In this promise we put our trust and pray: be thou pleased to send this servant of thy Word, Benedict, into thy harvest. Help him, bless his ministry and service, and open the ears of believers to the blessed course of thy Word, to the praise of thy name, the increase of thy kingdom, and the growth of thy church. Amen. Therefore, my dear brother, I wish for you, moreover, blessing and success, that you may walk in the fear of God and trust in the Lord!" Then "Now pray we all the Holy Ghost" was sung. *—Luther, Table Talk* (47)

* * *

Perhaps no better preparation for ordination could be suggested than to take the following passages of Holy Scripture and make a careful and prayerful meditation on each:

The call of Abraham. Gen. 12
Jacob's night of prayer. Gen. 32:24–30
The call of Moses. Exod. 3:1–4, 17
The power of intercession. Exod. 17:8–12
The gift of the Holy Spirit. Num. 11:18–23
The righteous and evil priests. I Sam. 3:1–21
Isaiah's call to service. Isa. 6:1–8
The man of God and his message. Jer. 20:7–9
The pastor's duty. Ezek. 3:16–21
The call of Amos. Amos 7:14–15
The consolations of Habakkuk. Hab. 3:17–19
Christ's invitation to quiet and prayer. Mark 6:31
Christ's prayer before calling his apostles. Luke 6:12–13
The pattern for every pastor. John 10:11–14
The coming of the Holy Ghost. Acts 2:1–4
The life of the missionary. II Cor. 6:1–10
A pastor's work. II Tim. 4:5   *—Peter Green* (48)

* * *

I did this day receive *as much honor and work* as ever I shall be able to know what to do with. Lord Jesus, proportion supplies accordingly.   *—Philip Henry* (49)

* * *

The minister who is troubled over his own life and wonders whether he is fit for his office should look back to his ordination. Everything depends upon the fact that men have laid their hands upon him and that through them God has given him the office that it may be exercised by him. Just as Luther overcame his misgivings by taking refuge in the First Commandment, so many a minister could conquer the doubts he has about the work of his ministry by putting his confidence in his ordination, the ordination which God's goodness holds before him and in forgiveness renews what was offered and committed to him.   *—Martin Fischer* (50)

213

Esteemed ordinands, since I have not the privilege of being a witness of your day of honor and joy, a day that should be a day of joy to the church, I take this means of saying to you what Melanchthon said:

"Christ as High Priest lays his hand upon his own, he chooses them through the voice of the church, he blesses them and anoints them with his gifts."

What riches, but also what responsibility! May both enter deep in your hearts and the church be made glad by your ministry.

I pray for you.

—Hermann Bezzel (51)

* * *

It gives me great pleasure to think that on Sunday next you will be made a deacon in God's church. I thank God that he has called you to one of the highest offices on earth, that henceforth you will be . . . "under" orders — God's orders —that you willingly renounce your life, your thoughts, your hopes, your ambitions to him. You will probably hear much and be told much at this time. I have nothing to say that you have not heard and will not hear said far better by others. Our church gives the keynote in the collect for Sunday: "We have no power." I never realized my weakness, my pride, my hollowness so much as I did at my ordination. God has been teaching me, even in the short time since I was ordained, wonderful lessons — lessons of strength being perfected in weakness. He alone knows the depths of our hypocrisy, our vanity, our atheism, and he alone can help us. To get nearer to him, to know him better — this is what I want, this is eternal life. As we believe in a Person who is by our side, who is helping us, training us, we shall be able to proclaim him to others. Do not mind about feelings. You may have beautiful feelings at your ordination time. Thank God if you have. He sends them. You may have none. Thank God if you have not, for he has kept them back. We do not want to *feel* better and stronger; we want to *be* better and stronger. And he *has* made us better and stronger.

And when all seems lost, Satan seems master, we are misunderstood; remember that "I believe in the Holy Ghost," who is stronger than separation or death, than feelings, than our hearts. All our feelings and thoughts and wishes are nothing. God is everything and in all. All our conceptions will be shattered, all our schemes overthrown, that a Great Person behind may be revealed. To know, to love, to make known, to make men love that Person is our work in life. . . .

We are men sent from God. We come to bear witness of a light. Do not let us confuse ourselves with our message. The message is everything; we are nothing. The light simply shines through us. We must be glad to be shattered, rejected, if so be that the Light shining through us may be manifested.

—Forbes Robinson (52)

* * *

DEDICATION

Send Me

Use me, God, in thy great harvest field,
Which stretchest far and wide like a wide sea;
The gatherers are so few; I fear the precious yield
Will suffer loss. Oh, find a place for me!
A place where best the strength I have will tell:
It may be one the older toilers shun;
Be it a wide or narrow place, 'tis well
So that the work it holds be only done.

—Christina G. Rossetti

* * *

A man can honor God's trust in him and fulfil his vocation only as he gives himself to God. If he knows that God's children in this world of time are and must be miserable misfits apart from God, that God longs only to lavish on them peace and "life to the full," and that, to an incalculable degree, it depends on the state of his own soul whether God will get through to them, then it would not be wonderful if he made, and kept making, a solemn vow — that by God's help he would never by any tampering with evil, any disloyalty, any scorn or affectation, any laziness or self-importance, hang a veil between his people and their one hope, that, indeed, no living soul would ever miss God because of him.

He will keep his vow not by hoping for the best, not by looking on his ordination as magic or manna that could last him all the days, not by the practice of continually testing his motives, but by worship only, by the regular habit of prayer.

—Adam W. Burnet (53)

* * *

The one need of your life, if you would serve God nobly, if through you the King of glory is to find his way to the people of his love, is your need of God. His faith in you, when at length he puts a congregation under your care, you will honor only by complete self-dedication to him. Who your people will be you cannot know. But you know this about them, that they need God above all things, and that God will need in you a consecrated man in order to reach them . . . and the Saviour will be there, in all the passion of his heart, as long ago, to feed his sheep. Is there anything more solemn than to think how much he depends on *you* for access to *them*? What can you do but by consecration give him the right of way through your life, that no self-born thing in you may hinder him, that his redeeming grace may have free course, and that every single soul may have the chance to be "abundantly satisfied"? *—Adam W. Burnet* (53)

* * *

At last, after all, to be unconditionally Christ's man, able at last to preach Christ crucified, not as a career, not for pay, but for love, to offer the Word of life to all these "hungry sheep" (and most of all these young ones whose calling tears my heart), to be God's "person" (not that dreary thing, a "personality"), to bear before his altar the sins and sorrows of one's own family of souls, to abide in his Holy Place, the "Innermost, where the flame is and the wings are throbbing" — how incredible, how shining a "port after stormie seas!" How small a price to "die daily," to "leave all that I have" (as for a while I must — yet how satisfying there at last really to fulfil that law which has sounded for so long in my soul!) — how small a price for so great a prize! "Lord, I am not worthy."

> "Love said, 'You shall be he.'
> I, the unkind, ungrateful?
> . . . 'You must sit down,' says Love, 'and
> taste my meat!'
> So I did sit and eat."

> —Nicodemus (Melville Chaning-Pierce) (55)

* * *

The Privileged Sacrifice

For my own part, I have never ceased to rejoice that God has appointed me to such an office. People talk of the sacrifice I have made in spending so much of my life in Africa. Can that be called a sacrifice which is simply paid back as a small part of a great debt owing to our God, which we can never repay? Is that a sacrifice which brings its own blest reward in healthful activity, the consciousness of doing good, peace of mind, and a bright hope of a glorious destiny hereafter? Away with the word in such a view, and with such a thought! It is emphatically no sacrifice. Say rather it is a privilege. Anxiety, sickness, suffering, or danger, now and then, with a foregoing of the common conveniences and charities of this life, may make us pause, and cause the spirit to waver, and the soul to sink; but let this be only for a moment. All these are nothing when compared with the glory which shall hereafter be revealed in, and for, us. I never made a sacrifice. Of this we ought not to talk, when we remember the great sacrifice which he made who left his Father's throne on high to give himself for us, "who being the brightness of that Father's glory, and the express image of his person, and upholding all things by the word of his power, when he had by himself purged our sins, sat down on the right hand of the Majesty on high."

—David Livingstone

* * *

What do I want? I want to serve. Whom do I want to serve? The Lord—in the person of his poor suffering children. And what is my reward? I serve neither for reward nor thanks, but out of gratitude and love; my reward is that I am permitted to serve. And if I perish in doing so? If I perish, I perish, said Esther, who, after all, did not know him who for love of me perished and who will not let me perish. And if I grow old in this service? Then my heart shall flourish like the palm tree, and the Lord will satisfy me with grace and mercy. I walk in peace and am careful for nothing.

—Wilhelm Löhe (56)

* * *

Beginning a Pastorate

Such servants of our common Lord as I have named are witnesses to the power of faith. They point beyond themselves to One who is at once the pattern and the object of our faith, and bid us run the race that is set before us, looking unto Jesus. Those words I should wish to take as my motto today. I come as a learner, with no policy to advocate, no plan already formed to follow. But I come with one burning desire; it is that in all our activities, sacred and secular, ecclesiastical and social, we should help each other to fix our eyes on Jesus, making him our only guide. . . . Pray for me, I ask you, not chiefly that I may be wise and strong, or any such thing, though for these things I need your prayers. But pray for me chiefly that I may never let go of the unseen hand of the Lord Jesus and may live in daily fellowship with him. It is so that you will most of all help me to help you. So shall we go forward together — not without stumbling, not without weariness — but always toward the loving welcome that awaits us in our Father's home, where the conflicts which now beset the earth will have vanished, where self-seeking cannot find entrance, where misery gives place to joy and quarreling to peace, because self is either sacrificed or forgotten in the realization of the love of God.

* * * –William Temple (57)

The Sacristy

The name itself expresses its nature. Sacristy means quite simply : the holy place. And if the exposition of the Word by the *Verbi Divini minister,* the minister of the Word of God, is always the center of evangelical worship, then it becomes clear what importance preparation for this proclamation has, not only with respect to the whole preparation of the preacher for his vocation but also with respect to every individual act of proclamation, every single service of worship. And here the sacristy has its peculiar place. . . .

You open the door . . . and cross the threshold. Where are you now — really? You are on the height of a mountain pass, or, to alter the metaphor slightly, in a defile or on a bridge between two banks, where beneath you the river of time goes swirling on, and above you, please God, the heavens are opened. For a few moments now you have in fact arrived at a strange wayside station. You are standing between workaday world and worship, between home and "office," between preparation for preaching and preaching itself, yea, also between the resting-place of the dead and the company of the living, or rather between the church triumphant and the church militant. And perhaps you sense something of the symbolic significance of this "betweenness." Perhaps never as in these moments in the sacristy is the interim character of our whole life so palpable, as it is described in that fugitive saying of our Lord on a bridge in North India : "The world is merely a bridge, ye are to pass over it, and not to build your dwelling on it." Then may you, too, realize afresh the interim character of our whole ministry, this ministry, which so easily entangles a person in the multiformity of life and equally easily isolates one in harsh loneliness, and yet is intended to keep building bridges from one bank to the other. . . .

So, through these and similar inner experiences, may there happen what a simply painted picture in a lonely sacristy is intended to express. The picture represents nothing more than a harp, but under it are the Latin words : *Nec unus dissonat,* not one string gives forth a false note. What a wonderful picture this is! Indeed, in this strange loneliness the harp of your soul may be so attuned that your sermon, even though it be quiet, may yet become a pure and rich-toned hymn to the praise of the great High Priest and his sufficient sacrifice. All the voices out of the past that mingle with the rumbling, muffled organ tones that filter through from the outside, all the thoughts which you may compress in a brief, sobbing prayer, all these open the way for the immediate impact of the Word, which you are to proclaim, upon your own heart. And if the experience of that impact is not exalting at all, not poetic at all, if it cast down the sheltering wall of the sacristy . . . and leave you completely defenseless and helpless before the holy God, a poor, despairing man, then remember the harp and what is written under it, and the imperishable truth of the recreative power of suffering, which is true particularly of spiritual suffering. . . .

Then go with God and step out of this world of ghostly voices and secret suffering in holy solitude, wherein the peace of God dwells nevertheless, and cross the threshold into the worshiping congregation, and do the work that is committed to you as a faithful man who is able to teach others also (II Tim. 2:2). —*Erich Schick* (58)

It is told of Robert Bruce, the great preacher of the days of James VI . . . that no man spoke with such evidence and power of the Spirit. "No man," the record runs, "had so many seals of conversion; yea, many of his hearers thought that no man, since the apostles, spake with such power." The secret of that unique inspiration is unveiled by what happened at Larbert once when he was in the vestry before service. Someone was sent to call him, but returned saying he did not know when he would be free to come. . . . "There was Somebody with him, for he heard him many times say with the greatest seriousness, 'that he would not, he could not go, unless he came with him, and that he would not go alone,' but the Other did not seem to answer." And they said of him when he came out at last to preach that "he was singularly assisted."

—Adam W. Burnet (59)

* * *

The Minister's Sunday

Does the pastor have a Sunday?

Or is it his calling to help other people to secure their Sunday at the price of giving up his own Sunday? Is it perhaps one of the sorrows of his calling that the pastor should be a *pontifex,* a bridgebuilder, who builds for others a bridge upon which he himself is not allowed to set foot?

Sunday, for the great majority of pastors, is the day of his most intensive, strenuous, and wearing labor. I know of many pastors who, Sunday after Sunday, conduct services in three or four perhaps widely separated places, and in addition perform baptism, marriages, teach in Sunday schools, and make sick visits that cannot be postponed. This is hard work, which demands a man's whole strength, and when it is continued for years, it saps the strength of the strongest before their time. When this day's work is done, a man's strength is no longer sufficient to fashion the evening for leisure, and Sunday sets in weariness and exhaustion.

But can the work of the pastor be compared with other work? Is not all the physical and mental toil of visiting and speaking counterbalanced by the fact that this work can always be a service of the holy, that in all these hours he can hold converse with the apostles and prophets, with the Lord himself in his gospel and sacraments, that he is privileged to stand at the altar, to pray and preach the good news, and administer the sacraments and fill himself and his hearers with the sweet comfort of the gospel? Is not the pastor's Sunday, with all its toil, nevertheless a day that is laden with rich freight, and is not he who is privileged to celebrate it favored above thousands of others who are sadly deprived of their Sunday, who struggle hard and perhaps unsuccessfully for a bit of Sunday, favored above all those who have lost Sunday altogether?

But, we ask, will the holy, the gospel, bear being made into this kind of work, a servitude, which no longer flows out of the fulness of a forgiven heart, but almost inevitably becomes a habit, an outward duty, a chore and imposition? Is it not the cunning deceit of the ancient enemy when, under the driving lash of duties, the holy service is transformed into an unholy drudgery, when the liberating truth is changed into a constant exertion of the will? Will not the glory of Sunday inevitably fade, if our Sunday ministry becomes a burdensome toil that cripples zeal and stamina?

Help and recreation can come only from Sunday itself; it will demonstrate itself in the Sundays of the pastor himself. Whether this work-filled Sunday becomes, despite everything, a real Sunday, depends essentially upon how the pastor goes into his Sunday. To have everything minutely prepared, well thought through and considered in mind and heart is in itself a great help. Only then will the pastor be able to meet the varied demands of Sunday with inner composure, his whole being filled with the greatness, the beauty, and the healing power of the ministry that is committed to him. Observing Sunday rightly — and this applies not only to the pastor — is like playing music rightly; the tones must be heard inwardly and formed with the voice of the heart before they are uttered; only then will the tones become a genuine melody. Or, to say the same thing in biblical metaphor, the thoughts and words must first be born in quiet conversation with God out of a devout stillness, the prayers must be prayed with the heart, in order that in the moment of execution the words of prayer and preaching may rise to the throne of God as a "sweet fragrance of Christ" (Eph. 5:2).

But the determinative thing must and can happen during the Sunday service itself. It is a singular experience of great significance that the pastor's liturgical service itself can become a genuine *recreatio,* a real recreation. It can happen that the pastor at the altar may completely forget not only himself but the external situation, including all that is disappointing and wearisome in his situation, be completely clothed with the glory and mercy of God, wearing Christ himself as light and strength, like a garment that covers and shelters him, so that he is revived, refreshed, nourished, and strengthened even physically. Indeed, it can happen that he may go to the altar fagged, overtaxed, and borne down, and all this falls from him; and he goes forth from his service renewed and refreshed, bearing the reflection of heavenly glory, if not upon his countenance, yet in his heart. Such experiences are a great comfort, but no cause for complacence or even self-conceit. But here the experience of Elijah in the desert, weary and dispirited, and the angel laying at his head the bread from heaven, becomes a living truth. Everything depends only on whether the Lord's servant is really a selfless servant of his Lord, really surrendered and devoted, completely committed to him whose messenger and instrument he is permitted to be; then he will not and need not any longer worry about what becomes of himself. No evil will befall him.

This is not to ignore the anxious question of whether the pastor has a Sunday, and we wish to guard against blunting the point of the question with pious phrases; but even a Sunday filled to the brim with work can be a real Sunday, a shining *dies domini*. In this domain, time is weighed, not measured by hours and minutes. And what are hours of strenuous work that weary the body and mind, if in them there has been the precious pearl of one moment that is completely filled? What power has darkness and gloom, if for one moment the lightning has flashed and filled the whole room with light and splendor?

—Wilhelm Stählin (60)

* * *

Mirror for Ministers

Have I had any illusions about my ministry?

In my ministry have I trusted in man and made flesh my arm (Jer. 17:5)?

Have I exercised my ministry in accord with the people's fleshly lust and the lust of the eyes in order to please them or gain advantage?

Have I loved my position, my prestige, my income, my family more than God and the truth of his Word and the salvation of my congregation?

Has the securing of my life and my possessions been more important than the exercise of my ministry and the growth of my congregation into Christ who is the Head?

—Max Lackmann (61)

MONDAY

The Ministry: Its Promise and Responsibility

* * *

Thus says the Lord God: Ho, shepherds of Israel who have been feeding yourselves! Should not shepherds feed the sheep?

—Ezekiel 34:2

———

Those who are wise shall shine like the brightness of the firmament; and those who turn many to righteousness, like the stars for ever and ever. *—Daniel 12:3*

By all the castings down of his servants, God is glorified, for they are led to magnify him when again he sets them on their feet, and even while prostrate in the dust their faith yields him praise. They speak all the more sweetly of his faithfulness, and are the more firmly established in his love. Such mature men as some elderly preachers are, could scarcely have been produced if they had not been emptied from vessel to vessel, and made to see their own emptiness and the vanity of all things round about them. Glory be to God for the furnace, the hammer, and the file. Heaven shall be all the fuller of bliss because we have been filled with anguish here below, and earth shall be better tilled because of our training in the school of adversity.

The lesson of wisdom is, be not dismayed by soul-trouble. Count it no strange thing, but a part of ordinary ministerial experience. Should the power of depression be more than ordinary, think not that all is over with your usefulness. Cast not away your confidence, for it hath great recompense of reward. Even if the enemy's foot be on your neck, expect to rise and overthrow him. Cast the burden of the present, along with the sin of the past and the fear of the future, upon the Lord, who forsaketh not his saints. Live by the day — aye, by the hour. Put not trust in frames and feelings. Care more for a grain of faith than a ton of excitement. Trust in God alone, and lean not on the reeds of human help. Be not surprised when friends fail you : it is a failing world. Never count upon immutability in man : inconstancy you may reckon upon without fear of disappointment. The disciples of Jesus forsook him; be not amazed if your adherents wander away to other teachers : as they were not your all when with you, all is not gone from you with their departure. Serve God with all your might while the candle is burning, and then when it goes out for a season, you will have the less to regret. Be content to be nothing, for that is what you are. When your own emptiness is painfully forced upon your consciousness, chide yourself that you ever dreamed of being full, except in the Lord. Set small store by present rewards; be grateful for earnests by the way, but look for the recompensing joy hereafter. Continue with double earnestness to serve your Lord when no visible result is before you. Any simpleton can follow the narrow path in the light: faith's rare wisdom enables us to march on in the dark with infallible accuracy, since she places her hand in that of her great Guide. Between this and heaven there may be rougher weather yet, but it is all provided for by our covenant Head. In nothing let us be turned aside from the path which the divine call has urged us to pursue. Come fair or come foul, the pulpit is our watchtower, and the ministry our warfare; be it ours, when we cannot see the face of God, to trust under the shadow of his wings.

—Charles Haddon Spurgeon (62)

* * *

Dare to Suffer for Christ

Therefore, O beloved brethren and fellow-laborers in Christ's vineyard, let neither the fears nor the waves of this troubled world affright you, that Christ may not rebuke you as men of little faith. For he is not sleeping; he is testing you to see how brave you will be. And if it so please him, he will command the winds to be still and so uphold you upon the waters that you will not sink. He will not let you be tempted beyond your strength, but always show you the way of escape, either out of the trouble or out of the world, and gives you power over dragons, lions, and basilisks that you may either escape them or tread upon them. You have declared your loyalty and love toward him in the answer of Peter, when he asked him whether he loved him and Peter replied, "Lord, thou knowest that I love thee"; or else you have entered the sheepfold by force or by some way other than through Christ. So now let us see who shall be first to suffer for love of his Lord!

What profit can you be to him if you work for him and guide the ship only in fair weather, but flee when the heavy weather comes? The princes of this world have soldiers who fight for them and suffer death for little pay. Should our heavenly Father and Lord have none who shall fight and suffer death for his sake, even though he bestows, not perishable rewards, but eternal joy, and has already saved and redeemed us through his own Son? So long as you confess Christ only when things go well and flee when they go wrong, none will believe you because of the example you give. For when you will not dare to face death for the Word you preach, everyone will conclude that you yourself do not put your trust in it. Therefore when you hear the rumbles and alarms of persecutions arising, let it be far from you to think of fleeing; but rather remember that God has summoned you to battle as weak men and stands ready to behold how brave each one will be. Shame upon him who thinks of flight and is not ready to stand in front of the sheep, when his Lord is leading and attacking! In this cause turn to God in earnest prayer, that he may perform the good work he has begun in you; that you may accomplish the end that his name and his Word may again be brought to the knowledge of the poor, misguided sheep and life be lived according to his will. For only those who abide to the end will be saved! *—Ulrich Zwingli (63)*

* * *

Authority

I was a pastor, ministering in a hospital. A patient said to me, "If you were a ditchdigger, you'd have a more useful calling than you have now." That was a long time ago, but I have not forgotten it. I thought so myself many a time as I watched the nurses performing their tasks which are so needed and desired by the sick, and surgeons and doctors performing the most wonderful operations — while I stood there making miserable attempts at pastoral conversation. If I were only a ditchdigger! But a pastor? An impossible figure! Impossible before God, the world, and even myself. For there is a tremendous gap between what is required of the pastor in his ministry and his authority and power. Does he have any authority at all? . . .

The pastor's authority is based solely upon the fact that Jesus Christ ministers to him through the forgiveness of sins.

What do I have to do in my ministry? I have to preach, and we say: Preaching is God's Word. And yet I know how these sermons of mine were produced. Often, it is true, with prayer and fear and trembling; but also by dint of coffee and tobacco, sometimes in a burst of effort, very sketchily and superficially, because I had seemingly more important things to do. Strictly speaking, an impossible thing — unless Jesus Christ himself is not ashamed to accept this preaching.

In confession I have to say: Thy sins are forgiven. But I myself am a sinful man. And when I consider before God all the clumsy blunders I have committed and all that I have neglected, precisely in this area of confession and the forgiveness of sins, I begin to understand the ancient saying that it is a miracle if a minister be saved.

The minister stands at an open grave and utters the words of Jesus Christ: "I am the resurrection and the life; he that believeth in me, though he were dead, yet shall he live." But an earnest minister said to me, "Hardly ever, when I have spoken those words in that situation, have I even approached the reality of death around me and within myself."

In a discussion among young people the question was asked, what did they expect of a pastor? One of them replied, "He himself must be convinced of what he says." And all the rest agreed. They perhaps did not know what they were saying. For who of us always believes? And who of us can guarantee our faith for even an hour? "I have prayer for thee, that thy faith fail not" — that is what sustains us.

When we consider the church and its existence, we can only describe it as God's great venture among us men, the venture of a divine *diakonia* with us, that does not balk at the utmost depths. The church of Jesus Christ and its history, Calvin once said, is nothing but a chain of resurrections from the dead. It is also a passion history of the incarnate Son of God. In everything that is taught and believed, loved and suffered, planned and thought in this church, Jesus Christ is venturing himself, daily repeating the washing of the feet of this church which have daily been soiled on its journey. And he must follow up everything that men do in this church, even the most shining deeds, and in some way set them straight and make something good out of them. But just because such a church really does exist, a church that lives by this ministry of Jesus Christ, the minister in his ministry is not merely an impossible figure, but a necessary representative, as long as God keeps his church among men.

–Hermann Dietzfelbinger (64)

* * *

Christ Dwells Only with Sinners

My dear brother, learn Christ and him crucified. Learn to pray to him and, despairing of yourself, say: "Thou, Lord Jesus, art my righteousness, but I am thy sin. Thou hast taken upon thyself what is mine and hast given to me what is thine. Thou hast taken upon thyself what thou wast not and hast given to me what I was not." Beware of aspiring to such purity that you will not wish to be looked upon as a sinner, or to be one. For Christ dwells only in sinners. On this account he descended from heaven, where he dwelt among the righteous, to dwell among sinners. Meditate on this love of his and you will see his sweet consolation. For why was it necessary for him to die if we can obtain a good conscience by our works and afflictions? Accordingly you will find peace only in him and only when you despair of yourself and your own works. Besides, you will learn from him that just as he has received you, so he has made your sins his own and has made his righteousness yours.

If you firmly believe this as you ought (and he is damned who does not believe it), receive your untaught and hitherto erring brothers, patiently help them, make their sins yours, and, if you have any goodness, let it be theirs. Thus the apostle teaches: "Receive ye one another, as Christ also received us, to the glory of God." And again: "Let this mind be in you, which was also in Christ Jesus: who, being in the form of God, thought it not robbery to be equal with God." Even so, if you seem to yourself to be better than they are, do not count it as booty, as if it were yours alone, but humble yourself, forget what you are, and be as one of them in order that you may help them.

Cursed is the righteousness of the man who is unwilling to assist others on the ground that they are worse than he is and who thinks of fleeing from and forsaking those whom he ought now to be helping with patience, prayer, and example. This would be burying his Lord's talent and not paying what is due. If you are a lily and a rose of Christ, therefore, know that you will live among thorns. Only see to it that you will not become a thorn as a result of impatience, rash judgment, or secret pride. The rule of Christ is in the midst of his enemies, as the psalm puts it. Why, then, do you imagine that you are among friends? Pray, therefore, for whatever you lack, kneeling before the face of Jesus Christ. He will teach you all things. Only keep your eyes fixed on that which he has done for you and for all men in order that you may learn what you should do for others. If he had desired to live only among good people and to die only for his friends, for whom, pray, would he have died and with whom would he ever have lived? Act accordingly, my dear brother, and pray for me. The Lord be with you.

—*Luther* (65)

Always there is one firm consolation — to know the source of our office and ministry. We have it in an order instituted by God. This order stems out of mercy. Because we have received mercy and because this happened and continues to happen, we can serve. This mercy stands not only at the beginning of our ministry, it accompanies us constantly, even in time of doubt. Only one who makes mercy in this sense the foundation of his ministry can go on working. On the gravestone of Bodelschwingh are inscribed these words of II Corinthians 4:1, "Therefore, having this ministry by the mercy of God, we do not lose heart." And so he instructed the young men who were to serve even where no human justification of their work might encourage them. They were made to understand that misery exists that it may bring forth the praise of God's mercy, so that, as Paul says, the bright light which God has shone in the heart may shine in the world (v. 6). Thus Jesus Christ becomes a reality on earth.

—Georg Merz (66)

* * *

He that intends truly to preach the gospel, and not himself; he that is more concerned to do good to others than to raise his own fame, or to procure a following to himself — that reads the Scriptures much, and meditates often upon them — this man, so made, and so molded, cannot miscarry in his work. He shall have his crown, and his reward for his labors. And, to say all that can be said in one word with St. Paul, "He shall both save himself, and them that hear him."

—Gilbert Burnet (67)

* * *

Encouragement

It may be granted, therefore, that we are called to difficult and costly service. Yet have we abundant cause to be satisfied with it, from the sustaining support and consolation provided for its emergencies. All, indeed, may be considered to be included in the single promise, "Lo, I am with you always, even to the end of the world." The officers he employs, in every age, are entitled to this treasure, as well as those of the first age. Keep your mind believingly attentive to this "always"—"Lo, I am with you," to qualify and succeed you in whatever work I call you to. "Lo, I am with you," to comfort you by my presence and Spirit, when your hearts are grieved. "Lo, I am with you," to defend and strengthen you in trials, though all men forsake you. While he stands with you, there can be no just cause of fear or faintness. You need no other encouragement. This you shall never want, if you continue faithful: and thereupon you may conclude, "The Lord shall deliver me from every evil work, and will preserve me unto his heavenly kingdom."—*Daniel Williams* (68)

* * *

Do What You Are Called to Do

There is a good saying that comes from Löhe: "Don't be ashamed to do what you are called to do." Even the awkwardly spoken word, if only it comes out of an obedient heart, is better than a word unspoken in disobedience. Even the prayer that seems ineffectual and may perhaps be ridiculed may have left behind a seed of blessing. Indeed, even if no fruit is created in the spiritual sense, so that a soul comes nearer to God, still there is one thing that has happened: a testimony has been given in the biblical sense. And this precisely is our task, a hard task, but a glorious task.

—*Erich Schick* (69)

* * *

The Ministry of the Shepherd

"Lift your drooping hands!" Anybody who receives ordination to the holy office of the ministry should know that he receives it in order that souls may be saved. This should fill his whole soul. Therefore let his hands never cease from reaching out for those who are sinking to rescue them from the whirlpool. Away with temporal comfort; away with earthly rest; away with the slumber and sleep of the slothful!

"Strengthen your weak knees!" Anybody who receives ordination to the holy office of the ministry should know that one's knees grow weak only when one runs with the world and after the world, but that the Lord's service does not make one weak and weary, that the Lord strengthens the weak and gives them the strength of youth when they call upon him. Strengthen your weak knees by constant prayer!

"Make straight paths for your feet!" Anybody who receives ordination to the holy office of the ministry should know that he dare not go limping between two opinions, trying not to displease either the world or God. He should know that he cannot serve two masters. He must make a straight path for his feet so that he will not preach a miserable message that pleases the world, but resolutely and fearlessly proclaim the foolish message of the saving gospel and deem it an eternal honor to be counted a fool by the world. With steady foot he will take his stand with these fools, for whom the eternal salvation which they do not see is more precious than the temporal pleasure which they do see, and with steady foot he will abide with them.

—August Vilmar (70)

* * *

Complete Surrender

If I were to write of the burdens that a preacher must bear and endure, as I know them and myself experienced, I would frighten everybody away from the ministry. For a devout, God-fearing preacher must be so minded that there is nothing he desires more than Christ, his Lord and Saviour, and the eternal life to come, so that even though he lose this life and all else, Christ would still say to him: Come unto me; you have been my beloved, faithful servant.

—Luther (71)

234

My experience as an evangelist has brought me three certainties. I am certain that to preach the gospel in season and out of season, and to believe that a man is able to respond to the power of the Holy Spirit is to live no easy life. There is a strain and a going out of virtue which is very real. The gospel always produces a division amongst the people; there is, therefore, ever present both in individual contact and in public assembly a note of discord. There are those who are for and those who are against; he who would preach the gospel cannot be insensitive to this. He must be prepared for criticism, some of it no doubt very fair and just, but much of it occasioned by a rationalization on the part of those who will not accept the gospel he preaches. Preaching the gospel is not a pastime of peaceful fishing, but rather a battle to land the fish.

Another certainty is the clear conviction of my own complete unworthiness to preach the gospel. The Spirit of God does not use a man to proclaim his gospel because of what he is, but in spite of him; and the more one sees the power of God to change people's lives the less one feels worthy to be used to proclaim it. There is a very real sense in which one knows beyond all doubt that the work of conversion is all of God and not of man. The words of St. Paul ring an echo in the heart of every true evangelist. "I was with you in weakness, and in fear, and in much trembling. And my speech and my preaching were not in persuasive words of wisdom, but in demonstration of the Spirit and of power."

Finally, however much, on looking back, one wishes that this or that had not been done or said, there is one thing I would never have altered; it is that on a day many years ago now the compulsion of Christ came to my heart and mind, and I knew that I must share the Christ that I had discovered for myself as Saviour and Lord. In that sharing, most fearfully and self-consciously begun, I started to discover what evangelism meant, and that discovery has been the greatest I have ever made. I would not have done anything else with my life than to seek with every power that I possess to share the gospel of Christ with all who will listen.

–*Bryan Green* (72)

* * *

Perfect Joy

One winter's day, as St. Francis was going from Perugia with Friar Leo to St. Mary of the Angels, suffering sorely from the bitter cold, he called Friar Leo, that was going before him, and spake thus, "Friar Leo, albeit the friars minor in every land give good examples of holiness and edification, nevertheless write and note down diligently that perfect joy is not to be found therein." And St. Francis went his way a little farther, and called him a second time, saying, "O Friar Leo, even though the friar minor gave sight to the blind, made the crooked straight, cast out devils, made the deaf to hear, the lame to walk, and restored speech to the dumb, and, what is a yet greater thing, raised to life those who have lain four days in the grave; write—perfect joy is not found there." And he journeyed on a little while, and cried aloud, "O Friar Leo, if the friar minor knew all tongues and all the sciences and all the Scriptures, so that he could foretell and reveal not only future things, but even the secrets of the conscience and of the soul; write—perfect joy is not there." Yet a little farther went St. Francis, and cried again aloud, "O Friar Leo, little sheep of God, even though the friar minor spake with the tongue of angels and knew the courses of the stars and the virtues of herbs, and were the hidden treasures of the earth revealed to him, and he knew the qualities of birds, and of fishes, and of all animals, and of man, and of trees, and stones, and roots, and waters; write—not there is perfect joy." And St. Francis went on again a little space, and cried aloud, "O Friar Leo, although the friar minor were skilled to preach so well that he should convert all the infidels to the faith of Christ; write—not there is perfect joy." And when this fashion of talk had endured two good miles, Friar Leo asked him in great wonder and said, "Father, prithee in God's name tell me where is perfect joy to be found?" And St. Francis answered him thus, "When we are come to St. Mary of the Angels, wet through with rain, frozen with cold, and foul with mire and tormented with hunger; and when we knock at the door, the door-keeper cometh in a rage and saith, 'Who are ye?' and we say, 'We are two of your friars,' and he answers, 'Ye tell not true; yet are rather two knaves that go deceiving the world and stealing the alms of the poor; begone!' and he openeth not to us, and maketh us stay outside hungry and cold all night in the rain and snow; then if we endure patiently such cruelty, such abuse, and such insolent dismissal without complaint or murmuring, and believe humbly and charitably that that doorkeeper truly knows us, and that God maketh him to rail against us; O Friar Leo, write—there is perfect joy. And if we persevere in our knocking, and he issues forth and angrily drives us away, abusing us and smiting us on the cheek, saying, 'Go hence, ye vile thieves, get ye gone to the spital, for here ye shall neither eat nor lodge'; if this we suffer patiently with love and gladness; write, O Friar Leo—this is perfect joy. And if, constrained by hunger and by cold, we knock once more and pray with many tears that he open to us for the love of God and let us but come inside, and he more insolently than ever crieth, 'These be impudent rogues, I will pay them out as they deserve'; and issues forth with a big knotted stick and seizes us by our cowls and flings us on the ground and rolls us in the snow, bruising every bone in our bodies with that heavy stick—if we, thinking on the agony of the blessed Christ, endure all these things patiently and joyously for love of him; write, O Friar Leo, that here and in this perfect joy is found. And now, Friar Leo, hear the conclusion. Above all the grace and the gifts of the Holy Spirit that Christ giveth to his beloved is that of overcoming self, and for love of him willingly to bear pain and buffetings and revilings and discomfort; for in none other of God's gifts, save these, may we glory, seeing they are not ours, but of God. Wherefore the Apostle saith, 'What hast thou that is not of God, and if thou hast received it of him, wherefore dost thou glory as if thou hadst it of thyself?' But in the cross of tribulation and of affliction we may glory, because this is ours. Therefore the Apostle saith, 'I will not glory save in the cross of our Lord Jesus Christ.' "

—*Francis of Assisi* (73)

* * *

Perquisites

The minister's office will often lead him to the bed of the dying and often he must go to the churchyard with the dead, often must he see the misery and affliction that is caused by death. There is no other office which in its performance presents such great compulsion to practice godliness as does that of the pastor. Therefore he must take the utmost care that the blessing and the high reward which the office itself will richly give him be not lost. One who preaches God's Word and is not himself comforted, strengthened, rebuked, and humbled by it is like a man who sits by a spring and goes thirsty, who has bread in his hands and goes hungry. One who performs his office mechanically receives only the perquisites and even that is rich recompense; even if they are only a few pennies he is getting too much. But one who lives and feels, suffers and rejoices with those to whom he has preached God's Word will at the same time be fed with them by the bread of life, and the Lord God will pay the perquisites in coin that moths and rust cannot consume and he never fails to pay.

—*Karl Büchsel* (74)

I have seventy-two children to confirm and among them some very big, strong, and tough ones. And often one's heart grows heavy and sometimes we become discouraged and say, what's the use of all this preaching and teaching? Then we also feel our weakness and the inadequacy of our work and to this too we attribute the fact that we see so little fruit of our labor. Then we grow fainthearted, despondent, and mistrustful of our own work, which has nevertheless been committed to us to do as best we can, and so we lose all joy in our work, the happy, hopeful spirit that is so necessary for good work.

Recently, I too had such an hour of weakness and dreariness, and at one sitting I read the first fourteen chapters of the Gospel of Mark. Suddenly it was like sunshine falling into my soul to find it said of our Lord again and again, "And he taught them." Never had anybody taught as he taught, no master in Israel, no prophet and no apostle, and one would have thought his teaching would have enlightened, converted, and inspired all the thousands who were his pupils, but what was the result? I shall not go into that. And yet he did not grow weary, and again and again it is said of him, "And he taught them," and he rejoiced when even a poor publican or a poor sinful woman was awakened by his message and drawn to him. Deep in the dust and with wet eyes I bowed before him, marveling at his humility, his patience, and his compassion; and since then I go to every session with these words in my soul: "And he taught them." It is like oil upon my head and I hold it high in that hour with my children, overflowing with joy, patience, and hope, and I cannot understand why this "and he taught them" was not long ago such an anointing and power as it is now. But, of course, we never have the Word of God until it is given to us (John 17), but when it is given, we see that we have received an infinite treasure. In so far as a man can give to another the Word of God, I give to you, my dear co-worker in the work of the Lord, this word as a comfort and cordial for you in your ministry, where you too are often heavy of heart. Go into church and your classes with this word; it is a rod and staff that will not let you down.

—*Friedrich Mallet* (75)

* * *

To a Discouraged Minister

When difficulties pile up before you like insurmountable mountains . . .

When behind you, you see nothing but failures . . .

When before you, you see nothing but trouble . . .

1. Do what is at hand to do. Consider each *single* day to be your appointed task. Leave to God the care of the future.

2. Don't desire to harvest. You are only a sower.

3. Remember that on the island of Nias the missionaries prayed for twenty-five years for an awakening.

4. If you can be comfort and strength to even one *single* person, then even fifty years of no success have not been in vain.

5. It is no help to an unrepentant one to be annoyed with him; what he needs is seeking love.

6. Even for Paul the "thorn in the flesh" remained. His grace is sufficient . . .

7. Christ can fight his battles even with broken swords.

8. It is not ability but faithfulness that counts (I Cor. 4:2). *"He dared to believe his way through the deepest gloom."*

—*Friedrich Zündel on Blumhardt*

* * *

Suffering is the highest action of Christian obedience and I call blessed, not those who have worked, but all who have suffered. Suffering is the greatest work in the discipleship of Jesus.
—*Hermann Bezzel*

God wounds deeply when he wills to heal.

–Hermann Kohlbrügge

* * *

Let us dry our tears and put out our mourning lamps for the Sun of Christ is shining.
–Wilhelm Löhe
–Walter H. Schulze (76)

* * *

The Secret of Joy

The whole secret of a preacher's power and joy and peace may be expressed in one word—"interpenetration." He must try to make his own every word of the seventeenth chapter of St. John's Gospel, with its central thought of divine interpenetration: "I in them, and thou in me." He must pray that at the close of his ministry he may be able to say: "I have given them thy Word." The Word he is to preach is the living and life-giving Son of God. He must find it first in sublime aloofness of eternal communion in the bosom of the Father. He must possess it by allowing it to possess him. He must surrender himself to it in order that through him it may become again incarnate and dwell among men. He must allow this Divine Word to control and fashion his life as well as his words, so that it may become in him a fountain of life for all men. "I live; yet not I, but Christ liveth in me." He must love the souls to whom he preaches as our dear Lord loves them. "The words thou gavest me I have given unto them."
–Paul B. Bull (77)

* * *

Come, brothers, march together: Jesus will be with us. For Jesus we took up this cross: for Jesus let us persevere in the cross. He will be our Helper: who is our Guide and Forerunner. Behold our King goes on before us.

–Thomas à Kempis (78)

Our office has now assumed a very different character from that which it bore under the pope; it is now of a very grave nature, and is very salutary in its influence. It consequently subjects us to far greater burdens and labors, dangers and temptation, whilst it brings with it an inconsiderable reward, and very little gratitude in the world. But Christ himself will be our reward, if we labor with fidelity. May he grant such mercy unto us, who is the Father of all grace, to whom be given thanks and praises through Christ, our Lord, forever! Amen.

—Luther (79)

* * *

Acts 20:17–36

O Brethren, write it on your study doors, or set it as your copy in capital letters still before your eyes! Could we but properly learn two or three lines of it, what preachers should we be! (1) For our general business, serving the Lord with humility of mind. (2) Our special work, take heed to yourselves, and to all the flock. (3) Our doctrine, repentance towards God, and faith toward our Lord Jesus Christ. (4) The place and manner of teaching, I have taught you publicly and from house to house. (5) The object and internal manner, I ceased not to warn every one night and day with tears. This is it that must win souls and preserve them. (6) His innocency and self-denial for the advantage of the gospel, I have coveted no man's silver or gold. (7) His patience, none of these things move me, neither count I my life dear. (8) And among all our motives, these have need to be in capital letters before our eyes. We oversee and feed the church of God, which he hath purchased with his own blood. . . . Grievous wolves shall enter in among you, not sparing the flock, and of your ownselves shall men arise, speaking perverse things, to draw away disciples after them. Write all this upon your hearts, and it will do yourselves and the church more good than twenty years' study of lower things, which though they get you greater applause in the world, yet separated from these, will make you but sounding brass and tinkling cymbals.

—*Richard Baxter* (80)

* * *

"*Resolves*—To try to learn to be thoroughly poor in spirit, meek and to be ready to be silent when others speak.

To learn from everyone.

To try to feel my own insignificance.

To believe in myself, and the powers with which I am intrusted.

To try to make conversation more useful and therefore to store my mind with fact, yet to be on guard against a wish to shine.

To try to despise the principle of the day, 'every man his own trumpeter'; and to feel it a degradation to speak of my own doings, as a poor braggart.

To endeavor to get over the adulterous-generation-habit of seeking a sign. . . .

To speak less of self, and think less.

To aim at more concentration of thought.

To try to overcome castle-building.

To be systematic in visiting; and to make myself master of some system of questions for ascertaining the state of the poor.

To listen to conscience, instead of, as Pilate did, to intellect.

To try to fix attention on Christ rather than on the doctrines of Christ.

To preserve inviolable secrecy on all secrets committed to me, especially on any confidential communication of spiritual perplexities.

To take deep interest in the difficulties of others so communicated.

To perform rigorously the examen of conscience.

To try to fix my thoughts in prayer, without distraction.
To contend, one by one, against evil thoughts.
To watch over a growing habit of uncharitable judgment."

—*Frederick W. Robertson* (81)

* * *

Ye, who your Lord's commission bear,
His way of mercy to prepare:
Angels he calls you; be your strife
To lead on earth an angel's life,
Think not of rest; though dreams be sweet,
Start up, and ply your heavenward feet,
Is not God's oath upon your head,
Ne'er to sink back on slothful bed,
Never again your loins untie,
Nor let your torches waste and die,
Till, when the shadows thickest fall,
Ye hear your Master's midnight call?

—*John Keble* (82)

* * *

The Accounting

His charge to the candidates on the eve of the ordination was always most impressive, "Tomorrow I shall say to you, 'wilt thou, wilt thou, wilt thou?' But there will come a day to you when Another will say to you, 'hast thou, hast thou, hast thou?' "

—*Charles Gore* (83)

* * *

In May 1849 Kierkegaard wrote of Bishop Mynster: "He is now 73 years old. Soon he will go in to—judgment. . . . His sermons are all right—but in eternity he is not to preach, there he is to be—judged."

—*Søren Kierkegaard* (84)

FIGHTINGS WITHOUT AND FEARS WITHIN

To be a Servant of God Means to be a Struggler
Ecclesiasticus 2

My son, if thou comest to serve the Lord, prepare thy soul for temptation. Set thy heart aright, and constantly endure, and make not haste in time of calamity. Cleave unto him, and depart not, that thou mayest be increased at thy latter end. Accept whatsoever is brought upon thee, and be long-suffering when thou passest into humiliation. For gold is tried in the fire, and acceptable men in the furnace of humiliation. Put thy trust in him, and he will help thee: order thy ways aright, and set thy hope on him.

Ye that fear the Lord, wait for his mercy; and turn not aside, lest ye fall. Ye that fear the Lord, put your trust in him; and your reward shall not fail. Ye that fear the Lord, hope for good things, and for eternal gladness and mercy. Look at the generations of old, and see: who did ever put his trust in the Lord, and was ashamed? Or who did abide in his fear, and was forsaken? Or who did call upon him, and he despised him? For the Lord is full of compassion and mercy; and he forgiveth sins, and saveth in time of affliction.

Woe unto fearful hearts, and to faint hands, and to the sinner that goeth two ways! Woe unto the faint heart! for it believeth not; therefore shall it not be defended. Woe unto you that have lost your patience! And what will ye do when the Lord shall visit you? They that fear the Lord will not disobey his words; and they that love him will keep his ways. They that fear the Lord will seek his good pleasure; and they that love him shall be filled with the law. They that fear the Lord will prepare their hearts, and will humble their souls in his sight, saying, we will fall into the hands of the Lord, and not into the hands of men: for as his majesty is, so also is his mercy.

Nulla tentatio pessima tentatio.
No temptation is the worst temptation.

—Luther

* * *

Nobody should ever look anxious except those who have no anxiety.

—Benjamin Disraeli (85)

* * *

The Preacher's Fundamental Sin

The preacher must learn that *his* fundamental sin is *not* to preach the gospel. He may be tempted by sins just as other people are, but the fundamental sin of his life is false preaching, false teaching, false theology. If the builder of a bridge were to build his bridge of pasteboard he would be prosecuted, he would be made responsible for the consequences, criminal action would be taken against him. But how about our preaching? What if our teaching and theology are like building bridges with pasteboard? What if the bridge we build here leads men to destruction instead of salvation? What if what we teach and proclaim is contrary to our ordination? What if the sole reason for our existence as preachers of the gospel be obliterated by ourselves? We preachers are capable of sinning in many ways like other people and it is good and right to remember this. But the work by which we must be tested as preachers and in which we must constantly examine ourselves is our preaching. There the question is, what is the substance and responsibility of our proclamation?

—Martin Fischer (86)

* * *

Professionalism

A corroding and deadening sin is professionalism, which shows itself in an affected tone of voice, a studied manner, a use of conventional phrases, and an unholy familiarity with spiritual things. When the minister of Christ falls into this state of soul, it is a woeful tragedy. Conceive it that a man should receive infants in the name of Christ, should dispense the Sacrament of the Lord's death, should minister by the bedside of the dying, should be witness of the supreme conflicts of the soul, should carry the message of the Divine Love, should intercede for the people with God, should live and work amid sacred mysteries—and should have lost all sense of their awfulness, their loveliness, their tenderness. If any man be able to leave the pulpit without fear, or administer a sacrament without being exhausted, or return from seeing one of his flock pass into eternity, and plunge into society, then he may well ask whether the Spirit of Christ has not forsaken him, and he has not been deposed from his office by the Lord's own hands.

—*John Watson* (87)

* * *

Familiarity with Holy Things

There are conditions in a minister's work which put him at a real disadvantage as compared with his people. In the exercise of his calling, he has, for example, continually to lead them in prayer; he may be depressed, irritated, anxious, secular, and yet he must give appropriate utterance to sentiments of a different level. He has to ascribe high praise to God in moments when his real view of life is sordid, he has to pour forth confident petitions for divine grace and assistance, though he never once has had experience of prayer as heard. As he grows expert in his profession he acquires an increased facility in the use of suitable phrases; but words thus used without an awe-struck sense of their reality are bound to work mischief in the nature, and thus for the mere professional the prayer in which his neighbors find expansion of soul may become an active means of hardening. The same is true of Bible reading which, for the common folk in all generations, has proved a source of comfort and refreshment, but for the professional the Bible tends to become a hunting-ground for texts. He does not deliberately explore its richness for his own profit, but makes incursions here and there, catching at what his ingenuity can employ for pulpit purposes. From of old, Scripture has proved itself a means of communion with the God who speaks in it, but for the merely expert craftsman it has no such dignity. And thus so far from devotion being easier for the minister it tends to be greatly harder, for in trafficking with the externals of religion he may readily delude himself that that is devotion which is little more than the dexterity of a trade. It is not safe for him to fall back upon his ordination, with the prayers and the laying on of hands, as if automatically a gift had then been conferred. *Cucullus non facit monachum* —the cowl does not make the monk; and the most regular and dignified ordination may leave a man exactly where it found him, a creature with heart unopened, a mere outsider in the things of God. The secret of the Lord is with them that fear him, and is discovered through dwelling with God, not through talking about him.

—William Malcolm Macgregor (88)

* * *

Nothing is so deadening to the divine as an habitual dealing with the outsides of holy things. *—George Macdonald* (89)

* * *

Disillusionment

Surely there are few figures so pitiable as the disillusioned minister of the gospel. High hopes once cheered him on his way: but now the indifference and recalcitrance of the world, the lack of striking visible results, the discovery of the appalling pettiness and spite and touchiness and complacency which can lodge in narrow hearts, the feeling of personal futility—all these have seared his soul. No longer does the zeal of God's house devour him. No longer does he mount the pulpit steps in thrilled expectancy that Jesus Christ will come amongst his folk that day, traveling in the greatness of his strength, mighty to save. Dully and drearily he speaks now about what once seemed to him the most dramatic tidings in the world. The edge and verve and passion of the message of divine forgiveness, the exultant, lyrical assurance of the presence of the risen Lord, the amazement of supernatural grace, the urge to cry "Woe is me if I preach not the gospel" —all have gone. The man has lost heart. He is disillusioned. And that, for an ambassador of Christ, is tragedy.

—James S. Stewart (90)

* * *

Conformity

Everyone who has ever occupied a position in life to which tradition and opinion, a long incrusted use and wont and habit of mind attribute a certain rigid pattern of behavior, knows very well the ponderous and incessant pressure of public opinion seeking to force the man into the mold. Such types as the statesman, the headmaster, the parson, the poet, are continually subject to this pressure to become what the public expect them to be rather than what they really are. That very expectation becomes the archenemy, the Satan of the soul. If it is not resisted the living person becomes a stylized statue; he is dead. . . . This is murder—murder of spirit—and the murderers are the victim's admirers and friends.

—Nicodemus (Melville Chaning-Pierce) (91)

* * *

Would-be theologians . . . must be on their guard lest by beginning too soon to preach they rather chatter themselves into Christianity than live themselves into it and find themselves at home there.

—Søren Kierkegaard (92)

No Escape in a Seminary

You cannot escape the temptations of the world or the flesh or the devil even in the cloister; all you can do is to change the form they take.

—F. R. Barry (93)

* * *

Hell is paved with priests' skulls. —*John Chrysostom* (94)

* * *

There is no true shepherd without temptation, as even the Great Shepherd, Christ, was tempted. The devil seeks especially, most frequently and most powerfully, to tear the Word of God out of the heart of that one who has it most really and most completely. The pastor must contend against the devil, not only for himself, but also for his congregation; a statement that is easily spoken, but which contains a veritable world of weight. Whoever knows nothing of these conflicts, knows not that the principal object of all the devil's attacks is the representative of the congregation and church of Christ, is not yet a true minister. . . . For all these it is necessary to arm oneself with the Word of God in a special way, so that it is available in every moment. The more deeply God's Word is rooted in us the more certain it is that we shall have peace.

—*August Vilmar* (95)

* * *

The conditions that have most aided me in the development of prayer are hardly due to architectural gems, mystical masterpieces, or aesthetic satisfactions. My education in prayer, so far, has sprung from shrinking inferiorities, startling, cowering fears, hopeless failures, blinding frustrations, and secret sins which have dogged my rationalizations, evasions, defiances, and deliberate self-deceptions until, spiritually breathless, I fell before the throne of grace and asked for absolution.

Other conditions to which I owe so much have been made possible by individuals, committees, and boards who have violently opposed my wilful desires. I have often thought that my ideas were God's ideas, but too often they were of my own impulsive and often egocentric whims. There have been those individuals with whom I clashed and conquered, many such, but the most helpful are those with whom I fought and was forced to forfeit my will and often bitterly resented as well as feared. Then there have been vestries which openly attacked my weaknesses in public meeting to such a degree that I was often ill before and after sessions. These belonged to the days when seldom did I ever face my shortcomings and failures, but projected them on the world and the people and the bad luck about me. . . .

It seems to me that the priest or layman who is not constantly harassed by thorns is underprivileged. His thorns may be in the form of browbeating little Hitlers, cynics, critics, and professional opposers, or they may be in the form of illness, impediment, scars, and disfigurations, or they may be in the form of lost love, betrayal, and disillusionment, or they may be in the form of wounded pride, humiliation, and ignominy, or they may be in the form of poverty, hunger, and destitution, or all of them put together. Most of us have never had more than one or two of the above combinations at once, but whatever they may be or have been, we must have thorns to learn to pray with power. A thorn usually leads to the cross, and the cross to the confession of sin, and thence to freedom and incomparable strength. But before we can feel the strength of Christ we must know that there is no health in us insofar as our own personal power goes—that of ourselves we can but eventually fail, but in Christ we can know nothing other than final victory.

—Austin Pardue (96)

I should think ill of any preacher who confessed himself untroubled by all those aspects of our experience summed up in what we call the problem of evil. I should expect him, if he were really a God-sent man, to be familiar with terrible visitations of doubt, to have moments when all solutions of the problem of evil, even those which he himself has attempted, seem to him vain; and I should expect those visitations to be more terrible for him than for others. Being the man he is, he must needs have his times of perplexity, nay, his times of extremity. They are among the conditions of his service and he must be willing to bear them as a good soldier of Christ. He enlists on the understanding that moments of despair are among the possibilities that await him, and when they come he must still say to himself, "for this cause I was born and for this I came into the world." No less is required of him by the traditions of the service. They were established in the Garden of Gethsemane.

—L. P. Jacks (97)

* * *

I was, on Sunday, the fifth, clearly convinced of unbelief, of the want of that faith whereby alone we are saved.

Immediately it struck into my mind, "Leave off preaching. How can you preach to others, who have not faith yourself?" I asked Böhler whether he thought I should leave it off or not. He answered, "By no means." I asked, "But what can I preach?" He said, "Preach faith till you have it; and then, because you have it, you will preach faith."

—John Wesley (98)

* * *

Jealousy

The man who has an awesome sense of God, the man who knows that what other men call their privacy is a region that lies forever in the white light of the divine scrutiny, is delivered, once for all, from such a vice as jealousy. The man in whose thought and prayer God ever looms greater knows that in the ministry no man is his competitor. With perfect humility he believes that no other can fill his particular niche in the economy of God. The man who cannot sincerely rejoice in another man's gift has no call to the ministry. Neither has he who has not learned, with his two talents, to work loyally with him who has five.

–*George Johnstone Jeffrey* (99)

* * *

Ambitio praedicatoris est ecclesiae pestis
The ambitious preacher is a pestilence to the church.

–*Luther* (100)

* * *

What Can a Pastor Give?

They all want something of me when they come to church. They all expect that I have something to give them. A pastor is a man who is beset by the expectation that he has something to give. And when they all expect that you have something to give, you finally get the idea yourself that you have something to give.

Do *you* have something to give? God help you never to grow so conscious of your ministerial office or your dignity that, as you grow older, more experienced, and mature, you come to be convinced in all "humility" that you have something to give!

What can *you* give to old R., who has been lying in the same bed for twenty years, paralyzed and shrunken, and yet is friendly, quiet, patient, even joyful in the Lord? What are you going to give to the dying young consumptive whose mother has called you to come, and you find him in utter despair? What are you going to give to those people in the pews who have been disciplined in suffering and patience for thirty years and more, much longer than you have? What are *you,* who are only a man, going to give to men like yourself?

But stop your questions! Tell me, what language are you speaking? Are you speaking the language of the poor in spirit or are you speaking the language of unbelief? Do you really have nothing to give? Don't you have something else to give? Don't you bring with you that Book from the pulpit, which is God's treasure for you and people like you? Has not the chalice and the bread been entrusted to you, so that you need not go to the hungering and thirsting with empty hands? Does not God have something to give? And can't you take as much as you need in order to be able to give?

Woe is me. Am I speaking the language of faith, or is it the voice of the Tempter that is whispering to me, "God's gifts are in your hand; just go ahead and use them?"

Get thee behind me, Satan! I have nothing to give, but God will give to me and my brethren, as he did yesterday and today, so tomorrow, out of the immeasurable riches of his grace. Amen.

—Heinrich Vogel (101)

* * *

Success?

We must make sure that we do not decide that we shall succeed. If we decide to succeed then we may succeed without succeeding in God's way. But if we go on from day to day seeking to do his will, then we shall be prepared to receive success from him if he wills it; and if he does not, then humbly to say—It is God's decision that David shall not build the temple, but he will raise up Solomon.

—W. A. Visser 't Hooft (102)

* * *

True Preachers Look Only to God

True preachers look only to God. True, they recognize God's light, power, and grace within them, but they also acknowledge that they receive all this not from themselves but from God. It is God who puts the Word in their mouths, it is God who through his Spirit presses the Word into the hearts of the hearers. Therefore they do all their work to his honor. They go out to scatter the seed of the divine Word, they spare no labor, they stretch their bodies, their life, their all in their ministry, as a faithful servant serves his lord with all his strength. And in this work they have good trust in God through Christ that he will give the increase to their sowing. If there is fruit, they give God the glory and say, "Thou hast wrought all our works in us" (Isa. 26:12). What the husbandman grows is God's doing, what good the teaching produces is God's work. If no fruit appears, they still do not cease to work and to trust and to pray, and they manifest their trust by keeping their happy courage.

–Heinrich Müller (103)

* * *

The Word of God knows no limits to its power. At any moment, if only your utterance gives it a faithful echo, souls may be born again, "begotten of the Word"; some sinner may be translated from the power of darkness into the kingdom of the Son of his life; a soul may awaken to hear God's call, who will bring tribes and nations into his kingdom; the heavenly vision may be unveiled to a blind soul, and the course of the history of the world may be changed. This will not be seen in its fulness till all is manifest on the day of judgment. But just as the pressure on an electric button may set in operation a long chain of antecedents and consequences, which will launch a ship, or explode a mine, or win a war, so in any spiritual preaching one can place no limits to the boundless possibilities. All we know is that, if we are faithful in our ministry, the Word which was in the beginning, which was with God, and was God, will issue forth once more from the bosom of the Father to plead with the men to whom we speak, and that no Word of God is without power, and that it will not return unto him void, but will accomplish that which he pleases.

—Paul P. Bull (104)

* * *

Although now both, viz. the planting and watering of the preacher, and the running and willing of the hearer, would be to no purpose, and no conversion would follow, if the power and efficacy of the Holy Ghost were not added thereto, who, through the Word preached and heard, enlightens and converts the hearts, so that men believe this Word, and assent thereto; nevertheless neither preacher nor hearer should doubt this grace and efficacy of the Holy Ghost, but should be certain, if the Word of God is preached, purely and clearly, according to the command and will of God, and men listen attentively and earnestly, and meditate upon it, that God is certainly present with his grace, and grants, as has been said, what man can otherwise from his own powers neither accept nor give.

—Formula of Concord (105)

* * *

If you would prosper in your work, be sure to keep up earnest desires and expectations of success. If your hearts be not set on the end of your labors, and you long not to see the conversion and edification of your hearers, and do not study and preach in hope, you are not likely to see much fruit of it. It is an ill sign of a false, self-seeking heart, that can be content to be still doing, and see no fruit of their labor. So I have observed, that God seldom blesseth any man's work so much as his whose heart is set upon success. But let all that preach for Christ, and men's salvation, be unsatisfied till they have the thing they preach for. He had never the right motives of a preacher that is indifferent whether he do obtain them, and is not grieved when he misseth them, and rejoiced when he sees the desired issue. When a man doth only study what to say, and how with commendation to spend the hour, and looks no more after it, unless it be to know what people think of his own abilities, and thus holds on from year to year; I must needs think, that this man preaches for himself, and drives on a private trade of his own, and does not preach for Christ even when he preaches Christ how excellent soever he may seem to do it. No wise or charitable physician is content to be still giving physic, and see no amendment among his patients, but have them all to die upon his hands; nor will any wise and honest schoolmaster be content to be still teaching, though his scholars profit not; but either of them would grow weary of the employment. I know that a faithful minister may have comfort when he wants success; and though Israel be not gathered, our reward is with the Lord; and our acceptance is not according to the fruit, but according to our labor.

*   *   *   —*Richard Baxter* (106)

It's true, my people in Twan do not pamper me. And when I am preparing my sermon on Saturday there are two who come to me. One of them says to me, "Albert, why do you bother yourself so much for the twenty or thirty people who come to your church? Take it easier." But then the second one comes and says, "Albert, look, I had only twelve who listened to me, and of the twelve one betrayed me and another denied me. Do you want to be better off than I was?"

Then I say to the first, "Get thee behind me, Satan; thou art an offense unto me." And to the second I say, "Thanks be to thee, Lord Jesus; help me to be thy disciple."

*   *   *   —*Albert Bitzius* (107)

If God be satisfied with a pastor, it is of little importance whether he please or displease men.   —*Thomas Wilson* (108)

The ministerial work must be managed purely for God, and the salvation of the people, and not for any private ends of our own. A wrong end makes all the work bad, as from us, how good soever in itself. It is not serving God, but ourselves, if we do it not for God, but for ourselves. They that set about this as a common work, to make a trade of it for their worldly livelihood, will find that they have chosen a bad trade, though a good employment. Self-denial is of absolute necessity in every Christian, but of a double necessity in a minister. —*Richard Baxter* (109)

* * *

Of Salary and Maintenance

If you say, this is hard measure, your wife and children cannot so live, I answer: (1) Do not many families in your parish live on less? (2) Have not many able ministers in the prelates' days been glad of less, with liberty to preach the gospel? (3) If still you say that you cannot live so nearly as poor people do, I further ask, can your parishioners better endure damnation than you can endure want and poverty?

And I must further say, that indeed this poverty is not so sad and dangerous a business as it is pretended to be. So you have but food and raiment, must you not therewith be content? and what would you have more than that which may enable you for the work of God? And it is not purple and fine linen, and faring deliciously every day, that you must expect, as that which must content you. "A man's life consisteth not in the abundance of the things that he possesseth." So your clothing be warm, and your food be wholesome, you may as well be supported by it to do God service, as if you had the fullest satisfaction to your flesh: A patched coat may be warm, and bread and drink is wholesome food. He that wanteth not these, hath but a cold excuse to make for hazarding men's souls, that he may live on a fuller diet in the world. —*Richard Baxter* (110)

Have I constantly remembered and been strengthened in faith and obedience by the remembrance of the divine gift and responsibility of my ordination, of the Lord of my ministry, and the mission of my ministry? Do I still believe in God? Do I still love the Lord Jesus Christ?

Have I confused the organizational busyness of my congregation with the discipleship of Jesus and the obedience of faith?

Have I promoted my own aims in the pulpit and at the altar instead of God's cause?

Have I disobeyed or disregarded the doctrine and confession of my church in my ministry?

Have I administered the sacrament of Holy Baptism and the sacrament of the Lord's Supper in the fear of God, as a steward of the mysteries of God, or without taking into account the faith and life of the recipients?

Have I instructed my catechumens and really brought home to them the sum of God's truth as it is presented in the catechism of my church?

Have I enjoined upon my congregation and sexton the duty of honoring, caring for, and using the church as the house of God and to see to it that everything is done decently and in order?

What is the appearance of my sacristy, the altar, and the font of my church?

Have I neglected the ministry of the organist and the music of the church?

Have I obeyed worldly and ecclesiastical authorities when I ought to have obeyed God more than men?

Have I tolerated or even approved social and political injustice in my community?

Have I contributed to war, to the class struggle, to hostility between parties and churches by what I have said or done?

Have I divided my congregation through my sinning against truth or love?

Have I avoided decision where God's Word and the welfare of the congregation demanded decision?

—Max Lackmann (111)

* * *

TUESDAY

The Minister's Life

* * *

A bishop, as God's steward, must be blameless; he must not be arrogant or quick-tempered or a drunkard or violent or greedy for gain, but hospitable, a lover of goodness, master of himself, upright, holy, and self-controlled.

–Titus 1:7–8

Set the believers an example in speech and conduct, in love, in faith, in purity. Till I come, attend to the public reading of scripture, to preaching, to teaching. Do not neglect the gift you have, which was given you by prophetic utterance when the elders laid their hands upon you. Practice these duties, devote yourself to them, so that all may see your progress. Take heed to yourself and to your teaching; hold to that, for by so doing you will save both yourself and your hearers.

–I Timothy 4:12–16

THE LIFE THAT PREACHES

Vita clericorum liber laicorum.
The life of the clergyman is the book of the laymen.

* * *

Vita clerici evangelium populi.
The life of the clergyman is the gospel of the people.

* * *

The Proof of Christianity

Order the parsons to be silent on Sundays. What is there left? The essential things remain: their lives, the daily life with which the parsons preach. Would you, then, get the impression by watching them, that it was Christianity they were preaching?

—Søren Kierkegaard (112)

* * *

Sacerdotis Christi os, meus, manusque concordent.
A minister of Christ should have his tongue, his heart, and his hand agree.

—Jerome (113)

* * *

The witness of the church's ministry belongs in the context of the witness of one's whole attitude. Jesus' own witness went forth, not only in words, but in the way in which he dealt with people. "The man receives sinners and eats with them." The message of forgiveness became incarnate in his association with "sinners," in that he had fellowship with them. It cannot be otherwise with the messengers of Jesus, with the church. The gospel is not an objective, universal truth, which one can pass on in the form of ideas, but rather the personal reality of God's sacrifice, the love that gives itself and bears our burden. So also this truth of the gospel can be proclaimed only in one's whole personal attitude toward people. The message of God's mercy, as it was a bodily, personal reality in Christ, must repeatedly become embodied in the love that seeks the lost. The credibility of the church when it preaches God's love for the lost depends on whether the church itself goes out to people in their lostness, identifies itself with them, and in a priestly way makes their predicament its own. In seeking, human love, God's love is understood. The incarnation can be preached and believed only to the degree to which it is lived in the preaching.

The Word and its embodiment belong together, not only in the individual preacher, but also in the church as a whole. The preaching church is at the same time the serving church, which takes upon itself the need of people and in every way seeks to set up signs of the love of Christ in the world. This is precisely the meaning and intent of its service. It is intended to be understood as witness.

It is in this comprehensive context that the preaching of the church's ministry stands. And there is still more to be said. Preaching also belongs in the totality of the church's "worship of God," all its forms and structures. This totality bears witness along with the preaching and thus sustains it. So it is with the liturgy, above all the word of the Bible in it, the songs of the church, its prayers and hymns, the order of every service of worship and the church year, the whole of the church's order and custom. But also the building, pictures and sculpture, liturgical music, the whole of Christian art, insofar as all this has had its impulse from the encounter with the gospel and is born of the Spirit of God, can become a witness that builds the church. For many people the gospel has been deeply written in their hearts by a picture, or the great Passion music composers from Bach down to the present day, or by a verse of some Christian poet of the past or present; and all this is speaking too when we listen to preaching. In a multitude of ways all Christendom is bearing witness along with the preacher. So, to be sure, it is true for

the life, the continuance, and the growth of the church that
it is the Word that does it. The church lives by the Word.
But this means the whole witness in all its breadth, not only
the preached Word by itself. The Word must do it—this does
not mean : the sermon must do it. Preaching in the service has
its indispensable importance for the building of the church
of Christ, but it is not the sole means by which the Spirit of
God creates the church; it is not the whole "Word."

–Paul Althaus (114)

* * *

It is true that the Lord . . . can work with the faultiest
kind of instrumentality, as he does when he occasionally
makes very foolish preaching to be useful in conversion; and
he can even work without agents, as he does when he saves
men without a preacher at all, applying the word directly
by his Holy Spirit; but we cannot regard God's absolutely
sovereign acts as a rule for our action. He may, in his abso-
luteness, do as pleases him best, but we must act as his plainer
dispensations instruct us; and one of the facts which is clear
enough is this; that the Lord usually adapts means to ends,
from which the plain lesson is that we shall be likely to
accomplish most when we are in the best spiritual condition,
or in other words, we shall usually do our Lord's work best
when our gifts and graces are in good order, and we shall
do worst when they are most out of trim. This is a practical
truth for our guidance, when the Lord makes exceptions,
they do but prove the rule.

–Charles Haddon Spurgeon (115)

* * *

The Windows

Lord, how can man preach thy eternal Word?
    He is a brittle, crazy glass;

> Yet in thy temple thou dost him afford
>   This glorious and transcendent place,
>   To be a window, through thy grace.
> But when thou dost anneal in glass thy story,
>   Making thy life to shine within
> The holy preachers; then the light and glory
>   More rev'rent grows, and more doth win,
>   Which else shows watrish, bleak and thin.
> Doctrine and life, colors and light, in one
>   When they combine and mingle, bring
> A strong regard and awe; but speech alone
>   Doth vanish like a flaring thing,
> And in the ear, not conscience ring.

–George Herbert (116)

* * *

To speak that we know and testify that we have seen, to speak it lovingly, to testify it boldly, never seeking to raise doubts, ever aiming to kindle faith and hope; to be receptive in the study, an empty vessel sanctified and waiting to be filled from the ever-open fountain, then in the pulpit to aim to take of this fulness and show it unto others; not primarily to proclaim a doctrine but rather to tell a story, to tell how it has affected our own lives; to have as the heart's desire the longing to give our people a taste of some precious blessing that we have found ourselves in the secret place; never to be trifling or self-advertising, ever to be tremendously in earnest and when possible at all, self-effacing; to bathe in the Book till it enters into the very texture of our speech. To love men, to be moved with a great pity at their presence, to see not merely a sea of faces, but rather a company of spirits, to compel their ears, to touch their consciences: never to allow ourselves to be turned aside to wrangle, negation or debate, to avoid technicalities and trivial things, to magnify the certainties and things of vital moment; to lift up Jesus to the eyes of men, to proclaim his love, his forgiveness, his cleansing power, his joy, his hope, his glory; thus to create in our listeners a hunger for holy living by backing up a great message with a great, noble, loving life.

–*M. J. McLeod* (117)

* * *

Of Example

Moreover, take heed to yourselves, lest your example contradict your doctrine, and lest you lay such stumbling blocks before the blind, as may be the occasion of their ruin; lest you may unsay that with your lives, which you say with your tongues; and be the greatest hinderers of the success of your own labors. It much hindereth our work, when other men are all the week long contradicting to poor people in private, that which we have been speaking to them from the word of God in public: but it will much more hinder, if we contradict ourselves, and if your actions give your tongue the lie, and if you build up an hour or two with your mouths, and all the week after pull down with your hands! This is the way to make men think that the word of God is but an idle tale, and to make preaching seem no better than prating. He that means as he speaks, will surely do as he speaks. One proud, surly, lordly word; one needless contention, one covetous action may cut the throat of many a sermon, and blast the fruit of all that you have been doing.

–*Richard Baxter* (118)

* * *

Divine Compulsion

Back of the office and ministry of the pastor a higher necessity must be evident, a constraint that comes from God. "If I preach the gospel, that gives me no ground for boasting. For necessity is laid upon me. Woe to me if I do not preach the gospel!" (I Cor. 9:16). Many ministers, it must be frankly said, do not indicate that this necessity is upon them. What they say in their preaching and pastoral work could just as well be left unsaid. It is idle talk. When we hear their preaching we get the impression of homiletical decoration, but it might just as well be omitted. Down underneath the preacher often feels this himself and is therefore uncertain in the depths of his being. But when we have become certain of a divine necessity in our ministry, even a chance meeting with a person on the street will be subject to that necessity. The pastor will always be ready to meet the unexpected and to say a word for which the other person is waiting. He will sense that God is guiding his pastoral care, that everything is going according to a purpose, a purpose which may perhaps be hidden from him, that there really are no "accidents" at all. Then, of course, he will no longer cherish the childish delusion that he can build the kingdom of God with his own hands or even build Zion by ecclesiastical or evangelistic methods. We may confidently rely upon it that God is not dependent upon us and that he can also work with people in the church and outside of the church without us. But we must, of course, be equally certain that God uses his church and its ministry. In the ministry of the church there are so many false notes : activism, vanity, and idle rhetoric, all the way down to the lying pastoral tone in conversation. To become practical and objective in pastoral care means, quite simply, to reckon seriously with God. One should therefore not push oneself upon others, but wait to be called. But when one has been called, then the unconditionalness of the divine necessity itself (not of church propaganda) must control one's conversation with the wounded worldling.

—Wolfgang Trillhaas (119)

* * *

Unconverted Pastors

An unconverted pastor is a great asset to the Adversary. Even a pastor may be unconverted. He may be so in such a subtle and hidden way that he may even be very zealous and active, without ever realizing that his real, chief sin is the innermost egocentricity and self-trust of his heart. He may also be unconverted in such an obvious way that people see it and take offense. When it comes down to it, the Adversary has no better ally than the pastor's own Old Adam. With his help the holy ministry can be transformed into something exceedingly unholy. The pastor becomes sensitive and power-hungry and insists upon respect for his position instead of cheerfully bearing the reproach of Christ. He becomes a master instead of a shepherd. His concern becomes not the salvation of souls, but his own position among men. Then the authority he has received "to build up and not to destroy" becomes an instrument of destruction that tears down the congregation and scatters the flock instead of gathering it. It is just as bad when the pastor, purely out of regard for his own person, does not dare to be a pastor, when he blunts the edge of his Lord's message and becomes a harmless cipher who says nothing and is content to hold his peace when he should be preaching repentance in the name of his Lord.

There is just as much egotism in a pastor's carnal pride as in his carnal modesty. Perhaps the most perilous temptations of his calling are these two. On the one hand, there is the egotism which always demands the center of the stage and the deciding vote, always craves the head table and wants to be the chief speaker of the evening. On the other hand, there is the craven complaisance which refuses to risk its popularity, which is careful to avoid declaring that nothing except faith in Jesus Christ can save a single person in this world and nothing but the Word of God can give us this faith. Or which says it now and then to satisfy its conscience, but says it in such an involved or abstract way that nobody who hears it would ever conclude that, without this faith and this Word, we shall in actual fact be eternally lost.

The pastor must be at once both fearless and unassuming; bold and frank in the name of his Lord, but humble in his own name; ready to turn the other cheek when he is exposed to personal affront, but of a holy stubbornness when it is a matter of holding fast to the Word of his Lord. His forehead must be adamant against the insults of the world, but his heart must be so sensitive that none in the congregation can fall or suffer misfortune without the pastor sharing his suffering.

Therefore, there is a somber seriousness in that saying of Chrysostom: *Mirum est si sacerdos salvetur.* It is a miracle if a pastor be saved. So serious is this, that it is best that we be immediately reminded of what the Saviour said to his disciples when it began to dawn on them how hard it is to attain to eternal life: "With men this is impossible, but with God all things are possible."

—Bo Giertz (120)

* * *

Every preacher should exhibit two things. First, a blameless life by which he can defy the world and no one have cause to slander the teaching, and second, irreproachable teaching, that he may mislead none that follow him. So he will be right on both sides: with his good life against the enemies who look much more at his life than at his doctrine; with his doctrine among friends who care more for the doctrine than about his life and will bear with his life for the sake of his teaching.

For it is indeed true that no one lives so perfect a life as to be without sin before God. Therefore it is sufficient that he be blameless in the eyes of the people. But his doctrine must be so good and pure as to stand not only before man but also before God.

—Luther (121)

A minister, wherever he is, is a minister, and should re
collect that he is on duty; a policeman or a soldier may be
off duty, but a minister never is.

—Charles Haddon Spurgeon (122

* * *

"The good Shepherd giveth his life for his sheep."

John 10:11

He gives his life by giving his labor, in taking all occasion
of instructing them; in employing his thoughts for thei
good; in praying for them continually, and rendering Go
propitious to them; in sacrificing his ease and peace for them
by delivering truths which the world will not receive withou
unkind returns; he gives up the dearest friendships, when the
stand in competition with truth and righteousness; he give
up all worldly satisfactions, when he does not look upor
what is lawful but what is expedient; he sacrifices his in
clinations, though never so innocent, rather than offend any
he submits to the humility and poverty of the gospel, that he
may give no example of pride and luxury to his flock; he
dares not be even a witness of disorders, lest he should en
courage them by his presence. It is true he must be the ligh
of the world, and without this he cannot satisfy the duties o
his charge; and it is thus he is to give his life for his sheep.

—Thomas Wilson (123

* * *

Many wear God's cloth that know not their master.

—Joseph Hall (124

* * *

"Everybody talkin' 'bout heav'n ain't goin' there."

* * *

God does not call those to feed the sheep of Christ, who
have no love for the Shepherd. For all who love not our

Lord Jesus are wicked; and unto the wicked God saith, What hast thou to do, to declare my statutes, or to take my covenant in thy mouth? How great a trust is committed to the pastor! Hundreds of precious immortal souls he is bound to watch over, as one that must give an account: And will you be able to give a good account of the souls of others, if unable to give a good account of your own? Is it not a most pitiable case, to be under a strict and awful charge, to affect the minds of your hearers with what never affected your own minds? Presume not, then, to undertake the care of souls, without personal holiness, until, by the blessing of God on your education, and your diligent attendance on prayer, reading, and meditation, you have attained a suitable furniture of gifts and graces for the service of the sanctuary.

–John Erskine (125)

* * *

The best books on pastoral theology are those which do not merely goad and terrify the pastor with the spur of the law: Pastor, you are lazy; you must be much more active; you must know all modern science and wisdom; you must give all your goods to the poor and your body to be burned. The first task of a Lutheran pastoral theology, before it lets him see the admittedly terrifying seriousness of his responsibility, is to show the pastor the beauty, the glory, the blessed promise of his office, to strengthen his faith in the true Victor, who stands behind his beggarly daily work, closer than to any other work of men.

Faith in this Victor is the decisive part of the pastor's sanctification. The Lutheran church and its ministry know of no sanctification that opens up a higher level of life beyond this faith. But we must be able to sense and see something of this sanctification of the pastor. This is the indispensable prerequisite of his priestly ministry. Sectarians are constantly twitting us about our conversion. We are thoroughly familiar

with the answers which we can give to these questions a.
Lutheran theologians; at this point we are all surprisingly
good "Lutherans." But the right, convincing answer to thi
question of conversion is not given in the form of a theo
logical statement, but rather in the life of a pastor lived i:
the fear of God. Lutheran theology cannot alter and has n·
intention of altering the fact that the life of the clergy is the
gospel of the people. There can be no line of separation between the office of the pastor and his personal life.

—*Martin Dörne* (126

* * *

The life of the preacher must be the prologue of the sermor
he would preach, the commentary on what he really teache:
and the epilogue, the seal of the sermons he has preached. Th·
preacher is not he who teaches for an hour on Sundays and
festivals, but he teaches by deeds, for whole weeks, months,
years, his whole life long, what he preaches on particular
days in words.

—*Johann Michael Sailer*

* * *

The "good news" must always be *incarnate*; that is, the
mistrusting person cannot be converted to make an act of
trust except he experience trustworthiness in personal encounter. That is the real business of a clergyman—to provide
the kind of personal encounters through which the mistrustful,
the anxious, the hostile, may experience and have revealed
to them the meaning of faith, hope, and love. And because
men who have been deprived of these spiritual necessities
find it impossible to accept the revelation of them easily, it
will be required of the "revealers," the ministers, to be strong
in these personal encounters and persist in *being* and *giving*
even to the point of their not being accepted. To accept another's mistrust and still to give him trust is to incarnate for
him the meaning "trust" and to save him from mistrust. Ob-

viously, this is a conception of the therapeutic relationship that can come only from religion and distinctively from Christianity. Only a relationship through which God is speaking and acting could hope to offer as much, but this is the kind of relationship for which separated, alienated, lonely man is looking.

—Reuel L. Howe (127)

* * *

Take heed to yourselves also, because there are many eyes upon you, and therefore there will be many observers of your falls. You cannot miscarry but the world will ring of it. The eclipses of the sun by daytime are seldom without witnesses. If you take yourselves for the lights of the churches, you may well expect that men's eyes should be upon you. If other men may sin without observation, so cannot you. And you should thankfully consider how great a mercy this is, that you have so many eyes to watch over you, and so many ready to tell you of your faults, and so have greater helps than others, at least for the restraining of your sin. Though they may do it with a malicious mind, yet you have the advantage of it.

—Richard Baxter (128)

* * *

For Self-examination

The natural description of a clergyman is a half-worldly, half-spiritual, wholly ambiguous official, a person of rank, who, in the hope of promotion by seniority and of becoming a knight in his turn (how completely in the spirit of the New Testament!), secures a living for himself and his family, supports himself from the fact that Christ was crucified, insisting that this deep earnestness (this "imitation of Jesus Christ?") is New Testament Christianity, sorrowfully complaining of the fact that there are so few true Christians in the community. For that the clergyman is a true Christian is certain enough, in spite of the fact that he goes about in long clothes,

273

which Christ has forbidden, when he says both in Mark and Luke (Mark 12:38; Luke 20:40) "beware of those that go about in long clothes."

—Søren Kierkegaard (129)

* * *

Occasionally one hears this saying of Luther's quoted: "Let no one give up the faith that God wants to do a deed *through* him." There is something inspiring about that. That saying is inscribed on the arch of the gate to the Wittenberg seminary but with this little alteration: "Let no one give up the faith that God wants to do a deed *in* him." This change, trifling as it may seem, is important. And, to be sure, it is the original reading. This is Luther's fundamental idea: that God has done something great *to* us. But then it was Luther who roused us to recognize that he wants to do something through us! This saying applies to every Christian, but it especially applies to ministers of the gospel.

—Hermann Werdermann (130)

* * *

The story of Mary and Martha, in which the Reformation saw the prototype of its evangelical understanding of the church, has a special message for the young theologian today. Just as in that extraordinary situation created by Jesus' visit, so in membership of the church, which is the body of Christ, hearing ranks above doing. The retribution comes if this order is reversed, if Martha's self-confident "busyness" prevails unchecked in the house of the church. And if, as in the case of the minister, that "activity" consists in "speaking," then it is almost certainly to be feared that the disregard of that evangelical rule of precedence will corrupt the future minister from the beginning and turn him into a mere "speaker," or even a "talker." In a truly evangelical interpretation of theological study the very opposite is meant. The purpose of this study is to help and guide the student so that in his future ministry also he will remain first and last a hearer. It is not his ministerial utterance and most certainly not his glib and fluent oratory which saves his congregation, but the Word of God. The living, occurring miracle of this Word makes pure hearing the fundamental law of human existence. And he himself, the messenger of this miracle, will never be done with hearing this divine Word. He must be glad to remain a hearer and a learner, a "child and pupil of the Catechism," as Luther declared himself to be, and therefore to the end, a student of theology. —*Martin Dörne* (131)

* * *

The Naughty Bishop

It is strange what little things will choke a youngster off religion. As an undergraduate I lost for a time what little faith I had because I saw a bishop unable to take a beating at tennis like a gentleman. A poor faith mine, you say. Yes, undoubtedly, but if Christianity does not prevent one of its leading exponents from behaving like a cad when he loses a game, it is a bad lookout for the rest of us.

—*H. R. L. Sheppard* (132)

* * *

Give yourself up to ever so many good works, read, preach, pray, visit the sick, build hospitals, clothe the naked, etc., yet if anything goes along with these or in the doing of them you have anything else that you will and hunger after, but that God's kingdom may come and his will be done, they are not the works of the newborn from above and so cannot be his life-giving food. For the new creature in Christ is that one will and one hunger that was in Christ; and therefore, where that is wanting, there is wanting that new creature which alone can have His conversation. —*William Law* (133)

ON TEMPERANCE IN EATING AND DRINKING

The noon meal may be as he wishes, but the evening meal should be frugal and brief, for this is good for the body and mind. As Horace says, *Coena brevis juvat, et prope rivum somnus in herba* (a brief supper in the evening and a nap in the grass beside a stream is beneficial); and Ecclesiasticus 31:20, "Sound sleep cometh of moderate eating; he riseth early, and his wits are with him." Therefore a proverb says truly: Jocund evening suppers make sad mornings. In short, long talk and drinking until late at night make a weak heart and a confused head and in the morning it is filled with catarrh and rheum and phlegm, which gravely hinders the priest in his office of prayer and service.

Therefore, that you may guard against this general evil, remember seriously that you cannot ruin an evening without at the same time partly or wholly ruining the next morning and, indeed, the whole of the following day. Believe those who speak from experience; if you do not believe them, then you will have to learn by your own experience.

CONCERNING THE PRIEST'S STUDY

At night always carry in your heart something from Holy Scriptures to bed with you, meditate upon it like a ruminant animal, and go softly to sleep; but this must not be too much, rather a little that may be well pondered and understood, that you may find a remnant of it in your mind when you rise in the morning. And in all study of the Holy Scriptures one must always despair of one's own ability and labors but only pray God with fear and humility for understanding. Therefore, when you approach the Bible, first lift up your eyes and heart to Christ in heaven and in a brief supplication implore his grace; which must also be done often during one's reading in order that you may think and say: Lord, grant that I may rightly understand this, but even more that I may perform it. But above all things guard against desiring to study the Scriptures only in order to know and understand them (for I believe that you are not such stupid scholars as to seek honor, gain, or glory thereby), nor even to be able to teach others. Your purpose must be adequately sure, for even here empty vainglory may lie concealed and hidden. Rather you must seek absolutely nothing but the glory of God, in such spirit that your one thought is: Behold, dearest Lord Jesus, if this study be not to thy glory, let me not understand a syllable of it; but grant unto me, a poor sinner, as much as in thy sight shall be to thy glory.

ON FAMILIAR INTERCOURSE

Only infrequent and brief social contacts are useful to the priest, for the proverb is true: Friends are thieves of time. And if friends are thieves of time, what shall outsiders, strangers, and those less familiar be? Nevertheless, here you will have need of great wisdom and care, lest, if you avoid too much the companionship of men, you fall into the society of evil spirits, or on the other hand, consorting too much with them, you are trampled by swine. Therefore when God calls you (that is, when it is necessary to serve, counsel, and speak with your neighbor when his salvation or other necessity requires it), then no law nor rule, no matter what institution you may belong to, dare keep you from it. All laws, even the rule of prayer and holding services, must give place to love. But when you are not called do not force yourself upon anybody, lest you begin to desire to gain the world and then suffer detriment to your soul.

ON PRAYER

Remember that you are a priest, that is, a public servant of the community; therefore you will earnestly pray, not so much for yourself, as for the sheep and especially the heads of the church, the bishops and rectors, for their salvation and the salvation of us all.

You will not always feel like conducting worship, but in order that you may become fit, you must sometimes enter upon it even though you are not fit. This you will do when you consider that you must hold services, not for your own sake, but for the sake of others who are caught in sin, for the sake of the innumerable needs of Christians. Therefore what you would not do for yourself, you will do for them. Do not begin now and then to rely upon the fact that you do feel fit.

ON HIS WHOLE LIFE

As Tobit taught his son to pray God to direct his life (Tobit 4:19), so you too should despair of yourself and pray that he may guide your steps according to his Word, just as Jeremiah says, "I know, O Lord, that the way of man is not in himself, that it is not in man who walks to direct his steps" (Jer. 10:23). But above all, clothe yourself with great gentleness towards sinners, for it is necessary to the priest that he despise none; but rather deem their sins and miseries as your own, as you see Christ has done toward us.   —*Luther* (134)

* * *

THE PASTOR'S LIFE OF PRAYER

Let the preacher labor that he be heard willingly, with understanding and with obedience; and let him not doubt that he can do this more effectively with the devoutness of his prayers than by skilfulness of speech. He should pray for himself and for those whom he is about to address, and be a man of prayer before he teaches. And before he puts forth a ready tongue, to God let him approach with a whole heart and lift up to him a thirsting soul, that he may pour forth only what God has given him to drink and utter that with which God has filled him.

I, therefore, cease not to ask of our true Lord and Master that he will deign so to teach me, either by the utterances of his Scriptures, or by discussion with the brethren, or by the inward and more sweet teaching of his own inspiration, that in those things which I am to put forward or assert I may ever hold fast to the truth; and I ask that from this very truth, himself, I may be taught many things and more which I do not know, for from him I have received the little that I do know.

I beseech him that he will go before me and follow me with his mercy; and that those things which I ought to know to my soul's health he will teach me; that what I know of truth he will guard me therein; that in those things in which, man-like, I am mistaken he will correct me; that in truths in which I am mistaken he will stablish me; and that from what is false and harmful he will deliver me; and that he will make to go forth from my mouth those things which are the most pleasing in the sight of Truth himself, that they may be received by all the faithful, through Jesus Christ, our Lord and Saviour.
—Fulgentius (135)

* * *

It is possible to be so active in the service of Christ as to forget to love him. Many a man preaches Christ but gets in front of him by the multiplicity of his own works. It will be your ruin if you do! Christ can do without your works; what he wants is you. Yet if he really has you he will have all your works.
—Peter Taylor Forsyth (136)

* * *

The Necessity of Private Devotions

Whoever must always give must always have; and since he cannot draw out of himself what he must give, he must ever keep near the living fountain in order to draw. Many a truth, when once appropriated, develops itself in life, but the development is twofold and threefold richer when the inner and the outer, the hidden and the public life are the same. The Divine Word and the theological sciences can become a devotional study, which is widely different from that dabbling and smattering of science which only estranges from the holy office and unfits one for it. This devotional study, on the other hand, fits, grounds, and strengthens for the work, clarifies the understanding and the experience, and gives ever new and ever deeper insight into the glory of the Word that is to be preached. It protects the pastor from the calamity of the indolent minister, who grows weary of his work and performs it in a halfhearted and mechanical manner, and confesses to his intimate friends that Christianity does not solve the deepest problems of life; whereas his lips could and should drop the honey of eternal life . . . Teaching is conditioned by experimental learning. Comforting is conditioned by noting and overcoming personal temptations. The fulness and consecration of life is a praying heart. Solitude is the fountain of all living streams, and nothing glorious is born in public.

–Wilhelm Löhe (137)

* * *

A Little Guide and Instructor for Future Pastors

To any young man who is studying theology and expects in time to become a pastor and minister, if he possesses or knows of nothing better, this brief summary is faithfully recommended.

I

First, you should know that those who would study the Holy Scriptures thoroughly must go through three gates or entrances.

The first gate belongs to *God the Father.* And here you must go up three steps.

The first is that you must learn to *know yourself* thoroughly; this is *cognitio sui ipsius*. For anyone who desires to study theology must begin his learning with himself and know who he is in the sight of God, where he came from, what he can do by his own powers, and also the powers of mind in things divine, what they are and their importance. For here is where we find nothing but sin, inborn, besetting, real, and daily sins. Here all our powers — wisdom, understanding, free will, all our thoughts and desires — are corrupted, darkened, weakened, and inclined to sin. Therefore it is necessary first of all to know yourself well; then through yourself you will be able to know and judge all other men.

Then the second step : learn to *humble yourself* and to count as nothing your own wisdom, understanding and discernment, your own piety and blamelessness, and cast out of your heart the proud idols that are there : your own wisdom, carnal understanding, natural piety, natural abilities and talents. Then honestly confess that you are nothing but a poor, sinful man in the sight of God, not worthy so much as to lift up your eyes to God in heaven. For to him who humbles himself the Lord God gives his grace and his Spirit, as St. Peter says (I Peter 5 :5).

Thirdly, you must *deny* and renounce not only *yourself* but all that you have and are and can be, your own body, life, living, honor, welfare, wife, children, house, goods, etc. Otherwise these earthly things may hinder you when they weigh upon you so heavily that you will pay little heed to God's Word and his kingdom. For the apostles, too, had to forsake, deny, and renounce what they had, as they themselves confess and declare : "Lo, we have left everything and followed you." But this is a hard, bitter, unsavory morsel for the Old Adam to swallow and it is hard to make him do it.

This, then, is the first beginning for one who desires to be a theologian, the first gateway to the Father with its three steps wherein you learn to fear God.

The second gate or entrance is to *God the Son*. Here, too, you must go up three steps.

The first is *lectio,* that is, you must diligently read and study the Holy Scriptures, the golden book, the Bible. Here you must employ your memory, so that you will know where every saying and story is to be found, the chapter in which it is located, in order that you may be commended as a good textuary and Bible student. For the Lord Christ himself bids us to search and read the Scriptures and before all else this foundation must be laid.

The second step or approach to God the Son is this : *repetitio,* that you begin to read the Bible from beginning to end in proper order and read it again and again, daily keeping in fresh remembrance what you have first read in the Bible. Here you will judiciously compare one saying and sentence with others. Where one explains another or more fully and clearly expresses the meaning and sense, note them down together and also write them in your memory. This will be of great profit to you.

The third step to Christ is *meditatio.* Here you take up your Bible a third time and read it through as before, but this third time with this purpose : to seek with special earnestness the right understanding of Holy Scriptures, applying yourself systematically to God's Word and the statements of Holy Scriptures. Here you may make your own *loci communes* or commonplaces, such as the righteousness and mercy of God, on fearing, loving, and trusting God, on obedience, chastity, good works, etc. Then you will have your previous passages at hand, fresh in your memory, and you will know where any particular passage belongs, under what commonplace it is to be entered and noted. Then you will soon find the real canon of theology in Holy Scriptures, that is, Christ, for it is he to whom all Scripture points. Here you will learn true faith in Christ.

The third and last entrance in the Holy Scriptures is to the *Holy Spirit,* who is the true teacher, the one and only doctor of the Holy Scriptures.

Here then you tread upon the first step, which is called *oratio.* There before all else you must call upon the Holy Spirit and pray for his divine grace and gifts, that he may inspire you with heavenly wisdom, reveal the mystery of Holy Scriptures, and lead you into all truth and godliness, in order that you may become a true catholic teacher and edify and guide the church of Christ by your doctrine and life.

The second step, however, is *experientia.* There you must undergo the discipline of the cross and be drilled and practiced in the school of the Holy Spirit, for experience contributes much. Therefore you must be dauntless beneath the cross just as a soldier is brave beneath his flag since he hopes to gain honor and recompense.

The third step to the Holy Spirit is *vocatio,* which means that you finally surrender willingly to your calling and then faithfully teach others what you yourself have learned in the Holy Scriptures.

These, then, are the three gateways, in which, as we have said, there are nine steps to be ascended. Thus you will come finally to the tenth step, which is life eternal, as St. Paul says (I Tim. 3:13). There you will learn what hope is.

We add what Mathesius said: an ambassador, preacher, and minister of Christ must pray not only when he is a student but also after he has been armed for knighthood and is in the ministry. Always he must pray, before he learns, before he preaches, after the sermon, for the sheep against Satan, against false brethren, heretics, tyrants. He should rise at midnight to pray with sevenfold petition, not according to rules, but like David and Peter. He who does not pray is not studying and whatever he does he accomplishes nothing that is good.

—Caspar Huberinus (138)

Christ came not to be ministered to, but to minister; and our first duty, therefore, is to be ministered to by him. First faith, then works.

—Peter Taylor Forsyth (139)

* * *

How did Jesus order his ministry . . .? What was his attitude, his method? . . . If as ministers of Jesus Christ we can imitate him, then our lives cannot be failures; and whatever the outward and visible results of it may seem to be, they must exert in some measure the same kind of influence and possess the same power of control.

We note . . . a certain detachment in Jesus' attitude toward contemporary events and the secular problems and policies of his day. He lived on a higher level and his mind was not overoccupied and concerned with the details and externals of outward circumstances. Rather, he lived a deep, personal, interior life that found its source and center in the life of God. Thus there appears a certain serenity and sense of security in his outlook upon the world. He was not harried or overborne by the problems presented by the conditions that confronted him because he lived in the constant realization of the strength and peace of God. The channels of communication between his own soul and the life of God were always kept clear and open so that his own life was being constantly reinforced by fresh supplies of divine grace and strength.

We do not need to be reminded of the prominent and consistent place which the practice and cultivation of the presence of God occupied in the life of Jesus. Because of this, his life was clothed with a certain spirituality which both delivered him from anxiety concerning the ultimate outcome of human affairs and at the same time lent him the authority which belongs only to those who are filled with the Spirit of God. How helpless the human life of Jesus appears to be before the great imponderable evils of his day. How little did his life and ministry appear to alter or overthrow them. Yet in the light of history we know that there was resident within his soul the moral forces that were destined to topple from their pedestals one hoary evil after another and to set in motion an irresistible power that recreated and is still recreating the moral life of the world.

We will do well, therefore, as disciples of Jesus, to imitate his attitude toward the external and contemporary and secular life of the world. We will not allow our minds to be too much occupied or enmeshed in the vexing questions of the day. We will keep ourselves informed concerning these, but we will not become so preoccupied with present-day problems which perplex, disturb, and harass the mind, that we shall cease to live on a higher plane, cease to be God-filled, God-inspired men. For only to the degree that we are this do we acquire real significance and become active moral factors in the life of the world and possess any powers of influence and control. Only the cultivation of the life of God, only the possession of the Spirit of God will equip us with the peace, the poise, the serenity, the power that will enable us to be in any degree to our world what Jesus was to his.

Thus we will take up our Bibles and seek to know God afresh in the plentitude of his power. We will read the glowing prophecies of Isaiah and of Daniel which so fortified the soul of Jesus. We will read the eighth chapter of Romans and the fourth and fifth chapters of Revelation until the magnificent hope enshrined within them becomes a living part of us, as well as the faith which comes so easily and so naturally out of the discovery of the divine life that we find in them. We must, in a word, become men of spiritual insight and live above the turmoil of the secular world. To move this world to better things, to lift it to nobler purposes, to be amongst those who are helpers and healers of mankind, it is necessary to have this vantage ground outside ourselves, outside the world, and that vantage ground is God.

–*Raymond Calkins* (140)

One thing you must learn to do. Whatever you leave undone you must not leave this undone. Your work will be stunted and half developed unless you attend to it. You must force yourself to be alone and to pray. Do make a point of this. You may be eloquent and attractive in your life, but your real effectiveness depends on your communion with the eternal world. You will easily find excuses. Work is so pressing, and work is necessary. Other engagements take time. You are tired. You want to go to bed. You go to bed late and want to get up late. So simple prayer and devotion are crowded out. And yet, . . . the necessity is paramount, is inexorable. If you and I are ever to be of any good, if we are to be a blessing, not a curse, to those with whom we are connected, we must enter into ourselves, we must be alone with the only source of unselfishness. If we are of use to others, it will chiefly be because we are simple, pure, unselfish. If we are to be simple, pure, unselfish, it will not be by reading books or talking or working primarily, it will be by coming in continual contact with simplicity, purity, unselfishness. Heaven is the possibility of fresh acts of self-sacrifice, of a fuller life of unselfishness. You are a man and a minister in so far as you are unselfish. You cannot learn unselfishness save from the one Source. Definite habits of real devotion — these we must make and keep to and renew and increase. Then we shall gradually find that we are less dependent on self — that even in the busiest scenes we dare not act on our own responsibility — that, be the act ever so small and trifling, when we are in difficulty we shall naturally, inevitably, spontaneously turn to that place whence help alone can come. But it is a wonderful help again and again to feel that we have been alone with him, that we are not working on our own responsibility, that he is the "Living Will" that rises and flows "through our deeds and makes them pure."

—*Forbes Robinson* (141)

ORATIO, MEDITATIO, TENTATIO

A Right Way to Study Theology

I will show you a right way to study theology, which I myself have practiced, and, if you adhere to it, you too shall be so learned that, if need should arise, you will be able to write books that are as good as those of the fathers and councils, just as I may make bold to boast in God, without pride, or deceit, that I would not acknowledge that some of the fathers had much on me when it comes to writing books, though I am far from being able to boast the same of my life. It is the way that King David teaches in Psalm 119 and which was without a doubt adhered to by all the patriarchs and prophets. There you will find three rules which are abundantly set forth in the whole psalm: *oratio, meditatio, tentatio.*

First, you must know that the Holy Scriptures is a book that makes foolishness of the wisdom of all other books, because none of them teaches eternal life, only this one alone. Therefore you must straightway despair of your own mind and reason, for you will not attain it by these. On the contrary, with such presumption you will cast yourself, and others with you, from heaven into the abyss of hell, as did Lucifer. Rather kneel down in your closet and pray to God in true humility and earnestness, that through his dear Son he may grant you his Holy Spirit to enlighten, guide, and give you understanding. You see how David in the above-mentioned psalm prays again and again: Teach me! O Lord, instruct me! Show me! and many other expressions like them. Even though he knew well the text of Moses and other books and heard and read them daily, he still desires the real Master of the Scriptures himself in order that he may not tackle them with his reason and make himself the master. For this produces those sectarians who allow themselves to think that the Scriptures are subject to them and easily mastered with their own reason, as if they were the fables of Markolf or Aesop, which require neither the Holy Spirit nor prayer.

Second, you should meditate, not only in your heart but also outwardly, repeating and comparing the actual, literal words in the book, reading and rereading them with careful attention and thought as to what the Holy Spirit means by them. And guard against being satiated or thinking that when you have read, heard, or said it once or twice you understand it fully; for this will never make an excellent theologian; it will be like immature fruit that falls before it is half ripe.

This is why in the psalm you see David constantly exulting that he would do nothing else, day and night and always, but speak, write, utter, sing, hear, and read God's Word and commandments. For God will not give you his Spirit apart from the external word. Be guided accordingly, for it was not for nothing that he commanded that his Word should be outwardly written, preached, read, sung, and spoken.

Thirdly, there is trial (*tentatio*). This is the touchstone that teaches you not only to know and understand but also to experience how right, how true, how sweet, how lovely, how mighty, how comforting is God's Word, wisdom above all wisdom.

So you see why it is that David so often in this psalm laments concerning all the enemies, the wicked princes and tyrants, the lying and godless spirits, which he must suffer by reason of the very fact that he meditates, that he applies himself to God's Word, as we have said. For as soon as God's Word goes forth through you the devil will afflict you and make you a real doctor [of theology] and teach you by his temptations to seek and to love God's Word. For I myself . . . must be very thankful to my papists for pummeling, pressing, and terrifying me; that is, for making me a fairly good theologian, for otherwise I would not have become one . . . .

So there you have David's rule. If you study well according to this example, you will also sing and praise with him in the words of the same psalm : "The law of thy mouth is better to me than thousands of gold and silver pieces." "Thy commandment makes me wiser than my enemies, for it is ever with me. I have more understanding than all my teachers, for thy testimonies are my meditation. I understand more than the aged, for I keep thy precepts." And you will find how flat and moldy the books of the fathers will taste to you; you will not only despise the enemy's books but the longer you go on the less will you be pleased with your own writing and teaching. When you have come to this point then you may confidently trust that you have begun to become a real theologian, who is able to teach not only young and imperfect Christians but also the advanced and mature; for Christ's church has in it all kinds of Christians, young, old, weak, sick, sound, strong, fresh, lazy, simple, wise, etc.   *—Luther* (142)

* * *

When we say, "Our Father" we have taken ourselves outside the realm of theology, and spoken the word that expresses the ultimate experience that man can have of God. It lies at the beginning of all theology and is its foundation; it lies at the end of it and is its pinnacle. The name expresses that simple and boundless faith which is the substance of our religion.

And so, my brethren, we need this daily prayer. I will not say that we need it more than others do, but I will say that we need it for the reason that others do not share. We need it to keep us conscious of the simplicity of faith. We who are students of theology and ministers of the gospel have the name of God continually upon our lips more often than any other men save those who use that name profanely. We have the thought of God continually in our minds. We think of him in this relation and in that. We make him an object of conscious reflection; we argue about him and discuss him. And in this constant occupation of our minds we run into the danger that God, our heavenly Father, may become to us a mere abstraction.

Therefore, we need, not now and then, but very often, to pray this prayer with all the humility and directness and simplicity of childhood, speaking as one person to another. When ye think, say, "Almighty, Everlasting, Everliving, Omnipresent, Omniscient"; when ye think, say, "Creator, Preserver, King of Kings and Lord of Lords"; but when ye pray, say, "Father."

—Charles Michael Jacobs (143)

* * *

It is a sad thing that so many of us do use to preach our hearers asleep; but it is sadder still if we have studied and preached ourselves asleep, and have talked so long against hardness of heart, till our own grow hardened, under the noise of our own reproofs. Though the head only have eyes, and ears, and smell, and taste, the heart should have life, and feeling, and motion, as well as the head.

—Richard Baxter (144)

* * *

We must for ever strive to keep an even balance between the practical and the devotional. The ceaseless whirl which is the modern ministry tends to destroy the possibility of possessing our own souls in tranquillity. Lord Morley has a striking passage in which he deals with a certain fundamental defect in the writings of Macaulay. After doing justice to the historian's gift of a picturesque and vivid style, he proceeds: "We can picture Macaulay talking, or making a speech in the House of Commons, or buried in a book, or scouring his library for references, or covering his foolscap with dashing periods, or accentuating his sentences and barbing his phrases, but can anyone think of him as meditating, as being possessed, for so much as ten minutes, by that spirit of inwardness which is the hallmark of the Kings and Princes of Literature?"

Substitute the career of the minister for that of the writer, and we have, in these sentences, a flashlight on the superficiality and ineffectiveness of much of our service for God's kingdom. Yet when this "spirit of inwardness" is blended with tireless practical service, it makes an irresistible combination. It is the explanation of the strange attractiveness of some men's character and preaching. In a thousand ways, what we are prevails over what we say. This has been noted in the case of two great contemporaries, Whately and Newman. "Whately," we are told, "required to bring to the mind of his listeners the clearest intellectual demonstration before he could lead them, whereas they were moved by anything Newman said, from the mere fact that it was he who said it." We must pray, then, for this "spirit of inwardness," that we may "take root downward that we may bear fruit upward." Here alone shall we find the resources that will carry us through the long years. The late Principal Cairns once drew a distinction between two kinds of Christians which is vitally applicable in the ministry. The first, he said, seem to live, as a nation is forced to live during a coal strike, on the bins at the pithead. The second are drawing regularly from the inexhaustible depths of the earth beneath. Sooner or later the difference will assert itself in our preaching as also in our lives.

—George Johnstone Jeffrey (145)

* * *

Any concern with the great and difficult subject of evangelical pastoral care leads us back again and again to the realization that the cure of souls, like everything else that is great and abiding, consists much less in speaking and doing than in being. This is precisely the reason why all pastoral care has its source and stay in the care of one's own soul. From the spiritual point of view, it is never our tasks that wreck us, only ourselves. It is possible that we may not be equal to a task, to fail, to be defeated, to come off badly, and yet to emerge from these defeats spiritually intact, even strengthened. And again it is terribly possible in success, even in seeming spiritual success, to gain the world and forfeit one's soul. But most often it is a case of an outward failure following upon a hidden, inner failure, a disobedience to a secret voice, a neglect of invisible and seemingly insignificant tasks within one's own soul, or also simple ignorance of the laws of spiritual life.

—Erich Schick (146)

* * *

Spiritual Disciplines

The preacher must practice discipline. A real preacher without "training" and discipline is inconceivable.

Above everything else, a part of the continuing discipline of an evangelical preacher is incessant study of Holy Scriptures. One must know the Bible and learn to think "biblically" and to see the world "biblically." Constant use of the Scriptures must not yield to any substitute, such as a devotional book. There are two things that are important for the pastor's reading of the Bible: to stick to complete passages, to read entire books in sequence, and to practice reading it daily as *lectio continua*, that is, to adopt a daily minimum as a rule. The evangelical pastor should not be put to shame by the Catholic priest who reads his breviary. But in all this one must not lose sight of the purpose of reading, which is to nourish one's thinking, feeling, and believing through reflection on what is read (*meditatio*).

Living and thinking with the people of the congregation is also a part of the pastor's discipline just because it is not easy for him. We know how Friedrich von Bodelschwingh the elder at the beginning of his ministry had to struggle against his aversion to meeting strangers. Personal disappointments, the demands that are made upon us, and realization of our own inadequacy, doubts that trouble our faith, the shaking of hope for the church which is necessary to our life — all this is hard, but it is part of the discipline of our office to fight our way courageously through all these temptations and trials (*tentatio*). Everything in personal and ministerial life that "goes against the grain of nature," the endurance of one struggle after another, this must be accepted for the sanctification of life and the strengthening of faith.

But there can be no discipline of obedience in faith without prayer. Prayer must be learned and practiced. In the prayer life of the pastor, like that of all Christians, there are many times of dryness, much irregularity, and sometimes years of neglect. To meet this the church in times past was wise enough to make use of prayer books, in order to learn discipline and for guidance in what we should pray. In particular, intercession for the congregation must have its place in the daily prayer of the pastor. Löhe said that the church register could be, among other things, "a great assistance to the pastor's memory and prayerful remembrance."

Thus at all times, *meditatio, tentatio,* and *oratio* have obtained and should obtain great importance in the church.

—*Wolfgang Trillhaas* (147)

* * *

Free!

Confidence in our ministry is, to use a Reformation distinction, not *securitas* but *certitudo;* and since it is not a matter of external security but solely a confidence made possible by the gift of God it is possible to possess it only on certain human conditions which demand self-denial and sacrifice.

"The work of God can be built only upon the ruins of our self," wrote Fénelon, the effective spiritual director in the time of Louis XIV. This applies to the pastor particularly, as it does to every Christian. There are, therefore, a number of fundamental features of his ministerial ethos in which this attitude must be manifest. We mention only three.

The pastor needs his own particular *ascesis,* using that word in its original sense of spiritual discipline and self-denial.

He needs to be free from the need for "success." There is something profoundly wrong when a pastor's joy in his ministry is dependent upon external success, and no pastor will be able to exercise a blessed ministry until he has once and for all renounced every temptation to achieve "success" in the ordinary human sense. At this point the difference between the ministry and every kind of worldly pursuit is clearly apparent. Every experienced pastor knows how quickly the young and able preacher can deteriorate spiritually from outward success, and older ministers are no exception. Certainty in the exercise of our ministry depends upon whether our hearts are independent of the ups and downs of outward success. Actually, the whole mission which the Lord has committed to his church is very obviously doomed to be unsuccessful in any outward, secularistic sense; this is in the very nature of the task and it cannot be otherwise. Consequently, our ministry must also reflect this fundamental law of the church.

On the same level is freedom from all comparisons between one brother and others. They have all received the same ministry from the same Lord, and no matter how natural may be the temptation to make these comparisons, it too must be once and for all overcome.

Then, too, there must be a fundamental freedom from all care, both material and spiritual. This is by no means to disparage outward concern for our life or watchfulness and faithfulness in the conduct of our ministry. But it is immediately apparent that the ministry cannot be exercised in certitude and gladness if it is all too manifestly overshadowed by outward and inner cares. Neither of these cares has any fundamental right to exist if there is any real certitude concerning our ministry. The Lord who calls and sends his messengers has indeed permitted his servants to bear witness to their faithfulness by giving up their lives and enduring many a trial, but never yet has he allowed one of his servants to go hungry. He who calls us also has the power to give us daily strength and a livelihood to perform it; and a pastor must learn before other Christians literally to believe the Lord's promise: "All these things shall be added unto you."

It is not at all a step from one category to another, but fundamentally and literally the same attitude to add that a pastor must also be free from all spiritual care. It is not we who sustain the church of God. This the Lord himself does. He can, and according to the very spiritual nature of his church, he often will ordain that it go through many trials. But as long as this earth endures there will be a church of God. Care would only be an evidence of a hidden want of faith.

Finally, in exactly the same way the pastor needs to be fundamentally free from all busyness, which is only another form of faithless care. One of the most flourishing congregations I know decided to reduce the number of its organizations —a sign of great spiritual strength! "He who falls from faith is hounded by the devil," said Luther in an exposition of Psalm 16 (v. 4). And freedom from bustle and rush can be a singularly shining testimony of faith precisely in our overbusy generation.

Besides *ascesis,* however, there is faithfulness.

This is to be understood in the first instance quite fundamentally. One who covets certitude and joy in his ministry must resolve upon a fundamental, completely unreflecting, I might almost say, blind loyalty. "One cannot belong half to God," said Fénelon. If even the ordinary Christian can find no blessing in trying to serve God only on certain conditions, then this is doubly true of the pastor. It is a dangerous thing when we begin to try and justify our weaknesses to ourselves on principle, and many a successful preacher has lost his power completely because of a hidden unfaithfulness. There can be no really blessed work in our ministry without this unconditional faithfulness.

This must apply not only to all matters of principle but also quite positively to our preaching. In his treatise, "Of the Difference Between an Apostle and a Genius," Kierkegaard pointed out that the preachers of his day were suffering a steady dwindling of their spiritual authority, because they were delivering "profound" discourses instead of passing on in the form of direct statement what is given to them in the words of Jesus and on his responsibility. "There is no question here of racking one's brains or philosophising, but simply that Christ said it, not as a profound thinker but with divine authority. . . . What Plato says on immortality really is profound, reached after deep study; but then poor Plato has no authority whatsoever."

May one say just this further word to remind us that this faithfulness must also determine the minister's private life? A pastor cannot and need not learn to know and experience every permissible pleasure of the world. It is the mark of great callings that they cannot do many things that Tom, Dick, and Harry may well permit themselves to do. The pastor should not fuss, much less complain, about what is simply taken for granted in the life of a soldier, a seafarer, a researcher, namely, that one's life mission simply includes the renunciation of many completely lawful pleasures in life. What he is, let him be wholly in this respect also. The faces of aged pastors, stamped by decades of faithfulness in the ministry, proclaim that the pastoral ministry is a noble service and that daily intercourse with the Word of God molds a man even outwardly. It is not even worth talking about the "sacrifices" we have to make, compared with the hidden, but sometimes altogether manifest glory of our calling.

One of the most precious and most apparent gifts of our ministry is the freedom which is a part of its most essential presuppositions. We live in the world. The Reformation did not merely make our vocation easy when it put the ministry back into the secular world. Now the pastor is the father of a family and in many other respects he stands in the very midst of those to whom he is to direct his ministry. No external, regulative piety limits his ministry. But this assumes that he rightly understands this freedom. It can be one of the most splendid outward virtues of our calling. *—Hanns Lilje* (148)

* * *

Preaching on the Verge of Prayer

For years it has become increasingly important to me that all our preaching should take place on the verge of prayer. Our preaching should be so near to prayer that it would require only a very slight transposition to turn our words into words of prayer. It is certainly an abridgment of our ministry for a preacher to think of himself primarily as a teacher. The center of the congregational sermon is an act of our priesthood, which we share with all believers, but which must first become manifest in us.

Therefore let us help one another to make progress in our praying. What we do in the pulpit is based not only upon the prayers we say during the service; rather it must be the prayers of the whole week that sustain the preacher. They create a spiritual atmosphere which is most in evidence when it is not obvious, and which accordingly makes of our sermon a work of art or a mechanical production.

—Hans Asmussen (149)

* * *

Busyness and Prayer

Yes, you could pray and, whatever you may think about it, using it as a poor makeshift of a thing much lower than a second best, not really a best at all, on which men fall back only when they can do nothing effective, and are too fidgety to be able to do nothing at all, Christ holds that prayer is a tremendous power which achieves what, without it, was a sheer impossibility. And this amazing thing you can set into operation. And the fact that you are not so using it, and simply don't believe in it and its efficiency and efficacy, as our fathers did, and that so many nowadays agree with you, is certainly a major reason why the churches are so cold, and the promises seem tardy of fulfilment. That mighty preacher, Thomas Chalmers, was once pondering over why, in spite of all his efforts and enormous popularity, there was not more spiritual outcome to show for it all, and came to this conclusion—that he was trusting to his "own animal heat and activity" rather than to the Holy Ghost. And is not that a shrewd and accurate diagnosis of the church's ailment in our day? Never was there a ministry so bustled and rushed and perspiring as ours is now. If things stick, we devise yet another type of meeting, and when this additional wheel is spinning round with all the rest of the complex machinery, and a wind is blowing in our hot faces, we feel better, and have a comfortable sense that something is going on; are tired and sticky, but happy engineers. But the whole point of the ministry, the reason why there is a ministry at all, is that people out in the press of life and finding that there they cannot keep in sight of God but get continually drifted away from him, that the little matters, to which it is their duty to attend, of necessity crowd him out of their preoccupied minds—lay hands upon a man, praying him, "Live in the secret of God's presence; and in the hush there, which we cannot know, commune with him face to face; and week by week, come out and share with us the message which, in that stillness, you have had a chance of hearing. We'll pay you for it, man, if you will only do it!" But now the ministry is every whit as busy as the rest of folk; and, in the roar of its machinery, can hear no more than anybody else. If only we would pray! But we, too, put our trust in our own animal heat and hard-breathing activity. Macaulay's fault, said that shrewd judge, Lord Cockburn, is "that he is always over-talking, and so always under-listening." So is the ministry these days. And, as Euripides reminds us, "even Zeus cannot reveal himself to a busybody."   —*Arthur John Gossip* (150)

* * *

Of Self-Preparation

Content not yourselves to have the main work of grace, but be also very careful that your graces be kept in life and action, and that you preach to yourselves the sermons that you study, before you preach them to others. If you did this for your own sakes, it would not be lost labor; but I am speaking to you upon the public account, and that you would do it for the sake of the church. When your minds are in a heavenly, holy frame, your people are likely to partake of the fruits of it. Your prayers, and praises, and doctrine, will be heavenly and sweet to them! They will feel when you have been much with God. That which is on your hearts most, is likely to be most in their ears. I confess, I must speak it by lamentable experience, that I publish to my flock the distempers of my soul; when I let my heart grow cold, my preaching is cold; and when it is confused, my preaching will be so. We are the nurses of Christ's little ones. If we forbear our food, we shall famish them; they will quickly find it in the want of milk; and we may quickly see it again in them, in the lean and dull discharge of their several duties. If we let our love go down, we are not likely to raise up theirs. If we abate our holy care and fear, it will appear in our doctrine. If the matter shew it not, the manner will. If we feed on un-wholesome food, either errors, or fruitless controversies, our hearers are likely to fare the worse for it. Whereas if we could abound in faith, and love, and zeal, how would it overflow, to the refreshing of our congregations, and how would it appear in the increase of the same graces in others!

More particularly: a minister should take some special pains with his heart, before he goes to the congregation: if it be then cold, how is it likely to warm the hearts of the hearers? Go, therefore, then especially to God for life; and read some rousing, awakening book, or meditate on the weight of the subject that you are to speak of, and on the great necessity of your people's souls that you may go in the zeal of the Lord into his house.   —*Richard Baxter* (151)

* * *

Personal Piety

He must have in his own heart an abiding sense of sin, sorrow for it, hatred of it, and longing for victory over it. He must have that trusting, resting, abiding, peace-bringing faith in a Saviour who has forgiven him all his sin. He must know by experience the blessedness of that inner peace which passeth all understanding. His heart must be so warm with personal love to the Saviour that he can look up and say, "Lord, thou knowest all things. Thou knowest that I love thee!"

—*G. H. Gerberding* (152)

* * *

It was Simon Magus' error to think that the gifts of God might be purchased with money; and it has a spice of his sin, and so may go for a kind of simony, to think that spiritual gifts may be purchased with labor. You may rise up early and go to bed late, and study hard, and read much, and devour the marrow of the best authors; and when you have done all, unless God give a blessing to your endeavors, be as lean and meagre in regard of true and useful learning, as Pharaoh's lean kine were, after they had eaten the fat ones. It is God that both ministereth the seed to the sower, and multiplieth the seed sown; the principal and the increase are both his.

—*Robert Sanderson* (153)

Only as hearers of the Word do we receive and keep our office.   —*Julius Schniewind* (154)

* * *

Prayer and meditation must be based on and bound to the Word of God, the written Word, in which God speaks to us. There are those of us who cannot pray aright unless we have the open Bible before us or at least a definite word of God in our mind. St. Jerome put it very beautifully in a letter to his friend, the abbot Pachomius—"Dost thou pray? Thou art speaking with the Bridegroom. Dost thou read? He is speaking with thee." (*Oras? loqueris cum sponso: legis? Ille loquitur tecum.*)   —*A. T. W. Steinhäuser* (155)

* * *

The ministry of helpfulness can come into being only through the power of the living God which constantly renews it. Ultimately all ministry in the church is a question of power. How much of our tremendous busyness, pure busyness would cease if we realized that genuine ministry can occur also in quietness and that real ministry is being committed to us when now and then we just stop and listen to the guiding voice of God. And how much of our tired ministry would disappear if only we dared to live by the ultimate power of prayer and obedience! For many this admonition may be a call to less work, but also for many it may be an encouragement to go on bravely and boldly in the manifold tasks committed to them, since God gives strength to those who dare to stand fast in his service.   —*Adolf Wischmann* (156)

* * *

THE PASTOR'S LIFE OF STUDY
Of Studies

It is common with us to be negligent in our studies. Few men will be at that pains that is necessary for the right informing of their understanding, and fitting them for their further work. Some men have no delight in their studies, but take only now and then an hour, as an unwelcome task which they are forced to undergo, and are glad when they are from under the yoke. Will neither the natural desire of knowing, nor the spiritual desire of knowing God and things divine, nor the consciousness of our great ignorance and weakness, nor the sense of the weight of our ministerial work, will none of all these keep us closer to our studies, and make us more painful in seeking after the truth?

O what abundance of things are there that a minister should understand; and what a great defect is it to be ignorant of them; and how much shall we miss such knowledge in our work! Many ministers study only to compose their sermons, and very little more, when there are so many books to be read, and so many matters that we should not be unacquainted with. Nay, in the study of our sermons we are too negligent, gathering only a few naked heads, and not considering of the most forcible expressions by which we should set them home to men's hearts. We must study how to convince and get within men, and how to bring each truth to the quick, and not leave all this to our extemporary promptitude, unless it be in cases of necessity. Certainly, brethren, experience will teach you, that men are not made learned or wise without hard study, and unwearied labors and experience.

—*Richard Baxter* (157)

* * *

I implore all Christians, especially pastors and preachers, not to be doctors too soon, and imagine that they know everything (for imagination and stretched cloth fall far short of the measure), but that they daily exercise themselves in these studies and constantly apply them to practice. Let them guard with all care and diligence against the poisonous infection of such security and presumption, and persevere in reading, teaching, learning, thinking, meditating, not ceasing until they have learned by experience and are sure that, by this teaching, they have killed Satan, and have become more learned than God himself and all his saints.

If they manifest such diligence, then I will agree with them, and they will receive what fruit they will have, and what excellent men God will make of them; so that in due time they themselves will acknowledge that the longer and the more they have studied the Catechism, the less they know of it, and the more they find yet to learn. And then only, as hungry and thirsty ones, they will truly appreciate that which now, because of great abundance and satiety, they cannot endure. To this end may God grant his grace! Amen.

–Luther (158)

* * *

The Parsonage

Next to the church comes the parsonage. The study window looks out upon the churchyard, and if the pastor wants to see the steeple near, he must raise his head and eyes higher than other people need. The bell that summons to prayer has, too, a louder voice for him than for the rest of the inhabitants, and the graves speak in deeper tones to his ear. The parsonage garden runs along the churchyard wall, and a door opens out of it to the bench under the old lime tree, from which one can overlook both sides of the village. Each one who passes up and down the street has an undying soul, and of each one the pastor must give account, as to whether he has sought, urged, and allured as a good shepherd should. On that bench under the lime tree, how much silent intercession must, indeed, be poured out! Nor is this intercession all. The Lord said unto Moses, "Wherefore criest thou unto me? Speak to the people, that they go forward."

Outwardly, the parsonage is a house like others, but whenever the devil goes about the village, seeking his prey, and planning where best he can spread his net, he goes about the parsonage thrice, and looks into every window. And most of all he rejoices if the door of that house be open to him and he cannot only make his way in accidentally, but rule there, and even hold his ground in the study, without being annoyed by prayer and the reading of the Scriptures. Watching and praying are the only bolts this thief fears. A parsonage is either a house of prayer or a very den of iniquity. There is no peace, indeed, for any of the ungodly, but a minister who lives without prayer and struggle is the poorest and most miserable man in the whole village.

–Karl Büchsel (159)

* * *

Of Studies

He was a very studious person and a very lively preacher: and one who therefore took great pains in his preparation for his public labors—with respect whereunto he once used these words: "God will curse that man's labors that lumbers up and down the world all the week and then upon Saturday in the afternoon goes into his study, whereas God knows that time were little enough to pray and weep in, and get his heart into a fit frame for the duties of the approaching Sabbath."

–Cotton Mather (160)

* * *

Not to read or study at all is to tempt God: to do nothing but study is to forget the ministry: to study only to glory in one's knowledge is a shameful vanity: to study in search of the means to flatter sinners, a deplorable prevarication: But to store one's mind with the knowledge proper to the saints by study and by prayer, and to diffuse that knowledge in solid instructions, and practical exhortations—this is to be a prudent, zealous, and laborious minister.

–Pasquier Quesnel (161)

One of the truly shocking facts about our present-day ministry is the way in which so many ministers are living lives of personal frustrations. The physicians of souls are lamentably unable to heal themselves. Much of the trouble lies in an almost constant conflict between the average minister's idealization of his own job and the actual life he leads. He feels in his heart that he ought to spend much time in meditation, in prayer, and in study, in order to bring creative insight to the needy people who are looking to him for help; but as the years go on, he finds that this side of his life becomes almost negligible. He feels he ought to be a prophet, but he knows very well that in fact he is a kind of business manager. His major energies are employed in conducting drives, planning promotional activities, answering letters, checking on printing, and general administration. The church becomes a kind of club, and the pastor is the manager of the club, looking after the details of organization. Some men rebel against this but do not know how to become free from it, while others, though they do some complaining, really welcome the chore-boy life they lead, because it protects them from that revealing encounter with the white sheet of paper lying on the study desk. They think they hate the telephone, but when the time for writing comes, they welcome the alibi which the steadily ringing telephone provides.

I know personally many ministers who actually use a study very little in any particular week. Most of them have what they *call* studies, but the real character of these rooms is that of offices. These rooms, whether in home or church, are places where the weekly calendar is prepared and some letters written, but they are not primarily scenes of struggle over big ideas. Seldom are they places where serious books are read, and still more seldom are they places where thoughts are laboriously put on paper. Many ministers must feel a twinge of conscience when they read in *Barchester Towers* the familiar description of Archdeacon Grantley in his study. The famous Trollope character wished to give the impression that his study was the scene of nothing but intellectual labor, but in fact he spent part of his time there, stretched on a couch, reading light novels.

—D. Elton Trueblood (162)

* * *

Study—the Seminarian's Calling

I never shall forget my first experience of a divinity school. I had come from a college where men studied hard but said nothing about faith. I had never been at a prayer meeting in my life. The first place I was taken to at the seminary was the prayer meeting; and never shall I lose the impression of the devoutness with which those men prayed and exhorted one another. Their whole souls seemed exalted and their natures were on fire. I sat bewildered and ashamed, and went away depressed. On the next day I met some of those same men at a Greek recitation. It would be little to say of some of the devoutest of them that they had not learnt their lessons. Their whole way showed that they never learnt their lessons; that they had not got hold of the first principles of hard, faithful, conscientious study.

—Phillips Brooks (163)

* * *

Watch, study, give attendance to reading! Verily, you cannot read too well; and what you read well you cannot understand too well; and what you understand well you cannot teach too well; and what you teach well you cannot live too well! *Experto crede Ruperto* (believe one who knows by experience.) It is the devil, it is the world, it is our flesh, that rage and rave against us. Therefore, dear sirs and brethren, pastors and preachers, pray, read, study, be diligent! Verily, there is no time for sloth, snoring, and sleeping in this evil, shameful time. Use the gift that has been committed to you and make known the mystery of Christ. If a man does not want to know, let him be ignorant, as Paul says in I Corinthians 14:38. We must not fail to proclaim the Word of mystery simply because we have baptism and the Sacrament. Things will be well when we have done our part. Amen.

—Luther (164)

* * *

The Study

A manse without a study would be comparable to a church without a pulpit, and the efficiency of the pulpit is commensurate with the efficiency of the study. When a minister settles in his manse, he should, before all else, be careful to choose as his study a fitting chamber and equip it for its sacred use. It should be a peaceful room, remote from disturbance; and it should have a pleasant outlook. The ideal is that chamber in the House Beautiful where Bunyan's Pilgrim was laid by Piety, Prudence, and Charity—"a large upper chamber, whose window opened toward the sun-rising: the name of the chamber was Peace." . . . Whatever lies without, a true study within is a hallowed place. You look around the walls, and there you see your familiar and treasured volumes, and find yourself in the presence of the immortals. "You see here," says Erasmus (*Colloq. Mil. et Corthus*) "the volume of the Gospels? In this he talks with me who once joined himself in eloquent companionship with the two disciples on the road to Emmaus, and made them feel no toil of the journey, but only a sweet burning of the heart as they drank in his honeyed discourses. In this Paul speaks to me, in this Isaiah and the rest of the prophets. Here talks with me the sweet Chrysostom, here Basil, here Augustine, here Jerome, here Cyprian, and the rest of the doctors no less learned than eloquent. Know you any who talk with you so pleasantly, any to compare with these? In such a fellowship, which never fails me, think you can the weariness of solitude creep over me?" For one who knows its use, a study is a precious place, a happy haven, a hallowed retreat.

—David Smith (165)

No man, and, consequently, no minister has ever been promised perfect happiness on earth. All ministers must be cross-bearers. "He that will be my disciple, let him take up his cross," saith the Lord, "and follow me." The whole of Scripture proves that God's children never yet were without tribulation here below. It is through much tribulation, indeed, that we enter his kingdom; they who do not share in it are bastards, not children; and the chastising of the Lord is no proof of his wrath, but his love.

What would the minister become if he led a life of mere comfort in a home where the cross, with all its various shapes and hues, had no place? His heart would grow dull and dead as stagnant water. His preaching would be barren and empty. His prayers would lack all unction and depth.

As it is, whenever the rest of the house is shaken, when the wind blows, or the waters rise, or the rains fall, the pastor must have his closet where he can be alone with God and his cross, some place apart which is only entered by those who wish to speak to him of pastoral concerns. Here he is "at home" in the narrowest sense of the word.

Let the minister's wife arrange all the rest of the house according to her own taste; the study must have nothing to do with domestic business or social visiting. *Oratio, tentatio, meditatio faciunt theologum* : that is the answer to what the pastor does in his study. *Oratio* has a very broad scope and includes every want, every desire of the whole congregation. *Tentatio*, too, applies to the whole world of the heart, all life's experiences in all their rich and broad extent. Therefore *meditatio* should not be limited to the lessons or excerpts from Holy Scriptures chosen as free texts. *Oratio* and *tentatio* find rest and satisfaction only in *meditatio*, and *meditatio* itself is dead and unfruitful without them. This *meditatio* must be distinguished from cursory reading of the Bible and also from exegetical studies . . . Real meditation must be learned from the Virgin Mary, of whom it is written that she "kept all these things, pondering them in her heart."

—*Karl Büchsel* (166)

* * *

Let us go forth now with the minister, who has the "mind of Christ", into that most sacred place, the study. Here is to be enjoyed a sweet and blessed fellowship with all that ennobles character and life. The best thoughts of the wisest and best men are the environment of the study, in the books that line the walls. The windows are opened toward Jerusalem. There is telephonic connection with the audience chamber of the King of kings, who is the Father of the minister. For this humble man is an heir of God. Prayers ascend, and messages of love descend in the sacred Word, in kindly providences, in the personal ministrations of grace. Here a man is alone with God; and that is just where he wishes to be. The study becomes the seclusion of Moses at Horeb, or of Elijah in the cave of the desert, or of Saul in Arabia, or of the Beloved Disciple on Patmos. Men who are to move their fellow-men must often be alone. Meditation precedes effective activity . . . The fire burned, while the psalmist was musing. Even Jesus of Nazareth, who had not where to lay his head, converted the hillsides into a study after sleep had fallen upon the world. Whatever else you neglect, no not neglect the opportunities of communion in the study. If they are improved, you will come from them with a radiance upon your countenance, which will convince men that you have been with God.

Upon the wall of the study, to catch the eye of the minister, as he enters, the student's promise is written: "If any man willeth to do his will, he shall know of the teaching." Obedience is the condition of knowledge. And another promise is also visible: "The Spirit of truth will guide you into all the truth." Submission to the leadership of the Holy Spirit is the pledge of spiritual discernment. These are the promises to the "mind of Christ." They may be trusted. God has given them. "All the truth" is to be grasped by him whose supreme desire it is to know the Incarnation of truth, who is the Way, and the Truth, and the Life, who reveals the Father, and who reveals mankind as well, who comes from God, who solves the riddle of existence, who answers the questions of the soul, whose control is love, who takes the whole world in his pierced hands and presents it at the throne of grace. "The mind of Christ" is expanding under these influences. The Redeemer of a sacred Book and of a far-off land and age is becoming a present and a personal Reality. This man of study and of prayer is losing himself, that he may find himself completely in Christ. He is seeing with the eyes of Christ, and is hearing with Christ's ears. Large, generous considerations are his.

—*Henry M. Booth* (167)

* * *

Study the Scriptures

Do you then, my son, diligently apply yourself to the reading of the sacred Scriptures. Apply yourself, I say. For we who read the things of God need much application, lest we should say or think anything too rashly about them. And applying yourself thus to the study of the things of God, with faithful prejudgments such as are well pleasing to God, knock at its locked door, and it will be opened to you by the porter of whom Jesus says, "To him the porter opens." And applying yourself thus to the divine study, seek aright, and with unwavering trust in God, the meaning of the Holy Scriptures, which so many have missed. Be not satisfied with knocking and seeking; for prayer is of all things indispensable to the knowledge of the things of God. For to this the Saviour exhorted, and said not only, "Knock, and it shall be opened to you; and seek, and ye shall find," but also, "Ask, and it shall be given unto you."

—*Origen* (168)

Reading

What has exceedingly hurt you in time past, nay, and I fear, to this day, is, want of reading. I scarce ever knew a preacher read so little. And perhaps, by neglecting it, have lost the taste for it. Hence your talent in preaching does not increase. It is just the same as it was seven years ago. It is lively, but not deep; there is little variety; there is no compass of thought. Reading only can supply this, with meditation and daily prayer. You wrong yourself greatly by omitting this. You can never be a deep preacher without it, any more than a thorough Christian. O begin! Fix some part of every day for private exercise. You may acquire the taste which you have not : what is tedious at first, will afterward be pleasant. Whether you like it or no, read and pray daily. It is for your life; there is no other way; else you will be a trifler all your days, and a pretty, superficial preacher. Do justice to your own soul; give it time and means to grow. Do not starve yourself any longer. Take up your cross and be a Christian altogether. Then will all the children of God rejoice (not grieve) over you.

—John Wesley (169)

* * *

Study hard, for the well is deep, and our brains are shallow. But especially be laborious in practice and in the exercise of your knowledge.

—Richard Baxter (170)

* * *

Prayer and Scripture Study

For any man solemnly to undertake the interpretation of any portion of Scripture without invocation of God, to be taught and instructed by his Spirit, is a high provocation of him, nor shall I expect the discovery of truth from any one who thus proudly engages in a work so much above his ability. But this is the sheet anchor of a faithful expositor in all difficulties; nor can he without this be satisfied that he hath attained the mind of the Spirit in any divine revelation. When all other helps fail, as they frequently do, this will afford him the best relief. The labors of former expositors are of excellent use; but they are far from having discovered the depth of this vein of wisdom; nor will the best of our endeavours prescribe limits to our successors; and the reason why the generality go in the same tract, except in some excursions of curiosity, is not giving themselves up to the conduct of the Holy Spirit in the diligent performance of their duty.

–John Owen (171)

* * *

Te totum applica ad textum: rem totam applica ad te.

Apply thyself wholly to the text; apply the matter wholly to thyself. *–Johann Albrecht Bengel* (172)

* * *

It is not many books or much reading that makes men learned; but it is good things, however little of them, often read, that make men learned in the Scriptures and make them godly, too. Indeed the writings of all the holy fathers should be read only for a time, in order that through them we may be led to the Holy Scriptures. We are like men who study the signposts and never travel the road. The dear fathers wished, by their writings, to lead us to the Scriptures, but we so use them as to be led away from the Scriptures, though the Scriptures alone are our vineyard in which we all ought to work and toil. *–Luther* (173)

* * *

No Time to Study?

We have plenty of time for all our work did we husband our time and hoard it aright. Did we work as many hours and as hard as the people who support us, work as early in the morning and as late at night and as hard all the livelong day? O, no! We cannot look seriously in one another's faces and say that it is want of time. It is want of intention. It is want of determination. It is want of method. It is want of motive. It is want of conscience. It is want of heart. It is want of anything and everything but time.   *—Alexander Whyte*

* * *

Mirror for Ministers

Have I prepared myself by prayer and attention to God's Word for every service (sermon, liturgy, administration of the sacraments)?

Have I been careless in preparation for my pastoral acts?

Have I lived in repentance and obedience by the power of my baptism, and have I taught the congregation to live by the same power?

Have I myself desired the Lord's Supper according to the command of the Lord and regularly offered it and magnified it to the congregation?

Have I allowed the Word of God daily to instruct, direct, admonish, rebuke, heal, comfort, and strengthen me unto repentance, faith, love, and obedience?

Have I been envious of the success and blessings of other ministers and congregations?

Have I taken seriously my responsibilities as a citizen and also urged these obligations upon my congregation?

Have I preferred to associate only with my friends?

—Max Lackmann (174)

WEDNESDAY

The Minister as Confessor

* * *

Receive the Holy Spirit. If you forgive the sins of any, they are forgiven; if you retain the sins of any, they are retained.

—John 20:22–23

———

Therefore confess your sins to one another, and pray for one another, that you may be healed.

—James 5:16

OF CONFESSION AND ABSOLUTION

What is Confession: Answer: Confession consists of two parts: the one is that we confess our sins; the other, that we receive absolution or forgiveness from the pastor as of God himself, in no wise doubting, but firmly believing that our sins are thereby forgiven before God in heaven.

What sins should we confess: Answer: Before God we should acknowledge ourselves guilty of all manner of sins, even of those of which we are not aware, as we do in the Lord's Pray To the pastor we should confess only those sins which we know and feel in our hearts.

What are such sins: Answer: Here examine yourself in the light of the Ten Commandments, whether as father or mother, son or daughter, master or servant you have been disobedient unfaithful, slothful, ill-tempered, unchaste, or quarrelsome, or whether you have injured anyone by word or deed, stolen, neglected or wasted aught, or done any other evil.

–Luther, The Small Catechism

* * *

Confession and Absolution

A Lutheran Statement

When I admonish to confession I am doing nothing else but admonishing you to be a Christian. If I bring you to become a Christian then I have also brought you to confession; for those who desire to become devout Christians and be free of their sins and possess a happy conscience already have the right hunger and thirst, so that they eagerly grasp for bread, as the harried deer burns with heat and thirst.

–Martin Luther

1. The great treasure of the church is the message of forgiveness of sins. Where there is forgiveness of sins there are also life and salvation. To dispense this treasure God not

only instituted the ministry and gave us the sacraments but also instituted the office of the keys. He bestowed upon his church the authority to remit or to retain sins in the power of the Holy Spirit. Only where this authority is exercised can the church live. For unforgiven sin destroys the fellowship; forgiveness creates it. Therefore every Christian is called to confession.

2. As Luther says in the Small Catechism, right "confession consists of two parts: the one is that we confess our sins; the other, that we receive absolution or forgiveness through the pastor as of God himself, in no wise doubting, but firmly believing that our sins are thus forgiven before God in heaven."

3. The church recognizes individual confession and common confession.

One who is seeking help and liberation in temptation and distress of conscience does well to make personal confession and receive the assurance of forgiveness. And when he does so he should frankly mention specific sins that burden his conscience. Nobody is forced to come to individual confession. We should seek it, however, and receive its special blessing with joy and thankfulness.

In common confession a person confesses his guilt as a sinner among sinners. And he receives the absolution as an individual by the laying on of hands or in the declaration that is made to all who are confessing. Everyone who confesses must know that the sins of the unrepentant are retained and that the gift of absolution includes the command to abandon the old sins and to live a new life.

Confession and absolution have independent importance apart from the reception of the Lord's Supper.

4. It is part of the ministerial obligation of the ministers of the Word to be available to all for the hearing of confession and absolution. They are obligated by their office to keep the seal of confession unbroken, before anyone else and also before

the law. Beyond this, every Christian, if he is asked to do so by one in need, can declare the forgiveness of sins in the name of God. This makes him, too, a confessor who is obligated to keep the seal of confession.

—Ordnung des kirchlichen Lebens (175)

* * *

Martin Luther, as he himself often acknowledged, could not do his work as a preacher and theologian by himself alone. It would have become too heavy for him. He needed the help of private confession. He is speaking from his own personal experience when in the Smalcald Articles he speaks of "the mutual conversation and consolation of brethren" as a particular divine means of grace. "I know what comfort and strength private confession has given to me. Nobody who has not fought often and long with the devil knows what it can do. I would long since have been strangled by the devil if I had not kept confession" (WA 10^{111}, 61 f, 1522). It is very remarkable that we pastors and theologians, at least the majority of us, have apparently been able to get along without private confession for two centuries. But who would seriously assert that we have not suffered from its loss? Therefore, a vital contribution to a renewal of the ministry will be that we begin again to take seriously the good, inherited practice of private confession wherever this is possible and, beyond this, seek new ways of developing ordered brotherly confession.

—Martin Dörne (176)

* * *

PASTORAL CARE OF THE PASTOR

Pastoral care of the pastor! None should think that this is a superfluous requirement. The pastor of souls must himself have traveled the road of repentance and confession. He must himself know what it means to have received the forgiveness of sins in a pastoral encounter. The pastor of souls, and particularly the minister as pastor of souls, must come to the pastoral encounter from pastoral care he himself has experienced. People sense whether we are speaking to them out of our own knowledge of the cure of souls. Only this makes us convincing to them.

—*Eduard Thurneysen* (177)

* * *

Who is My Pastor?

I

I begin with a deep lament, a lament for myself. I am a pastor of souls by reason of my calling. I must speak to people on the basis of their relation to God and I am supposed to lead them to God. I am not unaware of the great difficulty of this ministry and its great joy.

But who is *my* pastor? It may seem a contradiction, but often it seems to me that the loneliest man in the congregation is the pastor, who is always talking about fellowship, or at least should be. I have to preach and teach Bible classes, I am committed to proclaim the good news of the grace of God in Jesus Christ, who opens the eyes of the blind, delivers the captives and those who sit in darkness.

But who proclaims this good news to *me*? I too have often sat in darkness. . . . Where is my pastor? Many people come to me and each one wants something of me; frequently, though not often, they are even concerned about genuinely spiritual problems. But to each one, whatever his concern, I must say a friendly, encouraging word. I am with people the whole day. But I myself am completely alone.

II

The question is whether I can stop with that lament, whether the fault is not that of others, but my own, that I am a pastor without a pastor. To be sure, loneliness is our great trouble, but it may be that it is at least partly my own fault. Have we not, for example, almost completely lost the order which was intended to remedy this need, that of the *confessionarius* or confessor? But then I must ask myself, have I really sought out a pastor for myself, a brother? Do I not prefer to be alone? Am I willing to accept a criticism of the way I conducted my last young people's meeting or the way I do my work in general? May not the pastor of my soul, whose absence I lament, be already at my door, but I do not let him in?

The question, however, becomes a burning question when we consider what a perilous undertaking the cure of souls is. True, there is nothing greater than witness to the truth of God and nothing more glorious than to be able to speak God's forgiveness to another person, and "whoever brings back a sinner from the error of his way will save his soul from death and will cover a multitude of sins" (Jas. 5:20). But—"He that is near to me is near to the fire," says an apocryphal saying of Jesus. An experienced Christian once said to me that fundamentally only those things had a right to a place in preaching which would abide in the face of death and eternity; everything else, he said, was just talk. Since pastoral care is preaching, the same would apply to it. But what do I make of it?

Here I am supposed to comfort a person with the consolation of the living God. I know very well what is involved, but I only talk to him kindly and reassure him with fine, pious phrases. And when I do that I have given him stones instead of bread and substituted my human wisdom for the truth of God. Here is a person who comes to me seeking the light of God, which shines relentlessly but healingly into his life; and I, understandably enough, try to spare him and meet him with human lenience. And when I do that I have defrauded him of the disclosure of his sin and the forgiveness of his sin. Thus is the cure of souls debased into its caricature, the sedation of souls.

It can become even more perilous. The Word of God has power over spirits, said Vilmar, but its power can be exercised only through those over whom it has already achieved power. But what if I cut myself off from this power? I hear a person's confession of sin and am obliged to gaze down into a dark abyss. I myself may be infected if I am not in the sanctifying power of the Word; or I may become a Pharisee and despise the very person to whom the love of Christ belongs. I am asked for counsel in the most intimate concerns; I have the right to declare the forgiveness of sins—what an exalting privilege, and yet what a sinister temptation to gain ascendancy over the soul of another person! Knowledge is power, but knowledge about others gained in pastoral counseling can be dangerous to him who possesses it, and pastoral care is impossible without humility and dying unto self. Every day I have to visit the sick and speak to those who mourn. And every person must be taken seriously as a person. I know this, but how easily I get used to the hardest "cases"—already they are "cases," not people! And then the comforting, edifying words run like oil from my lips; for, after all, am I not a pastor, an expert on religious questions as others are in other areas? But when I do this I have forgotten that self-assurance and routine are the mortal enemies of all pastoral care. Yes, pastoral care is a perilous undertaking!

III

When Jesus sent out the seventy disciples to proclaim the message of the kingdom, he "sent them two and two" (Luke 10:1). The message was to come from the lips, not of one, but of two or three witnesses. This gives it greater power, but is it not also an unspeakable boon to the messengers themselves? Is not the very fact that we are set down in a brotherhood in itself a cure of souls, Jesus' own pastoral care of his messengers? Now the witness is no longer solitary. Perhaps it may not always be convenient; for now he must give up a part of his life, and the truth of what he says and how he lives is subject to the criticism of his brethren. But at the same time, this is the very help of God himself. In his ministry, its joys and failures, its successes and defeats, his preaching and pastoral work and all their perils, the witness of Jesus Christ is no more alone! His brother is with him, and in that brother the Lord who sent him to him is Himself present. The fellowship of prayer, of searching the Scriptures, of brotherly conversation is real and present. All through the New Testament church, in Peter (Acts 10:23), in Paul, who almost always had companions with him, we encounter this basic law of the Christian life. There is sound reason why Luther (in the Smalcald Articles, III, 4) should count among the ways in which God bestows the riches of his grace this *mutuum colloquium et mutua consolatio,* "the mutual conversation and consolation of brethren." For, as Luther says, "no man is to be alone against Satan; God instituted the church and the ministry of the Word in order that we might join hands and help one another. If the prayer of one does not help, then that of the other will."

We do not need to think that this brotherhood has died. It exists as long as there is a church of Christ. Often enough perhaps it is only because of our blind and faithless eyes that we do not see it. In every congregation of Christ there is a pastor for the pastor, even if he be some aged or sick person whom I visit and discover that he can give me more knowledge and certainty than I can give him.

The real secret of the brotherhood is that Christ himself is not ashamed to come to me through men. And here too lies the decisive help for the pastor. This is where he himself is constantly learning to know the reality of what he has to communicate in his pastoral work—the judgment and forgiveness, the consolation and counsel of God. How can he ever get along without this assurance? Is it not an absurdity that one who does not confess himself should hear confessions? Such a person must surely become hardened and callous, and the reality of the forgiveness he proclaims will become a pale, second-hand thing. Around him, confession, frankness, truthfulness, confidence must inevitably die. Often I myself am the least conscious of the dangers of pastoral care that threaten me particularly. Can I not ask a brother, a fellow minister to point them out to me, to warn me and restrain me? Can we not sometimes read the Bible together, possibly a portion on which I am going to preach in the near future? Four eyes see more than two and, besides, Jesus positively prefers to be present where two or three are gathered together in his name (Matt. 18:20). And all too often—I know from my own experience—I cannot even pray any more. Why should we not in our most intimate fellowship with one another drink from that fountain which we are always commending to the members of our congregations as the indispensable well of life? And what a blessing it is in such company not to have to talk, just to be able to listen! Am I able to do that any more, just to listen? But only a listener is a true pastor of souls. He who listens to God will also listen to the people who come to him. And every pastor knows that frequently more than half of all the help he gives comes from simply listening in the presence of God.

IV

One thing more must be added. It is true that Christ meets me in my brother, but that brother is not Christ. And brotherhood is not simply a formula that merely needs to be followed in order to be a good pastor. It cannot be reduced to a means, but it dare not be made a law. Therefore, in brotherhood there must also be solitude. But this will be a solitude quite different from that which we spoke of at the beginning. One of the mysteries of the Christian life is that it is realized in the polarity between solitariness and fellowship in the presence of God. Neither must be lacking. One who craves fellowship without solitariness falls into impersonality and lapses into a religious standardization that is far more legalistic than technical standardization. And one who seeks solitude without fellowship is close to the abysses of pride or despair. All pastoral care must be aware of this polarity.

Yes, flee from your solitariness into the fellowship and seek out your brother; but also stand alone before the Lord! Common worship and common prayer are indispensable to the Christian life; but the solitary hour of prayer is equally indispensable. There are many things that a pastor has to struggle through and suffer through in utter solitariness in the presence of God, and a man who has to confide everything to others and cannot keep anything to himself is no pastor of souls. The words we speak in pastoral care become worn, impotent, and feeble if they are not repeatedly cleansed and strengthened and renewed in the solitude of prayer. The brotherly counsel of others is good, but Jesus can care for our souls in silence and solitude too. Quiet listening to the Word is part of common study of the Scriptures, and it may well be that I can learn more about how to deal with modern secularized men from this solitary, face-to-face conversation at the well of Jacob (John 4) than from a whole course of lectures on this problem, just as all the psychology in the world cannot give to me the key to the knowledge of men that I find in John 1:4, 9: "In him was life, and the life was the light of men. The true light that enlightens every man was coming into the world." The way to learn other men's hearts is to know one's own heart in that place of solitude before God.

—*Hermann Dietzfelbinger* (178)

* * *

The Seal of Confession

Anybody who knows how strong is the compulsion to secrecy that is inherent in sin understands what it really means to speak out, confess, and reveal oneself in confession.

The deeper the consciousness of sin the less adequate is the general confession or private acknowledgment of sin to God in prayer, and the more elemental becomes the need to confide in a brother. Any baptized person may be called to perform this ministry, and anyone who is asked to receive confession is always in this case a rightly called minister of the church. In this instance the ordained minister differs from a brother who is called *ad hoc* only by reason of the fact that his calling is a fundamental one and that at his ordination he publicly pledged himself to keep the seal of confession.

One does not ask just any Christian brother to perform this ministry, but only one in whom we have confidence, one whom we believe is really able to receive the confession and keep silence. The worth of the true pastor of souls is measured, not merely by the gift of finding the right thing to say at the right moment, but no less by the great gift of silence. Only one who can keep the seal of silence deserves confidence. The evangelical pastor's obligation to preserve silence is always jeopardized by his marriage, since it is natural that a spouse should share everything with his partner. It is also endangered by the silly, vain desire to pass on to fellow ministers and other people tidbits from one's store of pastoral experience, and not least by the pulpit, which the imprudent preacher makes into a place of indiscretion.

But back of this temptation of the pastor to break the seal of silence there is something else. One who really receives and keeps secret what he has learned in the confessional finds that he has been called to bear a burden. A load has been dropped upon him. He may be shocked, disgusted, and outraged by what is revealed to him, and he will have to realize again and again that ultimately it is not his own ability to bear burdens that counts. He bears them in Christ's name. He should bear them because Christ took it all upon himself. He should bear them; he must even accept not only the tensions which arise from the understandable temptation to throw off the burden upon others, possibly making it public, but also those which arise from any sort of legal or ministerial obligations. Hearing confessions is hard because it can lead the pastor into conflicts of conscience, for which he must be prepared and which he must absolutely endure.

–Wolfgang Trillhaas (179)

* * *

FOR SELF-EXAMINATION

"We will give ourselves over continually unto the ministry of the word, and to prayer" (Acts 6:4).

Have I done so this day?

Have I been mindful of the duties of my proper calling?

Do I make it the great concern of my life to promote the eternal interest of my flock?

Have I read the Holy Scriptures, in order to instruct my people, and to preserve them from error?

Do I call upon God for the true understanding of the Holy Scriptures?

Do I deny all ungodliness and worldly lusts, so as to be an example unto others? . . .

Have I been charitable and kind to poor and needy people?

Do I make the gospel the rule of my private life, and Jesus Christ my pattern?

Do I endeavor after holiness??

Do I live as in God's presence?

Is my conversation unblamable?

Do I give the praise of this to God through Jesus Christ?

–Thomas Wilson (180)

* * *

The Mirror

Dear John:

So you want to be a pastor of souls? Absolutely necessary for this ministry is a mirror. But you, I know, are not fond of gazing into a mirror. And yet there are a lot of people who like to stand in front of a mirror because they are pleased with themselves. But you and I get no pleasure from looking into the mirror. I do not mean the mirror in the bathroom, but rather that unerring mirror of the Word of God that reflects the true picture of what we are. It reveals that latent anger within us as the source of murder. It exhorts us not to let the sun go down on our wrath (Eph. 4:26). And we take our hatred into the night and our dreams and drag it around with us for weeks. And our hard and heartless words? The Lord would have our hearts free of dust and dirt. And they are like an untidied drawer into which we stuff all kinds of rubbish to keep ourselves and others from seeing it. But we reproach others for their secret disorderliness. God's Word bids us to set our light on a stand that it may give light to all in the house (Matt. 5:15). But does our light shine in our own home? Sometimes in our homes one leaves the other to sit alone in the dark! How can one "who does not know how to manage his own household" (I Tim. 3:5) sow and cultivate love in the congregation? A look into that mirror paralyzes one's joy in this ministry. "Sweep before your own door!" You say it to yourself, and I say it to myself too.

My dear friend, don't be troubled. Don't avoid this mirror. If you shun its judgment, your pastoral care of souls will die, no matter how zealously you busy yourself with it. Then the worm is gnawing at its root. If you stand before the person who seeks your counsel as a paragon, how is the poor duffer going to have any trust in you? And do you not arouse his trust when he senses the fact that you too have to struggle and fight, that you too have your falls and the Lord's grace must constantly be picking you up again? We do not need to wash our dirty laundry in public every day, but in certain cases we can let those who seek our counsel know that their sin is also our sin. How can we ever hear confessions rightly without confessing ourselves? The other person gives us the key to his heart when we give him the key to ours. At the close of the service the pastor does not urge the congregation to pray for him simply to make a show of the terrific strain of his office, but because he too is not only a sinful man in general but also has to fight against evil every day and, like all the rest of us, always needs the prayers of the congregation. There is a legend of a little girl who had an ugly hump on her back, so deformed that she was either ridiculed or pitied by everybody. But when she died it turned out that the ugly hump concealed angels' wings. May it not be that all the ugly things in our lives that dismay us have in them angels' wings? We can make everything, literally everything, the subject of our prayer. So a look into the mirror of God's Word can become a blessing for us and for those to whom we minister.

My dear friend, don't avoid the mirror of the Word of God. If you do, your pastoral care is done for. Then you have ceased to care for your *own* soul. After all, it is not merely our own nature but the face of our Lord Christ that gazes questioningly at us from this mirror. And what more salutary could happen to us than this? His gaze kills our pride. Only a humble man can really be a pastor. His Word summons us to resist all evil to the death. Only a fighter can be a real pastor. The Lord's presence promises us forgiveness and gives us the courage again and again to make a new beginning. But how could our spirits be glad without his promise : "Behold, I make all things new." His Word is a call of alarm that keeps us from stiffening into self-satisfied security and saves us from the danger of fleeing into a deceitful double life. How often we try to put our best wares in the show-window while back of the counter there is nothing but junk. The mirror of God preserves us from being phony paragons. Real pastoral care requires truth. And that's what God's mirror gives us, in order that we two may care for others with unflinching and joyful hearts.

So we two shall hold on, you, dear John, and your friend
who greets you,   Christian

–Christian Lendi-Wolff (181)

* * *

Tailors in Rags

Many a tailor goes in rags, that maketh costly clothes for
others; and many a cook scarcely licks his fingers, when he
hath dressed for others the most costly dishes. Believe it,
brethren, God never saved any man for being a preacher, nor
because he was an able preacher; but because he was a justified, sanctified man, and consequently faithful in his Master's
work. Take heed therefore to yourselves first, that you be
that which you persuade your hearers to be, and believe that
which you persuade them daily to believe; and have heartily
entertained that Christ and Spirit which you offer unto others.
He that bid you love your neighbors as yourselves, did imply
that you should love yourselves, and not hate and destroy
yourselves and them.   *–Richard Baxter* (182)

* * *

The Blessing

I had a letter today from an ecclesiastic. He told me of
the death of his mother—a lovely old lady who was known
to me. The ecclesiastic bemoaned the fact that she died before
he could arrive to give her his blessing. Poor man! What a
condition of mind! Is it possible that he failed to realize how
he needed *her* blessing!   *–H. R. L. Sheppard* (183)

* * *

Starving Cooks

Take heed to yourselves, lest you should be void of that
saving grace of God which you offer to others, and be strangers

to the effectual workings of that gospel which you preach; and lest while you proclaim the necessity of a Saviour to the world, your own hearts should neglect him, and you should miss of an interest in him and his saving benefits! Take heed to yourselves, lest you perish, while you call upon others to take heed of perishing! and lest you famish yourselves while you prepare their food. Though there be a promise of shining as the stars to those that turn many to righteousnes (Dan. 12:3), that is but on the supposition that they be first turned to it themselves: such promises are meant, *"caeteris paribus, et suppositis supponendis."*

—*Richard Baxter* (184)

* * *

A man who has not tracked down the "old man" in all his erring ways and spied out his lies and self-deceptions, a man who does not know thoroughly the whited sepulcher of his own righteousness and the falsity of natural virtue cannot remove the blinds from others' eyes. A man who has not himself begun and continued daily to struggle with his flesh, a man who has not felt the helping hand of the Lord in the power of his holy Word and the sacraments, that man may go on talking and indulging in phrases about it, but no anxious heart will find peace through it. One who has not rested on the Lord's bosom and does not know the joy of his love cannot invite others to come and taste and see how merciful the Lord is. . . . It is quite unjustifiable to hold rationalism and its adherents in contempt when our own hearts have not been liberated from it. Only one who knows by experience that the Holy Spirit can make children of God out of poor sinners can also rightly beg and urge, lead and guide others to walk the same way.

—*Karl Büchsel* (185)

* * *

We have the same sins to kill, and the same graces to be quickened and corroborated, as our people have: we have greater works than they to do, and greater difficulties to overcome, and no less necessity is laid upon us; and therefore we have need to be warned and awakened, if not to be instructed, as well as they. *—Richard Baxter* (186)

* * *

He who can tell men what God hath done for his soul is the likeliest to bring their souls to God. Hardly can he speak *to* the heart who speaks not *from* it; *Si vis me flere,* etc. How can a frozen-hearted creature warm his hearers' hearts and enkindle them with the love of God? But he whom the love of Christ constrains, his lively recommendations of Christ and speeches of love shall sweetly constrain others to love him. Above all loves it is most true of this, that none can speak sensibly of it but they who have felt it. Our most elegant pulpit orators, yea, speak they with the tongues of men and angels, without the experience of this love, are no fit ambassadors for Christ. *—Robert Leighton* (187)

* * *

Penitence

Penitence must be the deep undertone of a preacher's life. No man can really see the heavenly vision, can hear the song of the seraphim, and look God in the face, without echoing the cry, "Woe is me! for I am undone; because I am a man of unclean lips . . . for mine eyes have seen the King, the Lord of Hosts." No man should dare to preach the Word of God unless by deep contrition, and sincere confession, and an earnest resolve to amend his life, his heart has been purified from sin, and his lips cleansed by the living flame of God's forgiveness. The nearer we come to the light of God's presence the darker will be the shadow of our sins. . . . This state of abiding penitence and humility will come readily to us if we are sincere in our desire to know ourselves. If we expose our soul to God, and allow the light of the Holy Spirit to shine down the long corridors of the forgotten past, and to bring to light the secrets of our hearts, the frequent inconsistencies of our lives which have so often denied the truth we have taught to others; if we remember that our present limitation and inadequacies are not chiefly due to lack of talent, but to hours of sloth from our schooldays onward, to days and years of selfishness or pride, to the refusal of the grace of the Holy Spirit in his gentle pleadings, to acquiescence in faults of temperament or of character, to the toleration of some lower standard of consecration than that which God placed before us, to the sloth or carelessness in preparation which has led to the loss of opportunity, we should not find it hard to win that habit of abiding humility and penitence which are the only appropriate vestments of a man who ventures to speak to others in God's name. This profoundly penitential memory of the past is not disabling to the preacher. The true penitence of one who is forgiven does not waste spiritual force in useless brooding, nor unnerve the soul for high endeavor. It was the secret of power in St. Paul whose loftiest songs of praise to God are accompanied and exalted by the deep undertone of the memory of his past.

> Also I ask, but ever from the praying
>> Shrinks my soul backward, eager and afraid,
> Point me the sum and shame of my betraying.
>> Show me, O Love, thy wounds which I have made!
> Yes, thou forgivest, but with all forgiving
>> Canst not renew mine innocence again;
> Make thou, O Christ, a dying of my living,
>> Purge from the sin, but never from the pain!
> So shall all speech of now and of tomorrow,
>> All he hath shown me, or shall show me yet,
> Spring from an infinite and tender sorrow,
>> Burst from a burning passion of regret:
> Standing afar I summon you anigh him,
>> Yes, to the multitudes I call and say,

"This is my King! I preach, and I deny him,
Christ! whom I crucify anew today!"

F. W. H. Myers' "St. Paul"

If we can win something of the penitence of St. Paul we may hope to know something of his power, and God can use the humble and the contrite heart. —*Paul B. Bull* (188)

* * *

A Preacher's Repentance

O Lord, I have been talking to the people;
Thought's wheels have round me whirled a fiery zone,
And the recoil of my word's airy ripple
My heart unheedful has puffed up and blown.
Therefore I cast myself before thee prone:
Lay cool hands on my burning brain and press
From my heart the swelling emptiness.

—*George Macdonald* (189)

* * *

The insincerities and the hypocrisies and the basenesses in our own characters take their true name, when we see them in the presence of Him in whom God was reconciling the world unto himself. We do not really know ourselves until we see ourselves before the cross of Christ.

When that self-revelation comes to you, do not shrink from it. You will be preaching repentance to others; how shall you preach it unless you have made trial of it yourselves? And the cross, which brings you self-knowledge, bitter and unwelcome though that self-knowledge may be, is the emblem, the pledge and token, of the reconciling love of God. It shows you your sin, but in the self-same moment it holds out to you the hope—nay, the certainty, if you will have it so—of forgiveness and a new life in God.

—*Charles Michael Jacobs* (190)

THE MINISTRY OF LISTENING
Listening, Understanding and Commanding

In this world in which all the external senses are over-excited, this world of noise, misunderstanding, suspicion, and haste, what a blessing it is to find anywhere a person who can listen, who is not deceived by appearances, but rather lets another person speak his best, who listens with a concentrated, attentive mind. It has taken psychoanalysis to impress again upon modern humanity, and to a large extent, Christianity too, the liberative value of listening.

Real listening takes time. But it is not merely an outward disposition; it also requires that one's own being be in order, at rest, that peace should be there, an inner harmony and detachment from one's own concerns. We well know that there is also a demonic caricature of this listening, a kind of listening that hankers after the secrets of others because it is motivated by lewdness and a secret lust for power, or the evil desire to feed on the heart's blood of another, or to escape one's own restlessness. Against the dangers of that caricature, from which we are never free once and for all, we must train ourselves in that genuine objectivity which is so critically important for every physician, and from time to time admonish ourselves: "Treat what is personal objectively and what is objective personally" (Heinrich Planck).

But the distinction between the objective and the personal is not the ultimate one. The standard of the holy must be added. Another person's lot, another person's trouble or guilt or joy is always something holy, because it is all of God and before God and only in his light can it be seen in its proper meaning and reference. All discussion, listening, questioning, all counseling and helping is justified only insofar as it serves to put everything under the light of God and there set to rights. What John says is pertinent in this connection also: "If we walk in the light, as he is in the light, we have fellowship with one another."

We all know the saying, "To understand all is to pardon all." This is a very dangerous half-truth. Certainly, understanding helps us to forgive. But when forgiveness comes only from understanding it usually means an abatement of the true standards, a lowering of goals, a false accommodation of the listener to the speaker; and this is the great danger that threatens all who are good listeners, who perhaps perceive what has not been expressed as with antennae that catch the finest vibrations. It is true that all lisening is an accommodation to what is heard and to the speaker. Provided that it does not contain a hidden delusion! We are dealing here with a hairline that cannot be indicated even theoretically. One can only feel it in one's conscience. Beyond this line, pastoral care becomes diplomacy, a kind of mimicry, a pose, a performance. These are harsh words, but we do well to visualize them. Here we become aware of deeply destructive powers; but light is also cast upon that great command of Jesus: "Be wise as serpents and innocent as doves." His command also contains the promise of a divine possibility, the possibility that all wisdom, all human understanding, all discernment of hidden connections can be combined with a God-given purity of heart, with simplicity. To protect ourselves and others, we must constantly fuse all our listening, discernment, sympathy, understanding, and counseling with the petition: "Make me simple, sincere, detached, gentle and quiet in thy peace."

In this way all listening becomes something other than mere passive reception. It enters into an alliance, so to speak, with "commanding." We do not mean "commanding" in the external sense of giving orders, but rather in the deep sense of faith in the victory, of knowing who the enemy is, of a call to struggle, of leading the way in all the things that really matter, and of secretly communicating power to others. Only he who commands in this sense can rightly be a listener, as perhaps only he who listens down in the depths can give

commands from the high watchtower. Listening and commanding—only the two together give promise of the great possibility that a man may not possess authority, but be authority.
—Erich Schick (191)

* * *

Listening

Christians, especially ministers, so often think they must always contribute something when they are in the company of others, that this is the one service they have to render. They forget that listening can be a greater service than speaking.

Many people are looking for an ear that will listen. They do not find it among Christians, because these Christians are talking where they should be listening. But he who can no longer listen to his brother will soon be no longer listening to God either; he will be doing nothing but prattle in the presence of God too. This is the beginning of the death of the spiritual life, and in the end there is nothing left but spiritual chatter and clerical condescension arrayed in pious words. One who cannot listen long and patiently will presently be talking beside the point and be never really speaking to others, though he be not conscious of it. Anyone who thinks that his time is too valuable to spend keeping quiet will eventually have no time for God and his brother, but only for himself and for his own follies.

Brotherly pastoral care is essentially distinguished from preaching by the fact that, added to the task of speaking the Word, there is the obligation of listening.

—Dietrich Bonhoeffer (192)

* * *

Listening to God

"Speak, Lord; for thy servant heareth." Even the very Pattern of all servants of God, Jesus Christ himself, performs his ministry only as "the Son can do nothing of himself, but what he seeth the Father do." He speaks what he has heard, and as he hears so he does. The pastor in his ministry can never be enough a listener. He is a proclaimer only to the degree that he is a listener. And he knows "how to speak a word in season to him that is weary" (Isaiah 50:4); he has "the tongue of the learned"; and this is the tongue of a disciple, the tongue of a listener and a learner. Through hearing the minister becomes a witness, not merely through experience, but by hearing with his whole being.

–Hermann Dietzfelbinger (193)

* * *

The Joy of Absolution

Twice does a minister learn beyond all question that the Bible contains the word of the Living God—once when he preaches the forgiveness of sins to the penitent, once when he sees a soul in the great straits of life lifted, comforted, and filled with peace and joy. *–John Watson* (194)

* * *

We Need our Brother

We speak to one another on the basis of the help we both need. We admonish one another to go the way that Christ bids us to go. We warn one another against the disobedience that is our common destruction. We are gentle and we are severe with one another, for we know both God's kindness and God's severity. Why should we be afraid of one another, since both of us have only God to fear? Why should we think that our brother would not understand us, when we understood very well what was meant when somebody spoke God's comfort or God's admonition to us, perhaps in words that were halting and unskilled? Or do we really think there is a single person in this world who does not need either encouragement or admonition? Why, then, has God bestowed Christian brotherhood upon us? *–Dietrich Bonhoeffer* (195)

It is altogether impossible for a pastor to exercise his ministry in joyfulness and certainty if he does so as an individual. There are no such things as theological stars and star performances. It is better to have four or five faithful members with whom the pastor prays than a hundred "interested" people who are attracted by his rhetorical abilities but disperse the next day. The pastor needs the ministry of brothers for joyfulness in his ministry, as a corrective for his calling which is always exposed to the dangers of individualism, and for the salvation of his own soul. A pastor without a real confessor simply cannot maintain his joy in the ministry.

—Hanns Lilje (196)

* * *

Of Patience

Another necessary concomitant of our work is patience. We must bear with many abuses and injuries from those that we are doing good for. When we have studied for them, and prayed for them, and besought, and exhorted them with all condescension, and spent ourselves for them, and given them what we are able, and dealt with them as if they had been our children, we must look that many should requite us with scorn, and hatred, and contempt, and cast our kindness in our faces with disdain, and take us for their enemies, because we tell them the truth; and that the more we love, the less we shall be beloved. All this must be patiently undergone, and still we must unweariedly hold on in doing good; in meekness, instructing those that oppose themselves, if God peradventure will give them repentance. If they unthankfully scorn and reject our teaching, and bid us look to ourselves, and care not for them, yet must we hold on. We have to deal with distracted men, that will fly in the face of their physician, but we must not therefore forsake the cure. He is unworthy to be a physician that will be driven away from a frantic patient by foul words.

—Richard Baxter (197)

Only he who continues in prayer will be victorious in the struggle to keep the pastoral encounter pure. Here prayer means that one makes the priestly act of setting one's listening to our neighbor as well as what he says into the context of listening and speaking to God. This listening and speaking in prayer evokes the mighty safeguard, the great aid, the liberating, penetrating, purifying clarity which must surround, permeate, and sustain the whole pastoral interview. Then the demons will be warded off, then will be created the atmosphere in which we shall meet each other without any false dependency, but in the true dependency upon him who is the Lord of this encounter, and whose one desire it is that our conversation shall become the place where we shall hear and communicate to one another his gracious and saving speech : All the wisdom we need in the care of souls is contained in Ephesians 6 : 18—

"Pray at all times in the Spirit, with all prayer and supplication. To that end keep alert with all perseverance, making supplication for all the saints, and also for me, that utterance may be given me in opening my mouth boldly to proclaim the mystery of the gospel . . . that I may declare it boldly, as I ought to speak."   *—Eduard Thurneysen* (198)

* * *

Mirror for Ministers

Am I humble enough to let members of my congregation speak the Word of God to me?

Have I heard confessions and granted absolution lightly?

Have I been chaste in thought and word and deed in all my associations?

Have I allowed the relationship between members or confessants to their pastor to become a human dependence?

Have I tolerated without protest generally known conditions of moral laxity within my congregation?

Have I been the advocate of an unhealthy, ungodly, and pernicious prudery?

Have I left the young people of my congregation to their own devices and views in matters of sex?

Have I knowingly tolerated social conditions in my community that contribute to the breakdown of marriage and family life?

Have I sufficiently declared and magnified in my preaching and teaching the greatness of God's gift of marriage, children, and the family?

Have I kept the seal of confession?

Have I been just as candid in private counselings as I have been in the pulpit?

Have I endeavored to help sinners into the right way?

Have I given comfort where God's comfort was not due?

—*Max Lackmann* (199)

THURSDAY

The Minister as Pastor

* * *

"Simon, son of John, do you love me?"
—"Yes, Lord; you know that I love you."
He said to him, "Tend my sheep."

John 21:16

———

Tend the flock of God that is your
charge, not by constraint but willingly,
not for shameful gain but eagerly, not as
domineering over those in your charge but
being examples to the flock. And when the
chief Shepherd is manifested you will
obtain the unfading crown of glory.

I Peter 5:2–4

PORTRAIT OF THE PASTOR

The Good Pastor

And this excellent man did not think his duty discharged by only reading the church prayers, catechising, preaching, and administering the sacraments seasonably; but thought—if the law or the canons may seem to enjoin no more—yet that God would require more than the defective laws of man's making can or do enjoin; the performance of that inward law, which almighty God hath imprinted in the conscience of all good Christians, and inclines those whom he loves to perform. He, considering this, did therefore become a law to himself, practicing what his conscience told him was his duty, in reconciling differences, and preventing lawsuits, both in his parish and in the neighborhood. To which may be added, his often visiting sick and disconsolate families, persuading them to patience, and raising them from dejection by his advice and cheerful discourse, and by adding his own alms, if there were any so poor as to need it; considering how acceptable it is to almighty God, when we do as we are advised by St. Paul (Gal. 6:2), "Help to bear one another's burden," either of sorrow or want; and what a comfort it will be, when the Searcher of all hearts shall call us to a strict account for that evil we have done, and the good we have omitted, to remember we have comforted and been helpful to a dejected or distressed family.   —*Izaak Walton* (200)

* * *

We were weary, and we
Fearful, and we, in our march,
Fain to drop down and die.
Still thou turnedst, and still
Beckonedst the trembler, and still
Gavest the weary thy hand!
If, in the paths of this world,
Stones might have wounded thy feet,

Toil or dejection have tried
Thy spirit, of that we saw
Nothing! To us thou wert still
Cheerful, and helpful, and firm.
Therefore to thee it was given
Many to save with thyself;
And, at the end of the day,
O faithful shepherd! to come,
Bringing thy sheep in thy hand.

—*Matthew Arnold* (201)

* * *

The Good Parson

The parson of a country town was he
Who knew the straits of humble poverty;
But rich he was in holy thought and work,
Nor less in learning as became a clerk.
The word of Christ most truly did he preach,
And his parishioners devoutly teach.
Benign was he, in labors diligent,
And in adversity was still content—
As proved full oft. To all his flock a friend,
Averse was he to ban or to contend
When tithes were due. Much rather was he fond,
Unto his poor parishioners around,
Of his own substance and his dues to give,
Content on little, for himself to live.
Wide was his parish, scattered far asunder,
Yet none did he neglect, in rain, or thunder.
Sorrow and sickness won his kindly care;
With staff in hand he traveled everywhere.
This good example to his sheep he brought
That first he wrought, and afterwards he taught.
This parable he joined the Word unto—
That, "If gold rust, what shall iron do?"

For if a priest be foul in whom we trust,
No wonder if a common man should rust!
And shame it were, in those the flock who keep
For shepherds to be foul yet clean the sheep.
Well ought a priest example fair to give,
By his own cleanness, how his sheep should live.
He did not put his benefice to hire,
And leave his sheep encumbered in the mire,
Then haste to St. Paul's in London Town,
To seek a chantry where to settle down,
And there at least to sing the daily mass,
Or with a brotherhood his time to pass.
He dwelt at home, with watchful care to keep
From prowling wolves his well-protected sheep.
Though holy in himself and virtuous
He still to sinful men was piteous,
Not sparing of his speech, in vain conceit,
But in his teaching kindly and discreet.
To draw his flock to heaven with noble art,
By good example, was his holy art.
Nor less did he rebuke the obstinate,
Whether they were of high or low estate.
For pomp and worldly show he did not care;
No morbid conscience made his rule severe.
The lore of Christ and his apostles twelve
He taught, but first he followed it himself.

—*Geoffrey Chaucer, tr. by H. C. Leonard* (202)

The Pattern of the Pastor

In the study of a very fallible and unworthy minister, and above the desk where he writes his sermons, hangs Andrea Del Sarto's head of Christ, the face of One whose passion is over, and who is now alive for evermore, full of peace and majesty. This minister has come to use that picture as a sacrament, in which the mind of the Lord is declared to his heart and conscience with secret approvals and saving judgments. If he consults his own ease and refuses some irksome duty, or through fears of man keeps back the wholesome truth, then is the face of the Master clouded with sadness and disappointment; if, being moved by the Divine Grace, that minister has during the day humbled himself or done some service at a cost to one of the disciples, then is the face lit up with joy, and the eyes of love bid him welcome on his return. The Christ is not in the poor print but in that minister's soul, and it is within we find the Lord before whom at every moment we stand to be approved or condemned. If God give us success, then to the feet of Jesus let our sheaves be carried; if it be his will we should fail, to the same dear Lord let us flee, who knows what it is to see his life fall into the ground and disappear. From his words let us learn to preach; from his example let us learn to serve; in his communion let us find our strength, comfort, peace, whom not having seen we love, to whom we shall one day render our account.

—*John Watson* (203)

The Excellent Herbert

At which time of Mr. Herbert's coming alone to Bemerton, there came to him a poor old woman, with an intent to acquaint him with her necessitous condition, as also, with some troubles of her mind; but after she had spoken some few words to him, she was surpriz'd with a fear and that begot a shortness of breath, so that her spirits and speech fail'd her; which he perceiving, did so compassionate her, and was so humble, that he took her by the hand, and said, Speak, good mother, be not afraid to speak to me; for I am a man that will hear you with patience; and will relieve your necessities too, if I be able; and this I will do willingly, and therefore, mother, be not afraid to acquaint me with what you desire. After which comfortable speech, he again took her by the hand, made her sit down by him, and understanding she was of his parish, he told her, he would be acquainted with her, and take her into his care: And having with patience heard and understood her wants (and it is some relief for a poor body to be but hear'd with patience) he like a Christian clergyman comforted her by his meek behavior and counsel; but because that cost him nothing, he reliev'd her with money too, and so sent her home with a cheerful heart, praising God, and praying for him. Thus worthy, and thus lowly, was Mr. George Herbert in his own eyes: and thus lovely in the eyes of others.

—*Izaak Walton* (204)

* * *

The Village Preacher

Near yonder copse, where once the garden smiled,
And still where many a garden-flower grows wild;
There, where a few torn shrubs the place disclose,
The village preacher's modest mansion rose.
A man he was to all the country dear,
And passing rich with forty pounds a year;
Remote from towns he ran his godly race,
Nor e'er had changed, nor wished to change, his place;
Unpracticed he to fawn, or seek for power,
By doctrines fashioned to the varying hour;
Far other aims his heart had learned to prize,
More skilled to raise the wretched than to rise.
His house was known to all the vagrant train;
He chid their wanderings, but relieved their pain;
The long-remembered beggar was his guest,
Whose beard descending swept his aged breast;
The ruined spendthrift, now no longer proud,
Claimed kindred there, and had his claims allowed;
The broken soldier, kindly bade to stay,
Sat by the fire, and talked the night away,
Wept o'er his wounds, or, tales of sorrow done,
Shouldered his crutch and showed how fields were won.

Pleased with his guests, the good man learned to glow,
And quite forgot their vices in their woe;
Careless their merits or their faults to scan,
His pity gave ere charity began.

Thus to relieve the wretched was his pride,
And e'en his failings leaned to virtue's side;
But in his duty prompt at every call,
He watched and wept, he prayed and felt for all;
And, as a bird each fond endearment tries
To tempt its new-fledged offspring to the skies,
He tried each art, reproved each dull delay,
Allured to brighter worlds, and led the way.

Beside the bed, where parting life was laid
And sorrow, guilt, and pain by turns dismayed,
The reverend champion stood. At his control
Despair and anguish fled the struggling soul;
Comfort came down the trembling wretch to raise,
And his last faltering accents whispered praise.

At church, with meek and unaffected grace,
His looks adorned the venerable place;
Truth from his lips prevailed with double sway,
And fools, who came to scoff, remained to pray.
The service past, around the pious man,
With steady zeal, each honest rustic ran;
Even children followed with endearing wile,
And plucked his gown to share the good man's smile.
His ready smile a parent's warmth expressed;
Their welfare pleased him, and their cares distressed:
To them his heart, his love, his griefs were given,
But all his serious thoughts had rest in heaven.
As some tall cliff that lifts its awful form,
Swells from the vale, and midway leaves the storm,
Though round its breast the rolling clouds are spread,
Eternal sunshine settles on its head.

–*Oliver Goldsmith* (205)

The Pastor's Credentials

A Christian man is a perfectly free lord of all, subject to none.
A Christian man is a perfectly dutiful servant of all, subject
to all.

—Luther (206)

* * *

Pastoral Authority

Genuine spiritual authority is to be found only where the
ministry of hearing, helping, bearing, and proclaiming is
carried out. Every cult of personality that emphasizes the
distinguished qualities, virtues, and talents of another person,
even though these be of an altogether spiritual nature, is
worldly and has no place in the Christian community. The
desire we so often hear expressed today for "episcopal figures,"
"priestly men," "authoritative personalities" springs frequently enough from a spiritually sick need for the admiration
of men, for the establishment of visible human authority,
because the genuine authority appears to be so unimpressive.
There is nothing that so sharply contradicts such a desire as
the New Testament itself in its description of a bishop (I Tim.
3:1 f). One finds there nothing whatsoever with respect to
worldly charm and the brilliant attributes of a spiritual personality. The bishop is the simple, faithful man, sound in faith
and life, who rightly discharges his duties to the church. His
authority lies in the exercise of his ministry. In the man himself there is nothing to admire. *—Dietrich Bonhoeffer* (207)

* * *

His people are ever in the pastor's heart, although this may
not appear in his ordinary manner. He claims identity with
them in their joy and sorrow and endless vicissitudes of life.
No friend is blessed with any good gift of God but he is also
richer. No household suffers loss but he is poorer. If one stand
amid great temptation he is stronger; if one fall he is weaker.

348

When anyone shows conspicuous grace the pastor thanks God as for himself; when anyone refuses his call he is dismayed, counting himself less faithful. He waits eagerly to see whether one who groped in darkness has been visited by the light from on high, whether another, who seemed to have gone into a far country, has set his face towards the Father's house. One family he watches with anxiety, because he does not know how they will bear a heavy stroke of adversity, and another with fear lest rapid success in this world may wean their hearts from God. He trembles for this merchant lest he fall below the rule of Christ and do things which are against conscience; he rejoices over another who has stood fast and refuses to soil his hands. He inquires on every hand about some young man of whom he expects great things; he plans how another may be kept from temptation. One thing he cannot do: criticize his people or make distinctions among them. Others, with no shepherd heart, may miss the hidden goodness; he searches for it as for fine gold. Others may judge people for faults and sins; he takes them for his own. Others may make people's foibles the subject of their raillery; the pastor cannot because he loves. Does this interest on the part of one not related by blood or long friendship seem an impertinence? It ought to be pardoned, for it is the only one of the kind that is likely to be offered. Is it a sentiment? Assuredly, the same sublime devotion which has made Jesus the Good Shepherd of the soul. If the pastoral instinct be crushed out of existence between the upper and lower millstones of raging sensationalism and ecclesiastical worldliness, then the Christian church will sink into a theological club or a society for social reform: if it had full play we might see a revival of religion more spiritual and lasting than any since the Reformation.   —*John Watson* (208)

* * *

The pastor should also rule the congregation, but the kingdom of God is not of this world and therefore it is to be ruled through the power of truth and the strength of cross-bearing love. He must guard the congregation not with the brittle sword made by human hands but with the ever victorious sword of the Word of God and with intercessory prayer to the Lord who has purchased the flock with his blood and who said, "Neither shall any man pluck them out of my hand" (John 10:28). He must lead the congregation into green pastures and feed it with the bread of life and the water of life which is the Word of God. He must also sit in constant judgment over the congregation, for he must preach him who says: He that believeth not in me is judged already, because he hath not believed in the name of the only-begotten Son of God; but he that believeth in me will not be condemned, for he has received the forgiveness of all his sins (John 3:18). The shepherd must not only feed and foster and guard the congregation; he must also seek the lost and follow after the erring until he find them. He must lift up his voice in the wilderness and plead and call, not as an indifferent hireling, but as a mother calls when she seeks her child. With heartfelt love for the souls of the erring he must plead and admonish. He must know that every soul that goes astray unwarned will be required at his hands. When a member of the flock is smitten half-dead by him who is a murderer and a liar from the beginning and left lying robbed, half-dead in the wilderness, he dare not pass by on the other side, but must wash his wounds with the wine of truth, ease him with the oil of grace, and also lead him home to the inn of Him who is the sole true Host of the house of God. He must have tears for Jerusalem even when it knows not the things which belong unto its peace. He who so waits on his ministry may call himself a pastor and be called a pastor, and he who sincerely desires to do so, but feels his shortcoming, may bear the name to his humiliation as a constant spur and thorn to make him pursue it that he may become so.

—Karl Büchsel (209)

It is our God-appointed office to lead men and women who are weary and wayward, exultant or depressed, eager or indifferent, into "the secret place of the Most High." We are to help the sinful to the fountain of cleansing, the bond slaves to the wonderful songs of deliverance. We are to help the halt and the lame to recover their lost nimbleness. We are to help the broken-winged into the healing light of "the heavenly places in Christ Jesus." We are to help the sad into the sunshine of grace. We are to help the buoyant to clothe themselves with "the garment of praise." We are to help redeem the strong from the atheism of despair. We are to help little children to see the glorious attractiveness of God, and we are to help the aged realize the encompassing care of the Father and the assurance of the eternal home.

—J. H. Jowett (210)

* * *

To have a cure of souls . . . is the highest task to which any minister can be called. To stand in the pulpit on Sunday and see the eager and expectant faces of the people turned toward you, and know they have come for worship and for the bit of bread that you have been preparing for them in the week; to feel as you look at them : "These are my people"; to know that in all the great hours of their life, when they want to be wed, when a child is born into their home, when trouble comes, when the doctor is going in and out, when bereavement robs them of every scrap of joy — to know that in that hour the door is open, and you not only may go but you must go; that the cry of their heart then is for their minister . . . to dwell upon that is to know a joy which, to my mind, not even the unquestioned delights of scholarly research can surpass. To receive the confidence of people, to know the secrets they have told to no other living soul; to blush with them over their sins and exult with them when the sin is flung under the table; to know their private affairs and to be the sharer of their highest ideals, is to have a joy of which not one of us is really worthy.

—*W. E. Sangster* (211)

* * *

Speaking of "the shepherds abiding in the field, keeping watch over their flock by night" (Luke 2:8):—

I would wish, that all clergymen, curates, parsons, and vicars, the bishops and all other spiritual persons would learn this lesson by these poor shepherds; which is, to abide by their flock, and by their sheep — to tarry among them — to be careful over them — not to run hither and thither, after their own pleasure, but to tarry by their benefices, and feed their sheep with the food of God's word, and to keep hospitality, and so to feed them, both body and soul. For I tell you, these poor unlearned shepherds shall condemn many a stout and great learned clerk: for these shepherds had but the care and charge over brute beasts, and yet were diligent to keep them and to feed them; and the others have the care over God's lambs, which he bought with the death of his Son, and yet they are so careless, so negligent, so slothful over them; yea, and the most part intendeth not to feed the sheep, but they long to be fed by the sheep: they seek only their own pastimes, they care for no more. But saith Christ to Peter—What said he? "Peter, lovest thou me?" Peter made answer, Yes. "Then feed my sheep." And so the third time he commanded Peter to feed his sheep, etc.

—*Hugh Latimer* (212)

* * *

The ancient form of the congregational "Call" in the Scottish church is significant: "We do heartily invite, call and entreat you to undertake the office of a pastor among us and the charge of our souls." This is the task to which a minister was summoned, and these were the terms on which the office and its emoluments were put into his hands; so if he leaves this work unattempted he is something worse than a lazy minister, he is a dishonorable, pledge-breaking man. And this Scottish form of "call" represents the general demand of all the churches, and it is surely clear that anyone who "undertakes the charge of men's souls" has pledged himself to a profession in which the initiative must always lie with him. The shepherd is not free to recline at his ease, waiting for some express summons; and in the shepherding of men none are in such grievous need of tendance as those who would never think of asking for it. In the background of the true pastor's mind there should always be the image of One who did not need to be sought but himself came seeking; for it is in the name of him who made himself of no reputation and who for our sakes became poor that all our ministry has to be exercised.

—William Malcolm Macgregor (213)

* * *

Some, on the contrary, undertake the charge of the flock, but wish to be so free for spiritual occupations, as not to give any time at all to external matters. Now, when such people wholly neglect to attend to what pertains to the body, they afford no help to their subjects. It is no wonder that their preaching is disregarded for the most part, for while chiding the deeds of sinners, and not giving them the necessities of the present life, their words certainly do not find sympathetic listeners. Doctrine taught does not penetrate the minds of the needy, if a compassionate heart does not commend it to the hearts of hearers; but the seed of the word does germinate promptly, when the kindness of a preacher waters it in the hearer's heart. Therefore, that the ruler may be able to plant within, he must also, with irreproachable intention, make provision for what is external. Let pastors, then, give their entire devotion to the inner life of their subjects, yet not neglect to provide for the exterior life also. *—Gregory the Great* (214)

Sometimes the pastor receives a sudden impulse to go to a certain house, and whether it come to him in his room or on the street, he obeys it with all possible speed. On the way he will sometimes reproach himself because he may be going on a needless errand, and he will be abashed on the doorstep because he has no excuse for calling. He needs none, as it appears, for he discovers in nine cases out of ten that he is needed in that house, and that his arrival is considered a providence. It is really something higher and finer—a guidance of the Chief Shepherd by the inward light of his Spirit. The pastor is convinced that if he had been more sensitive to the divine touch, and more watchful for the divine lead, he might have cared for the sheep with surer timeliness, and he remembers with regret many instances when Jesus called and he did not answer.

Telepathy is not a dream nor an imposture; it is a fact within the Body of Christ, whose members suffer one with another, through the Risen Head, who suffers with us all.

—John Watson (215)

* * *

Christ's Curates

Lest you be overwhelmed with the greatness of your task, remember no church is given to any man without the Saviour of the church and of him. After all it is Christ's church more than yours. He is the real Pastor of every real church, and the Bishop of its minister. You are but his curate.

—Peter Taylor Forsyth (216)

When Jesus handed over to Simon Peter the charge of the Christian church, he was careful to use the possessive pronoun "my." "Feed my lambs! Tend my sheep! Feed my sheep!" It is the mightiest pronoun in the New Testament for the saving of the minister from lordliness. "Simon, son of Jonas, feed my lambs. They are not yours, they are mine, but I wish you to look after them for a little while. I do not give them to you. They belong to me. Mine they always shall remain, but I ask you to tend them for a season for me. Feed my sheep. They are not yours. Not one of them shall ever pass from my possession, but I am going away for a few days, and I leave them with you. Guard them, feed them, guide them, be good to them for my sake. Follow me. Remember my gentleness, my watchfulness, my considerateness, my patience, my compassion, my readiness to help, my swiftness to heal, my gladness to sacrifice. Be the kind of shepherd to my lambs and my sheep that I have been to you. Follow me!"

—Charles Edward Jefferson (217)

* * *

CLOSE TO THE CHIEF SHEPHERD

The really vital question of the ministry is that every individual shepherd be constantly and earnestly concerned to remain in immediate contact with the Chief Shepherd, from whom he has received his office and to whom he will one day be accountable for it. . . . Only daily, direct encounter with the Chief Shepherd will keep the shepherd alert to the cares and needs of his flock. Only this will carry him across the abyss of proud or conceited self-satisfaction on the left or the abyss of tedium and resignation on the right. The shepherd needs the Chief Shepherd; if he is no longer conscious of this, if he constructs his own ministry, he is already lost.

For pastors, therefore, it must again become simply a matter of course that there shall be time set aside for daily Scripture reading and daily prayer, and this not only in the form of general family worship. The pastoral ministry requires pastoral study of the Scriptures and pastoral prayer. This is not merely a pious pastime which a few pastors indulge in alongside of their ministry. Because of his office and for the sake of his office the pastor must study the Bible. When a man knows of no more than texts of the pericopes and Bible class lessons on which he has to speak to the congregation it will soon be found, when his work is objectively tested, that he cannot preach rightly on these texts either.

And for the sake of his office the pastor must continue in prayer. He cannot be a real pastor to the endangered and suffering in his congregation without practicing priestly intercession for them. Here, too, there is a deep gulf between pastoral care with prayer and pastoral care without prayer. Let not the pastor tell himself that he is praying "without ceasing." Let him set aside a daily quiet time for Scripture reading and prayer. Many an error and scandal in the doctrine and life of our church would have been prevented if all pastors had kept this rule, if they had not allowed themselves to be led astray by the busyness of their Sunday and everyday life into the slothfulness of the inner man.

—Martin Dörne (218)

* * *

The Sheep Dog

We offer ourselves, one way or another, to try to work for God. We want, as it were, to be among the sheep dogs employed by the Lord Shepherd. Have you ever watched a good sheep dog at work? He is not an emotional animal. He goes on with his job quite steadily; takes no notice of bad weather, rough ground or of his own comfort. He seldom or never stops to be stroked. Yet his faithfulness and intimate communion with his master are of the loveliest things in the world. Now and then he looks at the shepherd. And when the time comes for rest, they are generally to be found together.

Let this be the model of your love.

—Evelyn Underhill (219)

The preacher has admiration for his peculiar reward, but the pastor has affection : if the preacher be ill there are paragraphs in the newspapers; if the pastor, there is concern in humble homes. No man in human society gathers such a harvest of kindly feeling as the shepherd of souls, none is held in such grateful memory.

—John Watson (220)

* * *

The deepest satisfaction in a minister's life is this constant, quiet, personal, and spiritual ministration to all kinds and conditions of men in every conceivable form of human need. There lies an inexhaustible source of happiness. To know it, one must idealize all these separate tasks and see in each one its eternal significance. A minister may lose the most precious part of his possible experience unless he look upon all of this as the best, the richest, the highest of all that is given to him to do. Some men serve parishes effectively by good preaching and skilful administration but have neither the will nor the ability to serve people individually. Such men never know the deepest and most subtle joys of the ministry. To the man who has once found the satisfaction of pastoral experience, nothing can compensate for its lack. To solve one human problem, though it may require days of his time, is a far more significant performance, will yield him in the end far deeper satisfaction, and will make a far greater contribution to human welfare than to stand on any eminence to be seen and known of men.

It is nothing less than sheer tragedy if through the lack of spiritual discernment, self-effacement, and love of men, a minister lose this, the crowning joy of his life. And also he loses the possibility of his deepest influence and the deepest gratitude of those to whom he ministers. To be loved, one must love much. The more one loves, the more he is loved. And the love that abides when all else has passed away is the

357

love that bears, believes, and endures all things. A minister ought to have no higher ambition than to qualify as a faithful shepherd of his flock. The word "pastor" must be his highest title of honor. Indeed, there can be no higher; for only he has fulfilled the divine commission of his Lord: "Feed my lambs, feed my sheep, not only publicly, but from house to house."

—*Raymond Calkins* (221)

* * *

LOVE FOR PEOPLE

So much pity and compassion had Friar Juniper for the poor that when he saw anyone ill clad or naked, anon he would take off his tunic, and the cowl from his cloak, and give them to poor souls such as these. Therefore the warden commanded him, by obedience, not to give away the whole of his tunic, nor any part of his habit. Now it fell out that Friar Juniper, ere a few days had passed, happened on a poor creature, well-nigh naked, who asked alms of him for love of God, to whom he said with great compassion, "Naught have I, save my tunic, to give thee; and this my superior hath laid on me, by obedience, to give to no one; nay, nor even part of my habit; but if thou wilt take it off my back, I will not gainsay thee." He spake not to deaf ears, for straightway this poor man stripped him of his tunic and went his way with it, leaving Friar Juniper naked. And when he was back at the friary, he was asked where his tunic was, and he answered, "An honest fellow took it from my back and made off with it." And the virtue of pity increasing within him, he was not content with giving away his tunic, but likewise gave books and church ornaments and cloaks, or anything he could lay hands on, to the poor. And for this reason the friars never left things lying about the friary, because Friar Juniper gave all away for love of God and in praise of him.

—*The Little Flowers of St. Francis* (222)

The Preacher's Mistake

The parish priest
Of Austerity,
Climbed up in a high church steeple
To be nearer God,
So that he might hand
His word down to His people.

When the sun was high,
When the sun was low,
The good man sat unheeding
Sublunary things.
From transcendency
Was he forever reading

And now and again
When he heard the creak
Of the weather vane a-turning,
He closed his eyes
And said, "Of a truth
From God I now am learning."

And in sermon script
He daily wrote
What he thought was sent from heaven,
And he dropped this down
On his people's heads
Two times one day in seven.

In his age God said,
"Come down and die!"
And he cried out from the steeple,
"Where art thou, Lord?"
And the Lord replied,
"Down here among my people."

—*Brewer Mattocks* (223)

* * *

The whole course of our ministry must be carried on in a
tender love to our people: we must let them see that nothing

pleaseth us but what profiteth them; and that which doeth them good doth us good; and nothing troubleth us more than their hurt. When the people see that you unfeignedly love them, they will hear anything, and bear anything, and follow you the more easily.　　　　　　　　　—*Richard Baxter* (224)

* * *

Agape

There are different ways of loving. Love of an immediate, instinctive kind seeks physical gratification. Another kind, not physical in origin, seeks ultimately to make the loved one dependent and to dominate him. An observer of human relationships will grant that this latter way of loving is the most common. Fundamentally selfish, it is a devious way of securing the upper hand; it forces, makes dependent, subjugates. But there is such a thing as genuine love which is always considerate. Its distinguishing characteristic is, in fact, regard for personal dignity. Its effect is to stimulate self-respect in the other person. Its concern is to help the one loved to become his true self. It seeks him for his own sake. In a mysterious way such love finds its purest realization in its power to stimulate the other to attain his highest self-realization. Thus its effect is to draw the other out into freedom. And if the loved one were called upon to give an account of what that love had meant to him, he would say, "I owe everything to it, most of all the fact that through it, alone, have I become my real self." A marvelous paradox! Truly, life's ultimate mystery!　　　　　　　　　—*Romano Guardini* (225)

* * *

Seeking and Saving Love

What makes the sermon popular in the right sense is the seeking and saving love of Jesus, which the pastor himself has experienced and which therefore also moves his heart and fills his mouth. The pastor who sincerely loves his congregation for the sake of the Lord Jesus is not discouraged by their sins and shortcomings. He does not lose patience, nor does he become bitter when it seems that he has worked in vain. Love hopes all things, bears all things, and endures all things. "If I speak in the tongues of men and of angels, but have not love, I am a noisy gong or a clanging cymbal." The sins that appear in the congregation must really trouble him and grip his soul, and he must not overlook his own fault in not having warned, prayed, rebuked, watched, and cried to God enough. The prayer of the pastor drives away Satan when he visits the congregation as light in a house drives away thieves. But when the pastor sleeps and does not daily bring the congregation to the throne of the Lord, then the devil can destroy the sheep unmolested. People very soon feel and note whether the pastor has a heart that burns with love or whether he is merely filling his office in a legalistic way.   —*Karl Büchsel* (226)

* * *

To Love All Men

Would Jesus Christ have mercy offered in the first place to the biggest sinners? then let God's ministers tell them so.

There is a tendency in us, I know not how it doth come about, when we are converted to condemn them that are left behind. Poor fools as we are, we forget that we ourselves were so.

But would it not become us better, since we have tasted that the Lord is gracious, so to act towards them that we may give them convincing ground to believe that we have found that mercy which also sets open the door for them to come and partake with us?

Austerity doth not become us, neither in doctrine nor in conversation. We ourselves live by grace; let us give as we receive, and labor to persuade our fellow-sinners whom God has left behind us, to follow after, that they may partake with us of grace. We are saved by grace, let us live like them that are gracious. Let all our things to the world be done in charity towards them; pity them, pray for them, be familiar with them for their good. Let us lay aside our foolish, worldly, carnal grandeur; let us not walk the streets and have such behaviors as signify we are scarce for touching the poor ones that are left behind, no, not with a pair of tongs.

Remember your Lord; he was familiar with publicans and sinners to a proverb. "Behold a gluttonous man and a wine-bibber; a friend of publicans and sinners" (Matt. 11:19). The first part, concerning his gluttonous eating and drinking, to be sure, was a horrible slander; but for the other, nothing was ever spoken truer of him by the world.

Now why should we lay hands cross on this text; that is, choose good victuals and love the sweet wine better than the salvation of the poor publican? Why not be familiar with sinners, provided we hate their spots and blemishes, and seek that they may be healed of them? Why not be fellowly with our carnal neighbors, if we take occasion to do so that we may drop and be distilling some good doctrine upon their souls? Why not go to the poor man's house and give him a penny and a scripture to think upon?   —*John Bunyan* (227)

* * *

PASTORAL OCCASIONS

The Funeral

You are standing now at the most shattering spot in the whole wide world — an open grave. There are others there with you, but how many are really standing there, how many will endure the gaping reality that opens here? The mourners, who are the most affected, are not, as it were, really standing at the open grave, but rather before their own pain, the grief of their hearts, the void that has been opened in their circle. And the rest of the funeral company, how quickly they will flee, as soon as it is over, back to their everyday life, to chatter, to the funeral baked meats, or perhaps even a bit of a spree! What are they fleeing from? They are fleeing above all from the open grave.

And in your soul too, my friend, there is something that would like to flee, something that feels how utterly impossible it is to endure standing here on the rim of the world. For down there, where they have now lowered the coffin, our world has come to an end, the world of everday and the world of heroic greatness, the world of passion and pain, of merriment and tears. This pit, little deeper than the height of a man, is the deepest abyss that eye can behold. No wonder you feel dizzy! But you dare not flinch; you dare not allow yourself to be drawn into a misty sea of emotion, you dare not take refuge in phlegmatic insensibility which would armor your feelings; you dare not do it for the others' sake and you dare not do it for your own soul's sake.

And because you refuse to flee, because you stick it out here, physically, mentally, and spiritually, death does something to you. It asks you now, as it will one day ask you in your last hour, whether you really believe that Jesus Christ is the conqueror of death. And if in your heart there is a joyful Yes, then death has lost its power; then there is no other power of eternal life, the peace of forgiveness, the omnipotence of Jesus Christ, and the death that is life. But if you cannot say this joyful Yes, if you can speak of nothing but the immortality of the soul, the grief, and the doubtful fame of the deceased, then make haste and save your soul! Then go and struggle for certainty and do not rest until you have found peace!

But the work of death is not finished with this question which it addresses to you. It is precisely when you can answer that question with the victorious joy of the redeemed that your being is in that moment changed by eternity itself. The standards are changed. You see through the material world to the eternal. It seems impossible for you to go on cherishing any thought of hate or dishonesty or evil lust; indeed, you become painfully ashamed of everything evil in your life. And though you know that the power of this new vision will not go on undiminished in the course of your days and nights, nevertheless you know far more deeply that what you have experienced here is the true, the real, the right, the authentic, and that everything else must be judged by this. Indeed, here you experience the judgment in anticipation, the judgment which is terror and blessedness; for even judgment contains within it a blessing. Blessing is found wherever truth is found. And behold, here you are standing at the door of truth as well as the door of peace.

It may be that at this place the inner reality of the soul whose body you are burying here will be revealed to you. In fear and trembling you realize what it means to commit a soul into the hands of God. Facing that soul, you feel, perhaps, a sense of shame, and thus in your own way learn what is the experience of all mourners, that the bitterest thing in our grief is regret. You regret that you did not know earlier and in his innermost being this person whose life is here brought to an end. You feel unworthy to bless his body for the last time. And in this very sense of unworthiness you realize afresh the divine commission and you know that this commission cannot be altered by men, nor you either.

It may be also that to your inner eye a veil, as it were, is removed from all the people who stand around the grave with you, as if grief had made their faces as open books. Not for long, since how should grief have power for very long over people who want to live! But that brief moment is enough to show you the real thing. And you vow to yourself that from now on you are going to walk, more than you did before, as a dying man among dying men, and in this moment you sense what great power can emerge from a right experience of death, what a saving, transfiguring, sustaining power it can be. When you stand there, how small so many things that have filled your days with labor and your nights with care become! And how other things loom up before your soul, great and mighty and with the majesty of the Eternal!

But in all this it becomes clear to you that it is not only when we suffer death that our Lord is the conqueror of death for us, but that he desires to be the conqueror of death at all times, in the midst of our life. There you sense something of the tremendous power that lies in that open secret of the Apostle: "As dying, and behold we live" (II Cor. 6:9). You begin to see how the last things invade this life; indeed, how they are actually the first things, upon which everything rests. You see, then why that last prayer of the Bible, "Amen. Come, Lord Jesus!" is in the real sense an everyday prayer, that is meant to be spoken in everyday life and will also be heard there.

It may be that not until you look back upon this grief you have borne with others, not until you reflect upon this life that is so full of riddles, that the full woe of transitoriness, the utter poverty of our death-doomed life, the infinite suffering of the world will fall upon you with concentrated impact, far more painfully than in those moments when you were actually facing all these forces—just as the terror of a sudden danger met on the road is fully felt only in recollection. Then you may look upon the whole of human destiny as John the Seer did, as a closed and sealed book, and in your way repeat his experience. "And I wept much that no one was found worthy to open the scroll or to look into it. Then one of the elders said to me, 'Weep not; lo, the Lion of the tribe of Judah, the Root of David, has conquered, so that he can open the scroll and its seven seals.' " (Rev. 5:4–5). And this truly heavenly comfort will go with you on every journey to an open grave that you still have before you and all your human pilgrimage. It will put into your heart and on your lips the praise of eternity, the new song of thanksgiving and adoration: "Worthy art thou to take the scroll and open its seals, for thou wast slain and by thy blood didst ransom men for God from every tribe and tongue and people and nation, and hast made them a kingdom and priests to our God, and they shall reign on earth."

—Erich Schick (228)

* * *

Visiting the Sick

He is always the priest, though he may not appear or act as one. For he bears as in an invisible chalice the very grace of God. He is himself the living medium by whom and through whom the healing strength of God passes into the life of the sufferer. Hence the visitation of the sick becomes one of his highest and holiest tasks. The minister to whom this visitation is a routine duty to be performed because it is expected of him; who is depressed himself by what he sees; who is not conscious of any divine mission and does not expect to accomplish any divine results, knows nothing of the possibilities that lie before him. But the one who enters this realm of suffering deeply aware of his great privilege and opportunity, who is filled with the spirit of reverence at what he finds there, who equips himself with all the resources at his command and exercises his calling with all the care and skill that knowledge of both God and man can give him, can repeat the miracles of grace of him to whom no sufferer ever looked in vain.

—Raymond Calkins (229)

* * *

Another part of our oversight lieth in visiting the sick, and helping them to prepare either for a fruitful life, or a happy death. Though this be the business of all our life and theirs, yet doth it at such a season require extraordinary care both of them and us. When time is almost gone, and they must be now or never reconciled to God, and possessed of his grace,

O how doth it concern them to redeem those hours, and lay hold upon eternal life! And when we see that we are likely to have but a few days or hours more to speak to them, in order to minister to their endless state, what man that is not an infidel or a block, would not be with them, and do all that he can for their salvation in that short space!

Stay not till strength and understanding be gone, and the time so short that you scarcely know what you do; but go to them as soon as you hear that they are sick, whether they send for you or not. —*Richard Baxter* (230)

* * *

How Luther Visited the Sick

When Dr. Luther came to visit a sick man, he spoke to him in a very friendly manner, greeted him very warmly, and first of all asked what was the matter with him, how long he had been sick, what doctor he had, and what sort of medicine had been given. Then he began to inquire whether during this illness he had been patient towards God. And after he had discovered how the sick man had borne himself while sick, and that he wished to bear his affliction patiently, because God had sent it upon him out of his fatherly goodness and mercy, and that he owned that by his sins he had deserved such visitation, and that he was willing to die if it pleased God to take him—then he began to praise this Christian disposition as the work of the Holy Ghost. And he praised the goodness of God in bringing anyone in this life to the true knowledge of himself, and to faith in Jesus Christ our Saviour, and to resignation to the will of God. He also admonished him to be steadfast in this faith by the help of the Holy Ghost, and he promised that he would diligently pray for him. If the sick then thanked him for visiting them, and said they did not deserve it, Dr. Luther used to say, it was his office and duty and he deserved no thanks for doing it; and he comforted them, telling them it would be well with them; they

367

need not fear, for God was their gracious God and Father; that he had given them good proof and assurance of this in his Word and sacraments; and, that he might redeem us poor sinners from the devil and hell, he had freely given his Son to die for us, and thus reconciled us with God.

—Table Talk (231)

* * *

Of Calls

If you would undertake it but for want of maintenance, then it is not unfitness, but poverty that is your discouragement; and that is no sufficient discouragement. We are all bound to dispose of ourselves to the greatest advantage of the church, and to take that course in which we may do God the greatest service; and we know that he hath more work for us in greater congregations than in lesser, and that the neglect of them would be the greatest injury and danger to his church and interest; and therefore we must not refuse, but choose the greatest work, though it be accompanied with the greatest difficulties and suffering. It must be done, why not by you as well as others?

—Richard Baxter (232)

* * *

Mirror for Ministers

Have I been afraid to suffer in the service of God and his church?

Have I subjected my congregation to my own indignation and love under the guise of God's wrath and Christ's love?

Have I encouraged my family in church attendance and have I had regular family worship with them?

In my congregation who cares for those who cannot or do not come to church?

Have I been a father to the poor, the oppressed, the sick, the sinners, the imprisoned?

Have I been contentious, contumacious, irascible, and uncharitable with the members of my congregation or with unbelievers?

Have I been hospitable and always ready to give help?

Have I complained and railed against my own congregation?

Have I sought out those whom the Pharisaism of my congregation has despised?

—Max Lackmann (233)

FRIDAY

The Minister as Intercessor

* * *

Like living stones be yourselves built
into a spiritual house, to be a holy priesthood, to offer spiritual sacrifices acceptable to God through Jesus Christ.

1 Peter 2:5

I urge that supplications, prayers, intercessions, and thanksgivings be made
for all men.

—1 Timothy 2:1

In the evangelical church we can speak of the ministry as a priesthood only in the context of, and in essentially the same sense as, the priesthood of all believers.

What is that sense? To be a priest in the permanently valid sense means to approach God—and particularly for others. So there is one element in the ancient priesthood that is retained in the gospel: men have mutual responsibility for the Christian condition of others. None is to stand before God only as an individual concerned only with his own petitions. All the members live by the Christian condition of the others; each one in his own Christian life has responsibility for the others, that they may be led to God through him. "Universal priesthood" definitely does not mean an individualistic dissolution of the church as a fellowship. It is just the opposite; it is the binding of every member to every other member in the inner structure of the fellowship. Priesthood, in the Reformation sense, means the "communion of saints."

—Paul Althaus (234)

* * *

Very early an interpretation pushed its way into the church according to which the primary function of the ministry ought to be that of a sacrificing priesthood, men who by virtue of their ordination were in a position to present an efficacious and purifying sacrifice. . . . It is wholly false. In other religions there is a place for sacrificing priests; indeed, there the offering of sacrifices is central in the priest's duties. But in the congregation of Christ there is no longer any place for such. The gospel signifies the great revolution in the religious world. The sacrifice which reconciles us to God is not our act, but God's. . . . Christ is the new covenant's only high priest, the offering brought by him is the sole, but also the eternally efficacious sacrifice. Until the time of Christ there was a place for the priest's continually repeated sacrifices, and for the high priest's atoning sacrifice. But with Christ the time of the high priest has come to an end. For when Christ offered himself he did it "once for all" (Heb. 7:27, 9:28). Here there is no place for a new offering. Here there is no longer any place for a sacrificing priesthood.   —*Anders Nygren* (235)

* * *

Priesthood is the possession of all Christendom, all baptized Christians. What then has priesthood to do with the ministry in particular? Every Christian is a priest according to his ability for those whom God has committed to him: man and wife in marriage for each other, father and mother for their children and others in the priesthood of the household, the teacher for his pupils, and so on. But the pastor is a priest for the whole congregation, called and set apart to perform a priestly ministry for the congregation as a whole. . . .

What does "true priesthood" mean in preaching, in the liturgy, and in the pastoral care of souls?

First, a minister is "priestly" who truly lives in the presence of God. One of Hermann Bezzel's friends said of him after his death, that he had never met a man who so impressed him as one who lived in constant, pervading consciousness of the presence of God. We have not all been given the same measure, but something of this must be discernible in every pastor. That pastor is "priestly" who goes to the altar, the pulpit, the sickbed from the sanctuary of complete concentration upon God, compelled by the hearing of his Word and earnest converse with God. Then what he does will be done in the sight of God himself, in the breath of his presence. This is what makes preaching, liturgy, pastoral visiting, and pastoral counseling "priestly." Priestly persons are those with whom we are conscious of God, who by their very being remind others of their relation to God. People want to receive from their pastors the sense of the reality of God. A sermon becomes priestly to the extent that its proclamation is sustained by the preacher's own real encounter with God and his gospel, to the measure in which the preacher, like Moses, comes from God's mountain and his speech about God flows out of the secret conversation of his heart with God.

Secondly, that minister is "priestly" who at the same time lives with and among men, like Jeremiah, like Jesus himself. To live in the presence of the Father of Jesus Christ will not lead a man away from people, but to them. If the pastor is to lead people to God he must *live* among them in every sense of the word. He must seek them out where they really live, inwardly and outwardly, as one who is himself at home where they live. To be a priest means to know the stresses and perils in the demonic bondages of these times, not merely from the outside, theoretically, apologetically, but as one who, like everybody else, is affected, captivated, and tempted by the atmosphere of despair and estrangement from God in our generation. The priestly pastor "dwells" (see John 1:14) in the midst of those who are bound by the law of this world, the imprisoned, the "outsiders." He is never the possessor of bliss, safe and secure within the walls of the church and its confession. He is acquainted with all the inner stresses and burdens of human existence, all the failures, all the guilt, because he shares it himself. It is a dreadful thing, a thing that accuses us in the sight of God, if people no longer come to the minister with their conflicts and their burdens because they can rightly say: he doesn't understand us anyhow.

—*Paul Althaus* (236)

* * *

Priest and Prophet

The prophet is compelled to go into the world, before the public; he must dare to fight, he must confront the enemy, he cannot escape having "enemies." He is obliged to draw sharp lines of difference; he must point his finger directly at those who are against God. He must openly brand those who appear to him to be ungodly and expose himself to the attacks of others whom he challenges in the name of God. In a sense he anticipates the Judgment in that he calls upon the Lord God to be the judge of the present. . . .

The priest does not need to take this way. His influence is exerted privately. The place where he works is that of brotherly and fatherly ministry in pastoral encounter. He calls people to prayer, his mission is the ministry of the pastor of souls in which heart addresses heart and conscience speaks to conscience. This may be the reason why so little is known in history concerning the work of the priestly man. Those who work in secret have no great name in public. . . .

In one of his earliest writings, Karl Barth gave classical expression to the essence of priestliness. "To uphold God's cause in the world and yet not wage war against the world; to love the world and yet be wholly faithful to God; to suffer with the world and be sensitive to its need, but at the same time open to the redeeming Word of salvation for which it is waiting; to lift up the world to God and to carry God down into the world; to be an advocate of man before God and a messenger of God who brings peace to men. . . ."

To be able to be an advocate before God he is forced away from the world into solitude before God. One who is not able to subject himself to the discipline of this solitude cannot be a priest. But at the same time he must be bound to men, keep in intimate contact with them, learn to know their cares and put himself in their place. He must be able to be a brother and a father.

But above all he must know the peace, the great reconciliation with God, the reconciliation that has been effected between God and men, which also makes peace possible among us men. . . .

Every ministry of the Word of Christ lives by the miracle of divine grace. Every ministry is a matter of the fulness from which we may draw grace upon grace, truth upon truth. Every ministry has its own peculiar task. Thus the teacher must endeavor to know the truth in its whole breadth and insist upon it in its stringency and exactitude. It cannot be otherwise than that he should become "fundamental," a stickler for principles; he must reckon with the insinuation that he is an orthodox pedant. With the prophet the situation is different again. He too serves the truth, but at any given time he must grasp the decisive point of the truth which is at stake at the great turning points in the history of the kingdom of God. By grasping it and holding to it one-sidedly, he lays hold on the decisive continuity of the past and foresees the fulfilment of the future. Thus he is able to link faith and hope together. "If you will not believe, surely you shall not be established," says Isaiah. "Faith is the assurance of things hoped for, the conviction of things not seen," reads the superscription of that great chapter of the Epistle to the Hebrews which sums up the whole of Old Testament prophecy. The Christian social worker, on the other hand, must devote himself to love. But in their work all of them are priestly, for priestliness has its place where peace is proclaimed, the peace which passes all understanding, the peace from which joy is born, which brings the presence of the Lord in the church. But this is why the "priest" too has his place and why he too must come to the fore at times, called as a "mediator" who bears witness to the great High Priest who mediated for us. —*Georg Merz* (237)

* * *

Intercession

Whether your congregation be large or small a great part of your task on its behalf lies in the realm of intercession. I do not simply mean asking God to bless your people collectively—though, of course, you will do that—I mean praying for every family, each separate soul, by name. Let me assure you that this suggestion is entirely practicable, whether you have a hundred members or two thousand. Method and system, of course, are necessary; but is there any reason why prayer should not be methodical? Take your communion roll. Use it as a directory of intercession. Single out, say, three families each day. Mention each member of these homes by name. Visualize their circumstances. Think of their work, their difficulties, their temptations. Remember very specially any who may have been growing indifferent to religious ordinances and drifting away from the church. Bear them individually upon your heart to the mercy-seat. From such concrete and particular intercession two results will follow. On the one hand, there will be a blessing for those for whom you pray. On the other hand, there will be revealed to you from time to time, even as you intercede for them, practical ways of helpfulness, new avenues of sympathetic understanding, opportunities of showing to this one or that other something of the kindness of God for Jesus' sake. And when you look into their faces on Sunday, as you lead their worship and proclaim to them afresh the all-sufficient grace of Christ, that background of your hidden intercessions, of your pleading for them name by name, will lift your words and wing them with love and ardor and reality. God will not refuse the kindling flame when secret prayer has laid its sacrifice upon the altar. And you will prove in your own experience the truth to which that great soldier of the cross, Samuel Rutherford, gave expression long ago: "I seldom made an errand to God for another, but I got something for myself."

—*James S. Stewart* (238)

* * *

The priest stands before the face of God and leads men to the face of God. Because he stands before God, he is apart from men. Because he leads men to God, he appears to men as the father and brother who seeks them out in their need and brings them to the Lord who turns away that need. Because he comes out of the sanctuary of God, he is surrounded by a power that repels all that is frivolous, all offense against God's holy law, every transgression of the limits set upon man, and therefore also a power that is able to pray with dignity, impressiveness, and force. Thus the priestly attitude appears in public worship primarily as a liturgical ministry, a ministry which is capable of stepping out of the sanctuary down into the chambers of the troubled and tempted to comfort them. With the power of prayer is the love that suffers and bears with others. The priest ministering liturgically at the altar is at the same time the devoted physician of souls, the true shepherd, the genuine pastor, and the discerning and, despite his sharp insight, understanding helper in every need, the server of our need, the deacon. For the sake of this liturgical, pastoral, and diaconal ministry and for one who is able to act in this way, the world and its allurements will become remote. The strength of his mind and senses is diverted from pleasure, he is able to fast, to practice self-denial, to turn away from this world's goods, to scorn influence and power, filled with only one concern, to remain faithful in the service in which God has placed him.

—Georg Merz (239)

* * *

Another part of our work is to guide our people, and be as their mouth in the public praises of God : as also to bless them in the name of the Lord. This sacerdotal part of the work is not the least, nor to be so much thrust into a corner as by too many of us it is. *—Richard Baxter* (240)

* * *

The pastor's private prayer is the heart of our ministry. Paul serves God in the gospel *en too pneumati mou* (Rom. 1:9), that is, in Spirit-prompted prayer. This prayer is unceasing, like breathing, and yet it has its definite hours of prayer. We know that Luther spent two hours daily in prayer. This includes the reading of the Bible : prayer originates and consists only in listening to the Word. I have heard bitter complaints that in an active parish there is no time for such meditation. Perhaps this must be overcome in faith in God, who, if we will only really hear and proclaim his Word, will give us helpers who will relieve us of other things.

How shall we read the Bible? I follow Asmussen's lectionary that covers the whole Bible in a year; but I am aware that this has value chiefly in providing only the necessary knowledge of the Bible. To what extent, in this quantitative reading, do we come to the point where we really hear, where we hear the Word spoken to us personally? One may choose shorter portions, such as the Bible readings which are available, despite their shortcomings. This hearing comes with practicing Luther's principle: *scriptura sui ipsius interpres* (Scripture is its own interpreter). Being at home with the Greek text of the whole New Testament gave earlier generations of ministers their power. The looking up of parallel passages in the Bible and concordance has opened up the Bible for many laymen, and for us, too, there is no better way of learning to hear, both scientifically and practically.

This listening passes over inevitably into prayer. Any application of the Word to ourselves can only be prayer. But prayer is "alert" to intercession. Ephesians 6:18 f: *"kai eis auto agrypnountes en pasee proskartereesei kai deesei peri pantoon toon hagioon kai hyper emou"* ("Keep alert with all perseverance, making supplication for all the saints, and also for me," RSV). And this intercession will be "alert" to the guidance of the first three petitions of the Lord's Prayer. Such intercession takes time. The concerns of our ministry, the people immediately committed to our care, the church of God, and all who serve it as pastors and teachers in the work of administration and of serving love, of the people of our own country and the whole wide world: intercession takes time, and we understand how the dying Polycarp prayed for two hours in intercession and could not stop.

For such intercession there can never be any set formula. And yet it is right that we have quite generally returned to formulated prayers, especially for corporate prayer. . . . The formulated prayer, as Bezzel said, is the "privilege of our poverty." There are needs so bitter, so deep, that there is nothing left but a Bible verse, a hymn stanza, a psalm. But in the use of formulated prayer we must again be warned of the danger of mere quantity.   —*Julius Schniewind* (241)

* * *

Altar Stairs

Much has been written about the Holy Communion and its celebration in our church, without, however, exhausting the full greatness and glory of this wonderful event. But there is one aspect of this holy act, it seems to me, about which little has been said or written, and that is, what goes on in the mind of the one who stands at the altar and administers bread and wine to the congregation.

There is good reason, it is true, for this silence concerning this interior event, for all this personal, mental experience is so insignificant compared with the objective event which is occurring there, so unpretentious in its glory, so glorious in its unpretentiousness. And yet it would seem that this personal experience must not be entirely passed over, for on the one hand it is possible that there may be some difficulties concealed here which should be brought to light, and secondly, this action at the altar is so great, so comprehensive, so exemplary of the whole compass of the life of the church and the office of the ministry that, from this point of view, even the personal experience of the one who administers the sacrament, though in itself inconsequential, becomes important. . . .

But how shall we speak of it? Whose pen can describe what happens in the soul in these holy moments? How much there is that stirs the heart, what secret tones resound, what marvelous perceptions traverse the soul!

When the congregation sings that venerable hymn of preparation,

> Lord, thou wouldst prepare us
> For thy Supper's joys;
> Be in our midst, O God,

must it not be to you, as you go to the altar with these words in your ears, as if the congregation were singing this hymn primarily for you, as if all these words, thoughts, prayers, and melodies were gathering about what you are doing? Of course, the blessing of the sacrament is not dependent upon your holiness and faithfulness—how miserable both flock and shepherd would be otherwise—and yet there sounds through the sublimely lovely melody of this noble hymn, like the sound of trumpets: "Purify yourselves, you who bear the vessels of the Lord" (Isa. 52:11), and it is as if this purification were now being performed in you, in judgment and grace, and you experience something of the greatness of that admonition born of holiest experience: "Let us go to the Table of the Lord as if we were going to meet death so that one day we may go to meet death as if we were going to the Table of the Lord."

Thus you learn in overpowering reality the deep, inner relationship between the sacrament and death. What is it that sums up this relationship? It is the experience of being known. Here at the altar, before the image of the Crucified, in the presence of the celebrating, praying, waiting congregation, before the elements of bread and wine, you are singularly awed by the realization of what it means to be known in the presence of the Eternal. Here, where the holy God makes himself known in Word and sacrament, you, too, are exposed to him in all your need and guilt, all your truancy, and all your nameless yearnings. For a few moments everything that is going on inside is brought to the surface and externals vanish in a mist. But this is also the very mystery of dying. How painful is this, how humbling, how bitter in the brief span of these moments that are filled with the thundering voice of eternity! But again how real is the presence of that holy power that again and again lifts your life beyond itself, that seems to burst its limitations and yet always draws them only tighter: the remorse of the dying. Hail, thou heavenly greeting on the altar stairs, praise to thee, thou holy Lord, for thy judgment even in the sacrament! O wonderful event in the remorse of dying!

So in these holy moments you stand alone before the altar, alone as only one power can make us men to be alone, the remorse of the dying.

But in earthly reality you are not alone, but in the midst of your congregation. And it expects of you first of all the decent conduct of the service for which you have been called. So here on the altar stairs the innermost experiences come into immediate touch with the necessity of fulfilling outward duties. How good this is and how deeply significant! Even in this is expressed a part of the nature of this sacrament, whose depths are rooted in the Holy of holies and yet reveals and veils its divine mysteries in the doings of bodily, everyday life. Therefore it is conformable to the sacrament that you should neither employ the external action to flee from the inward into the outward, nor also that you should disparage the outward for the sake of the interior event, but rather that here you should practice to maintain that holy oneness between faithfulness in little things and faithfulness in great things, that truly divine unity which the Master revealed to the disciples and committed to them when he bade them to celebrate the memory of his death with bread and wine.

Then the congregation comes to the altar, and you come face to face with one person after another, one soul, one destiny after another. There are those you know and those you do not know, those who are close to you, and those who avoid you, and perhaps those whom you avoid, young and old, believers and unbelievers, hallowed personalities and these clearly marked by sin, open faces and inscrutable faces. Who can count or name all the possibilities!

But there is one thing they all have in common; here they are all known and revealed. O the tremendous unmasking power of these altar stairs! It is as if here the person were quite involuntarily flinging back the visor that is otherwise so tightly shut and being constrained for a few moments by a hidden force to take off the mask behind which he normally hides himself from God and his neighbor. And in this holy disclosure at the sacrament, which no soul can wholly escape, there break forth hidden streams from these open visors, these unmasked faces, these souls that have somehow been stirred to the depths, all of which reach you who are there at the altar distributing bread and wine and the word of forgiveness.

How important it is for him who stands in this holy place that his attitude should be right and spiritual. What is this right attitude?

Right preaching must have, as it were, two voices, a *vox humana* and a *vox caelestia,* a human voice and a divine voice; and everything depends on whether the balance between these two voices is right. Similarly, we may say that the priest at the altar—for the administration of the sacrament is a priestly ministry—needs a double view into the depths of the human soul. This double view can be defined in the same way as the double voice. On the one hand it must be a lucid human view, the view to which nothing human is alien, which sees to the depths, candidly, calmly, completely anastigmatic, like the gaze of a physician, imperious, but very definitely not making any promises to give any human help or commands. Similar, indeed, to the view of an artist, who knows how to distinguish the essential from the nonessential, the real from the ephemeral, the hidden depths from the superficial and obtrusive, and yet in a way that avoids all meddling, personal and direct interference, even though it be only by the power of the most hidden kind of suggestion. Thus this human view is an understanding view in the broadest sense of the word, a look that throws a bridge between person and person, but not merely to create and cultivate personal relationships, but rather that the Word of God and the altar's gift may find its appointed way into the congregation.

What is the essence of the divine view? Its essence consists in our learning to see a person as God sees him. This we cannot do by nature; we learn it only to the degree in which we ourselves have been exposed by God. This means that we learn this holy way of seeing only as we live in the remorse of the dying. As we practice seeing a person as God sees him, we lay all the burdens which come to us spiritually because of him and also all the fetters that would cramp us before the throne of the Compassionate One. And this is precisely the priestly element in our ministry. Indeed, we might say that it is this that constrains us to priesthood, if we would not be lost with all the others, that we shall take what streams toward us from all these other souls and do with it what the Epistle to the Hebrews enjoins upon us:

"For we have not a high priest who is unable to sympathize with our weaknesses, but one who in every respect has been tempted as we are, yet without sinning. Let us then with confidence draw near to the throne of grace, that we may receive mercy and find grace to help in time of need" (Heb. 4:15–16).
—*Erich Schick* (242)

* * *

The secret of spiritual realism is personal judgment, personal pardon, and personal prayer—prayer as conflict and wrestling with God, not simply sunning one's self in God. There is no reality without wrestling, as without shedding of blood there is no remission. . . . For the preacher it is only serious searching prayer, not prayer as sweet and seemly devotion at the day's dawn or close, but prayer as an ingredient of the day's work, pastoral and theological prayer, priest's prayer—it is only such prayer that can save the preacher from histrionics and sentiment, flat fluency, and that familiarity with things holy which is the very Satan to so many forward apostles. . . .

A church of faith like Protestantism must always be what its chief believers make it. And these foremost and formative believers are the ministers. The real archbishops are the archbelievers. If a church has not its chief believers in the pulpit it is unfortunate. . . . The ministers are in idea the experts in faith. They are the élite of prayer. If the church is to be saved from the world it is the ministers that must do it. And how can they do it but as men pre-eminently saved from the world. And no man has the seal of that salvation on him except by action—by thought and prayer which become moral action. A man has the stamp of supernatural reality upon him only by such prayer. If another than the minister carries that stamp in any church he is its true minister.

A true minister, in the pulpit or out, does all his business in the spirit of this prayer. . . . And no man ought to take up this business unless he knows it. A preacher whose chief power is not in studious prayer is, to that extent, a man who does not know his business. . . . That of prayer *is* the minister's business. He cannot be a sound preacher unless he is a priest.

$\qquad$ —*Peter Taylor Forsyth* (243)

* * *

(1) You must pray for yourself that God would help you to bring your own spirit into a frame suitable to the work you are about to undertake—that the word you deliver may affect your own heart, or that you may first feel the holy flame you would communicate to others—that a *door of utterance* may be opened to you, and that you may speak

as becomes *the oracles of God*—that he would direct you to speak to the consciences and particular cases of your hearers, or that what you deliver may be a word in season—and that he will especially assist you in prayer, and give you *the spirit of grace and supplication*.

(2) You are to pray for your people—that their attentions may be engaged both to the evidence and importance of the things they are to hear—that God would open their hearts to give them a fair and candid reception, and that no bad prejudice may prevent the good effect of the word—that the grace of God may co-operate with his appointed means, to set home divine truths with power on their consciences —that they may be able to retain the *good seed* that is sown— that it may bring forth its proper fruit in their future lives— and finally, that their prayers for you, and behavior towards you may strengthen your hands, and make you more service-able to their souls.

—*John Mason* (244)

* * *

A True Pastor Prays

He who does not pray for the flock is not a true shepherd; intercession is at once an obligation of our office and of love. Yea, prayer is an invincible and inescapable passion of the true pastor's heart. A true shepherd prays even when he receives no answer. Nor does he pray only for his own visible activity. When Boos was pastor on the Rhine in the year 1820 he had a visit from a friend. He took him about the neighboring countryside and said: "Look around here, there is hardly a spot on this mountain where I have not many a time lain on my face and wept and prayed that the Lord would again give me the grace to open my mouth with boldness and preach his Word with success to the reviving of hearts, but I receive no answer." He could do nothing but pray. And he was heard, more than he knew. And what his biographer says is certainly true: "There is no doubt that

here in Sayn on the Rhine, the Lord did more through him
—at least in him—than anywhere else, but he would not let
him know it. It was to happen quietly." Let us mark that,
to our shame! May the Lord, however, mend his servants
and teach them in penitence to seek cleansing of their sins!
May his Holy Spirit teach them to pray!

—Wilhelm Löhe (245)

* * *

My Parish

This morning I prayed hard for my parish, my poor
parish, my first and perhaps my last, since I ask no better
than to die here. My parish! The words can't even be spoken
without a kind of soaring love. . . . But as yet the idea behind
them is so confused. I know that my parish is a reality, that
we belong to each other for all eternity; it is not a mere
administrative fiction, but a living call of the everlasting
church. But if only the good God would open my eyes and
unseal my ears, so that I might behold the face of my parish
and hear its voice. Probably that is asking too much. The
face of my parish! The look in the eyes. . . . They must be
gentle, suffering, patient eyes. I feel they must be rather like
mine when I cease struggling and let myself be borne along
in the great invisible flux that sweeps us all, helter-skelter,
the living and the dead, into the deep waters of Eternity.
And those would be the eyes of all Christianity, of all parishes—perhaps of the poor human race itself. Our Lord
saw them from the cross. "Forgive them for they know not
what they do."

—Georges Bernanos (246)

* * *

Priestly Men

The world is looking for priestly men who are not angry
with the world and also do not wail over it, but rather take

the burden of their brethren on their own hearts, men who put their whole soul into prayer for their brothers, who walk with the burden of their fellow-men's suffering upon them. Only on this painful road is there any real influence exerted from person to person. Only at this highest price can we win men. Not through police measures and not by great ideas are men constrained; only by the way in which Christ constrained us. Paul expressed the secret of his missionary success when in the first letter to the Thessalonians he looked back upon his missionary work and said, "We were ready to share with you not only the gospel of God but also our own selves, because you had become very dear to us." Whether we go out as missionaries or find our task at home, this is the feeble thanks that we can give to Him who healed our wounds: the image of his cross should be reflected in our lives.

–Karl Heim (247)

* * *

Priestliness

Only the "preacher," the servant of the Word, is able to meet the dangers that are concealed in the pontifical and the "priestish" figure, in the temptation of the abbé, even in the "ministerial attitude." The concept of priestly conduct, priestly life, priestly character is closely related to the discipline of the Word. The *presbyteros* had the responsibility of seeing to it that the Word was rightly proclaimed in the assembly. But it still is not this ministry alone, nor even this ministry primarily, which is referred to when we speak of priestly action. Nor is priestly action understood as something that is done by virtue of natural gifts or official authorization. It is rather a ministry of the divine Word which is exercised in fatherly responsibility and a discipline which claims a special dignity within the fellowship. This responsibility and this discipline is meant when we speak of "priestly conduct." This is why, in the language of our church, there is no such thing as priestly action in and of itself; the particular attitude which we call priestly is rather connected with all ministerial actions, indeed, it must be inherent in them.

A bishop must have in him something priestly; likewise the teacher of the divine Word must have something priestly about him, otherwise he becomes somewhat professorial. The evangelist must have something priestly about him, or he becomes something like a propagandist. The prophet must be priestly, or he will take on something of the agitator or the fanatic. When the church social worker lacks priestliness his ministry degenerates into professionalism; he becomes an administrator when he should be a helper. Thus the word "priestly" contains an unmistakable warning of the danger which we must guard against in our ministerial attitude. We must be fatherly, but certainly not like an abbé; watchful as a shepherd, but not clerical; mindful of the Word and its truth, as a true teacher, but not professorial; constantly ready to serve, but without being an administrator; responsible as a bishop, but always on guard against the temptation to dominate and use force. Thus in our church we mean by "priestly" that secret and mysterious power which directs a minister's action to preserve it from its dangers.

–*Georg Merz* (248)

* * *

About the office of priest in its technical sense, there will always be suspicion and debate, but there can be none about the priestly character. A Christian minister must imperatively be a priest in temper—one with his fellows, sharing their joys and fears, their hopes and sorrows and confusions, so that on their behalf he can present these before God; and, on the other side, he must be intimate with God, so that from the divine presence he can speak to men. Without this equipment he can have no strength or authority; the most regular ordination can give him none. Once for all this was declared by Jeremiah (23:22): "If ye had stood in my council ye would have caused my people to hear my words, and turned them from the evil of their doings." If his work is to be done a minister must know the way to that high and secret place where the world's turmoil is left behind and secrets are disclosed; and on all priests lacking this indispensable qualification Malachi (2:2–3) has pronounced a final sentence: "I will curse even your benedictions; I will rebuke your outstretched arm, and will spread dung upon your faces—even the dung of your feasts, and ye shall be carted away with it."

—William Malcolm Macgregor (249)

* * *

No one will have power with men who has not power with God for men. The victory may seem to be won whilst we persuade men, but it has to be previously won in the place of intercession. This place was to Jesus a place of agony and death, and there is no soul-winning without pain and sacrifice.

—James Stalker (250)

* * *

Nothing Accomplished Without Prayer

The true minister cannot forget or dispense with prayer. For what would he accomplish against Satan's power and craft by his own strength? And what can he do without God's grace and help? "Without me ye can do nothing" (John 15:5), said our Chief Shepherd, and his apostle said, "We are not sufficient of ourselves to think (much less accomplish) anything (that is, anything godly and good); but our sufficiency is of God" (II Cor. 3:5). But that must be sought of God in humble, sincere prayer for his help. To study diligently is good, but to pray diligently is still better. The holy apostles said, "We will give ourselves continually to prayer, and to the ministry of the word" (Acts 6:4). They put prayer first and then the ministry of the Word or preaching, because nobody will ever preach or accomplish anything that is good who has not first diligently prayed. Prayer can rightly be called a key to heaven, to the Scriptures, and to the human heart. Often what one seeks with great effort and much racking of one's brains and many books but still in vain is given to us quite unexpectedly after a few breaths of sincere prayer.

—Christian Scriver (251)

* * *

The Power of Intercessory Prayer

The prayer of power for his congregation is entrusted to the pastor who is called to be its shepherd. Through prayer he is the true center, the heart of the congregation; through prayer he brings them all to the throne of God; through prayer he holds them together in faith and confession, in hope and love; through prayer he stimulates prayer in the congregation, including prayer for him, of which he is greatly in need. He knows how to pray and he is sure he will be heard; therefore he must always have his congregation on his heart and daily he must take it to God in fervent supplication.

—August Vilmar (252)

* * *

Talking may be a great snare when it takes the place of prayer—and how easily it does! It is easier to talk with a man than to pray for him—in many cases.

—Forbes Robinson (253)

* * *

Persistent Prayer

We must learn to pray by praying, as we learn to read by learning the A B C. We constrain ourselves to prayer that it may constrain us, and will not let it go until it bless us and convince us that we have been heard. . . . Faithfully our prayer will strive to include every concern, from that of the smallest youngster in the care of the teachers to the sick and the aged. There is something so great in intercessory prayer, in which weariness so readily appears, that it must gladly flee to him who alone can say: I am the Good Shepherd.

—Hermann Bezzel (254)

* * *

I have prayed to be baptized into a sense of all conditions, that I might be able to know the needs and feel the sorrows of all.

—George Fox (255)

* * *

Intercession

At some time in the day or night think upon and call to mind all who are sick and sorrowful, who suffer affliction and poverty, the pain which prisoners endure who lie heavily fettered with iron; think especially of the Christians who are among the heathen, some in prison, some in as great thraldom as is an ox or an ass; compassionate those who are under strong temptation; take thought of all men's sorrows, and sigh to our Lord that he may take care of them, and have compassion, and look upon them with a gracious eye; and if you have leisure, repeat this Psalm, "I have lifted up mine eyes, etc. Paternoster. Return, O Lord, how long, and be entreated in favor of thy servants."

—The Ancren Riwle (256)

* * *

An Example of Intercession

Remember, O Lord, this congregation present, and those who are absent with good cause; have mercy upon them, and upon us, according to the multitude of thy loving-kindness; fill their garners with good things; preserve their marriages in peace and love; take care of their little ones; lead their youth; give strength to the aged; comfort the timid and afraid; bring home the scattered, restore those who have erred; and unite them all in thy holy catholic and apostolic church. Succor those who are vexed with unclean spirits; go with all traveling by sea or land; protect the widow, shelter the fatherless, deliver those in the mines; and those in exile; those in distress or poverty, or any kind of trouble. Remember all who stand in need of thy pity; those that love us; those that hate us; those who desire our prayers, unworthy though we be to offer them to thee. Remember, O Lord, all thy people, and pour upon them in abundance of thy goodness, granting all their prayers unto salvation. All those whom we have not remembered through ignorance or forgetfulness, or through the multitude of their names, do thou thyself call to mind, O God, who knowest the name and age of each even from his mother's womb. For thou, O Lord, art the Helper of the helpless; the Hope of the homeless, the Saviour of the tempest-tossed, the Harbor of the voyager, and the Physician of the sick. Be thou all things to all men. For thou knowest them all, their petitions, their dwellings, and their minds.

—Basil of Caesarea (257)

* * *

In the ministry of the gospel, prayer is no less powerful than preaching. He, therefore, who cannot pray, cannot be a perfect minister. For the things of God should be laid before men, but men's affairs before God.

—Johann Albrecht Bengel (258)

* * *

Mirror for Ministers

Have I prayed first of all for the gift of the Holy Spirit, for myself, for the congregation, for my fellow-ministers, for the whole church?

Have I regularly made priestly intercession for my congregation, for the weak, the sick, the tempted, for the young people?

Have I confused my own pious moods and feelings and those of the congregation with worship and prayer?

Have I helped erring members of the congregation to know and rightly use the name of God, the Word of God, the confession of the church, and the service of worship?

Have I given thanks for God's blessing upon me and my congregation?

Have I prayed for my enemies?

Is there strife and dissension in my own home?

Have I acknowledged my sins as such, struggled against them in the name of Jesus, the Chief Shepherd, and overcome them by the power of the Holy Spirit?

Am I ready to recognize my sins or do I make excuses for them?

Am I ready to confess that I lack everything that would make me a good shepherd, who can feed the flock of Jesus Christ?

Do I believe that I can bring all evil lusts and sins to my Lord and Chief Shepherd in confession, and in his Word receive the forgiveness of all my transgressions and the power of new life which will give me the strength not to fulfil the desires of the flesh and to feed the flock which God has committed to me?

I will believe,

for the Lord hath said:

"I will give you shepherds after my own heart, who will feed you with knowledge and understanding" (Jer. 3:15).

—*Max Lackmann* (259)

SATURDAY

The Minister as Preacher

* * *

What we preach is not ourselves, but Jesus Christ as Lord, with ourselves as your servants for Jesus' sake.

—II Corinthians 4:5

———

Faith comes from what is heard, and what is heard comes by the preaching of Christ.

—Romans 10:17

———

Preach the word, be urgent in season and out of season, convince, rebuke, and exhort, be unfailing in patience and in teaching. . . . Always be steady, endure suffering, do the work of an evangelist, fulfil your ministry.

—II Timothy 4:2, 5

IN PRAISE OF PREACHING

Among the means which the church uses to save souls, preaching stands first. It is the means by which those are called who stand afar off, and those who have been called are rendered steadfast in their calling and election. In preaching, the church does not aim to support the holy Word by human art, but the chief matter is not to hinder its power and operation and not to impose upon the Word any kind or manner of operation which does not befit it. The preacher proclaims salvation in Christ Jesus with the consciousness that not what he does, but the noble contents of the Word, must divide souls from the world and bring them near to God. Of course the preacher believes and therefore speaks, and it is a detestable contradiction to preach and yet not to believe; but a true preacher will not try to recommend the truth by imparting his faith and experience; that would be only to recommend himself; rather does he seek to bring his people to say with the Samaritans: "Now we believe, not because of thy saying; for we have heard him ourselves, and know that this is indeed the Christ, the Saviour of the world." An upright preacher does not purposely withdraw himself, nor does he purposely make him prominent, but he comes with the Word and the Word comes with him; he is a simple, faithful witness of the Word, and the Word witnesses to him; he and his Word appear like one thing. All his preaching is based upon holy peace. Even when he rebukes, and zeal for God's house eats him up, it is not the wrath of the restless world, but the wrath of the unapproachable God of peace, that burns within him. It is not he that speaks, but the Lord speaks in him and through him, and his execution of his office is worthy of the Lord. The churchly preacher always may be known by his manliness and maturity.

In great confidence in the divine Word he therefore despises every sort of machinery. He has a method, the method of simplicity. He does not seek to win friends for the Lord

Jesus Christ by means of human eloquence, nor by exciting the feelings, nor by a meretricious excitement of the nerves. His object is not a disturbed awakening, but the transformation of divine thoughts. Just as vocation goes on to enlightenment, and all progress in the inner life is conditioned by the progress of knowledge; so he seeks before all else to make the holy thoughts of the divine Word rightly known and to bring them before the memory, contemplation, will and inmost being of his hearers. He does not despise the feelings of men, but he awakens them by holding before them the heavenly light, or rather he sets up this light and is assured that with its ray warmth also will proceed from it. His watchwords are not *Awake* and the like, but those words of Scripture which refer to the gradual, silent growth of the divine mustard-seed. His insistence and compulsion are not the insistence and compulsion of human impatience, but a patient waiting on the Word. He gladly waits, knowing that precious fruits do not grow in a night. And he waits upon *all* his sheep, for he knows that the Lord has his own hour, his own haste, but also his own delays.

—*Wilhelm Löhe* (260)

* * *

The Pulpit

The pulpit is ever this earth's foremost part; all the rest comes in its rear; the pulpit leads the world. From thence it is that the storm of God's quick wrath is first descried, and the bow must bear the earliest brunt. From thence it is that the God of breezes fair or foul is first invoked for favorable winds. Yes, the world's a ship on its passage out, and not a voyage complete; and the pulpit is its prow.

—*Herman Melville* (261)

* * *

"Thirty Minutes to Raise the Dead In"

That hour when men and women come in, breathless and weary with the week's labor, and a man "sent with a message," which is a matter of life and death, has but thirty minutes to get at the separate hearts of a thousand men, to convince them of all their weaknesses, to shame them for all their sins, to warn them of all their dangers, to try by this way and that to stir the hard fastenings of those doors, where the Master himself has stood and knocked, and yet none opened, and to call at the opening of those dark streets, where Wisdom herself has stretched forth her hands and no man hath regarded,—thirty minutes to raise the dead in!—let us but once understand and feel this, and the pulpit will become a throne, like unto a marble rock in the desert, about which the people gather to slake their thirst.

—John Ruskin (262)

* * *

God in Action

Every Sunday morning when it comes ought to find you awed and thrilled by the reflection—"God is to be in action today, through me, for these people: this day may be crucial, this service decisive, for someone now ripe for the vision of Jesus." Remember that every soul before you has its own story of need, and that if the gospel of Christ does not meet such need nothing on earth can. Aim at results. Expect mighty works to happen. Realize that, although your congregation may be small, every soul is infinitely precious. Never forget that Christ himself, according to his promise, is in the midst, making the plainest and most ordinary church building into the house of God and the gate of heaven. Hear his voice saying, "This day is the Scripture fulfilled in your ears. This day is salvation come to this house." Then preaching, which might otherwise be a dead formality and a barren routine, an implicit denial of its own high claim, will become a power and a passion; and the note of strong, decisive reality, like a trumpet, will awaken the souls of men.

—James S. Stewart (263)

The Pulpit

The pulpit, therefore (and I name it filled
With solemn awe, that bids me well beware
With what intent I touch that holy thing) —
The pulpit (when the satirist has at last,
Strutting and vaporing in an empty school,
Spent all his force, and made no proselyte) —
I say the pulpit (in the sober use
Of its legitimate, peculiar powers)
Must stand acknowledged, while the world shall stand,
The most important and effectual guard,
Support, and ornament of virtue's cause.
There stands the messenger of truth. There stands
The legate of the skies; his theme divine,
His office sacred, his credentials clear.
By him, the violated law speaks out
Its thunders, and by him, in strains as sweet
As angels use, the gospel whispers peace.
He 'stablishes the strong, restores the weak,
Reclaims the wanderer, binds the broken heart,
And, armed himself in panoply complete
Of heavenly temper, furnishes with arms
Bright as his own, and trains by every rule
Of holy discipline, to glorious war,
The sacramental host of God's elect.
Are all such teachers? Would to heaven all were.

—William Cowper (264)

* * *

On Preaching

Were we not accustomed from childhood to hear the preaching of the Word of God, the tenor of preaching must surely seem strange to us. A man stands up before other men, many of whom are his superiors in station, prestige, intellectual gifts, scholarship, indeed, even in piety; and he can speak to them everything that in his estimation ministers to their salvation. They may accept or reject it, rejoice or grieve over it, they may censure or praise him, and regardless of all this he can speak to them thus, indeed, he must, and not seldom he does so. Where does he get this right? Does he assume it? But this would be a shocking presumption! Was it given to him by men? If men had given it to him they would long since have taken it away from him again. True, men installed him in his office in that they went through a certain prescribed form, but the office of the ministry itself was not instituted by men but by the Lord God through his Word.

This Word of God which endures for ever—this Word is the foundation of the evangelical preacher; upon this he stands solidly founded and everything that the Word speaks he, too, may speak, for the doctrine is not his but God's.

He may rebuke kings and beggars alike, he may reveal to all the deep corruption they bear in their bosoms and which yet so few can see; he may summon before the judgment seat of the law of God the wrongs and vices in vogue, these often-extolled wrongs, these often glittering vices. He may do this because he does not do it himself; the Word of God does it. He may proclaim mysteries which lie hidden upon heights to which no human spirit can lift itself. And when the Word proclaims these high things of faith through his mouth it is as the eagle who forsakes the earth, disappears from sight, seeks the sun, and greets it on high.

He may raise up the shattered sinner, crushed to earth by the thunder of the law, with the assurance of God's forgiveness, and this is his fairest privilege, this is the greatest benefit that one man can bestow upon another, this is the sublimest mission of his office. When those assembled before him appear as a heavy cloud from which tears will fall as drops, because of the many unfortunate ones among them, he may say to them, "Weep not." For those who ask him how best to manage their lives, inwardly and outwardly, he may, in accord with the sure precept of the divine Word, point to Christ the Pattern. He may entreat them to strive with the help of divine grace that Christ may live in them.

All this he may do. True, so long as his own faith is more a matter of mind than heart, he will make use of this high privilege only timidly and faintheartedly, but if his faith is strengthened and he has experienced the working of it in his inner life, then he will exercise his ministry with great joy and great boldness, and the Word of God will more and more manifest its own power in his mouth.

—*Franz Theremin* (265)

* * *

PRAYER AND TEACHING

As the minister reads the sacred writings on his knees— *betend lesend, lesend betend,* as Bengel puts it—he is reading them in the same spirit in which they were conceived and set down. In this mood the Holy Ghost, who is called in Scripture both the Spirit of truth and the Spirit of prayer, will be most likely to lead him into all truth.

What a new and fresh note will steal into his preaching! There will be no more dull and dry sermons, but the living, personal testimony of one speaking with authority. With cheerfulness and confidence he will say, "Thus saith the Lord," for the Lord has said it to him, and not to some ancient or modern commentator or sermon writer, from whom he got it at second or third or tenth hand. And in the daily round of pastoral work, warning and reproving, comforting and strengthening, he will draw on a rich fund of personal experience, and will deal with each member of his flock as lovingly and as truthfully as he has known God to deal with him.

—*A. T. W. Steinhäuser* (266)

Lo, we stand here, beseeching thee to bless thy word wherever spoken this day throughout the universal church. O make it a word of power and peace, to convert those who are not yet thine, and to confirm those that are. . . . O let not our foolish and unworthy hearts rob us of the continuance of this thy sweet love; but pardon our sins, and perfect what thou hast begun. Ride on, Lord, because of the word of truth, and meekness, and righteousness, "and thy right hand shall teach thee terrible things" (Psalm 45:4). Especially bless this portion here assembled together, with thy unworthy servant speaking unto them. Lord Jesus, teach thou me, that I may teach them; sanctify and enable all my powers, that in their full strength they may deliver thy message reverently, readily, faithfully, and fruitfully. O make thy word a swift word, passing from the ear to the heart, from the heart to the life and conversation; that as the rain returns not empty, so neither may thy word, but accomplish that for which it is given. O Lord, hear; O Lord, forgive; O Lord, hearken; and do so for thy blessed Son's sake, in whose sweet and pleasing words we say, "Our Father," etc.

— *George Herbert* (267)

* * *

THE SOLE SUBSTANCE OF PREACHING

Unum praedica: sapientiam crucis!
One thing you must preach: the wisdom of the cross!

— *Luther* (268)

* * *

Our heavenly Father said mankind was the salt of the earth, not the honey. And our poor world's rather like old man Job, stretched out in all his filth, covered with ulcers and sores. Salt stings on an open wound, but saves you from gangrene.

— *Georges Bernanos* (269)

"In him alone," as Calvin says, "is *tota materia salutis nostrae*—the whole stuff of our salvation." That might be accepted as the guiding principle of every evangelist: each may interpret, illustrate, enforce as his experience has taught him, but the center and substance is here. "I have only one sermon," said Hofacker, "Come, sinners, and look on Christ! and I have found that he who preaches Christ never runs alone." A comrade reported of Richard Cameron, the Covenanter in his ministry in the Killing Days, "The bias of his heart lay to the proposing of Christ and persuading men to close with him." Thus to exalt him as the sole Hope and Redeemer of men is enough—strong amid the broken, erect among the fallen, living among the dead and the dying, Jesus Christ, the Son of God, our Lord. It is thus the gospel should always be preached; and thus rejoicingly it should be received.

—William Malcolm Macgregor (270)

* * *

I preach what I myself need, repentance and forgiveness of sins.
—Ludwig Hofacker (271)

* * *

This is the Message!

We have a fixed faith to preach, my brethren, and we are sent forth with a definite message from God. We are not left to fabricate the message as we go along. We are not sent forth by our Master with a general commission arranged on this fashion—"As you shall think in your heart and invent in your head, so preach. Keep abreast of the time. Whatever the people want to hear, tell them that, and they shall be saved." Verily we do not read so. There is something definite in the Bible. It is not quite a lump of wax to be shaped at our will, or a roll of cloth to be cut according to the prevailing fashion. Your great thinkers evidently look upon the Scriptures as a box of letters for them to play with, and make what they like of, or a wizard's bottle, out of which they may pour anything they choose, from atheism up to spiritualism. I am too old-fashioned to fall down and worship this theory. There is something told me in the Bible—told me for certain—not put before me with a "but" and a "perhaps," and an "if," and a "maybe," and fifty thousand suspicions behind it, so that really the long and the short of it is, that it may not be so at all; but revealed to me as infallible fact, which must be believed, the opposite of which is deadly error, and comes from the father of lies.

Believing, therefore, that there is such a thing as truth, and such a thing as falsehood, that there are truths in the Bible, and the gospel consists in something definite which is to be believed by men, it becomes us to be decided as to what we teach, and to teach it in a decided manner. We have to deal with men who will be either lost or saved, and they certainly will not be saved by erroneous doctrine. We have to deal with God, whose servants we are, and he will not be honored by our delivering falsehoods; neither will he give us a reward, and say, "Well done, good and faithful servant, thou hast mangled the gospel as judiciously as any man that ever lived before thee." We stand in a very solemn position, and ours should be the spirit of old Micaiah, who said, "As the Lord my God liveth, before whom I stand, whatsoever the Lord saith unto me that will I speak." Neither less nor more than God's Word are we called to state, but that Word we are bound to declare in a spirit which convinces the sons that, whatever they may think of it, we believe God, and are not to be shaken in our confidence in him . . . If we had been entrusted with the making of the gospel, we might have altered it to suit the taste of this modest century, but never having been employed to originate the good news, but merely to repeat it, we dare not stir beyond the record. What we have been taught of God we teach. If we do not do this, we are not fit for our position. If I have a servant in my house, and I send a message by her to the door, and she amends it on her own authority, she may take away the very soul of the message by so doing, and she will be responsible for what she has done. She will not remain long in my employ, for I need a servant who will repeat what I say, as nearly as possible, word for word; and if she does so, I am responsible for the message, she is not. If anyone should be angry with her on account of what she said, they would be very unjust; their quarrel lies with me, and not with the person whom I employ to act as mouth for me. He that hath God's Word, let him speak it faithfully, and he will have no need to answer gainsayers, except with a "Thus said the Lord." This, then, is the matter concerning which we are decided.

–Charles Haddon Spurgeon (272)

* * *

Preach Christ

Preach Christ Jesus the Lord; determine to know nothing among the people but Christ crucified: let his name and grace, his Spirit and love, triumph in the midst of all the sermons. Let the great end be to glorify him in the hearts, to render him amiable and precious in the eyes of his people; to lead them to him as a sanctuary to protect them, a propitiation to reconcile them, a treasure to enrich them, a physician to heal them, an advocate to present them and their services to God; as wisdom to counsel, as righteousness to justify, as sanctification to renew, as redemption to save, as an inexhausted fountain of pardon, grace, comfort, victory, glory. Let Christ be the diamond to shine in the bosom of all your sermons.

–Edward Reynolds (273)

* * *

Messengers and Witnesses

The minister who keeps the word "message" always written before him, as he prepares his sermon in his study, or utters from his pulpit, is saved from the tendency to wanton and wild speculation, and from the mere passion of originality. He who never forgets that word "witness" is saved from the unreality of repeating by rote mere forms of statement, which he has learned as orthodox but never realized as true. If you and I can always carry this double consciousness, that we are messengers and that we are witnesses, we shall have in our preaching all the authority and independence of assured truth, and yet all the appeal and convincingness of personal belief.

—Phillips Brooks (274)

* * *

The Evangel

The "work of an evangelist" does not consist in proclaiming "ideals." It does not consist in criticizing man, his failures, his weaknesses, or his arrogance. It does not consist in the Kierkegaardian critique of the "religion man." It does not consist in *commanding* men to love God and each other, nor in preaching a social hope. It does not consist in giving a description of the evolution of this or that point of dogmatics, even if it is the best dogmatics.

The "work of an evangelist"—while he may make use of every possible material—is in what his name indicates. It consists in proclaiming the Evangel. The proclamation of the gospel is the proclamation of Jesus Christ. If Jesus Christ is the content, if it is "grace, nothing but grace, and the whole of grace," then there is no need of a supporting practical effect of some deed, because it itself is, and does, the one true deed. The church waits upon this deed, and the world awaits the action of this deed from the church. We must learn again to do this work sincerely and thoroughly. *—Karl Barth* (275)

* * *

The One Thing Necessary

Through the whole course of our ministry, we must insist most upon the greatest, most certain and necessary things, and be more seldom and sparing upon the rest. If we can but teach Christ to our people, we teach them all. Get them well to heaven, and they will have knowledge enough. The great and commonly acknowledged truths are they that men must live upon, and which are the great instruments of raising the heart to God, and destroying men's sins; and therefore we must still have our people's necessities in our eyes. It will take us off gawds, and needless ornaments, and unprofitable controversies, to remember that *one* thing is necessary. Other things are desirable to be known, but these *must* be known, or else our people are undone for ever. I confess, I think necessity should be a great disposer of a minister's course of study and labor. If we were sufficient for everything, we might fall upon everything, and take in order the whole Encyclopedia : but life is short, and we are dull; eternal things are necessary, and the souls that depend on our teaching are precious. I confess necessity hath been the conductor of my studies and life; it chooseth what book I shall read, and tells when and how long : it chooseth my text, and makes my sermon for matter and manner, so far as I can keep out my own corruption.

—*Richard Baxter* (276)

* * *

Thou art a preacher of the Word; mind thy business.

—*Old Puritan*

* * *

Christ Crucified

Nothing but godly wisdom must be the substance of our preaching, although to one it may be a stumbling-block, and to another, foolishness. . . . The word of the gospel is not weakened by age, it is an eternal gospel, and neither shall the fear of man, nor yet the wish to please men, hinder us from making this (after the example of St. Paul) the center of all our preaching, the alpha and omega of the whole gospel; viz. "Jesus Christ, and him crucified, who was delivered for our offences and raised again for our justification." That the government of the world is given into that hand which was pierced, is not this still to the Greeks foolishness, and that, not for the works which we ourselves have done, but through faith in the crucified, we must be saved, is not this still a stumbling-block to the Jews? Nevertheless, to us who are saved, it is the power of God. Brethren, if we look up to heaven with our naked eye, we see nebulous spots upon its face; but let us arm our eyes to view the stupendous works of the heavens, and we see these nebulae change into constellations. Thus, then, arm your eyes, ye to whom the preaching of a crucified Saviour of the world shows only clouds and darkness, arm yourselves, that is, give up yourselves, heart and soul, to the gospel; and it will become in your bosoms a godly light, and you will see the glory which floats over the cross of Golgotha.

—*August Tholuck* (277)

* * *

Evangelism is witness. It is one beggar telling another beggar where to get food. The Christian does not offer out of his bounty. He has no bounty. He is simply guest at his Master's table and, as evangelist, he calls others too.

—*Daniel T. Niles* (278)

* * *

We Must Serve the Word of God

We as preachers and teachers of the church are agreed, in fear but also in joy, that we are called to serve the Word of God in the church and in the world through our preaching, that it is not only we who stand or fall with the fulfilling of this calling but also that we see that absolutely everything that may be important and dear and great to us in his world stands or falls with it; and that therefore there can be no more urgent concern and more compelling hope than the concern and hope of our service, no friend more dear than one who helps us in this service and no enemy more hateful than one who would hinder us in this service. We are agreed that, besides this primary task, which is the meaning and purpose of our work and our rest, our zeal and our calmness, our love and our wrath, there is no secondary thing; but that everything secondary and tertiary that may and must concern us is comprehended and included in this primary task, given direction and blessed by this primary task. On this we are agreed, or we are not preachers and teachers of the church.

—Karl Barth (279)

* * *

The Text

The chief thing in the service of worship is not your opinion, as you may be inclined to present it in your sermon; the chief thing is and remains the text. Guilt is not absolved and the dying are not raised up by your believing and opining; here it must be: Thus it is written; this is what the messenger of Jesus is saying to you. For the ministry, therefore, the first and most important duty is to keep open the lines of communication and community with the apostles, in order that we may use their message at the right time and in the right way. To use it we must know it and to know it we must remain in communication with them.

—Adolf Schlatter (280)

* * *

One reads somnambulant sermons about coming into tune with the infinite, about cultivating the presence of God, about pausing in life to hear the melodies of the everlasting chime, and all the rest of the romance of piety breathed beneath the moon in the green and pleasant glades of devotion—all without a hint of the classic redemption, or even of the Christ, whereby alone we have access to any of the rich quietives of faith. The preacher has glimpses of the paradise, but no sense of the purgatorio. He has the language but not the accent of that far heavenly country. Oh! but we want men who have been there and been naturalized there. We want more than romantic and temperamental piety. We want the accent of the Holy Ghost, learned with a new life at its classic capital—the cross. We want something more than a lovely gospel with the fine austerity of a cloistered ethic. I do not wonder that the literary people react from self-conscious Galahad, sure and vain of his own purity, and turn to welcome the smell of the good brown earth. So also our virile sinfulness turns from the criticisms of fastidious religion to the *blood* of Christ and the cost at which we are scarcely saved. It was not Galahad or Arthur that drew Christ from heaven. It was a Lancelot race. It was a tragic issue of man's passion that called out the glory of Christ.

—*Peter Taylor Forsyth* (281)

* * *

Do not tell people how they ought to feel toward Christ. It is just what they ought that they cannot do. Preach a Christ that will make them feel as they ought. That is objective preaching. The tendency and fashion of the present moment is all in the direction of subjectivity. People welcome sermons of a more or less psychological kind, which go into the analysis of the soul or of society. They will listen gladly to sermons on character-building, for instance; and in the result they will get to think of nothing else but their own character. They will be the builders of their own character; which is a fatal thing. Learn to commit your soul and the building of it to One who can keep it and build it as you never can. Attend then to Christ, the Holy Spirit, the kingdom, and the cause, and he will look after your soul.

—*Peter Taylor Forsyth* (282)

* * *

Authority

If a man wants to be a minister, he must be in the power of Christ. If a man is sent to speak in his name, no half measures are sufficient. A minister is a slave of Christ. He should be ruled by his Lord, impelled by the Holy Spirit, and filled with a great passion to serve his cause. And that means also to be filled with a passion to serve and help the people for whom the Redeemer laid down his life. Only then can his authority become the authority of the Holy Spirit, which does not tear down but builds up. This authority does not find its expression in meetings of the congregation and church council. But it is felt so much the more in the pulpit. There it is patent that the pastor expects his preaching to do something, but also that he is not seeking to further his own will. He is the herald, who speaks in the name of his King, to waken the sleepers, to comfort the afflicted, and to strengthen the believers. The pastor has had them in his mind's eye when he was preparing his sermon. He saw their faces as he meditated. Their cares and temptations filled his thoughts. He was thinking of them, not of his reputation as a preacher. Again and again he has prayed for them, praying that through this sermon God would breach their indifference or kindle the flame of saving faith.

This genuine authority is always warm and compassionate. It never springs from hurt vanity or personal resentment. It may be, of course, that the preacher will be very gentle and forbearing as long as he feels he is esteemed and treated with friendliness. It is only when he is contradicted or challenged that he becomes sharp and bitter in his preaching. But that kind of zeal must really be called the zeal of anger and hot temper. It never brings forth the fruits of repentance and life. Anyone can see that the pastor is pressing his own cause and using the law as a weapon against his opponents. His admonitions make no impression when they are not wrung by the Spirit of God from a quaking heart that would have preferred to keep silence, but for love's sake is compelled to speak. It should therefore be the special concern of the pastor to preach repentance honestly and clearly, precisely when everybody is especially friendly and kindly disposed toward him. This is just the time when he has the greatest chance of helping them. Then it is easiest for them to understand that "we are ambassadors for Christ, God making his appeal through us."

Perhaps this confronts many a pastor again with the question which perhaps no pastor can escape. Have you ever preached without remembering your calling? Have you ever preached the Word solely for the sake of souls, without any thought whatsoever of the impression *you* were making, no matter whether you were pleased with your performance or whether you had feelings of inferiority?

In God's presence, this question can be answered only in one way: Father, I have sinned against heaven, and before thee. I am no longer worthy to be called thy pastor. Thou hast bestowed upon me the highest token of trust and the loveliest of all callings—and still, after all these years, I have the same proud, self-centered heart, greedy for praise and fearful of suffering and hardship.

The pastor who is in earnest with his ministry will inevitably feel the thorn in his flesh daily. The old Adam did not die at ordination. He continues to buffet us, this veritable messenger of Satan. But Christ's marvelous power is manifested perhaps chiefly in that he is able to transform our sins into means of sanctification and our defeats into victories for his cause. When the messenger of Satan buffets me it is in order "to keep me from being too elated." Every onslaught of the old man becomes a new occasion to turn to Christ, to hold fast to him, who alone can reconcile my wicked heart to God, who alone has the power to help a poor pastor through all his temptations. It is precisely when I realize that it is a great miracle if a pastor be saved that I can experience the full depth of the truth that Christ is a real redeemer for real sinners. So we need not stop with saying that it is a miracle if a pastor be saved. We can also say: Because I am a pastor, I know that even the greatest sinner can be saved.

—*Bo Giertz* (283)

Seeing that the ideas that people, philosophers and non-philosophers, thinkers and blockheads, weavers and statesmen, washerwomen and midwives, procurators, and preachers themselves have about the ministry are so diverse and mostly so unjust or at least inaccurate, here is a preacher who knows the dignity of his calling. He opens his mouth concerning his office, not to utter compliments and ceremonious comments, but sound words, with the noble frankness of a man who is conscious of his worth and the rightness of his cause and whom the truth makes bold.

A preacher is not *a product of an ecclesiastical academy;* he is not one of the seven wise men of Greece, not a peddler of truisms and teacher of wisdom and virtue, not a professor of morals, who must be tolerated by the state because by his discourses he can teach subjects obedience and increase the tax register and the cash box of the farmers-general. He is a sower who sows, not for these, but for a better world; a teacher of the great saving doctrine of God, a father and comforter of his congregation, a weak, unworthy, imperfect man, but with the lightning of God in his hand, which he has received, not from men, but from God and which he uses, not for petty vanity or anything trivial, but to pierce the bone and marrow of subjects and princes for their betterment that they may obtain a salvation glorious above all things.

It is not likely that anybody will argue against this conception, and it would have been well if this view had always prevailed.

—*Matthias Claudius* (284)

* * *

Heralds—that is the decisive word which designates the minister's *special* call and task. The Lord has a gospel which he will have brought to his congregation and to the world, and it is as such that he wills to use ministers. . . . *We are heralds*—that and nothing else. The gospel which we have received from God constitutes our whole beings as ministers. . . . We are heralds, heralds of gladness. We have received overwhelming, joyful news to proclaim to the world. This is central in all our diverse tasks, and that which in the final analysis makes them all come together into one single task. We have a teaching task, a nurturing task, the task of the cure of souls, but these we have solely as the consequence of the fact that we have been sent out as heralds to tell some great news which has taken place in our world, something which has to do with each and every one. . . . "The gospel is a power of God unto salvation for each and every one who believes" (Rom. 1:16). This is the gospel we are to give out. The power does not come from us; rather it lies within the gospel itself. We are but those who deliver it. We are heralds. That is the sacredness of our call.

—*Anders Nygren* (285)

* * *

Just as it was in the first century, so it is today: faith comes through preaching. But this preaching must then be done in the power of the Word of Christ. A man may be ever so brilliant and eloquent, moving and wise, but it does not become preaching until he himself is taken captive by God's Word and has no other desire except to let the Word itself speak.

Therefore the first duty of the pastor is to preach the message of the Bible as purely and clearly as he possibly can, without any abridgments and without any reservations. He is a steward of God to whom has been committed the mysterious power over life and death. What God expects of his steward is that he be found faithful.

The pastor is, therefore, not a prophet. He is not constantly waiting for a revelation and a message from the Lord which will be spoken to his heart. If he does not know what he should speak, he should not restlessly wait for the moment of inspiration. He should sit down and read his Bible, look up the parallel passages, make excerpts, and gather material.

He should read the old preachers who knew their Bible and see what they said on this text and what biblical truths they set forth in connection with it. The pastor is not a prophet. He is a teacher ordained to proclaim the old message "as he has received it."

Nor is the pastor a poet. He does not wait for an inspiration. He does not set himself up to say something that nobody has ever heard before or that has never been uttered before in this world. He does not prepare his sermons in some beautiful spot by the seashore or in a garden bower. He is the servant of the Word. His workshop is his study, where he works with his concordance, his Greek New Testament, and all the other helps he has in his library.

Least of all is the pastor a purveyor of talk and chit-chat. He is not there to tell little anecdotes picked up in the trolley cars or from the lips of children, or to deliver clever commentaries on the news of the day. His most zealous endeavor is not to make people come to hear him, but to have something to say to them, not to be original, but to be truthful, not to interest, but to help.

This is not to say that a pastor who desires to be a genuine preacher of the Word, has nothing to learn from the prophets and also the poets.   —*Bo Giertz* (286)

* * *

PLAIN PREACHING

The Apostles . . . were content . . . to tell the world in plain terms, *that he who believed should be saved, and that he who believed not should be damned.* And this was the dialect, which pierced the conscience, and made the hearers cry out, *Men and brethren, what shall we do?* It tickled not the ear, but sunk into the heart : and when men came from such sermons, they never commended the preacher for his talking voice or gesture; for the fineness of such a simile, or the quaintness of such a sentence: but they spoke like men conquered with the overpowering force and evidence of the most concerning truths; much in the words of the two disciples going to Emmaus; *Did not our hearts burn within us, while he opened to us the Scriptures?*

—*Robert South* (287)

* * *

All our teaching must be as plain and evident as we can make it; for this doth most suit to a teacher's ends. He that would be understood, must speak to the capacity of his hearers, and make it his business to make himself understood. Truth loves the light, and is most beautiful when most naked. It is a sign of an envious enemy to hide the truth; and a sign of an hypocrite to do this under pretence of revealing it: and therefore painted, obscure sermons (like the painted glass in the windows that keep out the light), are too often the mark of painted hypocrites. If you would not teach men, what do you in the pulpit? If you would, why do you not speak so as to be understood? At best it is a sign that he hath not well digested the matter himself, that is not able to deliver it plainly to another. —*Richard Baxter* (288)

* * *

Preaching: Its Difficulty

One part of our work, and that the most excellent, because it tendeth to work on many, is the public preaching of the Word. A work that requireth greater skill, and especially greater life and zeal than any of us bring to it. It is no small matter to stand up in the face of a congregation, and deliver a message of salvation or damnation, as from the living God, in the name of our Redeemer. It is no easy matter to speak so plain, that the ignorant may understand us; and so seriously, that the deadest hearts may feel us; and so convincingly, that contradicting cavillers may be silenced.

—*Richard Baxter* (289)

To preach a sermon I think is not the hardest part [of our work]; and yet what skill is necessary to make plain the truth, to convince the hearers; to let in the irresistible light into their consciences, and to keep it there, and drive all home; to screw the truth into their minds, and work Christ into their affections; to meet every objection that gainsays, and clearly to resolve it; to drive sinners to a stand, and make them see there is no hope, but they must unavoidably be converted or condemned : and to do all this so for language and manner as beseems our work, and yet as is most suitable to the capacities of our hearers; this, and a great deal more that should be done in every sermon, should surely be done with a great deal of holy skill.

So great a God, whose message we deliver, should be honored by our delivery of it! It is a lamentable case, that in a message from the God of heaven, of everlasting consequence to the souls of men, we should behave ourselves so weakly, so unhandsomely, so imprudently, or so slightly, that the whole business should miscarry in our hands, and God be dishonored, and his work disgraced, and sinners rather hardened than converted, and all this much through our weakness or neglect! How many a time have carnal hearers gone jeering home, at the palpable and dishonorable failings of the preacher! How many sleep under us, because our hearts and tongues are sleepy; and we bring not with us so much skill and zeal as to awake them!   *—Richard Baxter* (290)

* * *

The Venture of Preaching

It is a venturesome thing to preach; for when I mount to that sacred place [the pulpit]—whether the church be crowded or as good as empty—I have, though I myself may not be aware of it, one hearer in addition to those that are visible to me, namely, God in heaven, whom I cannot see, it is true, but who verily can see me. This Hearer listens attentively to discover whether what I say is true, and he looks also to discern (as well he can, for he is invisible, and in that way it is impossible to be on one's guard against him)—so he looks to see whether my life expresses what I say. And although I possess no authority to impose any obligation upon any other person, yet what I have said in the course of the sermon puts me under obligation—and God has heard it. Verily, it is a venturesome thing to preach! Doubtless most people have a notion that it requires courage to step out upon the stage like an actor and venture to encounter the danger of having all eyes fixed upon one. And yet this danger is, in a sense, like everything else on the stage, an illusion; for personally the actor is aloof from it all, his part is to deceive, to disguise himself, to represent another, and to transmit accurately the words of another. The preacher of Christian truth, on the other hand, steps out in a place where, even if all eyes are not fixed upon him, the eye of omniscience is; his part is to be himself, and that in an environment, God's house, which, being all eye and ear, requires of him only this, that he be himself, be true. "That he be true"—this means that he himself is what he preaches, or at least strives to be that, or at the very least is sober enough to admit that he is not. Alas, and how many who in mounting to this sacred place to preach Christianity are keen enough of hearing to detect the repugnance and scorn which this sacred place feels for him at hearing him preach with enthusiasm, in moving tones, with tears, the opposite of that which his life expresses.

So venturesome a thing it is to be the "I" which preaches, to be the speaker, and "I" who by preaching and in the act of preaching puts himself absolutely under obligation, lays his life bare so that if it were possible one might look directly into his soul—to be such an "I," that was a venturesome thing. Therefore little by little the parson found out how to draw his eye back into himself, indicating thereby that nobody had any business to look at him. In fact it was not (so he thought) about himself he was speaking, it was about the thing at issue; and this was admired as an extraordinary advance in wisdom that the speaker ceased to be an "I" and became if possible a thing. Anyhow, in this way it became far easier to be a parson—the speaker no longer preached, he employed these moments to introduce some reflections. Some reflections! You can perceive that in the speaker : his glance is drawn back into the eye, he resembles not so much a man as one of those figures carved in stone which has no eyes. Thereby he creates a yawning gulf between the hearer and himself, almost as wide as that between the actor and the spectator. And what he preaches are "reflections," whereby again he creates a yawning gulf between himself and what he says, as wide as between the actor and the poet or play-wright—personally he is as much aloof as possible while he "employs these moments to propose reflections."

So it is that the "I," who was the speaker, dropped out; the speaker is not an "I," he is the thing at issue, the reflection. And as the "I" fell out, so also the "thou" was done away with, thou the hearer, the fact that thou who sittest there art the person to whom the discourse is addressed. Indeed, it has almost gone so far that to talk in this personal fashion to other people is regarded as "a personality." By personalities (resorting to personalities, "taking the liberty to employ personalities") one understands unseemly and rude behavior—and so it will not do for the speaker, "I," to talk personally, and to persons, the hearer, "thou." And if this will not do, then the sermon is done away with. . . .

This fundamental change in the character of the sermon, by which Christianity was done away with, is also (among other things) an expression of the fundamental change which came about with the triumphant church and established Christendom, that as a rule Christ obtained admirers, not followers.

—*Søren Kierkegaard* (291)

Teaching is no joke, sonny! I'm not talking of those who get out of it with a lot of eyewash: you'll knock up against plenty of *them* in the course of your life, and get to know 'em. Comforting truths, they call it. Truth is meant to save you first, and the comfort comes afterwards. Besides, you've no right to call that sort of thing comfort. Might as well talk about condolences! The Word of God is a red-hot iron. And you who preach it 'ld go picking it up with a pair of tongs, for fear of burning yourself, you daren't get hold of it with both hands. It's too funny! Why, the priest who descends from the pulpit of Truth, with a mouth like a hen's vent, a little hot but pleased with himself, he's not been preaching: at best he's been purring like a tabby-cat. Mind you that can happen to us all, we're all half asleep, it's the devil to wake us up, sometimes—the apostles slept all right at Gethsemane. Still, there's a difference. . . . And mind you many a fellow who waves his arms and sweats like a furniture-remover isn't necessarily any more awakened than the rest. On the contrary, I simply mean that when the Lord has drawn from me some word for the good of souls, I know, because of the pain of it.

—*Georges Bernanos* (292)

* * *

There is in fact a tension between Him who spoke with authority and the speech of the scribes, a tension between the word of the Bible itself and our word of preaching. One who no longer feels this tension is in bad case. Or we might say, one who is not willing to bear this tension as a minister of the Word would better give up being a minister of the Word. This tension is bound up with the humanness of the preacher.

We are human beings after all, not merely those who sit in the pews. The preacher, too, has the right to be a human being. But the material with which we are dealing in our calling, the Word of God, is a fire. Christ came into the world to kindle a fire. The seeds he casts are fiery grains. But we men fear fire; and it is probably well that we do; better than to play with it. It is dangerous to take fire into one's hands, even in one's mouth. One actually has to be a real flame swallower to deal with God's Word, and this is just what we are not. And how easily it happens that we, who simply have to present this fire to the congregation, should be inclined, out of a mistaken consideration not only for our listeners but ultimately for our own flesh, to act like a mother who tempers the gobbets when they are too hot and blows on the porridge when it is too fiery to make it lukewarm for the child to take. Our greatest, our real difficulty in preaching is that the fire of God is always too hot for us and we cool it and temper it. Thus we falsify God's Word, perhaps not with malice aforethought, perhaps purely out of our own tenderness and consideration for those committed to our care. This falsification can be concealed just as well under the heavy, correct, and stately vesture of orthodox preaching as under the light and airy habiliment of liberalism.

Thus God's Word is corrupted in the preaching mouth of man. Therefore our concern, not, it is true, our sole concern, but certainly our most urgent, must be that the seed shall remain fiery in our hands, that the Word of God may be so preached among us that it may burn and give "light to all in the house."

—*Walter Lüthi* (293)

* * *

Unless the man in the pulpit has felt the deep hurt and heartache of humanity—its bitter, blinding tragedy—unless he knows the rough places, the dangerous turns, the dismal stretches of the old, winding road, and something of what the pilgrims carry in their packs, he cannot minister to our need, much less lead us far along the way whither we seek to go. If he is aware of his own heart and its yearnings, he must know that men do not go to church to learn about science, philosophy, or art, useful as such studies may be. They go sorely needing and sadly seeking something else—longing to hear a voice out of the heavens, telling them of the things eye hath not seen nor ear heard. They go seeking, as of old, the healing touch, the forgiving word, the hand put forth in the darkness, which makes them know that they are not alone in their struggle for the good. The preacher must live with the people if he is to know their problems, and he must live with God if he is to solve them.

—Joseph Fort Newton (294)

* * *

Qualities of the Good Preacher

A good preacher should have these qualities and virtues. First, he should be able to teach in a right and orderly way. Second, he should have a good head. Third, he should be able to speak well. Fourth, he should have a good voice. Fifth, a good memory. Sixth, he should know when to stop. Seventh, he should be sure of his material and be diligent. Eighth, he should stake body and life, goods and honor on it. Ninth, he must suffer himself to be vexed and flayed by everybody.

—Luther (295)

* * *

Qualities of the Preacher
As the World Would Have Him

As the world would have him, six things are necessary to the preacher: 1. He must have a fine accent. 2. He must be learned. 3. He must be eloquent. 4. He must be a handsome person, whom the girls and young women will like. 4. He must take no money, but have money to give. 6. He must tell people what they like to hear.

—Luther (296)

Affection

Would I describe a preacher, such as Paul,
Were he on earth, would hear, approve, and own,
Paul should himself direct me. I would trace
His master-strokes, and draw from his design.
I would express him simple, grave, sincere;
In doctrine uncorrupt; in language plain,
And plain in manner; decent, solemn, chaste,
And natural in gesture; much impressed
Himself, as conscious of his awful charge,
And anxious mainly that the flock he feeds
May feel it too; affectionate in look,
And tender in address, as well becomes
A messenger of grace to guilty men.
Behold the picture! Is it like?—Like whom?
The things that mount the rostrum with a skip,
And then skip down again; pronounce a text,
Cry-hem! and reading what they never wrote,
Just fifteen minutes, huddle up their work,
And with a well-bred whisper close the scene!
In man or woman, but far most in man,
And most of all in man that ministers
And serve the altar, in my soul I loathe
All affectation. 'Tis my perfect scorn;
Object of my implacable disgust.
What!—will a man play tricks, will he indulge
A silly fond conceit of his fair form
And just proportion, fashionable mien,
And pretty face, in presence of his God?
Or will he seek to dazzle me with tropes,
As with the diamond on his lily hand,
And play his brilliant parts before my eyes
When I am hungry for the bread of life?

—*William Cowper* (297)

423

He that negotiates between God and man,
As God's ambassador, the grand concerns
Of judgment and of mercy, should beware
Of lightness in his speech. 'Tis pitiful
To court a grin when you should woo a soul;
To break a jest, when pity would inspire
Pathetic exhortation; and to address
The skittish fancy with facetious tales,
When sent with God's commission to the heart.
So did not Paul. Direct me to a quip
Or merry turn in all he ever wrote,
And I consent you take it for your text,
Your only one, till sides and benches fail.
No, he was serious in a serious cause,
And understood too well the weighty terms
That he had ta'en in charge. He would not stoop
To conquer those by jocular exploits,
Whom truth and soberness assailed in vain.

—*William Cowper* (298)

* * *

Preaching is God's Work

In all simplicity seek only God's glory and not the applause
of men. And pray that God will put wisdom into your mouth
and give to the hearers a ready ear; then leave it to God. For
you must believe me, preaching is not the work of men. . . .
For to this day I, an old and experienced preacher, am still
afraid of preaching.

And you will very surely have these three experiences.
First, when you have prepared and outlined your sermon in
the best possible way, it will still fall flat. Second, on the
other hand when you have completely despaired of sermon
outline, then God will grant you to preach at your best, so
that the people will be pleased; but of course you will by no
means be satisfied yourself. Third, when you have no pre-

pared outline you will please both yourself and the hearers. Therefore pray to God and leave it to him; but let us study and carry on.

—*Luther* (299)

* * *

The Word, Words and Reality

The evangelical church is the church of the Word. This certainty is a common possession beyond many other differences. Inherent in it still is the power of the divinely effected origin of the evangelical church and a constant reminder of the spiritual, the creative, the divine which reigns victorious over all human effort. But there is danger in its greatness. It is the danger that the church of the Word may become the church of words. This danger is a constant threat because the Word of God always goes forth in the garment of human words. So, quite concretely, the church of the Word is always the church of words. And so words sound through our churches and meeting places. Who can count them? Who can grasp them? Who can name them? The little words and the big ones, the worn and the original, the contrived and the unconsidered, the words bought with heart's blood and those snatched up on the way, the words that are born of struggle and the inspired words, words freely ventured and words enjoined by inner compulsion.

And how various are the hearers of these many different words! But then, indeed, we have one listener among the others, one who is never absent and looks at us steadily as from a great distance, who not only reads the words from our lips but reads them as it were out of the depths of our hearts, without misunderstanding a single one of them. This one listener is our own soul. And then, afterwards, in the quietness, on the way home, this one listener speaks. Self speaks to self and says, "Those were the words, but what about your being? Have I the right to speak, being so uncertain, so small, so unfaithful? And when I speak, dare I, perhaps, say

425

only what I can back up with my own life? And what depths must be reached if I am to speak at all?"

The answer here, too, is: "Strait is the gate, and narrow is the way." But God makes it possible for the upright. . . .

We do not preach ourselves! What would become of us if we dared to say only as much as our lives represented? If only the perfect could speak, where would there be any preaching? Should not our speech itself be saying: There is something that is greater than my own life, something that is ever ahead of me and beyond me, shamefully far above and beyond me, but therefore also exalting, uplifting, and liberating—the truth of God! Is not this precisely the testimony of the Reformation, without which the church of the Word would not exist at all, the witness that must be declared again and again: God is greater than all, greater than our hearts, not only the proud, happy, contented heart, but also, and very definitely and specifically, greater than our hearts when they condemn us!

May not the desire to keep silent in the face of this dreadful contradiction between the greatness of the message and the smallness of our lives, may not this wish stem from weakness, from cowardice, from the urge to flee from the living God? It would be so much easier to keep quiet. It would be inwardly so much easier not to preach, not to worship, not to give moral instruction. But we cannot escape the living God. Somehow and sometime we have to go through the purgatory of our life. And part of it, for us, is this contradiction between our words and our being. Only if we endure it does this purgatory do its work. Even our own words should serve to make us grow; they should, so to speak, help to create a resistance by which our strength is increased. . . .

One thing, of course, is necessary; we must always submit ourselves to the power of truth and live by it. "When you communicate something that is existentially higher than your own existence you dare to communicate it only in such a way that it will serve your own humiliation" (Kierkegaard). It is not necessary to keep on saying this too often. "When you fast, anoint your head and wash your face." Time and again, of course, we shall be forced by our very preaching to come down a peg or two, or to make a confession, or to beg for forgiveness. But what harm is there in that? None. It only helps us to love the truth more than ourselves under every circumstance and really experience "the edifying in the thought that before God we are always in the wrong." But beyond this, we must steep ourselves again and again in the peace of forgiveness and then turn back to confident certainty. . . .

So the very distress of which we have spoken, instead of leading to depression or shallowness or spiritual paralysis or to a complete split in personality, can perform a great service for us. It can help us to get free from ourselves. In times of stress and doubt really plunge into the annealing bath of the Word and the preaching of the Word! Say to yourself: Why should I be anxious? Though I be ever so weak, so disheartened, so in need of human indulgence and divine forgiveness, so much the greater, more certain, and more powerful is the gospel, verily a power of God for salvation to everyone who has faith! Though my hand be too weak and unworthy to hold the banner, still it has its service to perform until God takes it out of my hand and gives it to someone who is greater and more worthy. It is not when we defy the whole world, but only when we defy ourselves in the power of faith that we have entered the decisive struggle which has the promise of victory.

"Each one was great in his own way, each in relation to the greatness of what he loved. For he who loved himself became great through himself, and he who loved others became great by his self-sacrifice. But he who loved God became greater than all.

"Each became great in relation to what he hoped for. One became great because he hoped for the possible, another because he hoped for the immortal. Yet he who hoped for the impossible became greater than all.

"Each became great in relation to the greatness of what he struggled with. For he who struggled with the world became great because he overcame the world, and he who struggled with himself became greater by overcoming himself. Yet he who struggled with God became greater than all" (Kierkegaard).

"Resist the devil and he will flee from you. Draw near to God and he will draw near to you. Cleanse your hands, you sinners, and purify your hearts, you men of double mind . . . Humble yourselves before the Lord and he will exalt you" (Jas. 4:7-8, 10).

—*Erich Schick* (300)

* * *

Preaching in the Presence of God

When you are going to preach, first speak to God and say: "Dear Lord, I would preach for thine honor, I would speak of thee, praise thee, and glorify thy name. Though I cannot do it well, do thou make it good." Don't think of Philip, Bugenhagen, me, or any other learned man, but consider that you are the most learned of all when you speak from the pulpit. I have never been troubled because I cannot preach well, but I have often been afraid and awed to think that I have to preach before God's face of his great majesty and divine being. Therefore only be strong and pray.

—*Luther* (301)

* * *

Qui ascendit cum timore, is descendit cum honore.
He who goes up with fear comes down with honor.

—*Ancient inscription on a pulpit stair*

* * *

The Parson Preaching

The country parson preacheth constantly; the pulpit is his joy and his throne: if he at any time intermit, it is either for want of health, or against some great festival, that he may the better celebrate it, or for the variety of the hearers, that he may be heard at his return more attentively. When he intermits, he is ever very well supplied by some able man, who treads in his steps, and will not throw down what he hath built; whom also he entreats to press some point that he himself hath often urged with no great success, that so, "in the mouth of two or three witnesses" the truth may be more established.

When he preacheth, he procures attention by all possible art; both by earnestness of speech—it being natural to men to think, that where is much earnestness, there is somewhat worth hearing—and by a diligent and busy cast of his eye on his auditors, with letting them know that he observes who marks, and who not; and with particularizing of his speech now to the younger sort, then to the elder, now to the poor, and now to the rich—"This is for you, and this is for you"; for particulars ever touch and awake more than generals. Herein also he serves himself of the judgments of God, as of those of ancient times, so especially of the late ones, and those most which are nearest to his parish; for people are very attentive at such discourses, and think it behooves them to be so when God is so near them, and even over their heads.

Sometimes he tells them stories and sayings of others, according as his text invites him; for them also men heed, and remember better than exhortations; which, though earnest, yet often die with the sermon, especially with country people, which are thick, and heavy, and hard to raise to a point of zeal and fervency, and need a mountain of fire to kindle them; but stories and sayings they will well remember.

He often tells them that sermons are dangerous things; that none goes out of church as he came in, but either better or worse; that none is careless before his judge, and that the Word of God shall judge us. By these and other means the parson procures attention; but the character of his sermon is holiness; he is not witty, or learned, or eloquent, but holy—a character that Hermogenes never dream'd of, and therefore he could give no precepts thereof.

But it is gained, first, by choosing texts of devotion, not controversy, moving and ravishing texts, whereof the Scriptures are full.

Secondly, by dipping and seasoning all our words and sentences in our hearts before they come into our mouths, truly affecting and cordially expressing all that we say; so that the auditors may plainly perceive that every word is heart-deep.

Thirdly, by turning often, and making many apostrophes to God as: "O Lord, bless my people, and teach them this point"; or, "O my Master, on whose errand I come, let me hold my peace, and do Thou speak Thyself; for Thou art love, and when Thou teachest, all are scholars." Some such irradiations scatteringly in the sermon carry great holiness in them. . . .

Fourthly, by frequent wishes of the people's good, and joying therein, though he himself were, with St. Paul, even sacrificed upon the service of their faith. For there is no greater sign of holiness than the procuring and rejoicing in another's good. . . .

Lastly, by an often urging of the presence and majesty of God, by these or such like speeches: "Oh let us all take heed what we do! God sees us; He sees whether I speak as I ought, or you hear as you ought; He sees hearts as we see faces. He is among us; for if we be here, He must be here, since we are here by Him, and without Him could not be here."

*   *   *   —*George Herbert* (302)

Give an Account of thy Stewardship!

The word of God! Give me back my Word, the Judge will say on the last day. When you think what certain people will have to unpack on that occasion, it's no laughing matter, I assure you!　　　　　　　　　　　　　　　　　—*Georges Bernanos* (303)

Everyone who can preach the truth and does not preach it, incurs the judgment of God.

—Justin Martyr

* * *

No man preaches his sermon well to others if he doth not first preach it to his own heart.

—John Owen

* * *

Star Preachers

I care not much for your stars; and for starring parsons least;

The better they are at that, they have less the true heart of a priest.

—Walter Chalmers Smith (304)

* * *

How easy is pen and paper piety, for one to write religiously? I will not say it costeth nothing, but it is far cheaper to work one's head than one's heart to goodness. Some, perchance, may guess me to be good by my writings, and so I shall deceive my reader. But if I do not desire to be good, I most of all deceive myself. I can make a hundred meditations sooner than subdue the least sin in my soul.

—Thomas Fuller (305)

* * *

Passionate Preaching

There is no prayer that ought to be more constantly on your lips than those lines of Charles Wesley, surely the most characteristic he ever wrote:

O Thou who camest from above
The pure celestial fire to impart,
Kindle a flame of sacred love
On the mean altar of my heart.
There let it for Thy glory burn.

431

Think of the news you are ordained to declare. That God has invaded history with power and great glory; that in the day of man's terrible need a second Adam has come forth to the fight and to the rescue; that in the cross the supreme triumph of naked evil has been turned once for all to irrevocable defeat; that Christ is alive now and present through his Spirit; that through the risen Christ there has been let loose into the world a force which can transform life beyond recognition—this is the most momentous message human lips were ever charged to speak. It dwarfs all other truths into insignificance. It is electrifying in its power, shattering in its wonder. Surely it is desperately unreal to talk of themes like these in a voice deadened by routine, or in the maddeningly offhand and impassive manner which is all too familiar. It ought not to be possible to conduct a church service in a way which leaves a stranger with the impression that nothing particular is happening and that no important business is on hand. "Went to church today," wrote Robert Louis Stevenson in his journal, "and was not greatly impressed." If that is the best we can do for people, is it worth doing? "Certainly I must confess," cried Sir Philip Sidney, "I never heard the old song of Percy and Douglas, that I found not my heart moved more than with a trumpet." And to you has been committed the infinitely more heartmoving story of the Word made flesh: "that incredible interruption," wrote G. K. Chesteron, "was a blow that broke the very backbone of history." "It were better," he declared, "to rend our robes with a great cry against blasphemy, like Caiaphas in the judgment, rather than to stand stupidly debating fine shades of pantheism in the presence of so catastrophic a claim."

—*James S. Stewart* (306)

* * *

Not Only the Pulpit Preaches

We have been accustomed by the Reformation to think of proclamation primarily as the preaching of the church, the public witness through which from the beginning the church was founded and continues to be grounded. "For the obtaining of this faith, God has instituted the office of preaching," says Article V of the Augsburg Confession. And today none of this is to be retracted or left out. But preaching dare not be taken by itself and removed from the context of the total witness of the church. The Reformation appreciation of the ministry of preaching does not justify making it an absolute and isolating it, as is commonly done in the present theological epoch. Preaching belongs together with the personal Word of pastoral care, the general with the particular. In any case, this particular, personal Word is building the church today at least as much as is the general. Preaching lives by its connection with the Word spoken from person to person and only so will it be constantly refreshed and gain authority and credibility.

But this particular, personal Word of pastoral care is proclaimed not only by the ordained ministry. Thus we are led to this further statement: preaching must be framed within the witness of the fellowship, the priesthood of all believers. Preaching does its work in us because fathers and mothers, teachers and friends have preached to us in their way and continue to preach to us, even though this may consist in nothing more than their leading and attracting us to listen to the preaching by their own listening. This puts preaching into a still broader context from which it must not be separated. The witness within the fellowship, to which we owe our being as Christians, went forth and continues to go forth, not merely in words, but through the whole Christian life of those with whom we live. The witness expressed in words lives by the witness of life without words (I Pet. 3:1 ff). And this latter without the former can mean more than the former without the latter. To live among people who really live in the fear of God, who demonstrate faith and love and Christian patience; to meet people who have been liberated by Christ to praise God and serve joyfully; to know people in whom the victorious power of faith in Christ is manifested in the midst of grievous suffering and in the face of death—these are the most powerful sermons we can ever hear. Through this kind of testimony the church makes its mightiest witness.

—Paul Althaus (307)

* * *

The Joy of Preaching

Preaching is the church in action. It springs from the act of confession itself. Every genuine act of confession is a venture of contradiction to the world. That is why there is no real preaching in the church that escapes the cross and no real congregation that does not share the suffering of Christ. But the assurance of justification makes our hearts glad and, like the apostle in prison, we do not grow weary of "declaring the mystery of Christ." The confessions of preachers in the recent past give the impression that the work of preaching is nothing but hard, heavy, slave labor. We never hear anything like that from the apostles. They preached the gospel joyfully. Not least the one who wrote his "Revelation" for the young churches threatened by the emperor of Rome. He heard the voice of his heavenly Lord: "Behold, I have set before you an open door, which no one is able to shut; I know you have but little power and yet you have kept my word and have not denied my name."

—Helmuth Schreiner (308)

* * *

The Word Unbound

We are all bound, bound to the traditions in which we have grown up, bound to certain political and economic views in which we have matured. Only one thing is not bound: God's Word. But it is precisely this Word that is committed to the church. Its power lies precisely in the fact that it is unbound. Only as the Word of God that is not bound is it living and active, sharper than any two-edged sword. If we bind the Word it will become a pasteboard sword with which we can help nobody and people will rightly laugh at it. We have been wielding enough of these pasteboard swords, particularly in our sermons. Preaching today means substituting the pasteboard sword with the sharp sword; it means proclaiming the unbound Word. Hermann Kutter, who knew something about this unbound Word, once said to me: "First I preached my church empty and yet it became full again." How can the Word fail to demonstrate its power if it is rightly proclaimed? Let us trust the Word and the Word alone and let us preach this way. This was true day before yesterday and yesterday, and it will prove to be true today. —*Günther Dehn* (309)

* * *

Listen to the Listener!

There are preachers who will suffer no criticism from their congregations, including criticism of the content of their preaching, and who react to even the most modest and well-founded remonstrance with an abounding pride. Their congregations are expected merely to accept what they say as if they were infallible and every congregation must simply accept everything the minister says. But true preachers find no pleasure in a congregation's simple acceptance of everything they utter as God's Word. They want their congregations to compare their word with God's Word; they themselves encourage the spirit of inquiry and examination. They teach their parishioners the holy duty of following the example of the Beroeans in examining the Scriptures to see whether what the preacher says is actually so. They admonish them: "Beware of false prophets"; "Test everything, hold fast what is good"; and their happy experience is that their congregations not only become more attentive and inquisitive but also, with increasing confirmation, gain more and more confidence in them. The true teacher can win people only if his teaching is questioned and tested in the light of God's Word, but the unfaithful should not win people at all. The sheep of Jesus hear his voice; they will not follow the voice of the stranger.

—Wilhelm Löhe (310)

* * *

Mirror for Ministers

Do I have any illusions about my preaching or the meaning of preaching?

Have I preached God's law and gospel without subjecting myself to the law of doing God's will and practising faith and love for Christ?

Have I set forth my own thoughts as God's thoughts?

Do I myself believe and do what I preach?

Have I kept silent concerning sin at the right time and spoken concerning sin at the right time?

Have I distorted the truth, failed to speak it, or failed to fight for it?

What do I love most, the preaching of the law or the preaching of the gospel?

Have I neglected to preach the law and the judgment of God according to our works?

Have I poured into the wounds of God's judgment the oil of his gospel when the time for it was right?

Have I feared the reproach of the world and its hatred?

—Max Lackmann (311)

* * *

THE CONCLUSION OF THE MATTER

How we should act and walk in the house of God, in the congregation of the living God, this we now know. But Thou, O Lord, have mercy upon us and forgive all the sins and transgressions by which we have sinned against thee and thy holy Word and ministry. But grant unto us and all thy servants great power, and strengthen thy life within us, that,

436

being shod with the preparation of the gospel of peace, we may go forward in patience, sowing the seed, and working and waiting for the precious fruit of the earth. Amen.

–Wilhelm Löhe (312)

* * *

And now, go thy way, O thou son greatly beloved, and work in thy lot lively, and prayerfully and cheerfully to the end of thy days; and wait and look for what the Lord will do for thee at the end of thy days; in those endless joys, wherein thou shalt shine as the brightness of the firmament, and as the stars for ever and ever. *–Cotton Mather* (313)

APPENDIX I

A SIMPLE WAY TO PRAY

For Master Peter, the Barber

By Martin Luther

Luther was asked by his barber, Peter Beskendorf, for some practical guidance on how to compose oneself for prayer. Luther complied with this request by writing this little treatise, which was published in the spring of 1535 under the title *A Simple Way to Pray, for a Good Friend.* It is counted a classic in Lutheran devotional literature. It should be noted that Luther always begins with a passage from the Bible or the Creed. First he carefully reflects upon the content of the passage and then meditates what the Holy Spirit is saying to him personally in and through the passage. The treatise is a pure illustration of evangelical meditation. (Text in *WA* 38, 351–373.)

Dear Master Peter:

I give you the best I have; I tell you how I myself pray. May our Lord God grant you and everyone to do better! Amen.

First, whenever I feel that I have grown cold and disinclined to pray, because of other tasks and thoughts (for the flesh and the devil always prevent and hinder prayer), I take my little Psalter, hasten into my room, or, if it is during the day and I have time, to the church where others are gathered, and begin to say the Ten Commandments, the Creed, and then, if I have time, some words of Christ, Paul, or the Psalms, saying them quietly to myself just as children do.

Therefore, it is a good thing to let prayer be the first business of the morning and the last of the evening. Guard yourself carefully against such false and deceitful thoughts that keep whispering: Wait awhile. In an hour or so I will pray. I must first finish this or that. Thinking such thoughts, we get away from prayer into business that will hold us and involve us till the prayer of the day comes to naught.

It may very well be that there are some works which are as good or better than prayer, especially if necessity demands them. There is a saying attributed to St. Jerome, "All the work of believers is prayer," and a proverb, "He who works faithfully prays twice"; but this can be said only if the work is done by a believing man who fears and honors God and remembers his commandments, so that he does not wrong anyone, nor steal, nor defraud, nor misappropriate. Then there is no doubt that such thoughts and such faith make of his work a prayer and sacrifice of praise.

However, the other side of the truth must be remembered also, that an unbeliever's works are nothing but cursing, and he who works unfaithfully curses twice; for the thoughts of his heart when he does his work must be such that he despises God and transgresses his commandments, and intends to wrong his neighbor and to steal and misappropriate. Such thoughts —what are they but curses against God and man, which make of his work and labor a double curse by which he curses himself? In the end such a man remains a beggar and a bungler. It is, of course, of this constant prayer that Christ is speaking in Luke 11, "Pray without ceasing," for one must unceasingly guard against sins and wrong, and this cannot be done unless one fears God and keeps his commandments in mind, as Psalm 1 says, "Blessed is he who meditates on his law day and night."

Yet we must be careful not to be weaned away from true prayer and finally come to interpret prayer to mean all kinds of works which are necessary but not true prayer after all, and thus in the end become careless, lazy, cold, and bored with prayer itself. For the devil who besets us is not lazy or careless, and our flesh is still all too active and eager to sin and inclined to be contrary to the spirit of prayer.

Now when the heart has been warmed by this recitation of the Ten Commandments, the Creed, etc., and it comes to itself, then kneel down or stand with folded hands and eyes lifted to heaven, and say or think as briefly as you can :

Heavenly Father, dear God, I am a poor, unworthy sinner, not worthy to lift up my eyes or hands to pray to thee. But since thou hast commanded us all to pray and promised to hear us, and through thy dear Son, our Lord Jesus Christ also hast taught us both how and what to pray, I come in obedience to this thy command. I come relying on thy gracious promise, I pray in the name of my Lord Jesus Christ with all thy holy Christians on earth, as he has taught us : "Our Father, who art in heaven," etc. Pray this through, word for word.

Then repeat a part, or as much as you wish. For example, repeat

The First Petition

Hallowed be thy name.

Then say : O Lord God, dear Father, hallow thou thy name both in us and in all the world. Root out and destroy the abomination, idolatry, and heresy of the Turk, the pope, and all false teachers and factious spirits who falsely bear thy name and who so shamefully misuse it, who horribly blaspheme and boast that it is in thy name and the church's commandment that they speak, when in truth it is the devil's lies and deceit under the cloak of thy name with which they grievously mislead so many poor sinners in all the world, even killing, shedding innocent blood, and persecuting, and thinking that thereby they do thee divine service.

Dear Lord, here do thou convert and restrain. Convert those who need still to be converted, that they with us and we with them may hallow and glorify thy name both with true and pure teaching and with good and holy lives. But restrain those who will not be converted, that they may cease to misuse, profane, and dishonor thy holy name and mislead the poor people. Amen.

The Second Petition

Thy kingdom come.

Then say: O dear Lord, God and Father, thou seest how the wisdom and reason of this world are not only profaning thy name and giving to lies and the devil the honor that belongs to thee, but are also opposing thy kingdom with all the power, might, wealth, and honor which thou didst give them in order to rule the world and serve thee. They are great, powerful, and many. They are gross, fat, and satisfied. They plague, hinder, and trouble the little flock of thy kingdom, which is weak, despised, and few in number. They will not suffer them on earth, and think they thereby do thee a great service.

Dear Lord God and Father, here do thou convert and restrain. Convert those who should become children and members of thy kingdom, that they with us and we with them may serve thee in thy kingdom in true faith and genuine love and come at last from this kingdom here begun into the eternal kingdom. But do thou restrain those who will not turn away their power and riches from the destruction of thy kingdom, that, being cast down from their seats and humbled, they may be made to cease. Amen.

The Third Petition

Thy will be done on earth, as it is in heaven.

Then say: O dear Lord, God and Father, thou knowest that the world, when it cannot frustrate thy name and wholly root out thy kingdom, employs tricks and frauds, carries on its many intrigues and strange plots, takes counsel, whispers, bolsters and fortifies itself, threatens and blusters, and proceeds with all evil will against thy name, thy Word, thy kingdom, and thy children to destroy them.

Therefore, dear Lord, God and Father, convert and restrain. Convert those who should still acknowledge thy good will, that they with us and we with them may be obedient to thy will, ready in this obedience to suffer willingly, patiently, and gladly all evil, cross, and tribulation, learning therein to know, and test, and experience thy good, gracious, and perfect will. But do thou restrain those who will not cease their raging, raving, hating, threatening, and wicked intent to do harm, and set to naught and shame their counsels, evil plots, and stratagems, that these may return upon their own heads, as Psalm 7 says. Amen.

The Fourth Petition

Give us this day our daily bread.

Then say: O dear Lord, God and Father, bestow thy blessing also upon this temporal, physical life. Graciously grant us blessed peace. Preserve us from war and discord. Give to our dear ruler success against all his enemies. Give him wisdom and understanding, that he may rule his earthly kingdom in peace and happiness. Give to all kings, princes, and lords good counsel and the will to preserve their lands and people in peace and justice, and especially help and guide our dear sovereign, under whose protection thou dost shelter us, that, being preserved from all evil and secure against deceitful tongues and disloyal people, he may rule in felicity. Give to all subjects grace to serve loyally and obediently. Grant to all the professions, to citizens, and farmers that they may be devout and show love and loyalty toward one another. Grant us good weather and the fruits of the earth. I commend to thee also my house and home, my wife and children; help me to guide them well, to provide for them, and rear them as befits a Christian. Ward off and restrain the destroyer and all evil angels who would work harm and hindrance. Amen.

The Fifth Petition

Forgive us our trespasses, as we forgive those who trespass against us.

Then say: O dear Lord, God and Father, enter not into judgment with us, for in thy sight shall no man living be justified. O account it not unto us also for sin that we are so ungrateful for all thine unspeakable benefits, both spiritual and physical, and that we daily stumble and sin many times more than we can know or see (Psalm 19:12). Look not upon our goodness or our wickedness, but rather upon thine own boundless mercy given us in Christ, thy dear Son. Forgive also all our enemies and all who do us injury or injustice, as we too forgive them from our hearts; for they hurt themselves most by provoking thee to anger and we are not helped by their destruction, but would rather see them saved with us. Amen.

(Here let him who feels that he cannot forgive pray for grace that he may be able to forgive. This, however, is a matter for preaching.)

The Sixth Petition

And lead us not into temptation.

Then say: O dear Lord, God and Father, keep us steady

and alert, ardent and diligent in thy Word and service, that we may not become satisfied, lazy, and indolent, as though we now had everything; in order that the grim devil may not creep in and take away from us thy dear Word, or sow discord and factions among us, or otherwise lead us into sin and shame, both spiritual and physical, but through thy Spirit give us wisdom and strength to withstand him bravely and gain the victory. Amen.

The Seventh Petition

But deliver us from evil.

Then say: O dear Lord, God and Father, this miserable life is so full of sorrow and misfortune, so fraught with danger, uncertainty, faithlessness, and evil (as St. Paul says, "The days are evil"), that we might well be weary of this life and desire death. But thou knowest our weakness, dear Father; therefore help us to walk safely through all this manifold evil and wickedness; and when the time shall come, give us a gracious death and a blessed departure from this valley of sorrow, that we may neither lose heart nor fear death, but with steadfast faith commit our souls into thy hands. Amen.

* * *

Finally, mark this, that you must always make the *Amen* strong, never doubting that God is surely listening to you with all grace and saying Yes to your prayer. Remember that you are not kneeling or standing there alone, but that all Christendom, all devout Christians are standing there with you and you with them in one unanimous, united prayer which God cannot ignore. And never leave off praying without having said or thought: There now, this prayer has been heard by God; this I know of a certainty. That is what "Amen" means.

You should also mark that I do not wish to imply that all these words need be spoken in prayer; for then in the end this would become a mere babbling of vain, empty words read from a book, as were the rosary of the laity and the prayers of priests and monks. Rather, my hope has been only to have stirred and instructed the heart as to the thoughts it should find in the Lord's Prayer. But the heart, if it is really warmed and disposed to pray, can well express these thoughts in words different from these, and, no doubt, fewer words or more. For I myself do not bind myself to these words and syllables. I say these words today and tomorrow I use some others, according as I am warmed and disposed. But I adhere as closely as I can to the same thoughts and the same sense. Often enough it happens that I so lose myself in the rich thoughts of one part or petition that I let all the other six go. And when such rich, good thoughts come, one should let the other prayers go and give place to these thoughts. Listen to them in silence and on no account suppress them, for here the Holy Spirit himself is preaching to us, and a single word of his preaching is worth more than a thousand of our own prayers. I have often learned more in one prayer than I could have obtained from much reading and pondering.

Therefore, everything depends upon my making my heart free and disposed to prayer, as the preacher says, "Before thou prayest, prepare thyself; and be not as one that tempteth the Lord" [Ecclus. 18:23]; for what else is it but to tempt God if the mouth babbles and the heart be wandering elsewhere? It is like the priest who prayed in this way: *"Deus, in adjutorium meum intende;*[1] Servant, have you unhitched the horses? *Domine, ad adjuvandum me festina;*[2] Maid, go milk the cow. *Gloria patri et filio et spiritui sancto;*[3] Run,

---

[1] Psalm 70: " Make haste, O God, to deliver me."
[2] " Make haste to to help me, O Lord."
[3] Glory be to the Father and to the Son and to the Holy Ghost."

boy, pox upon you!" I heard this kind of prayer often when I was under the papacy; and almost all their prayers are like that. This is only to mock God and it would be better just to play at it, if they cannot or will not do any better than this. Unfortunately, in my day, I myself prayed these canonical hours many a time in such a way that the psalm or the hour was over before I was conscious whether I was at the beginning or the middle.

Though not all of them blurt out the words like the above-mentioned priest, who jumbled his chores and his prayers together, they nevertheless do this in the thoughts of their hearts. They go rambling on and when they are done, they do not know what they have said or covered. They start off with *"Laudate"* and in less than no time they are off in lubberland. So it seems to me that one could hardly be presented with a more comical spectacle than one would see if it were possible to see the thoughts which a cold, irreverent heart will botch together. But now, praise God, I see that one has *not* prayed well when he forgets what he has said; for a true prayer is carefully thought through in every word and thought from beginning to end.

So a good, clever barber must have his thoughts, mind, and eyes concentrated upon the razor and the beard and not forget where he is in his stroke and shave. If he keeps talking or looking around or thinking of something else, he is likely to cut a man's mouth and nose, or even his throat, so anything that is to be done well ought to occupy the whole man with all his faculties and members; as the saying goes: *Pluribus intentus minor est ad singula sensus—*He who thinks of many things thinks of nothing and accomplishes no good. How much more must prayer possess the heart exclusively and completely if it is to be a good prayer!

This is what I have to say briefly of the Lord's Prayer or prayer in general, as I myself am accustomed to pray. For to this day I drink of the Lord's Prayer like a child; drink and eat like an old man; I can never get enough of it. To me it is the best of all prayers, even above the Psalms, though I love them very much. Indeed, it will be found that the true Master composed and taught it; and it is a thousand pities that such a prayer of such a Master should be babbled and gabbled without any reverence throughout all the world. Many people repeat the Lord's Prayer perhaps several thousand times a year and if they prayed it this way for a thousand years they would still not have tasted nor prayed a single jot or tittle of it. In short, the Lord's Prayer (as well as the name and Word of God) is the greatest martyr on earth, for everybody tortures and abuses it while few cherish and use it joyfully as it should be used.

But if I have time and opportunity after the Lord's Prayer, I do the same with the Ten Commandments, taking one part after another so that I may be as fully prepared as possible for prayer. Then out of each commandment I make a garland of four twisted strands. That is, I take each commandment first as a teaching, which is what it actually is, and reflect on what our Lord God so earnestly requires of me here. Secondly, I make of it a thanksgiving. Thirdly, a confession. Fourthly, a prayer—in these or similar thoughts and words:

I am the Lord thy God; thou shalt have no other gods before me, etc.

Here I consider, first, that God requires and teaches that I must have sincere confidence in him in all things, and that it is his earnest purpose to be my God. I must take him to be this at the risk of eternal blessedness. My heart must neither build upon nor trust in anything else, be it goods, honor, wisdom, power, or any created thing.

Secondly, I give thanks for his unfathomable mercy, that has in so fatherly a way come down to me, a lost creature, and that, unasked and unbidden, without any merit on my part, he offers to be my God, to accept me, and be my comfort, refuge, help, and strength in every time of need. We poor, blind mortals have sought after so many gods and would still be obliged to do so if he did not make himself so openly heard and offer in our own human language to be our God. Who can ever thank him enough for this?

Thirdly, I confess and acknowledge my great sinfulness and unthankfulness in so shamefully despising this beautiful teaching and great gift all my life and so enormously provoking his wrath with countless idolatries. For this I repent and pray for forgiveness.

Fourthly, I pray, saying: O my God and Lord, help me by thy grace, that I may learn to know and understand this thy commandment better day by day and with sincere trust live in accord with it. Watch over my heart that I may no longer be so thoughtless and unthankful, that I may seek none other gods nor comfort on earth or in any creature, but rather cleave only to thee, my only God. Amen, dear Lord God and Father. Amen.

Then, if I desire or have time, the Second Commandment, also twisted into a garland of four strands as follows:

Thou shalt not take the name of the Lord thy God in vain, etc.

First, I learn that I should keep God's name glorious, holy, and beautiful, not to swear, curse, or lie by it, not to be proud or seek my own honor or name, but rather humbly to call upon, worship, praise, and glorify his name, and let it be my whole honor and pride that he is my God and I his poor creature and unworthy servant.

Secondly, I give thanks for these glorious gifts, that he has revealed and given to me his name, that I can boast of his name and be called God's servant, creature, etc., that his name is my refuge, as a mighty fortress, as Solomon says (Prov. 18:10), to which the righteous man flees and is safe.

Thirdly, I confess and acknowledge my shameful, grievous sins, which all my life I have committed against this commandment, since I have not only failed to call upon, praise, and honor his holy name, but also have been ungrateful for these gifts and misused his name for all kinds of shame and sin by swearing, lying, deceiving, etc. For this I repent and pray for grace and forgiveness.

Fourthly, I pray for help and strength, that henceforth I may learn this commandment well and guard against this shameful unthankfulness, against misusing and sinning against his name, that I may rather be found grateful and in true fear and honoring of his name.

And, as I did above in connection with the Lord's Prayer, I admonish again; if the Holy Spirit should come while these thoughts are in your mind and begin to preach in your heart, giving you rich and enlightened thoughts, then give regard to him; let these written thoughts go, be still and listen to him who is better able to do it than you are. And note what he proclaims and write it down; so will you behold wondrous things in God's law, as David says (Psalm 119:18).

The Third Commandment
Remember the sabbath day, to keep it holy.

Here I learn, first, that the sabbath day was not instituted for idleness or fleshly lusts, but should rather be hallowed by us. But it is not hallowed by our work and activity (for our works are not holy), but rather by the Word of God, which alone is wholly pure and holy and hallows everything it touches, be it times, places, persons, work, rest, etc.; for through the Word even our works are made holy, as St. Paul says that everything created is consecrated by the Word and prayer (I Tim. 4:5). Therefore I learn here that first and foremost I should hear and ponder the Word of God on the sabbath, and then give thanks in my own words, praise God for all his benefits, and pray for myself and all the world.

He who so conducts himself on the sabbath hallows the sabbath. He who does not do this does worse than those who work on the sabbath.

Secondly, in connection with this commandment I give thanks for the great and lovely goodness and grace of God for having given to us and commanded us especially on the sabbath to consider his Word and message, which treasure no human heart can ever meditate enough, for his Word is the one solitary light in the darkness of this life and a word of life, consolation, and all blessedness. And where the dear, saving Word is not present there is nothing but dreadful, awful darkness, error, faction, death, all misfortune, and the devil's own tyranny, as is plain to be seen every day.

Thirdly, I confess and acknowledge my great sin and shameful unthankfulness in so disgracefully spending the sabbath in my life and so miserably despising his precious Word, and being so lazy, so loath, and sated to hear it, much less ever heartily desiring it or giving thanks for it. I have therefore allowed my dear God to preach to me in vain, I have let slip the noble treasure and trampled it underfoot. This he has suffered from me out of pure divine goodness and has not let this make him to cease preaching and calling to me constantly with all fatherly and divine love and faithfulness for my soul's salvation. For this I repent and pray for grace and forgiveness.

Fourthly, I pray for myself and all the world, that the dear Father may keep up steadfast in his Word and not take it from us because of our sins, unthankfulness, and indolence. That he may defend us from factious spirits and false teachers. That he may send faithful and true laborers into his harvest, that is, faithful and devout pastors and preachers, and that he may also grant to all of us grace humbly to hear, accept, and honor their word as his own Word, and also to thank and praise him for it from our hearts.

The Fourth Commandment
Honor thy father and thy mother.

First, I learn here to know God, my Creator, how wonderfully he has created me in body and soul and given me life through my parents, and how he it was who gave them the heart to care for me, the fruit of their body, with all their powers, to bring me into the world, to nourish, nurse, and rear me with great diligence, care, danger, weariness, and labor. Here too I learn to discern how to this hour he has guarded me, his creature, from countless perils and needs of body and soul and often helped me to escape them, as though every hour he were creating me anew. For the devil begrudges us even one hour of life.

Secondly, I give thanks to the rich and goodly Creator for myself and all the world, that in this commandment he has ordained and provided for the increase and preservation of the human race, that is, the households of home and state. For without these two households or governments the world could not endure for even a year, because without secular government there is no peace, and where there is no peace there can be no family life, and where there is no family life children can neither be born nor reared, and the estate of fatherhood and motherhood would cease to exist. But there stands this commandment, upholding and preserving both home and state, commanding obedience to children and subjects, and also insisting that it must be done, or if it is not done he will not let it go unpunished. Otherwise the children would long since have torn down and devastated all the life of the home by disobedience and subjects would have destroyed the state, because they are far more numerous than parents and rulers. Therefore this benefit too is unspeakable.

Thirdly, I confess and acknowledge my miserable disobedience and sinfulness, that, contrary to this commandment of my God, I have not honored my parents and been obedient to them, that I have often provoked and offended them, received their fatherly correction with impatience, murmured against them, disregarded their faithful admonitions, and rather followed that of loose company and bad fellows. And yet God himself curses such disobedient children and declares that their life will not be long; and the truth is that many do perish and die before they grow up! For he who does not obey father and mother must obey the hangman or else by God's wrath wilfully lose his life. For all this I repent and pray for grace and forgiveness.

Fourthly, I pray for myself and all the world, that God may grant us his grace and richly pour down his blessing upon both the home and the state. I pray also that henceforth we may be devout, hold our parents in honor, be obedient to our rulers, resist the devil and not follow his enticements to disobedience and discontent, and that thus we may by deeds help to improve our homes and our country and to keep peace, to the glory and honor of God, our own welfare, and the good of all; and that we may acknowledge this his grace and give thanks for it. Here there should also be prayer for parents and rulers, that God may grant them understanding and wisdom to guide and rule us peacefully and pleasantly. That he may guard them against tyranny, bellowing, and raging and turn them from it, that they may honor God's Word and neither persecute nor do wrong to anyone. For these great gifts must be sought in prayer, as St. Paul teaches (Rom. 12:12); otherwise the devil will be the top dog in office and things go to rot and ruin.

And if you are a father or mother yourself this is the time not to forget yourself and your children and servants, but earnestly to pray that the loving Father, who in his name has placed you in your honorable office and desires that you too should call him Father and honor him, may grant you grace and success to rule and nourish your wife, children, and servants in a godly and Christianlike way, that he may give you wisdom and strength to train them well, and to give to them good hearts and wills to follow your teaching and be obedient. For both are the gift of God, both children and their good development, both their turning out well and their remaining so. Otherwise a home becomes nothing but a pigsty, a school for scamps, as one sees among the godless, ill-bred people.

The Fifth Commandment
Thou shalt not kill.

Here I learn, first, that God wills that I should love my neighbor and therefore that I should do no harm to his body either by words or deeds. He also wills that I should not revenge myself upon my neighbor or do him harm by anger, impatience, envy, hatred or any kind of spite, but rather know that I owe it to him to help and counsel him in all his physical needs. For in this commandment God has commanded me to preserve my neighbor's body and likewise commanded my neighbor to preserve my body, as Sirach says (Ecclus. 9:14), he has committed to each of us his neighbor.

Secondly, I give thanks here for that unspeakable love, care, and faithfulness toward me by which God has built a great, strong shelter and wall around my body, so that all men should be in duty bound to care for me and protect me, and I should be bound to do the same toward all men. Moreover, he watches and when this is not done, he has ordained the sword for those who do not do it. Otherwise, if it were not for his commandment and decree, the devil would stir up such murder among us that nobody's life would be safe for an hour, as does happen when God is angry and punishes the disobedient and ungrateful world.

Thirdly, here I confess and lament my wickedness and that of the world, not only that we have been so terribly ungrateful for this his fatherly love and care for us, but also, what is especially shameful, that we do not know this commandment and teaching and do not want to learn it, but rather despise it as if it did not apply to us or we did not profit by it. And, what is more, we go on in our security, never letting it bother our conscience that, contrary to this commandment, we so disregard and forsake, yea, persecute, wound, or even in our hearts kill our neighbor. So we give in to our anger, hatred, and all malice as if we were doing what was right and good. Verily, here is the time to lament and cry over us bad fellows, us blind, wild, unkind people, who trample, kick, scratch, rend, bite, and eat one another like savage animals and do not fear this stern commandment of God.

Fourthly, I pray that the dear Father may teach us to know this his holy commandment and help us to conduct ourselves and live in accord with it. That he may defend us all from the murderer, who is the master of all murder and mischief, and grant his rich grace that people, and we with them, may become kind, gentle, and good to one another, that we may heartily forgive one another, and bear one another's faults and infirmities like Christians and brothers and thus live in true peace and harmony as this commandment teaches and requires of us.

The Sixth Commandment

Thou shalt not commit adultery.

Here again I learn what God thinks of me and what he would have of me, namely, that I should live chastely, decently, and soberly in thought and word and deed, each one putting no shame upon anyone's wife, daughter, or maid, but rather helping, saving, protecting, and doing everything that will preserve their honor and decency and also helping to stop the naughty mouths of those who injure or steal their honor. All this I owe, and God would have of me not only that I should leave unspoiled my neighbor's wife and family, but I am also in duty bound to help him to keep and preserve his respect and honor, just as I would wish that my neighbor should do this to me and practice this commandment toward me and mine.

Secondly, I give thanks to the faithful, loving Father for his grace and blessing, that by this commandment he takes under his care and protection my husband, son, servant, wife, daughter, and maidservant and so sternly and severely forbids that they be shamed. For he gives me sure direction and holds it over me and will not let it go unpunished, even if he must do it himself, if anybody transgresses and breaks this commandment and direction. None will escape him; either man must pay for it here or atone for this lust in the fires of hell, for he desires purity and will not suffer adultery, as we see every day that finally God's wrath catches up with all impenitent, profligate people and puts them to shame and ruin. Otherwise it would be impossible to preserve one's wife, children, and servants in chastity and honor from the devil of uncleanness for even an hour. What would become of it would be nothing but dog couplings and bestiality, as happens wherever God in his wrath withdraws his hand and lets things go.

Thirdly, I confess and acknowledge my sin and that of all the world for having sinned against this commandment all my life in thought and word and deed, and for not only having been ungrateful for this fine teaching and gift but even murmuring against God because he has commanded this discipline and chastity and not allowed all kinds of unchastity and villainy to go unchecked and unpunished and thus having despised, ridiculed, and condemned the state of matrimony. Sins against this commandment are above all others the grossest and most easily recognized and for them there is no cloak or cover. For this I repent, etc.

Fourthly, I pray for myself and all the world, that God may give us grace to keep this his commandment with our whole hearts and that we may not only live chastely ourselves but help and counsel others to do so.

So I continue with the other commandments if I have time and leisure or desire to do so, for, as I have said, I wish none to be bound to these words and thoughts of mine, but have merely set forth my example for him who may wish to follow it or improve upon it if he can. He may take all the commandments at one time or as many as he wishes. For the mind, when it lights upon a thing, be it good or bad, and is serious about it, is able to think of more things in a moment than the tongue can speak in ten hours and the pen can write in ten days. Such a nimble, subtle, mighty thing is the soul or the mind. Therefore it can soon go through the four parts of all ten commandments if it is so minded and is in earnest.

The Seventh Commandment

Thou shalt not steal.

First, I learn here that I should not take nor keep my neighbor's goods against his will either secretly or openly. I should not be unfaithful or false in my dealings, service, or work in order to gain my own by stealth, but rather support myself in the sweat of my face and eat my own bread in all honesty. Moreover, I must help to see to it that my neighbor, just like myself, be not deprived of his own in the way mentioned above. I learn also that through this commandment God in his fatherly care and great sternness is protecting and fencing in my property by forbidding others to steal from me, and if one does it nevertheless, he has imposed punishment and committed it to the hands of the hangman, gallows, and rope. Or, if the hangman cannot do it, he himself carries out the punishment, so that in the end they become beggars, as the saying goes, "Who steals when he is young will go begging when he is old," and again, "Ill-gotten goods never thrive" and "Evil gotten, evil spent."

Secondly, I give thanks for his faithfulness and goodness, that he has given to me and the whole world this good teaching and with it protection, for if he were not guarding, nobody would have a farthing or bit of bread in the house.

Thirdly, I confess all my sin and unthankfulness, wherever I have dealt unfairly, fraudulently, or unfaithfully with anyone throughout my whole life.

Fourthly, I pray that he may grant his peace, that I and all the world may finally learn and remember this his commandment and also let it improve us, that stealing, robbing, sweating, peculating, and unfairness may diminish and soon cease altogether through the coming of the Last Day toward which the prayer of all the saints and the whole creation is pressing (Rom. 8:20 ff).

The Eighth Commandment
Thou shalt not bear false witness, etc.

First, this teaches us to be truthful with one another, to avoid all lying and slander, and to be glad to speak and hear only the best concerning others. That sets up a wall and a defense between our reputation and innocence and malicious mouths and deceitful tongues, which God also will not leave unpunished, as has been said of the other commandments.

We should thank him both for the teaching and the protection which he so graciously gives us herewith.

Thirdly, we should confess and plead for forgiveness that we have spent our lives so ungratefully and sinfully, with lies and false, wicked tongues against our neighbor, to whom we rather owe the saving of his honor and innocence, as we ourselves would have others do to us.

Fourthly, we pray for help to keep this commandment henceforth and for a wholesome tongue, etc.

The Ninth and Tenth Commandments
Thou shalt not covet thy neighbor's house, his wife, etc.

This teaches us, first, that we must not under any pretense of right alienate, estrange, or extort from our neighbor his goods and what is his, but rather help him to keep them, as we would have done toward ourselves. And this too is a protection against the dodges and devices of the worldly-wise, who still get their punishment in the end. Secondly, we should give thanks for this, thirdly, confess our sins in repentance and sorrow, and, fourthly, pray for help and strength to become devout and to keep this commandment of God.

These, then, are the Ten Commandments treated in a four-fold way—as a little book of teaching, a hymnbook, a book of confession, and a prayer book. Hereupon a heart should come to itself and be warmed to prayer. But see to it that you do not undertake all of it or too much of it, lest your spirit become weary. Note too that a good prayer need not be long nor long-drawn-out, but rather should be frequent and ardent. It is sufficient if you can seize upon one part or even half of one part from which you can strike a spark in your heart. Well enough, the Spirit will and must grant this and will go on teaching in your heart if it is conformed to God's Word and cleared of foreign concerns and thoughts.

Then[1] if you have time left over or are so inclined, you may do the same with the Creed and make of it a four-stranded garland. The Creed, however, has three great parts or articles, according to the three persons of the divine majesty, as it has been divided in the past and also in the Catechism.

The First Article: Of Creation

I believe in God the Father Almighty, Maker of heaven and earth.

Here first a great light shines into your heart, if you desire to have it, and teaches you in a few brief words what all

---

[1] In the earlier editions Luther concluded with the following words:

"I shall say nothing of the Creed or the Scriptures here, for that would be an endless task. Anyone who is practiced in it can very well take the Ten Commandments one day and a psalm or a chapter of the Bible on the next and with this flint and tinder strike fire in his heart."

tongues and many books cannot express or inscribe, namely, what you are, where you come from, and wherefrom come heaven and earth. For you are the creature, the workmanship, the creation, the handiwork of God. That is, of yourself and in yourself you are nothing, you can do nothing, you know nothing, you are capable of nothing. For what were you a thousand years ago? What was heaven and earth six thousand years ago? Nothing, just as what has never been created is nothing. But what you are, what you know and are capable of, this is "God's creature," as you here confess with your mouth.

Therefore in the sight of God you have nothing to boast of except that you are nothing at all and he is your Creator, and that at any moment he can return you to nothingness. The reason knows nothing of this light. Many great people have sought to find out what heaven and earth and man and creation is, but they have not discovered it. But here it is declared: faith says that God created everything from nothing. Here is the soul's garden of pleasure to walk about in the works of God. But this is too long to write about here.

Secondly, one should here give thanks that by God's goodness we have been created out of nothing and daily preserved from nothingness—a fair creature of body and soul, reason, five senses, etc., and that we have been given dominion over the earth, fish, fowls, beasts, and so on. (Here we should think of Genesis, chapters 1, 2, and 3.)

Thirdly, one should confess and lament our unbelief and unthankfulness in not having taken this to heart, nor believed, regarded, or acknowledged it, much worse than the dumb animals, and so on.

Fourthly, one should pray for true, confident faith, that we may henceforth earnestly believe and deem that the dear God is our Creator, as this article declares.

The Second Article: Of Redemption

And in Jesus Christ, His only Son, our Lord, etc.

Here again a great light shines and teaches us that through Christ, God's Son, we have been redeemed from the death into which we fell after the creation through Adam's sin and otherwise must perish eternally. And this is the time when you remember this. Just as you had in the first article to count yourself a creature of God and never doubt it, so here, too, you must count yourself among the redeemed and never doubt it. Of all the words in it you must put first the word "our"; Jesus Christ, *our* Lord, suffered for *us*, died for *us*, rose again for *us*, so that everything is for us and applies to us, and you, too, are included in that "our." So the Word is given to us personally.

Secondly, you should give hearty thanks for this great grace and be joyful over such redemption.

Thirdly, you should bitterly lament and confess your shameful unbelief and doubt of this grace. Oh, what food for thought you will receive here; again how many idolatries you have practiced here, the numerous adorations of saints and countless works of your own which have opposed this redemption!

Fourthly, then pray that God will henceforth preserve you in true, pure faith in Christ, your Lord, to the end.

The Third Article: Of Sanctification

And in the Holy Ghost, etc.

This is the third great light, that teaches us where this Creator and Redeemer is to be found and met here on earth, and where it will all come out in the end. And this is the sum of it: where the holy Christian church is, there you find God the Creator, God the Redeemer, and God the Holy Ghost, who daily sanctifies through the forgiveness of sins, etc. But the church is where God's Word concerning this faith is rightly preached and confessed. Here again you have much to meditate upon of all that the Holy Spirit performs every day in the church, and so on.

Therefore give thanks here, that you too have been called and have come into this church.

Confess and lament your unbelief and unthankfulness in not having regarded all this.

And pray for the right, steadfast faith that endures and abides until you come to that place where everything will remain eternally, that is, after the resurrection of the dead in everlasting life. Amen.

* * *

Appendix II

THE LADDER OF DEVOTION

or

THE HEAVENLY LADDER

by Caspar Calvör

This is another simple illustration of evangelical meditation in the tradition of *Luther's meditatio, tentatio, oratio.* Caspar Calvör (1650–1725) published in 1691 three devotional works under the title *Christliches Kleeblatt (Christian Clover-leaf),* the third of which is entitled, "A Paved Way to Peace in God." The following is taken from this in the form reprinted in Wilhelm Löhe's *Der evangelische Geistliche,* Vol. I, pp. 126–131.

1) What do we mean by a ladder of devotion or ladder to heaven?

The proper and fruitful use of God's Word, the use that leads to devotion and to heaven, the use of God's Word as it is found in the Holy Scriptures and also in human books, such as the Catechism, etc.

2) I confess that I still do not know what you mean.

Look, this fruitful use of divine truth consists of three parts : 1) *meditation,* 2) *self-examination,* 3) *prayer.* One may read the Bible quickly and this has its advantages and is necessary. But one must also not neglect these three parts of a fruitful use of the Scriptures. Much depends on this!

3) Very well then, how does one practice *meditation*?

    a) I take a familiar text, a hymn verse, a portion of the Catechism, a prayer, or the like. I do not pass over a single word without pondering it, but consider and take to heart one word after another.

    b) In order that I may penetrate more deeply and thoroughly the meaning and sense of the word I have before me, I repeat them several times and ponder them slowly with reverent attention, also dividing the text into definite questions, inquiring into all the circumstances (who? what? where? why? etc.).

    c) I recall other passages from the Bible, the hymnbook, and the Catechism which correspond to this passage and ponder these also in my heart.

    d) I consider what teaching, admonition, or consolation I can derive from this passage or verse.

4) How do you practice *self-examination?*

I ask myself whether this passage applies to me. This I find out particularly by considering the persons of whom or to whom the passage is spoken. If I belong among them, then the passage pertains to me. Then I apply it directly to myself, just as if it were spoken directly to me. All the questions which I raised in the meditation I answer once more, but now with reference to myself. But if I am not to be counted among the persons to whom the passage refers, then I do not relate it to myself. Indeed, if it is a word of comfort, I do not apply it to myself until I have become the kind of person who can receive this consolation. I therefore begin at once upon my improvement by praying to God for mercy and conversion. If the passage which does not apply to me is a word of rebuke, then I give thanks to God for preserving me from the sin which is rebuked, but I also pray that he may continue to preserve me and graciously forgive my other sins and infirmities.

5) How do you practice *prayer*?

What I have discovered in meditation and examination I gather together in a prayer to God.

6) How do you then proceed from this preparation to the devotion of the heart?

The qualities of the inner life called to mind by the passage I employ at once in *the devotion of the heart,* the peaceful, blessed works of my interior Sabbath. I look at the sins and vices which are pointed out, curse them, and reject them, and pray God that I may be enabled with my whole heart to do this more and more, and that my soul may be liberated from the desire and love of them and find rest. Thus I have climbed the three rungs of the heavenly ladder and come to the fourth, that is, through preparation I have come to true worship of the heart. Then, having been strengthened by spiritual departure from evil and turning toward that which is good, by this blessed exercise of my soul in the prayer of the heart, I go to my daily work and practice the good outwardly, hating and refraining from evil outwardly.

7) Actually, you are not telling me anything new when you speak of this so-called heavenly ladder. One ought always to employ the Scriptures in this way and allow them to lead us to the festal hours of the inner life, to this foretaste of everlasting life.

Of course it is not new. But who uses the Holy Scriptures in this way? What is easier than this meditation, self-examination, and prayer, and what makes us wiser, stronger, more happy in that which is good? How it helps us to lay hold of the powers of the age to come which lie hidden in the Word! How sweet becomes the Word, sweeter than honey and the honeycomb! No, the thing itself is not new. But for many Christians the practice of it may be altogether new. Would God that this heavenly ladder, this use of God's Word were more common, more practiced, and more loved! The effect of it would be felt in every place and every way.

8) I wish that you would show me how to use the heavenly ladder by giving me one or more examples.

I would rather advise you first to make your own attempts. Perhaps later I could give you one or more meditations, self-examinations, and prayers. Here we learn more from examples furnished by others after we have discovered by trial and experience the points which are particularly difficult for us. Otherwise its practice according to the directions given is quite easy.

9) I beg you to give me only one example. How would you apply this meditation and self-examination, say, to John 3:16, "God so loved the world," etc.?

The questions for meditation are these:

Who has loved the world? *What* has he loved? *How, how much* has he loved it? *What* is the meaning of "He gave his Son"? For what *purpose* did he give his Son? What is meant by "perish"? What does "to have everlasting life" mean? Who is not to perish? What does "to believe in the Son" mean? Are any who believe in Jesus excepted from the promise of everlasting life? What other passages accord with this passage? And so forth.

In self-examination one might say something like this:

Does this passage apply to you, O my soul? It does apply to you, in part at least, for you are a part of the world which God so loved. Therefore this glorious "so" applies also to you. For you, too, the Son, the only-begotten, was given. Therefore you, too, shall not perish. But you will perish nevertheless, if you are not among the believers. The blessed promise of everlasting life does not apply to you if you do not believe in Jesus Christ. Does, then, this passage and its blessed promise really apply to you? Do you believe? Is your faith real?

10) But is not this but a catechism?

Yes, but a catechism in which teacher and pupil are one and

the same person. Here the questions sound entirely different and the answers too. This wells up mightily from the heart and goes to the heart.

11) And yet it could turn out to be nothing more than pure catechism.

It could, but that would be the person's own fault, in which case it would of course be pure pedantry. But just you practice it with real seriousness, in quiet solitude, as one who is seeking God. You will find a great blessing. Nor is it necessary to question every point, much less need everything be put in the form of questions. I put the questions only for the sake of brevity. Practice it yourself and you will soon note that a happy freedom will prevail; all that is meticulous and slavish will soon disappear.

12) But I still have not asked you to show me how, after this meditation and self-examination on John 3:16, to sum it all up in prayer.

You have done well not to do so, for this needs no pattern, especially since in prayer, even less than in meditation and self-examination, there should be no timorous precision.

13) You leave me, then, to my own practice and experience?

Absolutely. Here there is no room for any opinion except that which comes out of experience. *Go, try, test* what you have learned!

SOURCES OF THE PRAYERS

1. Ernst Glür and Kurt Jagdmann, *Orate Fratres, Gebetsordnung für evangelische-lutherische Pfarrer* (Göttingen: Vandenhoeck & Ruprecht, 1952), p. 14.
2. Hanns Lilje, *Der tägliche Gottesdienst, Alte und neue Gebete für jeden Tag*, 3rd ed. (Berlin: Furche-Verlag, 1939, pp. 57 f.
3. Karl Bernhard Ritter, *Pfarrgebete*, 4th ed. (Kassell: Johannes Stauda-Verlag, 1947), pp. 55 f. Adapted.
4. William Bright, *Ancient Collects and Other Prayers*, 5th ed. (London: James Parker, 1875), pp. 233 f.
5. Karl Bernhard Ritter, *Pfarrgebete*, pp. 57 f.
6. Otto Dietz, *Matutin- und Vesperbüchlein* (Neuendettelsau: Freimund-Verlag, 1937), pp. 57 f.
7. J. W. D.
8. Luther-Steinhäuser, Albert T. W. Steinhäuser, "Luther's Small Catechism as a Manual of Devotion," *Lutheran Church Review*, XLV, 3 (July, 1926), 283.
9. William Laud, from *Ecclesia*, in *A Summarie of Devotions. Lib. Ang. Cath. Theol. Laud's Works*, III, 68.
10. Michael Coelius, *Hanauische Kirchen- und Schulordnung* (1659).
11. Hanns Lilje, *Der tägliche Gottesdienst*, p. 58.
12. *Orate Fratres*, pp. 16 f.
13. Liturgy of Malabar.
14. J. W. D.
15. Lancelot Andrewes, *Preces Privatae*, Morning Prayers (Trans. Brightman).
16. Augustine.
17. *Book of Common Prayer, Canada* (Forms of Prayer to be used in Families: Evening). John Wallace Suter, Jr., *The Book of English Collects* (New York: Harper, 1940), p. 278.
18. Martin Luther, *Small Catechism*, Explanation of the First Article of the Creed.
19. *Evangelische Kirchengesangbuch*, in *Orate Fratres*, p. 18.
20. Hermann Bezzel, in *Orate Fratres*, p. 18.
21. G. C. Dieffenbach, in Georg Christian Dieffenbach and Christian Müller, *Evangelisches Brevier* (Gotha: Gustav Schloessmann, 1869), pp. 415 f.
22. Office of Compline, quoted in Frederick B. Macnutt, *The Prayer Manual* (London: Mowbray, 1951), p. 69.
23. Gelasian Sacramentary, William Bright, *Ancient Collects*, pp. 10 f.
24. William Löhe, *Werke*, VII, 1953.

25. Luther-Steinhäuser, *op. cit., p.* 283.
26. *Orate Fratres*, pp. 19 f.
27. *Book of Common Prayer*, Ireland. Suter, *The Book of English Collects*, p. 326.
28. *Common Service Book of the Lutheran Church, The Occasional Services, Order for the Installation of a Church Council.* Abbreviated.
29. *Agendenentwurf für die Altpreuss. Union, 1931,* quoted in *Orate Fratres*, p. 23. Altered.
30. *Pfälzisches Kirchenbuch, 1927,* quoted in *Orate Fratres,* p. 23.
31. Henry Parry Liddon, *Hours of Prayer for Daily Use through the Year,* Sext (1856). Quoted in Macnutt, *op. cit.,* p. 165.
32. William Bright, *Ancient Collects,* p. 237.
33. Frederick B. Macnutt, *op. cit.,* p. 71.
34. *Westminster Prayers* by P. Dearmer and F. R. Barry (London: Oxford University Press, 1936), p. 25.
35. John Hunter, *Devotional Services for Public Worship* (London: Dent, 1901), p. 52.
36. Martin Luther, *Small Catechism,* Explanation of the Second Article of the Creed.
37. Mozarabic Sacramentary.
38. Daybreak Office of the Eastern Church.
39. Dieffenbach and Müller, *op. cit.,* pp. 416 f.
40. Hermann Bezzel, *Gebete,* 1933.
41. John Calvin and Theodore de Beza, Strasbourg, 1539.
42. Wilhelm Löhe, *Seed-Grains of Prayer,* trans. by H. A. Weller (Chicago: Warburg, 1914), p. 67.
43. Luther-Steinhäuser, *op. cit.,* p. 283.
44. *Kirchenbuch für Baden,* quoted in *Orate Fratres,* pp. 25 f. Altered.
45. William Laud, quoted in Macnutt, *The Prayer Manual,* p. 144.
46. *Prayer for All Occasions* (Cincinnati: Forward Movement Publications, n. d.), p. 57.
47. Wilhelm Löhe, *Hausbedarf Christlicher Gebete,* 1859, quoted in Gerhard Molwitz, *Lutherisches Gebetbuch* (Chemnitz: Verlag Max Müller, 1938), p. 95.
48. Søren Kierkegaard, *Training in Christianity,* trans. by Walter Lowrie (New York: Oxford University Press, 1941), pp. 253 f.
49. Wilhelm Löhe, quoted in Karl Kampffmeyer, *Das teure Predigtamt. Gebete und Weisungen für den Dienst am Wort aus dem Schatz der Kirche* (Hamburg: Furche-Verlag, 1954), pp. 16 f.
50. *Tägliches Morgengebet,* quoted in *Orate Fratres,* p. 29. Altered.
51. Unknown, quoted in Macnutt, *op. cit.,* p. 215.

52. Unknown, quoted in Macnutt, *ibid.*, p. 215.

53. Office of Compline.

54. Gregorian Sacramentary.

55. Liturgy of Geneva, *Confession,* by John Calvin.

56. Martin Luther, *Small Catechism,* Explanation of the Third Article of the Creed.

57. Hermann Bezzel, quoted in *Orate Fratres,* p. 31.

58. Erasmus, *Precationes,* 1535, trans. by Frederick B. Macnutt, *op. cit.,* p. 12.

59. Dieffenback and Müller, *op. cit.,* p. 420.

60. Wilhelm Löhe, *Seed-Grains of Prayer,* p. 66.

61. The Swedish Liturgy, quoted in Paul Zeller Strodach, *Oremus. Collects, Devotions, Litanies from Ancient and Modern Sources* (Philadelphia: United Lutheran Publication House, 1925), p. 113.

62. James Burns, quoted in James Ferguson, *Prayer for Public Worship,* ed. by Charles L. Walker (New York: Harper, 1958', p. 13.

63. Luther-Steinhäuser, *op. cit.,* p. 284.

64. *Orate Fratres,* p. 32. Altered.

65. *Book of Common Prayer, U.S.* Suter, *The Book of English Collects,* p. 231.

66. *Orate Fratres,* p. 32. Altered.

67. *Gebete der Kirche,* quoted in *Orate Fratres,* p. 36. Altered.

68. *Westminster Prayers,* p. 24.

69. Thomas Wilson, *Sacra Privata.*

70. Gregorian Sacramentary.

71. Sarum Breviary.

72. Löhes' *Agende,* 1844, trans. by P. Z. Strodach, *Oremus,* p. 104.

73. Dieffenbach and Müller, *op. cit.,* pp. 418 f.

74. Gelasian Sacramentary, trans. by William Bright, *Ancient Collects,* pp. 10 f.

75. Unknown.

76. Dietrich Bonhoeffer, *Widerstand und Ergebung;* see *Prisoner for God* (New York: Macmillan, 1954), pp. 69 f.

77. Luther-Steinhäuser, *op. cit.,* p. 284.

78. John Watson, *Prayers and Services* (Publication Committee, 21 Warwick Lane, London, E. C., 1909).

79. J. W. D.

80. J. W. D.

81. Jeremy Taylor, *Private Devotions.*

82. William Temple, *Christian Faith and Life* (New York: Macmillan, 1931), p. 139.

83. Samuel Johnson, in Elton Trueblood, *Doctor Johnson's Prayers* (New York: Harper, 1947), p. 5.

84. Wilhelm Löhe, *Seed-Grains of Prayer*, pp. 355 f.

85. Hermann Bezzel, quoted in *Allgemeines Evangelisches Gebetbuch* (Hamburg: Furche-Verlag, 1955), p. 411.

86. William Temple, in A. E. Baker, *William Temple's Teaching* (Philadelphia: Westminster Press, 1951), p. 130.

87. Edward Meyrick Goulburn.

88. Dieffenbach and Müller, *op. cit.*, p. 419.

89. Michael Coelius, *Hanauische Kirchen- und Schulordnung*, trans. P. Z. Strodach, *Oremus*, p. 123.

90. John Cosin, *Works*, Vol. II, Prayers for the Evening.

91. Augustine.

92. Luther-Steinhäuser, *op. cit.*, p. 284.

93. J. W. D.

94. Based on prayer in *Tägliches Morgengebet*, in *Orate Fratres*, p. 46.

95. J. W. D.

96. Based on prayer in *Schwesternbrevier von Bethel*, *Orate Fratres*, pp. 50 f.

97. Traditional.

98. Sarum Breviary.

99. K. B. Ritter, *Pfarrgebete*, pp. 44 f.

100. James Martineau, *Home Prayers* (London: Longmans, Green, 1891).

101. Christina Rossetti, *A Poet's Prayers.*

102. Dieffenbach and Müller, *op. cit.*, pp. 417 f.

103. In *Das Gebet der Tageszeiten*, quoted in *Orate Fratres*, p. 60.

104. Luther-Steinhäuser, *op. cit.*, pp. 284 f.

105. Unknown, quoted in *Allgemeines Evangelisches Gebetbuch*, p. 378.

106. William Bright, *Private Prayers for a Week*, p. 12; slightly adapted by F. B. Macnutt, *The Prayer Manual*, p. 226.

107. Veit Dietrich, in Otto Dietz, *Die Evangelien-Kollekten des Veit Dietrich* (Leipzig: H. G. Wallmann Verlag, 1930), p. 85. XXIV S. after Trinity.

108. J. W. D.

109. J. W. D.

110. Based on prayer in *Tägliches Morgengebet*, quoted in *Orate Fratres*, pp. 59 f.

111. J. W. D.

112. *Weimarisches Gesangbuch*, 1873, quoted in Selina F. Fox, *A Chain of Prayer Across the Ages*, 6th ed. (New York: Dutton, 1941), p. 182.

113. Thomas Ken, quoted in Macnutt, *op. cit.*, p. 39.

114. K. B. Ritter, *Gebete für das Jahr der Kirche*, 1st ed. (Kassel: Bärenreiter Verlag, 1933), p. 35. Hereafter referred to as *Gebete* 1.

115. K. B. Ritter, *Gebete für das Jahr der Kirche*, 2nd. ed. (Kassel: Johannes Stauda-Verlag, 1948), p. 55. Hereafter referred to as *Gebete* 2.

116. Martin Moller, *Thesaurus precationum*, 1603; text in Gerhard Molwitz, *Lutherisches Gebetbuch*, p. 41.

117. William Temple in A. E. Baker, *William Temple's Teaching*, p. 128.

118. Veit Dietrich, *Kinderpostille*, 1549, in Gerhard Molwitz, *op. cit.*, p. 45.

119. John Wallace Suter, *Prayers of the Spirit* (New York: Harper & Bros., 1943), p. 18.

120. *Gebete* 1, p. 40.

121. *Gebete* 1, p. 41.

122. *Gebete* 1, p. 42.

123. *Gebete* 2, p. 80.

124. *Gebete* 2, pp. 71-72.

125. *Kirchenbuch für die Gemeinde (Isenhagen)*, quoted in *Orate Fratres*, p. 64.

126. Otto Schlisske, *Christliche Unterweisung im Jahr der Kirche* (Göttingen: Vandenhoeck & Ruprecht, 1949), p. 99.

127. Post-Communion in Sarum Rite, given in John Wallace Suter, Jr., *The Book of English Collects* (New York and London: Harper & Bros., 1940), p. 47.

128. Schlisske, p. 115.

129. *Gebete* 2, p. 180.

130. *Gebete* 2, p. 86.

131. *Gebete* 2, p. 87.

132. *Gebete* 2, p. 94.

133. Suter, *Prayers of the Spirit*, p. 22.

134. 1979 American *Book of Common Prayer*, pp. 216-17.

135. Eastern Orthodox, in Frederick B. Macnutt, *The Prayer Manual*, pp. 121-22.

136. *Gebete* 2, p. 249.

137. Suter, *Prayers of the Spirit*, p. 22.

138. J. W. D.

139. Charles M. Jacobs in Paul Z. Strodach, *Collects and Prayers* (Philadelphia: Board of Publication of the United Lutheran Church in America, 1935), p. 166.

140. *Gebete* 2, p. 114.

141. Prayer for Protection Through Life, *LBW* # 222, Minister's Ed., p. 113.

142. *Gebete* 2, p. 249.

143. *Kirchenbuch für die Gemeinde (Isenhagen)*, quoted in *Orate Fratres*, p. 70.

144. *Lutheran Book of Worship* #39, Minister's Ed., p. 138.

145. *Book of Common Prayer*, p. 221.

146. Martin Luther, *Klugsches Gesangbuch*, 1533; text in *Allgemeines Evangelisches Gebetbuch*, 1955, p. 430.

147. *Gebete 2*, p. 148.

148. *Gebete 2*, p. 144.

149. Primer, 1545 (adapted).

150. *Book of Common Prayer*, p. 223.

151. *Gebete 2*, p. 150.

152. Frederick B. Macnutt, *The Prayer Manual*, p. 117.

153. *Gebete 2*, p. 156.

154. Veit Dietrich in Otto Dietz, *Die Evangelien-Kollekten des Veit Dietrich*, p. 57.

155. John Dowden, *Book of Common Prayer, Scotland;* Suter, *The Book of English Collects*, p. 34.

156. *Gebete 2*, p. 170.

157. *LBW* #50, Minister's Ed., 52, 69; Andreas Althamer, *Katechismus*, 1528 (first Lutheran catechism); text in *Allgemeines Evangelisches Gebetbuch*, 1955, p. 435.

158. *Kirchenbuch für die Gemeinde (Isenhagen)*, quoted in *Orate Fratres*, p. 76.

159. Prayer for Trustfulness, *LBW* #204, Minister's Ed., p. 111.

160. *Kirchenbuch für die Gemeinde (Isenhagen)*, quoted in *Orate Fratres*, p. 84.

161. *Gebete 1*, p. 74.

162. *Gebete 2*, p. 185.

163. Christina Rossetti, quoted in Fox, *A Chain of Prayer*, p. 161.

164. *Gebete 2*, p. 152.

165. *Gebete 2*, p. 183.

166. *Gebete 2*, p. 193.

167. *Gebete 2*, p. 197.

168. *Gebete 2*, p. 199.

169. *Gebete 2*, p. 200.

170. Adapted from the Leonine Sacramentary by Frederick B. Macnutt, *The Prayer Manual*, p. 17.

171. Prayer for Those in Affliction, *LBW* #223, Minister's Ed., p. 114; Gelasian Sacramentary in Frederick B. Macnutt, *The Prayer Manual*, p. 221.

172. *Gebete 2*, p. 207.

173. *Kirchenbuch für die Gemeinde (Isenhagen)*, quoted in *Orate Fratres*, p. 82.

174. *Gebete 2*, p. 216.

175. *Gebete 2*, p. 219.

176. *Gebete* 2, p. 220.

177. *Gebete* 2, p. 221.

178. *Gebete* 2, p. 235.

179. Prayer of Self-Dedication, *LBW* #203, Minister's Ed., p. 111.

180. Veit Dietrich in Strodach, *Collects and Prayers*, p. 159.

181. *Book of Common Prayer, Scotland*, in Suter, *The Book of English Collects*, p. 264.

182. Father John of the Russian Church (nineteenth century) in Fox, *A Chain of Prayer*, p. 104.

183. *Lutheran Book of Worship* #194, Minister's Ed., p. 109; 1549 *Book of Common Prayer*.

184. Text in Dieffenbach and Müller, *op. cit.*, p. 474.

185. *Orate Fratres*, p. 96.

186. Wilhelm Löhe, *Liturgy for Christian Congregations of the Lutheran Faith*, trans. by F. C. Longaker (Newport, Ky.: 1902), p. 6.

187. *Ibid.*, pp. 6-7.

188. This prayer, always called "Luther's Sacristy Prayer," is not to be found in Luther's works or works on Luther. Diligent search has failed to discover its origin, though it breathes the spirit of Luther.

189. Lectures on Genesis, *WA* 43, 513.

190. From "Hymne to God my God in my sicknesse."

191. *Book of Common Order, Church of Scotland* (New York: Oxford University Press, 1940), p. 4.

192. In *A Preacher's Primer* (New York: Oxford University Press), p. 113.

193. John Underwood Stephens, *Prayers of the Christian Life for Private and Public Worship* (New York: Oxford University Press, 1952), p. 70.

194. Quoted in F. D. Coggan, *The Ministry of the Word* (London: Canterbury Press, 1945), p. 109.

195. Pss. 5, 119, 25, 26, 95, 99, 69.

196. Edward White Benson, *Prayers Public and Private* (London: Isbister, 1900), p. 39.

197. Dieffenbach and Müller, *op. cit.*, p. 475.

198. *Book of Common Order*, p. 3.

199. *Ibid.*, p. 3.

200. Form taken from *Gebete* 2, pp. 15-16.

201. Gallican; altered. See Bright, *Ancient Collects*, p. 185.

202. Gregorian Sacramentary, *Book of Common Prayer*, 1549.

203. Gelasian Sacramentary.

204. Roman; Joseph Oldknow and A. D. Crake, *The Priest's Book of Private Devotion*, ed. of 1909 (London: Mowbray, 1911), p. 214.

205. *Gebete 2*, pp. 16 f.

206. *Gebete 2*, p. 16.

207. Traditional; E. Milner-White, *After the Third Collect* (London: Mowbray, 1952), p. 111.

208. *Ibid.*

209. *Ibid.*

210. Adapted. Hubert L. Simpson, *Let Us Worship God* (London: Clarke 1928). Quoted in Noyes, *Prayers for Services*, p. 1.

211. Wilbur Thirkield and Oliver Huckel, *Book of Common Worship* (New York: 1932). Quoted in Noyes, *Prayers for Services*, p. 1.

212. *A Book of Offices and Prayers for Priest and People*. Compiled by two Presbyters of the Church (New York: Gorham, 1927). Quoted in Noyes, *op. cit.*, p. 1.

213. Dieffenbach and Müller, *op. cit.*, p. 477.

214. K. B. Ritter, *Pfarrgebete*, p. 18.

215. *Pfarrgebete zum Gottesdienst. Mit einem Nachwort hrsg. von der Lutherischen Liturgischen Konferenz Deutschlands* (Göttingen: Vandenhoeck & Ruprecht, 1950), p. 17.

216. George Herbert, *The Temple & A Priest to the Temple* (London: Dent, Everyman's Library), p. 292.

217. Dieffenbach and Müller, *op. cit.*, p. 482.

218. *Ibid.*, pp. 482 f.

219. Mozarabic Use.

220. George Herbert, *op. cit.*, p. 227.

221. Dieffenbach and Müller, *op. cit.*, pp. 533 f.; trans. Edward T. Horn, *The Evangelical Pastor* (Philadelphia: Frederick, 1887), p. 75 f.

222. R. F. Littledale and J. Edward Vaux, *The Priest's Prayer Book* (London: Longmans, Green, 1912), p. 37. Altered.

223. This and the following brief prayers are taken from various sources.

224. Often attributed to Melanchthon, who used it often; an echo of Bernard of Clairvaux, but not to be documented. Trans. by Theodore G. Tappert.

225. p. 20.

226. p. 20.

227. p. 4.

228. Bright, *Ancient Collects*, p. 185.

229. Adapted from *A New Prayer Book*, Easter III, by F. B. Macnutt, *op. cit.*, p. 131.

230. Wilhelm Löhe, *Liturgy for Christian Congregations*, p. 10.

231. p. 21.

232. p. 5.

233. Wilhelm Löhe, *Liturgy for Christian Congregations*, p. 11.

234. This and the following prayer quoted in E. Milner-White, *op. cit.*, p. 112.

235. In *A Book of Prayers*, 1932; quoted in E. Milner-White, *ibid.*, p. 113.

236. p. 4.

237. p. 17.

238. Quoted in *Orate Fratres*, p. 106.

239. Dieffenbach and Müller, *op. cit.*, pp. 509 f.; trans. Edward T. Horn, *op. cit.*, p. 156.

240. Dieffenbach and Müller, *op. cit.*, p. 499.

241. *Ibid.*, p. 500.

242. Quoted in Kampffmeyer, *op. cit.*, p. 172.

243. William Bright, *Ancient Collects*, p. 189.

244. Quoted in Kampffmeyer, *op. cit.*, p. 172.

245. p. 70.

246. *Prayers for the Minister's Day* (Boston: The Pilgrim Press, 1946), p. 30.

247. Dieffenbach and Müller, *op. cit.*, p. 520.

248. p. 28.

249. *Op. cit.*, p. 71.

250. pp. 33 f.

251. p. 79.

252. This and the following prayers from *Prayers for All Occasions*, The Forward Movement, pp. 54, 55, 52.

253. From Dieffenbach and Müller, *op. cit.*, p. 533.

254. *Sacra Privata*.

255. Trans by J. W. D.

256. Text in Dieffenbach and Müller, *op. cit.*, p. 531.

257. Trans by Edward T. Horn, *op. cit.*, pp. 45 f.

258. See *A Book of Prayers for Students* (London: Student Christian Movement, 1921), p. 123.

259. Quoted in Arthur W. Robinson, *Prayers New and Old* (London: S.C.M. Press, 1932), p. 77.

260. *Ancient Collects*, p. 234.

261. Source untraced, but ascribed to Thomas à Kempis.

262. In David Smith, *The Art of Preaching* (London: Hodder & Stoughton, n. d.), p. 217.

263. Quoted in Coggan, *op. cit.*, p. 124.

264. p. 23.

265. Luther-Steinhäuser, *op. cit.*, p. 286.

266. "The Minister's Morning Prayer of Recommittal," *The Pulpit*, XXII, 2 (November, 1951), p. 14.

267. *The Sickness unto Death*, trans. by Walter Lowrie (Princeton: Princeton University Press, 1941), pp. 212 f.

268. In *Das tägliche Wort* (Munich: Chr. Kaiser Verlag, n. d.), pp. 12 f.

269. Quoted in Mary W. Tileston, *Prayers Ancient and Modern* (Boston: Little, Brown, 1921), p. 80.

270. *Lift Up Your Hearts* (New York: Macmillan, 1942), p. 34.

271. Widely attributed to Francis of Assisi.

272. *Op. cit.*, pp. 234, 238; adapted.

273. In David Tait Patterson, *The Call to Worship*, rev. ed. (London: Carey Press, 1938), p. 200.

274. In *Christliche Gebätt, auf alle Tage in der Wochen zu sprechen*, 1567.

275. "The Parson's Prayer," in *Practicing the Presence* (New York: Abingdon-Cokesbury Press, 1936).

276. In *Venite Adoremus II*, World's Student Christian Federation Prayer Book, 1938, p. 79.

277. *Ibid.*, p. 74.

278. *Ibid.*, pp. 105 f.

279. Quoted in Kampffmeyer, *op. cit.*, p. 160.

280. *Sacra Privata*.

281. Quoted in *Allgemeines Evangelisches Gebetbuch*, 1955, p. 443.

282. Forward Movement, p. 38.

283. Adapted; in John W. Doberstein, *Prayers for Students* (Philadelphia: Muhlenberg Press, 1951), pp. 107 f.

284. *Ibid.*, pp. 108 f.

285. *Ibid.*, p. 109.

286. Quoted in Macnutt, *op. cit.*, pp. 142 f.

287. Quoted in Tileston, *op. cit.*, p. 109.

288. David Tait Patterson, *The Call to Worship*, p. 199.

289. pp. 117 f.

290. Written in 1950.

291. Paul Z. Strodach, *Oremus*, p. 74.

SOURCES OF THE ANTHOLOGY

1. *The Book of Concord* (Jacobs edition), pp. 38 f.
2. Article XIII, 13. Trans. from German version.
3. *Hedrabrev till prästerskapet och församlingarna i Göteborgs stift.* Trans. from German ed., Günther Ruprecht, *Sendschreiben an die Evangelische Christianheit* (Göttingen: Vandenhoeck & Ruprecht, 1951), p. 48.
4. Georg Merz, *Priesterlicher Dienst im kirchlichen Handeln* Munich: Chr. Kaiser Verlag, 1952), p. 31.
5. Report of the Commission on The Doctrine of the Ministry, *Minutes, The United Lutheran Church in America,* 1952, pp. 553f.
6. In a sermon on the Twenty-first Sunday after Trinity, 1524, *WA* 15 ,721.
7. J. W. D.
8. Quoted in Alexander Gammie, *Preachers I have Heard* (Glasgow: Pickering & Inglis, 1946), pp. 45 f.
9. Quoted in James Wareham, *The Priest and His People* (London: Mowbray, 1946), p. 17.
10. "A Sermon on Keeping Children in School," 1530, Phila. ed. IV, 146–150. Trans. by Charles M. Jacobs.
11. *Ein kleiner Spiegel für das kirchliches Amt, in Um Ordnung und Einheit der christlichen Kirche,* 1939.
12. In J. Rupprecht, *Ohnmacht und Kraft der Kirche im Urteil H. Bezzel* (1938).
13. *The Romance of the Ministry* (Boston: Pilgrim Press, 1944), p. 192.
14. *Ibid.,* pp. 251–253.
15. In *"Zeichen der Zeit,"* 1947; quoted in Karl Kampffmeyer, *Das teure Predigtamt* (Hamburg: Furche-Verlag, 1954), p. 19.
16. In *Der Weg zur Bruderschaft,* 1935; quoted in Kampffmeyer, *op. cit.,* p. 73.
17. *Sacra Privata. The Private Meditations, Devotions, and Prayers of the Right Rev. T. Wilson, D.D.* (New York: Appleton, 1841), p. 195.
18. Quoted in Thomas S. Kepler, *Spiritual Riches of John Bunyan* (Cleveland: World Publishing Co., 1952), pp. 300 f.
19. *Op. cit.,* pp. 19 f.
20. In *Die Kirche Jesu Christi,* 1926; quoted in Kampffmeyer, *op. cit.,* p. 35.
21. Quoted in Margaret Cropper, *Flame Touches Flame* (London: Longmans, Green, 1949), p. 223.
22. In *The Pilgrim's Progress* (The Interpreter's House).

23. *Gildas Salvianus: The Reformed Pastor; The Practical Works of the Rev. Richard Baxter*, Vol. XIV, 1830, p. 55.

24. *Ibid.*, p. 57.

25. *Ibid.*, p. 61.

26. *Ibid.*, pp. 63 f.

27. *Op. cit.*, pp. 80 f.

28. *The Taste of Death and the Life of Grace*, pp. 24–25; quoted in Harry Escott, *Peter Taylor Forsyth (1848–1921), Director of Souls* (London: Epworth Press, 1948), p. 68.

29. *College and Ordination Addresses* (London: Longmans, Green, 1905), p. 156 f.

30. From The Journals, quoted in Eduard Geismar, *søren Kierkegaard, Seine Lebensentwicklung und seine Wirksamkeit als Schriftsteller* (Göttingen: 1929), pp. 390 f.

31. *The Christian Ministry, with an Inquiry into the Cause of its Inefficiency*, 2 Vols. American edition (New York: Jonathan Leavitt, 1831), I, 14.

32. In *Apostolische Schlusskette und Kraftkern*, 1663; quoted in Kampffmeyer, *op. cit.*, pp. 19 ff.

33. Quoted in Charles Bridges, *op. cit.*, I, 121.

34. *Letters to His Friends*, Seventh Impression (New York: Longmans, Green, 1912), p. 96.

35. *For Christ and the Kingdom*, p. 34.

36. *A Commentary on St. Paul's Epistle to the Galatians* (trans. Erasmus Middleton), J. P. Fallowes, ed. (London: Harrison Trust, n. d.), pp. 2 f.

37. *The Shaking of the Foundations* (New York: Scribner's, 1948), p. 121.

38. *Op. cit.*, pp. 35 f.

39. *Letters to His Friends*, pp. 117 f.

40. *Die Lehre von der Seelsorge* (Munich: Chr. Kaiser Verlag, 1948), pp. 300 f.

41. From *Judge for Yourselves!* in *For Self-Examination and Judge for Yourselves!*, trans. Walter Lowrie (New York: Oxford University Press, 1941), pp. 126–128.
    Eduard Geismar says that this passage is probably read by every theological candidate in Denmark.

42. *Op. cit.*, pp. 67 f.

43. *This Grace Wherein We Stand* (Warrack Lectures, 1948) (London: Hodder & Stoughton, 1949), p. 86.

44. Quoted in Kampffmeyer, *op. cit.*, pp. 54 f.

45. Quoted in Rupert Hart-Davis, *Hugh Walpole, A Biography* (New York: Macmillan, 1952), p. 10.

46. John Watson (Ian Maclaren), *The Cure of Souls* (Lyman Beecher Lectures, 1896), (New York: Dodd, Mead, 1896), pp. 241 ff.

47. *WA*, TR, 5, No. 5376.

48. *The Man of God* (London: Hodder & Stoughton, 1935), pp. 25 f.

49. *Philip Henry's Life;* quoted in Charles Bridges, *op. cit.,* Vol. I, p. 11.

50. *Die Anfechtung des Predigers heute* (Bielefeld: Ludwig Bechauf Verlag, 1953), p. 50.

51. Quoted in Kampffmeyer, *op. cit.,* pp. 14 f.

52. *Letters to His Friends,* pp. 58 f.

53. *Pleading with Men* (New York: Revell, 1935), p. 109.

54. *Ibid.,* p. 105.

55. *Midnight Hour, A Journal from 1st May to 30th September, 1941* (London: Faber and Faber, 1942), p. 158. A layman who deeply desired ordination but was denied it.

56. J. Deinzer, *W. Löhes Leben,* III, p. 179; quoted in Wolfgang Trillhaas, *Der Dienst der Kirche am Menschen. Pastoraltheologie* (Munich: Chr. Kaiser Verlag, 1950), p. 66.

57. Part of Temple's address at enthronement as Bishop of Manchester, 1/25/21; quoted in F. A. Iremonger, *William Temple, Archbishop of Canterbury, His Life and Letters* (New York: Oxford University Press, 1948), pp. 290 f.

58. *Heiliger Dienst. Ein Buch von evangelischer Wortverkündigung und Seelsorge,* 4th ed. (Hamburg: Furche-Verlag, 1952), pp. 146–151.

59. *Op. cit.,* pp. 188 f.

60. *Das Buch vom Sonntag,* ed. by Wilhelm Stählin (Kassel: Johannes Stauda-Verlag, 1951), pp. 128 ff.

61. "*Beichtspiegel für Pfarrer,*" *Evangelisch-Lutherische Kirchenzeitung,* 4, 1 (Jan. 15, 1950), 6–7.

62. *Lectures to My Students,* First Series (New York: Sheldon, 1875), pp. 265 f.

63. In *Der Hirt,* 1524, quoted in Kampffmeyer, *op. cit.,* pp. 108 ff.

64. In *Deutsches Pfarrerblatt* (Feb. 15, 1955).

65. Letter to George Spenlein, April 8, 1516; *WA*, Br I, 33–36; quoted from Theodore G. Tappert, *Luther: Letters of Spiritual Counsel (The Library of Christian Classics,* XVIII) (Philadelphia: Westminster Press, 1955), pp. 110–111.

66. *Op. cit.,* p. 31.

67. Quoted in Charles Bridges, *op. cit.*

477

68. In *On the Ministerial Office*, 1708; quoted in Charles Bridges, *op. cit.*, I, 33 f.

69. *Op. cit.*, p. 241.

70. Quoted in Kampffmeyer, *op. cit.*, pp. 18 f.

71. E. A., 59, p. 243.

72. *The Practice of Evangelism* (New York: Scribner's, 1951), pp. 210 f.

73. *The Little Flowers of St. Francis*, chap. VIII, Everyman's Library, pp. 15-16.

74. *Erinnerungen aus dem Leben eines Landgeistlichen*, 9th ed. (Berlin, 1907), pp. 289 f.

75. *Neues und Altes*, 1869; quoted in Kampffmeyer, *op. cit.*, pp. 113 f.

76. In *Pastoralblätter*, 95 (1955), 6, p. 382.

77. *Preaching and Sermon Construction* (New York: Macmillan, 1922), p. 312.

78. *The Imitation of Christ*, IV.

79. Preface to the *Small Catechism*, 1529.

80. *Op. cit.*, p. 310.

81. Quoted in James R. Blackwood, *The Soul of Frederick W. Robertson, the Brighton Preacher* (New York: Harper, 1947), pp. 46 f.

82. *The Christian Year*, 1827, Second Sunday in Advent.

83. C. L. Prestige, *The Life of Charles Gore* (London: William Heinemann, 1935), p. 258.

84. *Journals* II, 20, quoted in Denzil C. M. Patrick, *Pascal and Kierkegaard, A Study in the Strategy of Evangelism*, II, 133.

85. In his last novel, *Endymion;* quoted in Hesketh Pearson, *Dizzy. The Life and Personality of Benjamin Disraeli, Earl of Beaconsfield* (New York: Harper, 1951), p. 294.

86. *Op cit.*, p. 8.

87. *Op. cit.*, pp. 298 f.

88. *Op. cit.*, pp. 77 f.

89. In *Thomas Wingfield, Curate*, chap. 74; quoted in C. S. Lewis, *George Macdonald, An Anthology* (New York: Macmillan, 1947), p. 113.

90. *Heralds of God* (New York: Scribner's, 1946), p. 20.

91. *The Kingdom of the Real, An Existential Study of the First Phase of the Fourth Gospel* (London: Lutterworth Press, 1951), pp. 112 f.

92. *Journal*, July 11, 1838; quoted in Walter Lowrie, *Kierkegaard* (New York: Oxford University Press, 1938), p. 169.

93. *Church and Leadership* (London: Student Christian Movements, 1945), p. 80.

94. In *De sacerdotio.*

95. *Pastoraltheologie.*

96. "Why Learn to Pray" in Charlotte M. Clough (ed.), *Partners in Prayer* (New York: Doubleday, 1953), pp. 13 f.

97. *Elemental Religion* (Lyman Beecher Lectures, 1933) (New York: Harper, 1934), pp. 40 f.

98. *Journal*, March, 1738.

99. *Op. cit.*, p. 67.

100. *W. A., Tischreden*, 6404.

101. *Traugott Untreu auf der Kanzel*, 1930; quoted in Kampffmeyer, *op. cit.*, pp. 89 f.

102. Quoted in Daniel T. Niles, *That They May Have Life* (London: Lutterworth Press, 1952), p. 38.

103. *Op. cit.*, quoted in Kampffmeyer, *op. cit.*, lest ed., 1939, p. 21.

104. *Op. cit.*, p. 83.

105. Part II (Solid Declaration), 2, 55.

106. *Op. cit.*, pp. 226 f.

107. Quoted in Kampffmeyer, *op. cit.*, pp. 95 f.

108. *Op. cit.*, p. 73.

109. *Op. cit.*, pp. 119 f.

110. *Op. cit.*, pp. 84 f.

111. *Op. cit.*

112. *The Journals of Søren Kierkegaard*, tr. by Alexander Dru (New York: Oxford University Press, 1938), p. 402.

113. *Ad Nepotianum.*

114. *Die Christliche Wahrheit, Lehrbuch der Dogmatik* (Gütersloh, C. Bertelsmann, 1949), II, 321 f.

115. *Op. cit.*, p. 11.

116. *The Temple*, Everyman's Library, pp. 63 f.

117. Quoted in Paul Scherer, *For We Have This Treasure* (Lyman Beecher Lectures, 1943) (New York: Harper, 1944), pp. 202 f.

118. *Op. cit.*, p. 58.

119. *Op. cit.*, pp. 56 f.

120. *Op. cit.*, pp. 48 f.

121. *Kirchenpostille*, on John 8:46.

122. *Op. cit.*, p. 270.

123. *Op. cit.*, pp. 195 f.

124. *Meditations and Vows*, IV, 1606.

125. "On the Qualifications Necessary for Teachers of Christianity," in John Brown (ed.), *The Christian Pastor's Manual*, 1st American ed. (Philadelphia, 1837), p. 142.

126. *Lutherisches Pfarramt. Rechenschaft und Wegweisung (Theologia Militans 10)* (Leipzig: Deichert, 1937), pp. 39 f.

127. "*A More Adequate Training for Ministers,*" in Paul B. Mayes (ed.), *The Church and Mental Health* (New York: Scribner's, 1953), p. 250.

128. *Op. cit.,* pp. 64 f.

129. *Samlede Vaerker,* XIV, 37; quoted in John A. Bain, *Søren Kierkegaard, His Life and Religious Teaching* (London: Student Christian Movement, 1935), p. 140.

130. *Der evangelische Pfarrer in Geschichte und Gegenwart* (Leipzig: Quelle & Meyer, 1925), p. 144.

131. *Grundiss des Theologiestudiums I* (Gütersloh: C. Bertelsmann, 1948), p. 118.

132. *Fiery Grains, Thoughts and Sayings for Some Occasions* put together by H. R. L. Sheppard and H. P. Marshall (London: Longmans, Green, 1929), pp. 156 f.

133. *Letters;* quoted in Charles Williams (ed.), *The New Christian Year* (London: Oxford University Press, 1941), p. 108.

134. *Tractatus de ratione vivendi sacerdotum,* Enders, *Luthers Briefwechsel,* 2, 46–50.

135. Bishop of Ruspe in North Africa, 508–33; quoted in Lancelot Andrewes, *Preces Privatae.*

136. Quoted in Harry Escott, *op. cit.,* p. 121.

137. *Der evangelische Geistliche,* Vol. I, 3rd ed. (Stuttgart: 1861), p. 132 f. Trans. G. H. Gerberding, *The Lutheran Pastor,* pp. 202 f.

138. "*Kleine Anleitung und Unterricht für künftige Seelsorger,*" in *Spiegel der Hausszucht Jesus Sirachs* (Nürnberg: 1552); text in *Evangelisches Hirtenbuch,* Vol. II, Dieffenbach and Müller, *Diarium Pastorale,* pp. 34–37.

139. Quoted in Harry Escott, *op. cit.,* 121.

140. *Op. cit.,* pp. 231 f.

141. *Letters to His Friends,* pp. 96–97.

142. Preface to Vol. I of the Wittenberg edition of his German works, 1539, *WA* 50, 658–661.

143. *Helps on the Road* (Philadelphia: United Lutheran Publication House, 1933), pp. 12 f.

144. *Op. cit.,* pp. 134 f.

145. *Op. cit.,* pp. 82 f.

146. *Seelsorge an der eigenen Seele* (Hamburg: Furche-Verlag, 1951), p. 5.

147. *Evangelische Predigtlehre,* 3rd ed. (Munich: Chr. Kaiser Verlag, 1948), pp. 208 f.

148. *Not und Verheissung unseres Amtes* (Nürnberg: Laetare-Verlag, 1948), pp. 14–19.

149. Letter to pastors, July 7, 1948.

150. *Experience Worketh Hope* (New York: Scribner's, 1945), pp. 58 f.

151. *Op. cit.*, pp. 223 f.

152. *The Lutheran Pastor* (Philadelphia: Lutheran Publication Society, 1902), p. 59.

153. Quoted in Charles Bridges, *op. cit.*, Vol. I, p. 45.

154. *Die geistliche Erneuerung des Pfarrerstandes*, 2 ed. (Berlin: Verlag Haus u. Schule, 1949), p. 20.

155. "The Cultivation of the Inner Life," *Lutheran Church Review*, XLIII, 196.

156. *Gott ruft uns* (Stuttgart: Ehrenfried Klotz Verlag, 1954), pp. 53 f.

157. *Op. cit.*, p. 181.

158. Preface to *The Large Catechism.*

159. *My Ministerial Experiences*, by Rev. Dr. Büchsel (London: Alexander Strahan, 1863), pp. 151 f.

160. On Thomas Shephard in Mather's *Magnalia;* quoted in Raymond Calkins, *op. cit.*, p. 161.

161. Quoted in Charles Bridges, *op. cit.*, I, 67.

162. In J. Richard Spann (ed.), *The Ministry* (New York: Abingdon-Cokesbury Press, 1947), pp. 171 f.

163. *Lectures on Preaching* (Lyman Beecher Lectures, 1877) (New York: Dutton, 1877), p. 44.

164. Preface to John Spangenberg's *German Postils*, 1543, *WA* 53, 218.

165. *The Art of Preaching* (London: Hodder & Stoughton, n. d.), pp. 100 f.

166. *My Ministerial Experiences*, pp. 155 f.

167. *The Man and His Message* (New York: Revell, 1899), pp. 116 f.

168. In a letter to Gregory; quoted in Hugh Thomson Kerr, *Preaching in the Early Church* (New York: Revell, 1942), p. 111.

169. To John Premboth, Aug. 17, 1760.

170. *Op. cit.*, p. 120.

171. Quoted in Charles Bridges, *op. cit.*, I, 84.

172. *Gnomon Novi Testamenti*, 1742.

173. *An Open Letter to the Christian Nobility*, Phila. ed., II, 151.

174. *Op. cit.*

175. A statement, covering all phases of the church's life, presented for discussion in the Lutheran church in Germany. The text from which this section on confession is translated is from

that presented by Bishop Wester to the Ev. Luth. Church of Schleswig-Holstein (1949), p. 18.

176. *Lutherisches Pfarramt*, pp. 40 f.

177. *Op. cit.*, p. 302.

178. In *Pastoralblätter*, 90, 9 (1950).

179. *Der Dienst der Kirche am Menschen*, pp. 106 f.

180. *Op. cit.*, pp. 66–67.

181. *Von Mensch zu Mensch. Seelsorgerliche Winke* (Zürich: Evangelischer Verlag, 1954), pp. 13–16.

182. *Op. cit.*, p. 54.

183. *Fiery Grains*, p. 243.

184. *Op. cit.*, p. 53.

185. *Erinnerungen*, pp. 224 f.

186. *Op. cit.*, p. 45.

187. Quoted in Ashton Oxenden, *The Pastoral Office* (New York: Protestant Episcopal Society, n. d.), pp. 155 f.

188. *Op. cit.*, pp. 76 f.

189. In *Diary of an Old Soul*, Jan. 31, quoted in C. S. Lewis, *op. cit.*, p. 119.

190. *Op. cit.*, p. 189.

191. *Seelsorge an der eigenen Seele*, p. 29.

192. *Life Together*, trans. John W. Doberstein (New York: Harper, 1954), p. 97.

193. In *Deutsches Pfarrerblatt*, LV, 4 (Feb. 15, 1955).

194. *Op. cit.*, p. 233.

195. *Op. cit.*, p. 106.

196. *Op. cit.*, p. 20.

197. *Op. cit.*, pp. 130 f.

198. *Op. cit.*, p. 306.

199. *Op. cit.*

200. *Lives*, 1673.

201. *Rugby Chapel.*

202. *The Canterbury Tales: Prologue.*

203. *Op. cit.*, pp. 299 f.

204. *Lives*, 1673.

205. From "The Deserted Village."

206. *Treatise on Christian Liberty*, Phila. ed., II, 312.

207. *Op. cit.*, pp. 108 f.

208. *Op. cit.*, pp. 216 ff.

209. *Erinnerungen*, pp. 222 f.

210. *The Preacher, His Life and Work* (Lyman Beecher Lectures) (New York: Hodder & Stoughton, 1912), p. 146.

211. *The Approach to Preaching* (London: Epworth Press, 1951), p. 72.
212. Quoted in Charles Bridges, *op. cit.*, I, 148.
213. *Op. cit.*, pp. 28 f.
214. *Pastoral Care*, tr. by Henry Davis (Westminster, Md.: Newman Press, 1950), pp. 72 f. (*Ancient Christian Writers. The Works of the Fathers in Translation.*)
215. *Op. cit.*, pp. 231 f.
216. Quoted in Harry Escott, *op. cit.*, p. 124.
217. *The Minister as Shepherd* (New York: Crowell, 1912), p. 176.
218. *Lutherisches Pfarramt*, pp. 28 f.
219. Quoted in Lumsden Barkway and Lucy Menzies (eds.), *An Anthology of the Love of God. From the Writings of Evelyn Underhill* (London: Mowbray, 1953), p. 213.
220. *Op. cit.*, p. 224.
221. *Op. cit.*, p. 175 f.
222. Everyman's Library, p. 140.
223. Source not found.
224. *Op. cit.*, pp. 128 f.
225. *The Faith and Modern Man* (New York: Pantheon Books, 1953), p. 31.
226. *Erinnerungen*, pp. 368 f.
227. Quoted in Thomas S. Kepler, *op. cit.*, pp. 298 f.
228. *Heiliger Dienst*, pp. 249 ff.
229. *Op. cit.*, p. 189.
230. *Op. cit.*, p. 101.
231. *Tischreden*, E. A. 61, 415; tr. by E. T. Horn, *The Evangelical Pastor*, p. 187.
232. *Op. cit.*, p. 86.
233. *Op. cit.*
234. "Evangelisches Priestertum," *Deutsches Pfarrerblatt*, 49, 3 (Feb. 15, 1949).
235. *The Gospel of God*, trans. L. J. Trinterud (London: Student Christian Movement, 1951), pp. 21 f.
236. "Evangelisches Priestertum," as above.
237. *Op. cit.*, pp. 12 ff.
238. *Op. cit.*, pp. 203 f.
239. *Op. cit.*, p. 16.
240. *Op. cit.*, p. 95.
241. *Op. cit.*, pp. 42 f.
242. *Heiliger Dienst*, pp. 151–157.
243. *Positive Preaching and the Modern Mind* (Lyman Beecher Lectures, 1907) (New York: Armstrong, 1907), pp. 108–192.

244. "The Student and Pastor," in John Brown, *op cit.*, p. 292.
245. *Der evangelische Geistliche*, I, 137 f.
246. *The Diary of a Country Priest*, trans. Pamela Morris (New York: Macmillan, 1938), pp. 28 f.
247. In *Das Wort vom Kreuz*, 1931, quoted in Kampffmeyer, *op. cit.*, p. 57.
248. *Op. cit.*, pp. 8 f.
249. *For Christ and the Kingdom*, pp. 15 f.
250. *Imago Christi.*
251. *Seelenschatz*, 1675–1692; quoted in Kampffmeyer, *op. cit.*, pp. 147 f.
252. Quoted in Kampffmeyer, *op. cit.*, pp. 149 f.
253. *Letters to His Friends*, p. 105.
254. *Der Dienst des Pfarrers, Mahnungen und Betrachtungen*, 2nd ed., (Neuendettelsau: 1916), pp. 77 f.
255. Quoted in Arthur John Gossip, *In the Secret Place of the Most High*, (New York: Scribner's, 1947), p. 155.
256. For English nuns, 13th c.; quoted in Willard L. Sperry, *Reality in Worship* (New York: Macmillan, 1925), p. 167.
257. Quoted in Arthur John Gossip, *op. cit.*, p. 155.
258. *Gnomon Novi Testamenti*, 1742, on Acts 8:15.
259. *Op. cit.*
260. *Three Books Concerning the Church*, tr. by Edward T. Horn (Reading, Pa.: Pilger Publishing House, 1908), pp. 181 ff.
261. *Moby Dick*, chap. viii.
262. Quoted in Newell D. Hillis, *Great Men as Prophets of a New Era* (New York: Revell, 1922), pp. 212 f.
263. *Op. cit.*, pp. 47 f.
264. From "*The Task*," Book II, *The Time-Piece*, lines 326–349.
265. Tr. from *Die Beredsamkeit eine Tugend*. See *Eloquence a Virtue*, trans. W. T. G. Shedd (Andover, 1850).
266. *Op. cit.*, pp. 200 f.
267. *A Priest to the Temple*, Everyman's Library, p. 292.
268. Words found in a fragment of a sermon on St. Martin's Day.
269. *Op. cit.*, p. 11.
270. *The Making of a Preacher* (Philadelphia: Westminster Press, 1946), p. 96.
271. In A. Knapp, *Ludwig Hofackers Leben;* quoted in Kampffmeyer, *op. cit.*, p. 47.
272. *Lectures to My Students*, Second Series (New York: Carter, 1889), pp. 70 ff.
273. *Works* (London: 1826), pp. 1039 f.
274. *Op. cit.*, pp. 14 f.

275. "The Ministry of the Word of God" in *God in Action, Theological Addresses* (New York: Round Table Press, 1936), pp. 80 f.

276. *Op. cit.*, p. 121.

277. In a sermon, "The Substance of Preaching and the Disposition of the Preacher," *A Selection from the University Sermons of August Tholuck, D. D.*, trans. Adeliza Manners (London: Seely, 1844), pp. 11 f.

278. *Op. cit.*, p. 96.

279. In *Theologische Existenz heute*, 1933; quoted in Kampffmeyer, *op. cit.*, p. 26.

280. In *Der Ruf Jesu*, 1913; quoted in Kampffmeyer, *op. cit.*, p. 31.

281. In Harry Escott, *op. cit.*, pp. 127 f.

282. *The Work of Christ* (London: Independent Press, 1938), p. 4.

283. *Op. cit.*, pp. 50 f.

284. *Werke*, Part III, 1778, pp. 74 f.

285. *Op. cit.*, p. 21.

286. *Op. cit.*, pp. 27 f.

287. Quoted in Charles Smyth, *The Art of Preaching*, p. 121.

288. *Op. cit.*, p. 123.

289. *Op. cit.*, p. 94.

290. *Op. cit.*, pp. 56 f.

291. *Training in Christianity*, trans. Walter Lowrie (Princeton: Princeton University Press, 1944), pp. 229 ff.

292. *Op. cit.*, p. 54.

293. Quoted in Kampffmeyer, *op. cit.*, p. 32 f.

294. *The New Preaching* (Nashville: Cokesbury Press, 1930), p. 40.

295. *W. A.*, Tischreden, V, 6793.

296. *W. A.*, Tischreden, V, 5338.

297. *Op. cit.*, lines 395–426.

298. *Ibid.*, lines 463–480.

299. *W. A.*, Tischreden, II, 2606 b.

300. *Seelsorge an der eigenen Seele*, pp. 17 ff.

301. *W. A.*, Tischreden, II, 1590.

302. *A Priest to the Temple*, Everyman's Library, pp. 226 ff.

303. *Op. cit.*, p. 60.

304. *A Pulpiteer.*

305. *Good Thoughts in Bad Times*, 1645.

306. *Op. cit.*, pp. 41 f.

307. *Die christliche Wahrheit*, II, 320 f.

308. *Die Verkündigung des Wortes Gottes, Homiletik*, 2d ed. (Schwerin [Meckl.]: Verlag Friedrich Bahn, 1936), p. 359.

309. *Unsere Predigt, Heute* (Stuttgart: Kohlhammer, 1946), p. 42.

310. *Haus—, Schul— und Kirchenbuch, Part II* (Stuttgart: 1859), pp. 57 f.

311. *Op. cit.*

312. *Der evangelische Geistliche*, I, 276.

313. Conclusion of *The Student and Pastor*.

INDEX OF NAMES

(Numbers in parentheses after the page numbers indicate the number given to the prayers in the first section of the book. Numbers are not indicated for selections in the anthology, since the authors' names are given in each instance.)

487